BABY RICHARD

A FOUR-YEAR-OLD COMES HOME

Dr. Karen Moriarty

Baby Richard — A Four-Year-Old Comes Home
By Dr. Karen Moriarty

Published by:
Open Door Publishing Inc.
P. O. Box 353311
Palm Coast, FL 32135 USA
Orders @ babyrichard.com or babyrichard.net

This book was printed in the United States of America.

Cover design by Alan Bernhard, Argent Books, Boulder, CO
Layout design by Vickie Swisher, Studio 20 | 20, Toledo, IL
Front cover photo with permission from AP/Wide World Photos
Back cover photo with permission from Scott Strazzante

Front cover photo: *His adoptive mother (center) hands Baby Richard to his biological father (left), while his adoptive father watches and a neighbor (right) participates in the transfer of the child on April 30, 1995.*

Back cover photo: *Otakar Kirchner holds his son Danny ("Baby Richard") for the first time after having met the child only one hour before.*

Library of Congress Control Number: 2003097282

ISBN 0-9745354-0-0

DEDICATION

To Danny,
   in the hope that you will know better
      who you are,
         that you were and are loved,
            and that a wrong was righted.

Each of us is born
into the world as someone;
we spend the rest of our lives
trying to find out who.

— *Dean Hamer & Peter Copeland*
Living with Our Genes

Oh I get by with a little help
from my friends.

— *John Lennon & Sir Paul McCartney*

ACKNOWLEDGEMENTS

WHEN I began this book, I underestimated the amount of time, energy, and emotional ergs that it would extract throughout the intense eight months of research, writing, and reliving the experiences herein. I discovered that writing is much like word weaving—first, a draft; then another and another; and thereafter, continuous meshing of more color, detail, and texture into its fabric.

It's difficult for me to express the gratitude I feel toward Otto, Daniela, and Danny Kirchner (f.k.a. Baby Richard), who started out as my clients and became so special that—perhaps ironically—I call them "my adopted family." Each one gave me permission, approval, and support in this undertaking. The Kirchner parents have survived, while ensuring that Danny has thrived. I have never known anyone else who has endured the level, intensity, and duration of opposition to their desire simply to have a family, to raise their own natural son, and to live a normal American life. Martin Luther King said, "The ultimate measure of a man is not where he stands in moments of comfort and convenience, but where he stands at times of challenge and controversy." The Kirchner parents are excellent examples of quiet personal victory over adversity and hardship.

My deepest gratitude is directed toward my husband Robert, who has "always been there" for me across three decades. "Life is made up of sobs, sniffles, and smiles, with sniffles predominating," wrote O. Henry. Robert has been consistently understanding and supportive through all of the sobs, sniffles, and smiles, through all seasons. He has helped me in overt and subtle ways through every page of this book.

My sister, Jo Addie, became a closer friend because of "Baby Richard." I appreciate all of her kind words and her caring through these roller-coaster years. Mike and Donna Foley encouraged me and contributed their insights and expertise from the time of my first written page. Bill Harte, in his quiet yet strong style, kept me afloat, without realizing his importance in my journey. Roberta Hennessy provided me computer and technical assistance, as well as her friendship, along the way. Norma Rumberger deftly and skillfully helped fill the gaps that needed attention during the final, sometimes difficult stages of preparing for publication, distribution, and marketing. I am grateful for the invaluable contributions of content and clarification from Judge James Heiple, Jeffery Leving, Bruce Boyer, Neil Steinberg, Adrienne Drell, and Enid Shortell.

To the journalists and other media persons who were professional, objective, ethical, and rational through the Baby Richard hysteria, I laud you for your efforts. You were self-destined to a lower profile, a smaller space, and a lesser spotlight, as you probably realized. If you were traveling the "high road," that was probably your reward. But thank you.

You are born with a pen and paper in hand, but you have to write your own story.

— Dean Hamer & Peter Copeland
Living with Our Genes

CONTENTS

Danny ("Baby Richard") and the author, Dr. Karen Moriarty, pause over a shared play activity for this photo, taken by the child's mother, Daniela, during his first weeks with his birth parents.

> The [woman] answereth:
> Nay, but thy child is dead....
> King [Solomon] therefore said:
> Bring me a sword....
> Divide, said he,
> the living child in two,
> and give half to the one,
> and half to the other.
>
> — *III Kings 3:23-25*

INTRODUCTION

__A REALITY BOOK....

Baby Richard — A Four-Year-Old Comes Home reveals the private events and truths under the camouflage created by mounds of speculation, falsehoods, and phony drama revolving around one baby, soon

> Our lives begin to end
> the day we become silent
> about things that matter.
>
> — *Martin Luther King, Jr.*

a child, unaware of his own celebrity and distorted public image.

Baby Richard—whose real name is Daniel ("Danny") Kirchner—was used by people from many walks of life for their own selfish purposes. Politicians from every level and branch of government, celebrities from coast to coast, journalists from every genre of media, a gang of attorneys, armchair mental health professionals, and others enthusiastically leaped into the public fray and onto the bandwagon, shouting vociferous protests for "his best interest." "Richard" became an easy topic for getting quick, prominent publicity; a forum for impassioned rhetoric to champion the cause of children; and a topic as safely embraced and widely popular as motherhood, the American flag, and apple pie.

Having written about himself as "a pathologically ambitious person..., the one quality that defines me most clearly," veteran columnist Bob Greene of the *Chicago Tribune* appropriated the Baby Richard story as his own from August 1993. In his unique resurrection of yellow journalism, Greene worked and reworked it, to his own taste and pleasure, across more than four years—with occasional sputters after that—fashioning more than one hundred columns about every imaginable aspect in his over-the-top, sensationalized coverage. He incorporated his own idiosyncratic "take" on the Baby Richard saga—which some writers more literary than Greene called Dickensian because of its circuitous history, dramatic and bitter conflicts, and interplay of raw, intense human passions at every step. Greene presented his imaginings about "Richard" as reporting facts, but like our modern-day "reality genre" of entertainment, he created a contrived, artificial situation in which real people were compelled to play out their real-life parts, at great personal expense and to life-altering outcomes. The public responded with an unprecedented outpouring of feelings, mostly rage.

Baby Richard was a story like none other. It inspired and spawned voyeurism, bad behavior, and just plain bad taste. The two protagonists, Otakar ("Otto") and Daniela Kirchner, having survived a rocky road in their relationship, came together to fight—through the Illinois court system—for their baby son. Their perceived crime was winning...and then retrieving him, at the age of four, from his would-be adoptive parents, Robert ("Jay") and Kimberly Warburton. Motivated by our human "biological imperative," they wanted to raise their own son, to become a family. For their understandable and yet courageous decision, Otto and Daniela were publicly vilified and excoriated in unprecedented ways and on a level surpassing the journalistic epithets and public furor usually reserved for those convicted of heinous crimes.

This reality book discloses, for the first time, the untold stories of "Baby Richard" (Danny); his birth parents Otto and Daniela; myself, as their therapist-turned-friend; and several other major participants. It also presents the real tragedy of Bob Greene, who grabbed the most visible and influential role in what was described as a Chicago-based morality play. Under the guise of deep concern and love for "Richard," whom he never knew, Greene molded the story into his own bizarre creation. Greene was later expelled from the *Tribune* for admitted sexual misconduct with a teenager, but more than a decade after the affair—a tragic and ruinous period of time for many who suffered from his vitriol.

Lest the reader assume that we are overreacting or overstating the effects of one columnist's journalistic campaign of destruction, please consider this. Imagine that you—or a loved one—are viciously attacked in the most widely-read newspaper in the Midwest by a prominent veteran writer, who has decided that his target is so reprehensible that he is unfit to be a parent to his own child. Although the target is law-abiding, never having been accused or convicted of any crime, the columnist assails his target's character in numerous ways. Not only are 2.9 million readers of the Sunday edition of the *Tribune* exposed to the piece, but "probably a number to equal or rival that"—according to the Tribune Media Services—in the nearly 200 newspapers around the country that syndicate the columnist.

That's potentially 5.8 million readers. Well, you say, that's not too bad—people soon forget what they read in the paper. Then, another column appears, repeating the assaults—another widespread opportunity to influence public opinion, 1.9 million readers on a weekday—well, actually, 3.8 million through syndication.

To get to my point, fold in 100 syndicated columns—on Sundays and weekdays—and do the math, and you have 430,000,000 hits, from coast to coast, ...and you also have the Baby Richard case, as promulgated by Bob Greene. He wrote with such vehemence and repetition that people thought he **must** be right. Of course, he never bothered to interview the child or his birth parents at any time. Why be confused by reality, the facts, or considering their side?

Sadly, other journalists looked to Greene—the self-proclaimed Baby Richard "knower"—as their definitive source. The real tragedy of Bob Greene is not that he was sacked by the

Chicago Tribune for "taking advantage of his position for personal gain" but that it was not done at the actual time of his sexual exploitation of a young girl. He got a "free pass" to exploit, through millions of newspapers, Baby Richard—an innocent child—and his parents, nearly destroying their lives.

This, then, is a reality book on two levels. First, presenting **real** people and events, we take the reader on a behind-the-scenes journey of human foibles, failings, toil, and triumphs, across more than a decade, into 2003. Second, we reveal the various parts played by the major Baby Richard participants by juxtaposing the misleading, phony, and fantasy material with the real-life facts and events that were concealed by a patchwork cloak of intermittent privacy and skillful media manipulation. We hope to dispel the effects of the hysteria and the hoopla, at long last, and to replace them with a better understanding of the extensive, unmitigated power of the press and rightfully to restore the dignity and honor of this beleaguered family. The real Baby Richard deserves no less.

W H Y   N O W ?

YOU MIGHT LEGITIMATELY ASK, WHY NOW? It has been eight years since "Baby Richard" burst onto the international stage through a live telecast of the weeping four-year-old boy being wrenched from the arms of his adoptive mother and passed to his biological father, a stranger to the child. This scene, the culmination of a highly-publicized four-year custody battle, touched the hearts and lives of millions. Described as "heart-wrenching," it set in motion events—both public and private—that would last for years and continue to this day. Baby Richard became not only the most controversial and widely publicized custody dispute and failed adoption in history—with theatrical media coverage of every aspect and development across **five** years—but also the most misinterpreted.

As timeless as the epic of Biblical King Solomon's feigned sword-splitting of the contested baby to determine his real mother, this modern-day version reveals a birth father and mother joining forces to regain their child, through the courts, from another set of parents who claimed him. The father would risk and lose everything...except, ultimately, his beloved son and his fondest wish, a family. The mother would successfully reclaim her first-born child, earning a second chance through a joyful reunion with him after four years of an anguished separation filled with painful regret. A relative's lie, born of a failed attempt at extortion, had led to the young mother's hasty, desperate decision to give up her infant, followed by immediate and profound remorse.

Over office water coolers, in church lobbies, and across grocery store aisles, people wondered how he would fare, how he would turn out. Echoing many other media portrayals, NBC *Dateline's* feature about Baby Richard climaxed with the prognosis that someday this child would have quite a story to tell.

This is the heretofore untold story of this smart, resilient, and beautiful child who would prove wrong the dire predictions for his future from a myriad of spotlight-seeking mental health experts, none of whom had even met him. Their prognostications included "an inability to develop as a normal child," his being "undoubtedly scarred for life," and "catapulted into mental illness," unlikely ever to overcome the devastating psychological effects of his traumatic, sudden transfer to his biological father. Ironically, the child's greatest triumph would be over the unique challenges in his toxic and threatening environment, created by hostile, relentless media, which whipped the public into a frenzy and jeopardized his right to a private, normal life.

Today, in spite of the doomsayers, Danny is a thriving twelve-year-old, who earns mostly A grades in school; plays soccer, basketball, and hockey with fervor and agility; deeply loves his parents and family; protects his two younger sisters; and would qualify as a contender for the Child of the Year Award. Sharon, 7, and Jessica, 5, are bright, bouncy little girls with long, flowing blonde tresses and charming personalities. The three siblings look and behave as if they have come straight from Central Casting as ideal, all-American kids—intelligent, attractive, healthy, and happy. They live with their birth parents, Otakar and Daniela Kirchner, as a typical suburban family, sharing solid, old-fashioned values and a fierce loyalty to each other.

As the psychologist who worked with Danny and his parents, I present an insider's view of the child's life from his first moments with his birth father and mother—strangers to him at the age of four when they showed up to claim him—to the present. A series of uncomplicated, effective parenting behaviors— expressions of love, praise, consistent expectations, focused interactive time, flexibility, patience, a sense of humor, and the teaching of values—have been responsible for Danny's remarkable, problem-free development. If the Kirchners have achieved an enviable level of success in parenting their children—in spite of ongoing economic hardship, a barrage of media attacks, and threatening, hateful public reaction—the average readers of this book, unencumbered by such a pervasively hostile environment, are even more likely to experience success by adopting similar approaches to their children.

This story discloses my professional and personal involvement in this complex tale of a mountain of make-believe from only a seed of truth. As typical of life-altering events, I experienced—during my thirty-year career—the greatest joys and the deepest sadness as the Baby Richard psychologist. Paradoxically, I felt that I was most empowering of others during times of overwhelming helplessness amid the flood of media venom.

This is also an exposé of the press gone awry, creating a legacy of destruction and wide-reaching ripple effects. Described as "incestuous" coverage by Illinois Supreme Court Judge James Heiple, who authored the unanimous Baby Richard decision, the media proliferated misinformation, distortions, half-truths, and lies—mostly without any first-hand sources—in newspaper, magazine, radio, and television stories across the country. Unrestrained and unchecked, the power of the media is alarmingly absolute, and it can be unleashed against anyone of its choosing.

THE IMPACT OF BABY RICHARD

"BABY RICHARD" prompted state legislatures around the nation into action. Within a stunning seventeen days, the Illinois General Assembly created, passed, and the governor signed into law an amendment to the state's Adoption Act. In spite of startling speed and bi-partisan support, it came too late to forestall the outcome of the state's Supreme Court decision awarding Richard to his biological father. Later, it was criticized by many for its potential threat to biological parents' rights to their own children.

"Though the [Baby Richard] case prompted passage of a new law in Illinois, spurred creation of a state paternity registry and drew attention to problems in adoption generally, its most obvious legacy, experts say, was to instill fear in adoptive and adopting parents.... [O]ther adoption experts say they are convinced that the case has prompted more couples to adopt from foreign countries." (Janan Hanna, "1 year later, legacy of Baby Richard case is fear," *Chicago Tribune*, April 29, 1996). Many Americans pursued international adoptions in order to avoid "another Baby Richard."

About thirty states, according to the *Tribune*, passed laws that have created paternity registries, and many cited the Baby Richard case as the impetus. Among the most recent, in 2002 the Florida legislature passed a controversial adoption law requiring mothers who cannot locate or identify the biological fathers of their children by a required exhaustive search to publish details of their past sexual relationships. The public notification is intended to give biological fathers the opportunity to preempt adoption proceedings and assert their parental rights.

"The erroneous idea that dads don't want to have anything to do with their children is exactly the attitude that has led to traumatic Baby Richard and Baby Jessica situations.... It is this kind of situation that the Florida adoption law is seeking to prevent," according to Jeffery M. Leving ("Florida Voices," *The Daytona Beach News-Journal*, August 31, 2002). Leving, the nation's most prominent fathers' advocate and author of the book *Fathers' Rights*, represented Elian Gonzalez's father in 2000, amid the political furor over the Cuban-born child who washed ashore in Florida and whose Cuban-American relatives tried to keep him.

Baby Richard is to Chicago as Elian Gonzalez is to Miami. Emotion-laden episodes about foreigner fathers reclaiming their sons, through legal authority, both cases gave rise to vociferous public outcries and, in some quarters, to a hysterical citizenry. Both cases were political hot potatoes, in different ways perhaps, but with permanent results. In 2003, Leving points to the profound, lasting effects of Baby Richard as the first public impetus to raising awareness of a father's rights to parent his child.

The Baby Richard case is often misinterpreted and misapplied as if his birth father first appeared after many months or years after the child's adoption. In reality, he filed his court petition before his son was three months old—eleven months **before** the lower court approved the child's adoption, based upon fraudulent affidavits claiming the father was "unknown." However, the case has nonetheless led to significant debate over the extent of fathers' rights in many forums. Baby Richard has spurred new awareness of the pervasive impact of the father upon a child's life. According to Leving, "As a society we must recognize and act upon the fact that dads love their children as much as mothers do."

Adoption agencies across the country have been compelled to deal with worried adoptive parents because of haunting memories of the unsettling Baby Richard custody battle and its outcome. Hundreds of agencies have revised their written materials and the content of their counseling sessions in order to clarify the widespread misconceptions regarding the case. Otakar Kirchner won his son in court because the child's adoption by the Warburtons (named the "Does" in legal documents) was not only privately arranged but based upon overt and purposeful deception of the father, who was told that his son had died minutes after his birth. Adoptive parents who do not engage in deceit and purposeful subterfuge aimed at preventing the biological father from knowing about his child need not worry about a "Baby Richard outcome."

The story also created widespread interest in the nature-nurture debate; in the issue of the child's rights vis-à-vis the parents'; and in the topic of the "best interests" of children versus laws that enforce parents' rights as the primary determinant. Many advocates of "Richard's" adoptive parents argued that, because the child was turning four when the Illinois Supreme Court issued its final ruling—denying a rehearing to the Does—he should be allowed to remain with the only parents he had known. His best interests, it was argued, required his being awarded to the Does/Warburtons because he had bonded with them and, implicitly, they could offer him the better home.

In heated discussions and impassioned "Letters to the Editor" from coast to coast, the Baby Richard story became a women's issue and an adoptive parents' cause. It also revealed an undercurrent of xenophobia, as the vast majority of the press and the public championed the adoptive mother as a martyr figure and condemned Otto Kirchner as "only a sperm dad." An immigrant who became an American citizen four days after he obtained his son, Otto suffered ongoing journalistic invective and public vilification both before and long after the highly-publicized transfer of his child.

At least one journalist raised the interesting question, If Baby Richard were an African-American—or other minority—child, would he have generated such long-term, intense public scrutiny and strong emotional reaction? He was, in fact, a "pretty little mite," blonde, brown-eyed child, adopted into "a nice Midwestern family"; the adoptive parents were "pillars of their community, providers of decent values…and, best of all, they were white" (Carol Sarler, "Parent Power," *The London Times*, May 18, 1997). If Richard were a child of the slums, would he have been responsible for generating so much camera film and newspaper print? If roles were reversed and the immigrant Kirchners were court-ordered to transfer the WASP, suburban Warburtons' natural child back to their custody and care, would there have been an "army of reporters"—as described by *People* magazine—at the event?

If Baby Richard's father had been African-American instead of Eastern European, would there have emerged such a significant number of visible, outspoken opponents to his claim to his child? Or, during the mid-nineties, would political correctness have obviated the media attacks and public outcry against him?

Some insightful individuals asked questions and debated regarding the media-fostered images of the two sides of the custody dispute—as well as the coloring of ethnicity, gender and journalistic biases in the case—but these rare, more rational voices were quelled by the vociferous, powerful outcries of many public persons who weighed in. Celebrities of the caliber of Tom Selleck from the entertainment world and Phil Jackson from the sports arena issued public statements in support of the adoptive parents and wanted Richard returned to them. Talk shows, both on television and radio, devoted programs to discuss the "tragedy of Baby Richard." Newspapers, radio programs, and NBC's *Dateline* conducted telephone polls to assess and publish the prevailing public reaction, which unsurprisingly revealed a significant bias against Otto and Daniela Kirchner. *Dateline's* exclusive story, "Home At Last?" on July 21, 1995, showed footage of the tearful, wrenching transfer of the child. Reporter Maria Shriver points out, "**Everyone** seemed to have an opinion" and "most opinions" were on the side of the adoptive parents. In their broadcast of an excerpt from WLS Talk Radio, a woman caller denounces the "child to be yanked from everything he knows to **nothingness**," an interesting term for his birth parents.

None of these media sources revealed that the adoption of Richard was based not only upon a lie to the father that his child was dead but upon untrue affidavits provided by the would-be adoptive parents. If the public knew these facts — clearly presented in the court documents but continually omitted by the media — would the reaction have been so condemnatory of Otto Kirchner?

In his "State of the State" address in January 1997, Illinois Governor James Edgar interrupted his speech to announce that he hoped that the judiciary would bring about "a happy ending to the 'Baby Richard' tragedy." This unprecedented act surprised many, not only because the Governor had released copies of his prepared address with no mention about "Richard," but because the state's highest court had issued its unanimous decision 2-1/2 years previous to these remarks. In addition, in accordance with the Supreme Court ruling, the five-year-old child had been living in his birth parents' home for twenty months! As early as 1994, Edgar had petitioned the court to let the child stay permanently with the Warburtons. It was that same year that the General Assembly hastily approved, and Edgar signed into law, the bill requiring courts, in certain circumstances, to elevate, above the biological parents' rights to their child, the subjectively-determined "best interests" standard for establishing custody. Mrs. Edgar, the Governor's wife, also became a frequent, visible, and outspoken proponent of the Warburtons' cause. The U.S. Senators from Illinois, Paul Simon and Carol Moseley-Braun, were counted among their numerous powerful allies in their quest to keep Richard.

Even the White House got involved. First Lady Hillary Rodham Clinton made an appearance on *The Oprah Winfrey*

Show, saying, "It's an outrage. That child had bonded [and]…was the child of an entire extended family and neighborhood." She provided her opinion again and referenced the case in her book *It Takes a Village*:

> …[T]here is the shadow of fear cast by uncommon but highly publicized cases in which birth parents sue to reverse an adoption. A forty-year-old newscaster I met in New Mexico wanted to adopt but was discouraged by notorious cases like that of Baby Richard, in which a child lived happily with his adoptive parents until his birth father won custody of him a few years later. However rare they are, **such cases undermine people's faith in our adoption system and encourage them to look to other countries for children, while so many of our own country's children go without proper care or love.** [Emphasis added] (1996)

Baby Richard also galvanized widespread public reaction against the court system. Not only was the Illinois Supreme Court criticized for its decision, overturning the lower courts' rulings and ordering that Richard be turned over to his father, but the nearly four-year process was appropriately viewed as unacceptably long. I was both surprised and dismayed, however, to discover that only a **handful** of persons (including the media), among dozens with whom I spoke about the case across a span of years, had actually **read** the Supreme Court decisions. The Court determined the adoptive parents as responsible for the prolongation of the litigation process:

> When the father entered his appearance in the adoption proceedings 57 days after the baby's birth and demanded his rights as a father, the petitioners [Does] should have relinquished the baby at that time. It was their decision to prolong this litigation…. (June 16, 1994)

The legal proceedings were dragged out by delays and machinations across the four years.

MEDIA POWER

The unmitigated power of the media to shape and determine public opinion, coupled with its ability to destroy, is perhaps the most compelling, troublesome characteristic and legacy of Baby Richard. British journalist Carol Sarler begins her article about the case by observing, "When Otto Kirchner came to reclaim the son he had never known…, he became America's latest hate figure. Would his critics have been so damning if they had known the whole, tragic story?" ("Parent Power")

Sarler suspected more of a story than was ever revealed in America, convinced her editor to send her to the States, and printed Otto's as yet untold story. At the time that her article was published, however, it had been more than two years since "[t]he image [of Richard's handover] burned its way through hearts and minds around the world…. The pictures flashed everywhere, first on television bulletins, then in the newspapers…. [A] story that had gripped the American imagination for months." Not only had it taken so long for the "other side" of the story to be featured anywhere—in sharp contrast with the purported standard of journalism to include both sides of a conflict—but the story ran only in Great Britain, and several other countries, but never in the United States. In her follow-up letter to me, Sarler writes, "[T]he response in this country has been fantastic; people are outraged and angry on [Otto's] behalf, and [the article] is also being syndicated as far as Australia…though not, as yet, in the USA (funny, that!)."

"Funny," maybe, but also pathetic. Meanwhile, denied a respectful opportunity to explain his side of the conflict or to defend himself, Otto Kirchner lost his American dream, his job, savings, good credit rating, apartment, a previously unmarred reputation, and his fair-weather friends, all because of the public hatred generated by one-sided media.

Lured by the fake promise that he would finally be afforded the opportunity to present his side, Otto traveled to New York City—as arranged by his attorney—to participate in a nationally televised talk show. Introduced to the audience as "the man who fought for his son and then abandoned him," Otto predictably became the target of the audience's outrage. It turned into an ambush.

"My only crime was that I loved my son and wouldn't give up fighting for him," he would tell me, "and I never told a lie or broke a law." Unemployed for two years and unable even to get job interviews after giving his name, Otto continued to suffer from the public's strong reaction, as described by Sarler in her article:

Those pictures of the handover [of his son] mean that now, two years later, Otakar Kirchner has only to enter a room to have it grow quiet; even in the discreet lounge of the smart hotel where we spoke, other guests looked, recognised, whispered, recoiled. "I feel," he says wretchedly..., "like the white O.J."

Since 9/11 and the wars in the Middle East, the reputation of the media has arguably improved; and the public perceive reporters and journalists with renewed respect, admiration, and, in many cases, gratitude. The vast majority of ethical, dedicated, and even courageous men and women who report the news and interpret it for their audiences and readers deserves this elevated public regard.

In contrast to these trustworthy professionals who provide an essential, reliable public service, there is occasionally an exception—as there is in all walks of life—an individual who creates material, presents it as real "news," and spins his own imaginings and fantasies into columns.

In his numerous Baby Richard columns, Bob Greene regularly and often savagely attacks the biological parents, while he both glorifies the adoptive parents and overtly elicits sympathy and support for them. So extreme was his Baby Richard coverage in both volume and obvious bias that other journalists mocked and mimicked him in their publications.

In the Chicago *Reader*, Neil Steinberg, using the pseudonym Ed Gold, created a monthly column about Bob Greene entitled "Bob Watch," with the expressed purpose and subtitle "We read him so you don't have to." In his December 22, 1995 article, Gold reviews the *Chicago Tribune* computer archives for the year:

A few keystrokes and we see that Bob had written 167 columns in 1995 as we went to press. And that 59 of those columns were about Baby Richard. A solid 35 percent of his entire output—with zero practical effect other than making certain people think that by focusing on one white boy who has two sets of parents fighting to love him, they were exercising supreme compassion....

In...11 years, Bob has written 1,923 columns. More than a third—723—involve children, a reminder that before Richard there were...other wee ones Bob has used to cynically fill his columns with pages of court transcripts and letters of reader outrage.

At the time of Steinberg's/Gold's analysis, Bob Greene had never spoken to Otto or Daniela Kirchner, and yet he wrote 59 columns about these people in 1995 alone. He would write **dozens** more, also without first-hand information. In column after column, for months, he wrote about Danny's progress in his birth parents' home without speaking to the child, his mother, his father, or me—the only professional working with the child. How did he get away with that? you might reasonably ask.

Greene has never yet interviewed any member of the Kirchner family.

In "Bob Greene's Richard File," the *Columbia Journalism Review* censured Greene and described the impact of his journalistic rampage:

...[N]o one has written more copy about Richard than...Bob Greene: more than 50,000 words...since May 1993.... For the eight weeks from when Richard was moved until the U.S. Supreme Court decided not to hear the case, Greene wrote about nothing else.

Readers have reacted by writing two to three thousand letters.... [E]ditors said this issue generated more letters than any story in recent memory, and that more than 90 percent agreed with the columnist. (September/October, 1995)

Quoting Richard Roeper, the article continues, "'This is the biggest journalistic meltdown I've ever seen.... It was like a broken record. It was the same thing, day after day....'"

"It was like pornography!" Neil Steinberg described his personal reactions to Greene's "mind-numbing," repetitive Baby Richard rampage during my interview of him in December 2002. "Greene turned people's private suffering into entertainment," and "he did it in incredibly bad taste and a nauseating style."

Columnist Phil Kadner wrote an article entitled "Bad Behavior and the Story of Baby Richard," in which he takes the unpopular but reasoned viewpoint, based upon the Illinois Supreme Court decision, in support of Otto Kirchner. Kadner not only actually read the Supreme Court decision but quotes from it:

> ...[T]he court concluded it would be wrong to reward the "deceit" and "subterfuge" of the adoptive parents by allowing them to keep Richard.

> That's what the decision was all about....

Kadner, as the anomaly among the press, presented this opinion:

> People behaving badly. That's the best description of the Baby Richard story....

> If you've been reading the newspapers or watching the television news in recent days, you would think there is only one side to the...case because that's all that's being told. (*Daily Southtown*, January 23, 1997)

In an ironic twist, however, Kadner—who otherwise seems to support Otto Kirchner—ends his column with "Being lousy father material is not a criminal act in our society. Not yet." Kadner, too, apparently chose to cater to the media-created majority opinion by slamming Otto Kirchner in his concluding sentiment.

Popular and iconoclastic Mike Royko of the *Chicago Tribune* enthusiastically joined the fray. He labeled Otto a "roly-poly Romeo," "Hungarian fiddler-cook," "some round-faced guy with a strange accent," and "a lover, a devil-may-care spender, ...and a riverboat gambler," with "a fiery gypsy personality." Referring to four-year-old Danny as Otto's "sperm-son," Royko wrote a column comparing the child to a putter that his father, a non-golfer, gave away and then decided blithely to reclaim.

People magazine covered the story in four issues. Although well written and factually accurate, the articles present a bias that is subtler than that of others. "The Homecoming" (May 29, 1995) tells the story of Danny's transfer and first days in his natural parents' home. It ends with an allusion to Otto Kirchner's "280-pound bulk hurtling toward the water's edge" as he attempts to retrieve a rubber ball for his son. The authors found it necessary to describe the child's father by his weight.

In "Sequels—This boy's life," the article concludes with a quotation from Bob Greene, following the statement, "[The Warburtons'] supporters, including...Bob Greene, continue to fear that [Richard's] abrupt removal from the only home he had ever known will leave lasting scars" (*People*, December 25, 1995/January 1, 1996). Omitting any reference to Otto's multilingual ability to speak five languages, the article quotes him as saying, "[Danny] doesn't want to do **nothing** without me" [emphasis added]. In this brief article, the author chose to highlight—and expose to ridicule—Otto's lack of mastery of the grammatical rules of English regarding double negatives. He could have chosen to paraphrase the quotation instead of using it to diminish the speaker.

"Apart Again," subtitled "Baby Richard's parents separate once more," presents the lamentable marital separation of the Kirchners, but it fails even to mention that Otto was visiting and providing care for his son three or four days every week and telephoning him daily (*People*, February 3, 1997).

Few, if any, of the multitude of news media that covered this separation story mentioned that Otto was visiting and caring for his children during many of the full-time work hours that Daniela was at her job. Numerous versions implied, and some stated, that the father who had fought so long for his child had abandoned him.

Although I cannot say definitively that there was no story ever printed about the Kirchners' reconciliation when it occurred, I have neither seen nor been able to find one. Otto and Daniela lived apart for eight to nine months during 1996-97 but have been together continuously ever since. However, if you were to ask the "man in the street," he would undoubtedly tell you that the father left his son and family and did not return.

Within days of Richard's transfer to his father, *The Oprah Winfrey Show* featured the Baby Richard case. Led by participant Bob Greene, the theme took on the tones of anger, sadness, and hand-wringing over the regretful fate of Richard, now in his father's home and care. With millions of *Oprah* viewers, Baby Richard hysteria among the general public grew and expanded markedly that day.

ABC's *20/20* show devoted several programs to the Baby Richard story. In the first, the Warburtons were allowed to appear under their pseudonyms, John and Jane Doe, for their interview with Barbara Walters. In the second, they once again presented their side of the dispute, this time using their real names. Otto and Daniela Kirchner were invited to neither program. The third show highlighted the marital separation of the Kirchner parents.

Even Australia's version of *60 Minutes* dedicated a program to this curious American controversy. The story surprised, startled, and intrigued people half way around the globe.

T O D A Y :
A   G E N T L E R   T I M E

Now, eight years later, the realities of Baby Richard may be revealed within a more temperate climate. Bob Greene—most responsible for the one-sided treatment by the media of the Baby Richard conflict—resigned from the *Chicago Tribune* on September 14, 2002, after he acknowledged sexual misconduct with a teenager "and other indiscretions." Greene's sexual relationship with the teenager occurred in connection with his job at the *Tribune*, shortly after the teenager's parents took their only child to his office for an interview in 1988. It occurred **before** he began his finger-waving, self-righteous tirade over Baby Richard and before he ruined the reputation of Otto Kirchner without even having spoken to him.

"The strange fall of a veteran columnist whose private life could not live up to his public voice" reads the subheading to "Bob Greene Gets Spiked" in *Time* magazine. This article describes Greene as "a local institution" and a defender of abused children, and it explains:

> To understand the apoplexy [his forced resignation] created is to understand what Greene had come to represent. He wrote for people hungry for moral clarity, for nostalgia, for a softer world.... It's just that he did not personally reside in that world....

> So far, four other women have publicly claimed that they had a sexual encounter with Greene, ...married for 31 years.... Says Neil Steinberg, a rival columnist at the Chicago *Sun-Times*...: "The defender of the purity of America [has] been using the [*Tribune*] newspaper as chick bait for 25 years." (Amanda Ripley, September 30, 2002)

The consummate irony and hypocrisy in Greene's sexual relationship with a teen-aged child—for which he admits guilt—are found in his accusing Otto Kirchner of "child abuse" for claiming his son after the Supreme Court decision. If the *Tribune* knew of his transgressions at the time, would the editors have fired Greene...years before the Baby Richard case? Would the newspaper have printed his more than 100 moralistic columns about Richard? If they had known of Greene's misconduct, would other members of the media and the general public have reacted in the same way and accepted his distorted take on the story? Would he have been a Pulitzer Prize finalist in 1998 for columns on children whose lives, in his opinion, were mishandled by the judicial and welfare systems?

Most people expect, or demand, their standard-bearers and spokesmen for morality to "walk their talk." In "Columnist Bob Greene resigns amid scandal," *USA Today* declares, "When it comes to ethics in the news business, a rule of thumb for journalists is: Don't do anything you wouldn't want to read about on the front page of your newspaper. The *Chicago Tribune* actually states that in its ethics policy...." (Peter Johnson, September 16, 2002). The *Tribune*, his 24-year employer, published in its Sunday edition—**on page one**—the notice, "To our readers.... Greene's behavior was a serious violation of *Tribune* ethics and standards for its journalists. We deeply regret the conduct, its effect on the young woman and the impact...on the trust our readers placed in Greene and this newspaper." (Ann Marie Lipinski, September 15, 2002)

Within a moral climate of scandal at the presidential level during the Clinton years, lawsuits against alleged pedophiliac Catholic priests, and daily front-page headlines filled with serious human failings and corruption, we all tend to become jaded. Greene's offenses seem minor to some, but their compelling significance relates to the obvious hypocrisy in his self-proclaimed role as the voice of voiceless children abused by the "system" vis-à-vis his own admitted sexual misconduct with a teen-aged child.

Today, having lost his journalistic forum through the *Tribune* and widespread syndication, Greene is unlikely to renew his maniacal Baby Richard marathon in response to this book—the other, quieted side of the story. In a safer world for the child, we are now able to disclose the stories of the main characters of "Baby Richard."

When I became the psychologist and therapist for the Kirchner parents and Danny after the Supreme Court ruling, I was considered to be "on the wrong side" by Greene. Swept into the debris created by Baby Richard hysteria, I received hate mail and threats; required additional police surveillance on both my home and my office; and, at first, lost clients and then my practice. I became part of the collateral damage. The most altruistic involvement of my career—I did all of my work on a *pro bono* basis—led to significant loss and a major life-style change.

However, it has also meant a special, ongoing relationship with Danny and his family, one that is unique and irreplaceable, as we have become family for each other. The 1997 *London Times* article accurately quotes me as saying that I would never do it again: "You can only give totally, emotionally like this, one time in your life."

If given a choice today, in spite of everything, I would do it all again.

This reality book attempts to set the record straight by presenting the true, untold Baby Richard story. It reveals the behind-closed-doors view of the child with his birth parents, as well as the effective parenting that resulted in his amazing adjustment; tells the stories of his father and mother; and dispels the myth of "Richard," a symbol and fairy-tale figure, in favor of the genuine child, Danny. Catapulted by editorial fantasies and imaginings into a pathetic figure, a curiosity, and a doomed victim, Danny not only survived but thrived in his real, private life. Deserving of a book in his own right, apart from his celebrity, Danny is a shining example of the resiliency of children, especially those who are loved and cherished, and of personal triumph.

This book is not intended to discredit or demonize the Warburtons, but simply and belatedly to effect journalistic balance by presenting the other side of the bitter custody struggle and its aftermath. They were involved in fashioning the lie, when Danny was four days old, intended to convince his father that the child died shortly after his birth, and they paid the court-imposed price of returning the child to his birth parents. The Warburtons have enjoyed the benefits of long-duration financial contributions from the public; of *pro bono* representation by one of the largest law firms in Chicago; of services by a public relations agency that shaped and advanced their image; of powerful allies in all three branches of state government, including in the governor's mansion; and of ongoing, supportive media coverage—all, unfortunately, at the expense of Otto, Daniela, and Danny Kirchner. In contrast, the Kirchners had a fledgling, storefront lawyer; little money, which they lost on the custody fight; with the media, only limited, occasional, and amateur representation that necessarily focused on damage control; and a flood of hate mail and death threats from a media-manipulated public.

Having led ordinary lives in oblivion, the Warburtons were propelled into the national spotlight by their intransigent fight to keep Otto and Daniela Kirchner's child. Suddenly they found themselves rubbing elbows with the governor and legislators, while First Lady Hillary Clinton, prominent journalists, movie stars, and other celebrities publicly championed their cause. While the child lived with them, the Warburtons were the recipients of street-corner, tin-can collections and solicited mail-in contributions from across the country to their Baby Richard Fund. Riding the crest of the wave of public sympathy and support, they announced their intention to establish a foundation "for children," within days of the United States Supreme Court's ending their legal options by declining their appeal of the Illinois Supreme Court ruling. Later, taking advantage of the first anniversary of "Richard's" highly-publicized transfer, they launched the kidsHELP! foundation at an event peopled by media representatives, politicians, and other prominent people. They created new opportunities for themselves while their currency with the public was running high. They formalized and capitalized on their perceived victimhood when the timing was ripe—fighting for Richard, losing at the U.S. Supreme Court level, and the first anniversary of losing the child.

For years, colleagues and friends have encouraged me to write this book, but my memories were too raw until now. After the Kirchners visited me this past summer for their two-week vacation, I felt deeply that my gains and theirs have finally exceeded our losses, not in monetary value, of course, but in the ways that count during a life review. From 250 pages of professional notes, a pile of newspaper articles so high that it would be considered a fire hazard in some households, a collection of videotaped programs, and vivid, full-color memories, I am now able to present our story.

Exclusive interviews with Danny Kirchner (f.k.a. Baby Richard), Judge James Heiple, Neil Steinberg, Jeffery Leving, Bruce Boyer, and many other principals in the story—conducted during 2002-03—have brought a special dimension and newly revealed information. The young woman responsible for the screeching halt to Bob Greene's career came forward, at the eleventh hour, to disclose details important to her, as well as her feelings, in an exclusive interview for this book. I am grateful to all of these individuals for their courage and candor.

Perhaps as a cathartic project to replace the career that I lost and to effect closure, this book enables me to share with others—with the permission, support, and encouragement of my clients, all three of the Kirchners—our private and public journeys together. Hopefully it will serve to demythologize the most publicized adoption and custody battle in history and to restore the image of Baby Richard's Danny to his rightful position as the normal, well-adjusted, happy, lovable—and loving—child that he is today.

The Transfer

There is always one moment in childhood when the door opens and lets the future in.

— Graham Greene

MILLIONS are watching as his adoptive mother carries the four-year-old child from their front door across the lawn, both of them sobbing and clinging to each other. At the street curb, his natural father takes the boy in his arms and places him into the waiting van.

Baby Richard met his father, Otakar Kirchner, only one hour before, when Otto and his wife Daniela, the boy's birth mother, walked through an agitated, shouting mob into the adoptive parents' home, and the couple saw their son for the first time. Before today, Otto and Daniela knew what he looked like only from a handful of photographs, recently provided them by Robert ("Jay") and Kimberly Warburton after they lost the last stage of the long custody battle in the Illinois court system.

Inside the house, the Warburtons had introduced the child to his biological parents, "This is Mr. and Mrs. Kirchner; you remember, we told you about them." Significantly they did not say, "This is your mother and father."

Dozens of television cameras and newspaper photographers, invited by the adoptive parents' representatives, capture the heart-wrenching scene, which is telecast and published across America and in other countries on several continents. Gathered around this most-publicized custody transfer in history are hundreds of reporters, strangers, neighbors, friends and relatives of the Warburtons, and uniformed police officers. Some of the onlookers jeer; some hold signs indicating their protest; and some call out derogatory and hateful names that are directed at Otto. A huge hand-written sign, "THIS IS CHILD ABUSE," leans against a nearby tree. "ASK RICHARD" and "REMEMBER RICHARD" appear on several of the placards being waved in the air by angry protesters. "Since when is true happiness judged?" appears on another sign, intended to address the Supreme Court decision. Reverend Fred Ade from St. Peter's Lutheran Church emerges from the Warburtons' house in order to calm the crowd, to encourage non-violence and restraint, and to request prayers for the child. Otto is prepared for a physical attack or even an attempt on his life, likely a shooting, but he has decided to risk his own safety as the price of his long-awaited introduction to his son.

"Monster!" is the most frequent epithet shouted by the mob. "Do you know what hell is? You're going there!" "Go back to where you came from!" "Bastard!" Spitting and sputtering their outrage, the men and women shout as Otto and Daniela, looking straight ahead, walk past them into the house. Otto is wearing his dark gray suit, a white shirt, and white-and-black striped tie; Daniela is dressed in her three-piece red wool outfit—pants, sweater, and matching large-lapel coat. They look their best for this first meeting with their child. Sharing the same values about attire, they wear clothing that reflects their deep-seated respect for the occasion.

At the street curb in front of the house, Baby Richard's bicycle, toys, and clothes are clustered together. By 2:35 p.m., Jay and Kimberly Warburton began carrying the items for viewing and waiting. The boy's silver bike, with training wheels, sits next to a blue toy box, suitcase, duffel bag, and a basketball and net. Among his toys is a blue stuffed frog with dangling hind legs. Exposed to the public through a dramatic removal ceremony, it is a pathetic display of the child's possessions. Yet, it is also an acceptable offering to the rolling cameras while the reporters and restless mob wait one hour for the emergence of both sets of parents and the four-year-old who has been turned into a curiosity and a pitiful victim.

The adoptive mother carries the boy through the front door to the street, at which point Otto takes his son into his arms. Shouts of "Monster!" fill the nearby air. What is the child thinking? Could these strangers be angry with him and calling him a monster? He knows the meaning of the word. Children of all ages are weeping, covering their eyes with their hands, and grabbing for their parents, who also weep and moan; some participants sink to the ground.

For days, weeks, and months, the picture of Richard in the arms of his weeping adoptive mother is displayed in newspaper columns and on television screens as reporters keep the story alive. The public, it seems, cannot get enough of this saga of a beautiful, blonde, brown-eyed, four-year-old boy from suburbia, wrenched from the arms, the home, and the love of the only mother and father he has known. The Warburtons are a church-going, WASP couple with a seven-year-old biological son of their own, Johnny. Jay, 38, is a fire fighter, and Kimberly, also 38, a mother, homemaker, and paralegal. The Kirchners are foreigners, immigrants from the former Czechoslovakia. Otto, 38, is currently unemployed and Daniela, 27, works as an esthetician. Baby Richard was born in March 1991; Daniela and Otto were unmarried and estranged at the time; and the Warburtons took the child when he was four days old through a quick, easy process arranged by their attorney. It was an "independent adoption," absent the benefits of counseling or the services of either a public or a private adoption agency.

The press has championed the Warburtons' cause since early in the custody battle, which began when the child was only 57 days old, although a large segment of the public believes that Otto only recently arrived on the scene. The Kirchners have been criticized and vilified as daily fare in the newspapers and on the airwaves, through subtle depictions and graphic assertions about their alleged unfitness to parent their biological son. Otto has been portrayed as inappropriate father material, labeled as "only a sperm dad," and Daniela as the callous woman who did not want her child.

Although reporters and journalists from across the country covered the case, step by step through the court process, the anti-Kirchner campaign was created, fostered, and advanced by *Chicago Tribune* columnist Bob Greene, who wrote many dozens of articles about the story. His editor called Greene "obsessed" with Baby Richard, and Greene was even censured by the respected *Columbia Journalism Review* for his over-the-top manner of commentary. The *Review* points out that Greene was hiding in the basement of the Warburtons' home on the day of Richard's public transfer to his parents. Many—if not most— journalists and reporters sought and received their "information" about the case from Greene, whose columns were syndicated in nearly 200 newspapers around the country, thereby spreading his bias against the Kirchner parents in a geometric progression through publications, radio broadcasts, and television programs in all fifty states.

Baby Richard's transfer to his father, telecast live and replayed across local, national and international channels, is anything but spontaneous. A Hollywood movie producer could not have staged the scene better, with the possible exception of adding musical background with violins and oboes. The event occurs on April 30, 1995, "a gray Sunday, chilled by a cold wind," at 3:00 p.m., the time selected by the adoptive parents. Capitalizing on Sunday afternoon as the ideal time for family television viewing, one of the Warburtons' cadre of attorneys— on behalf of her clients—invited the media to attend the send-off of Baby Richard. That morning attorney Laura Kaster held a press conference—in plenty of time for the media representatives to appear en masse at the mid-afternoon spectacle—at which she issued the invitation for them to attend and cover the story. "...[W]e think that Mr. Kirchner should not be shielded from the eyes of the world in doing this horrible act," Kaster announced in a righteous attempt to justify the wide-scale participation by the media, which opposing attorney Loren Heinemann labeled "atrocious."

This child's first moments with his natural parents play out amid a hostile, moaning, and voyeuristic audience—displaying "ghoulish curiosity," according to one columnist—and in front of a large contingent of aggressive, scrambling reporters and rolling cameras. "The crowd outside the O.J. trial has been dignified by comparison," *Chicago Sun-Times's* Richard Roeper would write, pointing out the similarity of the Warburton-created, "grotesque" scene to a sleazy movie.

"Their [Warburtons'] explanation that they had hoped to scare Kirchner away with the public scene does not hold water," the managing editor of Press Publications would publish. "The tireless Kirchner would have walked over broken glass or hot coals to get to his son at that point." ("'Richard' deserves a break," Kevin Beese, June 23, 1995) The "dog-and-pony show," as Heinemann termed it, was planned to shame and punish the Kirchners, at their child's expense.

The Warburtons—appearing ever-virtuous and donning the cloak of anonymity through use of their pseudonym "Does"—lost custody of Richard in the Illinois courts because of their complicity in the deception upon which his adoption took place. They were participants in creating and approving for his father the lie that the child died minutes after his birth. The reporters, however, ignore this fact in their coverage of the soap-opera-like transfer, even though it formed the basis of the court's decision to overturn the unlawful adoption and to award custody to Richard's natural father, the victim of the deception. This bizarre omission of such an important finding related to the case is an astounding example of emotionality overwhelming the reality of facts. It is also a prime example of media manipulation. If the full truth were told, would the adoptive parents have planned the transfer of the child in the same way? Would it have been perceived by the media and the viewing public in the same way?

Having lost at the Illinois Supreme Court level, the adoptive parents have in fact decided to take their case to the public. This is their last hope of forestalling, preventing, or overturning the Court's order directing them to turn over the child to his father, whom they had never even attempted to contact regarding their proposed adoption of his son.

The distressing sight of a mother losing her son is the focus of all cameras today, with replays to follow for a long time to come. Kimberly Warburton hands the weeping little boy to his father, assisted by a neighbor woman who pries Richard's hands from his adoptive mother's neck. The cameras move closer. Kimberly whirls around to her husband, the helpless Johnny at his side. Jay wraps his arms around her as she backs up to him, her eyes closed while she continues to face the sea of cameras. After her anguished expression is captured on film, she wheels around and races back into the house, leaving her distressed, wincing husband and forlorn son on the front lawn for more coverage.

Few recorders of the scene capture the joyful expression of a father in his first embrace of his son or of a birth mother in this long-sought reunion. Otto places the child inside the maroon minivan onto his mother's lap; follows him into the vehicle; and the driver, Otto's attorney Loren Heinemann, drives away to take Richard to his new home.

No one asks why, or if, a loving adoptive mother and father would arrange for such a large crowd, hissing and jeering, at such an important, frightening, and pivotal time for the child. No one asks why a mother would carry a big four-year-old boy instead of allowing him to walk the few steps to the curb, or why he is not carried by one of his natural parents, who are walking the same short path as well. No one asks why the newspaper picture that becomes an icon consists only of mother and child instead of father and son. Before this small group emerged from the Warburton home, Kimberly insisted on carrying Richard in front of the assembled crowd and media cameras to the waiting van. Otto and Daniela acceded.

No one asks why, or if, loving adoptive parents would orchestrate such a dangerous, dramatic, and traumatic separation of mother and son in front of hundreds of nearby gawkers and countless witnesses by television. No one asks why this transfer is so abrupt rather than progressive, as urged and planned by the Kirchner parents. No one seems to know, or remember, how or why the two months of efforts by a three-member team of mental health practitioners went so wrong and dashed the Kirchners' hopes of a pleasant, gradual transition of their son.

It was live; it was dramatic; it was painful to watch. One of my male clients described the scene, "Like an accident that you pass in your car; you don't want to look but you can't help staring at it." A female client described her reaction as extreme: "I couldn't stop sobbing all day; I couldn't eat my dinner; and it was difficult to sleep at all that night or the next, with the image of that poor child in my mind."

"Watching it was agonizing. It was supposed to be agonizing," *Chicago Tribune* columnist Eric Zorn would describe the event. "It was a horrifying moment, however orchestrated, of pure human pain...."

"According to my sources, the Warburtons and their supporters had for weeks been plotting to turn the transfer into a public spectacle," Richard Roeper would write on May 2nd. "That way they could continue to portray themselves as victims and complete innocents, and the Kirchners as cold and uncaring monsters." Roeper continues: "That was not a spontaneous demonstration.... Nice job of comforting the kid in his most vulnerable moment, folks." ("Adoptive Parents Took Low Road in Send-off," *Chicago Sun-Times*)

It could have been different. It could have been private. It could have been safer, dignified, more comfortable, less frightening, and more caring for the little boy. It **should** have been all of these things. And the media coverage could have been two-sided rather than bordering on hysteria and despair. The father's story could have been told. The story of the birth mother, who now, at long last, would be able to parent her child, could have been told. Balanced journalism is touted as the ethical standard of the industry. The Baby Richard case became the notable exception, and, in this country, the father's story—and the mother's—would remain untold. The controversy of a father's rights versus an adoptive mother's doesn't play out well for the father with the American public, especially when the conflict is shaded by a layer of xenophobia.

"If it bleeds, it leads," according to the old media adage. In this case, "If Richard cries, that flies..." onto front pages of newspapers and into lead stories of newscasts everywhere. Although several cameras capture footage of the child, smiling and holding his father's hand at the other end of the transfer one hour later, the weeping-child segment from that afternoon prevails across the airwaves. The public was left with no closure, no relief from the alarming portrayal earlier in the day.

Days before this most public of private events, the Kirchners' representatives—attorney Heinemann and I, as the psychologist who would be working with the child—pleaded with the Warburtons and their attorneys to transfer Richard in the privacy of a church or another home, away from reporters, onlookers, and strangers. The best interests of the child, we argued, would dictate that he be protected from a threatening and dangerous public event. The Warburtons refused and continued with the arrangements that ensured this as "the most publicized child custody battle of the century," fought as much in the press as in the court system. It would also be fought for a longer duration in the media than in the courts and in the opposite direction from the court rulings for the natural father.

The ripple effects of this Sunday afternoon would become wide and far-reaching for many lives. No one foresaw or predicted its lasting impact.

For years "Richard" would be forced to face a myriad of special challenges on a daily basis because of the continuous adverse publicity. He would be denied a private, normal life because of the media-generated toxic environment in which he was compelled to live, while his birth parents continuously struggled to shield him from harm and humiliation.

People everywhere would react to the case in ways that would reflect their own "unfinished business," their own emotional pain, their own personal histories. "Baby Richard" would become a type of Rorschach test—a larger-than-life version of the mysterious, evocative ink blots—eliciting in individuals various mixtures of suffering, fear, rage, sadness, and hatred.

"We don't see things as they are, we see them as **we** are [emphasis added]," said Anais Nin, the French-born American writer. Her insight would be proven accurate in the Baby Richard saga.

The Warburtons would be portrayed as tragic victims. Monetary contributions, which began by overt solicitation months previous to the final court decision, would continue and increase. They would benefit from a variety of collections in various names, among them the Baby Richard Legal Defense Fund, the Doe Family Support Fund, and the Warburton Family, the last of these undertaken and led by a Los Angeles talk show host. Bolstered by an outpouring of national public response, the Warburtons would begin fund-raising campaigns for children, the first launched soon after their legal options died at the U.S. Supreme Court level and another—named kidsHELP!—on the first anniversary of the highly-publicized transfer. They would continue to elicit and receive donations from a sympathetic public. Although they would work for new legislation for adopted children and other more nebulous goals, their ostensible and short-lived efforts would prove unsuccessful if measured by any tangible outcome.

Otto and Daniela Kirchner would receive an outpouring of hate mail and death threats from the public, spanning many months and requiring them to make "Richard's" safety the first priority in all of their decisions. They would live with the constant fear of a kidnapping attempt or other physical violence directed at their son. Dozens of anonymous hate letters would threaten to harm them or their child, in revenge for their having claimed him. Many would express the hope that their son would die, or disintegrate emotionally, as fitting and just punishment for his father's having taken him from his adoptive parents. The Kirchner parents would continue for years to struggle to overcome the pervasive effects of the four-year custody fight and of the vicious, biased attacks on them by a large segment of the media. Otto would continue to be unable to obtain employment, and they would be financially devastated. They would forfeit their social life and retreat to their home as a sanctuary from the hostile outside world. They would separate for several months, and Daniela would attempt to restore her legal parental rights to her own natural son, with disastrous results. Only the Kirchners' determination, steadfast courage, and intense love of their son and family would ultimately salvage their otherwise crippled, nearly destroyed lives.

The judge who authored the court decision that awarded Baby Richard's custody to his father would be forced to resign as Chief Justice of the Illinois Supreme Court in lieu of impeachment proceedings against him. The public outrage directed at him would be widely attributed to his role as draftsman of the unanimous (7-0) Baby Richard ruling. An otherwise reputable newscaster would display the judge's home telephone number on television in order to excite and direct the public's rancor against him. "I am still considered to be an enemy of children and anti-adoption," Judge James Heiple would tell me in 2002, after his retirement from the Court. "I received a bushel basket full of hate mail, including threats to my life, and at my home we received dozens and dozens of angry, vile phone calls while my wife was on oxygen and dying of fibrosis of the lungs."

The attorney who represented Otakar Kirchner in the custody fight for his son would lose his license to practice law. Publicity from the case would prompt a horde of new clients to seek him out for representation of their marital and custody disputes, so many that he would become unable to follow through on their behalf. A series of formal complaints against him would result in his forfeiting his license as the better alternative to the probability of the Illinois Supreme Court's publicly ending his legal career.

Another attorney, Bruce Boyer, Law Professor and long-standing child advocate at Northwestern University, self-initiated aggressive involvement in the Baby Richard case at the Illinois Supreme Court level on behalf of Otakar Kirchner. "I was alarmed at the lower and appellate courts' decisions," he would explain to me in 2002. "Their rulings for the Warburtons were in conflict with Constitutional protections of parents' rights to their children. If allowed to stand, those rulings would have led to wealthier parents' successfully claiming for adoption the children of poorer parents, simply by asserting a 'best interests' standard." To this day, according to Boyer, because of the Supreme Court ruling the rightful standard prevails, requiring that unfitness as a parent first needs to be proven before the "best interests" of the child are addressed to determine custody. A parent's child cannot be taken from him/her for adoption until that parent is proven unfit. Only then can the question be raised, "What are the child's best interests for custody?"

Adoption agencies across the country would formulate new policies and revise their informational materials to explain to worried, prospective adoptive parents the facts of the Baby Richard case and the laws upon which it was decided. Many people would opt to pursue adoptions of children from other countries rather than risk a "Baby Richard outcome."

Lawmakers across the nation would pass state legislation directed at preventing other "Baby Richard" cases. Although advocates for a federal adoption law would grow in number and intensify their efforts in the wake of "Richard," adoption would remain subject to state law with fifty different versions. Sixty percent of the states would adopt paternity registries, requiring mothers formally to attempt to locate and notify biological fathers about their newborn children as a pre-condition to adoption proceedings.

Politicians and celebrities, including movie stars, talk show hosts, and disc jockeys, would devote themselves to public attempts to remedy "the Baby Richard tragedy" through his return to the adoptive parents. These campaigns would span more than two years.

The United States Supreme Court would decline to consider a series of appeals of the case by the Warburtons, even after an unusual and ultimately unsuccessful campaign, on a nationwide basis, of citizens' signed petitions to the Court. The petitions would be circulated around schools, colleges, shopping malls, and workplaces with the expressed purpose of convincing the nation's highest court to undo the state court's Baby Richard ruling for the father.

The Illinois Supreme Court would intervene, within a matter of hours, in the lower court's unlawful **reopening** of the custody issue in 1997. Daniela's filing a petition to obtain a birth certificate for her son and to restore her parental rights after two years of raising him would prompt the grandstanding judge to "put everything back on the table." Although swiftly saved by the high court, she would retreat from her futile attempt because of bizarre repercussions.

Bob Greene of the *Chicago Tribune* would continue to lead and promote the anti-Kirchner campaign on a regular basis, to the point of "journalistic terrorism," the term used in the court ruling by Illinois Supreme Court Judge Heiple to describe Greene's "spread of so much misinformation." National sentiment would be "overwhelmingly on the side of the Warburtons," as assessed by *People* magazine. "**Everyone** would have an opinion," according to television's *Dateline*, and "mostly in favor of the adoptive parents."

Greene wrote seventy columns about Judge Heiple, relentless and critical—turning him into a controversial figure and a household name. The Judge became the lightning rod for public outrage on behalf of the unanimous Court of seven judges when he authored their decision. "Ironically, Baby Richard was among the easiest, least complicated cases in my thirty-year career as a jurist—it was a slam dunk, a direct application of law," Judge Heiple would tell me in an exclusive interview after his retirement. "But it was the most monstrous in terms of adverse publicity and the effects upon my reputation."

As Otto, Daniela, and Judge Heiple—among others of us—would learn, reputation is a great deal like Humpty Dumpty. Once broken, all the king's horses and all of his men surely cannot put it back together again. When a person attempts to restore his/her reputation, it's much like attempting to answer the proverbial question, "Have you stopped beating your spouse yet?" Neither "yes" nor "no" is a helpful answer, and the defensive posture into which one is cast only adds to the intensification of the damage.

As the psychologist employed by the Kirchners to assist with Baby Richard's transition and adjustment to them and to his new home, I would be forced—years before scheduled or age-eligible—into an unwanted, unplanned retirement.

The most recent public chapter of the story would be the forced resignation of Bob Greene from his 24-year career at the *Chicago Tribune* for "sexual misconduct and other indiscretions." Greene, incorporating his own idiosyncratic, obsessive bias, as well as lies, distortions, and fantasy material, wrote more than 100 columns about the Baby Richard story. He would repeatedly accuse Otto Kirchner of "child abuse" for complying with the Illinois Supreme Court decision to take his son and to parent him. On September 15, 2002, the *Tribune* would announce Greene's termination for sexual relations with a teenager, whom he met in connection with his job and about whom he wrote in one of his columns. The incident, admitted by Greene, occurred years **before** his morally self-righteous, highly indignant—and outrageous—four-year coverage of Baby Richard.

This untold, inside story of Baby Richard is a saga of betrayal and recovery; of the powerful and their victims; of the morally or otherwise corrupt and the courageous; and of apparent victories versus genuine triumphs. It reveals the roles of the court system, media, members of the legal profession, mental health professionals, and the public in this case, which took on epic proportions and became a modern myth. It is the story of a child who was treated like currency in a long, painful drama that played out in a variety of forums and of his metamorphosis from victim to victor amid the spoils....

When I accepted the job of psychologist and therapist for the Kirchners and their young son, I did so with two mutual conditions. Of necessity, their condition was that I provide services on a *pro bono* basis, as they had no money for professional fees. Mine was that I remain anonymous and avoid dealing with the media. The first condition would work out fine, as I would

The Private Side of the Transfer

"MY NAME IS DANNY!"

"Baby Richard" becomes a very real "Danny" to his parents, Otto and Daniela, during their 40-mile van ride to his new home in Mokena, Illinois. Called "Baby Richard" in the court documents by appellate court Judge Rizzi, who opted to use the name of his law clerk instead of "Baby Boy Janikova" (Daniela's maiden name), the child was given his legal name, "Daniel," shortly after his birth. He corrects his parents when they call him "Daniel," explaining that he likes to be called "Danny." Otto and Daniela, with Danny sitting on his mother's lap, smile over his head at each other and rejoice over his first communications with them as their son.

There is double irony in the child's name. First, his adoptive parents appropriately shielded him from the press, and the public neither saw a picture of him nor knew his name during his four years of anonymity. Yet, on the day that he is unveiled to an international viewing world—with the incumbent vulnerability and danger inherent in such widespread and dramatic exposure—his real name is also revealed, published, telecast, and

We are linked by blood, and blood is memory without language.

— Joyce Carol Oates

broadcast throughout the United States and other countries on several continents. Second, the adoptive parents named the child "Daniel," although they distanced themselves—and him—in every other way from his birth mother "Daniela."

Today unaware of the profound ramifications of this most public and controversial event, the Kirchners, on a daily basis across future years, would continue to live in fear of an attempted kidnapping of Danny and of physical violence. They had no way of knowing that this was not the end but only the beginning of their fight to obtain a normal family life with their son.

The ride back from Schaumburg, the sprawling Chicago suburb where Danny and the Warburtons were living, is different in every way from the trip there. Otto and Daniela are no longer tense and apprehensive; they are no longer childless; and they are relating as parents for the first time with their son, who has lived the past four years without knowing about their existence...until the past few hours. Loren Heinemann, who led the legal battle, is witnessing the culmination of his work by serving as the driver of the borrowed minivan, taking Danny "home"; he is feeling fulfilled and proud of his role. Adrienne Drell, reporter for the *Chicago Sun-Times*, is concealed inside the van as a witness for the Kirchners; she seems excited to be an insider to this event and is no longer worried about being discovered as a secret passenger. Adrienne will be the only journalist to observe the intimate details of the Kirchner parents' and Danny's first hours together. She is audiotaping these hours as evidence of the events as they unfold. The Kirchners may need the tape in the future if—within the current, prevailing atmosphere of bubbling hostility directed at them—there are charges filed against them for child abuse.

"I have never in my career seen such viciousness among my media colleagues as in this case," Adrienne would tell me. "It's unbelievable how biased they are, how angry they seem to feel, and how much they hate Otto Kirchner."

The Schaumburg authorities provided a police escort for the Kirchners on their ride to the Warburtons' home. Roads leading into the surrounding neighborhood were blocked off. Along the route, hundreds of people gathered, many wearing blue armbands and holding signs intended to show their disapproval and spell out their objections. For several miles, large baby-blue ribbons were tied around curbside trees, telephone polls, fence posts, and stop signs in a community-wide protest of the transfer of Baby Richard to his father.

On the reverse route, a caravan of media representatives in their vehicles, their cameras poised or rolling, follows the Kirchner van in the hope of capturing newsworthy pictures.

Inside the van, Otto puts his arm around Danny and hugs him. Both father and mother assure him that they are his parents and that they love him. He stops crying.

"Are you hungry?" Otto asks him.

"Yes," Danny responds; "I like the food at McDonald's." Otto directs Loren to go through the drive-in aisle of the nearest one, which appears in sight within seconds.

The parade of media vehicles follows them into the restaurant's drive-in lane and waits in line until the Kirchners receive their ordered food. The van's occupants, including Danny, laugh at the incongruity of the situation. The teen-aged attendant in the restaurant window must think they are celebrities. Smiling and nodding, he hands them chicken McNuggets and french fries, after which their van drives away, continuing to lead the unwelcome but determined entourage toward their home.

Sharing in the excitement and sense of relief, Otto's mother— holding her hands to her face—is watching the transfer of her only grandson on her television in Canada. Daniela's mother will also witness the telecast scene this evening in Slovakia. Both grandmothers may well be the only ones ever to witness their initiation into grandparenthood on international television. They both weep…, an ocean apart but united in their joy.

Days before, the Kirchners invited me to join them on their trip to get their son. I declined for two reasons. First, I clung to the belief that the Warburtons would not choose to turn the transfer into a media event, and the fewer people there, the less frightening and the better for Danny. They had stipulated that **only** Otto and Daniela would be allowed inside their home. I had informed the adoptive parents, on behalf of the Kirchners, that they would be allowed visitation with the child after his transfer if it was private, safe, and dignified. I had offered my own home or a church of their choice as the site of the transfer. If it became a media circus, especially at their arrangement, then it would be difficult, if not impossible, for the Kirchner parents to allow them visitation, as their ill intentions would be revealed. Although the Kirchners and I discussed and prepared for the eventuality of a mob scene, I predicted that the Warburtons would certainly choose "the higher path." As the proverb goes, I could not have been more wrong.

Second, I had committed to accompany my husband Robert on this Sunday afternoon to a reception for Charles Ferro, the retiring president of Morton College in Cicero. Ten years earlier my husband had been president of the college for a span of four years. Robert and Charles, then the academic dean, became good friends across years of daily working together.

Our plan today is for me to join the Kirchners as they arrive home with Daniel after an envisioned private, dignified, and pleasant introductory visit in the Warburtons' home. We planned their first approach toward the child and anticipated Daniel's reactions, talking about the possibilities with a mixture of excitement and trepidation across several days, including the previous Saturday night. Otto and Daniela were apprehensive but resolved; sorrowful over the many failed attempts to effect a gradual transition of Daniel to their home and their care; and prepared to deal with any challenge. The Illinois Supreme Court had ordered the adoptive parents to hand over his son to Otakar "forthwith," and it is now more than three months later.

If only the adoptive parents had allowed Otto and Daniela to meet their son, they would have waited patiently before taking him to live with them. The Kirchners had hoped for a series of visits, trips to the park, picnics, and other outings before effecting a change in the child's residence. The Warburtons' consistent refusal to allow a meeting—proclaiming "He's not ready"— prompted the exasperated Kirchners into an "Enough is enough" decision. Even if the Warburtons won the final round of the court battle, the June 1994 Illinois Supreme Court ruling irrevocably established Otto's rights to a relationship with his son—mandatory visitation, at the least—from that date forward. During the intervening ten months, the adoptive parents refused to allow the child to meet his birth parents. They kept insisting that the child did not even know that he had been adopted by them, thereby precluding the possibility of a meeting. This was the pivotal, critical conflict point that resulted in the sudden transfer of the child.

Having been at the reception for only fifteen minutes, I am approached by a college administrator who informs me that the handoff of Baby Richard has been telecast live on television just minutes ago. After offering brief apologies to Robert and the honoree, I leave immediately to drive to the Kirchners' apartment. Under these unpredicted, disappointing circumstances, I feel that I must get there as soon as possible to begin my work with the child and his parents during their first hours together as a family.

"We were on TV!" shout two children as I walk toward the door of the sprawling apartment building. It is one of nine multi-unit, brown-brick buildings, built around a pond, in Mokena, a safe, quiet southwestern suburb of Chicago. Across the street are acres of cornfields; the town, with a population of 10,000, is growing but still has a semi-rural feel to it. Adverse to publicity and controversy, the Mokena public library has recently removed a window display about Baby Richard, considering it inappropriate. Gathered on the concrete sidewalk are six boys of various ages, most of them jumping up and down, and all of them beaming smiles. "The cameras **just** left," announces ten-year-old Justin, who introduces himself.

Loren Heinemann comes out of the Kirchner apartment to greet me in the lobby in order to brief me about the pick-up of Danny and his current status. He describes Otto and Daniela's experience inside the Warburton house, Danny's meeting his parents, the good-byes, the mob's angry and threatening behavior, blue-ribboned trees, police escort, and McDonald's stop.

"To my amazement," says Loren, "Danny stopped crying seconds after he got inside the van. He was then silent while Otto and Daniela tried to engage him by asking questions, to which he gave only short, one-word responses. I told them that everyone could be silent and that would be okay. Then Daniela started playing with some toy dogs, treating them like puppets, and she began singing a song from *The Lion King*. She made a mistake in the song, and Danny corrected her. That seemed to break the ice; he laughed and so did she; and then he began talking more.

"By the time he exited the van, in front of the television cameras, he was smiling, holding his father's hand, and walking cheerfully into the building. He's now happy and unwrapping his toys. When he saw his bedroom, he just said 'Jeez!' and really seemed to like it."

Inside the two-bedroom apartment are Otto, Daniela, Danny, Adrienne, and a photographer named Dominic. Loren leaves to rejoin his own family; it has been a long, tense day.

Eager to meet him, I enter Danny's bedroom and find him sitting on his king-size bed, reviewing an assortment of toys and stuffed animals piled all around him. Clad in a red nylon jogging suit with black and white trim, he is an attractive little boy with military-cut blonde hair and big brown eyes. He is smiling and saying, "Jeez; I never had this before; this one is like Stevie's...." I realize that I am witnessing Danny's first comparisons between this place and his former life.

I introduce myself as "Karen." I don't want him to think that he needs a "doctor" or that there is anything wrong with him. The Kirchners and I are prepared to communicate, in a variety of subtle ways, our expectation that he will adjust well to these loving parents and this nice, comfortable, and safe home. He continues to play, picking up Power Rangers figures and toy cars.

His new bedroom has bright white walls, newly painted; beige wall-to-wall carpeting; and *101 Dalmatians* on his bedspread, walls, and window drapes. There are two large, white-laminate shelf units across from his big bed and a floor lamp, and a similar shelf unit on one side of the bed with a small table on the other. The shelves display dozens of items that Otto and Daniela have bought across four years to prepare for their son and to keep themselves believing that one day he would live with them: Dalmatians of various sizes, a Santa Claus, a dinosaur, other colorful stuffed animals, and theme figures from a series of recent children's movies.

A basketball hoop is visible in the closet, not yet hung on the wall. I learn that this was one among a large pile of Danny's belongings that the Warburtons had set out by their street curb for the photographers to film while they awaited the emergence of the child. Loren packed the boy's possessions into the van while Otto and Daniela—having been directed by the Warburtons' attorneys to enter the house alone—walked through the jeering, street-filled and front-yard mobs and sideline police officers. The Warburtons reportedly encouraged the morning churchgoers to attend the transfer event and passed out maps to their house.

"Why did they drop all of his things along the street for pick-up today if they intend to see him later?" I ask Otto. "Why would they expose his private possessions to the media and a gawking gathering of people in this way rather than delivering them later in a safer, more respectful manner?"

Otto shakes his head, lost for an answer.

"There are no medical records or any other documents for Danny among these things," he laments; "he came with no written history. We'll need to get them as soon as possible." I am thinking that medical records are not photogenic or dramatic; they would not evoke from a viewing public as much sympathy as the sight of his bicycle or toys.

Loren described the cluster of curbside belongings as having looked like a humiliating display of the ousted possessions of a rent-delinquent tenant who has just been evicted by an angry landlord. "It looked like he was being kicked out of the house along with all of his stuff," the attorney observed with disgust in his voice when he greeted my arrival.

Adrienne is writing an article for tomorrow's *Sun-Times* on her laptop computer at the dining room table. "Danny started cuddling with his mother in the van after only minutes; it was amazing," she tells me. "It made me marvel at the power of the biological bond, that instinctive connection between human beings who are related by blood, like we often see in the animal kingdom."

Dominic snaps some photographs and then leaves. Danny emerges from his room and moves around the apartment, looking inquisitively at everything. The living room, with standard-apartment white walls, is furnished with a long, black vinyl sofa and matching armchair; shiny black tables; and a large black shelf unit that houses the electronic equipment, including the television, stereo, VCR, and Nintendo computer set-up. Large black-and-white pictures of ballerinas adorn the walls. The beige carpeting lends some color to create a cozy room, brightened by sunlight through the sliding glass door during the day and by a floor lamp at night. The dining room, an extension of the main living area, holds a shiny black table with four matching high-back metal chairs. A small, typical-apartment galley kitchen adjoins the dining room, with a wide pass-through area between them. A small bathroom and sparsely furnished master bedroom complete the residence.

Danny touches the couch and the chair as he walks by them for the first time. An inquisitive inspector, he stops to survey the electronics, and his gaze settles upon the Nintendo remote control, with which, we soon discover, he is already adept.

He returns now and then to munch on one or two of the french fries on the living room cocktail table. Otto and Daniela are transfixed. They watch Danny with smiles and with frequent looks and knowing nods at each other. They are joyful. As we planned, they let him take the lead as he explores his new surroundings. They answer his questions and point out that these things are now his.

When it begins to get dark outside, Danny returns to his bed and begins to gather together his new Power Rangers toys and a few other presents. Otto and Daniela are by his side when he announces, "I'm going to take these home." Otto asks him if he would like to talk to Johnny. Danny continues to sort his toys and Otto repeats his question, to which the child, without looking up, answers "Yes."

"Of course, no problem; you can speak to him," declares Otto, who gets the portable phone from the kitchen and dials the Warburton home. Jay answers; Otto explains that he is calling "for Danny, who would like to speak to John." He hands the phone to his son.

"Hi, I got Power Rangers and...," Danny mentions a string of his other new toys. "My room is nice." He listens to what John has to say and then, without a goodbye or other words, he hands the phone back to his father. Otto explains to Johnny that Danny just stopped talking so that the boy does not think that anyone has interfered with the conversation.

Jay asks if Kimberly might speak to the child. Otto agrees, hands the phone back to Danny, and tells him, "Your mommy wants to talk to you."

Danny takes the phone and repeats the same conversation that he had with John. Then, once again, without a goodbye or other closing comment, he abruptly hands the phone back to his father. Otto tells Kimberly that Danny has returned to his toys and that they—the two sets of parents—should talk again later, perhaps tomorrow.

Otto and Daniela chat with Danny about his toys and his room. Although I talk to him also, I am careful not to interfere with his interactions with his parents.

An hour after his phone conversation, Danny announces, "It's dark; I want to go home," and he begins to cry. He sits silently on his bed and tears roll down his face. Otto and Daniela sit on the bed with their son between them.

They explain to Danny that they love him, that they are his "real" parents, and that they will take good care of him always. They tell him that he can see his "other parents" and brother when he asks to see them. Otto takes out his wallet and shows Danny a picture.

"See…, I always carry a picture of you with me, and you only do that when you love someone," he says. "I will never let anything bad happen to you. Please give us a chance, Danny; just give us a chance. We won't do anything that you don't want us to, and if you want something, we will get it for you. If you don't want to be hugged, we won't hug you, but if you want us to, we will. You just tell us what you want."

As I listen from the hallway to their conversation, I am thinking about the sign on the wall of a local family restaurant. "A father is someone who carries pictures where his money used to be," it reads. I realize that this bit of homespun irony is not only facetiously but also factually true in Otto's case.

Daniela leaves the bedroom to get the family album that she has prepared and returns with it to Danny's side. She and Otto explain to him a few photographs of themselves. "This picture was taken when we were married," Daniela says. Danny looks down at it and then up at each of his new parents. They show him photos from their honeymoon and early marriage.

I remain standing outside the bedroom door, listening so that I can counsel them about their next conversations. Adrienne listens also, as the door to the bedroom is open and she is sitting nearby.

Daniela picks up a framed photograph from the shelf and holds it in front of her son. "This is me, Danny, when I was nine months pregnant with you. This is my big stomach and here is you," she continues, as she points to the picture. Danny takes it in his hands and stares at it for a long time. He stops crying.

"Look at how much we look alike," Daniela continues; "we have the same hair, same mouth, same smile. You are my son…, **our** son."

"Why didn't I see you before?" he asks, looking first at his father and then at his mother.

"We wanted to see you **very much.** We were fighting to see you and to have you with us, but we had to do this in the court, and that takes a very long time. We have **always** loved you." Otto finishes his simple explanation and asks Danny if he wants to play a Nintendo game in the living room.

Danny jumps off the bed; heads for the television set in the next room; and begins to play a computer game. Otto and Daniela follow him; they both sit on the floor next to him, one on each side, and praise him for his skill. Genuine and frequent praise will continue to be a primary goal in their interactions with Danny. He is very intent, focusing on the screen while he manipulates the remote control. I realize that his parents are encouraging his play on the computer instead of risking his seeing himself on the television evening news.

Danny returns to the last of his french fries, still on the cocktail table, and has a few bites. He begins to play with his new remote-control-operated plastic car. Soon, inspired by this smaller one, he climbs into the nearby colorful, child-size car and starts riding it up and down the hallway until he has mastered steering it, after which he climbs out to look for another toy.

Danny begins shooting a toy gun that emits harmless sponge discs; starts aiming at us; and we all begin to duck away from the soft missiles with dramatic gestures. He laughs each time that one of us fends off the flying discs, and I marvel at his comfort level.

It's Christmas for Otto and Daniela. This is the day they longed for this past December, when they had not yet even seen a photograph of their son. This is the day they talked about more often than the weather, sharing their imaginings with each other about how it would be for him and for them.

Danny begins using "My room" when he refers to his bedroom. When I pick up one of his stuffed bears and start talking about it, he proclaims, "That's **my** bear." I am pleased that he is expressing and asserting himself; I am even happier that he is identifying these things as his own. He appears to be giving his parents "the chance" that his father begged of him.

Out of his hearing, Otto, Daniela, and I discuss the importance of letting him have his own feelings, whatever they are, and encouraging him to express them. I advise them to be natural, honest, and positive in their communications.

Today Otto and Daniela begin their pattern of allowing Danny to eat where and how he would like. During his first year with them, he would eat at the kitchen table or elsewhere—at the cocktail table or on the floor in front of the television or a computer game. He would eat as much or as little as he wished. His parents would avoid engaging in power struggles over household rules that appear insignificant when compared to his comfort-level and autonomy in his new surroundings.

"Everyone was crying in the Warburtons' house today," Otto tells me out of Danny's hearing. "It must have been very frightening for him. Jay said to me, 'Do you want to put him through this?' while he pointed outside the front window at the mob. It was like blackmail! Well, Danny can relax now. It will be safe and peaceful for him here."

Both Otto and Daniela speak by phone with their mothers to tell them about Danny. Otto's mother, living in Toronto, explains that she witnessed the hand-over of her grandson live on TV; she is upset and worried. What will this mean for his safety? What will it mean for the family's privacy and well-being?

Adrienne leaves at 8:30 p.m. with her article complete for tomorrow's edition of the newspaper, and Loren returns for another short visit.

"I need to calm my nerves," Loren sighs as he enters. He reports to us that he's gotten thirty-seven death threats on his answering machine at the office since shortly after 4:00 p.m. He paces back and forth in the living room, sipping an alcoholic drink that Otto has handed him.

The attorney informs us that he has issued a press release this evening. In newspapers tomorrow, it will be published:

> The problem which has arisen is that the Does
> [Warburtons] continue to make attempts to re-try the
> case they lost in the courts through a well-orchestrated
> media campaign.... We beg and beseech everyone to
> allow Mr. and Mrs. Kirchner to get about their lives and
> to allow them the time to set their family in order.

When I leave for the White Hen Pantry on an errand, I see a media van still parked at the street curb with a camera in the window, pointed at the front door of the apartment building. It would be there for several more days, arriving in the mornings and staying until dark. I decide that I will do all of my work with Danny and his parents in their home rather than my office. Danny's safety and privacy are at stake, and I don't want him to get the message that he needs to be taken regularly to a doctor for his emotional state or to be "fixed" in some way. In light of the frightening drama surrounding his departure and arrival experiences, I am not willing either to create or to risk additional fearful activities for Danny in their aftermath.

When I return with milk and a couple of food items, Danny is sitting between his parents on the living room couch. They are watching a videotaped movie, Disney's *The Lion King*.

Daniela asks Danny if he would like to get into his new pajamas and he replies, "No." She says "Okay" and they continue to watch the screen. Danny looks tired. He is leaning against his mother, his head on her shoulder, and his eyelids look heavy. He is starting to blink into sleep.

After whispered good-byes between us and expressed assurance that I will return tomorrow, I leave at 10:30 p.m. Danny is looking peaceful and content; Otto has his arm around his son; and Daniela is resting her hand on his head. *The Lion King* music plays.... "The Circle of Life".... "Can you feel the love tonight?... It is where we are." Such a fitting theme for this lovely scene. To me, this is the picture of a typical family, such as would be observed in thousands of other households, but it is neither expected nor taken for granted by this unique, newly formed, little family. Otto and Daniela sit very still and speak in hushed tones, afraid to awaken their son.

The next morning, immediately upon awakening, I would telephone Daniela. Danny fell soundly asleep in his clothes on the couch, with his head on a pillow that she brought from his bedroom. She and Otto debated as to whether she should let him sleep in his clothes or change him into his pajamas. They decided to put on his pajamas because, they reasoned, his father is a sound sleeper and he would probably be like his father. Danny never awoke; they carried him to his new bed; and he slept through the night. Daniela slept with him so that she would be there in the event of his awakening before morning.

I remember wishing that I could share with my clients—especially with those who described themselves as tormented by the television image of Baby Richard earlier that day—the cozy family scene that I witnessed that night. It would have comforted them.

While we had expected a quiet, caring exchange of the child between two sets of loving parents, working together to relax and comfort him, and a tearful, traumatic first night with a frightened child, we experienced the opposite. The transfer itself was so "scary" that Danny—sensing that his other home had turned very bad, with weeping parents inside, and "mean," threatening strangers all around—happily settled into the warm, soft, and safe comfort of his birth parents.

As mothers and other sensitive souls everywhere wept or, fearful of nightmares about Baby Richard, tossed and turned in their beds, Danny Kirchner—lying next to his birth mother overnight for the first time—enjoyed a deep and dreamless sleep.

CHAPTER THREE

My Story

Remember the good old days when only God could end the world?

— Anonymous

APPROACHING my home in the dark by turning onto Old Creek Road, I realize that I can't remember any of the 15-mile route that I have just driven from the Kirchners' apartment on their first evening together as a family. I have been engrossed in a reverie of thoughts about how I wound up as the psychologist and therapist for Otto and Daniela...and, now, for their newly arrived son Danny. As a private person who shuns public notice and dreads public speaking, I am committed to a whirlwind case of unprecedented media blitz, local frenzy, and national controversy.

Like the vast majority of my colleagues, I usually meet new clients when they walk through the office door. I seldom make home visits apart from the process of conducting child custody evaluations for the court system. This, however, is a unique, unforeseen set of circumstances, and I have met my new child client, now a celebrity, in his new home only five minutes after his first arrival there himself.

Minutes ago—after a six-hour visit—I left a little "instant family" that now includes a four-year-old child who has arrived with a largely unknown history as part of another family and neighborhood. I have been unable to reference any other cases of a child this age who is returned to his birth parents after so long a period in adoption. We will have to find our own way with Danny and meet his needs as they arise.

The Kirchner parents and I had hoped to effect a gradual, progressive move of Danny from his Schaumburg residence. We had decided on a tentative plan that included visitations and outings between parents and child across weeks or months.

The Illinois Supreme Court ruled in January, by granting a writ of habeas corpus, that the child be handed over to his father "forthwith." Since then, three painful months of efforts to begin the gradual process of bonding between parents and child have resulted in nothing more than Otto and Daniela obtaining a handful of photographs of Danny during February. They had not been allowed by the Warburtons to meet him, see him, talk to him by phone, or even send gifts to him on his birthday on March 16th. The adoptive parents insisted that they had neither yet told Danny that he was adopted nor that, living nearby, he had biological parents who loved him.

In late April, when it became apparent that there was no movement—not a single measure or action that involved Danny himself—toward compliance by the Warburtons with the court order, the Kirchners decided to get their son. The decision came as a surprise to me and, in fact, to themselves as well. Otto had announced in July 1994 that he wanted, at all costs, to avoid a Baby Jessica transition, which had been a recent public scene of a weeping child returned to her birth parents in front of menacing media and whirling cameras. Exhausted and desperate, Otto and Daniela had come to believe that their only hope to establish a relationship with their son was to remove him from the uncooperative, resistant adoptive parents and to become a family-in-process.

Loren Heinemann contacted the Warburtons' attorneys to demand compliance with the Supreme Court decision and to insist that they set a date and time—within 72 hours—for Danny's transfer to his parents. The adoptive parents' attorneys then arranged for the media circus, and the viewing world watched the pathetic spectacle as it unfolded.

Now I am committed to Otto, Daniela, and Danny as never before. They will need someone they trust to help with their adjustment to each other, especially in the wake of the frightening mob scene, the public scrutiny, and the acrimony through which they have come together.

"How did I get here?" I ask myself, reeling over the realization that I am a sole practitioner whose primary job is to assist this child—now widely perceived as more a part of the public domain than the son of two birth parents—within his new, unfamiliar family constellation. I know this is already the most publicized custody dispute in history. I wanted to work as one of the three-member team of mental health professionals that had been approved by both sets of parents in February. We did work together for weeks; successfully arranged for the four parents to sit at the table with us and with each other to begin to talk about Daniel; and collectively fashioned the Story that the child would be told about his adoption.

Then, when nothing more was happening and one member of our team left town for days—contrary to his promise to remain available—the process went awry. If only a timeline or date had been set for the achingly anxious birth parents to meet their son, they would have been willing to wait for custody, but the psychiatrist and the Warburtons refused even to discuss the matter "until later." Otto, feeling disappointed, discounted, and betrayed, fired the absent psychiatrist through Heinemann; and both he and Daniela asked me to work, without assistance from the other two, with Daniel and themselves.

I resolved to do my best and, as they requested, committed to work alone...unless, of course, Daniel would require psychiatric intervention in addition to my services as a psychologist. According to Illinois law, psychiatrists (who are licensed physicians) prescribe medication and oversee hospitalization of their patients, when necessary or advisable, while psychologists (who have earned doctorate degrees) specialize in verbal therapy, counseling, behavior modification, and similar interactions and interventions with their clients.

I know that I will need to address this situation in new ways, not only because of its unique circumstances but for Danny's safety.

During my ride home, I find my memory spinning into a life review, prompted by the intensity and anxiety of the day's events.

My own father, Rudy Meier, was an immigrant from Germany when he was eighteen years old. His parents Otto and Erna, his younger sister Edith, and he left their country of origin to escape the escalating Hitler regime. Living in Chicago with an uncle, he soon met my mother, born in this country to parents who had come from Hungary. She and her family were his new neighbors; she taught him to speak English; and they became sweethearts. Several years later they married.

Because he never spoke about his early years in America, I sensed that they were difficult. For most of his life, he worked in a bindery, beginning as a machine operator and, after years, earning a promotion to plant superintendent. He worked hard until he reached retirement age, but he died of cancer before having the opportunity to enjoy his planned leisure years.

"You're foolish for taking this job for no money," I could hear him saying in my imagination. "Foolish" had been one of his favorite words, and I am wondering if this attitude would be proven right.

My mother, Irene, worked as a secretary to top-level managers for most of her career; today she would be called an administrative assistant. She stayed home with me and my sisters for only brief periods of time, immediately after each of our births. When I was a teenager, she bought and ran a neighborhood secretarial service agency. Later, when I was well into adulthood, she divorced my father, after a thirty-year marriage; moved to California to start a new life; became a real estate agent; and met a life-long bachelor, whom she married within months of their first meeting. She always valued working and balanced her career and family at a time when all of my friends had at-home mothers. I was the exception and would later realize that she became a role model for me in my own zealous pursuit of a fulfilling career.

My childhood was uneventful except for the birth of my sister Jo after nearly a decade of enjoying life as an only child. Then, during my senior year in high school, when my focus was on shopping for luggage for my freshman year at college, my sister Lynda was born. We were like three different families because of our age differences.

It was an uncomplicated time in LaGrange, a peaceful, pleasant suburb of Chicago—tidy lives in tidy houses—when we got our first television set. I was six; Elvis Presley gyrated, upper torso only, on *The Ed Sullivan Show*; and married couples on sitcoms slept in separate beds. I knew *Ozzie and Harriet* households within my own neighborhood. The media consistently observed a tacit gentleman's agreement for celebrities and politicians that some private topics were off-limits to coverage. Elizabeth Taylor and Richard Burton's affair rocked the world and put Cabo San Lucas, Mexico on the map. The nuns at my Catholic school wore head-to-toe black habits with long, clinking rosary beads—which pre-announced their arrival—hanging from their thick rope belts. They taught us to name our children after saints, to stand up in respect when the parish priest entered our classroom to distribute our report cards, and to hate Communism.

My parents' responsibility to me, as their child, was defined as feeding and clothing me and providing a roof over my head. My father regularly announced, "I don't owe you a good time," which reminder surprised me because I don't recall ever having requested a good time. Theirs was a duty-based, joyless attitude toward parenting, it seemed to me then in an amorphous way I could not express in words but felt deeply. I remember only rare and limited interactive time with either of them. My father took me to a child's rodeo once, and my mother and I occasionally played Canasta together after she taught me the card game one rainy day when I was home sick from second grade. These memories are vivid as happy exceptions to an otherwise solitary life as a young child.

For brief periods of time, I tried ballet, horseback riding, and a local "charm school," but failed to excel at any of these activities and soon lost interest. Because my friends were generally unwelcome in my home—with one exception, Carol, a polite, quiet, and overweight child who lived one block away—I spent most discretionary hours at the houses of my friends, where I felt more comfortable and relaxed. I spent so much time at Carol's home that her parents and two brothers joked that they mistook me for a piece of furniture in their living room.

I remember vividly the day my father declared that if I intended to go to college, I would be on my own. He was not about to support "that kind of foolishness for a girl." If I were a boy, it would be different. Girls, he explained, attend college and then just get married and have children, clearly making college a waste of both time and money. I was thirteen.

Although my father made good on his promise not to contribute toward my college education, I qualified for a full academic scholarship to Mundelein College in Chicago. Mrs. Pidcock, my guidance counselor, initiated both my applications for admission and for an academic scholarship. Because of her faith in me and her assertiveness, I qualified for a tuition scholarship that, except for a token amount, would cover all four years on the condition of my maintaining at least an A- grade point average. With a $500 high school graduation gift from my maternal great aunt and uncle, I embarked upon my college career. I also decided that I wanted to become a counselor.

Attending a Catholic women's college, I found it easy to focus upon my studies with little distraction from competing interests. It was a time when the mission of the institution included the inculcation of values as well as the teaching of academic subjects. "To show respect" for ourselves and our studies, we were required to wear dresses or skirts to classes and to the dining room, appropriately named the "Tea Room"—pants and shorts were forbidden.

To support myself, I got a job as the secretary for the Missionaries of Africa—"White Fathers"—a Roman Catholic order of priests. I purchased a used, low-mileage, pastel-blue Ford Falcon from their elderly housekeeper, and devoted 25 hours each week, between classes, to my work for the good fathers and their cause. The White Fathers—some of whom were black—collected money for the missions, recruited young men into the priesthood, and assisted parish priests with hearing confessions and saying Mass. Working through all four years of college for them, taking additional jobs in the summer, I graduated *magna cum laude*, with some money in the bank but few memories of a social life.

Along with most of my roommates and close friends, I married within months of graduation; it was fashionable to become engaged before or during senior year. Glenn and I had dated each other in high school and, except for a period of six months—when we dated others—all through college. We seemed so compatible at the time of my junior-year high-school homecoming dance, when we already spoke about marriage and started making wedding plans. He was a good-looking football player, a quarterback, and an attentive, loyal boyfriend.

Six years later, married and living together for the first time, things were different. He loved sports and watching football games all day; I loved to read and study. I enjoyed travel and eagerly looked forward to seeing the world; he was a self-proclaimed, committed homebody. My idea of a great evening was dressing up and going out on the town with good friends; he preferred visiting his family, at least every weekend. I loved his family, too, but I would have preferred our spending the second day of our honeymoon on a sun-bathed Caribbean island rather than under his parents' roof forty miles from our new apartment. I loved and welcomed change at every twist and turn of life; he boasted that he had not changed at all since high school. After three years of marriage, he was ready to start a family; that summer I graduated from Northern Illinois University with a master's degree in counseling and wanted to continue for a doctorate. Except for these differences, we had a lot in common! Our one shared interest was based upon our chosen vocations; we were both teachers and loved working with children, especially pre-teens and teenagers.

After an all-night, marathon discussion, we agreed to divorce. My heart was elsewhere and he realized it. We shared an attorney, avoided a bitter struggle, and within three months obtained an oxymoronic "amicable divorce." Except for one brief, harsh telephone conversation regarding division of property, we maintained a posture of civility, courtesy, and friendship. When we parted, he told me that he would ensure that our paths would never cross; it would be painful for him ever to see me again; and he would avoid any future contact with me. I never did see him again.

In spite of our mutual success at separating and divorcing without rancor, it was a painful event because I realized that he was a good person; we had become members of each other's families in every way; and the future seemed fuzzy. I threw myself into studying and decided to work toward becoming a psychologist, specializing in marital and divorce therapy.

On my own and living alone for the first time, I continued to work as an English teacher to support myself. Although I enjoyed the students, especially the challenging ones, I always had more homework than they did, and I felt consumed by the required paperwork and recordkeeping.

Before long I obtained a job as a high school counselor, with the goal of following the example of my champion, Mrs. Pidcock, and also immediately began work toward my doctorate, taking classes at Northern Illinois University during evening hours and on a full-time basis during the summers. Commuting thousands of miles to and from the university and eating countless, tasteless hamburgers en route, I earned my doctorate degree in counselor education within four years. After another year of rigorous study, while I worked full-time as well, I took and passed the two-day, written state examination to become a registered psychologist in the State of Illinois. Later, under new legislation, I would become a licensed clinical psychologist.

My graduate studies resulted in more than an earned doctorate. Along the way, Dr. Robert Moriarty became my practicum instructor and supervisor, during the last stage of my master's degree, and four years later he became my husband. Robert taught me how to be a good therapist; at first, he became my mentor and then my friend. For the first year of our relationship, after the practicum ended, we maintained contact only by telephone. Robert was tall, handsome, intelligent, soft-spoken, patient, and so perceptive of people's feelings that his master's level students thought that he could read their minds.

"Sometimes I think he knows what I'm feeling before I get there myself," Robert Parker, a fellow student, would say to me during class. Because the course was about feelings, personal discovery, and counseling skills, the experience was powerful and transforming for all seven of us.

As a member of the baby boomer generation, I subscribed to the principle of delayed gratification, pledging to hard work and rigorous study toward the goal of a better, more fulfilling future. "Life is not all play," my father's favorite motto, meshed with my mother's, "Life is so short." My life-script, I discovered during self-assessment, was destined to play out by my focusing nearly exclusively on work...until an early, perhaps untimely, death.

While I was working on my doctoral dissertation, Robert encouraged and then convinced me that I could and would succeed in completing the tedious, demanding project that—before the widespread use of computers—required hours of research in university libraries and of wholesale revisions done by typewriter. Writing my dissertation the old-fashioned way, I spent seemingly endless hours in the university media center, reading, researching, and copying relevant material. One brutally cold, dark, windy winter day, as I sat in front of an imposing stack of books, I was feeling weary, uninspired, and listless.

"Remember the good old days when only God could end the world?" Into the old, worn, wood table top, someone—perhaps a fellow traveler down the dissertation path—had etched these words. I realized, at that moment, that I am among the generation of those who have witnessed our planet's profound and pivotal transition to human control of its very destiny. That day I decided that I wanted to make a difference in the world, small or large, but for the better.

Along the way toward my newfound goal, I discovered that Robert and I thought so much alike that we could finish each other's sentences. We shared an interest in reading, travel, ethnic food, and exotic places. We had the same political beliefs, sense of humor, and basic philosophy of life; our eschatological views corresponded; and we enjoyed the same activities. We were also both workaholics and shared a consuming passion for our professional involvements. At night we would talk for hours, regaling each other with stories about our pasts and the day's events. In college we had both majored in English and minored in philosophy and psychology. We had earned the same master's and doctorate degrees at N.I.U. We had both started our careers by teaching high school English and writing; we were soon promoted to the position of high school counselor. We discovered that we had even held the same dual position—English teacher and counselor—at the same high school in Dundee, Illinois, but five years apart! Early in our careers, we both advanced into administrative positions.

I became one of the fortunate who marry the love of their lives.

In 1975, during a whirlwind seven-week period, I married Robert, changed my name, began a new job, completed my doctorate, and became the stepmother of three great children. Eager to be a stepmom, I looked forward to new relationships with Robert, nine years old; Bridget, seven; and Sean, six. They lived with their mother, but my husband had been granted the customary, court-approved visitation schedule via his divorce decree.

From the time we first met, Robert worked as a counselor and a dean at the community college level; taught graduate courses at the university level; worked in private practice as a licensed clinical psychologist; and became the president of

Morton College in Cicero and then president of Forest Institute of Professional Psychology. Our lives revolved around schools, students, family, and each other.

Across nineteen years in public schools, I held administrative positions in which I worked directly with children and families and also in supervisory roles. As the chief student-services officer and later as the human resources administrator for a large high school district, I had multi-faceted roles that ranged from approving educational programs for the district's handicapped children to hiring all of the schools' teachers.

My favorite task was always counseling kids and their parents. From our earliest days of marriage, Robert and I talked about someday becoming involved together in private practice as psychologists. He had enjoyed private practice and felt happiest when helping people work through their personal and family problems. I shared with him a love of making a real difference in people's lives.

At the end of an especially bad day at work for either of us, we would commiserate with each other and plan the time when we could start a psychological services agency together. Maybe near retirement age, we reasoned, we could leave the security of pensioned positions in the public sector to become more entrepreneurial, while also helping people in need of psychotherapy. It was our dream, nurtured across two decades.

"Life is a series of compulsory adjustments" became my mother's motto during her later years. It turned out to describe the events that followed for Robert and me....

In 1992, after having served for seven years as the president of Forest Institute, a not-for-profit graduate school that offered master's and doctorate degrees for psychologists, Robert was advised by his doctor to leave his position and stop working. His medical condition had deteriorated to the point of his becoming impervious to the daily prescriptions that he took to manage his disorder. He had been diagnosed as having narcolepsy in 1969 and, with his doctor's assistance, managed his symptoms across twenty-three years so successfully that he could work long days and irregular schedules, including eleven years as a chief executive officer. Now the statistical probability of disability, long before the typical age of retirement, had caught up with him. The choice was clear, the doctor explained: either increase his medication to dangerous levels or accept disability status. Because his longevity was at stake, we decided within minutes of discussion in the doctor's office that he would choose the latter option. He left his position as graduate school president that same week.

This "compulsory adjustment" swept us into a review of our life-style and career directions. The position that I held, assistant superintendent of my school district, had changed in recent months by the departure of a respected colleague from our four-member, cabinet-level administrative group and by the inclusion of an individual who began pursuing his own personal and political agenda. His presence was destructive to group morale and functioning. For more than a decade we had been a great team; I had loved going to work each morning; but— because of dissension created by this newly arrived colleague—every new day became a struggle.

Although I had invested years of study and hard work into obtaining my state certifications as a teacher, a counselor, an administrator, and a school superintendent, it was time to pursue a different path.

I decided to leave the school district, where I had been happy for twelve good, fulfilling years. Now that Robert was no longer employed, however, my departure would need to be well planned and gradual. I applied for a part-time position with a local agency of psychologists and became the only practitioner there with extensive school-related experience. At first I was assigned children and teenagers who were having problems related to school, as well as a teacher client who required an elaborate remediation plan to keep his job. Later I had clients of all ages, who came with a wide range of presenting problems. I soon realized that I enjoyed therapy more than my other, school-based work, and I eagerly planned for a future with only one job, one that I truly loved.

Working full-time by day in the school district, I spent several nights each week and Saturdays doing therapy. When I met people in my private life and began introducing myself as a psychologist, rather than as an assistant superintendent of schools, I realized that my own emotional transition was complete. I was not only using my expertise and license in psychology, but every day I found myself looking forward more to working with my clients. My employment in the school district became a means to an end. I knew early on that it would take years of work as a psychologist to reach the point of earning my school district salary and benefits.

For three long years, I worked at both positions, typically requiring seven days a week; I wrote reports and filled out medical insurance forms for my clients on Sundays. Robert helped me with a myriad of tasks, and we decided that, although prematurely from our original timeline, we would refashion our dream of private practice together. In between my therapy sessions with clients, I set about learning the business of running a psychological services agency. I spent time with the agency's managers, reviewing with them procedures for medical insurance reimbursement, billing, managed care requirements, and other business-related activities.

Working intensely, I learned as much as I could absorb and became ready to launch my own small agency, Moriarty Associates. I hired a colleague, Dr. Raymond Lechner, psychologist for a neighboring elementary school district, to work for us on a limited, part-time basis. Dr. Lechner was not only skilled in working with young children and their parents, he was also adept at educational diagnostic testing for children. In March 1993, Raymond, Robert, and I became our agency; Dr. Lechner and I doing therapy and testing; Robert completing the business aspects that are required of a private sector agency.

To save on overhead costs, I sought and found a suite of three rooms in a modern, architecturally innovative building that was available on a shared basis. A Chicago-based law firm, with its primary offices downtown, used the second-floor suite only occasionally for its south suburban clients. For my share of the rent, I had a private office for therapy sessions with my clients, the second office as a testing room, and a shared, professionally-decorated waiting room.

Teal green was the predominant color of the suite; the walls, carpeting, and chair fabric were of varying shades. I liked the color green, symbolic of growth and healing, and expanded it into my office. We painted its walls green; retained the existing carpet; added a bright teal sofa, two armchairs, a large desk with file drawers, and a rosewood credenza to hold supplies. A bright yellow, kid-sized table and chair set in the corner was added to enable our children clients to draw pictures while I could sit at their level. The best therapy with little ones, I found, occurs over crayons on an eyeball-to-eyeball basis. We incorporated a cheerful theme by adding chair cushions and sofa pillows in fabric covered with sunflowers; hanging pictures of the big golden-yellow flowers on the walls; and filling vases with them. An ever-present bowl of M & M candies completed the purposefully homey look and feel of the office.

During the day I often used the lunch hour at my school district job and after-work time to meet with local attorneys, particularly those specializing in divorce and child custody disputes. I decided that I would continue these introductory meetings until I had come to know at least sixty lawyers on a first-hand basis. We would mutually refer clients; they to me when their clients expressed a willingness to try reconciliation before pursuing a divorce and I to them when my clients decided that their marriage was unsalvageable and divorce their next step. This systematic, person-to-person effort became the most significant marketing approach for Moriarty Associates.

On a sunny afternoon in November 1994, during one of my last planned meetings with local attorneys, I sat talking with Gary Felicetti, an established lawyer, in his Orland Park office. Apologizing for not having much time to spend with me, he asked if I had ever met Loren Heinemann, "the Baby Richard attorney." I had not, although I was familiar with the case because it had received constant media coverage during recent months. Mr. Felicetti recommended that, using him as my referral source, I call to schedule an appointment with Mr. Heinemann, whose office was located in the building next door.

Two days later I followed up, as suggested. Mr. Heinemann was very busy but agreed to meet me. He rescheduled our appointment several times, but on November 28, 1994, we met together in his office for nearly an hour.

Loren Heinemann greeted me at his door, shook my hand, and invited me to an armchair in front of his desk. He was a burly man with a moustache, short dark hair, and wide-set blue eyes. Wearing the traditional attorney garb of a dark suit, white shirt, and conservative tie, he looked professional and yet slightly disheveled. He talked openly about himself, his family, and his law practice; he was relaxed, self-disclosing, and congenial.

I liked his sense of humor, and we seemed to connect on a personal basis. David Sterba, one of my school board members and also an attorney, was Heinemann's office-mate; they shared the rent and a secretary. Stopping by the office while I was there, Mr. Sterba offered facetious, teasing remarks about his colleague for my benefit and compliments about me and the quality of my work.

Loren and I lapsed into a first-name basis with each other, and we seemed to establish an instant rapport and sense of mutual trust. He talked candidly about the intensity and frustration of the Baby Richard case, which had already spanned more than three tumultuous years. He and Otto Kirchner, the child's biological father, had become close friends. His other business was suffering, Loren explained, because of the incredible time commitment involved in the Richard case.

Soon, Loren continued, a mental health professional would be needed to work on a gradual transition of the boy to his biological father's home and care. He expected the Illinois Supreme Court to rule soon on the "Does'" petition for a rehearing; in June the Court awarded custody to Otto; and he expected another ruling in favor of his client. Loren asked if I might be interested in working on this case, on behalf of the child and his biological parents. I told him that I would find this kind of work both challenging and rewarding, and I would be interested. I left, feeling good about our meeting together, but with the belief that the attorney was simply chatting about the Baby Richard case, not really interested in me as a prospective therapist for Otto and his child. We had just met, and I was newly transitioning from my public sector job and part-time therapy to full-time private practice on my own.

My school district's seven-member board of education was supportive when I proposed that I continue there as a consultant but leave my full-time administrative position for my private practice. They granted me a six-year contract as a salaried consultant, which enabled me comfortably to transition to the work that I most loved, psychotherapy.

During my last days at the school district, I was joyful and excited about my new venture. With three years already invested in establishing my own agency, Moriarty Associates was doing well. We had established a good reputation among a significant group of domestic law attorneys and neighboring school district personnel, who were our primary sources for client referrals. With little money for marketing our agency, we specialized in "word-of-mouth" advertising. Clients referred their relatives, spouses, and friends, and individuals who knew me personally, including many of the lawyers whom I had met during recent months, made regular referrals.

Across three years of part-time practice, I was working progressively more hours with clients, sometimes scheduling on Sundays to meet everyone's needs. Although my clients spanned a wide range of ages—from three to eighty—and presented a range of problems, I was specializing in marital and divorce cases and in child custody evaluations. Early on, a number of attorneys and Cook County judges recommended me as a private, independent child custody evaluator in cases that had become difficult and acrimonious. I prided myself in objectivity and thoroughness. Several of my colleagues in the area had come to be perceived as "hired guns," and many of the judges reportedly questioned the credibility of these practitioners. It is the judges who review the reports and recommendations of the practitioner-evaluators and occasionally hear their testimony in court but who ultimately make the custody decisions. In addition to psychological testing and interviews of all involved persons, I insisted on making home visits—which very few of my colleagues performed—and on contacting school personnel, babysitters, and other individuals who knew the children well before I formulated my recommendations to the court for custody and visitation. I also enumerated in my reports, which averaged 25 pages, all of the reasons for my recommendations. Although I anguished over each case, I felt comfortable that my final findings were well explained and my conclusions based upon the best interest of each child. The feedback I received from both the judges and the lawyers was so positive and affirming of my unique, comprehensive approach that I planned to specialize in child custody evaluations.

With specific plans and dreams for my practice, regular referrals, and a steady clientele, I worked my last day and said my good-byes at the school district on January 25, 1995. Removing from the office my last two boxes of personal items and three potted plants, I left with the proverbial "song in my heart." Feeling a greater sense of relief than sadness, I was eager to start a new life-style with wider autonomy and more time for my husband, prospective hobbies, and travel.

That night I shared private thoughts with Robert, who understood. I told him that I was comfortable in accepting that I would never again see my name in the newspapers, as I regularly did in connection with my district job. I would become anonymous, a private practitioner with a small agency and the opportunity to begin a hobby of some sort, for the first time ever, and to replace part of my usual seven-day workweek with a social life. Over a chilled bottle of wine we celebrated those words and the new plan for our future.

Four days later, on Sunday, January 29th, Loren Heinemann telephoned me at home and asked if I would consider becoming involved in the transition of Baby Richard to his clients, the Kirchners. On Wednesday, the Illinois Supreme Court denied the "Does'" second petition for a rehearing of the case; the Court's ruling of June 1994 granted custody of "Richard" to his biological father, Otakar Kirchner; and the Does were now ordered to turn over the boy to his father "forthwith." Only the United States Supreme Court could now rule otherwise, an unlikely event.

Loren clarified that, if I accepted this job, all of my work would need to be done on a *pro bono* basis, as the Kirchners could not afford to pay fees. He added, "You'll be on the wrong side in terms of money." I would learn later that although Loren had been paid a retainer by Otto Kirchner, as well as some fees during the first two years of the court battle, at the state Supreme Court level—when his client was both unemployed and broke—the attorney's services also transitioned to a *pro bono* status. I realized, during this conversation, that implicitly Loren was also inviting me to join him "on the wrong side in terms of public opinion."

Accepting the job and the condition Loren offered, I presented my only condition for him and the Kirchners. "I would like to remain anonymous and to have no dealings of any kind with members of the media, Loren," I told him. "I believe that I will be both more effective and more comfortable in my work on behalf of the child and his parents under the condition of anonymity."

Loren readily agreed. I would soon realize that he was enjoying his role as the sole spokesman with the media and that the publicity was generating significantly more clients for his law practice. I would also learn, weeks later, that he had solicited many other mental health professionals on behalf of the Kirchners but with no success. Apparently no one was eager to accept a job that would require an undetermined but lengthy process, spanning many hours of both weekday and weekend time, on behalf of a pervasively reviled client, and for no payment of any kind.

The next day Loren faxed me a letter of commitment that incorporated our agreements on behalf of the Kirchner parents and "Richard." He and I spoke by phone; we exchanged all of our telephone numbers and approval to call each other at home; and he promised that, as a two-member team, we would maintain frequent contact on behalf of our shared clients.

"Are you ready to become involved in the black hole of this case?" he laughed. I thought he was exaggerating, but I would soon discover the case to be all-consuming and seemingly endless.

"Hostage Retrieval": February 1– April 29, 1995

__February 1, 1995

AWAITING the arrival of Otto and Daniela, I imagine her to be short and stocky with dark brown hair, brown eyes, and rosy cheeks. I have seen Otto many times on television and in newspaper pictures, and I know that I would readily recognize him if we passed on the street. He is a big man, both tall and heavy-set, with shaggy but short, straight brown hair, brown eyes, and a full face. He has a boyish look

A therapist's work is never over. Which isn't to say that patients don't get better. But the bond forged... —the relationship that develops when private eyes peek into private lives— can achieve a certain immortality.

— *Jonathan Kellerman*

but also premature facial lines that appear to reflect the hardship of recent years, during which he has fought in the court system for paternity rights to his son.

Long before my involvement in this case, I felt genuine sympathy and deep compassion for a man whose sincerity seemed so apparent. He loves his biological son, whom he has neither met nor seen, to the point of risking and losing everything and becoming a public hate figure. If his name comes up in a group discussion among my friends, several—if not most—of the participants express a level of rage that I have rarely witnessed in a discourse about current events. It is more like the reaction of an intimate, personal conflict than of an armchair view of a custody dispute between two sets of parents, all of them strangers. The frequency of media coverage, however, has eroded the feeling that these people are strangers; they seem more like members of an extended community in which every person has a stake.

At 2:30 p.m., as scheduled, Otto and Daniela walk through my office door and we meet for the first time. Otto had asked to change the session from 6:00 p.m. so that it would precede his press conference. Perhaps he does not want the press to follow him to my office and thereby discover my identity as the newly designated Baby Richard psychologist.

In stark contrast to my expectations, Daniela is no less than stunning. She is tall, thin, and willowy, with an hourglass figure, long, straight blonde hair, and bright blue eyes. She is wearing an all-black outfit—pants, boots, turtleneck top, and a vest with gold braid trim. She has a flawless, porcelain complexion, which I remind myself is not surprising because she is an esthetician by profession. She is self-possessed, graceful, calm, and sure of herself; not the insecure, defeated, anxiety-ridden person that I expected to meet. She looks and moves like a model.

Otto looks as I expected, except perhaps a bit larger in my small office. He is wearing a black and white checked suit, white shirt, and white-and-black striped tie. I sense that they have dressed in their Sunday clothes, prompted by their shared European values that reflect respect for me and my position. Few of my clients dress up for their therapy sessions, and even those who come directly from work appear more casual in their attire.

They seem relaxed and happy, not surprising in light of the one-week-old Illinois Supreme Court decision, issuing a writ of habeas corpus, which directs the Does to turn over his child to Otto "forthwith." Otto and Daniela sit close to each other on my couch and hold hands, or Otto shifts into resting his arm around his wife's shoulders, as we talk.

"This experience has brought us closer together," he explains, "but it has been very painful for both of us. Daniela was hurt by being made out as the bad person in this case, so much that she stopped reading the newspapers and watching television accounts."

While Otto does most of the talking, Daniela's face is animated. She smiles and nods in agreement at key points in his explanations. He appears to be the dominant partner in their relationship. He has also been the sole plaintiff in the lawsuit because Daniela signed away her parental rights.

Otto continues to talk about the basics of their relationship, its ups and downs, and their reunion and mutual fight to recover their son.

"This entire experience was like being dead for four years. It ruined my 'American dream,'" Otto declares. "Now we have hope.

"I can't live without my son," he continues with deep conviction. Otto explains his early longings for a relationship with his own birth parents, from which sprang a life-long commitment someday to have a family of his own to replace the anguished separation that he endured from the age of four well into his adulthood.

"After sixteen or seventeen years, I saw my father for the first time," Otto tells me. "I could never let that happen to my son. In my dreams and in my brain," he continues, "I keep thinking about what those people told Daniela—their reason for adopting was because their son wanted a brother to play with. It's a strange reason to me. I hope my son is not a second-class child in that house."

Otto pauses and then adds, "I feel like someone stabbed me from front and back. This is God's will—the Court's decision. I had rights to my son in June and we still haven't even been able to see a picture of him."

Otto explains that he and Daniela have voluntarily decided to exercise restraint by waiting for professional advice regarding the best process and timeline for meeting their son and becoming a new family. They devoutly hope for cooperation on the part of the Does, and they are both willing to suspend their feelings of anger in order to do whatever is best for Daniel.

Daniela concludes simply, "We are so happy that we will now see our son and have him with us."

As they prepare to leave after our two hours together, Otto assures me that he is pleased that I will become involved in the transition of his son. "I always preferred a woman to do this work," he says; "I think a young child relates better to a woman than to a man." They are interested in my having a great deal of personal contact with Daniel, and they want help in informing him about his birth history and their long fight for him.

The Kirchners hope to have their son within a matter of days.

As they leave, I realize that both Otto and Daniela are emotionally exhausted from their nearly four years of fighting through the court system for their child. "Their pain comes from their toes," according to the old saying, it is so deep. I hope for them that they will soon meet their son.

"Take good notes!" Loren Heinemann advises as we shake hands after our meeting in his office. He anticipates probable allegations of child abuse directed at his client some time in the near future. There is not much left in terms of realistic possibilities for court rulings for the adoptive parents in their determination to keep Otto and Daniela's son.

"If they allege abuse, they might keep their fight alive," he tells me. "Your notes and observations may become critical in our defense of any such allegations."

During the last week of January, the Does' attorneys petitioned Justice John Paul Stevens of the United States Supreme Court to grant a stay of the Illinois Supreme Court's January 25th order for them to turn over "Baby Richard" to his father. Judge Stevens, a Chicago native and the justice assigned to handle such appeals from Illinois, denied the request only one day after its filing and through a "rare weekend court order," according to the media coverage. The Does immediately presented the same petition to U.S. Supreme Court Justice Sandra Day O'Connor, the only justice still on the court who voted to delay enforcement of the Michigan

Supreme Court order two years ago that turned over "Baby Jessica" to her birth father.

The Does also agreed to produce one photo of the child for his father in a private session held in the chambers of Cook County Circuit Court Judge Stephen Yates. Requiring Otto to sign a statement that he would not show the photographs to anyone (except Daniela), they finally produced fourteen pictures of the child for Otto and Daniela in the privacy of the judge's chambers.

As I read the newspaper coverage about the photos, I was surprised that the adoptive parents retained full control in spite of the Supreme Court's precise, same-day ruling, ordering them to hand over the child to his father. "You are hereby ordered and directed to surrender forthwith custody of...Baby Boy Richard... to petitioner Otakar Kirchner," the majority wrote to the Does. Yet, days later, these people presumed to insist upon a written agreement signed by the father as their condition for merely showing him the first photographs of his son.

This past week, Governor and Mrs. James Edgar issued public statements requesting Otto to leave his son with the Does until he is grown. Brenda Edgar's letter to Otto, on the official stationery of the Executive Mansion, was photographed—like a historical document of special prominence—and reproduced in the newspaper. Her follow-up statement reiterates her position, "They're [the Judges] convicting a four-year-old child who committed no crime. That's not just." She reaffirms her appeal to Otakar Kirchner to "be a hero" and give up his son to the adoptive parents.

All aspects and angles related to Baby Richard are splashed across newspaper headlines, television newscasts, radio broadcasts, and talk shows. Every day during the latter part of January the story has been featured and highlighted.

A sole voice calling for a swift transfer of Baby Richard is reported—the advice of Lucy Biven, the therapist who supervised the successful transition of Baby Jessica to her biological parents. "It is an unpopular view, but swiftly is best," the Ann Arbor, Michigan psychoanalyst's recommendation is quoted by Adrienne Drell in the *Chicago Sun-Times*.

Across these media-saturated days, Loren Heinemann and I speak frequently by telephone to discuss the adoptive parents and their apparent, continuing refusal to become engaged in a process of transition. Loren believes that they provided his clients with the few photos of Daniel as a means of forestalling any real movement.

"It was as if they should be grateful and satisfied with finally seeing what he looks like," Loren tells me, "so now Otto should just wait and go away for a while."

Loren, on behalf of Otto, offered the Does visitation rights as a voluntary concession by his client, as well as a gradual transfer of custody of the child, if the adoptive parents would drop further legal appeals. The Does swiftly rejected the offer.

Loren informs me, "Otto and Daniela feel a strong rapport with you and they believe that their son will be comfortable with you also. They definitely want you to work with them and with him in the transition."

__February 7th

Otto and Daniela cancel their scheduled session for today because of Otto's "whiplash." He is suffering from a stiff neck and severe pain, Daniela informs me by phone. They both attribute his condition to the massive onslaught of media and public reaction directed against him during the past several weeks. They reschedule for next week.

__February 13th

Today the United States Supreme Court votes 7-2 (Justices Sandra Day O'Connor and Stephen G. Breyer dissenting) to refuse to grant a stay of the Illinois Supreme Court's order for the Does immediately to turn over Baby Richard to his father. The Does' attorneys announce that they still intend to petition the U.S. Supreme Court to overrule the state court's decision regarding the custody issue once the state court issues its written opinion. Such a petition will constitute the Does' **fourth** trip to the nation's highest court, which refused to take up their first appeal in November 1994 and has now twice rejected their petitions to stay the writ of habeas corpus.

__February 15th

Two men, private investigators, are reportedly making inquiries about Otto's character and personal background, according to the newspapers. The Does' lead attorney, Jerold Solovy, refuses to comment on any aspect of their litigation strategy. Ivan Kenessey, owner of the closed-down Chicago restaurant at which Otto worked most recently, was visited in his Hinsdale Cypress Restaurant by the two investigators. Peter Stanga, owner of the Riverside Restaurant, at which Otto worked during previous years, was also contacted for information. "Maybe one in 150 cases an investigator is used in an adoption or custody dispute," Joan Grant, a member of the state Bar Association's Family Law Council, is quoted as saying. (Adrienne Drell, "Richard's Dad Says 'Does' Have Hired Private Eyes," *Chicago Sun-Times*) It appears that the Does, in search of discrediting information, are preparing for more challenges to Otto....

__February 16th

The Kirchners arrive for their two-hour session looking calm and upbeat. They are both dressed entirely in white, looking like they might be ready for tennis.

"They have an investigator asking my friends questions about me," Otto says, shaking his head. "They're trying to get some kind of information to use against me. They say they will cooperate but there is no sign of any cooperation."

"We cried when we saw him," Daniela relates, alluding to the photographs of Daniel. "It looked like he was wearing poor clothes—maybe hand-downs from the older boy—and he had a terrible hair cut," she continues. "But he was beautiful," she murmurs with a tone that communicates a mixture of reverence and awe.

"It was incredible to see him for the first time," Otto exclaims, his eyes moist. "He looked so big, and it reminded me of everything in his life that I missed."

We discuss the various possibilities for the transition of Daniel. Otto and Daniela fear prospective renewed litigation by the Does. Both express their achingly intense desire to have their child with them and to begin to parent him.

"We trust you," Otto announces. "We want you to be the primary person to work on the transition." The three of us talk about involving other mental health professionals in the process. I encourage them to invite competent and caring individuals to work as part of a transition team on behalf of their son.

They discuss with me the development of their relationship. Otto has his arm around Daniela as they sit comfortably on my teal couch. "I met Daniela and I got crazy," Otto confesses in an attempt to summarize his feelings.

"Are you still crazy?" I ask.

"Yes," he confirms, with a smile and a nod toward his wife.

__February 21st

"Daniela is pregnant!" Otto proclaims as they enter my office today.

They are both enthusiastic over the prospect of another child. I think to myself, how sad and ironic it is that they have not yet been able even to meet their first child and now they are so excited about another birth. Fortunately, this one they will be able to share together, and they will have the opportunity to function as parents from this baby's first days.

They describe a freak automobile accident that Daniela had on her way to work this past Saturday morning. The steering mechanism malfunctioned, causing her car to spin around 360 degrees into the oncoming lane of traffic on the expressway.

"She was lucky she didn't have a serious injury and that another car didn't hit her head-on," Otto says. He suspects foul play; their car is accessible to anyone with malicious intent as it sits in the large, open parking lot in front of their suburban apartment building. It wouldn't take much for someone to sabotage their car under cover of night. Otto adds that recently they found marks, like gashes from a knife, along the exterior side of their sliding-glass patio door, as if someone had been trying to pry open the door and break into their apartment.

Daniela is afraid that their baby will be affected by her accident. She is suffering some symptoms of a problem, she tells me.

"I am getting scared about our son, too. I don't know when we will be able to see him," she says, her voice breaking. I realize that her heightened anxiety has understandably generalized to a variety of concerns in their lives. They are both visibly stressed and worried.

__February 23rd

"Daniela miscarried yesterday," Loren informs me by phone.

He and I speak nearly every day, calling each other at all hours. Loren encourages me to call the Kirchners to offer emotional support. "They are grieving their loss," he tells me; "they wanted this baby so much."

We also talk about involving other mental health professionals to work on the transition of Daniel. We both believe that a team approach is best. Daniel will soon be four years old and there is no precedent for us to consider for a child of this age to transfer to his birth parents from an adoptive home. In addition, the Does will likely become more cooperative, we agree, if they begin to work with a team of practitioners.

When I telephone Otto and Daniela to express my sympathy and inquire about their health, they are sad and disappointed over the loss of this baby. I am wondering about the layers of pain in these two individuals' lives. I am also feeling their loss.

Not having medical insurance, Daniela was turned away yesterday by the doctor who examined her. He would not admit her to the hospital, as she requested, and sent her home. She miscarried later that evening.

__February 28th

Otto and Daniela arrive on time, as usual, but neither one looks good. Daniela is pale and has deep circles under her eyes. Otto, for the first time, looks unshaven and solemn. They feel as if everything is going wrong. Still unable to find a job, Otto has been unemployed for months and money is a problem. They are excruciatingly anxious to meet their son; they talk about him all of the time; and they are tired of their pain and longing.

Both are disenchanted with the attorneys' unsuccessful attempts to resolve the matter of the mental health professionals who will assist in developing a gradual transition process for Daniel. There was discussion about Children's Memorial Hospital personnel becoming involved, but some private, confidential conversation was leaked to the press, according to Loren, and he discarded that option.

Loren is strongly encouraging closure on this decision with the Does' attorneys, Otto explains. He is issuing an ultimatum that the Does meet with me, as I will be serving as one of the professionals on a probable team of three.

Otto and Daniela talk openly and with passion about their feelings.

"How could you give up your first child?" Otto asks me rhetorically. "So many people—even the governor and his wife—are asking me to 'be a hero' and give up my son to the other people. What kind of request is that? I blame the media. It's not freedom of speech; it's freedom of lies. They make me out to be a stupid immigrant, a bad person. They can write and say anything they want, even if it's a lie. This never would have happened in Czechoslovakia. No one there would be able to take away my son and to keep him from me. Here, I don't have the right to live a normal life."

Otto continues, "My wife is bleeding and they turn her away. We have no insurance, and so she loses our baby. She miscarries. They stole my first child and now my second baby is dead."

During our two-hour session, we are unaware—until hours later—that the Illinois Supreme Court is issuing its written opinion for the January 25th writ of habeas corpus. The opinion provides the Court's reasoning for the writ and for refusing the Does' second request for a rehearing of its unanimous June ruling. Accusing the adoptive parents of "deceit" and "subterfuge" in getting and keeping Baby Richard, they write, "The Does do not have custody..., they have mere possession.... In simple terms Richard is in the Does' home without color of right." The 5-2 opinion cites the Does' having made false statements under oath "that the father was unknown," while having made no attempt to learn Kirchner's name or whereabouts in the adoption of his child.

The Does intend to appeal this ruling to the U.S. Supreme Court. The deadline for such an appeal is April 25th.

__March 6th

One of the Does' battery of attorneys, Laura Kaster, calls me to set an appointment for her clients. Loren has issued the ultimatum that the adoptive parents must meet with me or he will insist on compliance with the writ of habeas corpus, requiring them to turn over the child to his father. I offer to meet with them in a neutral setting near their home rather than in my office, which is located one hour by car ride from Schaumburg. I have arranged, through my brother-in-law priest, for us to use a private meeting room at the Alexian Brothers Medical Center in Elk Grove Village; it is minutes by car from their home; and Ms. Kaster agrees to this site. I want the Does to know that I will be considerate of their time and will try to accommodate their needs. Ironically, Daniel was born in this hospital four years ago this month.

__March 7th

Loren, Otto, and Daniela meet with me in my office to discuss my imminent meeting with the Does. Daniela arrives smiling and well dressed, as usual, today wearing red tights and boots, a red tunic top, leather gloves, and a brown faux-fur coat. Otto is wearing his black and white suit. They both look worried during our session; the tension and frustration are taking their toll; and they are running out of patience. They both desire, with every fiber of their respective beings, to meet their son. Daniela reports that she has not been able to eat since her miscarriage and she has noticeably lost weight. She is actually too thin; she looks gaunt.

We discuss my planned meeting with the adoptive parents. My principal goal is to assess their level of cooperation and attitude. My second goal is to obtain information about the child, his life-style, medical history, and cognitive and emotional functioning levels, as perceived by the Does.

Loren has been working to identify two other acceptable mental health professionals for our prospective team of three. The Does are likely to raise objections to me because they know that the Kirchners have already decided upon my involvement. In a case in which "taking sides" has been a primary determinant, they will perceive me as on the side of the Kirchners and will likely resist my recommendations on behalf of Daniel. I encourage Loren to include on the team a practitioner of the Does' choice in order to elicit a greater level of cooperation, thereby increasing the probability of a smooth, effective transition process.

All four of us agree to my stated goals, the upcoming meeting, and the concept of a three-member transition team for Daniel.

As we begin our good-byes, Loren mentions that dozens of people throughout the Chicago area are handing out flyers to the public, soliciting donations to the adoptive parents' Legal Defense Fund. They're also advertising in the *Chicago Tribune* for monetary contributions. Otto and Daniela are afraid of more legal machinations, although the Does' options are now limited by the Illinois Supreme Court's **third** ruling on behalf of Otto. Of course, another appeal to the U.S. Supreme Court is planned by the Does...and perhaps another attempt at a lower court, again petitioning for a custody ruling favorable to themselves, based upon an esoteric or convoluted application of some state law.

__March 9th

Loren informs me by phone that Ken Watson, a recently retired social worker with many years of experience in adoption cases, has agreed to become one of the transition team members. Watson has been a member of the board of directors of the American Adoption Congress and, for thirty years, the assistant director of the century-old Chicago Child Care Society. I call Mr. Watson in order to introduce myself and welcome him to the team. He is positive, forthright, and pleasant; and he expresses urgency toward beginning the team building process.

We lapse into a first-name basis with each other. Ken explains that, more than anything, he enjoys a challenge and considers this case both important and of special significance. Ken describes this situation as unique because it is a "reverse adoption" of a four-year-old—far from being a baby—transferring from his adoptive parents to his birth parents. Ken is also donating his services, and we concur that we share a great deal in common. We mutually pledge to do our best for this child as we begin our work together.

__March 10th

I stop by Loren's office this afternoon to pick up the written release that he has prepared for the Warburtons' (a.k.a. Does') signatures when I meet with them for the first time. This document clarifies the relationships. The Kirchner parents and their child are and will remain my clients; the Warburtons will not become my clients; and therefore confidentiality will be waived. This will provide for me freely to discuss information from them, especially about Daniel, with others, such as his birth parents, their attorney, and the team that will soon be formed.

Loren's attorney-colleague, Bruce Boyer, author of the *amicus* brief that was instrumental in Otto's winning the lawsuit for custody of his son, is now helping again as the liaison between Loren and Ms. Kaster. The level of animosity and tension between the two adversaries, attorneys Heinemann and Kaster, is high due to the history of litigation, strategies, and machinations throughout the nearly four-year case.

Loren informs me that Dr. Bennett Leventhal, a well-known psychiatrist at the University of Chicago, has agreed to become a member of the team. He is perceived as supportive of the adoptive parents and they appear to trust him. Otto and Daniela, who at first rejected Leventhal as inappropriate because of public statements that he made in strong support of the adoptive parents, have decided to give him a chance. I am delighted to hear this news; after weeks, we finally have a full team identified; and I hope that Dr. Leventhal's expertise will prove helpful to our work on behalf of Daniel. I telephone Dr. Leventhal and we discuss some preliminary ideas related to the team and our shared mission.

__March 13th

Laura Kaster calls to confirm my meeting with her clients at 5:00 p.m. this evening. She asks about the content of my questions for them; she is concerned that legal positions or strategy might be discussed. I assure her that my intent is to discuss the child's levels of functioning and personal history; to ascertain their wishes and goals, such as visitation with the child after his move to his birth parents' home; and to establish a rapport with them.

At noon I meet with Dr. Leventhal and Ken Watson in the psychiatrist's office at the University of Chicago. We spend an hour planning our approach to the challenge presented us as a team. We agree to the importance of establishing a relationship between the two sets of parents, admittedly a difficult and daunting task. We are well aware of the conflicting goals between the two sets of parents that will present an ongoing problem. The Kirchners feel urgency and want an expedited process, preferably across weeks or months, while the Warburtons desire a prolonged process, across months or years, and preferably ending with the child remaining permanently with them.

We discuss the need for a common story with regard to Daniel's circumstances, one that will be told to him by both sets of parents. The story must present all four parents in a positive manner, explaining to the child his adoption and its reversal in a way that clarifies that all of the participants love him and want what is best for him. The primary point of the story should be that everyone did the best that they could.

We speak about the desirability of our making a recommendation that the Warburtons put together a "life book" for Daniel with pictures of his life with them, of the hospital at which he was born, and of his biological parents. Ideally there will be a copy of the life book at each of the two homes.

We make a commitment to communicate with each other on a regular basis and then exchange our phone numbers. Dr. Leventhal is due to meet with the Warburtons next Monday. I leave our meeting to drive to Elk Grove Village for my appointment with the adoptive parents.

After introductions between us, Jay and Kimberly Warburton and I sit at a table together in the private room reserved for us at Alexian Brothers Medical Center.

"Why did you accept this case?" Kimberly asks, eager to hear my answer.

"I wanted to give something back," I explain. "I've had a good career as a salaried person, but now I can donate my services as I wish in order to assist people in a difficult and painful situation. I hope that I can be of help...."

In answer to my questions about Daniel, the adoptive parents describe him as a "happy boy, strong-willed, well-adjusted, and excessively active."

"He plays well with others, has good motor skills, and loves sports like basketball and baseball," continues Kimberly. "Danny loves the water; he dog paddles. He has a good memory for so young a child. He has a good imagination, makes up stories of his own, and likes all kinds of toys, such as Power Rangers figures and Pumba from *The Lion King*."

Kimberly and Jay describe Danny's relationship with Johnny, their seven-year-old biological son. "The boys are less than four years apart in age," Kimberly tells me. "They are in sync with each other; they play together and often sleep together, although they have separate bedrooms."

The Warburtons further describe Danny as a "confident, smart child who knows nothing about his adoption" or about the existence of his biological parents.

"He is good at thinking things through," they explain. "He can use a computer to play games like Sega. He's very venturesome; he takes risks and tries things; he loves to climb; and he's unafraid.

"Danny eats well and likes sweets; he's a great sleeper and sleeps through the night; he started speaking in full sentences very early. His fourth birthday is March 16th; he knows that is three days away and he is looking forward to it."

When I ask if he has any fears, Kimberly answers, "Maybe of the dark—he doesn't like it much; nothing else."

After our discussion of Danny, the Warburtons sign the release that has been prepared for them, and I clarify my relationship with them. Because the situation between the two sets of parents has been adversarial and there are conflicting interests involved, I will remain the advocate of the Kirchners, my clients, and of the child. I assure them that I will do my best at all times and will try to be sensitive to their feelings as much as possible. I thank them for their cooperation and inform them that our newly formed, three-member team has pledged to do our collective best for Danny.

Driving home in the dark, I mentally review my two-hour meeting with the Warburtons. Something was missing, I feel, but what was it?

Neither one of them ever mentioned the prospect of visitation with Danny after his transfer to his birth parents. I anticipated that this subject would have been foremost in their minds, probably their first question—will we be able to continue a relationship with him? It would have been my primary concern if I were in their situation. I wonder why they never even alluded to this topic. What does it mean?

__March 14th

Struggling to remain composed and professional, I am excited and eager to share with Otto and Daniela the information that the Warburtons provided me yesterday about Danny. I realize that this is precious data for the Kirchners, as they have waited four years to know **anything** about their son. He remains a mystery to them; they have fantasized about what he must be like; and they have discussed their imaginings with each other countless times. Now I have four pages of hand-written notes to share.

Otto and Daniela enter my office, sit down without greetings, and lean forward to hear the first descriptions of their child, who will turn four in two days from now. Through the majority of my verbal presentation to them about their son, Daniela steadfastly gazes at a photograph of Danny, which she holds in her hand in front of her. It seems as if she feels that he will come to life from that picture and appear in front of us if she stares hard enough. Recognizing the pathos in this situation, I am witnessing a rare combination of joy and pain.

Otto is looking agitated. He explains that hearing these reports about Danny makes him even more aware of his feelings of loss. "I have missed these important four years in my son's life, his first years, and we can never get those back," he laments.

We discuss the story that will be formulated by the team for both sets of parents to tell Danny about his birth, his adoption, and his biological parents. Otto and Daniela want to send birthday gifts to Danny. Otto suggests that the Warburtons explain to the child that the gifts have come from some people who care about him and whom he will meet later. I will follow up on this request. Hopefully the adoptive parents will accede not only for Danny's sake, to enrich his birthday experience, but to demonstrate their willingness to acknowledge the Kirchners' parenthood and to cooperate with them.

__March 15th

With excitement in his voice, Loren calls me to report that Otto has just called him with enthusiastic anticipation. After our session together yesterday, Otto returned home, sat alongside the backyard pond watching the ducks, and decided, "If Karen wants a 10, we'll do an 11!" He was referring to my encouragement for all of us to adopt a plan for Danny's transition that would be ideal for him—"a 10 on a 10-point scale"—even if it's difficult or painful for the adults. Specifically, Otto expressed to Loren his willingness not only to meet with the Warburtons, but "to eat cookies with them, to dance with Mrs. Warburton, if necessary," and to work together in peace toward a mutually acceptable transition plan. I am pleased with the Kirchners' faith in me, and Loren is both surprised and happy about our progress. I sense this as a pivotal point for Danny's birth parents in being able to set aside their anger and their fears related to a renewed court battle with the Warburtons in order to work with them in a cooperative mode.

Having gotten the Warburtons' home phone number from Dr. Leventhal, I call them to leave a message thanking them for our first meeting together and asking if they would accept gifts from the Kirchners for Danny on his birthday tomorrow. Within a couple of hours, Laura Kaster telephones me to say that the Warburtons were "not happy" that I called them at home and that communications should flow through the attorneys. I am disappointed that they are reverting to legal buffers between us. This insistence upon lawyers as interpreters and intermediaries does not bode well for the success of building trust and cooperation between the two sides.

__March 16th

This morning I write a recommended draft of the story about Danny's adoption that our team has decided will be our first step. Danny, whose fourth birthday is today, should know that he is adopted; he is functioning at a cognitive level to understand this concept; and he is old enough to have been told some time ago. According to some adoption experts, if a child can remember when he was first told about his adoption, he was told too late. I speak to Ken Watson by phone to elicit his input into the story, modify it, and then fax it to Dr. Leventhal.

In a follow-up phone call with Leventhal, I bring up the matter of birthday gifts that the Kirchners would like to send, on an anonymous basis, to their son. Leventhal, not supportive of this proposal, refuses to discuss the matter further and changes the subject. The outcome is that the opportunity is lost and the Kirchners are deeply disappointed. They had requested, through Heinemann, to send Christmas gifts "from Santa" to their son three months ago and were firmly rebuffed. With the passage of each holiday and special event, they are painfully reminded about the opportunities forever lost to them.

Leventhal and I decide that it is imperative that we get the two sets of parents together, along with our team, to begin discussions about Danny.

__March 17th
After seven or eight phone conversations among our team members about the Story and as many revisions, I fax the final suggested draft to Dr. Leventhal, who will have it when he meets with the Warburtons in three days.

__March 19th
I telephone Otto to say that I am delighted that he has become so willing and eager to meet with the Warburtons in a spirit of cooperation. I have only a partial understanding of his intense cumulative feelings related to the bitter custody dispute, I tell him, but I wholly appreciate and applaud his unselfish and caring approach. I read to him the final version of the story that has been formulated for Danny. It explains to the child that, in addition to his adoptive parents, he has birth parents who also love him. Otto likes the story and relates that Daniela will no doubt approve it also.

__March 21st
Dr. Leventhal informs me that his introductory meeting with the Warburtons went well. They appear cooperative, he tells me, but they were "not ready" to consider the story for Danny and accordingly he did not give him our draft. I phone Ken Watson and Otto to report the positive aspects of Leventhal's meeting, including his perception of the Warburtons' willingness to proceed with a transition plan.

__March 23rd
Walking into my waiting room carrying a cardboard tray with five cups of steaming coffee from the local McDonald's, I find Dr. Leventhal, already arrived and slouched in one of my teal fabric-covered chairs. He avoids eye contact with me as I greet him and offer him coffee. Unsmiling, he follows me into my office and takes a seat. He seems average to me in every aspect of his appearance—height, weight, build, and facial features—except that he has a graying beard and mustache. Leventhal ignores

my overtures toward friendly conversation, directing his attention instead toward Ken Watson, who has arrived and followed us into the office. It occurs to me before long that, based upon his behavior, Leventhal refuses to consider me at his level on the evolutionary food chain of mental health professionals.

Ken, a recent retiree, is tall, thin, and rugged-looking, with a lined but kindly face. He reminds me of Davy Crockett from late-night reruns of the old television program about the folk hero. Smiling and warm, Ken represents both a foil and a balance to Leventhal. Otto and Daniela arrive and pleasant introductions are exchanged. They are meeting Dr. Leventhal and Ken Watson for the first time. Leventhal emphasizes that he is a child psychiatrist with a great deal of experience with children.

During our three-hour meeting, Otto and Daniela candidly express their feelings about their son; Otto initiates most of their self-disclosures. He is honest and forthright, sharing with the two men some highlights of the couple's long, arduous struggle for their son and their plans for Danny. "We will give him lots of love," Otto summarizes his explanation.

It is clearly discernible that the ambiguity of the situation is wearing on Otto and Daniela. Little progress has been made in two months since the Supreme Court's issuance of the writ of habeas corpus, and Danny reportedly does not even know that he was adopted and that his birth parents exist.

Otto confronts Leventhal as having been quoted in the press during recent months, saying that it would be best for Baby Richard to remain with the adoptive parents. He questions the psychiatrist's intentions and discusses his fear that the doctor's loyalty has been pledged, in some way, to the Warburtons. Leventhal assures us that his work will be directed toward the best interests of the child at all times.

In response to specific, pointed questions from Otto, Leventhal promises not to discuss this case again with the media, now that he has been hired onto our team by the Kirchners, and not to participate in any court action that might be detrimental to Otto's interests. If subpoenaed, he explains, he must and will comply, but he will not become involved in the initiation of court action of any kind.

Leventhal also clarifies that he will be billing the Kirchners at his usual rate of fees for all of his services.

Otto and Daniela accept Leventhal's employment as part of our three-member team, based upon his assurances regarding his observance of practitioner-client confidentiality and his neutrality in any future litigation initiated by the Warburtons.

The Kirchners and I inform Leventhal that—now that a team has been formed—all three of us should meet with the Warburtons in order to begin our planning for their first meeting, outside of a courtroom, with Otto and Daniela.

__March 24th

On behalf of the Kirchners, I telephone Leventhal's office to remind him that I am planning to attend the scheduled meeting with the adoptive parents. I request that he call me over the weekend to inform me of its scheduled time. I then telephone Ken Watson to inform him of my communications with Leventhal's office and to confirm my plans to attend the important, imminent meeting.

__March 27th

Ken Watson calls to inform me that not only has a meeting been held with the Warburtons and Leventhal but that he himself also attended. Because the Kirchners, through attorney Heinemann, have assigned me as the coordinator of the team, my designated role is to become involved in all activities related to Danny on their behalf. The issue of trust is paramount with the Kirchner parents; Otto is the sole, court-ordered custodial parent of the child; and Danny remains with the Warburtons only because of Otto's decision for a progressive transfer process. When I speak to Loren about this situation, he is disappointed and angry. He is also suspicious of Leventhal's having excluded the Kirchners' representative from the first meeting with the adoptive parents concerning the transition process for Danny. Loren reports that Otto and Daniela are losing patience and are both depressed over the lack of any definitive progress.

"If Otto and Daniela do not meet their son within the next several days, the team process is likely to come apart," he informs me. I assure him that we will do our best tomorrow, when all seven of us—the four parents and three mental health professionals—are scheduled to meet together for the first time.

__March 28th

Otto and Daniela arrive in the parking lot of my office at 8:15 a.m. for the one-hour drive to Leventhal's office for their epic meeting with the Warburtons and our team of three. Both sets of parents will be asked to set aside the acrimony and animosity of their four-year legal battle that has been bitterly waged not only in the courts but in the media and public forums as well. As I am driving, Otto and Daniela talk, with great animation, about their anticipation, anxiety, and distrust. Why was a meeting held yesterday with the adoptive parents, Watson, and Leventhal, and not their named team coordinator? they ask. Why, especially after Otto had expressed clearly to Leventhal that he and Daniela were struggling hard to be able to trust him?

Otto and Daniela stand on the street corner in front of the steel-and-concrete office building, pacing and mentally preparing themselves for this meeting. They are committed to a positive tone and a promising outcome. I assure them that they will be fine, and I am proud of them for their willingness and commitment to meet with the Warburtons in a spirit of cooperation. Thinking to myself that this most difficult, voluntary act on their part speaks volumes in terms of their love for a child whom they have yet to meet, I admire their dignity and personal courage. After four seemingly endless years of longing for their son, who has been kept from them by this couple whom they are about to meet on amicable terms, they are examples, to me, of Ernest Hemingway's famous expression, "grace under pressure."

Before the full meeting, Watson, Leventhal, and I speak for several minutes in the psychiatrist's office to prepare ourselves. I explain my concerns, on behalf of the Kirchners, related to the unilateral meeting yesterday. I emphasize that this is not a matter of ego on my part but an issue of good teamwork, to which we had all pledged, and of trust.

Informing my colleagues, "It is imperative that some real progress be made today for Otto and Daniela," I assure them of my clients' dedication to a slow transition process if they can only meet their son. Once they meet him and he knows that they are his parents, they will be amenable to nearly any recommendations for the actual physical transfer of his custody.

We enter the conference room to join Otto and Daniela, already seated at the large table. Within a couple of minutes,

Jay and Kimberly enter the room, and the two couples greet each other, shake hands, smile, and sit down. The Kirchners are wearing their Sunday-best clothes, Otto in his suit and Daniela in a two-piece, crushed velvet outfit. The Warburtons are casually dressed, wearing shirts and denim pants. To the European-bred Kirchners, attire is symbolic of attitude and respect.

As pre-planned, Ken Watson—the member of our team who is perceived as neutral—serves as the facilitator of this meeting. Both sets of parents participate and remain cordial and polite. I am secretly amazed and relieved that all four of the custody combatants conduct themselves with mutual civility and courtesy. No harsh words are spoken by any of these four parents. In contrast to many of my other clients' sessions involving disputes over children, this encounter is a resounding success. At one such recent session, two men nearly came to blows, with fists poised, and restrained themselves only when one of the two wives jumped between them and screamed for them to stop. When their verbal threats of physical violence escalated, ignoring my entreaties to stop, and I feared for the safety of everyone present, I called the police, who promptly arrived. Our tension-filled session continued under the threat by the officers that they would arrest both men if their return was required. Here, however, to my surprise and delight, reason and calm prevail, and I am feeling newly hopeful that everything might continue to go well.

The tone and direction, however, turn negative during discussion of our next meeting. We are ending, after three full hours together, with the understanding that Leventhal is leaving town for eight days and, he insists, the participants' schedules do not allow for another meeting for nearly three weeks. I encourage another meeting this week before Leventhal leaves town, but, he asserts, his appointment schedule does not allow time for it.

During our car ride toward home, Otto and Daniela are unhappy and disillusioned. I lapse into playing cheerleader with them. "You were both so controlled and reasonable," I compliment them, genuinely and deeply impressed with their remarkably polite demeanor. "You both expressed yourselves well and made it obvious that you just want what is best for Danny."

"At this rate," Otto explains, "it will be months before we even meet our son. The older he gets, the harder it will be for us to begin bonding with him as his parents." Daniela forcefully nods her agreement with his assessment.

Otto and Daniela remind me that Leventhal had promised that he would be available to make this case a priority. They now wonder about his level of commitment and his willingness to move along the transition process for Danny.

"We have not even agreed to the story that Danny will be told about his adoption and about us," Otto laments. "There is no timeline for them to tell him that he was adopted and that he has birth parents who love him. He is already four years old and, they say, he knows nothing. If only we could see him...," he concludes wistfully.

As earlier agreed, I am assigned to revise the story yet again, making it shorter and more simple, and then to provide it to Watson and Leventhal for their additional input before the next meeting. After final modifications, the story is to be sent to both the Kirchners and the Warburtons for their review. Both sets of parents must agree regarding the content of the story for Danny about his adoption and his birth parents. Also, they need to be prepared to answer some likely questions from the child after he has been told the story. He should hear the same answers from his adoptive parents as, later, from his biological parents.

Amazingly, there is no media coverage of this first cooperative activity between the two sets of parents on behalf of Baby Richard. Apparently, all participants—including the cadre of attorneys on the sidelines—have observed the mutual agreement to exclude both the media and the lawyers. A "media blackout" has been decided as conducive to fostering cooperation between the two sides, as the war has been waged as much in the press as in the courts.

__March 30th

Ken Watson, Bennett Leventhal, and I speak by phone and fax the one-page story, with more suggested revisions, to each other until we are satisfied with it. Leventhal encourages me to contact the Warburtons directly in order to ask them by which means I should provide them with a copy of our final draft. I am willing to drive it to their home, fax it to them, or mail it, if they provide me with their address.

__March 31st

At 1:30 p.m. I call the Warburtons and leave a message on their answering machine, asking them to call me in order to tell me how to get to them the final draft of our team's suggested story for Danny. They do not return my call.

Meanwhile, Loren informs me that Otto wants to remove Leventhal from our team. The only harsh words during our parents' meeting were between Otto and the psychiatrist, when toward its end, Leventhal cut off discussion about the story, delaying this all-important topic for the Kirchners until another meeting weeks away. Otto and Daniela live every day focused on the prospect of meeting their son; each day seems to them longer than the previous one. The Illinois Supreme Court granted Otto custody in June 1994. Nine trying months have passed and their child still has no knowledge about his adoption or about his birth parents. He remains in the home of the adoptive parents only by Otto's refraining from an enforcement of the earlier court order and the writ of habeas corpus, issued in January. He and Daniela have chosen to engage in a gradual transition process that we all believe will be less emotionally disturbing and disruptive for the child. However, the prospect of three more weeks of waiting until another meeting of more talking seems unbearable to them. Loren believes that the most recent strategy of the other side is now purposefully to delay a meeting between Danny and his birth parents until the United States Supreme Court acts on their next appeal. The Warburtons will exercise psychological leverage if Baby Richard still resides with them and remains unaware of his adoptive status.

It is the psychiatrist, Loren emphasizes, who is most responsible for this postponement of the interactions that are necessary for progress. Also, Leventhal's cavalier attitude about his unavailability and another delay signals the likelihood of future impediments. Otto and Daniela are disgusted over the imposition of another long interval before any hope of movement toward meeting their son.

__April 3rd

Attorney Laura Kaster calls on Monday and tells Robert, who answers our phone, "Dr. Moriarty should not call my clients." She refers to the message that I left for them on Friday, three days ago. Kaster directs that the draft of the story be faxed to her. I am both surprised and disappointed to hear this directive, especially because we **all** decided—both sets of parents and our three-member team—that we would work together with no involvement by either the media or the attorneys. We agreed that we were now communicating on a different level, one that required privacy, directness, and mutual trust. The interpersonal relationship between the Warburtons and Kirchners—so recent, tentative, and fragile—requires that we act in accordance with our agreements.

Otto decides to release Leventhal from the process and from the team immediately. It was the psychiatrist who instructed me directly to contact the adoptive parents regarding the draft of the story. Now the attorneys must intervene and we have regressed several steps. Loren faxes a letter to Ms. Kaster, informing her that Dr. Leventhal's services are terminated, effective immediately.

__April 4th

The Warburtons are to call me by noon tomorrow if they wish to continue a team process for the gradual transition of Danny, Loren informs me. I meet with Loren, Otto, and Daniela in my office, and the tone is unchanged from two months ago. "We are so tired of waiting and nothing is happening," Otto says for himself and Daniela. Leventhal, purposefully or not, has been a buffer between the two sets of parents. Now the attorneys have returned onto the scene. This new setback—Leventhal's removal from the team—has slowed down an already torturously long process.

Musing over the similarity of this process to hostage retrieval negotiations, I wonder how many more machinations will be attempted before progress is made toward a reunion of Danny with his birth parents.

__April 5th

Robert and I keep our phone line free so that the Warburtons will be able to get through to us to express their willingness to continue a team process. Ken Watson is willing and ready to meet later this week, as I am, and we are hoping that the Warburtons will agree to a meeting. Instead of the awaited phone call, attorney Kaster sends Loren a letter stating that the Warburtons will remain involved in a process only if Dr. Leventhal continues to participate, that their full cooperation is contingent upon this condition. Loren responds by reminding Kaster and her clients that Otto had agreed to a gradual transition process on a voluntary basis; that he is not interested in Leventhal's continued services; and that he is rescinding approval for the Warburtons to keep his child, effective immediately.

__April 6th

Ken Watson informs me by phone that he is withdrawing from our team, "because the attorneys are now in the act" and the process has obviously broken down. He is angry that Kaster's letter to Loren threatens the opprobrium of the press and possible licensure implications for those who would advise Otto to take his child without continuing a transitional process. Kaster's threats of media retaliation and the prospective loss of licensure—directed at me—are clearly intended to manipulate and intimidate. This targeted approach makes the media into a weapon, enforcer, and avenging agent. Clearly, Kaster—as one of the agents of the Warburtons—believes in her power to produce these results. Her letter is faxed to me and copied to Leventhal and to Patrick Murphy of the Office of the Public Guardian.

   This evening, as arranged by Loren Heinemann, the sheriff's office delivers to the Warburtons a Writ of Habeas Corpus, along with a copy of the January 25th Illinois Supreme Court Order directing that Baby Richard be turned over to his biological father "forthwith."

__April 7th

Late in the evening, Bennett Leventhal calls me, stating that he has been informed that he has been fired from the transition team. He is "surprised" and "dismayed" and explains that he perceives this as "a problem between us." He proclaims, "It is your job to convince the Kirchners to trust me."

   "I have been doing a tap dance over here, trying to convince the Kirchners to trust you and the process, across weeks," I explain to him. "This was a process that required negotiations and trust. In my twelve years of experience in negotiations work, I have learned a most important lesson. Once the protocols break down, the process unravels like a ball of yarn. Our protocols excluded the attorneys; we agreed to remain available and you left town at the most critical point; and, although we pledged to work as a team, you held a meeting with the Warburtons that purposely excluded me, their designated representative. The Kirchners have lost both trust and patience. This is **their** decision."

"Well, I have decided that I **can** reconsider the matter of my professional fees," he responds. "I can now adjust them for the Kirchners if that will make a difference."

"As far as I know," I tell him, "the custodial parent has made a decision and his attorney has delivered that decision to you. I will relate your message to both of them and, if they change their minds, I am sure you will be contacted."

Leventhal is angry; his voice is higher by several octaves. He blames me for his having been fired, and I know that he will likely not forget this event. I realize, with a mixture of regret and sadness, that if the psychiatrist had ever articulated a commitment to Otto's meeting his son and someday living with him, we would be continuing our now-aborted process as a team. Even if Otto and Daniela had a projected date on which they could meet their son, they would have been amenable to almost any reasonable plan for a change in residence of the child. Now, it's too late to regroup as a team. Threats have been issued and attorneys are once again in charge....

Although I would welcome assistance from other supportive and caring professionals for a variety of reasons, I know that— in the aftermath of the failure of many options across months— it is inevitable that I will be working alone with Danny and his parents. I am now spending as much time on this case as on all of my other client sessions combined.

__April 8th, 9th & 10th

Otto, Daniela, Loren, and I speak by telephone numerous times. I inform them of Leventhal's offer "to adjust his professional fees" if he is allowed to continue to work on the transition process. Otto and Daniela are not interested.

The attorneys on both sides of the dispute continue to communicate through their intermediary. Bruce Boyer is relaying messages back and forth between Loren and the legion of Jenner and Block attorneys who represent the Warburtons.

__April 12th

The Warburtons' lawyers file with the United States Supreme Court their petition appealing the Illinois Supreme Court's most recent Baby Richard ruling. This is their **fourth** trip to the nation's highest court in eight months.

__April 13th

In our three-hour session today, Otto and Daniela are depressed, discouraged, tense, and anxiety-ridden. They both report difficulty sleeping, typically staying up through the night, talking, and then sleeping fitfully during early morning hours. They cannot eat; Daniela is pale and thin; and Otto is looking much older than when I met him less than three months ago.

"We're getting crazy over this!" he announces. "We never had a plan, never knew five steps ahead. We just wanted to do what was best for our son. It's now like a game for everyone.

"It was the most difficult decision of my life," Otto tells me, "for the Writ of Habeas Corpus to be served on the Warburtons. Only Mr. Warburton was at home, not Mrs. That may be a problem from a legal standpoint.

"We waited all these months to **avoid** an abrupt transfer of our son," he continues. "We hoped to avoid this, to have them cooperate enough for us to meet him, have visits with him over time, and then move in with us when he knew us and knew that we love him."

Because Daniela must leave for work, Otto accompanies her to drive her in their only car to the salon, but he returns less than an hour later. We meet in Loren's office to talk about the next steps. The attorney, too, is discouraged and weary.

Although the Cook County Sheriff's office served the Writ of Habeas Corpus, Loren informs us, high-ranking officials there have stated to reporters that they will not enforce the court order to retrieve the child.

Loren demands in writing that the Warburtons deliver Danny to his father by 3:00 p.m. tomorrow. Specifically, they must bring the child to Heinemann's law office.

At 11:00 p.m. Ken Watson calls me to ask what is happening regarding the case. He informs me that Bennett Leventhal has invited him to a meeting tomorrow with the Warburtons. I explain that I am surprised at this development because

Leventhal has been fired, in writing, by the legal representative of Otto, the custodial parent, and Watson told me days ago that he himself was withdrawing from the transition process.

"If there is a meeting tomorrow, it will be held without the consent or approval of the Kirchners and they will not be there," I notify him.

__April 14th

"My stomach is doing flip flops, thinking I'll have a four-year-old child here by 3:00 p.m. and I won't know what to do," Loren confesses to me by phone at noon. He adds that his "sources" have informed him that the Warburtons have left their home by car and are proceeding along the expressway with media vans and helicopter following them. Ken Watson left a message on my answering machine this morning, saying that I am welcome to attend the meeting with the Warburtons, scheduled at 1:00 p.m. in Leventhal's office.

Upon Loren's recommendation, I telephone Leventhal's office at 1:15 p.m. and, as soon as I identify myself, the receptionist transfers me into the conference room. Leventhal speaks to me, relating that he is surprised that I am not present. I remind him that he has been fired; it is inappropriate for them to be conducting this meeting about Otto's child against his wishes; and it would be unethical for me to attend without the Kirchners' approval. I request to talk to the Warburtons and I am transferred to the speaker phone.

"The Kirchners devoutly wish to continue a gradual process of transition for their son," I explain, "and they hope that you will agree to this. Dr. Leventhal has been fired by Mr. Kirchner. I will make myself available to you at **any** time to discuss this matter further on their behalf."

Jay asks me about Otto's intentions and wishes. I reply that he wants a "safe transition of his son, away from the media." He asks about a timeline and I answer "as soon as possible."

After giving the group my phone numbers, I reiterate my hope that the Warburtons will do what is best for Danny and agree to meet with me so that we might talk further. The Kirchners have requested that I represent them and their wishes in this capacity. They will talk among themselves, Leventhal informs me, and then get back to me.

At 4:30 p.m. I arrive at Loren's office, as planned, and, to my surprise and disgust, dozens of media representatives have gathered in the parking lot and inside the building. There are television cameras, flash cameras, and microphones in profusion. Otto has just finished making a formal statement.

"Did you intend your 3:00 deadline today, Good Friday, as an especially hurtful message to Mrs. Warburton, who is very religious?" yells the first reporter who can be heard above the noise of simultaneously shouted questions. "The time coincides with the commemoration of the crucifixion and death of Christ," he points out.

Otto assures the reporter that there is no connection, no special motivation, and merely a coincidence. He wants his son, in accordance with the order from the state's highest court, and he has waited beyond reasonableness.

By the reporters' questions, we discover that the Warburtons had taken Danny with them to Leventhal's office. Because they had not yet told the child about his adoption, they could have had no intention for the Kirchners to meet Danny this morning. Yet, the reporters query Otto, "If you wanted to meet your son so badly, why didn't you attend the meeting with the Warburtons and the team of mental health professionals?"

Otto tries to explain, but the reporters cut him off and ask more, yet similar questions. Clearly, they are enjoying the drama of Good Friday; the idea of specially targeted, symbolic messages; and the mystery of secret meanings. They seem to enjoy most the apparent disinterest of this biological father, who did not even bother to show up to what they were told was a scheduled meeting, thereby ostensibly forfeiting the opportunity to meet his son.

Loren joins his wife and baby daughter inside his office as most of the reporters pack up and leave with the stories they have garnered. Otto explains to two stragglers that he is disappointed and angry regarding this fiasco. His son was taken to the 1:00 meeting place as a media stunt and as yet another opportunity to demean him as an uncaring and undeserving father, as compared to the cooperative, loving adoptive parents. The reporters do not miss this opportunity, of course, to fashion Otto as the willful loser in this scenario. I am amazed that Leventhal and Watson would become participants, either willingly or unwillingly, in this charade…, to the unrefutable detriment of Otto Kirchner. His public image will certainly fall at least one more notch on the long, nasty measuring stick of media-fashioned public opinion.

After the last reporter has left, I invite Otto to my home to meet my husband and to discuss the disturbing events of the day. In the privacy of my living room, Otto, Robert, and I commiserate over the most recent, highly public triumph of the Warburtons, who brought Danny to the University of Chicago as a ploy and manipulation. Ignoring Heinemann's demand for enforcement of the court-ordered writ to present the child at his office by 3:00, the adoptive parents preempted compliance by a media witnessed and filmed journey to a 1:00 meeting that is painted as "the opportunity for the father to meet his son." The biological father failed to appear, they claim to the media, who then descend upon Otto in full force to ascertain why the father of Baby Richard is so uncaring as to miss a first meeting with his child. Not only is he discredited yet again but the Warburtons also deftly avoid delivering Danny by using this media-camouflaged subterfuge.

Leventhal calls me this evening to state that the group at the meeting decided that the Warburtons will meet with me, as I requested on behalf of my clients. Ken Watson will call me to make the arrangements.

__April 15th & 16th

The Warburtons have consulted their attorneys and will meet with me in their home this coming Tuesday, Ken Watson informs me by phone. I must come alone; Watson will be present as a representative of the Warburtons; and they will listen to what I have to say on behalf of Otto Kirchner.

When I speak to Otto and Daniela, their feelings are running high. It is Easter Sunday and they had hoped and expected to celebrate this holiday with their son. This is the fifth Easter since Danny's birth and they have never even seen him. We are making some progress, I assure them, because the Warburtons have agreed to meet with me. Perhaps, after all, we can continue to work toward a gradual transfer plan for Danny.

__April 17th

According to Loren, a lengthy petition has been filed in court today by Jenner and Block, on behalf of the Warburtons, requesting the court to order the appointment of Dr. Bennett Leventhal to oversee the transfer of custody of Baby Richard. The 16-page document—accompanied by an affidavit by Leventhal— consistently misspells my last name and also misrepresents my credentials, abbreviating my professional experience. "In the alternative [to the appointment of Leventhal]," the petition requests the appointment of an independent psychiatrist to "...prepare a report, to be submitted under seal to this Court, recommending an appropriate course of action for the transfer of Richard's custody...." In addition, "or in the alternative, ...this Court [should] appoint a Special Master to oversee the transfer...." This motion has been filed with the Illinois Supreme Court and Loren now has twenty-eight days to file a response on behalf of Otto.

This is the **fourth** ruling sought of the Illinois Supreme Court in the Baby Richard case within twenty months. I remember Leventhal's promise, made to Otto in my office, that he would not initiate any court action against Otto's interests.

The attorneys agree to accept the Writ of Habeas Corpus on behalf of Mrs. Warburton so that the sheriff will not need to serve it on her. Loren informs me that he has filed a petition with the Supreme Court requesting an order that authorizes and directs the sheriff to take the child on behalf of his custodial father.

The Chicago area newspapers publish reports that Otto Kirchner frequents gambling casinos. The various articles are tinged by a condemnatory tone. Columnist Michael Sneed of the *Sun-Times* refers to Otto as a "very, very frequent visitor" to the casinos. In other coverage, Heinemann is quoted as reminding people that "it's not a crime" to gamble in casinos and as saying that he himself has accompanied his client on more than one occasion.

Realizing that half of my work time every week is now devoted to this *pro bono* case, I schedule nine hours today in session with my other clients. It is a long day, but the pile of bills from my practice must be paid. I am having trouble sleeping at night and am awakened by frequent nightmares.

__April 18th

When I arrive at the Warburtons' home, as scheduled through Ken Watson, a television van and two cameramen are positioned across the street with their cameras focused upon me. The house, modest in size and plain in appearance, is a dark-brown tri-level with a side driveway that leads to a detached garage. I glimpse the fenced yard in back, from which a large black dog barks at my arrival. The front door opens immediately after my knock. As I enter, with a smile and a handshake for Kimberly and Jay, I ask them—nodding toward the nearby cameras—"Doesn't this get old?" Jay replies, "Today is a light day; there are usually **more** media people at our curb."

Ken Watson is sitting on the couch; I join him there; while Kimberly and Jay sit on chairs across from us. Kimberly explains that the furniture shows the wear and tear of children, and I notice that the dark-wood cocktail table in front of me is chipped and scratched. The blue carpeting, noticeably worn, bears an array of stains, presumably from the dog. Jay leaves to get coffee for us, and we attempt pleasantries while he is gone.

"May I meet Danny?" I ask Kimberly, as Jay returns with cups of hot coffee.

"No. He's not here; he's at a neighbor's house," she responds.

"If the Kirchners are allowed to meet their son," I explain on their behalf, "**all** things would be possible. They would be willing to wait patiently for a future time to move him to their home. They wanted to send him a bunny and a card at Easter, maybe take him to the park, or just make a phone call to hear his voice for the first time. Now they have given up on a 'gradual process' that has spanned three months with no progress at all."

I ask whether the Warburtons have informed Danny about his adoption. A copy of our team's laboriously-drafted recommended story was available to them weeks ago. Kimberly replies that they informed him during the past three days. "The first day we explained what adoption is; the second day, we told him that he himself was adopted; and the third day, we said he has other parents." When I inquire how Danny responded, Kimberly describes his attitude as "disinterested." She elaborates, "He asked to go outside and play."

To the all-important question, "May his parents meet him tomorrow?" the answer comes, "No; he's not ready." Both

Kimberly and Jay frown and shake their heads in harmony.

"May they meet him **soon**?" They respond again in the negative, adding that they want a slow, progressive transition, directed by the recommendations of a team of mental health professionals.

These responses direct me to the Kirchners' bottom line. "If they cannot meet their son, they want a transfer—as ordered by the Court—in a safe way, avoiding a media spectacle and a threatening public audience," I inform them. I offer my home as the transfer site or, if they prefer another option, a church of their choice.

"There is a lot of life that will be lived after several minutes of a transfer and, if it's done privately and safely, the Kirchners will promise you visitation with Danny after the physical transition is made. In the best interests of Danny, **please** consider his safety foremost and allow for a dignified, pleasant first meeting for him with his birth parents." I am pleading with them, on behalf of Otto and Daniela, to put Danny's welfare above anything else.

"If you create a media event, then it will make it more difficult—and unlikely— that the Kirchners will agree to your continuing relationships with the child. I'm not saying it will be impossible, but it will be improbable because you will have revealed your intentions not to help the child adjust to his natural parents."

Jay asks if the Kirchners are proposing a "reverse transition" for Danny, one that would place him in residence with his birth parents but allow his visiting with members of his adoptive family. I respond affirmatively and reiterate that, if they call in the media, they will be jeopardizing a continuing relationship with the child. "These are the messages from my clients."

Kimberly, leaning forward and looking into my eyes, asks, "In your opinion, between us, where do **you** think Danny should live?"

"Based upon everything I know as of today, I think he should be with his birth parents," I respond, knowing that this is not the answer that she either wants or expects. Perhaps she thought that I might apologetically respond, "I think he should remain with **you**; I am just doing my job on behalf of my clients." Kimberly looks as if I have struck her; she leans back in her chair.

Directing my further comments to her, I add, "I know that the media and the public overwhelmingly disagree with this position, except maybe for one columnist in my community's newspaper. But I know the Kirchners very well; they are good people; and they love their son more than anything else in life."

"Where did you see coverage supportive of the Kirchners?" she inquires. I am surprised by this question, considering all of the other topics that might be discussed about Danny's welfare. Obviously, the direction of media opinions is important in this house. I answer the question, informing her about a recent pro-Kirchner column by Phil Kadner in the *Daily Southtown*, a popular newspaper that covers south Chicago as well as all of the south suburbs.

After meaningful eye contact among themselves, Watson announces that the meeting is now over. Kimberly and Jay are frowning, anxious to show me to the door. We have met for two hours and the respective positions have been clarified. If the Kirchners meet their son, they promise to become engaged again in a progressive transition process. If not allowed to meet him, they will claim him, as court-ordered this past January. If the handover is private—no media or public audience—the Warburtons will be allowed visitation with the child. The Warburtons refuse to allow Otto and Daniela to meet Danny. They also continue to insist upon what amounts to the diversion of control to an intermediary "professional team" to make decisions about the child, thereby replacing his father's court-ordered authority and the custody decision.

When I leave, the curbside cameras are rolling. The news breaks later today about this meeting. "The child has been told about his adoption" is the focus of media coverage. I wonder who has informed them because I waved off their advances toward me and jumped into my car to head back to my office.

From my car phone, I inform Otto and Daniela—both waiting by their telephone—about my meeting. The Kirchners are convinced that, if they become engaged again in a process governed by a team of professionals, they may never have their son with them. They anticipate a series of begrudgingly scheduled meetings with Danny, across weeks or months, with the child crying, traumatized, and ultimately pronounced "unable to bond with his birth parents" by the adoptive parents and at least one of the "professionals." Layered with the continuing media attacks upon them, they would be expected "to do the right thing" by leaving their child with the Warburtons and disappearing from the scene.

Otto and Daniela decide that the Warburtons will probably work hard to ensure this predictable ending. Danny, at four, is no doubt impressionable and malleable; he will follow the lead and the wishes of his adoptive parents.

"They lost in court," Otto declares to me in an exhausted tone, "so they took their fight to the media and the public. That done, they are now taking it to the 'team of mental health professionals,' and the media blitz will continue on their side."

"We will never have our son," Daniela adds tearfully, "and we lose everything...in spite of the Supreme Court orders...."

Minutes later, I telephone Loren and we discuss the situation at length. "It is at an impasse," he pronounces, "and we have to proceed accordingly."

__April 19th

Otto and I discuss the possibility of his requiring a medical examination of Danny by a pediatrician. After being provided feedback from the medical doctor, my associate Dr. Lechner and I would then meet the child and assess the levels of his cognitive and emotional functioning. We would thereby be able to recommend the next steps of Danny's transition. Will the adoptive parents cooperate? We know that it is unlikely....

__April 20th

Loren Heinemann is insisting that the Warburtons turn over the child to his biological parents. He writes a letter requesting that they avoid a media circus and perform the transfer in a way that is sensitive to the child's privacy and dignity. If they do so, they will be allowed a continuing relationship with him. If they turn out the media, such a continuing relationship will be improbable. Their attorneys reply that it is in the child's best interests to continue a process with a panel of mental health professionals overseeing and directing it. They cite Leventhal as a strong proponent of such a process. He would like to be reassigned.

__April 21st

The Illinois Supreme Court issues its ruling in response to the Warburtons' petition for the appointment of Leventhal, or an independent psychiatrist and/or a Special Master, to oversee the transfer of Baby Richard to his father. In fifty-five terse words, the motion is denied, without comment. Heinemann has not even had time to construct or to file a response, which is rendered moot by the Court's amazingly prompt ruling within five days.

"It's not surprising," Loren tells me. "The Court has already ruled that Otto is the **only** one who should be making decisions on behalf of his son. It appears that the justices are losing patience with the Warburtons and their attorneys. It's sort of like they're saying, 'What part of "no" don't you understand?' or, regarding the writ of habeas corpus, 'Don't you understand that "forthwith" means "immediately"?' That was three months ago!"

__April 22nd

Otto and Daniela cancel their session in my office because of car trouble, but we speak on the telephone for an hour. They know about the Illinois Supreme Court's speedy denial of the Warburtons' petition to delay the transfer of "Richard" to his father by empowering mental health practitioners to formulate and direct a process and a timeline. They are genuinely hopeful and optimistic for the first time in many weeks. Again, the highest court in the state has issued a ruling—and an impressively swift one—reinforcing their decision in January: the child is to be turned over to his father "forthwith."

"Maybe we will meet our son soon," Otto says.

As explained by Loren, if the Warburtons do not comply with the Court order, they could face a contempt of court conviction, accompanied by a fine or jail time or both. In Illinois it is a felony to hold a child without his parent's consent. In addition, their continuing refusal to comply could result in kidnapping charges against them. They have "mere possession" of Baby Richard, not custody, according to the Supreme Court ruling. The adoption was invalidated and, technically, they are the **"former** adoptive parents" of the child. They have no more legal standing to him than their next-door neighbors have.

__April 24th

Loren informs us that the Warburtons' attorneys have finally conceded that the child will be transferred to his father. Otto and Daniela meet with me at my office for a two-hour session.

"We are tired of the media second-guessing us," Otto begins as they settle into the couch. He continues, "The press was waiting for Daniela in front of her workplace on Saturday. Every time I go to a store or a shopping mall, someone shouts out my name and screams something hateful." He relates that "Bastard!" and "Burn in hell!" are the current favorites.

Daniela expresses her concern about the media showing up at her salon. "I need to keep this job to earn a living for us," she explains. "I'm afraid that they will drive the customers away."

"Danny will miss his brother and the dog," Otto murmurs, staring straight ahead. "I wish we could do this another way, but there is no hope any more of getting cooperation from the other side."

We discuss various possibilities for Danny. According to Loren, a quick transfer is likely, consisting of one or two meetings during which Otto and Daniela would meet their son, they would become familiar with each other, and then they would take him to their home to stay.

Otto and Daniela are nearly vibrating with anxiety and eager anticipation.

__April 25th

The attorneys are discussing a meeting that might occur this week for Danny to be introduced to his parents. No specific date is set.

__April 26th

Loren informs me that, according to their attorneys, the Warburtons are willing to arrange a meeting in their home with only Otto and Daniela attending. They have set conditions for the introductory meeting. First, the child will determine the length of the meeting, whether that turns out to be minutes or merely a matter of seconds. Second, Otto and Daniela will not be permitted to touch or hug him at any time. Third, they will be introduced to Danny by their names, not as "mother" and "father." Otto perceives these conditions as another sign of bad faith. He and Daniela want to be introduced to their son as his father and mother. They believe that it would be confusing for him—and misleading—if, at the age of four, he meets them as "Otto" and "Daniela" or as "Mr. and Mrs. Kirchner."

At Otto's direction, Loren rejects these conditions. The Warburtons therefore "will not allow" this prospective meeting between Danny and his parents.

__April 27th

There is discussion between the attorneys about my meeting with another psychiatrist from the University of Chicago for us to plan together the first meeting of Danny with his parents. Upon Loren's recommendation, I make a series of telephone calls to her, leaving explanatory messages, but no meeting date is proposed. The psychiatrist is "not available until some time next week," and "there are objections" to my involvement, she informs me when we finally speak to each other directly by phone.

Loren, exasperated and taking courage from the most recent of four Illinois Supreme Court rulings in his client's favor, faxes to their attorneys a letter demanding that the Warburtons set a date and time, within the next 72 hours, for the child to be transferred to his parents.

__April 28th

Laura Kaster responds, by fax, that the child will be available to Otto and Daniela "alone" at 3:00 p.m. at the Warburtons' home on Sunday, April 30, 1995.

Making "one final offer," Heinemann writes to Kaster:

> Should the transfer proceed quietly and without any media, Mr. Kirchner would be more inclined to permit your clients to have continuing contact [with the child].... On the other hand, should your clients make a media circus out of this, the continuing contact could not be guaranteed.

Loren arranges to borrow a van, which he will drive, for the pick-up of Danny on Sunday. I will meet them at the Kirchners' apartment when they all arrive together later that afternoon.

Otto, Daniela, and I discuss our collective hopes that this transfer will be quiet, safe, private, and comfortable for the child. They have waited and planned for so long for this first meeting. They want it to be special. Aware of his probable confusion and discomfort, they are convinced that, if the adoptive parents are welcoming, the child will be correspondingly receptive. He will undoubtedly take his cues from the adoptive parents.

We discuss elements of a "reverse transition" for Danny. If the child continues a connection with his adoptive family, we believe, he will more easily and readily adapt to his new family and home. I recommend that every day, for at least the first week, we plan a tangible event for him. The first day he will telephone and speak with each of them. The second day, Otto and Daniela will take a photograph of Danny for him to place in an envelope to send to his other family. The third day, he will draw a picture or choose some piece of memorabilia or little gift to send them. On the fourth day, they will speak again by phone. The fifth day, the Kirchners will plan and discuss with the child a brief visit with the Warburton family for the seventh day. On the sixth day, Danny will telephone to confirm the visit, which will occur the following day. After the first week, contingent upon Danny's reactions and level of adjustment, we will plan specific activities for subsequent days. Otto and Daniela like this tentative plan. They will do anything that will help Danny adjust and that will comfort him. If he feels a continuing connection with his first family, he will settle in better and faster with his new parents, we reason, as we talk about his probable reactions.

The Kirchners invite me to accompany them in the van on Sunday. The Warburtons have communicated emphatically that Otto and Daniela are to come alone; my role would be limited to passenger status; and I am reluctant to intrude on the Kirchners' first moments alone with their son. I am due to attend a reception for the president of Morton College, with Robert, but I will join the Kirchners immediately upon their return from the Warburtons' home. They will then introduce me to their son, and I will begin my daily work with their new family in the privacy of their apartment.

__April 29th

By phone, Loren informs me that Adrienne Drell, serving as an eyewitness, will be accompanying the Kirchners and himself in the van on Sunday. Adrienne will witness the unfolding events as the Kirchners spend their first hours with Danny. Admittedly nervous about the imminent event, Loren is also anxious to meet the child over whom he has waged such a protracted, agonizing court battle.

Arriving at the Kirchners' apartment to prepare them for meeting their son, I walk in the door to find three men from the television program *American Journal* taking pictures of the various rooms. A tabloid program syndicated by King World, *American Journal* has obtained the Kirchners' permission, through attorney Heinemann, to cover the "coming home" aspect of Danny's transfer. They will not allow the reporters to see Danny or to speak to him, however, out of concern for his privacy and his probable discomfort. Otto and Daniela are interviewed by one of the reporters, who asks them questions regarding their anticipation of having their son at long last. They talk about their shared excitement and eagerness; describe the preparations they have made; and explain Danny's bedroom, filled with *101 Dalmatians* and toys of all varieties, waiting for him. The Kirchners hope that this coverage will serve as the last telecast episode of "Baby Richard." They want it to be the final scene of the final act of "Richard."

After the reporters depart, Otto, Daniela, and I discuss the various possibilities for tomorrow. Otto fears that the Warburtons will call out the media to compromise his first meeting with Danny. Daniela focuses solely upon seeing her son and bringing him home. I predict that the Warburtons "will take the high road" by avoiding a media extravaganza because of their professed love for the child, whom they will continue to see if they allow him a safe and dignified hand-over to his parents. Smiling, Otto accuses me of raging optimism in this matter.

We discuss the importance of their being patient, gentle, slow, and non-reactive tomorrow regardless of the circumstances into which they will be walking. We talk about the worst-case scenario, a mob reaction that may include threats and attempts to harm them or actual physical violence. Most of our time together centers on their relating to Danny. They agree that they will not rush him and will accept whatever feelings he demonstrates, from withdrawal to fear or rage. We agree that the child will most likely reflect the feelings that he witnesses in the adults around him, especially in his adoptive parents. If they are calm and relaxed, he is apt to feel and behave accordingly. If they are fearful, angry, or weeping, he will follow their lead. The Kirchners are ready, after my three-hour visit, to face any eventuality tomorrow.

At 9:15 p.m., I leave to drive to the airport to pick up Robert from a one-week vacation with his brother Ed and wife Jean in Florida. Although we had planned this trip together for several months, I cancelled my plans to accompany him because of the unscheduled yet imminent transfer of Danny. I decided to remain continuously available for the Kirchners' first days with their son; Robert understands. Ironically, I could have gone on vacation with my husband and returned on time for the Kirchners' first hours with Danny, but I had no way of knowing that across recent weeks, during which ambiguity has reigned.

My last words to Otto and Daniela are "We'll share a special day together tomorrow..., probably a quiet, pleasant transfer and a difficult first night with Danny."

Events would prove me entirely wrong. All three Kirchners would be subjected to a traumatic transfer event..., but we would enjoy a peaceful and joyful night together.

Danny's First Week at Home

__April 30, 1995

NEWS programs across the country feature "Baby Richard," highlighting footage of the front-yard transfer scene. The story plays throughout Canada and across Europe as an American tragedy. What will happen to this innocent child, torn at the age of four from the only parents and family he has known? The scene is termed "a four-hanky melodrama," "horribly upsetting," an "ugly spectacle," an "achingly lurid scene," and "like a grotesque scene from a made-for-television movie," among other emotion-laden descriptions.

> You can discover more about a person in an hour of play than in a year of conversation.
>
> *— Plato*

It would be difficult to exaggerate the hysterical nature of much of the coverage. Many on-air journalists weep; anchorpersons choke on their words; and word merchants of all kinds, among the media world, resort to creative hyperbole and expressions of protest and outrage.

It is the ideal story for projection. Both men and women, of all ages, interject themselves and their own children—or grandchildren, nieces or nephews—into the telecast image of a mother losing her four-year-old son, surrounded by a mob of moaning and weeping onlookers, uniformed police officers, and a horde of reporters and camera wielders.

As I am watching various versions of the transfer scene on news programs, I am haunted by the feeling that something is missing. The adoptive mother carries the weeping child from her front door to the waiting van at the curb. What is wrong with this picture? It is my sister-in-law, Mary Anne, the mother of two adopted children, who gives the answer to that question.

"If I were the mother of that little boy, I would be comforting and reassuring him **every** step of the way," Mary Anne tells me. "That woman walked silently with that frightened baby, offering him **no** emotional help at all. How could she do that?" Danny was alone during that terrible march; his adoptive mother chose to provide him only transport to the street curb.

My work with Danny begins today. Actually, however, it will soon turn more into play, as our most therapeutic conversations will occur while sitting on the floor together, engaging in activities such as talking through Dalmatian puppets, telling stories over the family album, and sharing between us the red crayon from a box of twenty-four colors.

__May 1st

In his new home, however, Danny is oblivious. Having slept all night without awakening, he arises cheerful and smiling. "It's morning!" he declares to his joyful new mother, who is surprised at the casualness and enthusiasm of his first utterance of the day.

Daniela has slept little. She spent this first night watching her regained son sleeping by her side, and, feeling a combination of excitement and trepidation, she was planning the next day. The television set will remain turned off by design in order to prevent her son from seeing the Baby Richard coverage. Living through the trauma of yesterday will not be repeated by a telecast replay.

Otto prepares sausage, pancakes, and orange juice for Danny's first breakfast at home. A firm believer in comfort food, Otto plans to cook most of Danny's meals; it is his way of "serving love" to his son. Tonight he will make roast chicken and mashed potatoes for dinner.

Walking past a curbside media van, its prominent camera focused on the door of the Kirchners' apartment building, I arrive at 1:30 p.m. This van will be parked here from morning to night-fall for a series of days.

To my delight when I enter, Danny is playing with his toys in the living room and laughing softly. When he sees me, he begins shooting the large, harmless sponge discs at me, as he did last night, and he laughs more loudly when I dodge them, with feigned drama, and run away to the other room. From this encounter, play will become a regular activity between us. We will have our best, most meaningful interactions during shared play sessions.

Otto's cousin's wife, Alena, and her one-year-old daughter, Veronica, are visiting. The baby crawls around on the carpeting and pulls herself to a standing position several times in an attempt to walk. Out of Danny's hearing, Daniela reports to me that he has told her that he likes her. She is visibly happy but disappointed that he did not say that he likes his father. I assure her that this behavior is remarkable for his first full day with them and that he should not be expected to like either one of them at this point in time.

Otto watches Danny in his play. He has decided that Daniela will take the lead in interacting with the child because he has already expressed positive feelings toward her.

Both parents took Danny outside briefly this morning to walk by the large pond in the backyard and to give him an idea of his immediate environment, the area that he will use for a playground. They came inside after a few minutes because of the cold but not before Otto discovered a flat tire on their car. In spite of extra patrols assigned to his building by local police, some malicious individual was able to inflict this damage under the cover of darkness.

Danny starts jumping on the furniture, from chair to couch and back again. Otto and Daniela are relaxed with his antics; the room is childproofed and safe. He is testing the boundaries in this new home with these new parents. He soon tires of this activity and begins stacking up his stuffed animals to create a fortress on the couch. The interactions between parents and son are relaxed and natural. Danny is trying to impress his new parents; he describes what he is doing as he plays. They smile their approval at everything he does; they are in awe of him and his abilities.

During my three-hour visit, I begin a routine that will become typical as I create some private time for Danny and me to talk. I ask him open-ended questions, such as "How are you feeling?" and "What would you like to talk about today?" My focus is upon listening, waiting for his responses, and encouraging him to say anything on his mind.

"This room is not scary," he tells me, looking mildly surprised, while we sit on his king-sized bed and play with his furry Dalmatians.

"No, this room isn't scary; it's a beautiful room with dogs, toys, and bright colors," I respond, and then wait.

Danny explains that his mother and Johnny had told him that his new room would be "scary." After a pause, he adds, "Daddy told me it would be scary, too, because he doesn't live there."

When the visiting baby crawls toward Danny's room, he exclaims, "This is **my** room!" He is already feeling ownership of his new surroundings and his own personal territory.

I advise the Kirchners to explain to the child the expectations, rules, and privileges in this new home. For example, he should never leave the apartment without one of them; he can help himself to certain items in the refrigerator; he can turn on the music at any time that he likes; and similar behaviors. Because of his most recent upsetting experience, his public transfer, I recommend that Otto and Daniela assure him as soon as possible that they will never leave him for any reason. He will need this assurance because, at the age of four, he may fear that these new parents might also give him to others.

In private, Otto informs me that Danny announced that his "other parents" told him that he should not shower in his new home or play with toys there. Otto goes on to explain that Danny plays readily and intently, and he demonstrates a good attention span, especially when engaged in a computer game. The only problem is that he refuses to shower. We decide to omit the shower, and Daniela is content to wash him at the bathroom sink.

As I leave their home, a reporter from the *Daily Southtown* newspaper approaches me on the front sidewalk for an interview and a photograph for tomorrow's edition. He asks me a series of eight questions about Baby Richard and how he is doing with his new parents. Although I had requested anonymity and no dealings with the media as my only requirements when I undertook this *pro bono* case, both of these privacy conditions have become impossible.

In order to shield Danny and themselves from the direct onslaught of the intrusive media, the Kirchners have asked me to provide information, as I deem appropriate, without limitation. They trust my judgment, they tell me, and sign a written statement, releasing me from therapist-client confidentiality so that I might feel free to respond to situations as they unfold. I realize that if I become a buffer between my clients and the press, both parents and child will be more comfortable and protected as they continue their bonding together as a family. Danny has already been the target of more cameras wielded by strangers than most children experience throughout their entire childhood. And, the curbside van and cameraman remain in place throughout the day, poised to film any glimpse of the child, now a celebrity and the subject of intense curiosity.

After engaging in three interviews today, I decline the invitation to participate in a panel discussion about the Baby Richard case on a talk show entitled *Chicago Tribute*. I explain that I have scheduled clients throughout the evening hours and cannot accept.

When I telephone the Kirchners at 10:15 p.m., Otto reports that Danny is sound asleep; he went to bed on his own initiative; and Daniela is sleeping by his side again. Danny has not cried or asked for his other family, and he seems more comfortable. When Alena and her baby left, Danny initiated conversations with Otto.

I predict to him that it will be "two steps forward, one step back" for some time yet.

__May 2nd

This morning I invite the Kirchner family to my house for lunch. I have interviews scheduled for Fox TV and Channel 5 News, but we can spend an uninterrupted two hours in the privacy of my home before the reporters arrive. His parents and I have already decided that I will not see Danny in my office for a host of reasons, including his safety as our first priority. The media van remains in its usual place on the street, its occupant observing their apartment building throughout daylight hours.

The Kirchners arrive shortly after 1:00 p.m., followed close-ly by the media van. The driver visibly takes pictures of my house. Danny is smiling as he enters, holding his mother's hand. Otto introduces him to Robert, and Daniela also meets my hus-band for the first time.

Danny is wearing new clothes—a white, burgundy, and navy-blue knit sweater, light blue jeans, sturdy brown dress shoes, and a belt adorned by a buckle with Power Rangers fig-ures. Daniela points out the belt to us, and Danny, grinning, looks pleased with himself and his attire. He is a handsome boy with perfect features and a slightly mischievous smile.

When we sit at the table for lunch, Danny becomes subdued and his parents encourage him to speak and to eat his soup. I realize that they are worried because of this first visible sign of discomfort. This is his first experience, in the care of his birth parents, of visiting other people, and they have arrived with obvious media accompaniment. It seems likely that Danny has become fearful of exposure to the media because of his unhappy experience on Sunday, when the aggressive newspeople were also surrounded by an angry and mournful mob. The child does not know what to expect in this new environment.

At one point, in response to entreaties that he eat his food, Danny says quietly, "Leave me alone." I am happy to see that he is able and willing to assert himself in this way and that his parents readily acquiesce. Within minutes, he begins to eat his food, and we adults purposely talk about happy things through-out the meal.

After we finish eating, Danny and I take a tour of all three floors of the house. From the guest bedroom window we see Adrienne Drell's arrival by car. Danny remarks, "I like that car," and his casual comment causes me to relax from a sudden onrush of anxiety over the prospect that he might become upset by an encounter with a stranger. Adrienne confines her contact to Otto, Daniela, and Robert in the living room so that Danny and I can spend private time together.

Danny and I make a game out of searching for the two cats. After looking behind drapes, sofas, and chairs, we find Sybil, our mysterious-looking black cat, lying between the two pillows on the bed. Danny and I both pet her; he is gentle and curious. "She is soft," he observes, looking up at me with a smile.

He and I proceed to the backyard, exploring together the screened gazebo and small pond with golden fish and pink water lilies. I ask him if, during his next visit here, he would like to eat hamburgers in the gazebo, play in there, and pet the cat again. He replies that he would like that. Now he has a second house in which he can eat, play, and feel comfortable.

Daniela tells me that they have bought all new clothes for Danny. "He especially likes his new pajamas," she reports. "He sleeps exactly like his father, in the same position, and soundly through the night." Her face and voice reflect her pride and delight in her son.

Earlier today, Daniela left home for three hours for a job interview, leaving Danny and Otto alone together for the first time. She has been granted a three-day child care leave-of-absence from her salon in order to remain with Danny on a round-the-clock basis during his first days of settling into his new family. Otto is pleased that the boy seemed relaxed with him while his mother was away. Especially when his father was working on tasks around the apartment, Danny initiated conversations with him.

The Kirchner family leaves my home just as Renee Ferguson and her crew from Channel 5 News arrive for our scheduled interview. Danny smiles as he climbs into the car in the driveway while the newspeople are parking on the street—by our design missing each other and sparing him another media encounter.

After introductions, Renee Ferguson shares with me her own recent story about a reconsidered adoption. Renee and her husband Ken Smikle, both African-Americans and the parents of a nine-year-old son, planned to adopt a baby girl from a teenaged unwed mother from a good family. "The teenager, also African-American, was still in high school, very bright, and had the realistic prospect of an Ivy League school in her immediate future," Renee reveals. "We made the arrangements with her and her parents; had the baby's room decorated and all set up; and hired an attorney to make the necessary legal arrangements. I always wanted a daughter and we were excited about the adoption," she continues. "However, when we went to the hospital to get the baby, the mother changed her mind. Her parents said that we could still proceed and take the child. I realized that my husband and I were very strong people and so were the young mother's parents. We could have imposed our collective will on the teenager, but I felt she would always keep reaching out for her baby. We couldn't go through with it. It was very difficult, but we just left," Renee explains. "The girl raised her baby, and her parents came to accept her as their grandchild. It was the Baby Richard situation—in the courts and in the media—that made me rethink adoption, its implications, and my own values. I didn't want that kind of complication," she concludes.

After the interview, which turns out to be more of a mutual sharing of information and feelings, Ferguson leaves to cover another story, and I hurry off to my office for a full evening of clients.

At 6:30 p.m. Loren telephones me from the Kirchners' home to ask my opinion. "Danny is playing basketball outside with the other children and having a great time. Should his parents interrupt him to take him to their scheduled appointment with the pediatrician for his first check-up or postpone it so that he can continue to have fun?"

My advice is for the latter option; I am delighted that Danny is already enjoying play with the neighborhood children; and Loren advises Otto and Daniela to reschedule the doctor's examination of Danny for tomorrow.

I had chosen the pediatrician carefully, interviewing her and warning her that the family might arrive at her office with unwanted but determined media accompaniment.

At 10 p.m. I phone Otto to discover that Danny played for several hours with five or six of the other children from the apartment complex. He was the center of attention, no doubt because of his status as the preferred subject of the ever-present television cameras. Not only were cameras rolling today but some of the media people interviewed the other children to elicit their comments about "Baby Richard." Meanwhile, Danny was riding his bike, playing basketball, and throwing pieces of bread into the pond for the ducks. Many of the neighbors from the apartment buildings that surround the pond were observing from their balconies; some were snapping pictures with their cameras; and several were talking on their portable telephones.

"I have six new friends!" Danny announced when he came inside. He has referred to Daniela as "Mommy" twice today. For the first time, Otto describes the situation as "remarkable." Until now, he has been anxiety-ridden and reserved about his own reactions to the child's adjustment. Danny is already sound asleep; he readily went to his bed alone tonight; his mother did not accompany him except to tuck him in and she joined him one hour later.

Today Loren brought over a White Sox tee shirt for Danny as a gift, explaining that he would need to shower before he could wear it. Daniela sponge-bathed him again, as he continues to refuse to take a shower. He says again that his other parents told him not to shower in his new house.

The end of Day #3 seems to be a resounding success, with neither tears nor requests for his other family. He has taken to calling Daniela "Mommy," at his own initiation.

__May 3rd

When I arrive at the Kirchners' apartment this evening, Danny is playing in the backyard with two eleven-year-olds, Jeffrey and Justin, the latter of whom "has taken Danny under his wing," according to Otto. Danny is riding his bike on the narrow concrete sidewalk that surrounds the pond. Otto retrieves a fishing pole from their patio and announces, with obvious pride, that Danny caught a fish earlier in the day.

Danny played outside today from 10:00 a.m. to nearly 7:00 p.m., with breaks for lunch and dinner. While we stand outside, watching Danny still at play, a neighbor, who introduces himself as Jim, comes over to tell Otto and Daniela that he knows what they are going through; he feels for them; and he will be available if they need any help. Jim is accompanied by his three-year-old daughter, a shy, attractive child. They are the only two people who have come forward thus far to express support of the Kirchners.

Later, Danny sits in front of the television set, drinks orange juice, and begins to play Nintendo games. Before long, he switches his attention to the collection of videotapes next to the TV and slides his favorite, *The Lion King*, into the VCR. Otto, Daniela, and I watch the movie with him, while he lies on the black couch. Daniela interrupts him to put on his pajamas; she returns with his *101 Dalmatians* pillow, which she places under his head on the couch. Otto places a blanket over him, and within minutes he is fast asleep. His mother carries him into his room and places him in bed, and he continues to sleep without stirring.

We discuss Danny's progress, and I advise Otto and Daniela always to explain to Danny where they are going, when they will return, and what to expect at any new place they visit. There should be no surprises for him. I also encourage them to explain that there may have been different rules at his other house, but at this new house his mom and dad need to have their own rules. Otto believes that Danny fears that his "other mother" will become angry with him if she discovers he has showered or bathed in their home. He is trying to engage Danny in discussing his other home so that he will become secure and trusting enough of his new parents to say anything on his mind.

Daniela is returning to work tomorrow, having taken off these first few days to spend with Danny. They need the money, however, and she is sad but resigned to returning to her full-time job as an esthetician at a modern beauty salon in Chicago. Otto will become the primary caregiver of Danny, a role that he welcomes after so many years of determined anticipation of fatherhood.

Loren telephones to report that the media, he has discovered, will be out in full force at the swearing-in ceremony tomorrow. Otto is due to become an American citizen. Otto and Daniela decide that Danny will not attend because of the frightening media bombardment that he has already endured this week.

Loren informs us that he has lined up a child psychiatrist at Loyola University, who has volunteered his services, to visit with Danny in his office. Otto believes this arrangement is merely a political gesture; reminds us that Danny has expressed a fear of doctors; and expresses his opinion that it would not be good for the child to be taken to a psychiatrist at this point. I perform a review of Danny's progress—he is eating well, sleeping through the night, playing with other children, interacting well with his new parents, calling Daniela "Mommy," and neither crying nor appearing either sad or depressed. His affect is appropriate; he laughs readily; his attention span is good, such as when he is playing a game; and he talks often, expressing his feelings and his wishes. He occasionally talks about his other parents, brother, and home, but he has not asked for them. One or both of his parents have been with him at all times, including his hours of sleep. Otto decides that a visit to the child psychiatrist might occur in the future, if and when needed.

We discuss the pros and cons of the possibility of Danny's continued involvement with his former adoptive parents. Otto's greatest concern is that the trauma of last Sunday will be relived by the child if he has contact with them; that Danny's emotional well-being and adjustment might be jeopardized by renewed memories of the media onslaught, weeping, mob jeers, and terror surrounding the transfer event. Danny retains a vivid, painful memory of it, and a renewed contact, Otto reasons, may well ignite a similar emotional reaction in him. How sad it is, I think, that their self-indulgent, orchestrated media blitz may well have backfired on the adoptive parents in terms of their relationship with this child. They had known the likely outcome of their decision, but they willfully chose to subject Danny to that most public, frightening scene of his life, which threatened his physical safety at the same time.

If Danny visits them, they are unlikely to approve of his bonding with his birth parents. All of the Warburtons' history demonstrates their unwillingness even to introduce the child to his parents. They reaffirmed their intentions of self-interest and retribution by calling out the media to witness Danny's suffering. Danny is smart enough to know that the two sets of parents have conflicting needs regarding his love and loyalty. He will probably experience worry, guilt, and confusion within such difficult circumstances. There are indications that he fears the prospect of the aroused anger of his adoptive parents if they discover that he has played and enjoyed himself in his new home with his new parents.

My visit today spans four hours. I leave at 10:30 p.m., still struggling with a weeklong illness, taking antibiotics, aspirin, and cough medicine. I am not sleeping or eating well, and I am also losing weight. Earlier today I agreed to a telephone interview from a news media service for radio broadcast in order to update listeners on the progress of Baby Richard. A reporter from the *Chicago Tribune* called to ask about the prospects of the child's meeting with his former parents; I explained that the child's needs are the first priority in this matter. Liz from Fox TV called to get information regarding my professional credentials. Several other media representatives have called and left messages. I am providing them information, at the request of the Kirchners, in the hope that they will be satisfied and the story will soon become "old news." Otto is dismayed that Loren seems continuously involved in media hype, perpetuating it. He has asked Loren to stop talking about the case so that Danny might begin a normal life.

The best news is that the media van and cameraman, stationed for days in front of the apartment building, are now gone. With Danny outside for hours, looking like an ordinary, normal boy at play with his friends, there is no bad news and therefore no story. When several of the neighbor children answered questions and declared they had never seen Danny cry or call for his "other parents," the reporters packed up their gear and disappeared.

With neither a tantrum nor a tear to capture on film, across the span of days, they vanish, presumably to move on to more propitious events, those with some photogenic adversity or travail.

__May 4th

A horde of media representatives, as predicted, appear to cover the story of Baby Richard's father becoming a United States citizen, as he is sworn in along with 120 others in the Dirksen Federal building. Daniela and Danny are waiting elsewhere in order to avoid the cameras and reporters.

I visit them in their apartment this evening from 5:00 to 7:00 p.m., bringing a bottle of champagne with me so that we might toast Otto's citizenship status. Loren appears for a half-hour visit and a glass of celebration with us. He announces that a representative from a philanthropic organization contacted him today to offer him $400,000 for his legal fees and Otto one million dollars, if he will relinquish custody of Danny to the Warburtons and settle for visitation rights with his son. In addition, he says, two other phone calls came in today, each pledging $50,000 for Otto and $20,000 for Loren if the child is returned to his adoptive parents. Otto responds that these offers are ridiculous and insulting.

The attorney reviews with us his conversations with a movie producer about the prospect of a "six-figure contract" for Otto for the rights to a movie about Baby Richard. "He is insisting on a **happy** ending as a condition of making the deal," Loren shares with us while taking his last sips of "bubbly." He continues, "That means you would have to return Danny to the adoptive parents, Otto."

Without words, Otto answers by a pointed look of disdain, directed at Loren, who recognizes his client's reaction as his time to depart. With a curt but friendly farewell, Loren leaves, smiling wryly, unsurprised by his client's reaction of indignation and disgust.

Danny goes outside to play again, after having eaten his dinner, while Otto and I sit on lawn chairs on the back patio to watch him. Before long, Danny comes up to ask permission to go to the hill nearby to play with his three friends, including Justin, who has become the self-proclaimed protector of his little playmate. We follow them to ensure that they are safe. Danny is hanging from the branch of an evergreen tree, laughing and showing off his climbing skills, while the other, older children seem genuinely amused by him and still in awe of his celebrity.

Earlier today, for the first time Danny referred to Otto as "Dad." After Daniela had encouraged Danny to try to fix a glitch in the electronic equipment himself, the child responded, "Only Dad can fix this." Otto is surprised and delighted that his son is now referring to him as "Dad." "This is my best day ever!" Otto declares as he relates the welcome incident. He informs me that he has assured Danny that they will never leave him or give him away to anyone, no matter what ever happens.

Danny has told Daniela that he would like her to stay with him during the day. She hates to leave him when she goes to work, but she has explained why she must work and has assured him that she misses him, too. Otto is still trying to find employment, to no avail. He would also like Daniela to be able to stay home with their child. Someone needs to bring into the household the funds to pay their bills.

__May 5th

At 2:30 p.m. I arrive for my daily visit with the Kirchners. Otto and Danny, returned from a tour of the local Toys Я Us store, bought more toys. Danny is excited about his new Power Rangers outfit, complete with belt and mask. He opens the box to show me the shiny costume; Otto helps him dress into it; and he reviews himself in the full-length mirror in the hallway. Then, with his father's approval, he leaves to show himself off to his new friends. Otto tells me that he and Danny also bought a pink, adult-size Power Rangers outfit for Daniela, with accompanying mask, for her to wear when she comes home. Danny is looking forward to playing with his mother this evening.

We join Danny outside, where there are no friends yet because they have not arrived home on their school bus. We all return to the apartment to await the imminent arrival of the neighbor children. Before long, Michael, a boy of Danny's age, appears at the front door and rings the bell. Danny is happy and animated, glad to be seen in his Power Rangers regalia. The boys go outside and begin riding their bikes together around the pond. Soon Justin returns from school and comes in search of Danny. I take this opportunity to ask Justin to talk to Danny about how nice it is to take showers every day.

When I talk to Danny today, his eye contact is good and he seems to want to talk to me more than usual. When Dr. Lechner arrives, as earlier planned, we introduce him to Danny as "Ray" rather than "Doctor Ray" because of the child's articulated fear of doctors. Ray will be available to the Kirchners during my two-week vacation to Indonesia, to which I had committed weeks before meeting Otto and Daniela, in early January. Ray provides Otto and Daniela with his various phone numbers, including his home number, so that they will be able to connect with him at any time.

Otto invites the three boys into the apartment, as it is getting chilly. They all follow us inside; Otto changes Danny's clothes into his two-piece, red-and-black windbreaker outfit; and the boys continue their play.

Ray leaves after assuring Otto that he will remain on call, as needed, while I am out of town. Otto invites me to review the daily mail, which includes a tall stack of hate letters and a smaller one of congratulatory messages. Every day the mail deliverer arrives with a pile of mail, most of which is addressed simply "Otakar Kirchner" or "Baby Richard's Father," "Mokena, Illinois," with no street address. The majority is hateful and includes obscenities, threats, and warnings. Occasionally I read some pieces, the most common theme of which expresses the hope that Otto "will burn in hell" for what he has done to his child and to the Warburtons.

Otto describes an incident today wherein Danny came inside, looking worried and nearly in tears, with mud on his shoes. Otto assured him that it was "okay—no problem," and he

visibly relaxed. He wonders to me about the rules and consequences in Danny's other house, as the child clearly expected to
be punished for getting dirty and bringing mud inside. Danny is
experiencing the first reactions of his parents to each new incident in his daily life.

__May 6th

Danny is talking today about his "other house," Otto reports to
me as I arrive for my visit. He refers to it as "John's house,"
demonstrating his understanding of his own situation and the
first articulated sign of detachment from his previous life. He
spoke about his friend Eric, whom he seems to miss. Otto
believes that he also misses John, but he has not yet asked to
see him or his former parents.

Danny is still getting daily sponge baths rather than bathing
in the tub or showering; he refuses to shower or bathe. Both Otto
and Daniela fear that, if they force the issue, Danny will begin
crying, which reaction they are trying to avoid at all costs. I
advise that they will need to require his compliance; crying is a
normal part of being a four-year-old; and, if he cries, it does not
necessarily follow that he will want to return to his former home.

During my three-hour stay today, cousin Lali, wife Alena,
and baby Veronica are visiting. They speak Slovak among themselves, and Lali and Alena mostly smile and nod at me. "They
are my only family here," Otto explains to me. "My father
returned to Slovakia years ago." I silently wonder about the
incongruity of Otto's settling in this geographical area in order
to be in close proximity to his father, who, before long, relocated
once again to another continent.

Otto and I speak about Danny's new testing behaviors. He
and Daniela have been trying so hard and consistently to make
everything perfect for him that he is becoming willful and
demanding. Danny is testing limits, normal behavior for a child
in a new environment, I assure him. If accustomed to a constant,
daily diet of perfection, served up by his parents, he will come to
expect a full menu of selections of his choice, not a realistic or
healthy situation for a four-year-old.

Danny is playing with Jeffrey and Melody, both eleven. He
appears comfortable with older children, both boys and girls, and
unintimidated by them. Otto explains that Danny always wants

to be outside with the other children, while he would prefer more interactive time between father and son so that their bonding process will be accelerated. Again, Danny's desires have been fully indulged throughout his first week in residence with his parents.

Daniela joins us as we begin to talk about their entering another phase with the child, in which they will need to insist upon his compliance with their wishes in certain matters. They will also need, from time to time, to impose consequences, such as a brief time-out if he expresses defiance. I advise them to condition certain privileges and fun activities upon his completing a required task. For example, they might condition his going outside to play upon his first taking a shower.

We talk about the importance of praise and positive reinforcement. When he complies with even the simplest of requests, they should say, "Thank you" or "Good boy" or "Nice job." A good goal is "to catch him doing something right" and then to praise him for it. Everyone wins and feels good with such exchanges; the child feels appreciated; and the adults bestow deserved acknowledgement. These behaviors also teach good manners and the importance of positive communications between family members. Daniela is visibly brightened by this advice.

As we lapse into talk about other issues, Daniela expresses discouragement about her work situation. Not only does she resent the time away from her son but, when traffic is heavy, her daily commute now takes one and one-half hours each way. She hopes to find a new position closer to home, but she wonders if a suburban salon will afford her the same level of salary and gratuities as her current job, located in a yuppie neighborhood of the city.

Danny and Jeffrey, driven inside by the cold, want to play computer games, but the adult guests are watching television. Daniela tries out her new assertive-mom skills by telling the boys they may play in Danny's room and they should not interrupt their company. Jeffrey readily responds "Okay!" and leads Danny to the bedroom.

Lali and his family leave for home after hugs all around. I have advised that, at least during Danny's first weeks, everyone who comes for a visit will be hugged upon arrival and again upon departure. This practice will demonstrate affection and trust within his new environment; will allay his fear of strangers; and will model for him loving gestures and interactions between his parents and their guests.

Minutes after Lali and his family have departed, Loren arrives, bringing a dozen cards and letters addressed to Otto and three letters for Daniela. Two contain $20 checks for the couple to use toward a gift for "Richard"; one individual has sent $100 with a complimentary note. The messages are positive and affirming, praising Otto for his perseverance, courage, and loyalty to his son. Loren has also brought a couple of toys, sent by strangers, which Danny happily accepts and begins to inspect and try out.

Loren, wearing a proud smile, informs us that he has been named "Newsmaker of the Week" by WGN and he will be featured on the front page of the *Daily Southtown* tomorrow. By phone this morning, he was interviewed for what had been pre-planned as one-half hour of a talk show for Seattle, Washington, but the incoming calls were so voluminous that he continued for two full hours of air time. Loren is exuberant about being a celebrity.

The big hurdle for tonight is Danny's prospective first bath or shower in his new home. Daniela gulps hard, rolls her eyes, and resigns herself to having to force a bath on her son. This is new behavior for her, having acquiesced to every one of his requests and whims this week in order to foster his getting used to his new family. I encourage her to proceed, as we discussed, and not allow herself to be deterred or controlled by crying. Daniela runs water for him in the tub.

From behind the closed door, we hear Danny crying, not frightened crying or sobbing, but the sound of a young child who is being made to do something he does not care to do. Daniela cajoles, coaxes, and reassures him, while she places him in the tub and washes him from head to toe. He says nothing but continues to cry his protest for several minutes.

Soon the door opens, and Danny emerges clean and dressed in his new two-piece, multi-colored pajamas. Looking calm and relaxed, he has stopped crying. His mother hugs him to her; he leans against her for a kiss; and then he returns to the living room, asking for his Power Rangers. Daniela explains that she chose a bath for him because he still seemed afraid of the showerhead.

Adrienne Drell and her husband stop by to give the Kirchners copies of the professional photographs taken of themselves and Danny on his first night with them. In the hallway, outside of the hearing of others, Adrienne talks to me about her colleagues. "In all of my career," she discloses to me, "I have never witnessed such viciousness among media people as I have seen directed against the Kirchners this past week."

After they leave, I tell Danny about my upcoming vacation; that I will be gone for two weeks but will see him every day again as soon as I return; and I will bring him a present from far away. I put a photo of myself on his bedside table, telling him that I want him to remember me while I am gone and that I will look forward to seeing him very soon.

Danny calls Daniela "mom" and Otto "dad" on a consistent basis today. Early this week the Kirchners taught him the Slovak words for "mom" and "dad," encouraging him to use those terms so as to avoid confusion by distinguishing themselves from his "other" mom and dad. Ignoring these alternative names, Danny proceeded on his own initiative to use "mom" and "dad," to the delight of his parents. He is now referring to the Warburtons as "Johnny's mom" and "Johnny's dad."

Otto informs Danny, "Soon it will be Mommy's birthday and we will have a nice cake for her."

"I had a birthday party, too," Danny relates to us, "but they took the cake away." Otto and I remember TV news coverage on Danny's birthday that featured a large, colorfully decorated cake, on which "HAPPY 4th BIRTHDAY, **RICHARD**" was displayed in frosting. The child himself was not shown on camera. Otto remarks, in a whisper to me, that it is most interesting that the cake did not wish a happy birthday to the real "Danny" and that it was probably just a prop, a part of the media campaign on the side of the adoptive parents. The story line tugged at heartstrings by emphasizing that this would likely be Baby Richard's last birthday with his adoptive parents.

__May 7th

During my daily check-in phone call, I plan my visit to the Kirchners' home for 4:30 to 7:30 p.m. "Danny spoke to me this morning about his other family," Otto says. Among other things, the child said, "My other daddy didn't want me to come here." After this conversation, Danny became affectionate and polite, using "please" and "thank you," and he hugged his father. Thus far, Danny has frequently shown affection toward his mother, leaning against her, hugging, and occasionally kissing her, but he has not initiated physical contact with his father until today. This conversation, directed by Danny, was an icebreaker between them. Shortly afterwards, he jumped onto his father's lap and snuggled with him. I am glad to hear this good news from Otto, who is joyful over this newest development. Danny is talking openly and in a trusting manner with his father.

Upon my arrival, three of Danny's friends—Jeffrey, Justin, and Jason—are playing with him in the apartment. Across three hours, they ride their bikes, fish in the pond, eat pretzels, and take turns riding in Danny's motorized car. Taking Justin aside, I thank him for his protective attitude toward Danny and request that he keep us informed of any development that seems unusual.

This evening Otto has prepared breaded pork cutlets for dinner, and he plans to call them "Dinosaur McNuggets" for Danny. Lamenting that the child prefers junk food, he hopes that Danny will develop a taste for home-cooked meals. In the meantime, he sometimes creates names for food that will appeal to the child.

When Daniela returns from work, she looks tired. She greets Danny and his friends, who are playing a Nintendo game in the living room. When we talk about my vacation and Dr. Lechner's availability to continue my work with them, Daniela says, "We will all miss you; you have become a part of our family."

We revisit the bath episode from yesterday. Daniela remarks that, although she expected Danny to remain angry with her after she forced him into a bath, he was neither angry nor upset once she put on his pajamas. He forgot the whole episode within minutes. She and Otto are no longer as fearful of the prospect of Danny's crying.

Today, as on every other day this week, I notice that Otto is always smiling as he watches Danny's every move around the apartment. He and Daniela gush their praises, "He is so smart...; he is so good at that...; he knows how to do it on his own." I realize that Danny understands that his new, "real" parents love and appreciate him in a special way. They have become instantly proud of him and genuinely delighted with everything he does, no matter how simple. When he throws stones into the pond, they remark, "He has such a good arm, he will probably be a great athlete." When he deftly uses the computer remote control, they say, "Look at how smart he is!" When he eats all of his meal, they exclaim, "You're an angel!"

Danny has become the epicenter of the universe for his mother and his father. He would have to be a stone not to feel these frequent eruptions of love from them.

Daniela makes me hot lemon tea soon after her return from work. I have a deep, lingering cough from a virus with flu-type symptoms.

Danny has so many toys now that both his bedroom and the living room are filled with them. He announces, "These are **my** toys!" when I admire them.

While Otto and I stand on the patio, watching the children play, he relates his most recent private conversation with Danny. "I told him I loved him very much and could not live without him." This seemed to make a big impression on the child. When I speak to Daniela about Danny's excellent progress, she speculates, "The power of flesh and blood is very great; even animals recognize each other and their own offspring in special ways."

As I am leaving for home, I feel ambivalent about my trip abroad, scheduled to begin in three days. When Robert and I made our plans for this vacation, I remind myself, I didn't even know Otto and Daniela, and I had no idea that I would be working with them and their son. Now, I would rather stay home and continue my daily visits with the Kirchner family.

However, Danny is adjusting better than we planned or even hoped; he is showing no signs of trauma or distress; and he is eating, sleeping, playing, and relating as a normal four-year-old. This is his eighth day in residence with his parents. In addition to daily phone sessions, I have visited their home every day for an average of three hours.

Every morning my first thought is of Danny and every night before I fall asleep my last concern is for his welfare.

> To be rooted is perhaps the most important and least recognized need of the human soul.
>
> — *Simone Weil*

The Story of Otto

> We are never so defenseless against suffering as when we love.
>
> — *Sigmund Freud*

"EVERY TIME an airplane flew over our soccer field, I would look up, excited, and wonder if my mother was coming for me." Otto, his voice low and eyes downcast, is describing the sharpest memories of his childhood. "Sometimes I would just stop playing and run home to wait for hours on the front porch, hoping to see my mother coming to reclaim me, like she promised....

"But she never came," he concludes after a long pause.

He and I are sitting in his living room, sipping coffee, while Danny and Justin are playing a game together in the bedroom. Now that Danny is settling into his new home after one week here—his comfort level increased by daily contact with friends from nearby apartments—his father and I can talk privately. Otto takes this opportunity to tell me the story of his own life, how he came to be here, in this country and in these circumstances of being detested by neighbors, acquaintances, and countless strangers.

Today, at his urging, I have read the most recent letters that have arrived in the mail, although I normally decline to read them. I know that Daniela refuses to read them. It is too upsetting and frightening for her to see daily reminders that so many strangers wish them ill to this extent. Nine of this batch of eleven letters are anonymous, either unsigned or signed "Concerned" or "A Parent," or some similar pseudonym. Nine of them would properly be called hate letters. Several express the sentiment—or a facsimile—"Go back to where you came from," and one rages, "I hope you burn in hell for all eternity." Only two of the letters are positive, one of them praising Otto for his courage in fighting so long and hard for his son and the other wishing his new family happiness.

None of the eleven envelopes includes a street address, as Otto and Daniela maintain an unpublished address and phone number. Addressed simply to "Baby Richard's Father, Mokena, Illinois," they are delivered by the dutiful postman—this daily fare of mostly anonymous, usually angry, and often vile mail.

Although **this** group does not contain threats, most of the early barrage of written hate missiles issue warnings, threaten physical harm, and liberally scatter obscenities. "When you least expect it, I will blow up your f——— ass" is an example that finds its way into my daily notes, in which I attempt to capture the relevant and the extraordinary aspects of my involvement with Danny and his family.

Otto has become immune to the invective and even to the death threats. Someone else would report these alarming warnings to their local police department. "What's the use?" he asks me when I suggest this course of action. "It won't stop the hate or the mail, and who knows what the police will do if I contact them? I can't trust...," his voice fades away and we change the subject. I understand his reluctance to invite authorities into his private life or to expose his family to intrusion. The heads of several state agencies, numerous legislators, and the governor have publicly taken positions attacking him. Any police officer would likely arrive with a predisposition of suspicion and bias against him, with a jaundiced eye. If Otto were to be arrested for an alleged violation of any kind, the arresting officer would be lauded as a hero.

"I knew my grandparents loved me," he continues, "but I couldn't understand how my parents could leave me behind.

All of the other kids were in contact with their parents, even if they were divorced. My parents didn't even write to me. I wondered if maybe I was adopted, and one day I asked my grandmother, 'Why else would it be like this?'"

Born in Bratislava, Czechoslovakia, in August 1956, Otto lived in a typical Eastern European extended family. Cousins ate together at his grandmother's table. She bartered her gold and diamond jewelry for food for her family during post-war communism years. Otto's parents and he lived with his maternal grandparents during his earliest years, but after his parents divorced, they both left the home and left behind their four-year-old son. He yearned for their return. Even before their departure, however, they were often not available to their young son. "They were always busy with other things, and not with me," according to Otto's memories of his early childhood.

"I remember one night in particular, my grandparents went to the house of a more fortunate neighbor, to watch the new invention, television. My mother had returned to the house to supervise me. But she wanted to go to watch television, too. I asked her not to leave me. She locked me inside my bedroom and left for the other house.

"At midnight I got very scared when I couldn't get out of my room," he relates. "I thought I saw green eyes everywhere. I even wet my pants. In a panic, I climbed out of the second-story window and from the ledge I jumped to the ground. I hit the sand and went unconscious."

Otto was rushed to the hospital, where he spent three days for treatment and observation. Fortunately, he had no broken bones but he was badly bruised.

Ironically, before long after Otto's accident, his mother became pregnant with the child of the owner of the "television house." She married him and gave birth to his son, a child who would replace Otto in her new life. Otto's grandparents assumed the custody and care of their abandoned grandson.

By the age of ten, Otto had lost contact with both of his parents. His mother, married to her much older second husband, who had forbidden her to bring her first son into their new family, not only complied with his bidding but discontinued communications with Otto. His father was sentenced to jail for his political activities in opposition to the Czechoslovakian regime, and he was forced to flee, for his life, to America. Occasionally, Otto recalls, his two maternal aunts would visit his grandparents' home. Pervasively, he felt discarded.

Although continuously lonely throughout his childhood years for his mother and father, Otto was loved and nurtured by his grandparents. Like his uncle and grandfather, he decided to become a proficient classical violinist. After seven years of music college, he began a career with the Slovak National Radio Symphony Orchestra, enjoying both status and recognition. Otto soon experienced another betrayal, however, this time by his trusted mentor. The conductor of the Radio Symphony Orchestra, a devout member of the Communist Party, reported Otto to the authorities as anti-Communist and a likely flight risk.

"Three soldiers came to my house, looking for me," he explains. "Then the KGB came for me, too. I felt I had no choice but to escape to Spain and from there to Germany." Because he could not safely return to his own country, Otto decided to emigrate to the United States. There, he reasoned, he would have the opportunities to rediscover his father and to settle into the best place in the world to raise a son of his own. He resolved that his son would have everything that he lacked, including—and especially—parents.

"We kids had more imagination than toys. I had two or three store-bought toys and that was it. We played ball and made up games to entertain ourselves," Otto recalls. "From early in my life, I wanted my child to have more than I did. I always wanted to be a good father, to be there for my son. I didn't want him ever to go through what I did. I promised myself at a young age to make a better life for my own son."

During his last year in his native country, Otto went to visit Piroska, an elderly Hungarian gypsy whose reputation for predicting the future was legend. Although others shared her career path as a seer with mixed reviews of their success, Piroska foretold—with widely-reported, remarkable accuracy—significant events in her customers' futures.

Otto vividly remembers her words to him. "Piroska told me, 'Otto, you will cross the ocean and there you will fall deeply in love with a beautiful blonde woman. You will have a son but at the same time not have a son. Then, the two of you will have two daughters.' I never understood the part about my son until now," he declares. "I believe in her powers, and I think that Daniela and I will soon have two daughters."

Before his emigration papers were issued, Otto was required to spend one year in a German refugee camp, where he lost forty pounds from work and worry. His grandmother wept when she saw pictures of him because—as she wrote him—he "looked like an entirely different person." Finally arriving in Chicago in May 1986, he was delighted to find his father, who appeared happy to see him. Otto was impressed and dazzled by the city skyscrapers and endless lights. He was also surprised and dismayed to see people begging in the streets, a new phenomenon that alarmed him. Had he made the right decision? he wondered.

With the help of his father, in two days he obtained a job as a host for the Riverside Restaurant in Riverside, Illinois, a nearby suburb of Chicago. He started in earnest to work on his English, learning the language mostly from his customers. After six months, he landed a job at the large, successful Kenessey's restaurant in the Belmont Hotel on Lake Shore Drive on the north side of Chicago. Starting there as a waiter, he soon progressed to assistant manager and then to manager. With his managerial position came the responsibility to hire and train his own staff. When Kenessey's went out of business in 1994, after months of unfavorable publicity directed at Otto, many people blamed its demise on the effects of the media storm. During the peak of its success in 1989, however, he hired another member of the local Czech community, Daniela Janikova, as a waitress.

Daniela was so new to the country that she spoke only limited English at first, but, a quick learner, she was improving daily. After hiring her, Otto taught her to become a waitress. She was the most beautiful woman he had ever seen, but she was also distant. She was eleven years younger than he and blessed with both grace and a quiet charm. He found himself trying to impress her, realizing that he was falling deeply in love.

"We were crazy about each other," he reminisces. "I could feel electricity whenever she appeared. I had never loved like that before."

A big complication for Otto was a long-standing relationship with his girlfriend Maria, who had come to America from Czechoslovakia to live with him. They enjoyed a close relationship, "but she was not interested in marriage or in raising children," Otto says. "That was a problem, but a bigger one was that she could not bear children. She had a medical problem as a teenager and never had it treated; it left her unable to have kids." Otto wanted a family more than anything else in life.

"Without children, life has no meaning for me; it's empty," he proclaims, revealing his foremost priority and motivational force.

On his birthday, August 26, 1989, Maria confronted Otto about his relationship with Daniela and told him to move out. He willingly left Maria for Daniela. Soon they were not only working together but also living together in his apartment on the north side of Chicago. With his emotional and financial support, Daniela left her waitress job at the restaurant to study at a nearby beauty school. Although already trained as an esthetician in her native country, Daniela found that she had to repeat her education in this country before she could qualify for a license to practice in her chosen field. Daniela became suspicious and jealous of Maria when she discovered that Otto's former girlfriend continued occasionally to visit Otto at the restaurant.

When Daniela discovered that she was pregnant with Danny, Otto was thrilled. "You can't imagine what the child meant to me," he exclaims. "During the pregnancy I talked to him and felt great joy in resting my head on Daniela's belly, listening to him."

In early 1991, during Daniela's eighth month of pregnancy, Otto received a call from Slovakia. His grandmother, who had raised him, was dying from Alzheimer's disease. If he wanted to see her again, he must go immediately. Daniela encouraged Otto to respond by going to see his grandmother for the last time.

"In the few days I was gone, my life and Daniela's changed forever," he sighs. Although he would be gone for less than two weeks, his life would be changed forever. Confronted by his maternal aunt, who was certain that life in America must result in instant wealth, Otto listened to her demand $10,000 from him, or, "I will make you very sorry," she warned. When he refused to pay, in spite she telephoned Daniela to say that Otto was honeymooning there with Maria. "It was a lie," Otto affirms, "but it did such terrible damage...."

Daniela, young, naïve, and alone when she received the malicious phone call, was devastated. She knew nothing of the unsuccessful attempt at extortion that led to his aunt's report about Otto's infidelity. While visiting his childhood neighbor-hood, he had in fact dropped in to see Maria's family, whom he had known for many years, but he did not reunite with Maria because Daniela and he were planning to get married.

"In fact," Otto tells me, "during my visit to Slovakia, I went to see Daniela's parents to request permission to marry their daughter." Otto, taking flowers to his intended in-laws, received their approval of his proposal of marriage to their youngest child.

"I tried to convince Daniela by phone that what my aunt told her wasn't true and I would be back soon," he relates with sad-ness and urgency in his voice. "She didn't believe me and became desperate. I tried to call her again and again, but she just hung up on me."

Bursting into tears at the beauty school, Daniela revealed the reason for her pain to a teacher, who attempted to comfort her. You must have this child adopted for his sake, said the teacher; you cannot have a baby with this kind of man! Conveniently, the teacher's friend was a lawyer who could arrange this adoption, and—as it turned out—the lawyer's for-mer paralegal, Kimberly Warburton, liked the idea of adopting him herself. There would be no need to deal with red tape or cumbersome agencies, the teacher urged; it would be easy…and best for the baby.

Within days Daniela met with Kimberly and Jay Warburton. The next day—while Otto was still abroad—she left the apart-ment that she shared with him. She went to a women's refuge, the Greenhouse, to wait until they could move her to a hospital, one that was far away from the hospital that she and Otto had planned for the delivery of their baby. Otto would be unable to find her there, she reasoned. She could give birth and hand over the baby to the waiting Warburtons, who could provide him with a good, two-parent home.

Without the benefits of counseling, family help, an attorney or time to think over her decision, Daniela found herself truly alone, vulnerable, and confused. Her only relative in the States, an uncle whose wife had recently left him, reluctantly told her that, if she had nowhere else to go, she could live with him. Otto explains, "Daniela couldn't bring a baby into his house. Her uncle said he wouldn't listen to a baby crying, and she felt then that she had no choice except adoption for the baby." She was living in a strange land, spoke little English, had no money, and was unfamiliar with adoption—a rare occurrence in her native country. The Warburtons were determined and Daniela succumbed to the plan.

In Illinois, there is a period of only 72 hours within which a mother may change her mind regarding giving up her child for adoption, Otto soon discovered. Daniela's decision became irrevocable on the fourth day after Danny's birth—so little time for such a monumental decision!

"My baby was gone!" laments Otto, visibly agitated as he relives his grief.

"A healthy, newborn white boy, the big prize, and the Warburtons...had it and they were not going to let it go, come hell or high water," attorney Loren Heinemann would describe the event. An infant, for free, only six weeks after their first meeting with Daniela; it was fast and easy.

"When I came home from Slovakia, Daniela was gone, brainwashed into not wanting to see me," Otto continues. "Once I saw her in a parking garage near the hospital and I started to run toward her. She saw me and began to run away. I stopped then because I was afraid the baby might get hurt. It was near her due date," Otto recalls. "A little later I tracked her down at the women's center, but she left there right before I discovered her whereabouts. I thought to myself, when she has the baby, we will make up. I will go to the hospital with flowers and we will then become a family at last."

Otto went to St. Joseph's Hospital in Chicago on March 16, 1991, Daniela's due date, hoping to hear good news and to see her and his baby. She had never checked in, he was told by hospital personnel. For days he telephoned the hospital and still no sign of Daniela. After realizing that she did not go to the hospital they had chosen, Otto telephoned all of the hospitals in geographical proximity during the days that followed. However, Daniela had delivered their baby at Alexian Brothers Medical Center in Elk Grove Village, miles away from Chicago but not far from the Warburtons' home. Otto did not find out about their son's birth on March 16th. Nor did he know about her signing adoption papers presented her 72 hours later, or about the Warburtons' sudden disappearance, with Danny, from her life.

"They changed their pager and phone numbers, and she had no way of contacting them," he explains. "Then she realized what she had done."

The Warburtons, their attorney, and Daniela had talked about the child's father. He wanted this baby, Daniela told them. Thus the decision was made to pass the word within the Czech community that Otto's child died an hour after his birth.

A few days after Danny's birth, Otto was in his office at Kenessey's restaurant when he received a phone call from a friend. "The baby is dead" came the bad news.

"I just covered my face in my hands and I cried," Otto declares as he visibly relives his loss. "I fell into a depression. It was terrible." Otto shakes his head as he remembers this saddest of times. "Then I got suspicious when I tried but failed to find a record of death so that I could visit his grave."

Desperate to know the truth, Otto searched through Daniela's garbage cans, hoping to find evidence of a baby, perhaps diapers or discarded bottles from baby formula. He was disappointed to find nothing to indicate that his child was alive and living with his mother. "When I telephoned her uncle's house, Daniela wouldn't take my calls. But her uncle told me the baby was dead," he tells me, frowning and staring blankly at the carpet.

"On Mother's Day I came home from work, and Daniela was there, asleep in the bed," he says. When she awoke, they reconciled. She told him the truth about their baby. To her surprise— and his own—he was not angry. "It was a time to celebrate—my child didn't die; he was alive!"

"We must get him back," I told her, "and she nodded and said 'Yes!'" They formed an instant alliance to regain their son. Danny was 57 days old.

Otto was referred to attorney Loren Heinemann by one of his customers at the restaurant. They met together that same week; the attorney heard Otto's story; and he reassured his new client. "This will take about four weeks," Heinemann announced. "There may be a blood test. The other side will see there's been a big misunderstanding and that will be that. You will have your son."

Heinemann knew Tom Panichi, the first lawyer who acted on behalf of the Warburtons in their adoption plan. He would discover later that Panichi filed false affidavits in court, stating that the father of the child was "unknown." In addition, the attorney had never asked to see any documents of identification from Daniela—driver's license, social security card, green card, passport, or resident alien card—that might have assisted him in finding the baby's father. Otto and Daniela shared their residence and their address. Otto could have been readily found if the adoptive parents and their attorney were truly interested in finding him in order to seek his consent to the adoption, as required by law. Heinemann called Tom and explained the situation. Panichi said he would recommend to the Warburtons that they terminate the adoption proceedings that they had already initiated in the court system. Three days later the Warburtons fired Panichi.

An adoption specialist, attorney Richard Lifshitz, took over the Warburtons' case and advanced their petition to adopt Danny. "This is going to be a little more complicated than we thought, Otto," Loren Heinemann broke the bad news. Otto asked how this could happen.

In the United States, an unmarried father has parental rights to his child, Heinemann told Otto. If a mother cannot or does not want to raise her child, the father can raise him rather than allow his adoption by others. In Illinois, Heinemann continued, the father must make his claim to the child within thirty days of the baby's birth. It is the responsibility of the adoptive parents to make certain that the father has in fact given consent to the proposed adoption or—if the father is unknown—to attempt to find him in order to determine whether he wants to exercise his parental rights. It is their responsibility to provide notice of their intention to terminate the unknown father's rights. They must do what they can to find the father of the child, including publishing notice of their intentions in a newspaper of general circulation for a period of six weeks. The Warburtons chose an obscure law bulletin rather than a mainstream newspaper. Of course, and predictably, Otto never saw it.

Daniela had disclosed to the Warburtons that she not only knew the identity of her baby's father but that he wanted this child and that he would never agree to give him up. Neither the Warburtons nor their attorney made any attempt to find Otto.

Heinemann filed papers in court on behalf of Otto when Danny was less than three months old, but within thirty days of his discovery that his child was alive. The Warburtons telephoned Daniela to ask if Otto was serious. "She told them that I would never give up," Otto says. "Kimberly Warburton responded, 'You cannot win; we are Americans and we will always win.'"

Heinemann describes the Warburtons' strategy as one of delay so that they might convince the courts that the child had been with them so long that he had bonded and therefore should not be removed. The Warburtons proceeded with the adoption process in full knowledge of the risk, but apparently confident that they would ultimately win. Heinemann would disclose his "sentiment that [he] felt throughout [the case], that it was Mr. and Mrs. White-Bread versus the Eastern European."

Listening to Otto and ruminating over his years of struggle, I fully realize that litigation can be prolonged for so long—and become so frustrating, painful, and wildly expensive—that not everyone will keep up the fight. It takes an incredible toll emotionally and financially—as dozens of my other clients have experienced—and many people give up along the way. Not Otto.

It took from June to December 1991 for a hearing to be conducted to determine that Otto was indeed the father, based upon a blood test and DNA matching. In May 1992, a Cook County judge ruled that Otto was an "unfit" father, a determination based solely upon his not having registered interest in parenting his child within thirty days of birth—even though during that time he did not know that the child was alive. Another fifteen months passed before the Illinois Appellate Court, by a 2 – 1 decision, upheld the lower court's ruling. Nearly another year passed—to June 1994—before the Illinois Supreme Court, in a 7 – 0 ruling, determined that Otto's rights had been ignored and violated and that his child should be returned to him. In the three-plus years, not one extra fact was added to the information available to the courts from the first days of the litigation process. "I predicted that the Supreme Court would rule in my favor," Otto summarizes. "It was my last hope."

As I am conversing with Otto, I remember frequently having heard and seen the statement in the media that he was determined "unfit" by the courts. Everyone I knew assumed, as I had also, that this meant that he had been deemed an unfit parent because of character flaws and his personal history. "Unfit" in his case simply meant the technicality—nothing more—that he had not come forward to express an interest in his son within thirty days. Much later, the Supreme Court ruled that he had done all that could be expected and, during those thirty days, he had not even known that his son was alive. Furthermore, because the Warburtons' adoption of the baby was unlawful and based upon deception in which they participated, the Court invalidated it. A majority of the general public still believes that this man is unfit as a father, unfit as a parent to raise his son.

"The most difficult decision of my life was to move Danny from the other house in a sudden way," Otto tells me, almost as if we have not walked the same recent paths together in his quest to claim his son. "I knew by all of their behavior and stall tactics that the Warburtons had no intention of assisting Danny to bond with me or his mother. They wouldn't even tell him he was adopted so they could keep saying, he's not ready to meet us, he's not ready to know about us.

"Once I realized that their plan was to delay until we gave up or until we were so badly beat up by the press and the public that we would just go away, I knew that I had to take action to get my son. If we had done a gradual process, as we hoped, I believe the Warburtons would have poisoned Danny against us. He would have cried and protested every time we went to visit him or take him to the park. They would then have announced to the world, 'See, he just can't bond with these people.'

"This way we can bond with him while he is under our roof. We planned to let him continue his relationship with them as much as needed to sustain him. When day after day he hasn't asked for them, I wonder how strong **their** bond could have been.

"During those hard years in court, some people would say to me, 'Otto, why don't you give up?' What kept me going was the haunting image of my son, at eighteen, saying to me, 'Why didn't you keep fighting for me?' That's what kept me from stopping...."

Now, however, Otto is paying the biggest price ever for his decision. We discuss his many recent but futile phone calls to local employers and his unsuccessful job applications throughout the area. His health is impaired; he has frequent chest pains, headaches, and insomnia; but he has no medical insurance and therefore seeks no treatment. His friends are gone; his ties with his ethnic community are severed. He has no money, a bad credit rating, and a ruined reputation. He has no privacy; neighbors try to eavesdrop and several videotape his family when they are outdoors; and strangers act out their hostility by yelling nasty, vulgar names and rude gesturing. Although he has been compelled to maintain an unpublished directory listing, the public finds him in other ways.

Knowing that Otto not only cannot obtain a job but not even an interview once he provides his high-profile name, I encourage him to consider a move to another state, for a fresh start and a better chance for employment.

"Daniela is afraid to move out of fear that we might **both** be unable to get work in a new, unknown place," he explains. "We have no money for a move. And, Karen, I have done nothing wrong. My crime is that I loved my son from the moment I knew Daniela was pregnant with him, and I wouldn't give up. I never broke a law or told a lie. Yet, I am like the white O.J. It's only in black or Mexican areas that people understand what this case was about. No one else wants anything to do with me."

"What happened with your playing the violin, Otto?" I ask him. "You have never spoken about playing in this country...."

"During the court fight I stopped playing the violin and haven't touched one since that time," he answers. "You have to have heart to play the violin, and the heart was taken out of me when my son was gone. I can't play again; I have no feeling for it."

Danny and Justin skip into the living room together in search of a snack. Otto, smiling at both boys, jumps up to oblige. He goes into the kitchen for juice and cookies for the two children. We stop talking so as not to be overheard by the boys, and I gather my purse and note pad to prepare to leave for my office.

On my drive toward Orland Park and a series of client sessions, I am engrossed in thoughts about Otto and his situation. I realize that he lives in a black and white world. For Otto, there is a right and a wrong in every situation, allowing only few and thin gray areas, if any at all. His attitude, based upon values he was taught throughout his childhood, drives his decision-making and colors his view of the world around him. To Otto, there was no other choice than to battle, with his last erg of energy and his last dollar, for his son. On a cognitive level, he had decided never to give up; and on an emotional level, he remembered too well the feelings of a child adopted by grandparents at an age ripe for loneliness, insecurity, and longing. He would have gladly walked into a burning building to get his child if it had come to that.

With no realistic prospect of a job, Otto worries continually and feels trapped. At least he has his son, I comfort myself with thinking, and Danny appears to be thriving in his father's full-time care. However, Otto is also receiving more hate mail than most people receive junk mail. I wonder, with trepidation, if threatened attempts at violence will come to fruition. What kind of toll will this level of hatred and contempt take on these people? How will it affect Danny?

How long can it possibly, realistically last?

Danny Settles In & Lies Abound: May 8 – June 18

__May 8, 1995

"THE telephone is ringing off its hook." This old expression will come to have new and real meaning for me today.

This Monday morning I am awakened by early phone calls that continue throughout the day. In fact, I have never received more calls in a single day than today, nor will I come close to equaling this volume again in the future....

A self-proclaimed "visitor," with an undisclosed identity, has reported to the press that, while listening at his apartment door, she heard "Baby Richard" crying hysterically and asking to "go home." "Richard" was also allegedly observed playing outside, unsupervised, with two other children and weeping over wanting to go home.

Media representatives from the major television networks, radio stations, newspapers,

> One of the most striking differences between a cat and a lie is that a cat has only nine lives.
>
> *— Mark Twain*

and the City News Bureau want immediate interviews and a response from me to these allegations about a traumatized Baby Richard, grieving and crying to be returned to his adoptive parents.

Amy from *The Oprah Winfrey Show* calls to request that I participate in their Wednesday morning program. Informed that I am leaving on vacation, Amy offers to cover the cost of my airfare to and from my vacation site if I will agree to participate in the Chicago-based show. I decline the offer.

I know that the secret visitor's allegations are unfounded, especially because at the reported time of her "discovery" I was at the Kirchners' home. I am amazed that the media representatives not only respond in frenzied, full force to this mystery person's news tip, but they apparently accept as truthful the word of a woman who has invaded the privacy of the Kirchner family by listening at their door to obtain her "inside information." As the reluctant but necessary spokesperson of the family, I find myself in a defensive posture, challenging the veracity of this woman's allegations, not even knowing her identity, her motives, or her whereabouts. Danny's Saturday night bath episode is the "traumatic event" that she has erroneously reported to the hungry media. I was present in the Kirchners' apartment for what would be—and should be—a private occasion in any other household in America.

To dozens of reporters throughout the day, I explain that Danny had refused to bathe or shower all week and that his mother appropriately gave him his first bath in his new home. He cried for five or six minutes like any four-year-old compelled to do something that he does not want to do, but he neither asked nor demanded to "go home." When outside, he plays with other children in full view of one—or both—of his parents or myself. He has made friends and is too busy playing to cry.

The majority of reporters and journalists respond to my explanation with incredulity; they range from skeptical to unbelieving. I realize that they choose to believe the allegations of an unidentified woman, who confesses that she was eavesdropping at the door of this child's apartment, over the explanation of the eyewitness, the psychologist who is working daily with the child and his parents.

There are so many calls that I am unable to maintain a written record of all of the callers. However, I consent to give short, taped interviews to set the record straight on this inaccurate, anonymous, and—no doubt—ill-intentioned report about Danny. I can remember no other story during my lifetime that has been reported by major networks and in reputable newspapers from an anonymous source who admittedly obtained her "information" by listening through the door of a family's private home. Because the Kirchners live in an apartment building with a security system, the intruder would have had to listen at their apartment door while standing in the private lobby between their unit and the locked front door of the building. Although to the media she called herself a "visitor," the stranger was most likely a trespasser as well.

When I arrive at the Kirchners' in mid-afternoon, Danny is playing with Jeffrey, Justin, and Jason in the backyard. Off to the side of the play area, I ask Justin, who has been with Danny all week, if he has ever witnessed his friend crying. Justin responds, "No, never yet."

Stacy Heinemann, Loren's wife, and daughter Lexi arrive for a visit. Otto invites the entire group for an excursion to Odyssey Fun World, the nearby, indoor amusement park. A favorite place for children of all ages, Odyssey Fun World—as its name suggests—is filled with attractions of various kinds as well as video and other interactive games. All four boys are excited at the prospect; Jeffrey, Justin, and Jason run off to get permission from their parents; and we travel to the Fun World in three cars.

Once there, the children run from one game to another, reviewing all of their options, and focus their collective desires on a self-contained, fenced area with colorful slides, tubes, ladders, plastic curvatures, and small sections filled with large multi-colored balls. The teenaged male attendant, in charge of placing identification tags around the arms of the children as they enter, says warmly and reassuringly to Otto, "This is a safe area and no one will take your child." Clearly, this young man has recognized Otto and "Baby Richard."

Stacy, tapping my elbow, announces, "Reporter Mike Parker and Channel 2 News have just arrived on the scene." The cameraman is filming Danny as he is sliding, jumping, and running through the plastic maze. Apologizing for the intrusion, Mr.

Parker shoves a microphone in front of Otto for an impromptu interview and then in front of me for my comments about Danny's progress. Fortunately, their mission accomplished, the media people leave us to enjoy ourselves without further intrusions.

Later, during my afternoon interview with Renee Ferguson, she informs me that the report that started today's media frenzy came from a "worried mystery visitor" to the Kirchners' apartment building. Warm and charming, Renee asserts that she is personally glad that I am working with Danny. She adds, "That psychiatrist would be presenting a paper about the child and giving speeches."

Tonight I have the rare opportunity to observe first-hand the Baby Richard coverage on the evening news. One channel shows an excerpt of my interview, wherein I allude to Danny's Saturday crying episode as a "minor crisis over his refusal to bathe." This footage is followed by the woman eavesdropper, her face blurred to protect her identity, giving her false report about Danny, embellished with articulations of alarmed concern.

"I will continue to monitor the situation," she promises, and I wonder if she intends to listen at the family's walls and doors on a regular basis. Even more, I wonder why a major-channel television program would present such a report of admitted privacy invasion of a minor, a four-year-old child, from an unnamed source. The commentator on the news piece concludes, "There are **definitely** problems in that household," obviously accepting the veracity of the mysterious, eavesdropping intruder over my eyewitness report, and dismissing my credibility. The juxtaposition of my smiling and making dismissive comments vis-à-vis the smugly concerned spy—reinforced by the correspondingly worried commentator—makes me look like a cross between Mary Poppins and Mary Tyler Moore…, except blonde. What a disaster! And this is only one of numerous coverages of "weeping Baby Richard," spun into a full-blown fantasy story about a desperate hostage-child screaming out for rescue and return to his adoptive family.

Yesterday Bob Greene's column was entitled "Bearing witness to a crime." It calls the Baby Richard court decision "a crime…committed against a child…. A child was sinned against, in the name of the people of Illinois." Today his column accelerates the crime theme and adds more bathos: "Having

been abandoned by the court, that's what this child is left with—
prayers for a miracle, and a brother frantically wondering
whether his brother's keepers will treat him with mercy." ("His
brother asks: Are they nice?" *Chicago Tribune*)

When I telephone Otto at 10:15 p.m., he informs me that
Danny and his friends continued to enjoy their Fun World outing together throughout the evening after I left for a series of
appointments in my office. "They tired themselves out with running around and playing all of the arcade games that they could
fit into the time," he says, laughing.

Upon their return home, another reporter was waiting for
them and demanded an interview, proposing, "Talk to me about
your son, and I promise to give you a chance...." Otto refused the
interview, upset over the arrogance of this man's offering him "a
chance" to be portrayed as a fit parent for his son in return for
exclusive, filmed comments.

Danny talked more today about "Johnny's house" and, in his
own words, described tension within the household. Otto shares
with me details of the conversation, and we agree that it is
healthy for Danny to talk as much as he likes about his other
home and family.

After watching the various Baby Richard news reports
throughout the day, Robert offers his opinion that the Kirchners
should consider moving away from Chicagoland. The coverage is
nonsense, theatrical and biased; the tone of it is cynical, judg-
mental, and sad or indignant. Both content and style are more
typical of tabloid sensationalism than of reputable journalism.
I share with Robert the recent observation of Adrienne Drell, who
described to me the unparalleled "viciousness" that she witnesses among her colleagues over every aspect of the "Richard" story.

__May 9th

Awakened at 7:45 a.m. by the phone ringing at my bedside,
I hear from the anonymous caller that I should not be allowed
near "Richard" and that I do not know what I am doing. This
turns out to be the kick-off for a series of assaults by phone and
mail—most of them anonymous—that will intensify in both volume and venom during the latter part of May and continue for
weeks. I will hear from adoptive parents, adopted children, and
assorted angry people from various situations and walks of life.

A few of them threaten violence directed at me. Four letters will be supportive of my professional work with Baby Richard, two of them from adults who, as adopted children, understand the advantages for "Richard" in being raised by his natural parents.

Later, during my usual, daily check-up call, Daniela relates that she and Danny are having fun together, making a marshmallow cake in anticipation of her birthday on Thursday. He is excited about the prospect of a celebration with cake and other treats.

After providing a series of interviews about Danny's progress, I head for the Kirchners' apartment. In spite of detesting these interactions with the media, I am acceding to as many requests as time permits. Otto and Daniela have asked me to refute the false reports about their son and have provided me will full approval to disclose any information that I deem appropriate. We have discovered that Loren Heinemann—their only other hope for representing their interests to the media—prefers the spotlight focused on his own role as victor of the court battle. Since the phony but widespread news broke about "Richard as hostage," Loren is effectively avoiding the role of discussing the unpopular and controversial aspects of the story.

When I arrive, Justin and Danny are playing in the living room, eating M & M candies and cheese balls, talking and giggling together. Danny is relaxed and conversational. We call him "bouncy" because of his exuberance and he laughs. In spite of their nearly seven-year age difference, the two boys have become close friends; Justin continues to express pride in his protectiveness toward Danny; and he refers to himself as "Danny's best friend."

Explaining to both boys that I will be gone on vacation for two weeks, I assure them that, when I return, Robert and I will host a barbecue at my house for them and they can pet Sybil and play in the gazebo. I ask Danny if he would like that. "Sure," he says, smiling and looking at Justin for approval. Justin responds, "I'll take care of him while you are gone."

Daniela speaks to me in private about her ambivalent feelings. "I am so happy that Danny is adjusting so well," she tells me. "But I feel like a fifty-five-year-old woman after all we've been through. On Thursday, I will be twenty-eight. I've lived in this country for seven years that seem like at least seventeen."

Daniela seems to me noticeably older than when I first met her, I am reflecting to myself without sharing the thought, and that was only three eventful months ago. I know that she has slept little since Danny's arrival. Overwhelmed by awe and joy, and fearful that he might have nightmares or awaken during the night, she only dozes for short spurts of time and mostly just watches him sleep by her side. She has returned to her full-time job, while her heart is at home full-time with her son. The turbulence of these four years has caused a permanent change in her. Daniela has matured from a young, protected, and naïve girl, reared in an uncomplicated European lifestyle, into a woman and a mother, wiser and worn-out from the harsh realities of unanticipated experiences in a complicated new country.

Otto decides that we should go to Odyssey Fun World again because the children had such a good time there yesterday. "This time, Daniela is home and can go also," Otto announces, "and we will probably avoid the media, who will not expect our return there this soon."

Justin obtains his mother's permission and, within an hour, we are at the Fun World. The five of us enjoy ourselves, uninterrupted by media. Daniela joins the boys in playing a series of their favorite games. After two pleasant hours, I leave the four of them, playing and laughing, to drive to my office for evening sessions with clients.

Interrupting my packing for our vacation, I call Otto and Daniela to remind them that Dr. Lechner will be available on a daily basis and, like me, he will come to their home rather than require their bringing Danny to our office. I also inform them that today I have spoken with Dr. El-Shafie, director of the child psychiatry department at Loyola University Medical School, who will work with Danny and them if the need should arise.

With ten successful days of Danny's experiences with his birth parents vividly in my awareness, I am now looking forward to a vacation abroad. Paradoxically, I feel both exhilarated and exhausted. Danny is doing better than any of us either anticipated or dared to hope. Robert and I agree that, by the time we return, the Baby Richard story will probably have ripened into "old news" and retreated into the archives of newspapers all around. Danny will be able at last to begin a normal, private life, away from media glare and lurid speculation.

Yet again, events would prove me very wrong. Tomorrow *The Oprah Winfrey Show* will feature "Baby Richard," with Loren Heinemann and Bob Greene among the participants. This program will result in even greater Baby Richard interest and hysteria among the public.

While away on vacation, I will become the newest target of Bob Greene's ongoing journalistic vendetta against the Kirchner family.

__May 12th

Damaged goods: Danny is portrayed these days as "permanently scarred" and "irreparably damaged" in newspaper accounts that keep the story moving along. It is the anger and indignation of writers, reporters, and mental health professionals who respond to Otto's claiming his son. How dare he...when we said he should forfeit the boy to his adoptive parents! Well, he turned a once perfectly good child into a traumatized mess of a kid. It serves him right! Although these sentiments are not expressed in words, connecting the dots from the actual coverage is easy to do.

"Child welfare officials have been told [Baby Richard] was left unattended for seven minutes outside his home," the *Daily Southtown* reports today. Loren Heinemann describes "a lynch mob mentality" directed against the Kirchners. Scott Hamilton, a spokesman for DCFS, announces that the agency has "initiated an investigation after...calls to the hot line."

In "HOT TYPE—Defending Otakar," the *Reader* today adopts a reasoned view about the story:

> "...This has been a shameful case, and many people were used. But none more than Richard, the innocent child whose public suffering we were compelled to witness...," [the *Chicago Sun-Times* wrote].

> "Coverage has been biased," that *Sun-Times* editorial properly observed. It was doubly skewed. We learned of Otakar Kirchner's love life, his gambling habits, his lack of employment, and his immigrant status. About John Doe we learned not even his name.... Those are the terms in which the conflict was most compellingly presented,

the predator versus the innocents besieged, and anonymity was the mantle of sympathy draped over the Does that immediately asserted their righteousness.

What's more, the story was put on the map by... Bob Greene, who...wrote early, often, and passionately on behalf of the side he favored. Greene crusaded.... Greene's partisan columns overwhelmed the other coverage.... Perhaps Otakar Kirchner deserved a Bob Greene of his own, for the sake of the balance the press sets such store by....

Unfortunately, the *Reader*, enjoying a readership of only a fraction of Greene's *Chicago Tribune,* will make little difference in the tide of public reaction against Otto Kirchner.

In "Richard coverage ugly at best," the *Southtown* today also evaluates the media's role under "Media Ethics":

...[B]y the morning after, some people were feeling a little dirty about the whole public spectacle [the child's transfer]....

Some of those asked to reflect on coverage of the Baby Richard case found it unbalanced and incomplete. And so the media circus...might be viewed as an ugly exclamation mark to a body of work....

Perhaps Kirchner's ethnic rawness and clumsiness with the language made it easier to pull for the Does....

It was the evil alien destroying the lives of people like us.... (Phil Jurik)

__May 16th

First Lady Hillary Rodham Clinton appears on *The Oprah Winfrey Show* for a live telecast of a discussion on "children in America" and Baby Richard. About Richard, the First Lady takes this nationwide opportunity to assert:

I think it's an outrage.... That child should not have been moved. Those were his parents.... It was as though a bomb had gone off and he was the only survivor. Now, think about it like that, because that's what's been done to that child in terms of the trauma.

Loud applause erupts from the audience. Phil Kadner will write about the wildly approving response that Mrs. Clinton easily elicited:

Think about that. The first lady, who was widely ridiculed for advocating national health care reform (after studying the issues for months) is cheered and receives national acclaim for an off-the-cuff remark about Baby Richard.

Does this make sense?

Is it any wonder that our elected leaders are experts at 30-second sound bites and photo opportunities but are unable to grasp complicated solutions to long-term problems?...

...[F]or a short time powerful people cared about him [Richard].

In the end, they merely used him for their own purposes.... ("Baby Richard and the power of the mighty," *Daily Southtown*)

Kadner will also "wonder if Mrs. Clinton read the Illinois Supreme Court's decision in the case, or if she was merely reacting to the one-sided reporting she'd read." ("Baby Richard and the outrage of lies, deceit," May 17, 1995)

Hillary Clinton's appearance marks the second "Oprah" program within one week to highlight the Baby Richard case, in support of the adoptive parents.

__May 21st

While the Kirchners are victims of ongoing attempts at intimidation, receiving regular threats, a mound of hate mail, and a scattering of ominous phone messages in spite of their unpublished number, the Warburtons are champions of the people. "Groups…have formed to raise money to help defray the adoptive family's legal expenses," the *Tribune* reported several weeks ago. "Organizers estimate that the fundraisers have collected about $40,000 in all." (Ray Quintanilla and Larry Hartstein, "Rallying behind Richard," May 2, 1995)

Drawing 350 attendees from 23 states, another rally is held today at the Village Green Amphitheater in Hoffman Estates, Illinois, for the Warburtons. Sponsored by the child-advocacy group, Hear My Voice, the rally is intended to raise funds for the adoptive parents and to influence the United States Supreme Court to take up the Warburtons' appeal.

__May 22nd

As one of Bob Greene's ongoing journalistic harangues about Baby Richard, today's version is entitled, "'I am ashamed to say I am from Illinois.'" From his alleged readers' letters, Greene quotes liberally. His portrayal includes elaboration of the "completely reprehensible and shocking" actions of the Illinois Supreme Court from a man, and "I have lost all faith in my country" from a woman. **Every** day that he writes, his coverage is about Baby Richard, with slightly varying aspects of the same tiresome theme.

__May 25th

At 20,000 feet, our plane beginning its final descent, I look out my window into the darkness. The millions of lights below look like golden-yellow and white rhinestones forming tidy patterns against a black velvet background. From such beauty, I forcefully drag my attention back to what awaits me upon my return home.

Jet-lagged and anxious to hear about Danny and his parents, I call Otto as my first priority. Danny is doing fine, even better than before, he reports. There have been no problems and no need to call the designated child psychiatrist. However, he informs me, charges of child abuse and neglect have been filed against him and Daniela with the Department of Children and Family Services. Dr. Lechner has handled the preliminary contacts in my absence, but Otto prefers that I become involved immediately. I assure him that I will be available to meet with the DCFS investigator at any time.

Immediately I telephone Loren, who reports, "**Many** accusations—dozens or even hundreds—have been made, and charges have been filed against the Kirchners and against **you** during the past two weeks. Adoptive parents' groups have accelerated their stand against the Kirchners and now against you as the advocate of the biological parents. A **lot** of other people, too, have gotten involved in this, including some very powerful individuals," he adds.

Loren tells me about rallies held in many states in support of Baby Richard's adoptive parents. Even the West Coast is heavily and visibly involved. A talk show host in Los Angeles is simulating Bob Greene's fanatical approach to the story. He is agitating the public and soliciting financial contributions to the Warburtons. Petitions to the United States Supreme Court, asking for a reversal of the Illinois Supreme Court decision in favor of Otto Kirchner, are circulating around shopping malls, colleges, offices, and other public places.

With late-night appointments scheduled, I brace myself for an evening of dealing with my clients' personal and family problems, and try to concentrate exclusively upon the long night ahead. In my typical workaholic mode, I had scheduled my regular clientele for tonight, beginning shortly after my return from abroad, until nearly midnight. Especially within the context of the alarming news from Loren, I feel ill-equipped to focus on my clients' troubles, but I also welcome the opportunity to forget, albeit for a short time, the special challenges in my immediate future. I will visit Danny and his parents tomorrow, and we will deal with the situation together.

__May 26th

Four pages of phone call messages await my response, I discover when I review the pile of materials and mail that accumulated during my absence. Two dozen messages are from media representatives. Three calls came in from DCFS regarding the child abuse and neglect charges against the Kirchners.

Ray Lechner phones to tell me that Danny was doing so well during these two weeks that he visited only twice, although he maintained nearly daily phone contact with Otto and Daniela. Ray also spoke to the DCFS representative, assuring her that I would soon become available to meet with her and to assist the

Kirchners in their response to the charges against them.

Minutes later, my friend Colleen, who had been house-sitting and caring for our cats, telephones. Weeping, Colleen blurts, "Please forgive me, please forgive me. I couldn't help myself. I had to leave your house and go to see my doctor. I couldn't stop crying," she sobs. Aware of Colleen's fragile condition, I know that she has been especially susceptible to stress-related emotional collapse during recent weeks. She was eager to stay at our home during our vacation for both a new perspective and a welcome distraction. In January 1995, Colleen—a tiny woman in her fifties—had undergone a craniotomy, necessitated by a freak accident at the DuPage County jail, where she had just begun her part-time position as a rehab nurse-counselor. Colleen had to learn to walk and talk again, through intensive therapy, and she was still healing, shaky, and unsure of herself.

"Whatever you did, I forgive you. It's going to be okay," I try to assure her.

"Bob Greene called on Mother's Day. I thought it was my son and picked up the phone. He asked questions, questions I didn't know how to answer," she stammers. "He wrote two columns about you. I am **so** sorry," she concludes, unable to continue.

"It's okay, Colleen. I know you did your best; you always do," I tell her.

She manages to explain that, after Greene's phone call, she broke down in an agony of guilt and despair. She feared that I would perceive her as having betrayed me. Knowing that she would be emotionally unable to remain in my house, she called my brother-in-law Gerald, who volunteered to feed the cats every day for a week, until our return. Colleen's doctor increased her medication, but her anxiety and agitation accelerated when she read Greene's columns, one on May 17th and the other on May 21st. Feeling responsible, she was overwhelmed by a flood of remorse and self-blame.

"Please know that I forgive you, even though there is nothing to forgive, I'm sure." I reaffirm our friendship and advise her to try to forget the entire experience.

Colleen, more calm now, informs me that she answered only Greene's question about my expected return. "I didn't say anything else, but I guess I said you would be gone for a total of two weeks," she confesses. Reaffirming "Everything will be all right," I hang up the phone and go in search of the newspapers.

As I am reading the *Tribune* columns, I feel a wave of cold sweep over me. My chills and rapid heart beat remind me of a deer caught in the headlights of an oncoming car. Months ago, when I narrowly missed hitting the majestic animal by swerving off the road, my heart pounded and I was nearly paralyzed by fear. Now I am feeling stunned, as if shot into a slower mode of thinking..., like an old-fashioned 33 RPM record, I think to myself. It is a mind-numbing experience, reading venomous attacks about oneself in the newspaper with the largest circulation and readership throughout the Midwest. Soon I will discover that Greene's columns are syndicated in nearly 200 newspapers throughout the country, from Atlantic coast to Pacific coast.

Considering me on the wrong side of the Baby Richard dispute, Greene attacks my credentials, integrity, ethics, and credibility. In addition, in the May 17th column, he criticizes me for having left town for two weeks. In the May 21st column, gathering more journalistic steam, he again attacks me, this time for having "left the country for a period of uncertain duration." Apparently in the full knowledge (on May 17th) that I was gone for a two-week vacation, Greene chose (on May 21st) to forget his awareness and to magnify my "badness" by spinning it into a departure from the country for an unknown length of time. To a casual reader, it seems as if I "left the country" in flight from the heat generated by Baby Richard backlash or as a criminal might flee to another jurisdiction after having committed a crime.

Greene, quoting the fired Leventhal, attacks my ethics and insinuates that I am serving as a puppet of Danny's parents, simply doing what they want me to do in my work with the child. Clearly, it seems to me, Greene would prefer Danny to be transported once or twice weekly in a steel car to a big concrete-and-steel building to talk for a clinical hour to a steely-eyed psychiatrist. When the child would act out his protest or display discomfort, fear, or symptoms of withdrawal, those behaviors would doubtless be interpreted as signs of his "ongoing trauma." Another great story for the self-appointed "Baby Richard columnist"! However, Greene has **already** established—and will continue for **many** months—his original theme about a traumatized Richard, suffering unimaginable pain, a victim of "child abuse." He will compare Richard to prisoners convicted of murder, to hostages, to children purposefully drowned by their mother, and to victims of the Holocaust and of the Oklahoma City bombing. He repeatedly calls upon child welfare agencies to investigate his parents' care of Richard, looking for child abuse.

Now that, as Danny's therapist, I have been discredited and dispatched by Greene, he will be free to accelerate his campaign of fever-pitch rantings about Baby Richard as irreparably damaged, emotionally distraught, and anguished—without the prospect of any credible contradiction. He will write dozens of columns, unfettered by any real information...or by the truth.

Across the days that follow, the most painful realization for me is that almost none of my relatives, friends, in-laws, or acquaintances mentions either of these columns to me. Apparently, even the most sensitive, caring, and articulate among them does not know how to discuss with me these journalistic attacks upon every aspect of my professional self and upon me as a person. I feel as if I have indeed been falsely accused of a crime, sentenced, and dismissed.

Resolving to continue my commitment to Danny and the Kirchner parents, I dedicate myself to proceed as if nothing has happened. Robert shares my anger and feelings of helplessness, and, more important, he supports my decision to continue my work with the Kirchner family. We both fully realize the prospective impact of these powerful journalistic missiles directed at my career and the likelihood of repeat attacks.

Greene has launched his several-times-weekly columns that are exclusively about Baby Richard. He is determined to write about nothing else until the U.S. Supreme Court has rendered its decision regarding the adoptive parents' appeal. His goals are to rally the public into petition signing on behalf of the side that he champions; to influence the decision of the nation's highest court; and, of course, to sell newspapers. Both his followers and his detractors are talking and writing about the bizarre, unprecedented situation of a well-known, mainstream columnist who has lapsed into writing, three or four times weekly, about only **one** topic. Within this context, I wonder why Greene did not wait until my return, only a handful of days after his anti-Moriarty columns were published, in order to provide me with the opportunity to address, or refute, his allegations about me. Typically, the ethics of journalism dictate that the writer obtain—and consider—both sides of an issue. Since he is writing **every** column about Baby Richard, nothing would have been lost by his waiting a few days..., except perhaps the melodrama and one-sidedness of his rampage. He has simply folded me into the villains' side of his favorite—and now exclusive—topic, and without affording me a chance to defend myself or to correct his distortions about me.

While people in my personal life avoid the subject as if it were a secret, fatal disease or a shameful crime, my clients telephone me about the content of the columns, some of them in a panic. "If you're not a psychologist, I am in trouble," Glen confronts me. "My insurance won't pay and the court will not pay attention to your opinions about my situation in the divorce," he shouts at me through the phone. I assure him that the State of Illinois has licensed me as a psychologist continuously for the past nineteen years, even if Bob Greene has decided not to recognize this reality. "I will have to think about this," he retorts. "I don't know if I will continue with you now."

I engage in a series of variations of this conversation with other clients. Nearly half of them cancel their next scheduled appointments.

After my abbreviated schedule of client appointments for the day, I await Otto's 7:30 p.m. arrival in front of my office building, as planned, so that I might visit with him and Danny during the car ride to pick up Daniela from work. Otto and Danny are both smiling when they see me, and we share happy greetings and hugs. "Give me five!" his father requests, and Danny responds from the back seat by leaning forward and slapping Otto's hand with his own, visibly proud of their new bonding ritual. After they repeat the "give-me-five" gesturing several more times, we begin our long ride to downtown Chicago.

Otto reports that Danny is now eating more nutritious, non-junk food that includes soup and home-cooked meats. We are careful not to discuss recent events that might be disturbing for the child. When Daniela gets into the car, Danny is all smiles; they hug and begin to talk, laugh, and play in the back seat together as we begin the trip back to Orland Park. Daniela and I are glad to see each other again. We both missed our daily private talks.

When we return to my office parking lot, I retrieve from my car a souvenir from Indonesia for Danny. He happily accepts the tee shirt with a big Dalmatian on the front and his tail on the back; I tell him that now he will match his bedroom. Daniela reminds him to say "Thank you," to which he immediately responds. As I have observed many times before, Danny is eager to please his mother.

Although we avoided discussion of weighty topics, I have satisfied my need to observe Danny's progress and to witness this new level of interactions between him and his parents. He is now fully animated and initiating on a consistent basis. He giggles and snuggles against his parents. Danny and his mother talk non-stop during the ride home except for a few minutes of shared singing.

Before I leave the family, I whisper to Otto, outside of Danny's hearing, that I have telephoned Ruth P. from DCFS in order to make her aware of my availability to attend and participate in her in-home investigation of the child's situation. She promised to get back to me soon.

__May 27th

Bringing Danny two more gifts from my trip, I arrive at the apartment at 4:30 p.m. to Otto's dinner preparations. He invites me to join them for dinner, but I decline, as Robert is planning for us to share our evening meal together at home. Danny inspects the hand-painted dinosaur mobile and small batik-cloth dog, and he takes them to join his other possessions in his bedroom. I show him a vacation photograph of me wearing a live python around my neck, in which he shows great interest and expresses it by a loud "Yuck!" and a laugh.

Otto reports that Danny has neither yet asked to see his former parents, nor has he even spoken about John during the past several days. He is talking about Justin regularly, and he asks to see his older best friend on a daily basis. The boys play together nearly every day, and Justin continues to watch over Danny as his self-appointed guardian.

When Daniela returns home from work, she announces her desire to visit Niagara Falls on their planned family trip to Toronto. They will take advantage of the Memorial Day weekend to enjoy their first vacation together as a family. She and

Otto begin to look at a map of the region, and Danny jumps onto the couch between them to review it also.

"I will see my grandma there," Danny announces to me. He knows that he will be meeting and visiting Otto's mother; he understands the biological relationship; and he is clearly excited over the prospect of this trip. I am pleased to see him interacting with his parents in such a relaxed, natural, and affectionate way. During my visit I observe Danny hugging both of his parents; he is comfortable initiating frequent hugs now.

"It seems as if Danny has been here forever," Daniela informs me. There is a pervasive sense of peacefulness about her that I have not witnessed before.

When Justin arrives minutes later, Danny asks if his friend can stay for dinner, and Otto sets another plate and utensils on the dining room table. The boys eat pork chops and french fries, talking with full mouths and laughing at each other.

Because Loren has reportedly been unable to get Danny's surname changed from Warburton to Kirchner on his birth certificate, the attorney has advised Otto and Daniela to take the most recent *People* magazine with them to Canada as documentation that he is their son. "The Homecoming" article includes full-color pictures of the child, the transfer scene, and his biological parents. In addition, they plan to take his certificate of baptism as a second document to offer as evidence of their parenthood and Danny's American citizenship. It is yet another bizarre dimension of "Baby Richard" for his parents to feel compelled to carry *People* magazine as proof of their legitimate claim to take their son with them into another country.

The City News Bureau and a myriad of reporters call me today in response to Bob Greene's vitriolic columns about me. I respond only to one, Eileen Pech from the Berwyn-Cicero newspaper, because she has become a friend of Robert's from her years of covering Morton College news while he was president. She interviews me for an article that is complimentary of my involvement with "Richard" and, as the only journalist with current, first-hand information, she reports details of Danny's remarkable progress.

__May 28th

Ruth P. and I discuss by telephone her imminent visit with the

Kirchner family. As the assigned investigator, she is providing the DCFS follow-up to charges of child abuse and neglect. I notify her that the family has traveled to Canada for a few days so that Danny might meet his paternal grandmother for the first time. She will schedule with me upon their return.

Bob Greene's column today quotes a "reader" comparing Richard's case to the drowning of two children by their mother in South Carolina; she concludes, "That's why I can't sleep at night." Greene ends, "This column, I am well aware, is supposed to be about a wide variety of subjects, is supposed to be occasionally amusing, sometimes entertaining. One of these days, I hope it will be again...." Regarding his promise [to champion Richard], "I don't intend to break it."

Greene's recurring theme has become the alleged "lie" that Richard was told by his father that he could see his adoptive family whenever he wanted. The child has not yet seen them, he virtually moans through the newsprint. It's easy, of course, to keep this angle going. Through the coming months in numerous columns, Greene will add the allusion to the precise amount of time that will have elapsed during which there is no contact between Richard and the adoptive family. He will not bother to find out if "Richard" has asked to see them or if he really cares.

__May 31st

The Kirchners return with happy reports about their trip to Toronto. Danny liked his grandmother; and, after having witnessed his transfer on TV one month ago, she was amazed that he looked so good. Danny has been gaining weight, and his blonde hair is growing out of the military-style cut that he had when he first came to his parents' home. It frames his face for a softer, fuller look.

Otto reports that their mail carrier has been approached by an unidentified woman who requested that she deliver mail directly to Danny. She declined, informing the strange woman that all mail must be processed through postal system regulations.

"It was a crime in broad daylight"—the Baby Richard ruling of the court—Bob Greene proclaims in today's offering to his readers. He quotes a teacher explaining why she decided not to include the Supreme Court building on her students' recent field trip to the state's capital: "It seemed sacrilegious to ask children to go in there." Referring to "Richard's pain and sacrifice," he concludes, "If we go down trying to save him, at the very least we keep faith with him, honor him in his suffering, and make ourselves fit to face our own children—and our maker."

Please! This from a man who has still not bothered to call to discover how the child is **really** doing..., the answer to which question, by the way, is "thriving."

__June 1st

There is a video camera visible in the window of a neighboring apartment. When I point it out to Otto, he explains that it has continued to be there on a routine basis, directed at the back-yard, pond area, and their patio.

Justin is visiting again, and Danny, with animation, tells both of us about his vacation. "My grandma was nice," he reports with a big smile; "she played with me." I envision the profuse hugs, tears, and kisses when she finally met her first grandson after a four-year waiting period.

Presenting it as a game, I ask both boys to tell me the rules about being outside. What are you allowed to do? What are you not allowed to do? What about the pond? For what activities do you need a parent's permission? Danny appears eager to show Justin and me that he knows the rules, and I start to relax as I become convinced that he is able to articulate his understand-ings. In preparing for the DCFS investigator's visit, we are focusing upon questions related to safety and security.

Justin's mother gives consent for her son to be present at my meeting with the DCFS representative. I have sought her approval so that Danny will be more comfortable and relaxed, in Justin's presence, with this stranger, who will be interrogating him about his new life.

__June 2nd

Justin and Danny are playing a Nintendo game when I arrive one hour before the scheduled DCFS investigation. Interrupting their activity, I begin to play "our game about the rules" again in order to prepare Danny. Although I am certain that he under-stands these rules, I fear that he may not communicate them adequately to the stranger. I am even more fearful that the DCFS investigator will feel obligated to find some evidence of child abuse or neglect because of the immense, mounting public and media pressure and scrutiny.

Danny takes my hand and leads me to his bedroom, which is tidy and organized. His new dinosaur mobile is hanging from the ceiling over his bedside table. His books, games, and menagerie of stuffed animals are displayed neatly in the various compartments of the shelf units. His closet has been outfitted with hooks and nails, from which hang some of his clothes, Power Rangers outfits, masks, and other toys too large for shelf storage. Danny shows me this new display of his possessions with obvious pride. "Look at everything!" he exclaims. "I can see it all at one time."

Sitting with him on the big bed, I engage him in play with the small furry Dalmatians, posing them to kiss and hug each other. Danny responds with his hand-held puppies, manipulating them to return the kisses and hugs. I am hoping that this acting-out of affection will pave the way for him to feel receptive toward the stranger's arrival.

At 3:30 p.m. I telephone Ruth P.'s office to inquire about the status of our appointment, scheduled for 2:00. She is involved in a meeting there, the receptionist informs me, but within seconds Ruth takes my call. She explains that a tornado has touched down in the vicinity of her office, and her supervisor would not allow her to leave the building under these weather conditions. We agree to reschedule for next week.

Loren arrives to share his perceptions of the *48 Hours* coverage of Baby Richard, which aired last evening. I am not surprised when I hear that Otto did not watch the program, because he and Daniela rarely turn on the television for fear that Danny will be exposed to news stories about himself, some of which are bizarre.

"The program included footage of Danny, smiling and 'giving five' by slapping his hand against the window from inside the car," Loren tells us while Danny is in his bedroom. The newscast that immediately followed the program, however, showed brief interviews with the Warburtons' neighbors, making incongruent comments. Statements like "It doesn't seem like him," "He seems to have a vacant stare," and "It looks like Daniel has had a personality change" cast negative and suspicious coloring over the preceding content of an apparently happy child.

__June 3rd

Before leaving for my office appointments today, I spend time with Danny in his backyard area to perform another review of the rules that govern his play.

"Who would you have to ask if you want to ride your bike around the pond?" I ask as my last question for today's drill.

"My dad!" he exclaims in a loud voice. Danny looks up to Otto for the expected smile that he is sure to elicit from his father.

We are ready for the DCFS investigator.

__June 5th

Ruth P. is scheduled to meet me tomorrow at 3:00 p.m. at the Kirchners' home. "I want to clear this matter up," she tells me by phone. I find myself ardently hoping that she is sincere and that there is no other, hidden agenda in the works. Dozens of powerful people have declared themselves in support of the Warburtons, including Governor Edgar, Mrs. Edgar, prominent legislators, and Patrick Murphy of the Office of the Public Guardian. These are individuals who, in their public roles, exercise control over state agencies, which include DCFS. Celebrities and politicians too numerous to list have announced their intentions to work toward the goal of returning Baby Richard to his adoptive parents. Might there be a behind-the-scenes plan to effect such a return of the child, in spite of the Illinois Supreme Court ruling? DCFS has the power to remove Danny from his parents' home and to place him in a foster home.

The U.S. Senators from Illinois Paul Simon and Carol Moseley-Braun, the American Academy of Pediatrics, the American Academy of Child and Adolescent Psychiatry, the Yale University Child Study Center, and Governor Edgar have joined the Warburtons' attorneys in petitioning the U.S. Supreme Court to consider the adoptive parents' appeal.

Bonnie B. from *People* magazine calls this afternoon to question me about my credentials. Bob Greene and a number of his readers have contacted the magazine to challenge my ability to work with Danny and to provide credible information about him, she informs me. I wonder about Greene's likely motive in trying to discredit me. If as reputable a publication as *People* quotes me as authoritative in relating that Danny is adjusting well and is happy with his birth parents, Greene's unrelenting columns about a deeply suffering, abused child, consumed by longing for his adoptive family, may be uncovered as merely his own fantasies and fabrications.

When I arrive at the Kirchners' apartment, Danny—at his insistence—is helping his father shave. Laughing, he pats both sides of his dad's face with his hands and then rubs noses with him. I secretly wish that others could observe these interactions, which reveal the amazing level of bonding that has occurred within five weeks between this child and his parents.

Danny and I play a board game together, during which I review with him the rules that we have been practicing for days.

As I leave, I assure Danny of my return tomorrow with "my friend Ruth."

__June 6th

After one more hour of verbal preparation with Danny and Justin, we are ready for the DCFS investigation. When the doorbell rings, both boys accompany me to answer the door to greet our guest. To my surprise, Danny is smiling, relaxed, and friendly; he acts like a young host to the visitor. I slept only two hours last night, worried that Danny might fear her because of his having witnessed hostility and threatening behaviors from so many strangers during recent weeks.

Ruth sits on the living room couch with me and explains the nature of her visit. Although Otto and Daniela are at home, I am serving as the facilitator in this investigation. Ruth had emphasized to me that she would be speaking with the child without his parents present.

Assuring Ruth that Danny is always supervised and never left alone, I describe the routines in the household. At least one of his parents is with him on a 24/7 basis. Because they always fear kidnapping or an attempt to harm him by some deranged individual seeking revenge, glory, or publicity, they are especially vigilant and cautious. If one of us is not outside when he is playing with his friends, we are continuously watching him through the sliding glass door of the living room.

Ruth produces a camera and requests photographs of the sliding glass door and of the view of the pond and backyard through it. I volunteer to take the photos for her. She steps outside with Danny and Justin in order to interview the boys in private. I hear Danny respond "My dad!" to two or three of her questions, the content of which I cannot hear through the glass door.

Speaking to Daniela about safety issues, Ruth makes recommendations that include the various neighbors taking turns in supervising the group of children at play. "That way you can help each other out with the kids," she explains.

After Ruth leaves, Daniela and I settle onto the patio to watch Justin and Danny playing ball, and we enjoy this opportunity to talk about recent events. We are both relieved that the DCFS visit seemed to go well. The investigator was a mature, experienced woman who appeared to be doing her job in a professional, conscientious, and thorough manner. Her questions to us were predictable and appropriate. Justin and Danny behaved well and answered Ruth's questions with apparent ease.

After Justin leaves for home, Danny makes a point of telling me, with concern in his voice, "My new grandma cried when she saw me." He adds, "Soon she will be coming to sleep over with us." Around his neck he is wearing a gold chain with three charms that represent faith, hope, and charity—a cross, anchor, and heart—an expensive gift from his other grandmother in Slovakia.

At my first opportunity, I notify Loren about the DCFS visit and our perceptions of it, and he shares our feeling of relief. Although we do not know the sources of the charges against the Kirchners, it is our mutual impression that there were literally dozens of complaints. The recent media hype has led to the general impression among the public that Danny is a pitiable and distraught child, likely the victim of child abuse or, at the very least, neglect.

__June 9th

During my evening visit with the Kirchner family, Danny brings me a photo of a tall, thin, good-looking nine-year-old boy with red hair and freckles.

"This is Mario," he beams, "and he's coming to visit me very soon."

Daniela explains that her sister's son will be coming from Slovakia to stay for eight weeks during his summer vacation. Since the boys spoke together by phone earlier this week, Danny has been looking forward to the arrival of his new cousin.

When I gesture toward the photograph so that I might see it better, Danny pulls it away, saying, "It's mine." Daniela and I exchange glances and, without articulating our shared thought, we both understand that it is good for Danny to feel ownership and a sense of belonging. He understands his biological relationship with this child, and he is eager for Mario to become a part of his family during the boy's summer hiatus from school.

Mario is one year older than Danny's former brother John. Not only has Danny lived for four years with an older sibling, he has demonstrated his comfort level and ability to relate to older children, including Justin, Jeffrey, and Jason from neighboring apartments. This will be another opportunity for him to function within his new extended family, many of whose members live thousands of miles away. Because Danny has been consistently indulged by his parents since his arrival, it will be beneficial to his development for him to learn, in this new home environment, to share his bed, toys, and parental attention with another child.

We eat homemade soup together, and Otto reports that Danny is eating well these days. "Yesterday he ate twelve little wieners, as well as bread and butter," announces the proud father, glancing at Danny, anxious for the child to overhear his praise.

After clearing the table, Daniela sits on the couch, and Otto, Danny, and I sit on the carpeted floor. Danny plops himself onto his father's lap, strokes his face, and hugs him with spontaneity and affection. He asks to see his father's watch, which Otto retrieves from the nearby etagere. Danny pulls the big silver watch onto his own arm, pushing it up toward his shoulder to prevent it from falling off.

"Daddy, can I have this watch someday?" he asks, looking up into his father's face.

"Of course, Danny, it will be yours," Otto answers him.

With a deep giggle, Danny adds, "I want to be **huge**, like my dad!" Smiling, he stretches his arms high above his head to demonstrate how big he wants to grow.

Daniela brings over the family album, which contains photos of their extended family on both sides and of their courtship period. Danny points to each picture and describes it, explaining to me his relationship with each new person.

Daniela tells me that she has gone over the album with him, relating stories about the pictured individuals on numerous occasions. "He now remembers everything. He is so smart and has such a good memory!" she exclaims. Danny straightens up, proud of himself, and we talk about the physical similarities between him and the others, including his parents.

Before departing, I invite the Kirchners and Justin to my house on Sunday, the 11th, for a cookout. During my car ride home, on the radio news program the announcer proclaims, "There are new reports of Baby Richard, now in his biological father's home for six weeks, traumatized and crying for his adoptive parents, who live in the suburb of Schaumburg. This sad story just continues getting sadder...."

__June 11th

Otto, Danny, and Justin arrive at 4:00, with Loren and his family close behind, as planned. Daniela will be coming from work, arriving shortly before 6:00 p.m.

Through the evening, we spend time both in and out of the house, in the screened gazebo, around the yard, and on the wrap-around deck. We share snacks, drinks, and a meal of hot dogs, Italian sausage, and hamburgers, followed by cheesecake. Danny eats well, has second helpings, and runs around the yard with Justin. Occasionally they participate in a token interaction with nineteen-month-old Lexi, who toddles around near her parents.

"I love this house!" Danny exclaims at one point during his play. He and Justin are especially enjoying their play with a small wooden airplane, propelled by a rubber-band apparatus, until it flies onto the roof of the house, landing there to remain until a later time when a ladder will be needed to retrieve it.

The day ends with smiles and fatigue as Loren declares, "Lexi is having a melt-down, she is so worn out." She sleeps all the way home in the car, closely followed by the Kirchner family in their vehicle, with Danny and Justin giggling together in the backseat.

__June 13th

My private practice is suffering and the telephone rings seldom. I have fewer clients now than ever before, except during my first five start-up months.

The Kirchners' home has become a place of refuge, I realize as I enter the cool living room from the warm, humid lobby and hear the soft hum of the window air conditioning unit. The place has a cave-like feel, drapes drawn for privacy from peeping neighbors and for protection from the relentless sun. It is clean and cozy, and it reminds me of a cocoon.

During my time with the Kirchners today, I spend the usual private time with Danny. He talks about his friends and his eagerness for cousin Mario to arrive. Danny takes baths now every day and sometimes doesn't want to get out of the water. He has a variety of bath toys now, arranged around the tub, including a big yellow duck.

"Danny has gained more weight," Otto reports. "You can tell it just by looking at him. His legs and tummy have filled out; he is no longer skin and bones!" Danny has also grown in stature, and his hair is noticeably longer.

Danny was excited today, his mother informs me, when she told him that she would not be going to work; she and his dad would both be spending the day with him. After hours of togetherness with his parents, Danny is playing a new Nintendo computer game by himself and nibbling on nearby food.

Having brought with me photos that I took on Danny's first night at home and during his first week, I sit on the floor to review them with him. He shows keen interest in them, staring for a long time at the picture of his mother and himself sitting on his bed during his first hours here. Although I expect some indication of distress from him, because of the wrenching scene on that painful Sunday, he appears relaxed and initiates conversation about various photos. He recognizes Adrienne and focuses on some of his favorite toys in the background of several of the pictures. I am discovering that Danny is especially attentive to details in his environment.

When I announce that I am leaving for home, Danny begs me to stay longer. I comply with his request until fifteen minutes later, when, attired in his pajamas, he has fallen asleep on the living room carpet. Otto and Daniela take this opportunity to update me on recent incidents that are alarming. Today a woman drove by the apartment in a car and yelled "Bastard!" at Otto, in Danny's presence, and then returned minutes later "to scream out more really nasty words." Yesterday, while in their car following behind a school bus, Otto and Danny looked up to see a cluster of young boys, scowling through the back window, pointing at Danny and demonstrating their understanding of the middle finger. Otto's greatest concern is for Danny, who, in spite of all of their efforts to shield him, witnesses on a nearly daily basis the rudeness and menacing behaviors of strangers.

__June 15th

Sandra A. from the City News Bureau calls me today for an interview in anticipation of the imminent U.S. Supreme Court ruling on the Baby Richard appeal. I telephone Otto to discover that he and Danny, tired out from the heat, are taking a brief nap. I invite myself there for an appointment tomorrow, as I realize that the Kirchners will need psychological support if the Court reopens the issue of Danny's custody. The Warburtons have requested a best interest hearing for Baby Richard.

I marvel that so many prominent individuals from across the country have championed the Warburtons' cause, especially now that he is settling in with his birth parents. There are rallies, letter-writing campaigns to the justices, and petitions under circulation, all in support of the adoptive parents. No one, to my knowledge, has pointed out the incongruity of the public's outrage over Danny's abrupt removal to his birth parents' home as compared to their current advocacy of a similar abrupt return of the child to his adoptive parents. If it was not okay, according to the majority public opinion, to remove the child from his former home, why is it now okay to remove him from his current home? If bonding is the issue, why is the question not asked, "Has he bonded with his birth parents during these past seven weeks?" The widespread assumption is simply that he has only bonded—and probably is only **able** to bond—with the adoptive parents. His natural parents are generally deemed unworthy of his bonding with them.

When I arrive for my three-hour visit, Danny, Justin, and Jeffrey are "rough-housing" in the living room. The boys run from room to room, yelling and teasing each other. Otto, as typical of him, is patient and smiling; he believes in giving children wide latitude in their play. It's a type of "Boys will be boys" attitude.

Having brought novelty balloons for the boys, I hand them the high-floating, helium-filled Dalmatian dog and soccer ball, and apologize for not knowing ahead of time that I should have brought a third balloon for Jeffrey. All three boys retreat to Danny's room, upon Otto's suggestion, and we are able to talk in private.

Otto discusses his improved relationship with Daniela. Parenting together has brought them closer; they talk more and understand each other better. There is much less tension than before, when each day was focused upon the uncertainty of the court outcome and upon their sadness and anxiety over their son's ambiguous situation.

Otto describes to me his earlier discussion today with Danny. He told his father that he does not want to return to the other house or to be sent anywhere else. Otto assured Danny that he would never permit him to be sent anywhere, that he and his mother have fought so long for him that they could never send him away for any reason.

When Danny and I speak privately, for the first time he is quiet and withdrawn, avoiding eye contact with me. Alarmed that he may be despondent over serious matters, I ask him questions, soothingly reassuring him that he can tell me anything at all and I will do my best to help. Tears start to roll down his cheeks. Hanging his head, he mutters, "Jeffrey can't go with us to pick up mom." This is a four-year-old's disappointment over a situational matter involving one of his friends, and I breathe a sigh of understanding and relief. Comforting Danny, I assure him that another time his friend will probably be allowed to accompany his father and himself on their ride to get mom from work.

Giving him a hug, I whisper that everything will be all right and that he will soon see his mother, who will be very happy to see him. He will probably see Jeffrey again tomorrow or the next day. Danny stops crying and leaves to join his father for their ride into the city. I note that this episode is the only time that I have witnessed Danny cry except for his first night here and during the bath episode one week later.

Many of the armchair experts on television predict dire consequences for this child, including life-long trauma, emotional crippling, and mental illness. Yet **none** of them has interacted with Danny, and I find myself wondering why mental health specialists would make such pronouncements, absent observation or first-hand information, about a real, flesh-and-blood child who is living among the viewing audience. Certainly spotlight grabbing is one motivation, as such woeful predictions fly into print and onto television screens, while contrary opinions are either ignored or dismissed as not credible. A defining moment for me was the quick disappearance of the media after Baby Richard's emergence as Danny Kirchner, playing happily with new friends in his backyard. When media personnel interview me and I relate to them Danny's excellent progress, they typically shelve any story on the subject or else they lapse into Bob Greene's version of abuse, agony, and despair, sometimes citing him as their definitive source.

Toward the end of my visit, two women who appear to be nineteen or twenty years old knock at the door of the apartment. Danny retreats to his bedroom and his toys, at his father's suggestion, before Otto opens the door. The visitors present themselves as selling magazines to earn points toward their college expenses. To my surprise, Otto invites them inside and, without further conversation, they sit on chairs at the dining room table and look up at us.

"An old man in another apartment made moves on us!" announces the dark-haired, wild-eyed, unkempt magazine salesperson. She explains that she has a large tattoo on the right side of her face, covered up by her long hair. If visible, I am thinking, it would be a fit companion to the large rhinestone in her nose, making her look even more like a protégé of Charles Manson.

Her companion, a more conventional-looking redhead, speaks about her brother regularly beating up their grandmother. "He is out of control," she exclaims, "and he is seeing a psychiatrist, but he's not making much progress." She alludes to "a problem with incest" in her family.

They both ask Otto questions about himself, his family, and the apartment. Do you have children? Where is your son now? What is he like? How is he doing? Does he like it here? Where is the lady of the house? Do you like living here?

We both avoid disclosing that Danny is playing in his bedroom. They are both histrionic, speaking loudly, and making exaggerated gestures to emphasize the content of their conversation. The more bizarre-looking woman begins to rub the table and chair legs with her hands as she talks. She is also rocking back and forth in her chair.

Otto makes two selections from their proffered list of magazines and hands them cash to pay for them. They cheerfully thank him and depart with "good-byes" delivered over their leather-clad shoulders. After Otto leaves the room to check on Danny, I follow the young women outside, but they have disappeared. Within minutes, I find myself lying on my back under the dining room table, scanning and feeling for an electronic "bug" that one of them may have placed there or under a chair. When Otto returns, he asks what I am doing, and I'm embarrassed to explain.

"With an unidentified mystery woman listening through your door to grab prime time news coverage, the media hungry for another story, and the U.S. Supreme Court ruling imminent, I'm thinking that a **lot** of people would love to hear **anything** that is happening in this apartment," I explain. "It would have been easy for one of those strange young women to place an electronic listening device under this table or one of the chairs."

Otto shakes his head and laughs benignly. I am surprised not only that he has accepted them at face value but, even more, that he has handed them cash for magazines that he may never see. This is not my business, I remind myself, and say nothing more about it. After setting an appointment time with him for tomorrow, I drive home in the dark, questioning my own mental health. Was my unsuccessful search for "bugs" a manifestation of blossoming paranoia or the realistic response to overly inquisitive, manic strangers?

Although it would take three months, the two publications would begin arriving at the Kirchner apartment, as promised by the two college aspirants. We would never learn whether they had another reason for their visit in addition to the sale of magazines.

Ruth P. from DCFS calls to request bits of data from me, including Danny's date of birth, so that she might complete her written report.

__June 17th

After completing a home visit for an ongoing child custody evaluation for the Cook County court, I drive to the Kirchners' apartment. Otto and Danny are suffering from the heat, trying to stay in the living room area, where the only air conditioning unit in the apartment does a barely adequate job at cooling. Tomorrow is Father's Day, but they have made no special plans because Daniela is scheduled to work on Sundays, including this holiday, Otto explains.

My visits with the Kirchners remind me of my work, during the seventies, for Maryville Academy, a residential home for abused, neglected, and abandoned children, all wards of the state. For two years, while also working full-time as a counselor in a public school, I held a part-time counseling job in the Maryville high school boys' building. As the first woman to be assigned to provide on-site counseling for these boys, my job description included socializing, interacting informally with the teenagers, and occasionally eating dinner with them, in addition to providing therapy. Similarly, my time with Danny and his family consists of various modes of interaction, including conversations about everyday topics, regular play activities, and shared meals. **Unlike** Danny, however, many of those teenaged children manifested symptoms of a troubled life, as real victims of adult irresponsibility or malevolence.

__June 18th

Today, in celebration of Father's Day, Robert and I visit my stepson and his wife at their home. Over dessert my daughter-in-law says, "I am so tired of being asked at work if I am related to 'that Moriarty woman' in the Baby Richard case...." Feeling a wave of vicarious embarrassment for her, I am profoundly sad that she is experiencing discomfort at work because of her relationship to me. However, realizing that there is literally nothing I can do to fix this situation, I choose to change the subject, and we turn to happier topics.

After arriving home, I telephone Daniela to hear about their day. I remember well Otto's description of his previous four Father's Days as "Grieving Days." "Danny is my life!" rings in my ears from my conversation with Otto yesterday. "If he's laughing and playing with the stuffed animals, it's the happiest moment of my day," he told me. Otto and Danny spent a quiet Father's Day together in play.

"They have gone to bed early," Daniela reports; "they were both tired from the hot, humid weather." She is weary from a full day at the salon. I will speak to her again tomorrow, which, we both realize, will be one of the most important days in their lives as a family.

Danny Thrives: June 19 – August 22

June 19, 1995

AT noon, my heart beating fast, I telephone Loren's office and hold my breath while I hear the report from his secretary. Issuing one word, "Denied," the United States Supreme Court has refused to take up the Warburtons' appeal of the Illinois Supreme Court's ruling. On the morning after Father's Day, Otto has received the best gift of all—the last chapter of more than four years of litigation—"with enough lawyers' paperwork to fill a storeroom," according to the *Tribune's* account. Loren must cancel his luncheon appointment with me, she continues, because he has been with reporters all morning and will continue giving interviews throughout the day.

Life consists of beauty, significance, and depth, which more often than not cannot be transmitted by means of words that we are constantly casting into the market places of the world.

— Gertrude Stein

My next call is directed at congratulating Otto and inquiring about his response. I cannot find the words to express my own sense of relief and joy.

"I am **very** happy," he assures me, "but I had to leave with Danny today by the back door because there was a **mob** of media people around the front door of the building. The Warburtons' prepared statement refers to Danny as '**our** son' and says they are committed to his receiving **qualified** mental health services." They have made abundantly clear that they are not going to walk away. Otto is upset over their strongly worded message and wonders if they are sending veiled threats our way.

After escaping by their back door, he and Danny were picked up by Stacy and driven to her home to avoid the media. Danny and Lexi played in the kiddie pool and ran through the sprinkler to get some relief from the oppressive heat. The press caught up with the little group, however, and snapped photos, one of which will appear on the front page of the *Sun-Times* tomorrow.

Hurrying home from my evening with clients, I channel surf on the remote control to catch as much of the Baby Richard coverage as possible. All of the major channels feature the story of the Supreme Court ruling. One of the news programs includes an interview of Bob Greene, who expresses his personal disappointment in having failed to effect a change on behalf of Richard through his multitudinous efforts. His coverage of the case will continue, he guarantees the viewing audience. Attorney Laura Kaster is featured, imploring that visitation opportunities be granted her clients. I marvel at the use of this public forum for such a personal request, especially because the Warburtons have never even called me. They know that I am the therapist for Danny and their liaison with the Kirchner parents. Every day I wonder why they do not call to find out how he is doing or to ask about visitation for themselves or Johnny.

Ruth P. now has all of the requested information, including birth dates and similar details, to finalize her report. We are hoping for a finding of "unfounded" related to the charges against the Kirchners. It would be both supremely ironic and tragic, in the wake of the U.S. Supreme Court decision not to hear the appeal, if Danny is removed from his home by authority of this state agency. Although I know that the charges of child abuse and neglect are indeed spurious, I fear the possibility of behind-the-scenes politics that may unduly influence the DCFS finding into a popular but grossly unjust outcome.

Greene's columns this past week, before the U.S. Supreme Court decision, have progressively elevated the level of hype. In "'How does this happen in America?'" he states, "The victim who is suffering the most, of course, is Richard—he is the child who has been forced to endure the maximum pain...." (June 12). "This is a very sad day to be an American," an attorney is quoted; "...my profession is forever soiled by the indelible stain...from the travesty [of the Illinois Supreme Court]...upon [Richard]" (June 13). "The only way I can live peacefully is to just not think about the constant ordeal that 4-year-old child is going through daily," Greene quotes from a Wisconsin man's letter to the U.S. Supreme Court. "[T]he governor...would be able to pardon[,] a person convicted of murder, but he cannot pardon Richard," writes an Illinois reader (June 14). Because of the Illinois Supreme Court, proclaims Greene, "Every value children are supposed to believe has been turned into a sadistic taunt." He concludes, "There is still time, though, to say a prayer for a little boy who never had a voice." (June 18)

"Journalism—an ability to meet the challenge of filling the space," observed Dame Rebecca West. Greene, it appears to me, is filling his space the easiest of ways, through writing about only one topic and using massive amounts of repetition, quotations from others, and excerpts from court documents. Other columnists, by contrast, are compelled to find different, interesting, and relevant topics and to do research. Greene probably taps out one of his columns in an hour, allowing plenty of time for his other pursuits, while his colleagues actually work.

__June 20th

Otto takes the family car to a repair facility today. There is a noticeable and alarming problem on the driver side with the steering mechanism or axle. The timing of this dangerous malfunction is interesting at the least. It is the day following the U.S. Supreme Court announcement. It would not be difficult for someone once again to vandalize the Kirchners' car while it is parked overnight in the large, open lot in front of the apartment building. Their street is lightly trafficked and dimly lit, making the car vulnerable to undetected tampering. Across weeks, a virtual flood of hate mail—some explicitly threatening physical violence or death—has poured into the Kirchner home. It would not be shocking to discover that one of its authors—or another enraged individual—has made an attempt to injure or even kill one of the Kirchners.

When I arrive, Daniela has set up bottles and other items in preparation to indulge me with a facial. She insists that she wants to do this for me as her only way to repay me for my work with Danny. I readily talk myself into agreeing with her, and Danny joins us to watch his mother using her professional skills. While she works, she explains that her training in Europe was more intensive and comprehensive than the corresponding program that she also completed in this country in order to obtain licensure as an esthetician.

During the cosmetic process, Danny darts in and out of the room in play. He picks up the bedside telephone to engage in pretend conversations. "Whom would you like to call?" I ask him and then recommend that he call Robert.

"Hi, Bob!" he says cheerfully, followed by some light comments about his day. "I love you; bye, Bob," he finishes and hangs up. Daniela and I laugh at his ingenuousness and spontaneous expression of affection. I notice today that Danny has been saying "also" on a frequent basis. It sounds authoritative as he uses it to punctuate the simplest of sentences. "My dad would like this also," he declares, and "I can carry this to the other room also." He seems to like the sound of this word, and it joins "huge" as another of his most common articulations.

Daniela has applied to a suburban salon for a job closer to home. Now working in a yuppie neighborhood and having cultivated a regular, loyal clientele, she is worried that her income will drop when she has to start all over again in another setting. Although she applied one month ago and the owner could not pay her requested salary, the woman calls this afternoon. She says, "My husband and I were talking about you and he believes we should not let you get away. We will pay your required salary for you to come work for us." I tell her that it is most interesting that this job offer comes today, when the U. S. Supreme Court decision, bringing the "Baby Richard" case to a dramatic halt, is front-page headlines in the *Tribune, Sun-Times,* and *Daily Southtown,* all of the major newspapers in the area.

Daniela's hesitancy to change jobs has little to do with the prospect of more publicity. It arises from her natural shyness and the requirement that she develop her own clientele once again by self-promotion.

"I have trouble approaching people and trying to sell my services and salon products," she explains. "My commute now is three hours each day, and it is hard on me to be gone so much from Danny. I will need to consider this job offer very seriously."

Otto relates to me that Danny, by phone today, gave his name to a relative as "Danny Richard Kirchner," demonstrating that he is comfortable with his true identity. Overhearing his father's praise, Danny struts over to me, announcing, "My name is Danny Richard Kirchner." He is proud of himself and looks for his dad's renewed approval.

Walter Jacobson from FOX-TV conducts a half-hour interview with me over the telephone this afternoon. He shares with me that, as a divorced father of two young children, ages three and five, he misses living under the same roof. "I can't imagine one of them being taken to another home and not asking for me," he asserts, referring to Danny's situation. I remind him that this is not his situation or his child and that, like him, the majority of people appear to be projecting into this story their own family dynamics.

Karen Gibson from a local cable-television talk show invites me to participate in her program tomorrow. Loren Heinemann has consented and will drive me there, she offers. I decline, as I am not interested in expanded publicity and Loren will be adequately representing the Kirchners on her show. The attorney is spending most of his time on television and radio programs.

__June 22nd

Auggeretto Battiste from the Illinois Department of Professional Regulation appears today, as scheduled, to conduct a preliminary investigation of me. In the wake of Bob Greene's columns attacking my credentials and competence, "Hundreds of complaints from readers tied up the office's phone lines," he informs me.

"The Department continues to receive several calls every day, most of which allege that you are incompetent," he informs me after we shake hands and he settles into an armchair in my office. A distinguished-looking, handsome African-American man, Mr. Battiste has a deep voice and a soothing style. He requests a copy of my resume` and a list of my professional activities and training since my first state licensure as a psychologist in 1976. I assure him that I will send him these items at my earliest opportunity.

Asking me about my Baby Richard work, he takes copious notes and nods occasionally. He has had experience with other media-created cases, he tells me, including "one in which the man did not have a chance when he became the target of animal rights advocates who went after him…, a nice man who didn't deserve it." I wonder if I will "have a chance," or if I will be catapulted into a legal and bureaucratic forum in which I will be compelled to struggle to maintain my professional license. Without my license, I am out of business and at the end of this career path.

After two intense hours of interrogating me, Mr. Battiste shakes my hand and wishes me well. With focused effort, I turn my attention to a series of afternoon clients. As soon as I complete my notes from the last hour with a divorcing couple, I head off to my in-home session with the Kirchners.

Otto informs me today that Loren and his wife have frequently observed the same car and driver in front of their home, once pulling into their driveway and taking photographs of their house. The Heinemanns continue to receive threats on a regular basis. Fearing potential violence, such as the recent firebombing directed at an attorney embroiled in a similar custody battle, Loren has notified the police.

On Monday, I will be meeting with child psychiatrist Dr. El-Shafie in order to discuss his performing a clinical evaluation of Danny. In the event of more litigation or adverse DCFS findings, such an assessment will be timely and perhaps preemptive of damaging action against the Kirchners' claim to their son.

During my two-hour visit with the Kirchners, Danny cheerfully takes his bath, emerging with dripping wet hair and a broad smile. He and Otto play a computer game together, and the child yells "Yes!" every few minutes when he scores a point against his dad.

Earlier in the day, Otto reports to me, a woman, three young girls, and a young boy, none of whom looked familiar, stopped in back of their apartment and purposefully started to approach Danny, who was playing on the patio. Otto brought Danny inside, avoiding the strangers, who then immediately retreated toward the front of the building. He followed, to observe them climb swiftly into a van and drive away.

When Daniela comes in from work, she and Danny exchange hugs and kisses. We look at photographs, recently developed from five rolls of film taken on their Canada trip. Danny, describing the pictures to me, is so delighted with them that Daniela brings out their camera and we take turns posing and snapping photos of each other in the living room.

Ruth P. from DCFS is completing her final report, from which a letter will be generated and sent to the Kirchners to inform them of her findings. I repeat her explanation of the process to Otto and Daniela. By phone this morning, she offered, "I was probably assigned by the Department to this high-profile case because I am grandmotherly and sensitive to the uniqueness of the Kirchners' situation." She made a point of telling me that she had seen Danny on television last night. "Isn't that what it's really all about?" she asked, referring to the child's welfare. I am hopeful that her comforting tone and message are reflective of an "unfounded" finding related to the spurious charges of child neglect and abuse against the Kirchners.

Daniela telephones the owner of the suburban salon while I am there; she accepts the new job and appears visibly relieved. She has become enthusiastic over the prospect of a new start and discusses with me various ways, consistent with her unassertive personality, to build a clientele. We talk about creating and distributing flyers, throughout the neighboring area, that highlight her extensive training and unique services. I encourage her to emphasize that she is European trained and has had nearly a decade of experience, four years in this country.

For the first time in months, Otto has a viable job prospect as the manager of a restaurant on the north side of Chicago. In spite of the distance, he is happy that someone, at long last, is interested in the possibility of hiring him.

Today their landlord was tracked down and interviewed by the media about Danny. How is he **really** doing? was the major question. Because he answered, "Just fine," it is unlikely that the interview will be aired anywhere.

__June 24th

Arriving with two large plastic cups in the shape of animals' feet, I greet Danny and newly arrived cousin Mario. Danny grabs the rhinoceros foot, leaving Mario with the black bear clawfoot, but both are happy and ask for beverages. At nine, Mario is much taller than Danny but he is also thin; he has freckles, bright blue eyes, and light red hair. He and Danny are already comfortable with each other, Daniela declares, although Mario knows only a few English words, matched by Danny's comparably limited knowledge of Slovak.

Daniela will remain at home with the boys for four days before she begins her new job. Mario will be sharing Danny's king-size bed, enabling her to return to her own room at night. Fearful that he might awaken during the night, she has been sleeping with her son since his arrival. She and Otto had decided that they would never leave him alone, not even for overnight hours, during his first months with them.

Playing Nintendo games together appears to be an equalizer between the boys. Danny is more proficient and shows his older cousin how to work the remote control. "Jeez!" exclaims Danny at regular intervals in their play; he is competitive and wants to win.

Only two letters addressed to "Baby Richard's Father" are delivered today. One of them praises him for his courage in claiming his son in spite of all of the challenges involved. The other contains the typical outpouring of hateful sentiments.

In my private time with Danny, after a minute of silence, he says, "The bad people took me away from the hospital when I was a very little baby. That's not fair." Looking up at me, he adds, "They can never take me again." As we talk, I become more aware that Danny has integrated his situation and has become confident and secure with his birth parents.

He has come to view his transfer to his "real" parents as a type of rescue mission, executed by his birth mother and father to retrieve him from John's parents.

__June 25th

Checking in by phone, I ask how things are going with Mario and Danny. Otto reports that the boys communicate through sparse words but many gestures. This morning all three of them fished in the pond and caught several fish.

Today Bob Greene's column, focusing upon the U.S. Supreme Court's ruling, quotes several alleged readers' outraged reactions. One unnamed middle-aged man is quoted, "'Maybe this day comes in every person's life—the day when he understands that everything he once believed in about his country is gone. I never thought I'd say those words.'" Greene continues, "Your patience in reading these stories—and the patience of my editors in publishing them—is very much appreciated. Now you will begin to once again see stories here that are about people other than this child...." He promises that, when there is a development about Richard, "it will appear here, but not every day."

The Kirchners and I hope that this column signals the end of the tyranny that has been so continuous and destructive. We will soon discover, however, that "Richard developments" will frequently continue to happen—or be created—by Greene, who, with the determination of a bull terrier, cannot let go of his most attention-getting and easiest topic.

__June 26th

Drinking the usual, strong Colombian coffee during my visit, I watch the two cousins at play and Otto remarks that I have become a member of their family. He serves us homemade meat loaf, rice, and applesauce that he has prepared for lunch. Often he serves a hot, cooked meal for lunch rather than dinner, which consists of lighter fare, such as sandwiches.

"Danny has gained three pounds since he arrived," Otto says, stroking the child's hair. Danny takes his third helping of applesauce. "You could see his ribs before, but now he is filled out and looking good."

Otto laments that they have still not received any of Danny's medical records from the Warburtons or their attorneys. "Danny has a scar under his lower lip," Otto points out. When asked about it, Danny explained that he had been hurt in a car accident and had to go to the doctor.

Meeting with Dr. Osama El-Shafie today at a restaurant, I explain that the Kirchners may request him to perform a clinical evaluation of their son. Dr. El-Shafie is an experienced, well-reputed child psychiatrist, recommended by Loren Heinemann. When I ask him if he would be willing to meet Danny in his home, he clarifies that he would prefer using his office. I realize that the Kirchners worry about continued media scrutiny and intrusiveness. If they take Danny for an appointment with a psychiatrist, they are likely to be followed or joined by reporters and cameras. Such an event would doubtless give rise to fatuous reports of Danny's "deteriorating emotional condition," an outcome that they will certainly try to avoid. Loren is interested in obtaining a written evaluation by a medical doctor that might be used in preventing further incursions into the Kirchners' lives by documentation of Danny's stability and remarkable adaptation.

__June 27th
In response to several weeks of incoming, harassing phone calls and mail, many with hate messages and threats, I telephone Chief Holub of the Palos Park Police Department. Loren has been urging me to request additional police surveillance of my home and property since the strange man and car have been regularly spotted in front of his home. The Chief tells me that he is "already aware" of my Baby Richard work, and he assures me that his department will take special precautions on my behalf, including increased patrolling of my street.

__June 30th
Mario, Danny, and Justin are riding bikes today when I stop by at 6:00 p.m. Justin's mother, Charlene, and Otto sit at a picnic table supervising the boys at play. Daniela arrives from her new job minutes later, and the four of us talk about the children. Danny passes by, pedaling fast, and calls out, "Hi, you guys!"

Daniela likes the new salon, its twenty-minute proximity to home, and the people there. However, she needs to buy new clothes, as uniforms are not worn there, and her wardrobe is limited.

__July 2nd
The Kirchners, with Mario, arrive at my home at 3:30 p.m., as invited yesterday. The children play in the small plastic pool, set up for them in our backyard. They grab the garden hose from each other, taking turns running through the gushing water and yelling. We enjoy a barbecue lunch together and play horseshoes. While Mario speaks his language, Danny speaks English, but they appear to understand each other. Mario is learning more English words every day, however, and Danny wants to do everything with his cousin. They have become inseparable.

__July 4th

According to the evening news, the Warburtons are planning to file another lawsuit. From a "reliable source," it is reported that they are due to file a petition in court, seeking visitation rights with Danny. I wonder once again why they have never contacted me, the child's designated therapist and liaison, regarding this issue. To seek judicial assistance in a sensitive matter so confounded by strong, human feelings and a bitter history of conflict seems like folly to me. A simple phone call, expressing genuine, heartfelt emotions, would go so much further in advancing their purported cause than more adversarial litigation. To the Warburtons, it seems to me, issues regarding Danny are a zero-sum game; there have to be winners and losers; and might is preferred over conciliation.

__July 5th

Mike Parker from Channel 2 calls to interview me about imminent, renewed litigation. "It is my understanding," he says, "that the Warburtons will allege psychological abuse of Danny if his birth parents do not allow them visitation with the child." He asks if I agree with this position, to which I respond, "No" and "No further comment."

__July 6th

During my private time with Danny, he initiates conversation about his former parents. He refers to them as "the bad people," and although I neither agree with this assessment nor encourage it, I listen without correcting or challenging him. Danny has processed and integrated his unique situation in his own, four-year-old way that includes "good guys" and "bad guys." Today I understand better why he has not asked to see them.

He is playing with Mario, as usual, and I leave for home to the sounds of their laughter.

__July 7th

Barbara Walters features the Warburtons on her *20/20* show this evening. "Tonight, the little boy who broke the nation's heart," the coverage begins. "You saw him torn from the only family he knew...," it continues. Barbara Walters introduces the

Warburtons, "It is a scene etched into the nation's memory—a confused and terrified little boy...."

Kimberly Warburton says, "We all only had one shot, one opportunity at doing it the right way, but Danny was going to be scarred. We thought the most important aspect was minimizing the scarring...." As I watch the program, I am wondering why any caring adult would want to describe any beloved child as "scarred" to the viewing nation.

The Warburtons discuss their disappointment and pain; they talk about their desire for a continued relationship with Danny, especially for their son Johnny. Jay says, "Does he feel that he was...kidnapped by the Kirchners and he's being held hostage?" He asks for visitation with Danny. Again, I wonder why they are making such a request on national television. Such a bizarre choice of medium for such a private, fragile matter!

On the evening news program that follows, a brief clip of Otto and Daniela is shown. Otto is quoted as saying that Danny would not be seeing the Warburton parents, but their son John would be welcome to visit his son in their apartment.

__July 11th

"Grandma is here!" Danny shouts as I enter the front door to meet Gabriela Berkey, Otto's mother, who arrived over the weekend from her home in Toronto. She is a robust, heavy-set woman with a strong handshake. We are introduced and she begins an animated conversation with me about her new grandson.

"Danny looks exactly like his father at this age! The way he walks, his hair, his expressions are Otto's," she relates to me, smiling the special pride of a grandmother. "You know, I saw the pick-up of Danny on television. Shortly after that, I got calls from relatives in Hungary and Czechoslovakia, who also saw it in their countries. The story was on the front page of our Toronto newspaper the next day. Otto, Daniela, and Danny were recognized by my friends when they visited me last month because of all the publicity!" she exclaims, shaking her head in disbelief of the international furor.

Danny reappears from his room, where he and Mario have been playing, to confess to me that he broke his bedside lamp. Penitent, he hangs his head as he tells the tale, and I imagine that the two boys probably got too boisterous, spurred on by the excitement of another visitor in the household. Daniela replaces the lamp with one from her own bedroom without so much as a "Be more careful next time." Both Otto and Daniela are casual and relaxed with regard to mishaps and little accidents.

"Mario is sometimes a difficult child," Daniela explains to me in private. Otto adds that the boy surprisingly asked to be spanked after engaging in a number of provocations. Both parents are worried that Danny may pick up some of his bad habits. He often becomes silly and laughs in a loud, attention-getting way, but the good news is that the boys continue to get along well together.

Danny brings out the growing family album again and points out favorite photos and describes them. He talks about his hero, Michael Jordan, to his grandmother and me. Through the afternoon Danny challenges Mario in their favorite computer games with the oft repeated, "I'll kick your butt!"

"I was in my mommy's tummy," Danny says to me as our little group sits in the living room together after sharing a Czech dish consisting of cabbage, dumplings, and bacon. "Can I listen to the baby?" he asks as he places his head against his mother's abdomen. He kisses her stomach, lifts his head, glances at me, and announces with a grin, "I kissed the baby."

Daniela confirms that she is indeed pregnant, and Otto joins in, "We are not telling anyone yet." I remember well Daniela's pregnancy in February and her loss of the baby due to having been refused medical treatment without health insurance. Otto and Daniela are both visibly happy about the prospect of another child.

"I will **have** to get a job now so that Daniela can stay home with Danny and the baby," Otto says with a worried look. Thus far no one will hire him; when he gives his name, he is typically refused an interview. Some people have attributed the failure of the once-bustling Kenessey's restaurant, for which he worked as the manager, to the continuously adverse publicity directed against him during the custody battle. The closing of Kenessey's tossed Otto into unwanted and long-term unemployment. Maybe someone will give him a break and hire him in spite of his notoriety, he and Daniela are hoping.

__July 16th

Daniela calls at noon to accept my invitation to visit at my home today. Gabriela, reacting adversely to the extreme Chicago summer heat, has left to drive herself back home, but the rest of the Kirchner family arrives late in the afternoon. Danny and Mario escape the heat by settling into our outdoor spa tub, filled with tepid water, and by splashing each other with the garden hose. The boys feed the fish in the small pond next to the gazebo, and Danny proudly reports this feat to his father.

We eat in the dining room today because it seems too hot to enjoy an outdoor meal. Danny talks about gypsies, repeating stories told him by his grandmother. He initiates discussion about the expected baby, and he seems genuinely excited about the prospect of a younger sibling.

Laura Kaster is scheduled to hold a press conference tomorrow, according to Loren's report earlier today. Otto and Daniela are worried about the uncertainty of the future, particularly in light of predicted renewed litigation. They inform me that they received the official letter from DCFS, stating that the charges of child abuse and neglect were "unfounded." We exchange meaningful looks without words. A small victory, justice prevailing, is vastly superior to the possible alternative of being compelled to fight to keep Danny from a politically motivated outcome.

__July 17th

At the Sheraton Hotel and Towers in Chicago, Jay and Kimberly Warburton hold a press conference today, in which they make prepared statements and answer only pre-planned questions. A professional public relations firm has reportedly advised them on their approach and format. They thank the public for all of the support they have received during their ordeal in trying to keep Danny, whom they call "**our** son."

Announcing that they are starting a foundation on behalf of children, they do not offer details or specifics. I am wondering about this new foundation and how it relates to the Baby Richard Fund, through which they have been collecting contributions for many months. According to Loren, they risk the loss of these funds now that Baby Richard's custody has been granted Otakar Kirchner by the Supreme Court. Conceivably, Otto could assert a claim to these funds because legally "Baby

Richard" is his son. Satisfied with having Danny with him, Otto has no intention of pursuing litigation toward the acquisition of these funds.

Kimberly makes an impassioned plea for her son John and Danny to be reunited. The Warburtons are interested in the formulation of a "psychological plan" for both boys in order to make their visitation with each other a workable possibility. Again, I am amazed that the Warburtons have chosen the media, rather than a phone call to me or to the Kirchners, to present their case. They have never telephoned me nor, according to Loren, have they contacted him about the issue of visitation. I also marvel that their apparent sense of self-importance has impelled them onto the airwaves and into viewers' homes in order to request another "psychological plan" for the children.

Adrienne Drell would tell me that she attended the Warburtons' press conference. "I was surprised and disappointed, however," she discloses, "when the announcement came that no questions would be taken from the media. I wanted to ask what they intended to do for children through the foundation and where the donated money would go...." The Warburtons' refusal to accept and answer questions is off-putting to many of the media attendees.

Meanwhile, Otto and Daniela have agreed to participate in a *Dateline* program in order to clarify Danny's emotional state. Even his former adoptive parents have labeled him "scarred" on national television. Worried about his projected image as pitiable "damaged goods," they want to refute this baseless, fabricated picture of their media-victimized son. If the public becomes aware that the child is genuinely happy and doing well, they reason, the story will die away and, hopefully, Danny will be able to begin a normal life in anonymity. As long as he remains a curiosity, a lamentable figure, and a hostage-like victim, the hype is likely to continue.

John Block, the producer of the segment, calls to ask me for an interview as Danny's psychologist, "the definitive source of information regarding how Danny is doing." Having successfully avoided the media for the past several weeks, I decline. Otto requests that I reconsider my decision, and accordingly I call Mr. Block and schedule with his crew for tomorrow at my home.

__July 18th

Four technicians, John Block, and Dawn, the interviewer, arrive at 10:00 a.m., one hour earlier than scheduled, to begin preparing for my interview for *Dateline*. Carrying in more than thirty cases of equipment, which includes lights, microphones, cameras, backdrops, and other items, they set about turning my great room into a studio. They move all of the furniture to another room and set up two chairs in the center of the area, one for Dawn and one for me. From 12:30 to 3:00 p.m., Dawn asks me a multitude of questions from a prepared list held on her lap out of view of the rolling camera. Toward the end, John passes over to her two more sheets of further questions.

A sound technician pins a tiny microphone under my jacket lapel and a similar one on Dawn's collar so that the two of us might walk and talk outside, in front of my home, to continue the interview. The cameraman precedes us, filming and taping our conversation as we walk together across the lawn and up the paved driveway. After Dawn thanks me for my time and candor, I excuse myself to head toward my office and evening sessions with clients. Robert oversees the crew's packing of equipment, their return of our furniture to the proper places, and their leave-taking at 4:15 p.m.

Six hours of process result in four minutes of program time on the July 21st *Dateline* program. The Baby Richard segment, "Home At Last?", runs for a total of sixteen minutes, which include an interview of Otto and Daniela, footage of Danny at play, and a review of the history of the case. As usual in Baby Richard coverage, there is no mention of the Warburtons' involvement in the original lie that was created for the biological father about the child's having died at birth. I am pleased, however, that I have been afforded the opportunity to set the record straight about Danny's remarkably fast and comfortable adjustment to his birth parents and new home.

Just when I am thinking that this program may serve as the punctuation mark to end the story, allowing me to return to my pre-Richard life without media, I hear from Otto that a variety of reporters, journalists, and program producers have contacted Loren Heinemann to request coverage of a prospective meeting between Johnny Warburton and Danny. The media representatives would like to arrange for a reunion of the two boys as a special feature for their respective programs and publications. Otto informs Loren of his position that this is a private matter and, if and when it occurs, it will **not** be a media event.

A fundraiser will be held in Lansing, Illinois, in four days for the Warburtons—the *Southtown* reports today—specifically for the "Doe Family Support Fund." For the dinner 600 tickets have been printed at $15 each, and 2,500 raffle tickets will be sold for $1 each; the goal is to raise a total of $11,500.

__July 20th

Having cut his finger on a knife from the fishing box, Danny presents me with his bandaged "owie" when I arrive. Otto played nurse to him earlier when the child frightened himself by accidentally administering a deep cut to his own finger; it was his blood, dripping on the carpet, that most alarmed him. Otto tells me that Danny asked his father to hold him tight. That reassurance provided, he went off to seek out Mario for a safer play activity.

Danny, now used to reporting to me on his own the highlights of his day, takes me by the hand to show off his new, jazzy, silver Power Rangers bicycle, a two-wheeler with training wheels. Mario has inherited Danny's old bike, and now the cousins no longer have to share but can ride together "like Batman and Robin."

Otto shows me a newly arrived letter, anomalously directed to his full, accurate address, urging him to be a "truly good father" by returning Danny to the Warburtons. It is forcefully worded and well-written, postmarked from New York, causing us to wonder about the author. Having maintained an unpublished address, he has received only a small handful of letters, among hundreds, that are correctly addressed.

Mario and Danny invite Otto to join them on the living room floor where they are playing the card game "War." Danny claps his hands in glee when he wins and eagerly gathers his cards in a pile, sometimes insisting that he has won when the cards say different. His father explains, "You can't win all of the time," to which he responds, "I **want** to win all of the time!" Danny's competitiveness corresponds with his otherwise strong personality, which has no doubt contributed to his rapid, comfortable adjustment in his parents' home.

__July 21st

Today Danny lost the gold chain with its faith, hope, and charity charms that he has worn daily since receiving it from his maternal grandmother. He hung his head and mumbled to his mother that he lost it at Justin's house. Expecting to be punished, Danny was subdued and quiet until she reassured him, "Accidents of all kinds happen to little boys and it is okay."

Justin is leaving for Las Vegas for several weeks to visit with his father, who lives there. Danny and Mario will play by themselves in his absence.

This evening *Dateline* covers "Baby Richard" as the program's feature story. Maria Shriver narrates the segment, which includes footage of Danny at play, interacting with his birth parents, and throwing a ball with the interviewer. He **seems** normal and well adjusted, runs the theme of the piece, and several minutes of my interview are shown. Ms. Shriver states, "**Everyone** seemed to have an opinion…, most on the side of the adoptive parents." At its conclusion, viewers are encouraged to give their opinions by telephoning the number displayed on screen, as the "Feedback" portion of the show. I wonder why the "majority" opinion of the public is already announced, followed by a call-in opportunity for viewers.

__July 24th to August 9th

My visits with the Kirchners continue on a regular basis, three times per week, with phone calls nearly every day to check on their progress. Mario and Danny are constant companions; Otto continues to apply for jobs; and Daniela works full-time at the salon, progressively expanding her clientele.

Since Bob Greene's columns about me in May, I have not received court-referred child custody evaluations and my telephone has nearly stopped ringing from new clients. My client sessions have dwindled to less than half of last year's number. In an attempt to recover my losses, I begin to advertise pre-marital counseling and private mediation services. I mail out flyers to judges, local attorneys, and other prospective referral sources, hoping that clients in search of these services will replace the lost work.

As I will soon discover, there is no response for pre-marital counseling services, while mediation results are better. Through mediation, couples often resolve their child custody disputes in a faster and less adversarial manner than through the court system. In mediation, the individuals decide their own fate and that of their children, while in court the judge makes a binding decision for them. The Cook County Court offers three sessions with a mediator for divorcing parents and many disputes are thereby settled. The mediator, as the facilitator, works with both individuals to help them create an agreement with each other regarding the issues of custody and visitation. Many disputes remain unsettled after three sessions, however, and the parents are free to decide their next course of action. They can reconcile, postpone further action, revert to an adversarial legal process through their attorneys, enter into counseling, or choose mediation with a private practitioner to continue to work toward a resolution of their issues. With my training in labor negotiations and win-win bargaining, I have developed a structured process that is intended to expedite agreement between individuals.

Many attorneys, however, seem reluctant to refer their clients for mediation services because they perceive the mediator as usurping their role and because such referrals result in a direct loss of income for them, a diversion of fees to another profession. A few hundred dollars paid to one mediator will often replace thousands of dollars paid to two opposing attorneys for the same—or a better—outcome and in less time and with less anguish for the individuals. I will soon discover that attorneys refer only their clients with limited funds for mediation services. However, with shared motivation to work toward successful resolution of their differences, we usually reach agreement of all presented issues within four or five sessions, and protracted litigation is avoided.

Since I began my Baby Richard work, I have been spending at least half of my professional time, including weekend hours, with this case. I schedule my other clients around my in-home visits with Danny and his parents, and I now work more hours on Saturdays and Sundays.

__August 1st
Second City, the popular, live Chicago comedy show, launches its new offering, "Baby Richard's Got Back, or It's Not Easy Being Bob Greene." With parody, puns, and pomp, the troupe performs its satire to less-than-glowing reviews. Even the theater is

reflecting the talk of Chicago and the inexorable linking of Baby Richard and Bob Greene.

__August 10th

Otto, Daniela, and the two children are spending more time in their apartment. Not only is the August heat a factor, but they continue to be recognized, followed, and sometimes confronted in public places. People whisper, point, and frequently make rude comments. There are "Baby Richard sightings," which result in calls to Bob Greene and the *Tribune*, providing information about the child's whereabouts and his appearance. "He looked sad while standing at the grocery counter," a caller will report.

Bob Greene, seeking any information, will write a column about anything related to "Richard." Absent first-hand accounts—he has still never spoken to Otto, Daniela, Danny, or me—he is writing from strangers' input, the child's former neighbors, his readers' letters, mental health experts who have never worked with Danny or even met him, and fantasy material.

From time to time, Otto and Daniela speak wistfully about a future when their family will be able to live a normal life. They talk about the prospect of normalcy with a level of enthusiasm that other people evince when they talk about winning the lottery.

Mario has learned sufficient English to talk in simple sentences and to ask for what he wants, using his second language. Danny has learned a number of Slovak words to use with Mario and his own parents, who now regularly speak both languages with the boys.

Adding to the family album, I bring with me two rolls of developed photographs from the family's recent visits to my home. Danny reaches for them, proclaiming "These are mine," and then examines each one, with Mario at his elbow, sharing in the inspection.

__August 11th

Having been unemployed for one year, Otto is experiencing sleeplessness, lack of energy, chest pains, and flu symptoms. His recent, sole job prospect has not materialized, and he is unable even to get interviews. Realizing that it is unlikely that he will obtain another managerial position, he has been regularly applying for a variety of different jobs. He is eager for almost any kind of work. It is demoralizing, of course, not to be hired but even worse to be rejected for an interview once he provides his name.

Extending my visit to four hours today, I spend private time with each member of the family. Danny starts by telling me that he is getting "huge." Raising his arm and making a fist in the air, he exclaims, "See my muscles! I am getting very strong!" He shows me his new toy saxophone and a hand-held viewer with slides of "Lion King" characters, each of which he shows me while he tells me their names.

To music playing in the living room, Danny begins to dance for our small group. Daniela praises his natural rhythm as he adjusts his movements to fit the tempo of the changing music. I remark that Danny has inherited his father's musical talent and Otto smiles his obvious pride in his son's graceful, uninhibited dancing.

When I ask Otto, a classical violinist in Czechoslovakia, if he might resume playing, he answers, "I don't have the heart for it here; there is no inspiration for me." He informs me that there are new neighbors in the apartment complex who are continually looking for Danny. The fourteen-year-old boy regularly comes to their patio, asking to see Danny. In another apartment, a large camera is often visible in the window between the curtains.

An alarm clock buzzes at 9:30 p.m., triggering the time for Mario and Danny to take their baths in preparation for bedtime. After Danny has emerged in his pajamas, I say my good-byes and leave the family as the boys are jumping into bed.

This evening, *Dateline* presents some of the specific viewer feedback to its earlier program about Baby Richard. "Most of those who responded" support the adoptive parents; three of their responses are quoted. On the Kirchner side, only one man's letter about the child is excerpted, "...He is now where he belongs."

__August 12th

Mario is writing postcards home to his mother and other family members when I arrive. Tonight I notice that Danny is saying "please" with regularity. His parents are making special efforts to teach him manners. Daniela is also teaching Danny to count to one hundred. Remarkably, for an intelligent child, he could not count correctly to twenty when he first came to live here.

Both Otto and Daniela continue to be child-focused in all of their behavior. They routinely stop what they are doing when interrupted by one of the children to attend to his present need. They interact with the boys in a variety of ways and, in fact, their social life revolves around them. Because of the Baby Richard hysteria and sightings, they have all but withdrawn from their former friends and associates, leaving them with limited social interactions outside of their home. Daniela has friends at work; they entertain Otto's cousin and his family; and they interact with the few neighbors whom they know and trust. Activities within their little family, now including Mario, anchor them happily at home together.

We speak about the *American Journal* coverage of Baby Richard that was replayed on television this week. Daniela feels strong sympathy for celebrities who have no privacy and experience intrusion into their daily lives by the media and the public. She stopped reading articles about the case months ago and now watches television only rarely and selectively, avoiding all programs that might feature the "Richard" story.

I share with Daniela my newly developed sense of detachment from the media coverage. There is the epic Baby Richard saga, which has become a story of fabrications, distortions, and speculation, while there is the real Danny and his loving family, who bear little or no resemblance to the other.

Loren Heinemann continues to discuss the case and the Kirchner family, basking in the glory of his legal victory and newfound, widespread celebrity. He drives hours to radio talk shows; provides regular telephone interviews; and seems to accept every invitation from the media that he receives. Otto has requested that Loren desist from talking about his family so that their ability to begin a private, anonymous life will be accelerated—but to no avail. Loren not only enjoys the attention and publicity but it attracts more clients. He could never afford to pay for the level of advertising that he receives for free from his frequent exposure as the Baby Richard attorney who single-handedly won the case by beating one of the giant law firms in Chicago. It is a modern-day David and Goliath story, and Loren tells—and retells—it well.

Otto laments that Loren has seemingly lost their phone number, as he rarely calls or stops by these days.

__August 18th

This evening I arrive with note cards and matching stickers that I promised Danny and Mario several days ago. Intrigued by the variety of animals pictured on the cards, they begin to write on them, Mario in Slovak and Danny in scribble.

Otto, still unable to find a viable job prospect, discusses his ruined credit rating. Before the custody battle, which has sapped his resources, he was able to buy two new cars within a few years on credit. Now, unemployed, he cannot get a loan and his economic picture is bleak. Although working full-time, Daniela is bringing home less pay because gratuities are typically lower from suburban customers and she is still cultivating a regular clientele.

Danny, in good form, shows me his new karate moves, proud of his accomplishment. Otto believes that Mario's long-term visit has been beneficial overall for Danny, who seems relaxed and carefree from morning to night in his cousin's company. Mario's earlier pattern of silliness, including making faces and noises, has decreased in frequency, and he communicates more appropriately now.

__August 20th

While attending my cousin Mark's open house in Chicago, he shows me a copy of today's *Tribune*, in which Bob Greene's column presents as factual his imaginings about Danny longing for his former brother and adoptive family. Mark, a member of the Viatorian order of Roman Catholic priests, expresses his concern for me as inextricably wrapped up in a fly-paper story that won't go away. The misinformation and distortions in Greene's articles continue unchallenged, and he writes without checking the accuracy of his content with the child's parents or with me, as their therapist.

__August 21st

Today's Bob Greene column presents intimate, personal information about Danny's lost "crucifix"—in reality, the anchor, heart, and cross charms on a gold chain, the gift from his grandmother. He accuses Otto of lying and Daniela of giving away her baby, two of the recurring themes in his writing. He cites his source for this latest reported episode as Loren Heinemann.

I am amazed that Loren would provide this type of private information to Greene about his clients, especially after he has been requested by Otto to stop discussing his son with the media, particularly with Greene.

__August 22nd

With strong feelings of trepidation, I telephone Otto to ask how everyone is doing. He has not seen the latest Bob Greene missiles, and he is content that the boys are doing fine and having fun together. I schedule a visit tomorrow to offer support in the wake of accelerated, impassioned media coverage that will doubtless damage the Kirchners even more in the eyes of the public, thereby impairing further Otto's chances to land a job.

For the first time ever, I speak with Bob Greene when he calls my office while I am awaiting the arrival of my next evening client. I explain that I am unable to speak with him because of a series of appointments until 10:30 p.m. He calls three more times, leaving messages.

I wonder why he is bothering to contact me now, after months of writing in a definitive, misleading manner about Danny's progress—absent information from the only mental health professional who has been seeing and working with the child. Surely it cannot be to pose the question, "How is he doing?" He has not cared to ask that even once across the nearly four months of my time-intensive work and contact with the child. I realize that if he put himself into the position of knowing real information, he could not very well continue to write the fantasized drivel that elicits a flood of reader response and sells more newspapers..., or could he?

As I am leaving my office at 11:00 p.m. to go home, I decide to tell Greene to leave my clients alone, to allow them normal lives, and to write about other cases where he might actually do some good instead of inflicting this outrageous level of damage upon Danny and his parents. I will have my chance tomorrow, but I will also pay a big price....

...We must be true to our beliefs,
dare to be ethical,
and strive to be honorable.
For integrity
is the highest ground
to which we can aspire.

— *Anonymous*

Don't compromise yourself.
You are all you've got.

— *Janis Joplin*

Good name in man and woman, dear my lord,
Is the immediate jewel of their souls:
Who steals my purse steals trash;
'tis something, nothing; 'Twas mine, 'tis his,
and has been slave to thousands;
But he that filches from me my good name
Robs me of that which not enriches him
And makes me poor indeed.

— *William Shakespeare*

NOT realizing that today would plunge me into a media feeding-frenzy over the manufactured desire of the public for a Danny-Johnny reunion, I consent to an interview with Bob Greene. He is at fever pitch, I soon discover, when we begin our telephone conversation....

__August 23, 1995

If you speak the truth, have a foot in the stirrup.

— *Turkish proverb*

Direct Hits & Survival: Aug. 23 – Dec. 31

Calling at 7:50 a.m., Greene leaves a message on my answering machine, followed by another call at 10:20 a.m. His fifth call to me within fifteen hours signals an unusual level of urgency, one that I typically encounter with suicidal or hysterical clients. I don't expect this sudden volume of contacts from him, especially in light of the fact that he has never bothered to speak to me before. He has written dozens of columns about "Baby Richard," never having interviewed Danny, either of his parents, or me. Therefore, Greene knows from little to nothing about the real child. However, this lack of contact and of first-hand information has not deterred him from writing from ignorance.

Having this opportunity at last, I tell Greene today by phone, "You are just spinning your fantasies and imaginings in your columns, which bear **no** resemblance to the reality of how Danny is doing." The child is thriving and enjoying a nearly stress-free home life, no thanks to him and his phony propaganda. I point out that he is still using over and over again, as the companion picture for his articles, the four-month-old picture of adoptive mother and child from the transfer day, and he should probably update his material. Informing him that I have a pile of current photographs of Danny, smiling and laughing, in contrast to the one he is using as an icon, I offer to send him one of these photos to use in updating his material. Predictably, he ignores my offer to provide him with a current picture, which would contradict his established theme of the tormented, pathetic Richard.

"This is now **old** news—or it should be," I assert. "Let this child begin a normal life; he deserves it; and you are doing no one any good by continuing to write and write about what should now be a non-story."

When Greene asks about the prospect of a "reunion" of Richard with Johnny Warburton, I clarify for him that the real child Danny no longer talks about John and that it is unlikely that he thinks much about him. "He spends every waking hour with his cousin Mario from Slovakia, who has been here now for the past six weeks," I tell him. "They are inseparable. They eat, sleep, and play together all day."

Having been authorized by the Kirchners to speak openly to the media on their behalf, I am free to share this information with Greene, foolishly hoping that he will now divert his journalistic attentions elsewhere. I avoid telling him that Daniela is three months pregnant, as I have not explicitly received the Kirchners' approval to share this news. I know that they would not want it revealed to the entire country, in nearly 200 newspapers, by Bob Greene. What I know and Greene doesn't is that the Kirchner parents are preparing Danny for a new sibling, and they do not want him confused or emotionally torn by premature contact with his former sibling John. They are creating a family, bonding, and joyfully anticipating another birth, this one to be shared with each other. It is a regained opportunity for all of them to experience the miracle of birth...as a family.

Emphasizing to Greene, "This is not the time for a contact with his former sibling for a variety of reasons," I tell him that a reunion will take place when the child is ready, not when the media dictate. "Again, Danny does not ask for John; he asks for Mario or his neighborhood friends, Justin, Jason, and Jeffrey," I convey to him.

"Please go away," I implore, "and write about children who really need help and intervention. This child needs neither. You can do some good by advocating for real abused children. This child is loved and cherished."

After nearly one hour of conversation, we say our good-byes and hang up. I feel content that I have said everything important about Danny. I hope that Greene, now informed about Danny's real situation, will take the high road and move on to other subjects, especially now that I have clarified Danny's real current status as opposite to Greene's hyperbolic creation.

One hour later, Greene calls again. This time he suggests that the Kirchners agree to engage in a mediation process with the Warburtons, facilitated by Cardinal Bernardin, toward the goal of getting the two boys together. "What part of our previous conversation did you not understand?" I ask him. "Danny is not ready for a meeting with any member of his former family; he does not ask to see them; and the media's desire for a reunion will not be the controlling factor. His parents are determined, also, that any meeting of these two boys will not become a media event. Timing is everything in these matters," I explain, "and the parents are the best judges of the readiness of their child for such potential encounters.... Are you a parent?" I query.

"I **never** talk about my personal life," Greene responds tersely.

Now angry and obviously frustrated, Greene questions my credentials to work with this child. I inform him that I am a licensed clinical psychologist and that I have worked with children and on behalf of them, in schools and in private practice, for twenty-seven years. Clarifying that I am providing all of my services to this family on a *pro bono* basis, I affirm that my motivation is to do my best for Danny and his parents. "I am not involved for money," I tell Greene, "and my only condition for accepting this case was anonymity, as I wanted no contact with the press and no publicity. This is a case of helping a family who cannot afford to pay professional fees for therapy or for public relations. Unlike the Warburtons, for whom funds have been collected across many months, the Kirchners have neither sought nor received an outpouring of public contributions." In fact, months ago when Loren Heinemann suggested the solicitation of donations for the Kirchners' legal expenses and for mental health services for "Richard," both the Kirchners and I declined his offer.

"It is time for Danny to be able to live a life that is private and dignified, like any other child," I insist to my unreceptive listener. "A media-controlled meeting with his former adoptive brother would not be conducive to an intimate human experience between two children."

As in our earlier conversation, I suggest, "You should consider directing your journalistic efforts to benefit children who could use advocacy, such as children at Maryville Academy, where I worked part-time, or inner city kids, who have no spokesmen. Your columns are the greatest impediment to Danny's life and you are harming—not helping—him."

Naïvely believing that he might care or that it might make a difference, I inform Greene that the real tragedy is his making the child into a curiosity and a pathetic public figure. "You have created a wholesale invasion into this four-year-old boy's private life," I tell him.

"Regarding the Warburtons, if they want to see Danny or arrange for their son to see him, why don't they call me?" I add. Greene offers in response, "Some people have asked me, if the Warburtons love him so much, why don't they just appear at his door to see him? That would probably be a bad idea, I suppose...."

Greene persists, "Cardinal Bernardin is willing to try to work this out as the mediator for both sides...." He is attempting yet again to establish his position as the media mogul who successfully brings about a perceived happy ending to this chapter of the Baby Richard story. As early as his June 4th & 7th columns, Greene recommended—and arranged—intervention by the much-loved Cardinal, Archbishop of Chicago. Greene is creating news, and he is determined. He has already gone public by declaring the Cardinal's willingness, elicited by himself, to serve as the mediator for the purpose of reuniting the two boys.

"Feel free to have the Cardinal or his representative call me, and I will give him the same information that I am providing you," I respond. "Danny's parents have decided that it is not the right time for their son to reunite with his former family. It is **their** decision, based upon his best interests. It's not a media decision."

Our conversation ends, and I know that he will retaliate against me because he probably not only hates the message but the messenger.

Naïvely, I am consoling myself with the belief that at least Greene will have to bring to an end his self-initiated mission to effect a dramatic reunion of the two boys. Now made aware that four-year-old Danny is understandably focused on the "here and now" of his new family, cousin, and daily life, Greene may even admit to his readers that the child has moved along, I am thinking. Correspondingly, Greene may finally move on to another subject, perhaps one for which, in contrast to Baby Richard, he might actually do some good for a child or multiple children.

I would soon discover once again how wrong I could be. Greene would not only decide to continue his made-up story of the intensely suffering Richard, clinging to his past and longing for a reunion, but he would ratchet up the pathos another notch or two. He would also decide to discredit me so that any of my reports of reality about "Richard" would not get in his way or expose him as a spinner of false tales. He would simply paint me as ill-intentioned and not credible.

"And if thou tellst the heavy story right, Upon my soul, the hearers will shed tears," Shakespeare wrote in *Henry VI*. Bob Greene would decide to tell his gold-mine, "heavy story right" to tug on the heartstrings of his readers and to draw their tears, but it would be unreal, wrong, and just plain exploitative.

__August 24th

Holding up four one-dollar bills when I enter the apartment today, Danny is grinning his anticipation of spending this small fortune at Toys Я Us, a frequent destination. "He loves having money and also spending it," Otto chuckles, as he watches Danny present to me the symbols of his daily activities.

"See, I have a key **also**!" he exclaims, showing me a large, old key that his father gave him so that he might feel like a big boy with responsibility. In addition to "also," "jeez," and "huge," "difficult" has joined his favorite words. Now that he is learning more each day, from reading a simple word to playing a new computer game, he often describes the challenge of the day as "difficult." I am happy to observe that he persists in his efforts and rarely gives up. I always make a point of praising him for his perseverance.

Today Danny calls himself a "gypsy," a word bequeathed him by his paternal grandmother. Otto laughs and explains, "He **has** some gypsy blood."

Mario has now learned enough English words to communicate with Danny at his four-year-old level, and the boys play as peers. Having had an older brother in his other house, Danny is undaunted by the more aggressive Mario, who is seven years older. He interacts with his cousin with apparent ease and self-confidence. I note today, as on many previous occasions, that Danny's emotional flow is even, with only rare and fleeting episodes of anger or sadness; he seldom cries.

When I return home, I call Loren to inquire why he has been disclosing intimate details in Danny's life to Bob Greene. "To keep the story alive," he answers unabashedly. Greene has been writing in his usual malicious manner, attacking the Kirchners' judgment and parenting, although he has never witnessed them in action. Loren is feeding Greene tidbits, in spite of his clients' repeated requests that he cease talking to him. Loren directed Greene to me, however, to deliver the "bad news" that the reunion, over which the columnist has been regularly beating his journalistic drum, would not soon be held. Loren's decision, I will discover, is a purposeful one; Greene will direct his ire at me. The attorney continues his pursuit of the "good guy" role, happily turning others into the "bad guy."

__August 27th

The entire family is helping Mario pack his belongings for his return to the Slovak Republic in time to start another school year. Otto announces that more of their relatives will soon be coming to stay with them, including Daniela's mother and Otto's cousin.

In his Sunday column today, Bob Greene writes a typical, impassioned version about Baby Richard's pain and betrayal. There has been no reunion, and "'this is how mental illness begins,'" Terrence Koller is quoted as saying. Koller is a child psychologist and the executive director of the Illinois Psychological Association. Greene continues, "Richard was observed this summer in a grocery store with his biological parents; the person who saw him said that he was standing alone and appeared to be talking to himself." He concludes, "...[A]s we will report Monday, there is another voice helping to keep [the reunion] from happening."

__August 28th

This Monday morning, when I awake, I call to wish Mario a safe trip home and to tell him how much I enjoyed spending time with him during these past weeks. He understands me and responds loudly, "Yes!" and "Okay!" I walk downstairs from my bedroom in pursuit of breakfast to discover Robert on the landing, still at home on his golf day, holding the *Chicago Tribune.*

Having realized years ago that Robert misses golf only for one of the three D's—downpour, death, or destruction—and not always then, I sense that the precipitating event today fits comfortably into one of these categories. It's not raining and no one has died. He hugs me tightly for a full minute and then hands me the newspaper, open to Bob Greene's column.

In "Doctor's trust has a catch," Greene states, "...[S]ome leading national authorities in child psychiatry are appalled by what was done to Richard under Moriarty's sudden-removal plan." Blaming me for Danny's "abrupt" transfer in April, he writes, "...Karen Moriarty, the woman who came up with the plan to take Richard from his adoptive home suddenly, with no transition period." Of course, he ignores the months that I worked trying to implement a progressive transfer for the child. Greene further attacks my credentials and accuses me of planning to exploit the child for my own financial profit. And I am **the** person, according to Greene, who is preventing the reunion of the two boys.

The stark reality is that Otto Kirchner has provided mental health services for his son on solely a voluntary basis. He could have used a neighbor, anyone, or no one to assist in Danny's adjustment. As a licensed clinical psychologist, who is working more like an old-fashioned social worker—providing all of my services in a home environment—I am spending ten to twenty times the number of hours in interaction with the child and his parents than would a psychiatrist. Greene has taken the position that Richard needs a child psychiatrist, as would a child who is mentally ill or emotionally disturbed or a child who requires medication or hospitalization.

This is Greene's way of punishing me, I am thinking, for his frustration and anger over failing to bring about the prospective reunion that he has raised to epic proportions and that he has so ardently wanted to claim as his own.

I feel myself go numb as I read the column and sink onto the stairs. It is so bad that I don't even like myself after I've finished reading. How could any other reader respect me after this onslaught? In my mind, I see—as in a kaleidoscope—a myriad of images of my clients' faces, men and women, individuals of a wide span of ages, all looking disappointed, wondering about my integrity.

"I want to spend the day with you," Robert tries to comfort me, without even alluding to the venomous portrayal in the newspaper. "We'll get an attorney and we'll stop this ————!"

Overwhelmed and gushing tears, I cannot respond. Frozen on the stairway, I finally nod in assent. I feel clammy and my heart is racing as I seek another hug.

After Robert settles me on the couch, my appetite gone and my head still filled with visions of my clients' reactions to Greene's fabrications about me, I am absorbed in the realization that he has retaliated in full measure. He was thwarted in his plan to force a reunion of two young boys and claim the soap-opera encounter as his victory. He had already climbed onto the proverbial limb by offering the Cardinal to mediate the event, and now he cannot deliver. And he chooses to present mine as the voice of "no" on behalf of Danny's parents, my clients, who are only doing what is best at this time for their son.

A deluge of thoughts floods my consciousness. "Never fight with a guy who buys his ink in barrels," the motto of a prudent superintendent of schools, reverberates in my memory of better times, when my colleagues and I laughed over this nugget of wisdom. Loren, who otherwise has been providing Greene with fodder for his columns, chose not to serve as the bearer of this piece of bad news for the "obsessed" journalist. A flash of recent memory shows Danny, in full smile, hugging his mother's tummy and exclaiming, "I can hear the baby!"

Media representatives have been circling for another sensational story. It's a competition as much as any sport in town. Who will successfully create the reunion? Who will photograph or film it? Who will report it first? If Greene could not deliver, after publishing preparatory columns, then he will resurrect a villain. What else can he do? He unveiled me to the public in May, crippling my once-healthy private practice, and I am an easy target once again, a sole practitioner whose lifeblood is integrity and reputation. My sin is that I have chosen the "wrong side," the Kirchner family, including the controversial, mythical Baby Richard.

Robert leaves my side to telephone his college roommate and attorney friend, Ross Tyrrell. He asks Ross to recommend an attorney who would be willing and able to take on Bob Greene and the *Tribune* on my behalf. "William Harte!" is his immediate response. "He is known in my circles as 'the attorneys' attorney.' He knows the law, he has integrity, and he does his homework. He is the best, a hero to me," extols Ross, who promises to pave the way for us to meet Mr. Harte.

Agreeing by phone to meet with us tomorrow morning, Bill Harte saves me from drowning in misery today. I decide to put all of my emotional energy throughout the day into focusing upon our strategizing together, within twenty-four hours, not too long a time to wait. Meanwhile, unable to eat or to concentrate on the report that I intended to write for a client today, I fight the urge to call the Kirchners, aware that they will probably feel responsible for my misfortune. I want to spare them more grief; they have enough to handle without mine. After all, I am supposed to be the strong one, the therapist, the professional, their advocate. Now I have transitioned into their intimate friend who shares their pain on more than cognitive and empathic levels. I find myself weeping for them, myself, and the career for which I have worked so hard and which I risked for the privilege of helping a little boy and his friendless family.

__August 29th

Watching an amber sun come up over the dewy, grassy field behind my home, I try to draw comfort from the predictability, calmness, and beauty of nature. Before becoming immersed in "Baby Richard," I had seen more rainbows than sunrises, having inherited the nocturnal gene from my ancestors. On my best days, I sleep until noon and unwillingly succumb to bedtime at 4:00 a.m. With a private practice, I have earned the luxury of setting my hours around my energy peaks and sleep cycles. For the past few months, however, I have become familiar with the sound of the first bird chirping at dawn, having wrestled with sleeplessness at one or both ends of my night.

This morning Robert and I arrive one-half hour earlier than scheduled at Bill Harte's office in downtown Chicago. While we wait in the large, well-decorated reception area, Ross Tyrrell walks in to greet us. He has read the Bob Greene column since his phone call with Robert yesterday. Ross looks down at the carpet as he calls it "scurrilous." He is embarrassed for me, and I feel my eyes start to burn once again, but I swallow hard to avoid tears.

When Mr. Harte enters, I am impressed by his appearance. He is well over six feet tall, thin, and distinguished, dressed in formal attire. His eyes are penetrating. He leads us into his private office, where he trades his navy-blue suit coat for a burgundy sweater before he sits down to discuss my situation. He listens intently and he says little, which I will discover is his usual pattern, but when he speaks his words are direct, precise, and meaningful.

After Mr. Harte reviews the four *Tribune* columns about me that I have brought and we discuss the related facts, he agrees to take my case. Tomorrow he will write a letter on my behalf to Bob Greene and his Editor-in-Chief. I am relieved that there will be a swift response to Greene's defamatory statements about me, although, as we all know, the damage has been done. Robert and I thank him profusely for his time and support.

We head for the nearby Illinois Department of Professional Regulation Office to meet with Mr. Battiste, who is welcoming, warm, and congenial. He explains that his office is having a busy day with all of the incoming calls in response to Greene's column.

"It has been nonstop!" he declares. "People are outraged and many want to file formal complaints against you." He is happy to hear that I have sought legal representation in this matter. Having already reviewed the case with his supervisor, Battiste notifies me, "There will probably be an informal hearing at a first level regarding the content and allegations of the columns." I will be receiving a letter about that hearing, he informs me, and my attorney will be welcome to attend with me. My license to practice psychology is at stake, and I assure him that I will comply with all required procedures.

Mustering the courage to call Otto as soon as I return home, I hear from him that he is physically ill from reading the columns about me. He and Daniela are hurting for me; it is so unfair; and he would feel terrible if he were in my place with regard to my profession. Otto will sign a release for me so that I might speak freely and intimately about the case with the investigators, and he offers to testify in my defense.

__August 30th

Danny is sitting on his favorite "huge" chair in the living room, playing a "difficult" computer game. He has already spoken by phone with Mario, safely arrived back home with his parents in Slovakia. Danny requests that I play opposite him and, handing me a remote control, he teaches me how to use it to move the characters on the screen as we enter into vigorous competition.

Otto commiserates with me as I describe my meetings yesterday. He signs the written release and volunteers to go anywhere that would be helpful for me in the investigation that will be conducted. I have become one of the "bad guys"— as Danny would say if he knew what was going on—in this complicated story for which there is no end in sight.

As I am leaving, Danny requests "gypsy music" of his father, who complies by turning on the stereo. He begins to dance in rhythm with the beat and to giggle, pleased with himself and oblivious to the adult-level public furor about him outside of the shelter of his home. I am feeling uplifted by the vision of him with his father, both laughing, as I reenter the outer world of "Richard" fabrications and fantasy.

__August 31st

Nancy Glass, moderator, and Kathi Johnson, producer of *American Journal*, arrive at my home to film the Kirchners and me today. Four technicians follow the women to set up cameras and microphones. Otto and Daniela had long ago consented to do one segment for this program in April and another in August. Because Daniela informed Loren that she was not interested in participating beyond August, the agreed-upon month, the *Journal* producer immediately flew in this crew from New York so as not to miss their last opportunity to cover the story. I have offered my home as the site of this taping session in response to the Kirchners' landlord refusing more media invasions at his apartments.

During their six-hour filming process, I entertain Danny so that Otto and Daniela can participate in their interview without interruption. He and I are playing together outside when I observe my new neighbor walking across her front lawn. Danny and I approach her so that I might introduce myself. After we exchange names and I welcome her to the neighborhood, I suddenly realize that Danny is no longer at my side. Panic ensues as I imagine myself explaining to his parents that Danny has disappeared, followed by a vision of prospective headlines, "Psychologist Loses Baby Richard to Kidnapper!" I throw off my high heels and run barefoot at full speed around the house, screaming "Danny! Danny!" into the air. I am wondering how far away a kidnapper might have gotten with the child, within these elapsed two or three minutes, while his parents are chatting on camera inside my house. Rounding a corner of the house, I see him standing at the birdbath, splashing water with his hand. I experience a new level of cosmic gratitude. Hugging him and taking his hand, I lead him to retrieve my shoes from the neighbor's front yard and then to reenter the house. Together we sneak up the stairs as the camera is rolling in the great room, directed at the seated interviewer and Danny's parents. We find and pet Sybil, who has retreated to a guest room sofa in avoidance of the strangers and hot, bright lights on the first floor.

Hand-in-hand we tiptoe downstairs to the basement family room, where Danny and I begin to play tic-tac-toe on the cocktail table, one of his favorite games. He looks around the room and announces, "Some day I want a house like this one!"

I marvel at his maturity, speaking prospectively about his own future as an adult and a homeowner. Recently he has demonstrated a deeper understanding of the concept of time, including days, weeks, and months, and of future activities, such as starting school and having more visitors at his house.

As the Kirchners leave, I give a thumbs-up signal to Danny while the car begins a slow roll down the driveway. He flashes a broad smile and returns the same signal to me through the back window. Ms. Glass turns to me and says, "You are their best friend and they're lucky to have you."

__September 1st

As a birthday gift to myself today, I telephone Chief McCarthy of the Orland Park Police Department to request increased surveillance of my offices, Moriarty Associates, in the center of town. Notifying him that I have been receiving hate calls and threats again as the result of the renewed Bob Greene attack, I explain to the Chief that I work most weeknights during hours after the other offices in my building have closed. I am often alone or with one or two clients at a time, some of whom are emotionally disturbed. He agrees that I would be an easy target for violence by a client or an inflamed Bob Greene reader. Sympathetic to my situation, Chief McCarthy assures me that he will order additional police surveillance of my office building and parking lot during weeknights and Saturdays. A couple of days ago I contacted Palos Park Chief Holub once again to request similar surveillance for my home, to which he readily agreed. I am more careful and vigilant now when I leave the empty office building in the dark to walk to the only car in the parking lot. Threats of violence directed at me have become commonplace during recent days. Greene's making me into the originator of the sudden transition plan for Baby Richard has agitated both men and women into fierce reactions of rage and desires for retaliation.

I call Otto this evening to invite him and his family to my home on Sunday for a shared birthday party. His birthday, earlier this week, was overshadowed by Greene's journalistic onslaught against me and its resultant complications. I am determined not to miss an opportunity for celebration, especially because we have little reason for partying these days.

__September 3rd

Our cake reads "Happy Birthday, Otto and Karen!" in blue and pink frosting, and Danny is excited to attend a party. "I want a birthday, too!" he exclaims. His father promises him that he will have a party in March, when he turns five, which seems to satisfy him.

During dinner, Otto and Daniela play their new mealtime game with Danny. Instead of cajoling him to eat, they call him an angel if he finishes his plate. Becoming an angel is accompanied by vigorous hand clapping and praise from both of his parents; it appears to be a successful strategy. His parents sometimes feed him a forkful of meat or potatoes, and he enjoys the special attention. I can't help but think that they enjoy this little shared ritual because they missed out on their son's helpless baby stage.

Daniela whispers to me that when she was combing his washed hair this morning, Danny said, "You're doing this so I will look nice for Karen!" He has become well accustomed to presenting to me anything new or special about himself or his daily activities. Today he points out his new clothes, a blue long-sleeve shirt and matching pants.

When it's time for cake, we invite Danny to blow out the candles. After singing "Happy Birthday to You," all four of us adults—Otto, Daniela, Robert, and I—spontaneously begin to hug each other, and Danny jumps in the middle of us to get hugs too. We know, without words, that together we have experienced unique, unforgettable events and have traversed parallel emotional paths.

After dinner, Danny feeds fish in the pond, pets our cats Sybil and Tom Riley, and plays soccer with his father and mother in our backyard with a new ball brought from home.

After the Kirchners leave in the dark, I remember that my curbside flowers need watering. Approaching the street with my filled watering can, I notice the front of a black car that is parked yards from my driveway, mostly shielded from view by a line of tall flowering bushes. Because our country road is lightly trafficked by only residents and their visitors, I have never seen a car parked in this unusual place before. I drop the watering can, spin around, and run back to the house to report to Robert the presence of a strange, silent vehicle. Is it media? "Baby

Richard" and his parents have just left. Is it the author of one of the threatening letters that I have received? Is it someone who intends to inflict damage? "The lights are off and the motor is not running," I inform Robert, who is calling the police. Two squad cars, one from each end of the road, arrive within ten minutes. The four officers jump out of their vehicles to confront the occupants of the parked car.

Holding an axe from our garage, the only weapon available, Robert waits on our driveway as Officer Mattingly walks up to report their findings. "It's just two sixteen-year-old lovers," he announces. "It's just ironic that they chose **your** house to park in front of. We have been doing special patrols here at least three times every day. They were so scared when we came upon them, at an intimate moment, that you can be sure they won't return," he assures us.

We inform the officer about the Kirchners' all-day visit and their departure only seconds before I spotted the parked vehicle. The Kirchner family has been followed regularly and, under these circumstances and the continual outpouring of hatred from the public, we all have grown more vigilant, concerned, and cautious. Until recently, I often left my car and house doors unlocked. I have spent a lifetime of fearlessness, now gone forever.

Relieved, Robert and I retire to bed but I find myself starkly awake, listening to the nighttime noises outside, trying to distinguish between the sounds of nature and a potential intruder.

__September 6th

Sharing the usual Colombian coffee during my visit, Otto and I discuss the continuing public reaction to him and Danny whenever they go out and about together. Many people approach Otto to make nasty comments, to tell him to return his child to the adoptive parents, or to call him "monster," "bastard," or "a—hole." He tries to shield Danny from this acting-out behavior as much as he is able. Some people continue to contact Bob Greene to report Baby Richard sightings, knowing that almost anything, no matter how trivial, will likely be considered welcome news.

On a more pleasant topic, we review Sunday's party, and I share with him the troubling experience of the parked car, now a funny episode after the passage of three days. Otto smiles in sympathy and reminds me that his car—always parked in an open, accessible lot—had a punctured tire on the morning after the transfer of Danny and has also needed major repairs twice during recent months. He suspects tampering but cannot prove it.

Danny joins us, freshly scrubbed by his mother and wearing his pajamas, eager to participate in talk about the party. I share with him photographs from the event and provide Otto with a duplicate set for their family album. Danny studies the pictures, commenting on each, and tries to remember every activity from the day. He especially likes the photos of Sybil and Tom Riley and the four that he asked to take all by himself with my camera. We are trying to dispel his lingering apprehensiveness about cameras, and he seems less fearful of them.

Daniela remarks that Danny asked before the party if "strange people" were going to take pictures of his dad there. She answered "no," and he seemed more casual and relaxed about the subject than he was only weeks ago. His sense of security is growing in spite of the media blitz, intensified public scrutiny, and hostile reactions from strangers. Danny thinks that always being the focus of public attention is normal for children everywhere.

__September 7th

This afternoon my former colleague, David Binotti, drops by my office without an appointment. With fewer clients these days, I am doing paperwork when he arrives, and I am happy to spend time with him. Dave is the controller of District 230, and when I was the chief personnel officer there, we worked together on a daily basis across fourteen years. He is one of my favorite people, a competent, sensitive, caring, and dedicated man, with whom I shared both the good and the trying times.

Dave has come by to inform me in person that Walter Jacobson recently contacted the school district to find out about any skeletons in my professional closet. He asked some pointed questions, including whether there had ever been a problem involving my employment with the district. Dave assured Jacobson that there were none. I explain to Dave that private investigators have been probing into Otto Kirchner's life and Loren Heinemann has reported similar intrusions. Dave should be prepared for more inquiries about me, I tell him.

After we talk about more pleasant topics, Dave leaves, expressing his concern for my welfare and safety. Later I would remember this as my last contact with Dave, who, at the age of fifty-one, succumbed to cancer in October 1998. I would feel sorrow not only over his death but over my not having told him how much I respected him and valued our friendship—one of the lost opportunities in my life.

__September 8th

Today Danny is taking more photos of his family and me with his parents' camera, oversized for his small hands. He chuckles, proud of himself, after each snapshot that he takes. Otto describes him as bouncy and exuberant. Now that Mario is gone, he gets all of the attention once again from his parents.

"Danny is very interested in the baby," Daniela says, "and he asks often when the baby will arrive so that he can have a new brother or sister."

On cue, Danny asks, "When **will** the baby get here?"

"The baby has to grow bigger first before he or she will come out," she responds. To his follow-up question, "Why?", she explains, "This is how it works with babies, and it was the same with you when I carried you as a baby."

We discuss the prospective costs of childbirth. Because the Kirchners still do not have medical insurance, Daniela, now in her fourth month, has not undergone an examination by a gynecologist. Having suffered a miscarriage in February, she wants to ensure that everything is going well with this pregnancy. I will attempt to find them a doctor who is willing to provide services either on a *pro bono* basis or for reduced fees.

Otto laments the recent court judgment against him in the amount of $7,000 for rental fees allegedly owed for his previous apartment. When the Kirchners moved to the suburb of Mokena in preparation for the arrival of their son, the landlord claimed that Otto owed six months of rent for an early termination of his lease. Loren represented Otto in this matter, but he questions the attorney's handling of the case. Due to the circumstances surrounding it, this judgment may well have been prevented, but Loren did not communicate well with Otto, who now wonders whether his lawyer did as poorly in court. He rarely comes around any more, Otto informs me, but he is still active on the publicity trail and in accepting new clients and their retainers for his services.

Wearing a new football jersey and matching pants, Danny watches a videotape of *Jurassic Park* and questions his parents about the fate of the dinosaurs. He asks "Why?" and "How come?" frequently during my visits. Danny has an inquiring mind, and both of his parents are patient and enjoy providing him with explanations at his level of understanding.

After the movie, Danny brings out of his bedroom an interactive computerized game that teaches letters of the alphabet, shapes, and numbers. He becomes engrossed in the learning game, demonstrating a good attention span for a four-year-old. "When I told him that he needs to know these things before he can start school," Daniela tells me, "he got **very** serious." Danny became instantly motivated to learn all of the concepts and figures and to concentrate on giving the correct answers.

Otto has talked to a representative of the Department of Professional Regulation, who called to ask him questions about my therapeutic services. My attorney has informed me that we need to make my license to practice psychology our first priority. Otto recalls the conversation to me, especially emphasizing that he told the investigator, "This is more nonsense, created by Bob Greene, who has been trying to hurt anyone connected to the Kirchner side of this case." Otto continued by praising my commitment to his son and family and the quality of my work. What Otto lacks in political niceties and tact, he more than makes up for by his forthrightness and honesty. I thank him for his support in this worrisome business.

Danny gives his father a hug and a kiss tonight as he passes through the living room. I observe that he is often spontaneously affectionate with both of his parents. He still regularly asserts, "I'll kick your butt!"—a borrowing from the Power Rangers—when he challenges anyone to compete with him in computer games. Tonight we laugh as Danny tries to use a white crayon in his coloring book and declares, "It doesn't work!" when no color appears on the page. I explain that the crayon works but doesn't show up on white paper. On that happy note, I say goodbye and leave for home.

__September 10th

My friend Colleen calls to report that the *Tribune* has now placed Bob Greene's column on page 2 of the Sunday edition. His own brand of yellow journalism, at the expense of Danny and his family, has won him another reward, a type of promotion by page placement. "Where is the truth?" Colleen asks rhetorically. I feel discouraged and fearful that Greene's Baby Richard tirade will only continue or even escalate, if that is possible. For eight weeks before the U.S. Supreme Court decision this summer, he wrote about nothing else. He has been prominently rewarded.

When I telephone the Kirchners, Daniela answers on her way out the door to do the weekly laundry in the utility room across the hall. Otto is sleeping and she is concerned that he is depressed over their continuing problems. He still has no job and no good prospects. They have not heard from Loren for two weeks, and Daniela suspects that he may be feeling guilty about providing Bob Greene with information about Danny's private life for his columns. I have not heard from Loren either, I tell her. I recall Mark Twain's observation, "It takes your enemy and your friend, working together, to hurt you to the heart: the one to slander you and the other to get the news to you," and I am struck by its appropriateness now.

I ask to speak to Danny, and when he says "Hi," I become aware that I have never spoken to him by telephone. Across nearly five months I have visited Danny so frequently that telephone contact with him has never occurred. He informs me of the highlights of his day, and they become mine, too.

My appointment calendar is sparse, as I have gotten no new clients during recent weeks and several of my ongoing clients have terminated their therapy.

__September 13th

After divulging my problems with shallow, erratic, and night-mare-laden sleep to Dr. Linda J., my gynecologist, I explain that another reason for my appointment today is advocacy on behalf of the Kirchners, my clients. Daniela is pregnant but has no doctor, money, or medical insurance, I tell her. I describe their plight, created by an unprecedented level of adverse publicity that is both destructive and undeserved.

After she excuses her nurse assistant from the room, Dr. J., to my delight, agrees to become Daniela's physician and to adjust her fees to a level that she and her husband can afford. She conditions her assistance on "no media coverage of any kind," emphasizing that this is a big concern for her. I guarantee her that the Kirchners are not interested in publicity; that their participation with the media has occurred only when necessary and on a defensive basis; and her involvement will be protected from public knowledge. I thank her heartily and depart, feeling happy and yet apprehensive about the promise I have made her. What if a media van, undetected, should follow Daniela to the medical office and its occupant confronts the doctor for an exclusive interview? I can't allow myself to worry about this eventuality, but I determine to warn Otto and Daniela to exercise caution at a special level in order to prevent being followed when they appear at their appointments with Dr. J.

__September 14th

During our conversation today, Otto wonders if he will ever find work in the Chicagoland area, which has been saturated by the *Tribune* columns to the point that he is recognized—and rebuffed—almost everywhere he goes. The weekly amount of Daniela's tips from her new clientele is only a fraction of her previous level at the downtown salon. They don't know whether this difference is due to customers' awareness of her identity as the Baby Richard mother or to the suburban clientele. Otto will accept any job of any kind, having lost all hope for a managerial position. He worries that if he returns to a restaurant, customers may protest and leave, as they did at his last job. Many observers attributed the failure of the Belmont Hotel Kenessey's restaurant to Otto's media-generated notoriety and his being easily recognized.

Otto is still enjoying the role of "Mr. Mom," he tells me, smiling and nodding in Danny's direction. Daniela also likes his being an at-home father, who cooks, cleans, and plays with his son. Danny spends more interactive time with Otto every day, while most of his friends, older by several years, are in school.

To my informing Otto and Danny about my imminent trip with Robert to celebrate our anniversary, the child exclaims, "No fair!" and jumps up to hug me. I am pleased that he has become comfortable in spontaneously initiating affectionate gestures with me. Ensuring that he understands that I will return in two weeks, I hug him again and leave for home.

__September 17th to 29th

On a vacation to celebrate our twentieth wedding anniversary, Robert and I join a tour group, sponsored by the Palos Hospital Auxiliary, traveling to Thailand, Singapore, and Hong Kong. During one of our initial waiting periods at the airport, James O'Connell, a fellow traveler, approaches me to reveal his awareness of my involvement in the Baby Richard case. "Others in the group have expressed their concerns to me about you," he sputters. "I have some strong opinions regarding the case that I will share with you sometime over a beer," he adds and then walks away. A group of twelve men and women, gathered around their luggage, are silently watching O'Connell and they greet his return. He has been their emissary, I realize, and the message has been duly delivered. The proposed beer event never occurs, and Robert and I share all of our meals as a twosome throughout the trip, as our traveling companions, avoiding us, find other places to sit at each eatery on our tour.

__September 29th

Upon my return from the Orient, I telephone the Kirchners to hear that Danny is doing well. My second call, made to my attorney, finds Bill Harte in his office, having filed my lawsuit against Bob Greene and the *Chicago Tribune* earlier today. The charges are defamation and false-light invasion of privacy. The focus, in layperson's language, is upon damage to my reputation as a professional person. Although my caseload is at a low point, I take comfort from the belief that this action will serve to stop Bob Greene from writing about me again. It will accomplish that goal, but the deathblow to my practice has already been administered. I will soon discover that a sole practitioner—with a miniscule budget for advertising and with clients from word-of-mouth referrals—does not have a realistic chance of survival after having been targeted and vilified by a widely-read columnist who is syndicated in almost 200 newspapers...and who "buys his ink in barrels." Unaware of my future, however, I slide into a welcome, deep sleep of six hours for the first time in many weeks.

__October lst

Having become ill with serious flu symptoms at the end of my vacation, I am suffering from a relapse. Phoning Danny and his father from the comfort of bed, I inform Otto about my lawsuit. He hopes that it will now cause Greene to find, or create, subjects other than Baby Richard for his columns. Danny is happy that I am returned from my trip, and I promise to visit him in a day or two, when I am feeling better.

__October 3rd

Entering with small souvenirs for Danny, I notice that the apartment is dark, its blinds drawn to block out sunlight and voyeuristic neighbors. Otto explains that local public interest in Baby Richard has seemingly increased during the past two weeks. It is likely the cumulative effect of so much publicity across so much time.

Today, in front of Danny, a young woman approached Otto in a store and asked how his son was doing because she heard "from the media" that he was "falling apart." He responded that she probably heard this report from Bob Greene, who didn't know what he was talking about. She scowled at him and then at Danny, pivoted, and strolled away. These occurrences are now commonplace. Many people in the apartment complex and their visitors go out of their way to observe Danny, while strangers in stores, parks, and other public places unabashedly examine the child and his parents and often follow them. The more subtle expressions of hostility—frowns, grunts, pointing, and head shaking—are often directed toward the child himself, while name-calling, vulgarities, and obscenities are aimed at his father.

Although I am unaware of any published article that asks, What is all of this publicity doing to the **child**?, the Baby Richard hysteria, perpetrated by Bob Greene, does not escape the notice of the highly reputed *Columbia Journalism Review*. In its September/October 1995 issue, "Bob Greene's Richard File" censures the journalist for his extremist and biased approach:

> Few legal cases have generated as much passion and outrage from the media, public officials, or citizens as Chicago's adoption case known as "Baby Richard." Few columnists and commentators in that city haven't

written about the boy, now four years old, who was transferred April 30 from the family he had lived with since he
was a few days old to the biological parents he had never
met. But no one has written more copy about Richard
than *Chicago Tribune* columnist Bob Greene: more than
50,000 words (66 columns) since May 1993.... Most of the
columns, syndicated to more than 200 newspapers, were
written this year. Greene blasted the Illinois Supreme
Court for...awarding Richard to his biological parents....

Readers have reacted by writing two to three thousand
letters.... [E]ditors said this issue generated more letters
than any story in recent memory, and that more than 90
percent agreed with the columnist. Among his colleagues
in the media, however, Greene's obsession with the story
has been characterized as overkill....

Richard Roeper, a columnist for the...*Chicago Sun-Times*
who wrote five columns on Richard, says..., "This is the
biggest journalistic meltdown I've ever seen.... It was
like a broken record. It was the same thing, day after
day, to the point of obsession.

Greene and his editors insist that he was prepared to
stop writing about the case when he was no longer able
to provide new information. But he seemed to be creating some of his own news when he ran comments from
readers and went as far as asking Chicago's Roman
Catholic Archbishop, Joseph Bernardin, to negotiate
some sort of compromise between the two sets of parents.
When Bernardin responded that he would like to help,
Greene ran that in his column.... [N]othing has come of
the offer....

Greene...said he won't stop writing columns about it
until the boy is allowed to visit the family that raised
him: "I'm not going away."

This lone journalistic plea for rationality makes no difference in Greene's "over-the-top," inane coverage, which continues

unabated, as promised at the end of the article. Although scholarly, this publication cannot compete with the readership of the *Chicago Tribune*, the newspaper with the largest circulation and readership in the Midwest, and its message goes unnoticed by the general public.

Talking with Otto, the primary victim of Greene's rampage, I listen to the only good news in an otherwise grim picture. He informs me that the neighbor who lives directly across the street from Loren Heinemann's house is willing to rent his home to the Kirchners for eighteen months with an option to buy after that period of time. The man is quoted by Heinemann as saying, "Otto deserves one break and I'd like to provide it." Most important among Otto and Daniela's considerations is the prospect of more privacy for their family in a freestanding home with a fenced yard. The Kirchners will need to find someone to rent their apartment in order to be released from their current lease. They can obtain occupancy of the little, three-bedroom starter home on December first.

Daniela is elated by this welcome news, which corresponds with her renewed ability to eat and the cessation of morning sickness and daily nausea. To my surprise, the magazines that Otto ordered weeks ago from the two bizarre college aspirants have begun to arrive at the apartment. Perhaps things are looking up.

Otto remembers to tell me about a significant and disturbing event that occurred several days ago. A Lutheran minister, who looked like the clergyman at the Warburtons' house on April 30th, appeared at his front door, without an appointment, "to talk about Danny's religion." Otto responded that he was not interested in a conversation and the man, after one more attempt, left. The prospect of Otto's appearing at someone's front door, unannounced, is equally probable to his applying for a passenger trip to the moon, he explains to me. He considers this type of behavior presumptuous, disrespectful, and insulting. Otto has since received a packet of information from the local Lutheran church, including sign-up forms. I am aware that Otto and Daniela decided months ago to raise Danny in the Roman Catholic religion, in accordance with their own upbringing.

Loren remains distant, even during the Kirchners' inspection of the neighboring home that they have been offered. Stacy has told Otto and Daniela that people on the street still approach Loren to say things like, "How can you sleep at night after what you did to that little boy?"

This week, I relate to Otto and Daniela, I have spoken to seven attorneys in connection with current or prospective clients, and every one of them was aware of Greene's columns about me or of my lawsuit against him, which was reported in the *Law Review Bulletin*. I am compelled to struggle to maintain my professional credibility on a daily basis. The Kirchners feel helpless and I reassure them that this is not their fault. I am buoyed up by Danny's reaching out for a hug and a kiss during my departure ritual, and, having no clients scheduled this evening, I head for home.

__October 6th

Danny is eating waffles, syrup dripping from his chin, as I begin my visit. He appears to be experiencing "cabin fever," as he and his father have stayed close to home for the past two weeks. His improving manners are apparent by his frequent use of "please," "thank you," and "excuse me," but he also glibly refers to himself as "boss" of the house. "Danny wanted to visit Karen and Robert's house yesterday," Otto informs me, "and he got really insistent about it. I had to talk him into doing other things here."

Daniela has cut her hair short, and this new style gives her an elegant look. As she returns from work, she is wearing a red dress and matching sweater. Otherwise thin, she is now obviously five months pregnant, and the couple has announced their good news to family members and a small number of people whom they consider friends or colleagues.

Danny leaps into her arms and, returning his embrace, she cautions him, "Be careful because the baby gets scared." She often uses this explanation to discourage his boyish roughness, and I realize that she is ever conscious of her miscarriage only eight months ago. She and Otto want this child, and happily the doctor has confirmed that both baby and mother are doing well.

Otto requests that I sign a form application to verify that Danny is their dependent. They have been unable to get a birth certificate for Danny; Loren tells them that he has encountered "impediments" to his efforts to obtain one. With embarrassment, Otto takes back the form after I have signed it.

Daniela murmurs that they must apply for public aid: "There is no other way...."

We discuss the verdict from the O.J. Simpson criminal case, and Otto relates similarities between the media's sensationalized, divisive portrayal of the outcome and the media's unique slant on his own case. "**My** only crime is loving my son and being unable to live without him," he points out as the defining difference between the two situations.

__October 13th

Having no scheduled clients today, I have more hours than usual to spend with the Kirchner family. Otto feels that their plan to relocate to a house is well timed; they need to get away from this apartment complex. There are two boys, whose family has just moved into a neighboring unit, who have sought out Danny. They destroyed his motorized mobile car by pounding on it with hammers, Otto informs me. Danny tells me about the incident in his own words, referring to the children as "the mean kids." He talks about the police, who might help him if needed, and I realize that his parents have discussed with him the role of the local authorities in enforcing law and order.

Danny takes me by the hand to his bedroom window, and he points to a large broken stick on the ground outside. "The mean kids broke that stick and looked at me with mad faces when they did it," he reports to me, sadness in his voice.

Although the two friends play together outside, Danny is no longer allowed to go to Justin's home, because Otto and Daniela believe that he is too vulnerable to the malevolence of strangers when he is not under their supervision. Danny confesses to me that he got so angry over this decision by his parents that he kicked the wall in his bedroom.

At his suggestion, Danny and I walk out to the patio together, while his father has left to do some shopping, and we watch the ducks swimming in the pond. We play ball together in a game of his creation, while we sit on plastic lawn chairs facing each other. I discovered early on that he readily talks about his feelings and important matters when we become engaged in a play activity together. Our focus on a mutual task lessens inhibitions, and he shares more intimate information than he does in eye-to-eye contact. Danny mostly wants to be permitted to visit Justin in his apartment.

"Are you ready?" I ask, stalling, with the ball poised in the palm of my hand, up in the air.

"Yes!" he yells. I repeat the procedure, still holding the ball, and adding, "Are you sure?"

This routine escalates—"Are you absolutely sure?"—until he is squealing from laughter. He teases me back, as we continue to withhold and then throw the ball to each other in this erratic way.

"I was just joking," he excuses himself when he tells a fib about the ducks and I challenge him with the truth. I am delighted to observe such a well-developed sense of humor in so young a child. He enjoys the banter as much as the ball tossing.

Danny disappears into the apartment and returns with an orange popsicle from the refrigerator for himself and another for me. "This one is for you," he says as he presents it to me. I praise him for his thoughtfulness in front of his father, who has returned from the store with a bag of groceries.

"Why do the birds stay outside all of the time?" Danny asks. He is developing a pattern of trying to figure out the causality and meaning of things in his environment. "How does that work?" and "Why?" are his most common questions, and he often becomes engrossed in studying everyday things, such as how a new toy is put together.

__October 16th

Tonight in session, I interpret a personality inventory for one of my ongoing clients, Judy, a mother who is allowed visitation with her son only under the supervision of his therapist. After she was found guilty of child neglect in court, this prohibition was imposed by the judge for an indefinite duration. Two hours each week, across the past eight months, she has interacted with her ten-year-old son in my office. I counsel, guide, and sometimes direct their communications with each other.

Judy announces that her stockbroker brother has informed her that I do not have the credentials to administer or interpret her personality test, according to Bob Greene. While I assure her that I am both qualified and licensed, I realize that my credibility, not only with her but other clients, is weighed against the volume and venom of Greene's attacks on me, made in reputable newspapers of wide circulation. To most readers, if it is in print, it must be true. After she leaves, I sink back into my chair, fearing that months of difficult work together and real progress are now jeopardized by a malicious journalist. Perhaps the "most unkindest cut of all," as Shakespeare wrote, is this pervasive threat to my effectiveness, which has nothing to do with my skills and competence, but rather with a crisis of confidence purposely created by a columnist with no first-hand information or knowledge about my work.

__October 17th

Joe, one of my court-referred clients, appears with his daughter Zoe for an update session about the child's progress within the context of his custody dispute with the child's mother. He is aware of the Bob Greene columns about me, and we discuss their potential implications at such time when I am called upon to report to the court my recommendations about Zoe. To his expressions of "concern and worry," I provide him with a copy of the letter from Bill Harte, which challenges Greene's allegations, clarifies my credentials, and counters the columnist's distortions and lies. Joe says that he will consult with his attorney about this matter and let me know their decision.

By telephone I speak to Daniela and then to Danny, who talks about his newest toys, which include a car wash game. When he is finished providing a summary of his day, he ends with "See you later, alligator."

I inform Daniela that later this week I will bring the book *What Color Is Your Parachute?* for Otto to assist him in his job search. Her take-home pay is less than it was one year ago, she discloses, and they are both anxious for him to obtain employment as soon as possible.

__October 18th

When I return the phone call from Karen Spring of *Newsweek* magazine, she relates that she is preparing a 1995 year-in-review piece about Baby Richard for an imminent issue. She has already spoken to Bob Greene, but she would like input from me as the child's psychologist. I provide her with a status report of his surprisingly comfortable, rapid, and easy adjustment. She thanks me and ends the conversation.

Bill Harte has been in contact with the attorney at the Department of Professional Regulation, who now has my file, including the investigators' reports and the requested materials that I have provided. She has not yet had time to review the file, she told Bill, but "there is at least one more question remaining" about my work with Baby Richard/Daniel Kirchner. Bill shares with me that his own daughter is a clinical psychologist, who, like me, performs a variety of services for clients. He seems reassuring, but I have trouble sleeping again tonight, as I toss and turn, reviewing in my mind other possible options for employment.

__October 21st

Before my scheduled office appointments, I stop by the Kirchners' apartment to find Danny whirling around in his new costume for Halloween. He is Batman, complete with black shirt, pants, flowing cape, and mask with pointed ears. Excited, he shows me a game board in the middle of which is a large button with the Joker's face on it. When he pushes the button, peels of demonic laughter fill the living room. If his parents have $1, I am thinking, they spend 90 cents of it on Danny. They are determined that he will not be deprived of anything that they can find a way to provide for him. He asks me to take a photograph of his Batman self, and I promise that next time I come I will bring my camera. Danny then begins to watch the movie *Free Willy*, while his father and I talk about the family's planned relocation to the house across the street from Loren.

"The bad people are taking him from his mother and it is very sad," Danny says as he turns to me during a moving scene in the movie. I wait to see if he will articulate a comparison to himself, but he becomes engrossed in watching the animal action without further comment.

When I begin to head for home, Danny exclaims, "It's not fair," and invents an excuse for me to accompany him to his room to show me his array of toys, games, and stuffed animals. He is stalling to extend my visit, and I assure him that I will return soon.

__October 22nd

My sister Jo has a baby crib, mattress, linens, and a diaper-changing table that she wants to give the Kirchners for their expected baby. I inform Daniela that Jo sympathizes with their situation and understands what they have gone through. She is the only person, except for Robert, who regularly seeks from me updates on their progress. At family get-togethers or parties with friends, people seem to avoid the topic, as if it is some dread disease. Jo says she feels as if she knows the Kirchners herself, having heard from me so much about the family, and she considers these gifts as a token of her esteem. Daniela's voice breaks as we make arrangements together for their delivery to her house.

__October 23rd

Today two of my clients initiate discussions about Bob Greene columns. Katie S., who comes for weekly therapy, describes his most recent article. When she leaves, Rose L. enters my office for a return session, upon the recommendation of her attorney. I worked with Rose, her husband, and daughter two years ago. Her teenage daughter is both depressed and socially withdrawn, Rose explains, but her husband does not want her or the child to resume as my clients.

"He is telling everyone that you have ruined this little boy's life—Baby Richard; he's read this in the newspaper. He is now of the opinion that you are neither a good therapist nor a good person, because of the columns," she asserts, looking down and avoiding eye contact while she speaks.

Rose continues, "You helped us before, though, and I think you can help again.... All I care about is my daughter, and she likes and trusts you," she clarifies, raising her gaze. I will speak with Rose's attorney, as she requests, and we will decide the best course of action for her daughter.

__October 24th

Bringing Danny a big pumpkin carved into a smiling cat face with whiskers and pointed ears, I present it to him when he opens his front door. He accepts it with a "thank you," adding, "but scary pumpkins are best." Otto lights a candle to illuminate the non-scary vegetable, and Danny correspondingly beams.

Otto is doing the laundry this afternoon so that Daniela can relax when she returns from work. Danny is drawing numbers and letters on paper, practicing for school. He appears to be ambidextrous as he shifts the pencil from one hand to the other. Drawing a number five, he talks about turning that age at his next birthday.

Otto has been attempting to reach Loren, with no success. He has a traffic ticket, along with the hope that the attorney may be able to reverse the recent judgment in the amount of $7,000, entered against Otto for the early termination of his lease agreement on his Chicago apartment. Although Loren promised to represent Otto in these matters, he has not returned phone calls.

"I just don't get it," Otto laments. "I will go to court by myself and explain my side to the judge. I will tell him that my attorney did not do what he promised in these two matters."

__October 25th

Karen Spring from *Newsweek* calls again to check one last piece of data. Her New York editor, she tells me, is reluctant to quote me in the magazine because of Bob Greene's portrayal of my credentials. I assure her that I am a licensed clinical psychologist, and my license has been renewed continuously by the State of Illinois—every two years across the past nineteen. "Well, I am not sure whether you will be quoted," she says. "The article will be brief."

__October 26th

Financial problems weigh heavily on Otto's mind. The phone has been disconnected because of an outstanding balance due. He is experiencing chest pains that sometimes travel down his arms. We talk about the advisability of increased exercise. He is trying to lose weight, at least 25 to 30 pounds, so that he will not be as easily recognizable in public places.

Meanwhile, in his bedroom Danny is preparing his Batman costume for Halloween. I remark, "You are so cute," to which he responds, "I know." I ask him how he knows that he is cute, and he answers, "My daddy told me."

Otto expresses more ambivalence toward Loren; still no word from him.

__October 30th

Frank, the stockbroker brother of my client Judy, comes to our scheduled session for their celebration of John's eleventh birthday. Judy longs for the day when the court will allow her to visit her son without therapeutic supervision. John's teenage sister, Ellen, arrives along with Frank's wife, turning the event into a small family reunion. Frank questions my credentials, as I expected, and I clarify for him the inaccuracies in Greene's columns. He is not only satisfied but he thanks me for my work with his sister and nephew. I am feeling tired out, as all of my contacts by phone and in session today have required self-defense in the form of explanations regarding the offensive, defamatory newspaper columns.

__October 31st

Instead of trick-or-treating, Danny is lying under a blanket on the living room couch with his head resting on his *101 Dalmatians* pillow. Having planned a three-hour visit, I am glad to be here to listen to his disappointment as a crashed Batman. Pale, listless, and feverish, he is sick for the first time since his April arrival. He sleeps deeply for one hour while *Batman 2* plays on the VCR to its conclusion. When Justin and several other boys, attired in full costumes and masks, arrive at the front door, Danny is energized and calls out their names. He asks wistfully to be allowed to join them, and I accompany him and the others to the landlord's apartment for one handout of candy and then back to the couch for Danny.

Otto takes the opportunity of my presence with Danny to leave for ten minutes to inform his landlord about the prospective move. The landlord demands an additional month of rent, on top of the security deposit and rent for the last month of occupancy. Otto is disappointed.

__November 2nd

Danny has recovered from his illness on Halloween, but Otto is sick today with stomach problems and continuing chest pains. He looks gray, while Danny is bouncing around the apartment, happy and entertaining himself with his battery-run toys. Danny is singing into his new cordless microphone as he walks around, gesturing with his arms, like a singer in a nightclub.

To Otto's surprise, Loren showed up in traffic court yesterday. As Otto stood in line waiting his turn in court, Danny asked to be picked up and held. Danny clung to his father's neck, while people stared, and some nudged others and whispered. Otto thinks that Danny is getting used to reactions from strangers, but understandably he is still often uncomfortable with their attention. It is as if this child is experiencing another kind of social existence—different from that of his peers—as in a *Twilight Zone* episode.

"It's not fair," Danny responds when I announce my departure for the day. After I explain that I need to go to work "like your mom," he nods and hugs me goodbye.

__November 3rd

This evening I accompany Robert to his annual golf dinner, held at a local restaurant. Pat Walsh, one of my former school board members, is there and greets me warmly. He has read Greene's columns about me and has wondered how I am holding up under this media onslaught. He asks if my friends are providing any support or initiating calls. "It must be hard for them to do that under these circumstances," he adds, shaking his head. I realize that, in fact, no one has called, but I am too embarrassed to admit it.

"You must have lost business," he ventures, and I affirm that indeed I have.

__November 4th

My friend Lupe calls at 10:00 p.m. to say that a major television news channel just announced that it will feature a six-month update on Baby Richard tonight. Switching from the movie *Maverick*, I catch the solemn tone and regretful message from the news commentator that, using the *Chicago Tribune* as their source, "There is bad news to report." Baby Richard is not enrolled in school; his father is still unemployed and "is experiencing dark moods"; he is talking about the possibility of moving with the child out of the country; and there are financial problems to the extent that the telephone is disconnected. They show on screen a clip of Danny from his first visit to Odyssey Fun World. Danny appears behind a large wire-mesh fence, making it look like he is confined in a cage; there is no mention of his whereabouts, no explanation of the context. Then a piece of footage from April 30th—weeping child in the arms of adoptive mother and handoff to father—plays as a summary. I feel a wave of nausea as I envision even more intense public reaction against the child's father and increased scrutiny of Danny by strangers. More than anything else, I realize that he, his family, and I are helpless to do anything about this ridiculously trivial and yet massively intrusive media coverage.

What a cheap shot, I am thinking to myself, when the media disclose an embarrassing event such as the loss of a private citizen's phone service for financial reasons. I know of no other case like this during my lifetime. What a tasteless and mean-spirited invasion of privacy! This is discriminatory and misleading reporting, at the least. With regard to Danny's not attending school, at four years of age, he is not yet eligible for kindergarten until fall 1996.

The Kirchners' struggles are largely attributable to the media. It is a vicious cycle: troubles, media spotlight, more troubles, more media exposure. Meanwhile, I am aware, the Warburtons are receiving contributions from across the country from a sympathetic public. Talk show hosts, journalists, and special interest groups are soliciting donations for them.

Robert goes out at 11:00 p.m. to buy the *Tribune* to assess the damage. True to form, Greene has written another vitriolic, biased, and distorted picture of the situation, yet again criticizing the Supreme Court and the Kirchners for their alleged vile acts and lies. No contact yet with the ex-brother, Greene rants.

I resolve to visit the Kirchners tomorrow to offer my support and discuss alternatives. I believe that their best option is relocation to another state, but I am aware that their financial condition is a serious impediment to a move away from Daniela's current job.

__November 5th

When I arrive at the Kirchners' apartment, no one is home. Passing an hour at a local restaurant, where I take my time with a sandwich and a cup of coffee, I know that I cannot get through to them by phone and decide to return for another try. Again, there is no sign of life inside; I leave a note promising a visit tomorrow; and drive home to prepare for a social evening with friends at a benefit dinner for the homeless.

__November 6th

In good spirits and smiling, Otto and Daniela are playing a game with Danny as I arrive on her day off from work. Neither has read the *Tribune* column, but Loren told them about it yesterday. They were invited for dinner at the Heinemanns' home for the first time in months. Now that they will soon be neighbors, Loren explained, they should be friends and socialize more often. Loren's attempt to reconcile comes in the wake of his feeding Bob Greene private, confidential information regarding the Kirchner family.

"I had a good time playing," Danny reports, "and a good time eating." He holds a doll, a significant departure from his Power Rangers and Batman toys, and I assume it is a gift from little Lexi Heinemann.

Daniela brings out the vacuum cleaner and runs it across the dining room floor, picking up the remains from the haircut she has given Otto earlier today. I decide not to share with them the *Tribune* column, deciding that sometimes ignorance **is** bliss. I head for my office, leaving behind a content, little family who will soon be facing even more big problems.

Phoning from her home in Palm Springs, California, my mother shares the latest news, which includes a visit from her cousin Fran and wife Arden from Barrington, Illinois. When the subject of Baby Richard came up in conversation, her visitors mumbled their disdain, reluctant to talk about it. Realizing they felt deep-seated sympathy for the adoptive family, my mother dropped the subject and refrained from discussing me at all with them.

__November 7th

Brad, a long-term client who has struggled with his obsessive-compulsive disorder since the age of five, interrupts our session to allude to Greene's Sunday column. "Why doesn't he stop?" he asks me, and I am tempted to say that the journalist may share his disorder, but I refrain.

Scheduled to participate in a local book-signing engagement, Greene will be coming to Brad's neighborhood bookstore. Brad is tempted to appear there, he informs me, in order to advocate on my behalf and to encourage Greene to halt his Baby Richard marathon. "I am tired of reading about this subject over and over; it's ridiculous that he continues to harp on this case," Brad relates. I thank him for his good intentions but dissuade him from acting on his noble urges, and we revert to discussion of his own problems.

During lunch with my long-time friend and colleague from a nearby school district, Ray expresses sympathy for me. He has read all of the columns and volunteers the opinion that people believe what they read in the newspaper, particularly a reputable paper of wide circulation. "This is not the *National Enquirer* or some rag; it's a big-time publication," he points out. "Greene has attacked your ethics and abilities; I just hope you can overcome it."

__November 9th

Arriving in their parking lot minutes after I pulled in, Otto, Daniela, and Danny jump out of their car to greet me. Danny takes out his special key and opens the door for us. Otto laughs and pats him on the head as we enter and take off our winter coats. Danny looks taller and more mature today; he is wearing blue jeans with a red, white and black sweater, and gym shoes with thick socks.

Otto shares with me that he is feeling more optimistic about the future. A stranger approached him yesterday to make a reassuring comment. He takes it as a sign that not everyone wishes him ill or perhaps public opinion is changing a bit in his direction. He lost his temper with Danny and raised his voice for the first time, he confesses. "The sky did not fall down," he comments, "and Danny didn't even cry." Otto continues, "He must have realized that I was doing it for his own good and he immediately wanted a hug." He is content in the belief that Danny knows that he is loved and that he feels secure. Otto has assumed the traditionally maternal role with Danny as his primary caregiver, with a nurturing, indulgent style, and he knows now that he has been both competent and successful.

Otto lapses into a story about the happiest day of his own childhood. "My father took me fishing and we spent the whole day together. I saw him infrequently but I always sensed that he loved me more than my mother did. I have never forgotten that day and I hold it dear." Otto believes that, to this day, his mother's love is more superficial and his father has deeper feelings for him.

As I depart, I feel better knowing that both Kirchner parents are looking forward to living in their first home, having another baby, enjoying a recovered relationship with Loren, and, hopefully, benefiting from a lapse in negative public opinion to enable Otto to land a job.

__November 10th

Insisting on becoming a paying customer, I arrive for a facial treatment by Daniela at the beauty salon. She escorts me into her private room, which is set up for comfort and efficiency; I feel myself relax immediately. I decide to forgo the more typical silent enjoyment of the experience, and we talk the entire two hours while she administers creams, lotions, and hot towels.

"Otto is **so** anxious to work again," she shares, "and I would **love** to stay home with the children. If he can work again full-time, my wish would come true, to be able to be home with my kids. The baby is due in February and by then we might be able to exchange roles. We're moving to the house at Thanksgiving, and Loren is giving us his extra refrigerator, which will help."

His cousin Lali is scheduled to help Otto move their furniture and other possessions. Loren may help also, as they cannot afford professional movers.

__November 13th

In a "small world" incident today, I see Gary Felicetti exit the elevator and walk to an office on the same floor as mine. As I follow him inside, he recognizes me in a friendly greeting and invites me to sit and talk. With a free hour between clients, I can leisurely speak with him about my involvement in the Baby Richard case. Gary chortles, clearly enjoying the knowledge that he was the one who first pointed me in Loren Heinemann's direction one year ago, thereby beginning my immersion in "Baby Richard."

"You changed my practice and my life," I mockingly accuse him. "I will probably never be the same." We laugh as we enjoy together the ironies of the situation. I have experienced an outpouring of public hatred in the form of letters, phone calls, and threats; extra police surveillance on both my home and my office; and a dwindling clientele. Some days I drive to my office for only one or two appointments. Last Saturday all three scheduled clients cancelled or were "no shows," and I sat alone for nearly four hours before I left to return home. My phone rings rarely; my family and friends avoid discussing the topic of my work...or avoid **me**; and my professional license is in serious jeopardy, as I am currently the subject of an investigation by the state licensure board. I worry about my ability to survive, both professionally and personally. I have developed a fierce, secret envy of the baggers at the grocery store, all of whom seem to me to be carefree and happy. I have become the plaintiff in a lawsuit for defamation and false-light invasion of privacy pending against Bob Greene and the *Tribune*. Having regular difficulty sleeping and having shed my former sense of fearlessness, I find myself looking over my shoulder every time I walk to or from my automobile. My mother is embarrassed to discuss me with visiting relatives. "Other than these things," I tell him, concluding the litany of changes in my life, "everything is fine."

"I think you should consider writing a book about this case," Gary suggests, "as a knower and a person who is sympathetic to the birth parents. Your revealing the behind-the-scenes story would provide a service and would dispel Bob Greene's mythology about the boy."

Revealing that it would be too painful to relive the experience by writing about it, I congratulate Gary on his new office and welcome him as a neighbor. Maybe we will talk again soon over a cup of coffee....

__November 14th

Danny is sweeping snow and ice from the patio with a straw broom today. Bundled up in layers of clothing, he comes inside every few minutes to report his progress to his father and me, as we sip hot coffee and watch him through the glass door. The pond is now frozen and neighbors occasionally walk along its edges.

Loren is more accessible now and Otto is pleased. They have formed a special bond from the intense time spent in court and in preparation of legal documents across four stressful years. Loren confided to Otto that a woman in his neighborhood was offered money to reveal "some dirt" about the attorney or his family. He complains to Otto that he is under continuous scrutiny by neighbors, colleagues, and clients.

People magazine is preparing an update on Baby Richard. Brian Alexander, already aware of the family's imminent move to a house, has contacted Otto for an interview. Otto worries about the effects on Danny of the unrelenting media hype. With his media-created reputation as a traumatized, disadvantaged, and abused child, who is likely crossing the threshold into mental illness, what will be its impact as he begins school, attempts to establish relationships, and tries to be just a normal kid? I remind Otto of some recent incidents in which Danny acted out his anger, and I encourage him to continue to support such expressions as healthy—and perhaps especially necessary—for a child with his unique history and media-packed baggage. Otto is comfortable with and non-reactive to Danny's occasional expressions of anger, which are short-lived and normal. Danny is not only self-confident but he is intelligent, competitive, and sometimes willful; he is blessed with a strong and stable personality.

Before I leave, Otto helps me carry inside, from my car trunk, some gifts from my sister Lynda, including a stroller, baby blankets, and a book of baby names, all items that she no longer needs. While outside, he shows me deep scratches in the sliding glass doorframe near the latch; these are new and troubling. Anonymous mail has arrived again in response to Greene's most recent columns. People, mirroring the columnist, are demanding a "happy ending" to the story through a meeting of Danny with his former adoptive family or through his permanent return to their home.

Danny and his father are throwing snowballs as I scrape ice off my car windows and then, having no client appointments today, set off for home.

__November 17th
When I arrive today, Otto is sick and I offer to make a run to the local convenience store to get a few items that he needs, including coffee and cigarettes. Upon my return, Danny is stubborn and demanding; he is testing his father, who takes it in stride.

"I am being a mean kid," Danny admits to me as if making a confession. "Don't laugh!" he says, addressing my response. Otto and I agree that his obstinacy has resulted from several days of confinement to the apartment. Not only is it too cold outside for him to play comfortably but his father has been ill for four days and unable to face the typical, nasty confrontations by strangers.

Otto shares with me his disappointment with his cousin, who has refused him financial help. "I paid for his and his wife's airfare from Slovakia and helped him with one year of rent payments, but he has forgotten these things now that we need assistance." All of his recent attempts to find a job have been unsuccessful and disheartening.

__November 19th

Having accepted an invitation this evening to a family dinner hosted by a sister-in-law, Robert and I sit down at the dining room table among twelve adults. The conversation is lively and animated until one of the guests alludes to the "sad Baby Richard situation." Another guest, a social worker, asserts, "I have **very** strong feelings about the case," as she looks down intently at her plate. Her sister changes the subject, and, uncomfortable and embarrassed, I decide that our visit here will be brief today.

__November 20th

Preoccupied by my acute awareness of the devastating effects of the skewed media coverage upon the Kirchner parents and Danny, I decide to take the only action that seems likely to do some good. I telephone Loren to request that he discontinue his leaking information to Bob Greene, who long ago assumed the leadership role in the media battering of this defenseless family. As Otto's attorney, he should respect his client's expressed wishes regarding his representation of him and his family to the media. There are compelling ethical issues involved, which include his client's right to confidentiality.

"Please stop talking about Danny with the press, Loren," I implore him. "Otto tells me that he has asked you on several occasions to discontinue revealing information about the privacies of his son and family. They can't even **hope** to begin a normal life until the coverage ends. Danny deserves a private life; he is entitled to live like a normal, anonymous child now that the court battle is over." I lapse into pleading with him for his cooperation.

To my surprise and disappointment, Loren responds, "How **dare** you tell me what to do! I will do whatever I... please. It's none of your business.... Don't ever call me again, at home or at my office. If you do, I will report you to the police for phone harassment." He hangs up the phone without a goodbye.

Otto has shared with me recently that he will never file a complaint against the attorney. "I could never do **anything** that might harm his child, directly or indirectly," he emphasizes, "now that I am Lexi's godfather. Where I was raised, a big responsibility comes with being a godparent. No matter what he does, even if he continues to betray us to the press, I could never do anything to threaten his livelihood or to hurt his daughter or family."

Although Loren would continue to provide information to the media, to the point of the eventual dissolution of his relationship with the Kirchners, Otto would never initiate any action adverse to the attorney or his family. In the fullness of time, however, a series of Heinemann's other clients would file formal complaints against the attorney for various infractions related to his legal representation of their cases. He would turn out to be "his own worst enemy."

__November 21st

Danny greets me at the door to show off his Chicago Bulls uniform, a red nylon jacket with its prominent logo and matching pants. He is grinning and happy with himself. Otto confirms that Danny is now back to being his "usual self," recovered from a bout of "cabin fever" and restlessness. Danny pulls out the family album and begins reviewing the newest additions, photographs of himself with his parents in various settings.

"When I was a child, there were maybe twenty pictures of me for all of those years, usually one at each birthday," Otto says, nodding toward Danny. "We already have dozens of pictures of him, seven rolls just developed this week." Danny also wants everything that he sees advertised on television, Otto reports. He is playing today with a new Batmobile, purchased as soon as it became available at the local toy store.

Otto and Daniela are worried about scraping together enough money for their deposit on the new house. They have also decided that Daniela's willing mother should come from Slovakia for an extended visit to help with the new baby and

Danny, especially when Otto returns to work. He is confident that someone will risk hiring him, perhaps as a waiter in a local restaurant. With $2,000 they will be able to cover their bills and pay for the airfare of Danny's grandmother.

Robert and I have discussed our savings account, I explain to Otto, and we can't think of a better destination for $2,000 of our money. Within three days, Otto and Daniela will make arrangements for Grandma to come for her extended stay after the baby is born.

Otto has decided that Danny is ready to spend some time with his former adoptive brother Johnny. In anticipation of the holidays, Otto and Daniela have agreed to a reunion of the two boys. If the first meeting between them goes well, a series of play sessions will be planned.

"Will you supervise their visits, Karen?" Otto asks. "Maybe they could be held at a neutral place, like your house...?"

"Of course, I'll be glad to do it," I assure him. "My house would be a good place because Danny likes it, and he feels comfortable and secure there."

Loren has recommended to the Kirchner parents another mental health professional for this role as the liaison and supervisor for the boys' visits, Otto tells me sheepishly. Indignant and angry over my appeal to him to honor Otto's requests to stop fanning the flames of the media with tidbits of personal, private information about his clients, Loren has unilaterally decided to remove me from the case. "But Danny would be comfortable only with you and might refuse to go with someone else," Otto reasons. After having heard Otto's rationale, Loren readily agreed. The attorney will make an official announcement about the proposed reunion at a press conference this week, in honor of Thanksgiving.

__November 22nd

"Daddy told me to stay in my room!" Danny calls out to me from his doorway as I enter their apartment. Otto explains to me that he asked Danny to play in his room, out of hearing of the television, while he is in the living room, switching channels, looking for coverage of Loren's press conference. He hopes that Loren presents the announcement in a positive and sensitive manner. A blurb comes on Channel 5, promising the latest development in the Baby Richard case.

Entering Danny's bedroom, I compliment him on his Power Rangers costume, which he has chosen to wear today. "Your room looks like a toy store," I tease him. He tries to convince me that he could use even more toys and reminds me that Christmas is coming. He is working on a coloring book on the floor, and I join him by picking up a red crayon to begin a picture of my own. We continue to have our best talks over shared activities, during which Danny blossoms into full conversations.

After the news program that covers the story of the prospective meeting of Baby Richard with his former brother, Otto invites Danny back into the living room. We leave our crayons and join his father for a few minutes, until I realize that it's time for me to leave for my office. Reminding them of their invitation to share Thanksgiving with Robert and me at our home, I hug Danny goodbye as he approaches me with open arms.

"You will sleep two times and then we will go to Karen's house," his father assures him in terms that he and Danny use often to interpret the passage of time.

__November 23rd

Loren Heinemann has fashioned the news about the proposed reuniting of Danny and Johnny as "the result of terminated therapeutic services" for Danny. Implicitly it seems now that Danny's therapist has been the impediment to the reunion across past months. Loren, ever the hero, presents the "good news" as if he is the originator of the reunion plan, long awaited by Bob Greene and a large segment of the public. Loren discouraged Otto from participating in this press conference, ensuring that he would become the sole champion at the event.

I wonder how my few clients will receive this news. All of them know about my involvement in the case, and I fear that this latest, self-serving, and slanted portrayal by Heinemann will result in the loss of more of them.

Marveling at Loren's arrogance in publicly announcing the termination of my services without discussing with me the progress of my treatment plan for Danny, I realize that he is grabbing this opportunity to keep the "Richard" story alive at my expense and his gain. It is effective, of course, and impossible to counter. It would be inappropriate for me to insist that Danny needs continued therapy, as he is symptom-free of emotional problems, and yet my support of him and his family remains beneficial, if not even necessary. Otto and Daniela, my clients, have not terminated my services. Bottom line, however, it is difficult to determine professional services from personal friendship, support, and advocacy when no fees are charged and no billings are generated.

Loren has projected me, in the most public way, into a limbo status with all three of my clients, Danny, Otto, and Daniela. His anger toward me has played out in a public forum, through a press conference, and ultimately across airwaves and newspapers. Because Baby Richard's therapy has been terminated, he can now be reunited with his former brother.

__November 24th

Otto is cleaning the empty apartment and Danny is eating pizza as I arrive.

"I don't like this place any more," declares Danny. "I like the new house. I have my own room there and a playroom, too."

"It took only a few hours to move our things to the new house," Otto says with relief. "We have lost our privacy here completely, so it is a good time to move away. We will all have a new start."

__November 29th

Adrienne Drell calls me about the prospective reunion for her article for the *Sun-Times*. "I am not from the school of melodrama regarding this matter," I tell her. "This is a good will gesture for the two boys to get together and play. It should be a simple, private event with milk and cookies."

I do not disclose to any reporter that Danny is at best nonchalant about this reunion. At the age of four—always focused on the "here and now"—Danny has been continuously immersed in his everyday activities, which have included his friends, his visiting cousin Mario, and his parents. When his father asked Danny this week if he would like to see Johnny, he paused for several moments before answering with a casual and tentative "yeah." He then resumed playing with his action figures.

Kathi Johnson from *American Journal* calls to inform me that the program's Baby Richard update is due to air and she has revised her lead-in to the coverage. Hoping that this reunion will change the tide of public opinion to the extent that Otto will become employable once again, I have guaranteed the Kirchners that I will make myself available at any time and will gladly offer my home as the neutral site for the boys' meeting.

__December 1st

Today, at the request of my client Sandy S., I speak with Richard Eisaman of the Family Counseling Agency in Frankfort. Sandy's son is going to Mr. Eisaman on a regular basis for therapy, and I explain the mother's reasons for having requested my input on behalf of her son. Mr. Eisaman interrupts me to say that he knows about my Baby Richard work, and I find myself once again attempting to clarify misunderstandings about my role in the case. I am discovering that once I disclose that I am providing all of my services on a *pro bono* basis, my colleagues resume their willingness to interact with me. They appear less inclined to believe the sinister motives attributed to me in the *Tribune.*

It is a rare occurrence for me these days to converse with anyone who does not know that I am the Baby Richard psychologist. I haven't gotten a new client in weeks, and some of my long-term regulars have cancelled their sessions or discontinued their therapy altogether.

__December 2nd

Otto carries Danny, still sleepy from his nap during the car ride, into my house, with Daniela following behind them. Otto winks at me while Danny clings to his father, his arms wrapped around his neck. We are celebrating a delayed Thanksgiving dinner together. On the actual holiday weekend, I was overcome by exhaustion and flu symptoms, sleeping on and off through both daytime hours and overnight.

Now living in their new rental house, Danny has had his first reported nightmares since his transfer to their custody, Otto tells me. It is another adjustment for the child, but the three-bedroom house affords him, in addition to his own bedroom, an adjacent playroom that contains all of his toys, games, and stuffed animals. It will become a bedroom for the baby next year but for now it is Danny's special place for play. He mostly likes the big back yard, and his parents are grateful for the cyclone fence that surrounds it, providing security with a locked gate.

After turkey dinner and trimmings, Danny excuses himself from the table and Otto suggests that he thank Robert for having prepared this good food for them. Danny walks over to Robert, offers a handshake, and says, "Thank you, Bob." He grins, proud of his display of good manners, while his parents look at each other knowingly and praise him for being so polite.

Once the child is preoccupied with toys in an adjacent area, Otto informs me that, according to Loren, the Warburtons are setting conditions for the prospective meeting of Danny and their son Johnny. They would like Danny to meet with their minister beforehand and to include both the clergyman and a psychologist of their choosing at the event. They do not consider my home a neutral site and prefer a different setting, such as a hotel room. Discouraged by this complicating, off-putting response to his simple, straightforward offer, Otto reflects that they have never called me, Danny's therapist, to inquire about how he is doing or to request visitation with him for themselves or their son.

__December 8th

Their new home is a solid, little ranch-style house, with gray shingles, black roof, and white trim. Its one-car attached garage is filled with boxes from the move. The small living room holds the black furniture from the apartment; it will become the family room, the center of all activity. A large separate kitchen holds the dining room table, its four chairs, and the big black-vinyl armchair. At one end of the L-shaped laminate counter sits the refrigerator; the microwave is perched on the countertop; and, at the other end, there is an empty space instead of a stove, as the owners took theirs with them. I decide that Robert and I will send the family a new stove as our early Christmas present. On my way home today I will order a stove from Best Buy, and the Kirchners' kitchen will be complete and functional within a few days.

All three white-walled bedrooms are modest in size, but adequate for the Kirchners' possessions. The playroom, bright and colorful, looks like a tiny toy store; all of Danny's white shelves are overflowing with toys, books, games, and furry animals; and his child-size table and two chairs occupy a corner. The room is outlined by a double string of Christmas lights, hung from the ceiling and blinking merrily.

A special feature of the house is the walk-through bathroom, accessible from the bedrooms on one side and from the utility room on the other. A washing machine for their clothes will afford them convenience and privacy while doing their laundry. Their charitable next-door neighbors will soon give them a clothes dryer so that Daniela will not need to hang wet laundry in the bitter cold outside or to struggle with it, through snow and ice, to a Laundromat. I notice that the house is without air conditioning, which will become a problem during the hot, humid summers in Richton Park, Illinois.

Grinning, Danny greets me in the living room, grabs my hand, and leads me to the kitchen window so that he can point out the spacious back yard. The large wooden deck, outside the back door, will be turned into a play area for him, and the picnic table will allow the family, in good weather, to eat outside. The small, nearby storage shed, a birdhouse hanging from its front eve, will become a playhouse for Danny in addition to holding tools and a lawn mower.

"Can I go out to play for only two minutes?" Danny begs his father, as they both look through the kitchen window at the snow-covered lawn. Otto acquiesces; bundles up his son in his snowsuit, wool hat, gloves, scarf, and boots; and Danny skips outside. We watch him roll in the snow, make snowballs, and run around, enjoying his freedom in his very own yard.

Otto will be fixing up the house across the coming weeks, removing dark wood paneling and painting the walls a semi-gloss white. In the hope of returning to work by January, he will continue his job search. The telephone is now connected and working. They have gone without phone service for the past several weeks in the apartment, but now I am able to call once again to check in with them regularly and to announce my visits.

Before long the house fills with visitors—Lali, his wife and daughter, Loren, Stacy and Lexi, and two friends from the Slovak community. Danny and Lexi squeeze themselves onto the bay window ledge behind the couch in the living room; they gently touch the Christmas window decals and little winking lights that outline the area; and their eyes are as wide as their smiles.

Soon tiring of that activity, baby Lexi and Danny become involved in parallel play with their respective toys on the floor, while the adults talk around them. Taking that image with me, I excuse myself to drive to my office for two client sessions.

__December 9th

At Father James Moriarty's reception in honor of his retirement, held at St. Joan of Arc Parish in Skokie, Robert and I wish him a long and happy new life. Robert's oldest brother, Jim has been a Roman Catholic priest for forty-five years and, because of a shortage of clergy throughout the Archdiocese of Chicago, he will continue to offer Mass, hear confessions, and perform funeral services on a regular, part-time basis. The event is well attended by parishioners, family members, and friends of the honoree.

One of Robert's cousins, an upbeat and lively middle-aged woman, approaches us on her way to the buffet table. After greetings, she immediately indicates that she is aware of my Baby Richard work. When I begin to speak about it, she summarily closes the conversation, "I can't even **talk** about that child because of my deep feelings; you'll have to excuse me." She turns and walks away, and thus ends another social gathering.

__December 15th

Otto's mother is arriving from Canada this evening for her holiday visit. Daniela's mother will be coming early in the new year for an extended stay; Otto and Daniela have purchased her airline tickets. Danny is looking forward to seeing both grandmothers. I join him and his father tonight for a Hungarian dinner, prepared for us by Otto, and followed for me by the usual robust coffee.

Their five-foot-tall Christmas tree, adorned with lights, ornaments, and tinsel, stands prominently in the center of the main wall of their living/family room. Otto has already removed the dreary paneling, repaired the walls, and covered them in snow white. The room is now brighter and yet cozy and warm.

Danny leads me to his playroom, where a whistling black train with a winding, circular track occupies the floor. He explains that this is a gift from Grandma, "the one that is coming today." We talk about Christmas and when I mention that Santa Claus will be coming, he corrects me, "Baby Jesus comes on Christmas Eve; Santa comes before." To clarify for me, Otto relates that he and Daniela have taught Danny the Slovak version of the holiday: Santa visits on December 6th and the Baby Jesus on Christmas Eve; both are occasions for gift-giving.

Otto has received a letter today from a woman in Virginia, who beseeches the Kirchners to allow Danny to visit with his former brother during the holidays. She writes that she will sleep better at night if this reunion takes place, and she will be sending Christmas gifts to Danny. Otto shakes his head as he marvels aloud at this combination of intrusiveness and generosity from another stranger. Letters from the public continue to arrive, forwarded to their new unpublished address by the Mokena post office.

__December 18th

In her Christmas card greeting, Shirley H., one of my former school board members who has relocated to Wisconsin, writes about Baby Richard. She has been reading about my work in the case, and, "in spite of sympathizing with the adoptive parents," she sends her good wishes. Messages in several other cards from family and friends allude to the "poor child," "tragic situation," or a similar term of sympathy related to "Richard."

I am wishing for a respite from Baby Richard—not from Danny and his family but from the warped media version. It would be my best Christmas gift.

__December 22nd

Thrusting a shiny wrapped and ribboned gift in front of him as he enters, Danny exclaims, "This is for you!" Following him inside from the cold and wind, Otto, Daniela, and Gabriela arrive with hearty expressions of Christmas cheer. Otto introduces his mother to Robert, and after coats, hats, and scarves are hung up in the guest closet, the six of us settle onto sofas in our great room. The tall, thin Christmas tree, trimmed with strings of small sparkling bulbs of mixed colors, lights up the room and fills it with the woodsy smell of evergreen.

Daniela's pregnancy is proceeding well, but she is tired. She continues to work full-time at the salon and then many evening hours setting up their new home.

We exchange gifts; Danny rips open his presents, slowed down only by tight ribbons; and we share our holiday dinner together. Gabriela is delighted to have a family and a grandson to celebrate the holidays with her. We toast our wine glasses to a better year ahead. Danny is using his new fork and spoon, both engraved with his name, and, studying his shiny Christmas utensils, he proudly announces himself as "Daniel

Richard Kirchner!" We all laugh our affectionate response.

After our dessert of German-sweet-chocolate cake, Otto tells me that, according to his latest information from Loren, it is "now acceptable" for the two boys to meet in my home rather than a hotel or other neutral site. "The other side is supposed to call you to set up the meeting," he says. I assure him again that I will look forward to their contacting me. Nothing more is said about this matter, as we return our attention to the celebration of Christmas.

"Silver bells..., silver bells..." melodiously reverberates through the house, and we feel at peace.

__December 24th

Churning out another maudlin column today, Bob Greene bemoans, "You can break a child like a dog." Referring to Baby Richard, who has not been reunited with his former brother, he writes, "[S]till he waits, and the days go by. This is sinful." The companion picture to his column is that of the weeping child on the April 30th transfer day...once again. Greene, enamored with Governor Edgar's statement from months ago, ends his column with it: "Frankly, I cannot imagine how the justices who prevailed in this case will be able to sleep at night." ("For two betrayed boys, one more night of silence," *Chicago Tribune*)

__December 25th

Returning tonight from a restful three-day get-away in a rustic but comfortable hotel, Robert and I bask in the realization that an escape from hostility and suspicion feels wonderful. With the reunion of Danny and his former brother imminent, perhaps this holiday will signal the onset of normalcy for us. The media and the public, to be told only that the boys' visit with each other has occurred, will hopefully move on to other concerns. We are yearning for closure to the ceaseless media coverage, led by the seemingly ever-present, determined Bob Greene, who has vowed not to go away until the two boys have been reunited.

I telephone my mother in California to wish her and my stepfather Jack a happy holiday. She informs me that her friend from Chicago sent her a card in which the terse, hand-written greeting referred to Baby Richard: "Your daughter is on the **wrong side.**"

"Merry Christmas."

Danny celebrates his first Christmas with his joyful parents in 1995.

__December 26th

This evening Robert and I attend the annual Boxing Day party of our neighbors, Albert and Doreen Crewe, both originally from Great Britain. Every year Albert wears the same red-velvet tuxedo jacket, bow tie, cummerbund, and black pants as the colorful host of this merry commemoration of the unique, post-Christmas holiday of their country-of-origin. Doreen wears a different, but always elegant, formal dress each year.

Their long, unpaved driveway is lined with dozens of luminaria, flickering in the wind. The house smells of good food and of pine from the large Christmas tree. The Crewes serve a nearly lethal military punch from a huge crystal bowl along with dozens of meats, cheeses, breads, and fruits. Professional servers, hired for the day, circulate through the various rooms of the house, carrying trays of hors d'oeuvres and napkins for the dozens of guests. With a fire crackling in the massive stone-front fireplace, people take turns at the piano as a large, enthusiastic group gathers around each pianist to sing special-request holiday songs. The regulars—those who attend every year—update each other on the changes in their respective lives since the last party.

Robert and I arrive in festive spirits, happy to see familiar faces and to greet our neighbors, most of whom we see only once or twice during the typical year. This event, however, is colored by constant allusions to Baby Richard, initiated by other guests, who adopt serious looks and frowns while they share their feelings about the case.

"I can't help thinking all of the time about that unfortunate child and what he must be going through," blurts a middle-aged woman who lives on our road. "I can't bear reading about him any more; I keep thinking about my own grandson who is his age, and it breaks my heart." She looks at me as if I am responsible for her vicarious suffering.

"The **real** child, Danny, is doing fine and enjoying Christmas with his parents," I begin in an abortive attempt to ease her discomfort. She wheels around, glass in hand, and walks away before I can add another thought to my simple explanation of "Richard's" current status.

Several other conversations are similarly uncomfortable. It occurs to me that some of the attendees have carried to this party their personal agendas to vent their rage and disappointment upon me. Perhaps they believe that I can or will do something to enable Danny to return to his adoptive parents. Some think that I am making a bundle of money from so prominent and controversial a case, and at the expense of "Richard," who they believe is living an agonized, prisoner-like existence. When I attempt to assuage their concerns with the truth, they raise eyebrows, give quizzical looks, purse their lips, and fold their arms across their chests. **They** read the newspapers, they tell me, some of them indignant in their righteousness. **They** know how he is **really** doing, and it's pitiful, tragic, and unforgivable.

I am feeling like a small beehive in the room and the conversational buzz around me is "Baby Richard," accompanied by frowns, furrowed brows, downcast looks, and heads shaken in disapproval. Elsewhere in the room, people are smiling, laughing, singing, and hugging each other.

Char Blount, our realtor's wife, approaches and, after a cursory greeting, alludes to Bob Greene's "disgusting" columns about me. Char is an anomaly among this gathering tonight, as she appears genuinely sympathetic as opposed to hostile. I suddenly feel a gush of gratitude, followed by embarrassment as I realize that my eyes have welled up with tears. Choosing to look away rather than speak, I decide that it is time to go home. I am more fragile than I expected.

Turning back to embrace Char quickly, I wish her "Happy holidays" and then retreat to seek out Robert in another room. As soon as he sees me, he puts down his glass on the nearest table, gives me a silent nod, and walks to the cloakroom to retrieve our coats and scarves. After hasty good-byes, we leave our hosts and their guests for an early but welcome departure.

"Next year will be better," Robert promises me, squeezing my hand in his. I hope that he will be proven right.

__December 30th

Having been invited to the Kirchner home for dinner, Robert and I settle into the living room with Danny, while Otto and Daniela prepare our meal in the kitchen. They have arrived only twenty minutes earlier; Otto, accompanied by Danny, had driven Daniela home from work.

Danny begins teaching Robert how to play his Nintendo game with dual remote controls. He is laughing and leaning against Robert on the couch. I am delighted to see that he is both self-confident in playing against a new adult competitor and affectionate. Danny greeted both of us with spontaneous hugs when we arrived.

Daniela appears with cheese and crackers, and after placing the appetizers on the cocktail table, she beckons Robert and me to accompany her so that he might see their new home. Danny joins us to show Robert his playroom, liberally strewn with twinkling holiday lights. Danny points out one of his favorite Christmas presents, a Star Wars spaceship with small movable parts. When we proceed to Danny's bedroom, Dalmatian-themed and tidy, he declares gleefully, "I have **two** rooms now in this house!"

Returning to the living room, Danny unwraps his gifts from Robert and me. One of them is a walkie-talkie set, and he is excited to see that he can give and receive messages between rooms. After mastering the concept of holding down the "send" button before speaking, Danny is visibly pleased with himself.

Our dinner consists of Hungarian stuffed cabbage with sausage and for dessert a dobos torte, similar to my favorite home-baked cake from childhood days. Otto's mother prepared the main dish yesterday and then left for her return trip to Toronto; Otto bought the torte at a local ethnic food store. Sitting at the table, I notice that Otto has painted over the plastic, imitation-brick wall in the kitchen; has removed the old-fashioned wallpaper from the other walls; and has covered them all with bright white paint. Everything looks clean and shiny.

After dinner I give Otto a certified letter that I have received, addressed to him but sent to my office. He opens it to find a typed letter of seven pages from Mr. Carlson, the Kirchners' former landlord, along with several pictures of the apartment and a check for $224. Carlson presents his rationale for failing to refund the entire security deposit of $600; he cites problems with the condition of the apartment. Otto is surprised to receive anything, not because of the apartment's condition when they vacated it, but because he would have little recourse to getting no refund at all. Daniela, in contrast, is disappointed and angry; she was counting on a larger refund. I had visited the apartment while Otto was completing his tasks of filling wall nicks and nail holes, touch-up painting, and cleaning. The place looked good and in rentable condition to me.

We collectively turn our attention to more pleasant activities. I present Otto and Daniela with photos from our Thanksgiving celebration together from recently developed rolls of film. Danny reaches for them and reviews each one, studying the pictures of himself, after which he walks over to the cabinet and brings out the latest family album. Robert and I listen as he explains the newest additions; his parents have recently gotten back photos from months of accumulated rolls of film.

Otto whispers to me that, according to Loren, the Warburtons were supposed to have called me this past week about the prospective visit between Danny and Johnny. Bob Greene has written yet **another** column on the subject.

"No one has called me," I respond, "but as soon as I hear anything from either the Warburtons or their attorneys, I will let you know immediately. I wonder why they have not called me once during these past eight months, especially since I gave them all of my phone numbers last April and told them that they could call me any time. They know I am seeing Danny regularly, and I thought that they would call to see how he is really doing or to ask directly about the possibility of seeing him."

Otto shakes his head in a silent response. Robert and I say our good-byes and leave for home at 9:30 p.m., Danny's extended bedtime during the holiday season.

__December 31st

Today, the front-page article in the *Daily Southtown* provides a recap of the biggest stories of the year. A picture of Otto and Danny from the April 30th transfer is featured, along with a concise summary: "No story all year seemed to rile people more than the custody fight...'Baby Richard.'" It reminds readers that "the public's sentimental un-favorite, biological father Otakar Kirchner of Mokena...took a heavy pounding in the media." (Phil Jurik, "1995: A scary year") I telephone Otto and Daniela to wish them "Happy New Year!" and to inform them of the unsettling newspaper coverage. Danny takes the phone to wish me a New Year greeting.

My New Year resolution is to begin serious work on marketing my practice in new directions. Court-appointed child custody evaluations have stopped coming; my clientele has decreased to only nine or ten contact hours per week; and the office phone is generally silent. Most of my current clients are long-term, having continued from weeks or months before my Baby Richard notoriety, or referrals from former clients, who know me from first-hand contacts and successful therapy.

I resolve to advertise more widely my services in mediation and testing as well as consulting work. With twenty-seven years of successful experience in education, I will seek jobs as a consultant for school districts in the areas of human resources and counseling.

Tomorrow the major newspapers will publish the "Top Ten stories of 1995," according to the annual poll of Associated Press member editors and broadcasters in Illinois. "Baby Richard" is third among the ten. The *Chicago Sun-Times* will print results from "A Year in Morning Line," its reader poll service, including—under "Hot Topics"—the Baby Richard response:

To the question, "Did the Illinois Supreme Court rule correctly in awarding custody of Baby Richard to his natural father?", 85% of 3,304 calls said No, while only 15% said Yes.

As I become engrossed in a personal review of the past year, I reflect upon the impact of "Baby Richard" on my career. My private practice in psychology, having become focused on Danny and his parents, has been reduced, in terms of billable hours, almost to the level of a hobby. My personal life has been colored by various shades of hostility from strangers, neighbors, friends, and acquaintances. My "family" now includes a four-year-old boy and his parents. I realize that, for me, family has become more a function of choice than of birth and bloodlines. I have come to love these people who were first merely newspaper headlines, then my clients, and now my closest friends.

Turning my attention to the year ahead, I convince myself that it will be better, less stormy, and happier than the past twelve months.

Judge not by appearances but give just judgment.

— St. John 7:24

The Reunion Fiasco

**Appearances
are often deceiving.**

— "The Wolf in Sheep's Clothing," Aesop

**Beware, as long as you live,
of judging people
by appearances.**

— Jean de La Fontaine

TIGHT-LIPPED, tight-laced, and gripping tight his locked briefcase, Dr. Barry Childress enters my home to meet with me about the Reunion. After a series of telephone calls between us, he has agreed to come to my house, where we might discuss the prospect of Danny and his former adoptive brother Johnny getting together once again. It is a cold and windy Saturday, January 20, 1996, at 4:00 p.m. when the Warburtons' designated psychiatrist and representative in this matter arrives.

Since the day of his transfer to his biological parents' home last April, Danny has not seen the former adoptive parents or their son John. During the first days in his new surroundings, Danny spoke often about Johnny. He talked about play activities that the two boys shared and Johnny's preferences for certain foods. Although he never asked to see the other child, he seemed to miss him. From his first night with them, Otto and Daniela told Danny that if he wanted to see his "other parents" or his brother, he should ask them and they would arrange for a get-together.

His parents and I were surprised that, although he seemed comfortable with speaking about the other family, Danny was not requesting to be reunited with them. It appeared that the child decided to give his "real" parents the "chance" that his new father had begged of him as they sat together on his king-size bed that first night. They had showed him the photograph of Daniela, taken when she was nearly nine months pregnant with him. Danny studied that picture and he realized that this woman was his birth mother.

Days passed and turned into weeks until the memories of his past dimmed for the four-year-old, whose time was spent in the care of one, or both, of his parents on a 24/7 basis. His mother continued to sleep in his bed at night; his father cared for him while Daniela worked full-time; and both parents shared in his care during his mother's off-work time. The hours that they spent with their son were mostly interactive, always loving, and observably supportive. He was never left in the care of a baby-sitter or other individual. Otto and Daniela not only feared the possibility of a kidnap attempt or violence from an emotionally disturbed, publicity-seeking individual, but they jealously relished and preserved their time with him. They both felt as if they were making up for lost time, for the four torturous years during which they only imagined what he was like and ached to meet him and to be with him.

Otto and Daniela gushed their surprise and delight over his smallest accomplishment; they sat and watched him in play; and they engaged in a variety of games and activities with him. His mother would don her pink Power Rangers out-fit and chase with him around the apartment; his father taught him to play cards and to fish; and they would compete with him in computer games. During his earliest weeks, Justin and Jeffrey were his constant companions. The children loved participating in typical boys' activities—bicycle riding, fishing in the backyard pond, climbing and running around outside, playing ball and Nintendo games. During the summer, throughout which cousin Mario lived with the Kirchners, Danny and he were inseparable, eating their meals together, playing, swimming, and sharing the huge bed at night. They laughed and giggled; Mario, six years older than his American cousin, assumed a protective role toward Danny; and sometimes they would "get silly together," as Otto described their mischievous exploits.

With continuous attention and fun activities within a warm, affectionate environment, Danny thrived in seemingly every way and started gaining weight as early as his first month. The days and weeks that he spent in the Warburtons' home immediately preceding his transfer were undoubtedly tense ones. Danny spoke about the stressed atmosphere in four-year-old terms. To him, the household turned bad and scary with so many people there who were nervous, weeping, and agitated.

The actual day of Danny's meeting his parents and leaving with them for his new home was especially frightening. There were a lot of strangers outside, frowning and weeping, yelling and calling names. He most remembered them shouting "Monster!" and that was scary. Inside, his "other parents" were crying, sad, and angry. Gathered there were a lady psychiatrist, several strangers—we learned from the newspaper that Bob Greene was hiding in the basement—and neighbors and relatives who came to say goodbye. The adults were embracing each other and talking with a combination of pain and alarm. Although he did not want to go anywhere, Danny was uncomfortable and becoming progressively more frightened throughout the day. During the ride to Mokena, sitting on his new mother's lap, he could relax for the first time and snuggle against her.

Danny's parents decided early on that they would arrange a meeting between their son and the Warburtons only if he asked to see them. Jay and Kimberly revealed in numerous ways that they were not interested in fostering parent-child bonding between the Kirchners and Danny. Even when they introduced Danny to his biological parents, Kimberly said, "This is Mr. and Mrs. Kirchner...," rather than acknowledging them to the child as his parents. Unless a continuing relationship became necessary to sustain him emotionally, Otto and Daniela chose to avoid contact between Danny and the Warburtons so as not to confuse and upset their son, or to subject him to an emotional tug of war between two sets of parents.

Many adoption experts believe that when a young child is adopted into a family, he should discontinue regular contact with his birth parents. Danny was in the opposite situation. A child cannot readily or easily adjust to two sets of parents except in rare circumstances. I marveled at the incongruity of Danny's unique situation when so many media representatives and a vocal segment of the general public vehemently argued for "Baby Richard" to rejoin his adoptive family or to maintain an ongoing relationship with them. He was a child who left adoptive parents, whose adoption of him was court-ruled as null and void, to live with his natural mother and father. In addition to their genetic bond—the strength and significance of which was hotly debated in some quarters—they were now bound together by both legal authority and a continuously deepening love and affection. Some would argue that he was also bound to his birth parents on moral grounds. Why, I wondered, was it assumed by so many that this one child should be shared by four parents, two of whom had taken him from the hospital of his birth, wrapped in deception? It seemed unlikely that these same two adoptive parents—whose court-filed affidavits claimed the child's father to be "unknown"— would become suddenly supportive of his bonding with that father. If prospective renewed interactions with them would be destructive to his comfort-level and emotional well-being, why would his birth parents seek or initiate such contact?

Johnny, at the age of eight, was different. As a child, he would not likely carry an agenda of disruption between Danny and his birth parents. I had never met Johnny Warburton, but Otto and Daniela had seen him for the first and only time on the day of Danny's transfer, when they spent one hour in the Warburtons' home.

"It might be good for Danny and Johnny to get together again," Otto told me as Thanksgiving 1995 neared. "I want to do the right thing by God. I think that Danny is now strongly bonded with his mother and me. The timing is probably right, especially during the holidays. Danny is also looking forward to a biological brother or sister in this house. It will now be less confusing for him to spend time with Johnny."

"I agree with your assessment and your decision," I confirmed with Otto as we began to discuss the particulars of a child-to-child reunion. Daniela shared our perception that it may be beneficial for the two boys to resume a relationship.

Loren Heinemann happily turned Otto's decision into another media event. The imminent reunion of Baby Richard with his adoptive brother Johnny was covered in newspaper, television, and radio stories. Like a cat in catnip, Heinemann savored the opportunity to take center stage once again, this time with news that was heralded as joyful by those who had followed the case for months or years. Bob Greene's constant reminders, via impassioned columns, prevented the public from forgetting about the long, uninterrupted separation of the two boys.

"If their reunion is a good one and goes well, they can get together often, even every week," Otto proclaimed to me as he visibly became more receptive to the idea of an extended family for Danny. "It still would not be good for him to see Jay and Kimberly Warburton," Otto reasoned. "We can't trust their motivations and we can't risk opening up old wounds for Danny. At the least he will be confused and at worst he will be traumatized. I feel sorry for Johnny; he didn't do anything wrong. He's an innocent victim in this situation."

Otto shared with me that when he asked Danny if he would like to see his adoptive brother again, "I had to remind him about Johnny." At the age of four, after more than six months of no contact, Danny had foggy memories of the other child.

To my amazement, the Warburtons never call me. I anticipate that Jay or Kimberly will telephone me at their earliest opportunity after Heinemann's announcement in order to arrange for the reunion of Danny and their son. I often wonder why they have never attempted to speak to me about Danny; to ask how he is doing; or to register their desire for resumed contact. For that matter, for months they could have telephoned the Kirchners, whose unpublished phone number was provided them in April 1995. The Warburtons never called the Kirchners after Danny's first week with his birth parents. The attorneys have consistently been unwilling or unable to make any progress toward cooperation across recent months.

Although Otto's declaration of his willingness to arrange for a Danny–Johnny reunion is widely publicized, weeks pass and New Year 1996 begins before the Kirchners or I hear any response from the Warburtons. In mid-January, Dr. Childress calls me on their behalf. He has been authorized to discuss with me, Danny's therapist, their concerns and conditions for any prospective renewal of contact between the two boys. I invite the psychiatrist to my home, because it will likely be more comfortable and conducive than an office to foster trust and cooperation between us. We will also be less apt to attract media attention if we meet in a private, secluded setting.

Speaking with the gravity of an international ambassador, Dr. Childress informs me, "This is a difficult and complex matter." We are sitting in my family room, across from each other, and Robert has left the room after introductions between us and our guest. "We don't know how the boys will react to each other," he warns. "There may be anger or sadness, resentment or confusion," Childress continues.

Flashing across my mind is the vision of two ambassadors from opposing kingdoms negotiating a sensitive meeting of their respective princes, who might become responsible for the outbreak of hostilities between their countries if they fall into a dispute.

"You can prepare Johnny beforehand," I offer for his consideration, "while I will work with Danny. I think that Danny will be fine. He seems relaxed about the idea."

Dr. Childress strongly cautions me against optimism. He is speaking in a deep, solemn voice, his gaze fixed downward at the carpet, as if he is discussing a patient who has made three attempts at suicide.

"You and I are professionals, Dr. Childress," I say to him. "Between us, we can probably deal effectively with two children. We can have milk and cookies for them, and we can separate them if it becomes advisable. We just need to prepare the boys before their get-together and then work together...."

He interrupts, "There are certain conditions that need to be met for the Warburtons. They have serious concerns and will agree to a meeting of the children only if their requirements are addressed."

"The Kirchners have approved a reunion of the children—without any parents present—which may well lead to regular get-togethers between them," I explain. "Their **only** stipulation is that it cannot be a media event. They will not permit any reporters or journalists to be present.

"They would like a mutual but simple announcement to be made **after** the reunion to say only that it has occurred,"

I continue. "The Kirchners hope that this event will end the publicity so that Danny can finally begin to lead a private life, which he deserves. That is their fondest wish."

Both Otto and Daniela devoutly hope for an end to the story of Baby Richard. Every day they are forced to deal with the toxic fall-out from the continuous, adverse publicity. Since Danny's transfer, it has focused on the prospect of a melodramatic episode of two little boys, formerly brothers, coming together in a tearful, joyous explosion of emotion and relief. In contrast to another media circus, a simple, private, and pleasant get-together of the two children may effect a final chapter. After such closure, the media will hopefully pick up their journalistic tents and move on to another battlefield.

"A concise statement—agreeable to both sides—could be released to the press, confirming that the boys have had renewed contact with each other," I urge. "That could serve as the culmination of the story, its final punctuation mark. We want Danny to be able to become a private person once again; he deserves a normal life."

"I will have to discuss this further with my clients," Dr. Childress responds, shaking his head with increased solemnity. He recommends that the site of the boys' meeting should probably be a downtown hotel, a neutral place. I suggest my home as a possible site.

"Danny is comfortable in my home," I explain to him. "He has been here numerous times and he looks forward to returning. You and I can both work toward Johnny's being comfortable here as well. We would have the safety, security, and resources of a home environment for the two boys here."

Guaranteeing me that the chosen site will be an important consideration—among others—for his clients, the psychiatrist begins to prepare to leave. We have spent nearly two hours and have made some progress in terms of communications, but no agreements about the reunion.

"I will get back to you after I have discussed this matter further with my clients," Childress promises. "I don't know at this time what their response will be to the Kirchners' proposal."

"They just want the two boys to be able to get together to play and to be friends," I try to assure him. "Because the media are hungry for the story, **after** the reunion we can mutually issue a brief prepared statement that it has occurred."

"I will ascertain what would be acceptable to Mr. and Mrs. Warburton in this matter," the psychiatrist summarizes, his jaw set and his lips tight.

I accompany him to my front door. Bundled in his heavy, tailored wool coat, he shakes my hand, and departs at dusk.

"We have never seen our son since he left that day," Kimberly Warburton addresses the media as the cameras whirl, click, and flash.

She is taking the lead for the official kick-off of their newly-created kidsHELP! Foundation at the Hyatt Regency Chicago Hotel. It is April 30, 1996, the first anniversary of Danny's internationally publicized transfer to his biological father. It was the Warburtons' representatives that invited the media to cover that event. Today donations are sought from the public for the Warburtons' third and most recent fund-raising campaign. During their protracted court battle, the Baby Richard Legal Defense Fund solicited contributions for their legal fees incurred in fighting for Otto Kirchner's child. Large ads in the *Chicago Tribune* encouraged mail-in donations from the public; their supporters passed around tin cans in offices and blue buckets on street corners; and collections were taken in shopping centers and church lobbies. After they lost the last stage of the Baby Richard litigation when the United States Supreme Court refused to take up their appeal, they announced the imminence of a foundation which would collect contributions from the public; and donations were taken for the Doe Family Support Fund. Kimberly Warburton will work full-time for the new foundation, which comes with the prospect of an opportunity to draw a salary. The fund-raising "nationwide crusade" will receive the benefits of donated office space in Chicago.

Choking back tears at the microphone, Kimberly announces, "It's a tough day for us, so you'll have to bear with me"; her voice is breaking. I am watching this excerpt from her address on my television. "We lost our son" just one year ago, she reminds her audience. She and Jay will continue to work toward the benefit of **all** children **everywhere** through this new vehicle, this new foundation. Its logo includes the underlined phrase "Remember Baby Richard."

The room is filled with politicians and celebrities. The Warburtons have long-standing, visible, and outspoken supporters, and many are attending this event. The governor's wife and a number of other prominent individuals become directors and trustees of the foundation.

Sympathy is running high. "Isn't it awful that these people have not been allowed to visit with their son? It just breaks my heart!" Attendees shake their heads. "These poor, sad people...."

No one knows about the aborted attempts to arrange a reunion of the two children. Otto is widely depicted as a liar. He promised Danny on the day of his transfer that he could see his adoptive parents again and he announced at Thanksgiving that the two boys could reunite. Yet it has never happened. Kimberly says, "We resolved issues so that the boys could just play and be brothers...but we have not heard back from them." (Anne Bowhay, "Baby Richard case leaves legacy," *Daily Southtown*, May 1, 1996) Everyone who has an opinion says it is the biological father's fault.

No one asks if Danny still remembers the Warburtons. No one asks if he has asked to see them. No one asks if the whole matter should properly be a private one rather than a public spectacle. Riding the crest of the wave of public sympathy and compassion, the Warburtons are benefiting from the well-planned, widespread exposure of their loss and their pain. They are victims again; this is the anniversary of their victimhood. It continues by virtue of their family's loss of contact with the Kirchners' son.

Again I am amazed that Danny is considered by so many to be part of the public domain rather than a private citizen, the son of his natural parents who are now raising him. I also wonder about the dynamics of turning personal suffering into a formal occasion. This particular event, held on the anniversary of Danny's transfer, is intended to solicit money.

The Warburtons have created a unique career path for themselves. As the couple who publicly lost a child, they self-qualify to continue their dual role as victims and as leaders of a sanctioned cause. They have segued from the Baby Richard fund to the Doe Family Support Fund to this at-least-third fund, kidsHELP!

"...I was openly pessimistic about being able to provide a truly neutral 'media-free' setting for the reunion of these two boys," Dr. Childress' letter to me states. Having taken five weeks after our meeting to send a response to my invitation, on behalf of the Kirchner parents, to a simple milk-and-cookies get-together between the two children, the psychiatrist relates:

> The idea of saying "the boys are meeting; it's over," is obviously unacceptable as it implies that much has been made of nothing —it is not "over", and the outcome of this decision and its surrounding actions may not be clear for years, if ever.

> I can find no neutral statement that both sides could make to the media. You indicated that both you and Mr. Kirchner would like to end the media's involvement with Danny and yourselves.... I think that a signed confidentiality agreement would neutralize these concerns.... (February 23, 1996)

Purportedly unable to find any "neutral statement that both sides could make to the media," Childress rejects the possibility of cooperative mutuality between the Warburtons and the Kirchners regarding a child-to-child reunion. If there were to be a shared statement, the Warburtons would lose their pronounced advantage with the sympathetic media, while the Kirchners might be portrayed in an atypically positive light. The powerful, rolling engine of media engineers would lose its steam....

With his letter, the proposed Confidentiality Agreement is enclosed. It requires **nine** signatures, including those of Dr. Childress, the attorney for each side, both sets of parents, my husband Robert, and mine. There are four conditions that pertain to nondisclosure of any particulars or circumstances of the reunion by any of the signatories. One of the four conditions stipulates: "[O]ther than to those listed below [signatories], none of the signatories will disclose his or her own or the boys' reactions, impressions, or recollections of the meetings to anyone, including but not limited to any member of the public or the media."

As I am reading the proposed document, I cannot help but wonder if the representatives of princes and other nobility engage in such contractual agreements before they get together for a social event. Do they execute such confidentiality agreements when they come together over milk and cookies or similar fare?

Otto and Daniela are disappointed—though not surprised—that this latest representative of the Warburtons is advancing another legal impediment to Otto's good faith offer for his son and their son, former siblings, to begin, or renew, their friendship.

The Kirchners are unwilling to accede to a contractual agreement for a social event between two young children, a five-year-old and an eight-year-old. This legal document, if signed and executed, may well serve to pave the way toward another round of litigation. Otto and Daniela proposed a play session, supervised by an individual of the Warburtons' choice and by me, that could easily serve as the springboard to continuing, regular contacts between Danny and Johnny. The Kirchners perceive the Warburton/Childress formal response as pessimistic, arrogant, and fraught with litigious intimidation.

No further attempt of any kind would be made by the Warburtons or their representative to arrange for renewed contact between the two boys. They never even propose a modification of their position that would have turned a simple social event into a legally enforceable matter with contractually stipulated conditions.

The media leap onto the opportunity to label Otakar Kirchner a liar once again when the reunion does not happen. The Warburtons are yet again both the heroes of the non-event and the victims of the "continuing tragedy of Baby Richard." The path was well paved for the launch of their new fund-raising campaign, intelligently scheduled on the first anniversary of their widely telecast and highly-publicized loss.

"Like a seed that will grow" with love and nourishment, "the children will be the ones to harvest it," Kimberly declares, describing kidsHELP! at its initiation luncheon.

As president of kidsHELP!, Kimberly Warburton would file with the Illinois Secretary of State its required 1996 Annual Report, under the General Not for Profit Corporation Act, in April 1997. Of ten listed trustees, I was successful in contacting six of them during early 2003. None of them remembers having seen a financial statement; several reportedly "dropped out" after a brief time; and only **one** could cite any accomplishment of the organization by suggesting a generalized "increased awareness" of the needs of adopted children. One trustee said the foundation's goals were "vague and overly ambitious"; he discontinued his involvement early on because "it didn't have legs." Incredibly, the listed treasurer of the foundation refused even to speak to me after stating curtly, "I was only involved very peripherally." kidsHELP! was "involuntarily dissolved" on May 1, 1998, for failure to file its 1997 Annual Report.

Unfortunately, it appears that there wasn't much for the children to harvest.

1996: Year of Changes & Challenges

__January & February

BRIDGET? ISABELLE? DANIELLE? INGRID? SHARON? SOPHIA?

Choosing a name for their baby, due in mid-February, becomes a favorite topic for Otto and Daniela during the first weeks of 1996. It is a joyful subject, taking their minds off problems of financial hardship, Otto's inability to land a job, and hateful media coverage, led by Bob Greene, who continues to beat his journalistic drum about "Richard."

You may give them your love
but not your thoughts,
For they have
their own thoughts.
You may house their bodies
but not their souls,
For their souls dwell
in the house of tomorrow....
You are the bows
from which your children
as living arrows
are sent forth.

— *Kahlil Gibran*

The unique aspect of the Kirchners' lives, I realize, is that they are the helpless victims of continuously bad press. Who else, among private citizens, has had to suffer this level of public excoriation? Who else is discredited, loathed, and reviled to this extent? During my lifetime, I have never seen another example of individuals who have received this type of treatment by the media. Unsurprisingly, they pay a price every day of their lives. They continue to fear a kidnapping attempt upon Danny, perhaps by a deranged newspaper reader seeking recognition as a "righter of wrongs" or craving guaranteed high-profile publicity. They are struggling to pay their bills, Daniela working full-time at the salon, Otto working as an at-home dad for his son. They share a broken-down car and worries about the future.

Together Otto and Daniela prepare for the birth of their second child, a baby whom they will raise from his or her first day of life—vastly unlike their experience with their first child, raised in another home for four years while they fought for him and wondered what he was like. Painfully aware that they missed all of the "firsts" in Danny's life—first gurgle, smile, hug, laugh, word, and step—they eagerly anticipate these joys with Danny's sibling. They both look forward to an enlarged family and resolve themselves to doing their best. Their greatest hope is for the media to lose interest in Baby Richard; they crave a private life; they long for anonymity.

Visiting the Kirchner family two or three times every week, I come and go around my schedule of clients. Typically I visit for three hours, a pattern established from my first week of working with Danny. When I arrive, Otto makes me a cup of strong coffee; Danny shows me his newest toy, game, or accomplishment; and Daniela provides me an update on Danny and on her pregnancy. Otto and Daniela continue to share with me their fears, dreams, goals, worries, pain, and joys.

Danny is thriving. He regularly greets me with hugs and spontaneous reports about his day and his feelings. He eagerly anticipates the birth of a brother or a sister. In four-year-old terms, he tells me how his mother is doing with her pregnancy. Danny has not mentioned John—or the Warburton parents—to me, or in my presence, for months now. I wonder if it would be good for him to visit with Johnny or if it would reopen wounds and confuse him; if it would unnecessarily divert his attention from his own family, soon to change with the addition of a baby. After Otto publicly promised a reunion between the two boys, I have remained ready to serve as a facilitator of the proposed get-together. Until a meeting is actually scheduled, however, we are not discussing the matter with him.

Since our heated phone conversation just before Thanksgiving, Loren Heinemann and I have not spoken. He directed me not to call him again, and he has not contacted me.

In their new neighborhood, the Kirchners live directly across the street from Loren and his family. All of the neighbors, of course, know who the newcomers are, and reactions have been mixed. The couple next door, Peder and Enid Shortell, have been friendly, welcoming, and sympathetic to Otto and Daniela's status as unwillingly-public private people. Danny plays often with Peder and Enid's three daughters, and I am pleased to observe his obvious comfort level with them. These relationships have appeared to soften his approach with other children; he plays various games with the girls, including hopscotch; and he turns less often to Power Rangers and other symbols of aggression.

Otto and Daniela frequently talk to Danny about the new brother or sister that he will soon have. They have decided not to question their doctor about the gender of their baby, but they both assume they will have a girl. They describe to Danny the importance of being a big brother—he will be able to play with the baby and also help to protect him or her. Danny often leans his head against his mother's stomach and says something to the baby. Daniela purrs with approval; she invariably hugs him and reassures him of her love; and he pats her tummy and feels part of the eager anticipation around him. Otto looks forward to fatherhood with two children; he has wanted a family from the time when he was a young child; and since Daniela's miscarriage last year he has been hoping for a healthy baby.

Daniela's approach to childbirth is relaxed and pragmatic. She has not only given birth before but she has read books and magazines to prepare for the birth of her second child. On February 20th, she delivers a healthy, six-pound fifteen-ounce baby girl, twenty-one inches long, with more-than-fuzz brown hair. The baby's large brown eyes remind me of the children painted on black velvet backgrounds with eyes that seem to fill their faces. Daniela's labor and delivery are apparently so easy that, years later, she has difficulty remembering details. She recalls only that Sharon Danielle was beautiful. Most mothers, of course, say the very same thing, but after Robert sees Sharon for the first time, he confesses to me privately that he has never seen such a beautiful and serene baby.

Because the doctor is worried that Sharon might develop jaundice, he decides to keep the baby in the hospital for an additional two days of observation and care after releasing Daniela the day following the birth. Otto and Daniela visit the baby for hours each day, anxious to bring her home.

Danny eagerly awaits his first introduction to little Sharon, who has been named after the actress Sharon Stone. Daniela had chosen "Bridget" from her list of potential names, but after seeing her baby's face for the first time, she declared, "She doesn't look like a Bridget! She is Sharon!"

I realize that Danny has had a sibling for most of his five years, an older brother, and he is used to sharing the attention of parents. Although he retains only a partial memory of that brother, in behavioral terms he has been conditioned to expect the presence and influence of another child within his family constellation. This time, however, he is the older sibling. He will be the leader and trendsetter in his new family; the model of behavior for his sister; and one of her protectors.

"I have my own baby!" Danny exclaims as I enter his warm house from the blustery, damp cold. Danny and his parents are palpably joyful and excited. They have just returned from the hospital with their new family member, and she is wrapped not only in a large white blanket but in her parents' arms. They take turns holding her and inspecting her—gazing at her face for long minutes in the way that new parents seem almost unable to look away—and Danny eagerly takes his turn. Daniela places the baby gently in his arms after he has settled securely onto the couch and has reached out for her. She teaches him how to hold her; how her head must always be supported; and how he must be careful and still when he holds her in his lap.

Danny is gentle with his little sister. It is apparent from her first day at home that he expects to play a significant role in her life, and the priority for him is to shield her from harm. It is an endearing characteristic for so young a boy.

Although there is media coverage of Sharon's birth—"Baby Richard gets a sister"—it is relatively minor in terms of emphasis and placement. Typically a few lines in the newspapers—in the middle section of each paper—are devoted to this new chapter of the "Richard" story. Otto and Daniela have done all that they could to protect their privacy, but word got out to the media, probably from hospital personnel. Although they wish for anonymity for themselves and their children, they realize by now that the media has jumped on any story, no matter how mundane, for the opportunity to spin another Baby Richard episode. This birth is **real** news.

As I review the coverage, it occurs to me that in a number of other countries that I have visited, the "big news"—front-page stories and highlighted reports on television and radio—consists of positive, happy, and successful events. In China, for example, the government-controlled media highlight the good deeds of its citizens. A tribute to the donations of time and money from altruistic Chinese businessmen to flood victims was featured as the foremost story of the week. In this country, it seems, a lead story about the good deeds of citizens is the anomaly. "If it bleeds, it leads...."

Otto and Daniela welcome the mild response to their "blessed event" by the media. Maybe this is a sign of better times ahead.

"The anniversary of Danny's transfer is only two months away," I remind them as we speak in hushed tones while Sharon sleeps in her mother's arms. "I think it would be a good idea for us to take the initiative by releasing to the media a photograph of Danny with his new sister. This should discourage the rampant speculations that Danny is long-suffering and the similar rumors about him and your family."

Otto and Daniela like the idea. Without a publicist or anyone officially to represent them with the media, they continue to be fair game for those who present fiction and fabrications about them as facts. Even though he lives directly across the street, Loren Heinemann has distanced himself from the Kirchners. He spends more time at his office now that his clientele has expanded from the publicity that he received for having won the Baby Richard case against one of the most visible and successful law firms in the Midwest. Because Otto and Loren's formerly close relationship has cooled, the attorney would not be a good choice to serve as the liaison between the Kirchners and the media.

Bringing a camera with me on my next visit, I pose Danny with his sister and snap some photos of them. Danny is proud of her and comfortable holding her, although he is unaware of the purpose of these pictures.

"Can I go back outside to play?" he asks his father after the photos.

"Yes, if you get bundled up; it's cold outside," Otto responds. Danny pulls on his blue winter jacket and wool hat, while his father wraps the long plaid scarf around his neck and insists that he wear his mittens. Danny leaves the house to seek out Leah and Alisa from next door.

"My mother will soon be here to help out with the baby so that I can return to work," Daniela informs me. She and Otto, still unemployed, are both home now, sharing in child care activities. Although they both enjoy their time with the children, they worry about money. Daniela is frugal, of necessity, and Otto rarely purchases anything for himself; he buys cigarettes but little else.

Sharon is pink, plump and pretty, even as an infant. As I watch her lying on her back in her bassinet, I ponder her place in this little family. She represents a new, welcome opportunity for Otto and Daniela to parent their baby from her first days. I recall Otto frequently expressing deep regret over everything he was forced to miss during Danny's infancy and first years, all of the birthdays, holidays, and just "everydays." Danny, who otherwise might be overindulged, will need to share once again with a sibling. He will also have a playmate and companion. During recent months he has not only bonded with Peder and Enid's three daughters but has grown accustomed to various kinds of gentler play activities with them. Before this experience, Danny played with boys—his cousin Mario, Justin, Jeffrey, and others from the apartment complex—and only rarely with girls. He demonstrates both versatility and self-confidence, never appearing intimidated by older children, and he readily initiates conversations with other children, boys and girls of all ages. Having a sibling, three years older, during his earliest formative years has contributed to his ongoing comfort level and sense of security with other children. Justin, six years older than Danny, was his best and constant friend last year

Danny (five) holds his one-month-old sister Sharon in his living room during March 1996.

across the seven months that the Kirchners lived in their Mokena apartment. The two boys interacted largely as peers. Justin prided himself on looking out for Danny when they were together, but Danny could keep up with his older friend when playing ball or computer games, riding bikes, and fishing in the backyard pond.

During each of the following weeks, I continue to visit the family regularly, scheduling around my office appointments and other commitments. The Kirchners are expecting the imminent arrival of Greta Janikova, Daniela's mother, from the Slovak Republic. She is leaving her family for a span of months in order to help out with the baby and Danny so that Daniela will be able to return to her job and Otto will be able to resume work if he is successful in getting hired. He has contacted Ivan Kenessey, owner of the restaurant-bar at which he worked in Chicago before it permanently closed its doors nearly two years ago. His prospects for a job at Kenessey's Cypress Restaurant in Hinsdale, a nearby suburb of Chicago, look good. Because the owner already knows and trusts Otto, he is not unduly influenced by the adverse publicity.

Otto and Daniela are co-parenting, both of them at home on an around-the-clock basis during Daniela's maternity leave-of-absence. They are more relaxed and content than I have ever seen them.

"As long as our children are happy and healthy, and I can be with them, nothing else really matters," Daniela tells me while she breastfeeds Sharon. The baby sleeps through the night most of the time; she has adjusted well and easily to breastfeeding; and she seldom cries. She gets non-stop attention from her parents and brother, who take turns holding her.

Otto changes Sharon's diapers and carries her around the house, talking to her in soft tones. He is at his best as a father. He is comfortable with his nurturing nature as a parent; unashamed to show affection by frequently hugging and kissing his children; and always ready to bathe, dress, feed, or diaper as the need arises.

__March, 1996

"I'm going to be working again!" Otto announces as I walk through the front door on a frigid, windy afternoon. "Mr. Kenessey called to tell me that he will hire me as a waiter. I won't be a manager any more; there is no opening for one; but I can work full-time, and maybe even more."

Danny is playing a board game with his mother; Sharon is napping; and Otto is pacing, propelled by a mixture of excitement and relief. The restaurant—an upscale, well-situated establishment just yards from a major expressway exit—is doing well and enjoys a steady clientele for both lunch and dinner.

"I should make enough money there to pay off our bills before too long," he shares with me. "Maybe Daniela can even stay home with the kids after a few months."

"That would be great," Daniela adds, smiling. "I've liked Otto staying at home with the kids, but it's now time for **both** of us to work so that we can get out of debt. When my mother comes, we can both work and not worry about Danny and Cicka."

"Cicka?" I query her. This name—pronounced "Sis´-kah"—is familiar to me, but I have not heard it for two decades. Meaning "little kitten," it was my great-uncle's nickname for my great-aunt; after she died in 1977, he never used it again in my hearing. It brings back fond memories of a blend of security, affection, and tenderness.

"I love that name," I tell Daniela and explain to her and Otto its special meaning to me.

"Reporter Anne Kavanagh is writing an article about 'Baby Richard,'" I tell them when Danny has left the room. "She is asking why Danny is not attending pre-school as if there is some sinister reason. I explained that he is home with both of his parents and his infant sister; that he plays regularly with neighbor children; and that his mother is teaching him the alphabet, numbers, and similar pre-school subjects. She seemed to be looking for a major flaw or a dark secret."

"Danny is learning well," his mother happily reports. "He can count to one hundred; has learned shapes and pre-school vocabulary words; and he knows the alphabet. When I told him that he needed to know these things before he could start school, he got very serious about learning them."

Bob Greene is still writing his inflammatory columns, and most of the Kirchners' neighbors avoid them. Peder and Enid have become their only real friends in the neighborhood, and they try to help out in small but significant ways.

By the end of March, Otto has worked seventeen consecutive days. When offered the opportunity to work extra days at the restaurant, he always accepts. Daniela is still at home with the children, and they need the money that he earns.

"It's feast or famine for you, it seems," I tell him as he joins Daniela, the children, and me in the living room. It's 7:30 p.m. and he has just awakened from a nap.

"I have lost nearly thirty pounds," Otto says, "with all of the walking and working every day. It's difficult being a waiter after I was in charge of the other restaurant for so long, but it's a job and I'm glad to have it. Everyone recognizes me, though, and I never know **how** they will react to me. Some are angry and ask for a different waiter, or they just walk out, but some are nice and ask how my son is doing."

Danny holds Cicka on his lap for a few minutes and then asks for his father to take her. He sometimes gets bored with just holding her, and he often asks his parents how long it will be until she can talk and play with him. Daniela is pleased to report that Danny has not shown any signs of jealousy; he likes the baby and wants to help with her care.

"I think Danny tested me the other day," Daniela whispers to me, "when I was breastfeeding Cicka. He announced that he was hungry, something he rarely does, and he looked for my reaction. I put the baby down immediately and made him a sandwich. He looked very happy, as if he realized then that he is as important to me as the baby." To Daniela, this was a pivotal event for her son.

Soon Danny will lose his playroom, when it is converted into a guestroom for his grandmother. His train set, toys, games, and stuffed animals will be moved into his bedroom. Cicka sleeps in her parents' bedroom; her crib is placed next to their bed. The baby's theme has become Mickey and Minnie Mouse; her sheets, comforter, blankets, and other items are covered with the famous Disney mice.

Daniela is delighted to relate a good experience that Otto had yesterday at work. He had waited on a table of teachers, who left him a sizable gratuity, but more significantly, one of them called the restaurant the next day to compliment his service and to leave the message, "He did the right thing for his son."

"Otto felt very good," she explains to me, her voice breaking. "And I did, too. It's been really hard on him dealing with the public because many people are so angry and rude to him."

Back at my office, I continue to be challenged to answer to prospective and ongoing clients about my Baby Richard involvement. Rita S., a young woman with a six-year-old daughter, has resolved to eliminate the child's father from her life, in spite of his demonstrated devotion to the girl. She interrupts our discussion about her failed marriage in mid-session. "I am offended by your Baby Richard work, and I'm leaving," she announces, grabbing her purse and coat in haste and heading for the door. Her husband later telephones to inform me that they will transfer to another therapist. His wife refuses to return, not because of the quality of my services, he is quick to point out, but because of what I have done to "that poor child Richard."

At lunch with Marilyn Wood, an attorney for one of my clients, she shares with me her awareness of my situation vis-à-vis Bob Greene and the "Richard" case. Ms. Wood had been an attorney for DCFS for six years and became involved in the Baby Sarah case. "Greene also wrote many columns about that case — a whole series," Marilyn tells me. "He condemned the birth parents, the judge, and the therapist. He misrepresented the biological parents by referring to the mother and 'her boyfriend.' They were a married couple, but he didn't acknowledge that. Greene ruined the Baby Sarah therapist. She recommended that the five-year-old girl be placed with her biological parents, who had rehabilitated their lives, instead of the foster family that wanted to adopt her." Allegedly it was Bob Greene's vitriolic attacks upon the "Baby Sarah" judge that led to his leaving the juvenile court. The parallels between the cases, Baby Richard and Baby Sarah, are striking; and Ms. Wood is sympathetic to our victimization by a columnist who specializes in sensationalism.

Even at the dentist's office, there is talk about Baby Richard. The dental assistant asks whether I am still seeing the child and how he is doing. Dr. Michel, my dentist, greets me and alludes to the Greene articles, which he has read.

"The columns about you were about as bad as they possibly could be," he says in an attempt to show empathy. "If I had been maligned like that, I would have wanted to fight back."

Leaving some of my business cards, I encourage referrals for therapeutic services. The dentist and his staff members seem supportive and encouraging, and nowadays I am seeking clients from sources that know me personally.

Something has to be done about the continuing adverse publicity from Bob Greene's writings. With only occasional, sporadic coverage by other journalists during recent weeks, the "Richard" story is now carried almost exclusively by Greene. I schedule a no-cost consultation with Steven Garmisa, an attorney at a Chicago-based law firm. Mr. Garmisa has recently authored an article in our local newspaper about defamation cases.

When we meet, I explain to him that I am representing the interests of the Kirchners and describe the unending travail in their lives—including Danny's—because of Greene's journalistic campaign against them. In essence, I am requesting him to pursue a lawsuit on behalf of Otto and Danny against Bob Greene and the *Chicago Tribune* for defamation and invasion of privacy. Such action may compel Greene to stop his attacks, and the Kirchners may be entitled to recover monetary damages through litigation. It should not be too difficult for a competent attorney to prove the deleterious effects upon Otakar Kirchner of dozens of Greene's columns, especially as related to his long bout of involuntary unemployment. Of course, Garmisa would need to undertake the case on a *pro bono* basis or on a contingency, the former option meaning he would donate his services and the latter resulting in his getting a stipulated percentage of a monetary award if the lawsuit prevails. The attorney responds with articulated sympathy and a well-reasoned negative answer. I thank Mr. Garmisa for his time and, still determined to find an attorney to advance the Kirchners' cause, I begin a mental review of all of the attorneys whom I know—nearly one hundred—for a likely candidate for this Herculean job.

Mike Foley, who has worked for my school district for many years, is a smart, aggressive, conscientious attorney and we have become friends. He and his wife Donna, also an attorney, have started their own law firm, Foley & Foley. Mike may be interested in representing Otto and Danny. He is a man of integrity and he exhibits a rare level of dedication to his clients.

While I am at attorney Garmisa's office, Daniela, dressed in her best clothes, and Sharon, wrapped in blankets to protect her from the biting cold, visit the beauty salon so that Daniela's colleagues can see her baby. Accompanying her is Danny, the proud brother, who enjoys showing off his little sister.

At the end of the month, Otto, Daniela, and their children attend a birthday party for the two-year-old son of Mr. Kenessey. Guests are invited to enjoy the indoor pool, and Danny, excited about being able to swim inside a house, fearlessly enters the tepid water.

"He walked into the deep water," Daniela explains to me during my next visit, "and he panicked. He doesn't know how to swim yet, so I got scared and just jumped in, with all of my clothes and shoes on, and grabbed him to pull him out. Everyone around looked so surprised at me because no one else saw that Danny was struggling, it happened so fast. He didn't want to go back into the water after that, so he didn't. I just hope that he isn't always afraid of the water after that frightening event."

Otto won enough money this week at the gambling casino, they tell me, to cover their rent of $600. Although Daniela feels ambivalent about Otto's gambling, he often does well and his winnings help to pay their bills.

__April, 1996

Danny's favorite activity these days is using his new baseball machine, which shoots out the balls in a regular rhythm while he practices his batting skills. Now that it is spring, he can play outside more often. Self-confident and proficient, he hits more than one-half of the balls while I am watching him. Every few minutes, he pauses to hit his bat on the ground, like the professional players, and he looks to me for my approval. He has mastered the pitcher stance, and he seems both aware of his good motor skills and eager for praise.

Sharon wears pink knit booties with "Daddy" embroidered on them. The baby looks like her father. I share with Otto and Daniela that a recent research study demonstrated that a significant majority of babies look like their fathers. The researchers hypothesized that, through evolution, human babies have developed this characteristic, perhaps because newborns who look like their fathers are more likely to be claimed, protected by them, and therefore more likely to survive and reproduce. In any event, Otto beams with pride when any similarity between him and his children is pointed out.

The Kirchners inform me that they have declined an interview with Anne Kavanagh, who is writing a "Baby Richard" story for a summer issue of the *Ladies' Home Journal*. It will be an article about the Warburtons' suffering and loss, including an allusion to their alleged six-figure debt for legal fees.

On a bright Saturday morning, Otto and I meet in my office with Mike and Donna Foley for nearly two hours. We discuss the ongoing impact upon the Kirchners' daily lives from the continuing *Tribune* columns by Bob Greene. Among numerous examples, Otto describes an incident on St. Patrick's Day, when a party of seven came into the restaurant for dinner, but once they recognized him, they left in protest. Another customer said to her waiter in a loud voice, "Bring me my check; I don't want to throw up," after having announced that she recognized "Baby Richard's father." Donna Foley, a mother of two young daughters, is especially sympathetic to the Kirchners' situation. Mike may assume legal representation of Otto and Danny, he tells us. He and Donna will discuss the matter, weighing the pros and cons as well as the likelihood for success.

Otto informs me that he and Daniela will avoid the media and refuse interviews. The one-year anniversary of Baby Richard's transfer is imminent, and I am receiving phone calls and inquiries about Danny on a daily basis. Otto requests that I provide information about Danny, reaffirming that I might speak openly, without limitation, to reporters. My involvement will hopefully keep the journalists away from Danny and Sharon and yet satisfy what will likely be a voracious media hunger for news. If we don't provide some news, there are those who will create it. Based upon recent history, the themes of such "news" will range from curious and pessimistic to damning and "heart-breaking."

Through the night, on a series of consecutive days, I am working on my written response to the formal complaint against me that has been filed with the American Psychology Association, my professional organization. Dr. Marlin Hoover, whom I have never met, filed this complaint based solely upon Bob Greene's columns about me. Dr. Hoover has no other information or knowledge about me as a practitioner except that one of his female clients transferred permanently from him to me, and she and her six-year-old daughter have become two of my ongoing, long-term clients. In his complaint to the Ethics Committee of the A.P.A., Dr. Hoover writes:

> I have no direct knowledge of this case, and rely only on information offered in the newspaper. However, the

accusations raised by the columnist, Bob Greene, in the Chicago Tribune raise serious questions about...Dr. Moriarty.... (October 12, 1995)

My response must be filed within thirty days. I complete a draft and send it to Bill Harte for his review and recommendations. I continue to battle frequent headaches, probably attributable to stress and worry. Thus far, I have heard nothing from the Illinois Department of Professional Regulation, which began their investigation of me one year ago. I was told to expect a hearing, conducted by their office, but so far nothing at all has happened. Not only is my case presumably still under review in that Department, which has the power to suspend or revoke my license to practice psychology, but now the A.P.A. is beginning an investigation, based upon Dr. Hoover's complaint.

The A.P.A. has a series of sanctions that it might impose if an accused psychologist is found guilty of an ethics violation. These include a reprimand; censure; expulsion from membership; a stipulated resignation; issuance of a cease and desist order; a supervision, training or tutorial requirement; and probation.

In essence, this psychologist has presented Greene's columns as the sole formal complaint against me, alleging amorphous ethical violations on my part—all related to my "Baby Richard" work.

"The **child** is the best psychologist," Gabriela declares when I visit the Kirchners' home on Easter Sunday. Referring to Danny, she clarifies, "He could tell that he was loved and wanted here from his first hours and he has responded to that." I agree with her assessment, which captures the reality of the situation in succinct terms. With flashback memories to last year, I recall Danny jumping onto his father's lap on the living room floor and spontaneously hugging his mother during those first days. Today I have brought a silver picture frame, a gift from my sister Jo in honor of the new baby. Daniela puts a photo of Sharon into the frame and places it on the etagere shelf among other pictures of the family.

"We all went to Easter Mass together," Gabriela reports. "Danny looked so cute all dressed up in his suit. He talked about the 'Jesus guy' and made up songs to sing to me. And he looks out for his little sister; he reminded his mother that she should wash her hands before picking up the baby!" His grandmother is virtually oozing with praise about Danny, and, overhearing her, he grins and stands a little taller.

Several days later when I visit, Danny greets me at the front door. He opens his mouth to show me his first lost tooth, a front bottom one. Long accustomed to offering me information about himself from the first moments of each of my visits, Danny has become conditioned to report anything new or significant before I even ask. He shows me his new roller blades and a child-size, plastic golf club set. Danny takes my hand to lead me to a large colorful board with numbers and letters inserted into slots, and he demonstrates his ability quickly to count to twenty and to recite the alphabet. I praise his achievements and compliment him on his hard work in learning these important lessons.

Daniela's commitment to breastfeed the baby requires frequent and focused attention to their new addition. I notice that she is careful to balance her time between the children, however, so that Danny will not feel neglected. Often, while she is feeding Sharon, she will say to Danny, "As soon as I finish here, I will come over there to see how you are doing," and she is dutiful in following up on her promise. Danny exhibits no need to compete for attention. He seems comfortably established in his niche as the older child, who is needed to assist in the protection of his new, helpless sibling.

Danny is regularly using Slovak words now, becoming bi-lingual. He knows the words for some animals, certain foods, and several parts of the body. His mother recites the words for him as he points to objects, and then he repeats them. Danny has also spontaneously begun to call Daniela "mama" instead of "mom."

"It's a higher term of endearment, I think," Otto explains to me, "more than 'mom.' Danny is more bonded with his mother than ever. The birth of Cicka made him understand better his own birth, and he realizes now the real meaning of being his mother's son...and my son." Otto is both perceptive and sensitive to any changes in his son's behavior; he analyzes with me every significant new development.

Gabriela returns to Canada after her one-week visit. Otto and Daniela have sent the airline ticket to Danny's other grandmother in Slovakia so that she might arrive here as soon as she completes the necessary arrangements to leave her husband and home for the months ahead.

One of Danny's continuing favorite activities is to bring out the family album and to review the photos. Even though I have seen most of the photos before and have been the photographer for a good number of them, he likes to explain to me the people and settings. It's his way of storytelling without a book. When I give Danny a child's tennis set as a gift, it turns out to be a duplicate of one that he has already gotten from his parents. *Toy Story* and *Winnie the Pooh* have replaced the Power Rangers and Star Wars as his preferred movies, books, and toys. His interests are now less traditionally masculine and aggression-oriented. With a baby sister in the house and three girls next door, his most frequent playmates, his behaviors have noticeably softened and quieted. He is not only happy in the company of girls but is also often solicitous for their well-being. His parents effusively and frequently compliment him for his caring and concern.

Daniela tells me about their recent trip to the store to buy new shoes for Otto now that he is on his feet so much at work. The salesman gave Otto a rebate of $5 in cash from a pair of shoes that he exchanged for less expensive ones.

"Otto gave Danny the five dollars so that he would have his own money," Daniela describes the event. "But Danny gave it back to his father. He said, 'You take it because you might need it, dad.' I was so impressed over his concern for his father. He probably knows that we have been worried about money; for a five-year-old he is so caring." Daniela's eyes moisten as she remembers this little—and yet big—incident.

Danny wants to wear to bed his new red-and-navy striped sport shirt that he says is "just like Robert's." He demonstrates the ability to identify the titles of thirty of his videotapes. Although he does not know how to read, he has memorized the pictures and can retrieve any movie that he wants to watch.

Prominently placed on a new shelf mounted on the living room wall is a shrine to the Blessed Virgin Mary. Daniela has purchased the statue of Mary and has placed silk flowers and a large votive candle in front of the virgin mother. She burns the candle every night and it flickers its pale light around the small room.

Otto has signed a contract with Mike Foley, now his attorney, who will prepare a lawsuit with Otakar and Daniel as plaintiffs against the defendants Bob Greene and the *Chicago*

Tribune. Hopefully this action will bring to an end Greene's obsessive and malicious columns about Baby Richard. He may be forced to find another case or cause to champion, perhaps one that would actually bring about some beneficial result. Trying to be objective, I wonder what good has resulted from his ravings about "Richard." So much ink and so many trees and what has come of it? The Warburtons are well-known symbols of perceived victimization; the Kirchners are widely despised; and Danny has become a public curiosity and a pathetic, tragic figure. There are new laws, including a putative fathers' registry for adoptions in Illinois, but are these attributable to this columnist? The laws were passed some time ago, and yet Greene continues to write about his trademark story, his primary focus on Richard's "longings" and continuing lack of contact with his former family.

Otto and Daniela approve two of my photographs of Danny holding his one-month-old sister for our release to the members of the media who request them. Following the adage, "A picture is worth a thousand words," we have agreed among ourselves that photographic evidence of these two thriving children might mitigate the media-promulgated depictions of Danny as a devastated, miserable hostage. He has noticeably grown and filled out from last year, the time of his transfer event; his longer blonde hair and rosy cheeks contribute to the look of a healthy child; and his beguiling smile represents his usual facial expression.

Next-door neighbor Enid, who continuously saw Danny on a nearly daily basis, would tell me, "My nickname for him was 'Dan Dan the Sunshine Man' because he was always smiling and happy. He was always going and seemed to never stop, he had so much energy. He was so vibrant and fun to be around."

In sharp contrast to Danny's content frame of mind, I find myself struggling on several levels. My private practice has diminished to the point of ten to twelve billable hours weekly; my income has decreased to the level of one decade ago; and my physician, Dr. Stavinga, has prescribed medication for my recurring headaches. He encourages a less stressful life-style and strongly recommends my taking the medication on a regular basis. After watching the movie *Babe*, about a charming pig, I wept for several hours; my emotions are raw; and I am feeling uncharacteristically vulnerable and hating it. I often watch children's movies because discussing them during the first minutes of a therapy session with a young child serves as an ice breaker, as a shared experience between therapist and client, and as a topic that tends to relax apprehensive youngsters. For the time being, however, I decide to forgo watching movies that are likely to trigger a strong emotional response.

Clare Korinek telephones me to share a good news/bad news story with me. Clare had worked for Robert at Morton College for many years until she accepted a position in the private sector, but she and her husband have remained friends of ours. Clare attended a shower with a group of friends at the Cypress Restaurant this week. Otto was their waiter; Clare recognized him immediately; and she told him, "We share a common friend, Karen Moriarty."

Otto responded, "She helped me keep my sanity during the struggle to get my son...."

Clare continues, "Several people among the group were going to say confronting and insulting things to him, but I cautioned them not to. I told them that they don't know the whole story, and they shouldn't spoil this shower for others. So, a very unpleasant scene was avoided.

"My neighbor looks just like Otto Kirchner," Clare elaborates, "and he and his kids have received a lot of grief from people who mistake him for Otto. It has been a **very** difficult situation for them. I can just imagine what it must be like for Otto to experience these kinds of reactions from people. And I came close to witnessing an embarrassing example at the shower."

I thank Clare for her kind words to me and for her supportive actions at the shower.

As a member of the Palos Park Zoning Board of Appeals, I attend a regularly scheduled meeting, as usual. This voluntary, uncompensated position provides a means of performing community service. The board hears and acts upon residents' petitions to deviate from zoning ordinances for special circumstances. At this meeting one of the cases involves a young couple's request for approval to build a garage that exceeds the ordinance-prescribed boundaries.

As I arrive and take my assigned seat at the front table, the chairman of the board confronts me, in a booming voice, "Have you received any publicity from the media lately?"

The hush in the room, among the thirty persons gathered there, seems palpable to me. Embarrassed, I respond, "Not recently," but I realize that there will soon be more publicity due to the imminent one-year "Richard" anniversary. Several people send dirty looks my way; several others look away; and one says, "I wouldn't want to be **you**." An elderly woman in the front row informs her husband, "That's the woman who's responsible for Baby Richard's sudden removal from his nice family in Schaumburg." Fortunately, the meeting begins and normalcy settles into the evening's format.

On my next visit with the Kirchners, Danny is playing with three neighborhood girls in his backyard. They are running around, throwing a large beach ball to each other. Otto, Daniela, and I are sitting on lawn chairs on the backyard deck, watching the children. Danny trips and falls down; he starts to cry, unusual behavior for him; and Otto gets up to check him out. As Daniela and I observe the interaction, Otto sits on the ground next to Danny and inspects his leg. After he gently pats his son's head and leg, Danny stops crying and springs upright to resume his play. The worried girls, who have gathered around the younger Danny, voice their approval that he is uninjured.

"I think Danny is showing off for the girls," a broadly smiling Otto whispers to us. "He is trying to impress them."

Otto informs me that several reporters have appeared in their neighborhood and at Kenessey's in order to get a story about "Richard." "They seem to know everything about our lives and where to find us," he laments. "I don't know where they get their information, do you?" he asks me.

Although I have been interviewed by more than one dozen reporters in anticipation of the anniversary coverage that is inevitable, I have been careful not to disclose the whereabouts of the Kirchner home or Otto's place of employment, or to reveal other information that would be invasive of their privacy. I am providing the media with an update of Danny's current status — at the Kirchners' request — and nothing else.

A newspaper article about Loren Heinemann's troubles is the subject of conversation between Otto and Daniela, who have not spoken with the attorney for weeks. The story in the paper is about a recent case for which Heinemann reportedly failed to appear in court, as scheduled. Before long, similar stories about alleged misfeasance will be reported.

As I leave, I walk across the pink and yellow chalk drawings—a hopscotch board and several other, creative figures that include wide-petaled flowers—that cover the Kirchners' asphalt driveway. They provide a colorful testimonial to Danny's more artistic bent now that he is playing with girls on a regular basis.

Telephone calls have resumed, as early as 4:15 a.m., consisting of assorted silent hang-ups and hateful messages, such as "You **will** be sorry you became the Baby Richard psychologist!" and "How can you live with yourself...?" I cannot determine whether they are placed to my office or my home, because the office telephone forwards calls to my house. Upon my attorney friend's advice, I contact the Chiefs of the Orland Park and Palos Park Police Departments in order to report the renewed calls and threats. Both Chiefs of Police express concern and assure me that they will order increased police surveillance on my office and my home for a period of thirty days.

A representative of the *Chicago Tribune* contacts me for a picture of "Baby Richard" for "anniversary" coverage. Because the Kirchner parents and I have decided that we will distribute the photograph that they selected to any member of the media who requests it, I agree to provide a copy. A messenger is sent to my office; he offers to pay for the photo; I refuse to accept payment and hand him the picture for unlimited use and distribution.

During late April and early May, Baby Richard's transfer anniversary is featured in newspapers and magazines, on radio and television. The photograph that we provided is widely used. Although the real information about Danny and his family is positive—the child is thriving, as is his infant sister; both parents are working; and they live in a comfortable home—the coverage, to say the least, is tinged with sadness and alarm. How is he **really** doing? reporters query.

Back at the real Kirchner home—as opposed to the media's more lurid imaginings—everything looks and feels like a normal, healthy environment except, of course, for the incursions by strangers. Enid and Peder notice that unmarked vans drive slowly by the Kirchners' home; sometimes they observe the driver snapping photos of the house. At other times, a dark van—occupied by an indistinguishable man wearing sunglasses—parks for long periods of time at the street curb.

Anxious to escape the renewed Baby Richard frenzy, Robert and I embark upon a one-week visit to Palm Coast, Florida, to spend time with his brother Ed and wife Jean and to sightsee. On impulse we decide to drive down the east coast to look at condominiums. Thinking that some day we might buy an ocean-front condo as a vacation place, we inform the realtor who greets us at his building's front door that we are "only looking, not buying." Donald Webb takes us to view seven units, all located on the beach in a little community called Ormond-by-the-Sea. One of them is a newly constructed two-bedroom, two-bathroom condo on the seventh floor; it has a small balcony overlooking the Atlantic Ocean.

As soon as we cross the teal-colored carpeting, passing gleaming white tile and matching white cabinets in the kitchen, to the sliding glass door through which we marvel at the great expanse of turquoise ocean and the white foam of swooshing tides, we are sold. Within hours we become the surprised but happy owners of our own little escape haven on the ocean. This place will afford us the opportunity to get away from the pressures of my practice whenever my schedule permits. It has been only one month since the media blitz over Baby Richard's anniversary, and I am sharing the Kirchners' emotional exhaustion and irritation over the story that won't go away.

Within days of our return from Florida, Greta Janikova arrives in Richton Park to join her new, expanded family. A tall, thin woman with short, ash-blonde hair, she looks intense and serious, as if smiles have become sparse from a hard, dutiful life course. She would appropriately be described as a "handsome woman," with bright, penetrating blue eyes and high cheekbones. She knows only a dozen English words, but she nods and gestures to make up for her limited vocabulary when she talks to English speakers, such as me. Greta speaks Slovak with her daughter, Otto, Danny, and Sharon. The adults understand her completely, of course, while the baby, six weeks old, is oblivious to language differences, and Danny, five, understands her only partially and sporadically. Danny is certain to learn his second language well, now that he has a live-in grandmother who uses it exclusively. Their situation reminds me of my own grandmother—with whom my parents and I lived until I turned five—who spoke Hungarian most of the time. I learned to understand her, but because I could speak only a few words of her native language, communications between us tended to be one-way. She supervised me while both of my parents worked full-time, and I remember struggling to try to explain things to her. However, because she was both nurturing and attentive, she overcame our communications difficulties in other ways, which included cooking and baking for me as well as force–feeding me soft-boiled eggs and bananas for breakfast because they were "Goo-ood!" for me.

Greta has looked forward to meeting and hugging her grand-son Danny since she watched him one year ago on her television, when Otto and Daniela retrieved him from his adoptive family's house. Now she can also hug and cuddle her new granddaughter. Greta coos with delight, tears spilling down her worn cheeks, as she begins her grandmother role with these two beautiful children, who look so much like her and her daughter. Greta is eager to be loving and helpful; she came to do a job; and she embraces it wholeheartedly.

When we are first introduced to each other, I can tell from her knowing smile, enthusiastic nodding, and firm handshake that she knows who I am and who I have become to her family. From that first day, we would come to share a continuing sense of rapport, communicated with few words and mostly on a nonverbal level, but renewed and reinforced through annual Christmas cards and messages sent to each other across the Atlantic Ocean.

__May through December, 1996

Greta does her job helping with the children and the house so well that Otto begins to feel alienated. She assumes the lead role in caring for the children through daytime hours, while Otto works more than the traditional forty-hour week—trying to earn as much as he can for his family—and Daniela also works full-time. Otto was Danny's primary caregiver for his son's first year in their home. He fed, bathed, and dressed him; played with him; and took him places. They were inseparable. That year, Daniela was with Danny whenever she was not at the salon or commuting, but her work and required travel time consumed an average of fifty hours per week, making Otto the central figure in his son's life.

The Kirchner family constellation has changed three times within one year: Danny arrived, Sharon was born, and Grandma Greta moved in. Daniela and her mother—always emotionally close, even when separated by an ocean—together, as a new team, dominate the household, a predictable and understandable outcome. The change in dynamics and its suddenness cause a distressing, unsettling, and painful disruption for Otto. I have witnessed similar problems within my own extended family and with several of my other clients. It is frustrating to realize that while this family is suffering significant, daily stresses and strains, everyone is a good person; everyone loves the children; everyone wants to do the right thing; and yet the individuals tend to get in each other's way. Paradoxically, if each individual was less involved and committed, it would result in less discomfort and conflict among them.

Each of these adults fiercely desires to nurture, to love, and to do for the children and the household. Otto is making up for lost years with his son; Daniela is savoring her long-awaited second chance with her son; and Greta is embracing her opportunity to be needed and helpful with her two new grandchildren and their family. And everyone wants to hold the baby, feed her, and take care of her. Greta takes over the everyday running of the household, including the outdoor gardening; she is tireless.

The more everyone tries to do, the more the marriage suffers. Greta and Daniela spend hours together with the children, talking about the children, and planning for the children. Otto begins to feel like an outsider. At work during evening and weekend hours, the times when a waiter earns the largest part of his income, he comes home to discover that he missed out on most of the children's activities. Tired from spending so many work hours on his feet, he often sleeps during daytime hours. He and Daniela spend less and less time together.

The children, always the central focus of the household, continue to grow and to thrive across months. Unfortunately, their parents' marriage is not correspondingly thriving.

As I arrive for a visit, Danny greets me on the front porch. His head bowed, he confesses, "I was mean to Grandma today." I realize that he is telling on himself, he is so conditioned to reporting to me anything meaningful in his daily life. Danny explains that he was disobedient; he knows that he is wrong to defy his grandmother. When I enter the house, she frowns deeply, shakes her head, and looks discouraged. I smile, intervene by explaining to each the feelings of the other, and the tension dissipates. Grandma realizes that Danny feels sorry for his defiance.

The children's everyday lives are typically pleasant, happy, and comfortable. Except for normal glitches—such as Danny's occasional acting-out as a normal five-year-old boy "with a mind of his own"—the weeks pass peacefully as they do in countless suburban homes. Both parents work at their jobs, the children grow and develop, and Grandma cooks, cleans, and helps in countless ways.

When Daniela returns home from the salon, she breastfeeds the baby and exercises her. She holds Sharon's feet and flexes her legs several times and then repeats the activity with the baby's hands and arms. Then she turns to Danny, reviewing his day with him and engaging in his most recent favorite activity. On Otto's only day off from work, he spends time with the children, often finding himself in competition with Grandma's plans for them.

"I have been writing a newspaper column for 25 years; what the five prevailing justices did to those two boys is the single most brutal act I have ever seen a branch of government commit against totally helpless and voiceless people," Bob Greene wails in his August 25th column. Alluding to "Richard" and his former adoptive brother, he tells readers about "his [Richard's] pain" from not having been reunited with the other child. I am thinking that it must be a slow day and no creative juices flowing for Greene; he is back to ascribing feelings to Danny, about which he knows nothing. He continues: "Sixteen months. Not a word." The next day, he writes more of the same. If the result of the court's decision, to Greene, is "the most brutal act" he has ever seen, the man has led a sheltered life indeed. He should spend two or three weeks in my office; visit an orphanage; or spend some time with a DCFS caseworker.

Danny starts kindergarten in the early fall. My visits continue on the basis of once or twice weekly. Sometimes the Kirchners come to my house for a barbecue or other occasion. We celebrate all of the holidays, birthdays, and other important events together.

"One of the boys told me my mother is very stupid," Danny informs me during his first month of school. He is upset and perplexed as to how he should respond to this affront by one of his peers. He tells me that he just said, "She is **not**," and walked away. Danny does not understand how other children know about his mother; they have not even met her.

On one crisp but sun-drenched day during the fall, Greta and Daniela are speaking in hushed tones when I arrive. They both greet me with what appear to be forced smiles.

"Otto has left and is living somewhere else," Daniela blurts in response to my quizzical look. "He comes to spend time with the children whenever he can, several days a week."

As I sink into the living room couch, I feel profoundly sad. Not surprised to hear this news, I review to myself the most recent events in their family that I have observed. There has been noticeable tension between the two parents and between Otto and his mother-in-law. Sharon, eight months old, is too young to sense anything, and Danny appears calm. When I speak to him privately, I discover that he is secure in the knowledge that his father will be spending time with him as before. Clearly, both Otto and Daniela have spoken with Danny, assuring him that he will continue an uninterrupted relationship with his father. In his short life, Danny has learned remarkable coping skills. I feel relieved at first and then worried about the future of this troubled family.

When I speak to Otto several days later, I discover that he is troubled and conflicted. He feels like a stranger in his own home. His role has been reduced to an ancillary figure who is home for only a few of his children's waking hours and one day per week. His more-than-full-time work schedule keeps him away much more than he would prefer, and when he is home, he mostly sleeps.

"Daniela and I are having serious problems," he shares with me. "She is totally involved in being a mother, which I understand; it's great that she is so devoted to the kids. The rest of the time she spends with her mother and they both criticize what I do. We have no time together. Everything has changed since her mother came. I know her mother wants to do the right thing and works hard, but it's too much, and I'm just an outsider now." He confides in me that it was Daniela who asked him to leave.

Promising both Otto and Daniela that I will remain neutral and avoid taking sides between them, I genuinely empathize and sympathize with each one. I have come to understand intimately their feelings and their perceptions regarding their relationship, which has been repeatedly challenged in so many ways during the past tumultuous five years. I become successful in serving as a liaison between them in subtle ways and in maintaining a supportive relationship with both of them.

Just before Christmas, Bob Greene dusts off one of his columns from last year's holiday for a recycling. He wails, through the print, "All a lie. Not a single phone call; not a single visit" between Baby Richard and his former brother. "[I]t has now been one year and eight months since... Richard was carried in tears from the adoptive home...." Last year Greene wrote, "This is sinful." This year he opts for a noun, "This is a sin," and this is a "kind of cruelty" that no child deserves. Just as he did in last year's Christmas column, Greene concludes with Governor Edgar's words from long ago: "Frankly, I cannot imagine how the justices who prevailed in this case will be able to sleep at night." ("Another Christmas—Not a visit, not a word," *Chicago Tribune*, December 22, 1996) The reality is that Danny, at the age of five, barely remembers John Warburton, whom he has neither seen nor spoken to for twenty months.

At Christmas, Daniela, Greta, and the children come to our house for a gift exchange and dinner. Robert and I miss Otto's presence, but the event is still festive, if subdued. Danny loves visiting at my house, and he enjoys wandering from room to room. Having recently lost both of his front teeth, he smiles ingenuously, but soon realizes that he looks especially charming to all of us in the room. He responds by flashing an even bigger smile. Sharon, ten months old, crawls around on the carpet and pulls herself to a standing position by holding onto the edges of furniture. She has wispy, platinum-blonde hair and has filled out to the point of what I describe as "cherubic chubbiness." Robert, Daniela, and I take turns snapping photographs to preserve this special occasion.

"Both of the children are healthy," Daniela says, with a wan smile, to Robert and me. Wearing a red velvet outfit that nearly matches the baby's, she is thin and pale but also seems more relaxed than in recent weeks. "Otto calls Danny every day and he still comes to the house to visit the kids several times a week. I think things are better this way," she continues.

Greta knows more English words now, and she can communicate with us in a basic, simple way. She now speaks a combination of Slovak and English with Danny; he appears to understand everything she says to him.

"Danny can speak to his grandmother in Slovak," Daniela exclaims with pride. "He has learned a lot of his second language from listening to us talk and from his interactions with her."

As 1996 is coming to an end, I realize that my private practice has become sporadic in terms of clients and cash flow. Sometimes it takes us months or even more than a year to collect from medical insurance companies on behalf of our clients with coverage. During the holidays my weekly sessions are reduced to eight or nine per week. People typically suspend their therapy during the Christmas season. Deciding to work on Christmas Day, however, I spend several hours in the home of Judy, convicted of child neglect, who continues to spend time with her eleven-year-old son only under the direct supervision of his therapist. If I am not present, she will be unable to see her child on Christmas.

My court-assigned work has dwindled to an insignificant level, and local attorneys refer clients to me only infrequently. Most of my current clients are word-of-mouth referrals from former clients, who have recommended my services to their spouses, relatives, or friends. I realize that I should consider other options, such as a possible return to school district employment.

My ties with family and friends have been weakened by the complex, unforeseen circumstances of the past two years. Robert and I have begun to escape to Florida on a regular schedule; every seven to eight weeks we spend a long weekend or even a week at our new condo. Life feels better there for us—no unwelcome phone calls; no media; and no visible threats to a pleasant, normal life-style. There is always a slower pace there, anonymity, a "vacation feel," and warmer weather. It is becoming more and more difficult to return to the difficulties in Chicagoland.

Now that I am no longer a therapist for the Kirchners, having transitioned into a unique combination of friend, ally, and family member, I know that I can continue a close relationship with them from near or far.

Dispirited and tired out on New Year's Eve, I achingly wish for a better year ahead. Most of all, I hope for a reconciliation between Otto and Daniela. If the media—and especially Bob Greene—will graduate from the Baby Richard story to other cases and causes, this alone will contribute significantly to the probability of the Kirchners' reuniting and beginning a life of normalcy, which they have never been allowed to experience together.

I had no way of knowing that things would just get worse...and soon.

Cheer up! The worst is yet to come!

— Philander Chase Johnson

At Christmas 1996, Danny—missing his
front teeth—sits on his mother's lap, next
to his grandmother (Greta) in my home.

The Talk Show Ambush

> In the future everyone will be famous for fifteen minutes.
>
> — *Andy Warhol*

> Avoid, at all costs, spending your fifteen minutes on a talk show.
>
> — *Dr. Karen Moriarty*

"The man who left the son that he fought for...." The announcer's voice resonates through the studio. The audience is electrified. Thus begins the introduction of Otto and me as we walk onto the *Saturday Night Live* stage for a taping of the nationally televised NBC talk show, *In Person*, hosted by Maureen O'Boyle. We have been lured to the program as the highlighted guests so that Otto will be able to tell his side of the six-year Baby Richard story for the very first time. It is the first week of February 1997, during the most frigid part of winter.

Mike Foley called me three days before the taping to request, on Otto and Danny's behalf, that I participate in the talk show, as an eyewitness, so that the public will hear the other side of the "Richard" story. We hope that this opportunity will pave the way for an improved image for Otto. Perhaps he will be able to obtain employment if a segment of the public sees the real, human side of the man and learns that he has been a victim, on several levels, rather than a worthless, evil character, as he has been portrayed. He and his family will benefit from such exposure; possibly they will be able to begin a more normal life. Again, Otto is desperate for work; the Hinsdale Cypress Restaurant permanently closed on New Year's Eve; and he has no realistic prospects for another job. He worked at the Cypress for only ten months before it went out of business.

Mike has paved the way for our participation in the show by establishing conditions with Larry Garrison, his liaison. I have agreed to appear as a guest, along with Otto, so that I can set the record straight regarding Danny. "He is a healthy, thriving, normal child in every way," I envision myself telling the viewing audience. "Contrary to reports by the media who have never met Danny, he is **not** a long-suffering, scarred, emotionally damaged child."

Reporters and columnists have repeatedly sought prognoses about Baby Richard from mental health professionals who also never spoke with the child. Since my first day with Danny, when I would be asked about his progress and respond in positive terms, the interviewers would typically disregard, minimize, or entirely omit my comments from their stories. Instead, they would seek out "an expert" who would offer opinions of serious concern for his mental health; strongly express skepticism that he could be happy and doing well; and issue dire predictions about his future. Those hand-wringing, furrowed-brow prognostications would find their way onto television screens and newsprint. They became the story; they became the myth of Baby Richard; they were imaginings and speculations by people who were strangers to the real Danny.

Most of my clients believe that Danny has been irreparably traumatized by his "brutal transfer" and his current "hostage-like captivity" within his biological parents' home. They envision him longing to be with another family in Schaumburg, doomed never again to be able to trust, to love, and to bond with others. They read about him; they hear about him on call-in radio shows; and they believe what they read and hear. If asked, they admit that **no one** who is giving these alleged progress reports about the child has actually claimed to have met him or talked to him since the day of his transfer. "But, of course their reports **must** be **true** or how could they print and say these things?" they assert.

Now, however, I will have the opportunity to refute the reports of the spotlight-seeking "professionals" who, absent first-hand information, simply give the media what they want.

"Danny deserves to be known as the great kid that he really is," I tell Mike Foley. I am making arrangements to postpone my scheduled clients' sessions in order to travel to New York City for the taping. "He has the right to be treated, not as a curiosity or a pawn in a melodramatic make-believe tale, but as a real flesh-and-blood child. What are our conditions?" I ask him.

"They have guaranteed that Otto will be able to tell his side of the story at last; the only other guests will be the natural parents of one similar adoption case, and no spokesperson for the Warburtons will appear," Mike responds. "Also," he continues, "the audience will consist of fewer than forty people and audience participation will be discouraged. They agree not to describe Otto and Daniela's marital separation as Otto's 'having left or abandoned' his son."

With these assurances, I feel more optimistic about the Kirchners' future than I have in many months. I envision Otto and Daniela together again, with the two children, as a family; Otto working in a good job, perhaps hired by a sympathetic Chicagoland viewer of this imminent program; and Danny's image beginning to change from a troubled and tragic figure to a normal little boy.

Otto and I meet at the airport, as planned. On the plane we discuss the possible ramifications of this opportunity for national coverage of the untold story. Maureen O'Boyle appears to be an articulate, attractive, and assertive interviewer. *In Person* seems to represent an appropriate forum for our disclosure of the behind-the-scenes story, for Otto to present his side at last, and for us to dispel the myth of Danny's disintegrated mental and emotional state.

During the early morning hours, pacing back and forth in my hotel room, I contact Bill Harte by phone to ask him about the parameters of my disclosures on national television. "You continue to do what is best for your clients," he says in a succinct summary, "and don't worry about anything else." Bill's directness and integrity dispel my concerns and contribute to my readiness to do this onerous deed—to become a talk show participant.

The producers of the program have arranged for payment of the airfare, hotel accommodations, and limousine transportation for Otto and for me. On our way to the NBC building, the limo driver picks up several more people, who share the ride with us. I wonder what connection these four individuals might have to the *In Person* program. When Otto and I introduce ourselves to them, we discover that the married couple and two women are scheduled to appear as guests on the show.

Could there have been a mistake? Mike Foley ensured that the program would cover Baby Richard exclusively, except for minor, secondary participation by a husband and wife, natural parents of a child whose adoption was also ruled invalid. Could it be that two programs will be produced today—the one on "Richard" and another, separate one?

As we exit the elevator, several attractive young people greet us, pair up with each of us, and lead us to separate dressing rooms.

"We will be using the dressing rooms and stage of *Saturday Night Live*," my perky, platinum-blonde usher-greeter declares.

After we enter my assigned dressing room, she assesses my appearance, her head tilted to one side. She rearranges my hair with her bejeweled hands and explains the format of the program.

"You will walk on stage and sit on a chair next to Otto Kirchner and facing Maureen O'Boyle," she explains, gesticulating with giddy enthusiasm. "She will ask you both questions. You will have lots of time to answer them. There will be give and take, too. Just relax and say anything you want," she instructs me.

Ms. Enthusiasm thrusts at me a two-page document entitled "Participant Agreement." She waves a shiny pen and chirps, "Just sign this, please. You don't have to read it; it's just the standard wording. We'll have to hurry. You're due to be on stage in a few minutes." She begins to strut toward the door, glancing over her shoulder to see if I have signed the agreement and have begun to follow her.

"I'll read this document before I sign it," I explain. Her smile disappears and she returns to the dressing room table.

As I am reading the two-page contract, I am not surprised to see elements that guarantee River Tower Productions ("Producer") the sole and exclusive rights to all or part of the program "throughout the world in all media now known or here-after devised." I am surprised, however, to read "Producer may, at its sole discretion, edit, rearrange, and/or change said Rights and Materials and combine same with other material." I realize that the program's editing process will probably result in the telecast of an entirely different product from the original taping.

"We should really get going," my usher-greeter, no longer bubbly, interjects. "You can sign that now and then read it later," she suggests with a frown.

As I read further, ignoring her apparent impatience, #5 is troubling, as it requires my acceptance of an unknown surprise on stage:

> I may experience a surprise…in connection with my appearance on the program, the parameters of which have been told to me. By initialing the adjacent box, I confirm the foregoing and I agree to voluntarily participate therein.

"What are the parameters of the potential surprise?" I ask my usher-greeter, who has already started again to head toward the door. She stops in her tracks.

"Oh, I don't really know," she sighs dismissively. "Probably nothing," she adds, looking down at the pen. "Well, if you have a problem with that one, we can just cross it out," she spurts after realizing that I am not signing this version of the contract. With several flourishes of the pen, she lines out the surprise clause.

"Is that okay now?" she says in a petulant tone of voice.

After I sign the Agreement, she breaks into a full smile once again, renews her bounciness, and twirls around to lead me to the stage.

We approach the elaborately draped backside of the stage. Otto, escorted by his exuberant, Tom Cruise look-alike usher-greeter, joins us. Tom's chalk-white teeth glint, like Bucky Beaver's in the toothpaste commercials of yore, in the bright, sterile lights of the studio. We stand awaiting our pre-taping introductions to the audience that will signal our entrance onto the stage.

Two beautiful young women and one handsome young man, all of whom are wearing tight jeans and enjoying a "good hair day," spring onto the stage minutes before the taping begins. They work the audience into a frenzy by repeatedly exhorting,

"Let us hear you shout!" "Give us some applause!" "Now boo for us! Come on, you can do better than that! Boo-oo-oo! Boo-oo-oo! That's it! Now more applause! Put your hands together!"

Against the backdrop of the stage on a huge screen is a picture of Danny, unsmiling, sad, and eyes downcast, his gaze directed at the guests' chairs below. In spite of Mike Foley's having provided more than a dozen photos of a smiling, happy, actively-engaged Danny in various settings, the producers chose this one picture of a pensive child to form the visual background of today's program.

The announcer's voice booms, "...This is Otto Kirchner, who fought so hard for his son Baby Richard and then left him!" Otto walks onto the stage and takes his pre-assigned seat. "And Dr. Karen Moriarty, the psychologist in the case." I walk to my chair beside Otto. Angry about the introduction that directly violates one of the conditions of our appearance on this program, I force myself to smile. Members of the audience are agitated, murmuring and jeering. I am hoping that, in the editing process, this inflammatory introduction of Otto is omitted from the televised program.

"The image was devastating," Maureen O'Boyle pronounces, "a four-year-old child torn away from the only parents he'd ever known.... America wept through the headlines.... Much of the public is outraged.... The home is shattered again. Many people say...the Kirchners are unstable." On the big screen Danny's stationary picture fades out, replaced by footage of the painful transfer scene wherein Baby Richard is wrenched from his adoptive mother's arms.

O'Boyle, looking grave and deeply concerned, asks Otto about his son. Otto responds that Danny is doing well and he begins to explain the current situation regarding his separation from Daniela. Within the context of the purposely condemnatory introduction and this hostile audience, nothing good can come of this topic. I look out upon a sea of angry, scowling faces. There are more than one hundred people—perhaps as many as two hundred—in the audience, three to five times the number promised by the producer. The bright lights beam down upon us; it is hot and uncomfortable.

Otto attempts to explain his motivations and perspective, but O'Boyle interjects questions and comments that communicate her disdain. "I know you want to blame the media," she says in an accusatory tone, followed by her opinion, "The media simply report the news."

"We invited the Warburtons, but they declined," she adds as a type of rebuttal to Otto's credibility. This invitation of the Warburtons violates another pre-condition of our appearance on this program.

Before Otto has the opportunity to explain the events that led to the unlawful adoption of "Richard," the lies and deception, stalling and manipulations, Maureen O'Boyle introduces her next guests. To my amazement, a series of individuals appear as guests, resulting in **seven** segments about adoption during this one-hour show. Bob and Beth Joice, the unsuccessful adoptive parents of Austin, describe the unfitness of the child's biological father, who won custody of his two-year-old son. An adoptive mother and a birth mother discuss their amicable resolution of a dispute over a bi-racial child, born to the seventeen-year-old who later reclaimed her infant son. Millie, a woman who has unsuccessfully struggled for seven years to adopt two boys whom she has been raising, criticizes the court system and the allegedly drug-addicted birth mother.

Carol Sandusky, adopted at the age of four, discusses the emotional upheaval resulting from her birth parents' appearance after twenty years. Alluding to her conversation with Mrs. Warburton "last night on the telephone," Sandusky is an advocate of "Richard's" adoptive parents; her participation is another violation of the producer's guarantees to Mike Foley. Addressing Otto, she continues, "I don't think you did a real great job of parenting, pal!" The audience loudly applauds and yells approval of her verbal attack on "Richard's" father.

Dr. Jerome Smith, the clinical social worker who served as an independent expert in the Baby Jessica dispute, joins the other guests. He explains his recommendation, which went unheeded by the court, for the DeBoers, Jessica's adoptive parents, to be granted custody of the girl instead of her biological parents.

As a summary to the show's theme, attorney Nancy Ericson emphasizes, "Adoption laws need to change to keep up with the times." She urges a nationwide standard for adoption to replace the state-by-state array of laws with varying requirements and conditions.

As if to prevent the program from fulfilling even one of its promises to us, Maureen O'Boyle, microphone in hand, sashays into the audience to get reactions from some of the more emotionally-aroused individuals.

"I am absolutely appalled at this Otto guy!" spits out a middle-aged redhead, her face distorted by disgust. "I can not imagine you saying that your child was the most important thing and you fought through hell and everything...to get your son back and now the most important thing in your life, and you don't even have him in your custody...," she continues. "He's with the mother who didn't even want him! **What kind of father are you?**" she yells, squinting with rage.

"Wow!" shouts O'Boyle. The audience applauds wildly and hoots its agreement with these expressions of outrage directed at Otto.

Beth Joice, from the second segment of the show, jumps in to criticize Otto. "Where were you...? Why didn't you...?" She is on a roll.

"You **did** remove him ['Richard'] from the stable home he was living in," chimes in O'Boyle, now blatantly joining the direction of the audience's ire and evoking more enthusiastic applause for her assertion.

Answering the questions directed to me about Danny, I assure the audience that he is happy and thriving. I share with them the best summary that Danny himself offered: "During his first week, he told me, 'I like this house; I can eat here; I can play here; I have friends.'"

Shortly before the end of the hour, I begin to assert myself to present the input for which I made the long trek to New York City. "What disturbs me is the allegations that Danny is...emotionally disturbed.... That's why I'm here...."

"We're not talking about that now," O'Boyle abruptly interrupts me. She directs the focus back to the negative theme that is flowing like a river. I am denied the opportunity to refute the pervasive public assertions about Danny's mental and emotional health as a "doomed child."

With only minutes—instead of the promised one hour—allocated to the carrot offer of Otto's first opportunity to tell his story, the "Baby Richard" segment turns into a collage of anti-Kirchner accusations, confrontations, and hostile reactions.

Even television viewers who leave the room for a drink of water or bathroom break are unlikely to miss seeing the gut-wrenching Baby Richard transfer scene. It is shown **three times.** It is more overt and more effective, and yet similar to subliminal advertising—against Otakar Kirchner. Six other stories are incorporated into the program, creating the general theme in favor of adoptive parents and decrying the raw deal that many have suffered. Otto's story after all is just the lead, the grabber, and, as pre-planned by the producers, the best example of an adoption gone wrong. The program exploited him; violated every condition that was promised; and turned an opportunity for vindication into an ambush.

As soon as the taping of this orchestrated attack is over, I rush off the stage, into the dressing room to grab my coat and purse, and head toward the elevator. Otto is not far behind. I feel soiled, used, and foolish. My personal and professional goal—to establish Danny's image as normal and thriving as opposed to "damaged goods"—remains unfulfilled in spite of promises, guarantees, and nine hundred miles of travel to New York City. I have rarely felt this intensely angry during my lifetime and I feel confused as to how to deal with it.

As I fleetingly pass by Maureen O'Boyle, who is grinning and looking self-satisfied, I say to her, "This has been a betrayal. The program has been the **opposite** of everything we were promised."

"Oh?" is her sole response, hand on hip and eyebrows raised as if ingenuously surprised.

"We should have known better than to trust these people," I tell Otto that evening over drinks in the plush hotel bar. Otto, who does not drink alcoholic beverages except for one glass of wine or beer on a rare special occasion, sips a glass of white wine while I down three glasses. Although I am furious, sputtering my words as I struggle to control myself, I realize that Otto, sitting across from me, is calm.

"This is the way it always goes," he says with resolve. "I am used to it. Don't get so upset, Karen," he advises; "there is nothing that we can do."

"It will be a nationally televised show, Otto," I remind him. "They guaranteed certain conditions for us to fly all of the way here and participate as guests, but they violated every one of them. The show had its own agenda and it was directed against you. Although they issued promises, they had no intention of allowing your agenda. We need to talk to Mike Foley as soon as possible. Maybe he can stop the airing of the show. It will surely have the opposite effect from what we hoped for. They made you look like a jerk and a demon, and I feel like a sidekick moron."

As I try to relax in the dimly lit lounge, I am feeling over-whelmed by the pathos in this situation: Otakar Kirchner is so accustomed to betrayal that he is beyond surprise, beyond anger. He is controlled, philosophical, and resigned. He has learned to expect very little from people, especially those with power, cre-dentials, and status…, and he is consistently proven right.

This is a man whose offenses have consisted of loving his son and refusing to give up the struggle to parent him. He is vilified and despised on a nationwide basis. With a reputable, honest, and caring attorney, Mike Foley, this most recent fiasco could not have been predicted. Mike sought and received all of the appro-priate assurances from one of the producers before Otto and I left for New York. Would he be able to avert further damage to his client's reputation by preventing the airing of the show?

Returning to Chicago the next day, Otto and I part ways at the airport. As soon as I walk into my office, I call Mike Foley to inform him of the disaster. He drops his other work to follow up by writing a letter, sent by both fax and mail to Michelle Mazur, producer of *In Person*. The document concludes with the formal revocation of our permission to be included in the final program:

> Since the show has not honored the conditions of their appearance, Mr. Kirchner, Dr. Moriarty, Daniel and Daniela Kirchner hereby revoke permission for the Maureen O'Boyle Show to broadcast, convey, or other-wise use their images, names and words at any time. (Michael J. Foley, Foley & Foley, February 7, 1997)

The program is televised on February 25, 1997. From the edit-ing process, it turns out worse than the live, on-stage experience. I avoid watching it and hope that no one I know will see it. Unfortunately, many people watch the program, and two members of our family, one in Illinois and one in Virginia, decide to videotape the show and send me copies. I feel embarrassed and ashamed; we should have known better. It would take me more than three years to bring myself to watch a videotape of the show.

My clients and family members who watch the show think it is very damaging to Otto's already-sullied image. "Although it was designed to be more like a soufflé, it turned out to be a mud pie," I would offer as a type of explanation to my friends. I don't want to talk about this fiasco, one of the most humiliating and infuriating chapters of my career. I find myself musing over the irony of the only condition that I had set when I began my work on behalf of Danny and his parents—anonymity. Although I successfully avoided contact with the media for months and declined more than a dozen invitations to talk shows, circumstances changed and Otto explicitly urged me—as the only continuous first-hand witness—to provide the media with accurate reports about Danny's progress. *In Person* became the unfortunate exception to my avoidance of talk show participation. The producers had guaranteed us an exclusive opportunity, but they provided a public flogging.

Mike Foley would explain that our experience with talk shows is not unique. Many of them are characterized by false promises that lure guests to participate and then, during the taping, spring upon them formats, conditions, and questions that surprise, embarrass, and humiliate. The Participant Agreement of this program included a surprise clause, which— to no avail—I insisted be stricken.

"For your fifteen minutes of fame, never spend them on a talk show!" I laughingly advise my sister Jo after I have recovered from the experience sufficiently to discuss it.

Mike's attempts to abort the program on behalf of the Kirchners and me were predictably unsuccessful. He would have had to travel to New York to file a petition with a court of competent jurisdiction to forestall or prevent the program from being televised. The necessary time, expense, and uncertainty of the outcome served to discourage legal action in the matter. Otto and Daniela could not afford to pay legal fees and travel-related expenses. Another media-created nightmare was added to the library of anti-Kirchner publicity.

Otto will continue to look for a job through the winter, spring, and summer months of 1997. As before, he will experience difficulty even getting an interview once he provides his name. Robert suggests that he consider changing his name, and I recommend that he reconsider moving to another state, preferably Florida.

"I have broken no law, told no lies, and done nothing evil to run away from," Otto appropriately reminds us. He won a highly visible custody case and complied with the Supreme Court ruling. He is proud of his surname, his father's name, and he has no intention of changing it. He will persist in seeking a job; he is honest and willing to work hard. He is now an American citizen; has a family to support; and will find a way.

This combination of perseverance and steadfast commitment—unswerving in spite of his long-standing pattern as the victim of betrayal by the powerful and the ill intentioned—has served to win him both his son and his pride.

Robert and I respect his decision...and we admire him.

CHAPTER THIRTEEN

The Separation

This is Chicago, Kid. You can't beat fresh blood on the walls.

— Richard Gere/Billy Flint
The movie Chicago

"'BABY RICHARD'S' FATHER LEAVES HOME," the headline of *USA Today* announces the breaking news on January 21, 1997. I am walking by an airport newsstand, while Robert is guarding our luggage, on our way home from a long weekend in Ormond-by-the-Sea, Florida. Glancing at the front-page blurb, I stop in my tracks, grab a copy of the newspaper, and hastily read the article. During my brief absence from Chicago, the "scandal-loving Windy City," the news about Otto and Daniela's separation has made headlines around the country and received coverage on both national and local television channels.

"I'm **gone**!" a voice in my head shouts. I don't know if I can bear to witness any more of this media bashing and especially the pain and upheaval that it causes Otto, Daniela, and Danny. I need to move away and to talk them into moving also. They need a new start in another place, where they have a chance to become anonymous.

"The article doesn't even mention that Otto continues to see his son," I tell Robert. "It sounds as if he has abandoned the son he worked so hard to claim. I can't believe this!"

The *USA Today* article, by Debbie Howlett, begins:

Two years after the courts awarded custody of the child
known as "Baby Richard" to his biological father, the father
has moved out of the family home and left his son behind.

The father, Otakar Kirchner, is living in a motel room registered to a woman he worked with at a local restaurant....

It continues:

"Baby Richard"...was taken sobbing from the Warburtons
in April 1995 as supporters of the Warburtons taunted
Kirchner with cries of "monster!"....

...[A] former family lawyer, Richard Lifshitz, said
Kirchner's actions are outrageous...."

Opening the newspaper that I brought that same day from
Florida, *The Daytona Beach News-Journal*, I find the article,
"Father walks out on Baby Richard." Again, there is no mention
that the father is continuing frequent contact with his son; it
reads like an abandonment.

For Bob Greene it is yet another welcome opportunity to
attack Otto in a cluster of *Tribune*—and syndicated—columns.
"Biological father departs, leaves Richard behind" ends with the
lament, "...[T]his may have ominous consequences for that little
boy" (January 19, 1997). The next day, his article, "Another
assurance—'The child stays with me'—broken," attacks
Richard's living with his mother: "[H]e did not ask to be born, he
did not ask for any of this to happen" (January 20, 1997). The
next day, in "Now's the time to give Richard what is due him,"
Greene virtually moans:

You would think that the courts of Illinois would feel
some sense of obligation to him [Richard]—some sense
of, to use a word that applies to the heart instead of the
head, devotion. Devotion is owed that child.... [N]ow,
after what has happened as a result of the Illinois

Supreme Court's decision to dissolve the [adoptive] family, the boy appears in danger of being in limbo. Devotion is owed him—in all of our names.

...A child is powerless.... (January 21, 1997)

Feeling a bottomless sadness, intermingled with anger and an overwhelming sense of helplessness, I telephone Mike Foley as soon as I arrive back at my home. He is working on a press release on behalf of Otto and Daniela. Mike faxes me a copy, which communicates Otto's reaction:

PLEASE LET US LIVE OUR LIVES

Yesterday, I was saddened to see that Bob Greene and the Chicago Tribune had once again invaded the lives of my family. Although I do not consider myself a public figure beyond the confines of my son's case, the Tribune has apparently decided that my privacy, the privacy of my wife, and of my children need not be respected. Because I cannot cancel what Greene and the Tribune have done, it is necessary for me to respond and set the record straight.

My wife and I have separated after many years together. The separation is amicable and we are cooperating in raising our children. I visit the family frequently and for extended periods of time....

....We ask for your prayers. To the media, we ask that you respect our family's privacy, so that we can work through our problems. (January 22, 1997)

There is widespread speculation, reported by the media, that the Warburtons will attempt to capitalize on this situation by renewing their efforts to obtain custody of Danny. In general, the theme in the media's coverage is the desirability of Baby Richard being returned to the adoptive parents—even after having lived nearly two years with his birth parents.

Eric Zorn writes a column in the *Chicago Tribune*, entitled "'Baby Richard' story now has sadly familiar ring," in which he proclaims:

> Voices of sympathy and outrage were loud this week— Look at what this man [Otakar Kirchner] has done!....
>
> If you are heartbroken at this boy's current circumstances, good. You should be. For now he is a symbol not of his own extraordinary and Byzantine plight, but of all the ordinary kids everywhere beset by the ordinary failures of the adults who love them—a genuine and ongoing tragedy. (January 23, 1997)

How many married people who separate—whether they are celebrities or private, anonymous individuals—are victimized by this kind of vitriolic attack by the media and the public? A significant number of the journalists who cover this story are separated or divorced parents. Yet everyone seems to be casting stones at Otto Kirchner, and no one knows the circumstances that led to this separation. It should be a private event, as it is for millions of Americans who opt for a trial separation from their spouses. If it is not private, if the media converge to get a story, then there should be equitable, balanced reporting. Although it is really nobody's business, and a detail undisclosed to the press, it was Daniela who initiated the separation by asking Otto to move out of the family home. Yet he bears the brunt of the attribution of guilt in this titillating matter. At the least, in their reporting the media should clarify that the father has not abandoned his son; that he spends many hours every week with both of his children; and that the problem is a marital one between the two adults.

Half of American marriages end in divorce. In 1997, does the media condemn the separating or divorcing individuals? As usual, however, there are neither rules nor perspective when it comes to Baby Richard coverage—not even rules of good taste, fairness, or objective, impartial journalism.

With a spurt of rationality, combined with anomalous support for the child and his mother, the *Chicago Sun-Times* editorial takes a position expressed in its title, "For once in his life, let Danny be Danny":

...Now Kirchner has moved out of the family home, once again giving rise to public debates over Danny's best interests.... Through it all, Baby Richard has grown into Danny Kirchner, a beautiful kindergartner who is the spitting image of his mother.... He doesn't need more lawsuits or speculation about whether his adoptive parents should try to regain custody. Enough is enough. Leave the boy with his mother. (January 23, 1997)

Expressing my concern about his welfare, I talk to Otto on the phone. I have known for weeks about the Kirchners' separation, but the media have broken the news in a way to coincide with reports of Judge James Heiple's traffic violation and alleged attempt to avoid receiving a traffic citation. Although disclosure of the Kirchners' separation is not timely, it is dramatic. We would never come to know whether a segment of the media—or a behind-the-scenes instigator—timed the latest Baby Richard "crisis" with Heiple's plight for political reasons, or whether it actually took **four months** for any reporter to discover that Otto and Daniela Kirchner had separated.

"I'm being followed again," Otto relates in our conversation. "There are several people, probably private investigators, trying to find out details about my private life. I'm doing my best to avoid them. I won't stop visiting my kids, though. I try to lose them before I get anywhere close to the house."

When I visit Daniela, Grandma, Danny, and Sharon, I feel comforted by the immediate sense of normalcy within the house. It is "business as usual" for the two women, who happily share their child care responsibilities. They welcome Otto to the home on a regular basis so that he can maintain and foster his relationships with the children, both of whom look forward to his visits.

"I don't pay attention to what the newspapers and television are saying about us," Daniela affirms. "I just avoid seeing it at all. My mother and I spend all of our time and attention on Danny and Cicka."

Knowing that Greta, as a novice in learning to speak English, does not read the language, I realize that there is a natural, shared commitment between the women to ignore the incursions into their family's private lives by the media. Greta and Daniela purposefully and successfully avoid all exposure to the publicity. They have opted for self-protection through avoidance and a healthy version of denial.

They are strongly bonded to each other, as friends in addition to being mother and daughter, and Greta has become totally absorbed in her activities of caring for the children and the house. As the intimate friend of the family, who has lived through many bad times and fewer good times with them, I understand the dynamics of Greta's presence within this family unit. It is a mixed blessing in that her assertiveness and control benefit and influence the family in many observable ways, and yet it is a curse to Otto and Daniela's marriage. Greta has assumed the role and duties that Otto had held with his new and growing family. Daniela, still nursing Cicka while working full-time, welcomes her mother's help and advice. Danny continues to receive constant attention as the beloved older child, never taken for granted after the gruesome conflict that was required to reclaim him.

All three of the adults—Otto, Daniela, and Greta—are well intentioned and loving, but as a family trio they repeatedly get in each other's way, especially Otto and his mother-in-law. He is not ungrateful; he simply feels unneeded.

Before long, I decide, I will broach the subject once again of their possible relocation to Florida. Perhaps they will decide to reconcile, move with the children to another state, and begin a new life in a neutral environment. Robert and I, now planning to leave Illinois once our home is sold, hope that they will choose to live near us so that we can help them and continue to see them as often as we have come to expect.

During January, the news breaks about the complaint filed against Loren Heinemann by the Attorney Registration and Disciplinary Commission in Chicago for repeatedly failing properly to respond to malpractice charges. Judge Heiple, well recognized as the author of the unpopular Illinois Supreme Court decision that found in favor of Otakar Kirchner, finds himself embroiled in escalating controversy that threatens his position as Chief Justice. His January 1996 traffic violation, turned into a media blitz during January 1997, gives rise to a series of events that grow in intensity and public attention. Over weeks, the furor would grow to the point of creating a statewide legislative movement toward impeachment proceedings. Governor Edgar, also in January 1997, interrupts his "State of the State" address to register his hopes that the judiciary will correct the "Baby Richard tragedy." He wants the child returned to the adoptive parents.

When the Cypress Restaurant closed down on New Year's Eve, Otto was left once again not only without a job, through no fault of his own, but with no prospects for another. Both of Kenessey's restaurants have now gone out of business—the one on the near-north side of Chicago in 1994 and this one in Hinsdale at the end of 1996. No one would ever know to what extent Otto Kirchner's visible presence in each establishment contributed to its demise. When he began employment at each restaurant, it was brimming with regular customers and requiring waiting lines for service. Threats of boycotting and picketing of the Hinsdale Cypress were commonplace during Otto's employment there; even a Catholic nun vociferously led a movement to get Otto fired. Ivan Kenessey twice demonstrated his faith in Otakar, based upon first-hand knowledge of the man's integrity and work ethic, but he has lost both of his restaurants within three years. Who will take a risk by employing Otto now? I wonder.

Unfortunately, the timing of these new developments—Heinemann's and Heiple's—coincides with the resurrected media spotlight on the Kirchners' separation. Otto is again described as out-of-work, an unemployed loser. Danny is living with his mother, a suspicious parent at best, according to media portrayals. Daniela is continually referenced as "the woman who did not want her child."

My clients—like everyone else I encounter—discuss the pros and cons of these various events. Radio talk shows focus on these most recent issues, invariably intertwined, and recreating Baby Richard hysteria. They are emotionally loaded topics. Judge Heiple is blamed for a "bad," "awful" Supreme Court decision in the case. Daniela is blamed for the well-intentioned but disastrous mistake she made in 1991, six years ago, as if these subsequent years have not provided ample evidence of her redemptive behavior and exemplary parenting. Otto is blamed for nearly everything, including the decayed state of marriage in America today.

"Opinion is ultimately determined by the feelings, and not by the intellect," observed Herbert Spencer during another century. Applicable today, this truism is reflected by individuals everywhere who react strongly and relate these media-shaped events to their own circumstances.

"They should give that boy to his adoptive family in Schaumburg," Gloria S., a middle-aged client and mother of four, insists to me. "If he were my son, I know he would want to go back there. That adoptive mother is like me," she continues, lapsing into a recitation of the perceived similarities between Mrs. Warburton and herself. "That birth mother is too pretty to be a good mother; she is a femme fatale type and probably cares more about her hair style than she does about that poor little boy."

I am beginning to think that I would rather be a bagger at the local grocery store than a practicing psychologist. Each day is becoming more difficult than the one before.

When I speak to Otto in February, he informs me that he is still being followed regularly by unidentified individuals. Mike Foley confirms that there are surveillance activities on his client. Afraid to lead strangers to his family home, Otto continues to visit his children often but he is taking labyrinthine routes.

In various conversations with each of them, I encourage Otto and Daniela to move to Florida, a potentially warmer climate for them in more ways than one. Robert and I are planning the necessary details of a permanent move for ourselves. Robert fully supports the idea of our relocation—he is also disillusioned and tired of Baby Richard mania—and we meet with our financial adviser three times to discuss our options.

When I spend time with Otto at a suburban restaurant, I learn that a variety of reporters and strangers have been snooping around the motel where he is staying. Because he is residing in a public facility, he has even less privacy than before. While Otto was living in his Richton Park home, his privacy was compromised by passersby on the street or sidewalk, but the patch of front lawn, as private property, served as a buffer to direct intrusion. Now, strangers are able to perch just outside the front door of his room at the motel. He has no recourse to prevent it.

He has begun another job search, but his prospects—especially within this generalized climate of hostility directed at him—appear dim. Daniela continues to work full-time, paying the household bills to the best of her ability, while the children's grandmother takes care of them during their mother's work hours. When Otto visits three or four days per week, the women defer to him so that he can enjoy his interactions with Danny and Sharon. Ironically, his access to them has improved because of the clarity of the separation and his visitor status. Daniela and he generally avoid each other as much as possible; they both appear to need this time apart.

The emotional atmosphere within the house is similar to the pre-separation months except for newly decreased tension between the parents. Enid has volunteered her help to Daniela and Greta. She has superceded her neighbor status and become a genuine friend. Daniela's initial reluctance to trust anyone has faded across the months, as both Enid and Peder have given of themselves in a variety of ways to assist the sometimes frustrated grandmother and the struggling Daniela.

"Although I was pressured by some of the neighbors to shun the Kirchners, I chose to ignore them," Enid would explain to me. "I have really pulled back from many of my other neighbors. In fact, before the Kirchners moved in, my husband and I were good friends with Loren and Stacy Heinemann, but no more.

"I'm very proud of Daniela and the way she has dealt with everything," Enid relates. "It was hard on her after Otto left. She is a really strong woman. If I had her troubles, I wouldn't handle them very well," Enid discloses as she recalls those months of her intensified involvement with the family.

Robert and I slide into a state of disengagement from the Chicago area before we fully realize it. I no longer read the newspapers and generally avoid watching television news programs. We travel to Florida every six to seven weeks, and by mid-April we put our house, once our dream home, on the market for sale. Real estate is selling slowly in our quasi-rural community, especially because sewers and city water will soon replace the septic systems and private wells, at the assessment cost of $25,000 – 30,000 per household. Home buyers are unsurprisingly discouraged upon hearing about this imminent encumbrance, and most of them opt to look for houses in other neighborhoods, where sewers and water have been long-established amenities.

Expecting a prolonged period of waiting for our home to be sold, we connect with Ellen Nash, a realtor in Palm Coast, Florida, who shows us dozens of houses in the area. During June we find a like-new, two-story home on a saltwater canal; it has soaring ceilings and room in the backyard for a swimming pool. We execute a contract on it, contingent upon the sale of our Palos Park house. Because its owners are expecting their second child during the fall season, they are happy to wait for eight or nine months before the closing process and moving out.

Although I am focusing upon our prospective move, I continue providing services for my ongoing clients. My caseload is generally light, and much of my time is spent preparing for a long-distance move. We donate hundreds of books to our local library; dispose of boxes of college papers and old personal records; and haul a significant portion of our winter clothes, as contributions to a worthy cause, to GoodWill Industries. Family members and friends, including the Kirchners, stroll through our house, laying claim to certain pieces of furniture that they will use after we move away. Robert and I are taking less than half of our belongings from our thirteen-room house to Palm Coast. We are downsizing to a three-bedroom stucco house with limited storage and only one-half of the living space of our current home.

"We are **right**-sizing, like a lot of major companies nowadays," I jokingly tell Robert, as we begin to pack our accumulated assortment of cardboard boxes. "It's occurred to me that our new Florida **house** has the same square footage as our **driveway** at this house."

"We will have fewer things to worry about and to take care of," Robert philosophizes, adopting the most positive viewpoint toward our imminent changes.

When I accelerate my encouragement of Otto and Daniela to join us in our long-distance geographical move, each of them expresses strong reluctance. Neither one will move any significant distance from the two children, of course, and—with their marriage on shaky ground—they are unwilling to move as a family. Daniela is comfortable in knowing that she can support the household with her income and gratuities from the upscale salon at which she has worked for the past two years. She is afraid that she will not be able to approximate her current level of compensation in another state. Otto chooses to remain optimistic about his prospects for employment within the Chicagoland area. He is willing to commute a long distance, if necessary, and he has demonstrated that he is a loyal and dedicated employee. He has resigned himself to a job as a waiter, having abandoned hopes of obtaining a high-paying management position like the one he held when he first met and hired Daniela at the first Kenessey's restaurant.

Robert and I are disappointed to accept the reality that the Kirchner family will not be moving with us to Florida. They will come to vacation with us, however, and we will return to Chicago often to visit them and other members of our families, including our grandchildren [whose number will joyfully increase from four in 1998 to nine in 2003].

Having been a chronic workaholic, I frequently wonder how I will adjust to an early retirement—long before I am age-eligible—in a new state and a new neighborhood. My work with clients has been fulfilling. From the telephone call on New Year's Eve from an attempted suicide, saved by an ambulance ride to the hospital for emergency treatment, to the recovered obsessive-compulsive client, able to resume work after two years of unemployment and intensive psychotherapy, I find satisfaction in helping people in meaningful ways. I care about every one of my clients; worry about them during my leisure hours; and struggle to maintain professional objectivity and emotional detachment. With my own small agency and no one to pressure me into focusing on the economic bottom line, I often function like an old-fashioned social worker. I have often donated my services, such as by maintaining regular contact with school personnel for troubled adolescents or by accompanying a child on supervised visits to the home of his mother. When marital therapy succeeded and the troubled couple decided to stay together, I rejoiced. When an anguished father resumed his relationship with his alienated child, I shared his relief and happily accepted his gratitude. I have perceived my role as the advocate of my clients; the office phone forwards to my home, and I personally receive their calls at all hours; and I also routinely accept and return their calls when I am away on vacation.

What would I do without a job? I have been employed continuously for three decades, most of those years holding two jobs or working by day and attending graduate school by night.

A forty-hour workweek has been a rarity for me until recent months, when it became an involuntary, unwelcome development. I became accustomed to fifty and sixty-hour workweeks early in my career. How will I adjust to a life of leisure?

Through subsequent weeks, Otto and I often discuss Judge Heiple's plight, the disturbing repercussions from his identification as the "Baby Richard judge." We hear rumors about Loren Heinemann's problems; his license to practice law is in jeopardy; many of his clients have filed formal complaints against him. In separate conversations, Daniela and I discuss these issues. Neither Otto nor Daniela has spoken to Loren or Stacy for several months. The neighborhood is divided. Their only real friends are Enid and Peder Shortell.

Daniela's increasing worries about her marriage are exacerbated by the ever present, gnawing realization that she abdicated her legal rights to her only son. She telephones Bruce Boyer, who refers her to Susan Haddad, a seasoned attorney who is likely to accept Daniela's case to seek restoration of her parental rights to Danny. Otto readily supports Daniela's decision. As their son's sole custodial parent, Otto has been concerned about Danny's status in the event that something should happen to him. If he were to become incapacitated or to die, Daniela would have no legal claim to her son. Would the Warburtons resurrect their claim to Danny?

By Easter Greta returns to her family in Slovakia. She has been a part of her daughter's family for one turbulent year. Greta's husband has missed her and he joyfully welcomes her home.

After lunch, Danny puts his plate in the kitchen sink, during the week of his sixth birthday in March 1997.

What do you call a mother who has given birth to a child; who has been raising that child for two years; who is married to the biological father and custodial parent of the child; and yet who has no legal rights as a parent to her child?

Answer: Daniela Kirchner.

Daniela finds herself in a situation that is conducive to a clever, challenging, and cruel riddle. And yet it is too true...and worrisome.

Having signed away her parental rights to Danny when he was four days old and she was

Daniela's Fight for Legal Rights to Danny

Who is a mother and yet not a mother?

— Riddle

alone, desperate, and malleable, Daniela discovered almost immediately that she had made the biggest mistake of her life. The Warburtons had left with her child, with Otakar Kirchner's child, and had changed their phone and beeper numbers and disappeared from her life. Any hope of maintaining contact with her son vanished, and she realized the enormity of her decision to give him up for adoption.

She didn't even understand adoption in this country. In Daniela's experience in her native land of Czechoslovakia, adoption was rare; relatives typically assumed the responsibility for rearing a child in need; and it was accomplished without legal sanction. By contrast, laws governing adoption in Illinois, her state of residence, provided for irrevocable decisions by mothers after 72 hours of their child's birth. A biological father was required to assert his claim to his child within thirty days of birth, after which passage of time an adoption of the child is allowed to proceed under the assumption that the father is disinterested or "unfit."

When Daniela reconciled with Otakar Kirchner, Danny was less than two months old. Upon learning from her that his baby was alive and living with a couple in Schaumburg, Illinois, Otto was overjoyed. Immediately he sought an attorney to pursue the recovery of his son. Daniela joined forces with him, not as a plaintiff in the lawsuit but as his moral support and ally.

"I knew I made a mistake right away," she would tell me years later when we discussed the turbulent period during which she signed away her son. "I had no counseling; no friend or family nearby; no lawyer; I felt so alone. I was just learning English; I had no money and no medical insurance. I only wanted what was best for my child. Teachers at the beauty school told me I would be doing the right thing to let the Warburtons raise him."

Daniela longed to have her baby back; to be able to raise him; and to create a family. She and Otto married on September 12, 1995, six months after Danny's birth, and the central focus of their union became the fight to regain their child. Paradoxically, the experience fused their commitment to each other and strengthened their bond in what became an all-consuming shared goal, and yet it created ever-present daily tensions, comprised of anxiety, worry, pain, and sometimes despair. Some days during the protracted court process Otto would feel optimistic over his prospect of winning custody of his son, while Daniela would be overcome by regret and hopelessness. Other days their feelings would switch, and they tried—but not always successfully—to buoy up each other. As anyone who has been in a similar situation can attest, it was the **not knowing** that was the worst part for them across the weeks that turned into months that turned into years. Would they ever see their son? Would they ever become eligible to raise him? Would the court award custody to Otto, his father, who had always wanted him from the moment of his conception? Would he then become her son once again? They wondered and they worried on a daily basis. Sometimes they wept together.

When the Illinois Supreme Court first ruled on behalf of Otakar Kirchner in July 1994 and again in January 1995—denying a rehearing of their unanimous earlier decision—Daniela, through her marriage, received a second chance with her son, then four years old. It was an opportunity for redemption, for undoing, for making up for lost time, and very simply, for unspeakable joy.

Although I saw her or spoke with her nearly every day for months, Daniela did not talk about her happiness in having regained her son. She did not need to—her joy was ever apparent in her face and in her tireless behaviors in caring for Danny during the hours that she was not at her full-time job. In European fashion, she chose to sleep with him in his king-size bed for months so that she would be available if he awoke during the night, a rare occurrence. When home, she interacted with him; played with him; and taught him numbers, shapes, letters of the alphabet, and other age-appropriate lessons.

My favorite recollection involves her frequently donning an adult-size, pink Power Rangers costume to play with Danny, who wore his own costume often, at the four-year-old's level. They would run around, laugh, hide from each other, tickle, and sometimes roll around on the floor. She became a child with him, and Danny beamed and bonded and blossomed.

Even though Otto was Danny's primary caretaker, while Daniela worked and commuted for fifty hours each week, the child connected with his mother in a special, immediate way. From their first hour together in Loren Heinemann's borrowed van, through the first honeymoon-type days between parents and child, and on through subsequent weeks, Danny's bond with his mother was apparent. He spontaneously began to call her "mom" on his third day in his new home. He sought physical contact and affection with her from the first day, when, sitting on her lap in Heinemann's van, he snuggled with his birth mother for the first time. Later that day, she and Otto pointed out to him the striking physical similarities between mother and son.

"Look at how much we look alike," Daniela told Danny during his first evening in his parents' home. "We have the same hair, same mouth, same smile." She held in front of him her favorite photograph, taken when she was nine months pregnant, and pointed to her stomach. "This is you."

Danny stared at that picture; then looked up into his mother's eyes; and he understood. From that point in time, everything would seem different to Danny. This was indeed his mother. This man with her, the man who had fought for him and had come to claim him, was his father.

By spring 1997, Daniela decides that she must restore her parental rights to her son. The startling and troubling reality is that she has **no** legal rights to her child. What if Otto should die? What would happen to Danny? What if she should die? Because she has become the primary breadwinner of the family, her death would be devastating for the child in many ways, including financially. Would he qualify for her Social Security death benefits? What if she and Otto should divorce? They have been separated for several months and divorce is a realistic possibility. Otto not only has sole custody of Danny—granted by the highest court of the state—but Daniela signed away her parental rights to her son more than six years ago. Would she ever become eligible for custody? Would she qualify for visitation rights with her son in the event of a divorce or legal separation from his father?

During this anxiety-filled time, neither Otto nor Daniela is willing even to think about the prospect of limited access to their son, of reduced time with him, of diminished parenting opportunities. For both of them, Danny, now six, and Sharon, his one-year-old sister, are the focus of their lives. In spite of marital problems with each other, Otto and Daniela readily and heartily concede that the other parent is loving, consistently devoted, and totally committed to their children.

What happened to them? I ask myself. As their therapist and now their friend, I understand, but it is nonetheless painful and disappointing. They have been through so much together. Now they are apart...except for their mutual unswerving, steadfast dedication to Danny and Sharon.

On the stress scale, Otto and Daniela would easily win the highest score among my clients and my acquaintanceship.

Within **two years**, they have experienced multiple and profound changes and challenges. They have suffered a miscarriage and have had two children—a four-year-old who came suddenly and yet through an agonizing battle, and a baby, now one year old. They have lost not only the little money they had worked hard to accumulate but also their good credit rating. They have moved their residence from a hostile, glass-bowl setting into an ambiguous one; have lost their friends; have undergone two bouts of long-term unemployment for Otto, interrupted by a short-lived job; and have absorbed a mother-in-law into their household. Otto's health has deteriorated, and without medical insurance, they both fear serious illness in their family. They have suffered through a dreadful, protracted, and highly public litigation process; have inadvertently galvanized the state legislature against them; have discovered that their enemies include powerful individuals in all three branches of state government; and have become the targets of frequent, non-stop attacks in the press. This last factor alone—continuous media viciousness—accounts for an unbearable level of marital stress. They are the victims of media-fostered public outrage and a resultant barrage of hate mail, which includes death threats and other warnings of violence and vengeance. What other couple is compelled to deal with this unique phenomenon? I know of none. And, they have been powerless to prevent it...or to stop it.

How many couples could withstand these unique challenges and hardships? I wonder. Yet, they have borne it all with shared determination to protect and nurture their children and with basic civility toward each other, even in the worst of times.

Daniela is at a crossroad. Several months into her separation from Otto, she telephones Bruce Boyer. Daniela knows Bruce from his having initiated and authored the *amicus* brief at the Illinois Supreme Court level in support of Otto's parental claim to his son. He had publicly championed the Kirchners' side of the custody fight. Boyer refers her to Susan Haddad, a mature, experienced attorney who might accept Daniela's case.

Following up on Boyer's recommendation, Daniela contacts Ms. Haddad, who agrees to advance her cause. Just as Daniela, as a non-plaintiff ally, had joined Otto in his legal fight for custody of their son, Otto joins her in seeking the restoration of her rights to Danny as his mother. There is a second, related compelling issue for legal representation by Haddad. Otto and Daniela have never gotten a birth certificate for Danny. Across months, attorney Loren Heinemann had attempted to obtain one, to no avail. Danny's kindergarten, a public school program, had accepted him on the basis of his unique circumstances. Otto and Daniela explained to the school principal their inability to produce the required birth certificate. Already aware of their situation from the prolific media coverage, the principal agreed to enroll Danny in the kindergarten class when the school year began in late summer of 1996. Absent the flexibility and compassion of this school official, however, Danny would have been barred from attending public school without the requisite birth certificate.

"We have two options," Susan explains to Daniela during their first meeting. "You can adopt Danny or you can file a petition to restore your parental rights to him. With adoption, there will probably be a home assessment, a court-appointed guardian for the child, and a judicial inquiry into his best interests. Restoring your parental rights will mean voiding your 1991 consent to the child's adoption. We could proceed with either alternative."

After deliberation and further discussion, Daniela and Haddad, with Otto's support and concurrence, decide for the second option. It is too risky, within the context of the political climate against the Kirchners, to proceed with a petition for adoption. This option would open the gates to renewed, biased scrutiny of the Kirchners' perceived fitness to parent their son. An impartial, fair, and non-political review of their situation would be nearly impossible. The highest placed officials in state agencies, including Patrick Murphy of the Office of the Public Guardian, who inserted himself into the case early on, have been active and vocal supporters of the Warburtons. The former adoptive parents are likely to resume their legal maneuvers if Daniela seeks to adopt her own son.

"The birth certificate should be an easy matter," Ms. Haddad tells Daniela. "Otto should have received it long ago, immediately after the Supreme Court ruling when he won custody of Danny. It's just a simple administrative act to issue it. I will apply for it in the Office of Vital Statistics."

To Haddad's surprise, her request for the birth certificate, on behalf of her client, is rejected. "It should have been an everyday type of routine matter," Susan would explain to me years later. "When they saw my client's name, they told me that I would need a court order to get a birth certificate for the child. The file was flagged as a special case. It was a politically motivated decision." Haddad experiences her first legal roadblock.

Still unaware of the extent of her clients' dangerous and precarious environment, Susan proceeds by filing a Petition to Establish Parent/Child Relationship in the Circuit Court of Cook County on behalf of Daniela Kirchner. The primary goal is for Daniela to establish a legal mother-child relationship with her son Danny by voiding the "irrevocable consent" that she had signed in 1991 for his adoption by the Warburtons. Because the Supreme Court invalidated the adoption, Daniela's consent to it should be likewise voided, Haddad reasons. Otto, as Danny's father and custodial parent, has signed a petition seeking to have Daniela's adoption consent voided and requesting the issuance of a new birth certificate, naming both Kirchners as his parents.

"If anything happens to me, this whole case could be reopened," Otto explains to reporters, who appear again in full force after the news about Daniela's petition is leaked to the press. Baby Richard is once again front-page headlines and lead television news.

Swiftly the Warburtons' attorneys file a petition with the court on their behalf, arguing that Daniela "intentionally inflicted severe emotional harm" on them by allowing Danny's adoption and then trying to undo it. They request the court to appoint a guardian for the child; to conduct a best interests hearing; to approve scheduled visitation between them and the child; and, "if appropriate, [to grant] a transfer of the child's custody to them." Having been denied a best interests hearing by the Illinois Supreme Court, the Warburtons are attempting, two and one-half years later, to obtain a more favorable ruling from the lower court!

"The pain they [Warburtons] have suffered can never be erased, but its ongoing impact may be alleviated in some small measure by providing them with court-ordered routine visits...or in awarding them custody," attorney Jerold Solovy writes in their petition. Some observers among the legal community express their surprise because the state's Supreme Court has ruled that the Warburtons have no legal standing to Daniel

Kirchner, and yet they are choosing actively to engage in this litigation as if they maintain a legal relationship with the child.

Attorney General James Ryan files a petition asking the
court to deny Daniela's request to void her adoption consent.

The Illinois Department of Children and Family Services, after
being contacted by the Warburtons, decides to enter the case to
oppose the Kirchners' request. DCFS Director Jess McDonald is
quoted as saying, "Our concern was obviously for other adoptions....
The Baby Richard case created a real anxiety for families that had
adopted or were considering adoptions." The agency officials fear a
"chilling effect" on all adoptions if Daniela is allowed to revoke her
adoption consent. (Mark Brown & Adrienne Drell, "Baby Richard
battle back in court," *Chicago Sun-Times*, July 17, 1997)

As I read the newspapers, I am baffled as to why DCFS and
politicians who have sought to take a public stand in this matter fail to point out that Daniela's case is genuinely unique. Hers
is a one-of-a-kind case, unlikely to be replicated by others.
Because the state's highest court invalidated the Warburtons'
adoption of Danny, a number of legal experts opine that the
birth mother's consent for that adoption should be correspondingly voided. Daniela is not only the birth mother but she is
married to the biological father, who is also the court-ordered
custodial parent of the child. How likely is this situation to be
repeated? The Illinois Supreme Court, in its written decision,
had clarified that adoptive parents who do not use deceit and
subterfuge to adopt a child have nothing to fear. Yet, the quoted
public officials sound the alarm for all adoptive parents and the
potentially precarious state of their adoptions. Unsurprisingly,
adoptive parents' advocacy groups are roused into aggressive,
vocal protest: Daniela Kirchner must be stopped!

Bob Greene enthusiastically jumps onto the issue once
again. In his July 27th column, "After 819 days, Richard gets his
chance Monday," he writes:

> Since the day Richard was put into that van—since the day
> he and his adopted brother were promised...that they could
> be a part of each other's lives—819 days have passed....
>
> This state [of Illinois] owes those children something.
> Even prisoners are permitted to see and speak with

loved ones. What has been done to those boys in the name of the people of Illinois is one of the cruelest acts a branch of government can commit against the most helpless and voiceless of its citizens. And—obscenely—it was done by a court of law....

Now a court of law has been given the unexpected opportunity to help those boys.... Judge Gay-Lloyd Lott has been assigned the case.... Richard and his brother may finally begin to get their day in Court before a judge who is willing to listen. The case will be heard at 9:30 a.m. Monday in Judge Lott's courtroom on the 14th floor of 32 W. Randolph St. (*Chicago Tribune*)

Before publishing this most recent, impassioned portrayal, Greene never bothered to inquire whether Danny even remembers his former adoptive brother!

However, responding to Greene's exhortations, the public and media representatives pour into the courtroom the next morning. It is standing room only. "By the time I entered, all of the seats were taken," Haddad would tell me later. "It was almost a lynching, and everything that took place was so mean-spirited."

Frightened at the prospect of a reopened court battle, along with another round of media and public hysteria, Daniela and her attorney formally request to withdraw her petition. Daniela chooses to retreat rather than to fight this new battle. She had hoped for a simple, straightforward response by the court, and she expected, if not media disinterest, at least a mild, unintimidating reaction. In startling contrast to her expectations, a variety of state officials have initiated involvement by taking a public stand and by filing petitions with the court. And, Bob Greene—alleging the court's having separated Danny and "his brother" as "one of the cruelest acts a branch of government can commit"—used the *Tribune's* Sunday paper to fill the courtroom with Warburton supporters, media representatives, and members of an agitated public.

Judge Gay-Lloyd Lott, playing to an overflowing courtroom and rolling cameras, refuses Daniela's request to withdraw her petition, an action that many legal experts label "unprecedented." In this type of civil case, the plaintiff has the absolute right to withdraw a petition, under state law.

"I think that when you put this case back in court, you put everything back on the table," announces Judge Lott in a resounding voice to a pleased audience. He orders the Cook County Department of Supportive Services to visit the Kirchners' home, to conduct an immediate evaluation of the child's home life, and to report back to him in court by Friday, four days away. The prospect of the lower court's reopening the custody issue, settled by the state's highest court, astounds many observers, especially those who are engaged in the practice of law.

Bruce Boyer courageously declares, "There is absolutely no legal authority whatsoever to support what Judge Lott did.... This is a private matter between [his] parents. The court has no business using Daniela's request as a basis of exposing this child and his family to a contentious hearing that cannot possibly be in this boy's interest, no matter the outcome."

Under the Illinois Adoption Act, biological parents cannot revoke consent for an adoption unless they can prove that they issued their consent under duress or were coerced into surrendering their child. That argument must be made within twelve months of the adoption. However, Daniela's case is one of a kind, as explained in the *Chicago Tribune's* front-page coverage:

> ....[S]ome legal experts say that because the adoption [of Baby Richard] was invalidated, a court could rule that her [Daniela's] consent for adoption also was invalidated.

> But legal experts noted that there has never been a case that matches the facts of this one, and it's hard to know what the courts would do. (Robert Becker & Janan Hanna, "Ruling might reopen legal door on 'Richard'," July 29, 1997)

Two of the Warburtons' attorneys, Robert Byman and Laura Kaster, praise Lott's ruling as an enormous victory, adding that an official review of the child's circumstances is long overdue. Susan Haddad protests the judge's ruling, labeling his refusal to permit a plaintiff to withdraw a civil action "stunning."

Bruce Boyer leaps into an advocacy role once again, appropriately directing the case to the Illinois Supreme Court. In the most forceful and critical statement that he has issued related to the court system, Boyer proclaims: "It is unfortunate to see yet another judge unable to withstand the pressure of public scrutiny and do the right thing.... I only hope the higher courts of Illinois will correct him before any more damage is done to Daniel Kirchner." Susan Haddad and her appeals specialist colleague, attorney Paul Bargiel, begin drafting an appeal to the Illinois Supreme Court.

"I declined to speak to Bob Greene or other journalists about the case," Susan Haddad explains during an exclusive interview with me in early 2003. "I successfully avoided them. Regarding the media, it's okay for them to attempt to understand a case, but it's an entirely different thing for them to attempt to determine its outcome. The latter is what happened in Daniela's case. The media demanded the outcome they wanted. No one was interested in the child's well-being. Everyone was interested in the spectacle of it and the energy they got from it...and in the Warburtons."

Having practiced as a family law attorney for nineteen years, Susan Haddad was still not sufficiently prepared for the fall-out from this case, "which should have been routine," she emphasizes. Paul Bargiel refers to Daniela's petition as "innocuous," a simple request to formalize the child's mother as his mother.

"It was like tabloid coverage for all of the mainstream newspapers!" Haddad continues. "They made a circus out of the courtroom, and the judge responded to their expectations, to their demands." The atmosphere was charged with insistence and indignation. Again, the media were attempting to create the story, to ensure that it would continue along the thematic path that they had established and promulgated from years before.

Having accepted the case on a *pro bono* basis, Haddad explains her motivation: "There was a travesty of justice visited on these people [the Kirchners], and I appreciated that. They were never fairly or critically examined by anyone; the negative coverage was all-pervasive. When I took their case, I wanted to do something to help them and their son."

Susan describes Danny, whom she met in her office, as "an exquisitely nice child, very much in love with his parents."

Judge Lott ordered Haddad to turn over her client's phone number and address to the court and to the Department of Supportive Services, due to investigate the child's circumstances within his home that same week. "I refused," she informs me. "I was ready to go to jail, but I wouldn't give them the information. Everything was so politically motivated and I knew where it was headed."

Regarding Danny's birth certificate, Susan's theory is that it was denied the Kirchners for sinister but obvious reasons. "A birth certificate is typically required before a child is admitted to school. Without it, the expectation is that Danny would be turned away. If he was not in school," she explains, "DCFS could take him away from the Kirchners and he might then be placed with the Warburtons again.

"I also tried to get Danny's medical records for his parents," Haddad adds. "The Kirchners had been unsuccessful in attempts to get them, so I called Jenner and Block to request them....

"We never got them."

Arriving at the Kirchners' home at dusk, I have already heard the news of Daniela's legal defeat in court on my car radio and on television. The Baby Richard custody case is reopened: "Everything is back on the table." I park my car near a curbside media van and run to the front porch. Unlocking the door, a visibly shaken Daniela lets me in and quickly shuts it behind me. She is pale and trembling.

Stepping over black wrought-iron numbers on the carpet, I realize that she has torn them off the front of the house and thrown them down. "I don't want them to show the public where we live; I don't want them to know our address," Daniela offers as explanation to my quizzical look. "If they televise pictures of our house and street number, who knows what might happen? The crazies could come here and try to harm us or take Danny. I won't put the numbers back up. There have been other media vans, too; they followed me here."

Last night, after I heard from a friend about Greene's inflammatory, rallying column, I offered to accompany Daniela to court today. Robert and I would drive her there and protect her from the gawking and hostile assembly. She declined, stating that everything would be all right; she was not even required to appear in court; and Ms. Haddad would represent her there and "take care of everything."

"I heard…." I tell her, taking her hand. "You and Otto and the children need to leave the state. You can go to our condo in Florida and stay there as long as you need to."

"You're probably right," she agrees. "The judge will probably take Danny away from us on Friday. He wants to be the judge to make things right for the public and the media, to give them what they want. He will get a lot of publicity for himself all across the country. But what will happen to Danny?" She begins to cry.

Before long, Otto arrives at the home. After embracing Danny and Sharon, he sits down in the living room with Daniela and me. His jaw is firmly set and he is shaking his head.

"Nothing surprises me in this case," he exclaims, "but this can only mean bad things for us. They will use this situation as a way to take Danny from us, maybe as soon as Friday. We may not get him back."

Together we begin planning their departure to Ormond Beach, Florida, to go to my two-bedroom condo on the ocean. Robert and I bought it as our escape destination; now it will be literally that for this besieged family. Otto and Daniela will pack up the children and enough clothes for a few weeks and leave, under the cover of dark, during the wee hours of the morning. Hopefully their car will make it all of the way there without a breakdown. The condo is furnished, equipped, and ready for occupancy, and no one will know their whereabouts except for their attorney, Robert, and me.

After we agree on this plan, I head for home. Worried and tired, I am reviewing the latest turn of events, deplorable and astonishing, and yet resulting in Otto and Daniela's reconciliation. Otto has returned to their home. They are reunited in a renewed, fierce battle to keep their son and their family intact. Regardless of their marital problems with each other, the dangers to them from outside forces—a grandstanding and powerful judge, his deleterious and unlawful rulings, a resurrected public outcry, and resumed media fury—are far worse. The prospect of losing Danny has diminished and overshadowed their other concerns; they are now parents first and foremost.

Watching the sun rise the next morning, I am pacing and wondering about the various possibilities for Danny and his family now that the court has "put everything back on the table" and ordered an emergency home visit. Any investigator assigned to this case would realize that the pervasively held expectation is for him to find and cite problems within Danny's home environment.

Mike Foley has advised me that, especially if the Kirchners become unavailable, I may be subpoenaed into court to testify as to their whereabouts. If I refuse, the judge has the power to send me to jail until I comply. Will I choose to reveal their location? I resolve to withstand pressure to disclose information that would be detrimental to them; they have been my clients and now they are more; and Danny's welfare is in serious jeopardy.

Preparing for an afternoon of scheduled clients, I find myself absent-minded as I begin to dress and gather my files. The telephone rings and I jump.

"Karen, the Supreme Court has ruled for us!" Otto blurts out as I say "hello." "I just heard the news," he exclaims, triumph in his voice. "Judge Lott has been stopped in his ruling. He has to explain to the high court why he refused to permit Daniela to withdraw her petition. The home visit and hearing on Friday are postponed."

Otto had predicted to me that the Illinois Supreme Court would intervene, but I had considered his expectation overly optimistic. Now, that Court has not only called a halt to Judge Lott's ruling but the response has come within twenty-four hours, truly amazing speed.

Specifically, the highest state court has stayed Lott's ruling, canceling the emergency home visit and court hearing scheduled for Friday, and has further ordered the judge to explain in writing the reasoning behind his rulings. Issuing an emergency order, signed by Justice Michael Bilandic, the Supreme Court has directed Lott to postpone any further action until its subsequent review of his written submission.

This highly unusual move by the Illinois Supreme Court proves that the justices watch television news and read the papers. Their immediate, preemptive ruling has been made on an overnight basis.

In an uncharacteristic editorial, the *Chicago Tribune* assumes a position of support for Daniela's cause in an article entitled "The madness Baby Richard induces":

> Something about the so-called Baby Richard case has a way of making people who ought to be sensible adults behave foolishly. The latest to fall under this spell is Cook County Circuit Judge Gay-Lloyd Lott, who on Monday decided it wasn't enough to do his job in the Richard case; he had to DO JUSTICE. Fortunately, the Illinois Supreme Court stopped Lott before he could do any serious damage. One hopes the court will make permanent next week its temporary stay of the judge's meddlesome ruling....

> Lott had his teeth into a good one and wasn't going to let it get away. He ordered county social workers to visit the Kirchner home and evaluate "Richard" and his circumstances, which could include anything from whether he is enrolled in school to whether he puts the cap back on the toothpaste....

> It's time for Lott and everyone who has popped off about this case, from Gov. Jim Edgar down, to grow up and butt out. "Baby Richard...doesn't need saving or rescuing or even Justice. He needs for himself and his family to be let alone. ("Editorials," July 31, 1997)

Unfortunately for the Kirchners, several of the major area newspapers and radio programs create a series of call-in polls for the public to register their opinions on the case. As an example, on July 31st, the *Sun-Times* asks its readers, "Should the Baby Richard case be reopened?" A majority—51.6%—respond "Yes," an interesting outcome when considered in light of the fact that "Richard" has been in the care of his biological parents for twenty-seven months.

Once again, the ire of the public has been resurrected and inflamed. Otto and Daniela are forced again to deal with widespread harassment and rancor. Everyone has an opinion. Most of my therapy clients are quick to share their feelings with me. The bad news is that nearly all of them support the Warburtons' renewed legal efforts; but the good news, in a perverse way, is that my clientele is limited these days and my need to respond to these opinions is likewise limited. My weekly caseload is hovering at a dozen hours.

The Warburtons file another petition with the Illinois Supreme Court, requesting its ultimate support of Judge Lott's ruling. They are determined to pursue their own agenda for the Kirchners' son.

In a twelve-page document, Lott's attorney files his judge-client's response to the high court's order directing him to explain his rulings. Lott explains that he perceived Daniela as trying to sidestep normal adoption proceedings, which require a home assessment and a judicial inquiry into whether such a proposed adoption is in the best interests of the child. It appears that the judge took it upon himself to fast-forward to the alternative process—adoption—the one that was **not** initiated or requested by the plaintiff, Daniela Kirchner, who had sought a simple revocation of her 1991 adoption consent.

The Kirchners' response to Judge Lott's ruling and rationale—filed by Susan Haddad and Paul Bargiel—addresses the Supreme Court:

> ...One has only to pick up a newspaper or turn on a television set since the...ruling...to become aware of the circus-like atmosphere that envelopes every aspect of this case. Once again all of the feelings associated with the initial case have come to the front. The Kirchners are villified [sic.] and their son is the object of undesirable attention.... If she [Daniela] was naïve enough to believe her petition would escape attention, she has learned otherwise and has paid for it if this matter is allowed to continue. Shining the spotlight on him for the next weeks, and months, perhaps years, will serve no good purpose, and is certainly not in his best interests....

In addition to the devastation which will be wreaked on the Kirchners and their son by continuing this matter in the trial court, there is also the credibility of the judicial system to consider....

...[T]he clear public perception that rulings in high-profile cases in general and this high-profile case in particular often turn on public opinion rather than the law and the facts.... But none can deny, in light of what has occurred in the media since [Lott's ruling], that the public confidence in an independent judiciary guided by the rule of law has been seriously eroded....

In a prompt, three-sentence order, the Illinois Supreme Court rules that Judge Lott must take no further action except to dismiss Daniela's petition, as she has requested. In a one-party civil action, the legal right to withdraw a petition is absolute. The Warburtons' standing—or lack thereof—remains unaddressed during this latest round of legal maneuvering. The Supreme Court established and clarified the former adoptive parents' **lack** of legal standing in its ruling two years ago.

Ironically, Daniela's relationship to Danny remains unchanged. Her victory is simply to retain the status quo; she remains Danny's *de facto* mother but not his legal one. Baby Richard continues to lack a legal mother. Daniela now understands "that she will never be just another litigant and that this will never be just another case," Susan Haddad summarizes as she describes the tarnished triumph of the bizarre outcome. "Daniela was naïve to believe that she could pursue a legal parent-child relationship with little or no notice."

Predictably, Bob Greene expresses his outrage, and the media marathon continues. Attorney Robert Byman is quoted in the *Sun-Times* as saying regarding the Warburtons, "It is not their intention to give up." Further legal options will be reviewed on their behalf.

At their home, Otto and Daniela cancel their plans to flee to Florida now that there is no compelling need. They have been rescued—Danny has been spared—by the Supreme Court...with both dispatch and forcefulness.

"I am afraid ever to go to court again," Daniela sighs as we sip coffee together at their kitchen table.

Otto nods his agreement. "The Warburtons will not leave us alone. They are determined to interfere with Danny's peaceful life."

"I'm just happy that the two of you are back together," I try to console them. "Maybe there is a silver lining in this dark cloud." They look at each other and smile.

From our conversation, I can tell that Otto feels a need to remain in the home for many reasons. He is understandably fearful for Danny's safety and security, especially now that his family has become so visible and exposed once again. The question of how Danny is doing has been raised far and wide, and surely people will resume amateur surveillance attempts as in the past. It will take two parents to ensure round-the-clock protection of their family.

"Daddy, can you fix this?" Danny queries, running into the kitchen from his bedroom and thrusting a mangled plastic action figure into Otto's hand.

"Sure I can," his father assures him, as he twists the figure back into its original shape and returns it. Danny grins and whirls around to return to his play.

"At least Danny is unaware of all of the trouble, and he is happy, especially with his father back home," Daniela says, smiling. She is holding eighteen-month-old Sharon in her arms, rocking back and forth.

"You're Danny's mother in all of the important ways, Daniela," I assert in my attempt to comfort her. "Nothing will ever change that."

Daniela has never ventured into another attorney's office or into a courtroom since the terrifying events during the summer of 1997. The prospect of losing her son again has outweighed her desire for legal closure. "The madness that Baby Richard induces" has served as a permanent disincentive for her to pursue re-establishment of her parental rights to Danny as his mother.

Susan Haddad never went to jail; the Supreme Court firmly and permanently prevented further action by the lower court. Judge Lott would tell me in April 2003 that he was astounded by the media madness over Daniela's petition. "It was horrendous for days," he recalls. "Every newspaper covered the story as well as television and radio all around. Some said that I was a knucklehead and others praised me for 'doing the right thing.' I had to get a lawyer to represent me and my ruling to the Supreme Court; it put a stop to everything."

Although it took more than two more years and occurred only after changes in political office of several individuals in state government, Susan Haddad successfully obtained for the Kirchners a birth certificate for Danny on September 20, 1999. Through a "tip-toe-quiet" trip to the Cook County Clerk's Office, she requested and got the birth certificate that should have been quickly and routinely granted long before, in 1995. On it, Otakar Kirchner is designated as Daniel's father and Daniela Janikova Kirchner as his mother.

Danny has subsequently been able to travel with his mother and siblings to Slovakia to visit with his grandmother and other relatives. Fortunately, his passport, made possible through his birth certificate, was issued without protest or visible impediment.

Otto and Daniela's reconciliation was successful; they remain together; and they share a deep and wide appreciation of their parenthood above all else.

Although Danny's pediatrician—in addition to attorneys Heinemann and Haddad—has also attempted to obtain the child's medical records, they have never been received.

> Pride goes before disaster,
> and a haughty spirit before a fall.
>
> — *Proverbs 16:18*

CHAPTER FIFTEEN

The Story of Loren Heinemann

An intriguer sows discord, and a talebearer separates bosom friends.

— *Proverbs 16:28*

LOREN HEINEMANN agrees to be disbarred in Illinois. It is another dramatic turn of events in the unending saga of Baby Richard. It is September 24, 1997. Heinemann is registered as "disbarred on consent" and his name is summarily removed from the state's list of attorneys.

During the weeks surrounding the summer of 1997, the "Baby Richard curse" is plaguing individuals intimately involved in the case. Judge James Heiple is besieged by attacks upon his integrity to the point of a statewide movement toward impeachment. He voluntarily steps down as Chief Justice of the Illinois Supreme Court after painful media and public excoriation, attributed by most observers to his role as draftsman of the unpopular, unanimous court decision that awarded the child to his biological father. Baby Richard's birth mother, Daniela, attempts to restore her parental rights to her son with disastrous results. She retreats, frightened and grateful to maintain the status quo of raising her son absent any legal claim to him. Otto is again unemployed, through no fault of his own, after the second, formerly bustling Kenessey's restaurant at which he worked permanently closed its doors. My private practice has declined in both clientele and income to the extent that I am making arrangements to close down, years before reaching an eligible early retirement age, and to move away, with my husband Robert, to a quiet, simple life in Florida.

Having suffered through months of travail related to his practice of law, Loren Heinemann finds himself in legal trouble on a regular basis. The media are prompt to report each stumble and fall, always pairing his name with the allusion to his having been the victorious attorney in the Baby Richard case. It was the kind of high profile case "that can make a lawyer's career." However, one year after the long, arduous court battle ended, Loren Heinemann is served "with the kind of papers that can end a lawyer's career."

The Illinois Attorney Registration and Disciplinary Commission files a complaint against Heinemann alleging five counts of misconduct, none of which pertain to the Baby Richard case. The detailed complaint accuses the attorney of lying to clients, fumbling their cases, and, in one case, suggesting "that a client thwart a court's order by diverting asserts to offshore banking accounts and leaving the country." The cases include a divorce, a child custody dispute, and a personal injury lawsuit.

Alleging that Heinemann counseled a client to do something illegal or fraudulent, one count details his advice: the client "could avert complying with a court order to turn over approximately $391,800 to his wife" by transferring the money to offshore banking accounts and permanently leaving the United States. This alleged offense occurred in September 1995, while he was representing a man in a divorce case. The complaint further alleges that Heinemann allowed clients' legal rights to expire by failing to file court documents by required deadlines and that, in one case, he failed to appear in court eight times. In addition, he is accused of lying to clients, telling them "he had filed legal papers on their behalf when he had not" done so. (Ken Armstrong, "'Richard' attorney accused," *Chicago Tribune*, June 19, 1996)

During the winter, spring, and summer months of 1995, Loren had confessed to me that he was having trouble keeping up with his other cases. His Baby Richard involvements were "all-consuming," he complained and celebrated at the same time. Not only was he the only visible attorney for Otakar Kirchner, the child's father, but he also served as spokesman, friend, advocate, and public relations liaison for the Kirchner family. On the other side, the Warburtons were blessed with dozens—if not hundreds—of individuals in similar capacities to Heinemann's one-man juggling act. The Warburtons enjoyed the services of professional spokespersons; a horde of attorneys; the ongoing and forceful advocacy of a large, well-organized adoption-based group; and supporters from all walks of life and all fifty states. By contrast, Loren became a one-man show.

Some of his clients understood, he told me, while others did not. "Some people are proud to say, 'My attorney is on TV!'" he boasted.

Loren and I spoke on a nearly daily basis across months. We would telephone each other at all times of the day and night to talk about breaking news and to plan, on behalf of the Kirchners, the best response to legal, political, social, and media maneuvers during their most turbulent times. From my first therapy session with Otto and Daniela on February 1, 1995, to September of that year, Loren and I met in each other's offices, in our homes, at local restaurants, and at the Kirchners' home on dozens of occasions. We became a two-person team, both working on a *pro bono* basis during those harrowing months, and sharing our primary focus upon the welfare of Otto, Daniela, and Danny. We participated in barbecues, birthdays, and everyday social events with the Kirchner family; sometimes our spouses would also attend. Our professional and social relationships mixed and blurred because of the unique, intense circumstances.

Loren and Otto had become close friends during the early weeks of their attorney-client relationship. It was 1991; Danny was an infant, only a few months old; and it became apparent early on that the Warburtons' fight to keep Otto's son would drag on for a long time. Heinemann had first predicted to his new client that it would take "only a few weeks" for Otto to have his son, because the other side "would realize that there had been a big misunderstanding about this child and that he was not eligible for adoption." Within days, however, the Warburtons fired Tom Panichi, the attorney who initiated adoption proceedings on their behalf, and hired Richard Lifshitz, an attorney who specialized in adoptions. Clearly, they were gearing up for a battle. Neither Heinemann nor Otto, however, had any idea that the conflict would become so prolonged, ugly, and destructive, progressively involving powerful individuals at every level of government and across the country. At each step and with every new, disturbing surprise, their friendship grew. They were spending hours of time together, in and out of court, planning and debriefing, preparing and commiserating.

Loren Heinemann was a sole practitioner with a small, unimpressive office; he was labeled "a storefront lawyer" by several reporters. Practicing general law, he began to spend most of his time with domestic cases, including divorce and custody disputes. Ironically, after his own divorce, he had vowed never to practice family law. "You become what you loathe and fear the most," Loren was quoted as saying about his diverted career path. (Meg McSherry, "Heinemann ignores villain tag," *Daily Southtown*, May 7, 1995)

Loren was routinely answering most of his own incoming telephone calls when I met him in his Orland Park office in November 1994. He was sharing a secretary with another lawyer and engaging in other efficiencies to limit his overhead expenses. His wife Stacy and he had a one-year-old daughter, Alexandriana (Lexi), and he was contributing to the support of his sixteen-year-old daughter Zhenesse from his first marriage. Loren and Stacy's simple home in Richton Park, Illinois, a suburb of Chicago that is mostly peopled by blue collar and low-to-middle income workers, was modest in both its size and furnishings. At 38, Loren was described as little more than a novice, suddenly thrust into a bright spotlight by virtue of his representation of this one case, and he was largely unprepared for the celebrity and the notoriety.

Loren Heinemann grew up in Minneapolis, Minnesota, the son of a police officer and a homemaker. After his high school graduation in 1977, he entered the Army and served for a span of seven years. He took Russian language classes in California in preparation for working in the National Security Office in West Germany. He was transferred to Augsburg, where he took courses at a branch of the University of Maryland, from which he got his bachelor's degree. As an Army intelligence officer, he worked on a high-tech system, listening in on Russian generals and residents and working on breaking Russian codes. There he met Denise, a native of south suburban Chicago, who was doing similar work. They married; their daughter Zhenesse was born;

but the marriage soon deteriorated and ended in divorce.

Heinemann decided to accept a scholarship offered to him by Hamline University School of Law, a small Jesuit school in St. Paul, Minnesota. After he graduated, he moved to Chicago—alone, depressed, and short on cash—and found himself sharing office space and overhead with a succession of other lawyers.

By then, most of Heinemann's plans for himself had failed. His first marriage lasted less than three years. His original hopes for a career in business never came to fruition. A series of unsuccessful attempts to establish law partnerships with other attorneys in Chicago's south suburbs, along with a brief bout of unemployment, prompted Heinemann to branch out into a one-man office of his own. He married the attractive, young secretary, Stacy Musich, who worked for the Palos Heights law firm that he left in order to establish his own practice.

Before Baby Richard, his biggest case was reportedly "negotiating a deal for a 19-year-old who was caught with 8 pounds of heroin." Heinemann undertook Baby Richard "with a mixture of bravado and insecurity." He often sought reassurance from his professional colleagues and from reporters. "Did you read my brief?" he would ask the media representatives, seeking their encouragement. (Janan Hanna and Louise Kiernan, "Kirchner lawyer pays price," *Chicago Tribune*, February 7, 1995)

It was "Baby Richard" that introduced him to the harsh realities of public rancor and the unique stresses and strains of a high-profile legal controversy. "This case has shown me everything that's good about the law and everything that's bad about being a lawyer," Loren confessed to me on the day that we met.

Loren and Otto, both 38 when they met, shared other traits and directions in common. Both were stocky, heavy-set men, who smoked cigarettes together when stressed by the complexities and intrigues of the legal process. During the same month, September 1991, both men married beautiful, intelligent women, each more than a decade younger than their new husbands. Both couples loved and wanted children. The Heinemanns, with baby Lexi, and the Kirchners were vacationing together at a friend's condo in West Palm Beach, Florida, when the unanimous Illinois Supreme Court ruling was announced in mid-June 1994, ordering Baby Richard to be turned over to his biological father. All four parents celebrated the joyful news, speculating among themselves about the real name of "Baby Richard," not yet disclosed to them. The Baby Richard pseudonym, conferred by the appellate court, hid the boy's name from the public...and also from his birth parents.

Otto Kirchner not only became Lexi Heinemann's godfather but also her "Uncle Otto." Loren would tell me early on that Otto was "like a big teddy bear" with his baby daughter, who loved Uncle Otto and even sometimes called him "Da Da."

When we spoke during our first days of working together, Loren was quick to remind me about the bad—and worsening—image of his client. "He's such a sweet guy," he would say, "but the media hate him and the public too." It was obvious that Loren—in spite of weak protestations to the contrary—wanted to be liked; he hated to be hated; and as time passed, he started to distance himself from his client-friend, at first subtly and then overtly.

Loren became the master of the sound bite. He was always ready for the media with a quip and a retort. He was gutsy and outspoken, but he sometimes came across as brash, glib, and uncaring. Employing sarcasm and misdirected humor at times, Loren's comments did not reflect well upon his immigrant client, who had his own conversational problems that included lapses into ungrammatical statements when his native language translated in an awkward way into English. Both Otto and Loren were often portrayed and described as thugs. Their opposition, in contrast, was polished and refined; all of the lawyers used excellent diction, dressed impeccably, and exercised strategic restraint. The adoptive parents, "John and Jane Doe," remained mysterious and unavailable, protected by a cloak of anonymity across years, and buttressed and buffered by a tag team of sophisticated lawyers—men and women, young and old.

Adrienne Drell, a journalist with a master's degree in law and one of the few reporters who appeared to sympathize with Otto Kirchner and his plight, actually read all of the Baby Richard court documents. Covering all of the unfolding chapters of the story for the *Chicago Sun-Times*, Adrienne interviewed Loren dozens of times, and he was especially candid and self-disclosing with her. In "Controversial Case Takes Emotional Toll on Attorney," she reveals not only the painful aspects of his representing Otto Kirchner, but the reason for his instant celebrity as a David-versus-Goliath figure:

Attorney Loren Heinemann stood alone before the Illinois Supreme Court last Wednesday, arguing Otakar Kirchner's right to Baby Richard.

Lined up against him in Springfield were more than a dozen attorneys, led by Cook County Public Guardian Patrick Murphy, Edward J. O'Connell, the court-appointed guardian for the child, and Jerold Solovy, managing partner of the mammoth Jenner and Block law firm.

And he won.

But being on the unpopular side of a controversial case has exacted a price—in dollars and cents and emotional isolation....

The case has affected Heinemann's relationships with several close friends who sympathize with the adoptive parents, and...he has received anonymous hate calls and letters. (January 29, 1995, *Chicago Sun-Times*)

Heinemann is quoted by Drell as saying that he could not even afford the cost of the paper required to respond to continuing challenges by attorneys for the adoptive parents. "'I still owe $2,000 in reprint costs for last month,' said Heinemann, who stopped billing Kirchner a year ago when the fees topped $175,000." If it were not for his wife working, he states, his "office would be in a cardboard box on Lower Wacker Drive.... Otto and I are legal pariahs."

Two months previous, in mid-November 1994, the powerful law firm of Jenner and Block publicly announced its assumption of the adoptive parents' case on a *pro bono* basis. Carrying 400 attorneys on its payrolls and advertising "an international scope," Jenner and Block was contributing "more horsepower" and "additional resources" to the Does' side:

...Jerold Solovy confirmed Tuesday that he will personally argue the Does' side before the Illinois Supreme Court. Solovy will head up a five-attorney team, with 15 other lawyers available for help.

Still representing the Does is attorney Richard Lifshitz....
(Adrienne Drell, "Law Firm to Work Free On Baby
Richard Case," *Chicago Sun-Times*, November 23, 1994)

This virtual army of attorneys on the side of the adoptive
parents gave the term "lawyering up" a new level of meaning.

Against twenty-one high-powered attorneys on the Does'
side—more than O.J. Simpson had on his team—Heinemann was
alone on Otto Kirchner's side, with his only help provided behind-
the-scenes by Bruce Boyer from the Northwestern University
Law School's Family Law and Justice Center. Boyer readily
donated his services by telephoning Heinemann and offering his
legal assistance after the appellate court ruling for the adoptive
parents. Heinemann needed Boyer's help and legal expertise, and
he wisely accepted it, but he also kept quiet about it.

In spite of the cadre of attorneys present on the Does' side in
the courtroom in January 1995, while Heinemann appeared
alone, the Illinois Supreme Court—within four hours of hearing
oral arguments—ruled:

You are hereby ordered and directed to surrender forthwith custody of the child known as Baby Boy Richard,
also known as Baby Boy Janikova, to petitioner Otakar
Kirchner. (January 25, 1995)

Many legal experts were stunned at the speed and brevity of
the Supreme Court's same-day ruling. The written opinion
would be issued weeks later. Some observers opined that the justices believed that the Court's authority and previous rulings in
the case had been disregarded. The Court had awarded custody
of Baby Richard to his biological father in June 1994, and then
denied the Does' petition for a rehearing in July 1994. Now the
adoptive parents were asserting **another** claim to Richard, this
time based upon the new Illinois law that was passed in an
attempt to pave the way for a preemptive "best interest" hearing. Otto Kirchner was requesting a writ of habeas corpus in
accordance with the June and July rulings. He wanted his son
turned over to him.

In any event, this was another highly-publicized, dramatic
episode that spread Loren Heinemann's name, as the underdog-

victor, across the country. Loren's celebrity rose to a new level. He could not have afforded to pay for even a small fraction of the publicity that his victory earned him. Bruce Boyer—whose quiet, behind-the-scenes work as the major draftsman of Otto's appeal to the Illinois Supreme Court was largely responsible for its success—chose to remain unknown and unrecognized. Loren basked in the glory and the limelight by himself. He deserved it, he reasoned, by virtue of his having spent so many hours of uncompensated time on behalf of his client.

As I would learn much later, Loren was more than delighted to accept the only condition that I requested when I assumed the position of the Kirchner family's therapist—anonymity. I clarified to him that I wanted no contact with the media and that my identity should remain undisclosed while I would be working with the Kirchner parents and their son. These stipulations were readily and heartily endorsed by the attorney, whose favorite role at the time was serving as the exclusive public relations representative of the Baby Richard parents. Loren was not interested in sharing with anyone his control or the favorite aspects of his self-fashioned job as front man with the media.

The January Supreme Court ruling, signaling the imminent move of the child to his father's custody, began Heinemann's elevated status as the highly-sought Baby Richard spokesman, public person, and supremely successful attorney. He was admittedly having trouble keeping up with his ongoing, everyday clients now that his days were filled with Baby Richard interviews, requests for interviews, and related hoopla. He held press conferences, drove many miles and long hours to participate in television programs, and provided frequent telephone interviews for radio broadcasts. Before his departure for a two-hour drive by car to a radio studio interview, I saw Loren one afternoon, his eyes wide with eager anticipation. "They begged me, pleaded with me to come and tell my story on their program," he boasted. "I'll go and give them what they want!"

Although he was already unable to keep up with his work on behalf of his other clients, Loren was accepting new clients, who pressed him to take their cases. Certainly, many reasoned, if Heinemann could beat the odds and strong public sentiment, in spite of having been astoundingly outnumbered by his opposition, he must be able to win their cases as well.

While Heinemann was accepting new clients, he was also collecting retainers from them. He continued as a sole practitioner, however, and with the influx of a new clientele, he became hopelessly stretched beyond his means to deliver.

Although it does appear that Heinemann's lapses and offenses caused the demise of his own legal career, the media cynically chose to portray his troubles in a manner that highlighted petty and tawdry aspects. "Former Kirchner Lawyer Cited After 3 No-Shows" in the *Chicago Sun-Times* begins:

> Hmmmm. Attorney Loren Heinemann, who once represented the Otakar Kirchner family in the Baby Richard case, appeared in court Friday on a contempt citation— and left behind his jewelry as collateral! (Michael Sneed, May 5, 1996)

"Heinemann has failed to appear in court three times!" writes the snide Sneed, who outlines the major facts. A doctor claiming that Heinemann owed him $350 was suing the attorney in small claims court. "Cook County sheriff's deputies were ordered to bring him before the judge," but "shortly afterward, Heinemann showed up on his own." He was permitted to pay his bond by turning over his watch, bracelet, and a gold band.

The doctor, a Chicago plastic surgeon, had filed the claim for a seven-year-old debt that "stemmed from a personal injury case Heinemann handled while with another law firm," according to the *Daily Southtown's* article, "Baby Richard lawyer settles small claim against him" (Jack Beary, May 7, 1996). Heinemann is quoted as saying that the law firm owed the fee, but he paid it in compliance with a court order. The doctor's fee was for "services as an expert in evaluating a claim from one of Heinemann's clients." The attorney paid court costs in addition to the surgeon's fee and got his watch back from the court.

On April 13, 1996, the *Daily Southtown* covered a small claims court case against Heinemann in an article headlined "Richard lawyer loses in court":

> The Orland Park lawyer who won custody of the child known as Baby Richard...suffered a courtroom loss

Thursday, when a former client sued him for not showing up in court.

...Monee resident Angelo Triolo[,] lost his bid to win custody of his child in November 1994 because Heinemann
missed a scheduled court date in the case.

Triolo filed a small-claims court case against Heinemann
in February, and on Thursday won $715 from the attor-
ney—a refund of almost all of the retainer he paid on the
case. (Adam Lisberg)

"'Baby Richard Curse' strikes again; dad involved in car
crash" covers three unrelated incidents, intertwining them in
Chicago Tribune fashion:

No sooner did we write about a "Baby Richard Curse"
than Otakar Kirchner got a ticket after a traffic accident.
Kirchner's brush with the law follows an embarrassing
scrape with police for James Heiple, the Illinois Supreme
Court justice who wrote the unpopular...decision, and a
bankruptcy declaration for Loren Heinemann, the attorney who won custody of the child for Kirchner. (Hevrdejs
& Conklin Inc., September 10, 1996)

It would seem that the Baby Richard curse started early on
for lawyers involved in the case. Thomas Panichi, the attorney
who initiated adoption proceedings on behalf of the
Does/Warburtons, deservedly received a public sanction for his
role in filing knowingly false affidavits:

Attorney Thomas Panichi, running for Cook County
Circuit Court judge..., was found "not qualified" by a
local bar organization because of his conduct while representing the adoptive parents of Baby Richard.

The Chicago Council of Lawyers said Panichi...signed
petitions with his clients "asserting that the natural
father was unknown, a statement that was knowingly
false."

In 1993, Illinois Appellate Court Justice John Tully took Panichi to task in a court document for handling the adoption when he knew that the biological mother knew the identity of the father. Tully said Panichi never made any effort to find the father, Otakar Kirchner, "who was still living in the same apartment on Lake Shore Drive," and he signed affidavits with the court that "the father on due inquiry cannot be found." (Adrienne Drell, "Case Gets Lawyer Bad Rating," *Chicago Sun-Times*, November 8, 1994)

Panichi was also "not recommended" by the Chicago Bar Association, "with no reason cited," according to Drell. Furthermore, he "acknowledged that the Illinois Attorney Registration and Disciplinary Commission was asking questions about his role in the [Richard] case," but he "was confident 'nothing will come out of that.'"

Otakar Kirchner took no legal action against any attorney. His sole focus remained continuously upon his son. Even when Loren Heinemann lapsed into a good guy/bad guy mode with the media and continued to disclose private details related to the Kirchner family, Otto refused to file a complaint against his former friend.

"When I became the godfather of Loren's daughter Lexi, we became like family to each other, according to my values and upbringing," Otto asserted when he and I discussed Heinemann's apparent refusal to honor attorney-client confidentiality. "In Czechoslovakia, we took these matters seriously. A godparent's responsibility is important. I could never bring any harm upon his child and, therefore, I could not harm him either, even though he continues to stir up trouble that causes us pain."

During the summer of 1995, when Loren Heinemann routinely accepted invitations to discuss his famous case with the media, he decided to respond to the wrath of the public. His explanations for having represented Otto in successfully claiming his son turned apologetic. Several times I heard him say that even a criminal, such as a murderer, is entitled to representation by an attorney. "I was just doing my job," he would shrug, looking both innocent and resigned. This discrediting explanation from his own attorney served to place—or more accurately to keep—Otto in a bad light with the media and the public.

"If his own attorney talks about him that way, what kind of man can he be?" Many of my clients would express these, or similar, sentiments about Otto Kirchner after having heard or read Heinemann's words. The attorney was distancing himself from his client Otto and his new little family. He stopped making regular visits to the Kirchners' home, and when he did drop by, he was eager to leave.

"Loren has no time for us any more," Otto would often lament to me. However, he continued to value his relationship with the attorney and to remain loyal to him. Otto realized that Loren chose to ignore his repeated requests to discontinue discussing the case so that the story might fade away and Danny might at last have the chance to begin a normal life. Not only did Heinemann continue to talk about the case and his victory at every opportunity, but he took what became his own media campaign to a new stage. He began disclosing personal and private information about the Kirchner family, against their expressed wishes, to keep the story alive.

As deftly as Shakespeare's scheming Iago dropped a telltale handkerchief, Heinemann revealed tidbits from the Baby Richard family's lives. Bob Greene jumped on any dropped morsel of information like a dog on a bone. In a maudlin article, "'They said I should come over,'" Greene quotes Heinemann as saying that "the crucifix" that Richard's biological father had given him was gone. (*Chicago Tribune*, August 21, 1995). "When the biological father asked him where it was, Richard said: 'Johnny took it.'" Greene continues by alleging that this is the child's way of asking for his other family; the biological parents told lies to the child that "he could go back home whenever he wanted"; and "they lured him into a false sense of security with a room full of presents."

"Is there no one with the mercy to help these boys?" Greene ends his column with typical hyperbole, after reminding readers that it "has been almost four months since he and his brother were told the cruelest lie of all: that they could see each other, talk to each other, visit with each other whenever they wanted."

Although the private, behind-closed-doors event within the home of the Kirchner family is none of either Bob Greene's business or his millions of readers', Heinemann assisted him in weaving a distorted and damning story out of a simple, harmless incident. And they got it wrong.

Danny had received—rather than a crucifix from his father—a gold chain with gold faith, hope, and charity charms from his maternal grandmother from the Slovak Republic. She had bought this expensive, symbolic gift for her new grandson so that he might know that she loved him and longed to meet him. Danny wore his chain-and-charms around his neck every day. One afternoon he returned home from playing at Justin's apartment without it. When his parents asked where it was, he blamed Johnny—whom he had not seen for months—for its loss. "Johnny took it," he offered as his explanation, shifting the blame. A four-year-old's response to having lost his grandmother's precious gift is turned into fodder for an obsessed columnist's presumptuous interpretation of incorrect details related to an intimate exchange between the child and his parents.

Otto and Daniela are mortified over the realization that their family's privacy is invaded and betrayed by a friend, by their attorney who has won their trust. Their relationship with Heinemann is damaged by this most public of betrayals, his disclosure of intimacies in their child's daily life to their biggest self-proclaimed enemy. In the pages of the *Chicago Tribune* and dozens of Greene-syndicated newspapers, their private events and conversations are portrayed—and incorrectly in order to advance the theme of attack against them—for anyone to read and to judge. They are accused of being liars once again by Greene, who has never even talked to either of them.

Across weeks and months subsequent to the erroneous "crucifix" column, Heinemann would continue to discuss Otto, Daniela, and Danny with the media, in spite of entreaties from his client-friend to desist. More columns would be written by Bob Greene, incorporating Heinemann's morsels of trivial "events." During Thanksgiving week, I telephoned Loren to request him to discontinue his inappropriate disclosures.

"Please stop talking about the Kirchners to the media, Loren," I implored him. "Otto and Daniela want Danny to be able to begin a private, normal life without public outrage directed at them and at him at every turn. You can talk about the legalities of the case, of course, but please stop talking about their private lives."

Angry and apparently determined to continue his agenda of self-promotion, Loren explodes, "Who are you to tell me what to do? I'll do whatever I please." He concludes, "Don't ever call me again or I will report you to the police for phone harassment!"

Thus ended my relationship with Loren Heinemann. At his insistence, I never spoke to him again. The Kirchners continued to socialize, although less frequently, with the attorney and his family for several more months, during which their relationship grew progressively cooler and more distant. Otto and Daniela tried to guard Danny's and their own privacy as much as possible; they became cautious in their conversations with Heinemann. The Kirchners had moved to a home located directly across the street from the Heinemanns' house on Thanksgiving weekend 1995. During early 1996, however, not only did contact between the two households cease but the neighborhood became divided. The Kirchners found themselves once again living in a palpably hostile environment.

By the time the Kirchners' marital separation becomes front-page news in January 1997, Heinemann is openly critical of his former client, his former friend. He is quoted in the *Daytona Beach News-Journal*, as well as other media sources, saying, "It's not the way I'd pictured it ending.... It hurts a lot." Heinemann is no longer either the Kirchners' attorney or their friend, but he is center stage once again to provide his opinions for the "quotable quotes" and cameras of the swarming media. Mike Foley is Otto's capable attorney and spokesman, but Heinemann presumes to promote himself again as a knower and an important person. For example, he relates that he recently saw Danny on his way to church. Although he has lacked any substantive information, as well as permission to discuss the Kirchner family, since the break-up of their friendship, Heinemann is readily available to tell the media that he is "disappointed" and "hurt" by the latest events. It is another good guy/bad guy portrayal.

Six months later Heinemann forfeits his licensure as an attorney. His action comes only weeks before a scheduled hearing by the Attorney Disciplinary Review Commission on the charges against him from a series of clients.

Heinemann would blame the loss of his law career on the Baby Richard case.

A lawyer with his briefcase
can steal more
than a hundred men with guns.

— *Mario Puzo*

My mama always said
you gotta put the past behind you
before you can move on.

— *Forrest Gump*

CHAPTER SIXTEEN

Striving for Normalcy: 1998 – 2002

The strongest
and sweetest songs
remain to be sung.

— *Walt Whitman*

"LET ME DO THE MOVING FOR YOU," Otto suggests on the telephone on New Year's Day 1998. Feeling nostalgic, with a twinge of sadness, I am looking outside my kitchen window at a cover of white snow. Robert and I signed a contract to sell our "dream home" two days ago. We have lived in this spacious, California-style, light-filled house since 1986, when it was newly constructed as a "spec" home by an entrepreneurial local builder. We must vacate now in less than one month, by January 29th.

"You can rent a big truck. I'll take time off from work and load up your furniture; drive it down to Florida; unload it; and then come back home," Otto recommends. "You'll save a lot of money, and I want to do this for you...and Robert. It's all that I can do to pay you back for everything you did for me and my family," he concludes with an assertion that I know is heartfelt.

Holding three written estimates from professional moving companies, I was poised to sign the lowest-bid contract when the phone rang minutes ago and Otto, hearing the good and bad news about our imminent plans, offered to do the physical work of our across-the-country move. He steadfastly refuses financial reimbursement of any kind, and Daniela makes arrangements to miss a day of work also. She will care for the children while Otto is away for two days of truck driving.

A small army of relatives on Robert's side of the family—his son Bob, nephews, nieces, and spouses—show up to carry furniture and boxes to the rental truck during our last Sunday in Illinois. Robert and I have lived in Chicagoland for all of our lives. Now we will begin a new life together in the Sunshine State.

Otto arrives, jumps onto the driver's seat of the long truck, and leaves with map in hand. Equipped with cat carriers that hold Sybil and Tom Riley—both crouching, stiff, and silent, at a high level of feline apprehension—Robert and I depart by limo for the airport. We fly to Orlando, drive to Palm Coast—the site of our new home—and await the arrival of Otto and the rental truck. As we soon learn, he drove all night—without a stop for food or sleep—because in his otherwise-correct calculations of estimated time of arrival, he did not include the reduced rate of speed, due to the truck's governor, set at sixty miles per hour. In addition, he drove through severe rainstorms for most of the trip. Upon arriving at our new home, Otto gulps down a quick meal—his first in more than twenty-four hours—and we speed to the airport, taking one wrong turn and missing his plane by thirty minutes. After an overnight at the Orlando Sheraton, Otto boards the first morning plane to Chicago—necessitating Daniela's late arrival at work—and he gets home to his children and his own job. Ending a long period of unemployment, Otto landed a job three months ago as a waiter for a family-owned Italian restaurant in a western suburb of Chicago. He returns on time for his next scheduled shift at work. Robert and I are profoundly grateful for his unselfish act in replacing the professional movers and undertaking the tiresome, cross-country truck drive.

January was a harried month. We lived amid dozens of boxes on all three floors of our home, the possessions acquired across twenty-three years of marriage. My last social event was the baby shower that I hosted for Daniela, nearly eight months pregnant with the couple's third child, Jessica Daniela. Although the original plan had been for the shower to be held at my home, the prospective move compelled a quick reconsideration and the booking of a private room at a neighborhood restaurant. It turned out to be a special celebration, bittersweet for me, while Danny, nearly seven, and Sharon, almost two, frolicked around the room and the guests.

Watching *Good Will Hunting* at our local movie theatre turned into an embarrassingly tearful situation. Like Robin Williams' character in the film, I was also saying goodbye to my own clients, some of whom I had worked with for years. I found myself sobbing from the time I left the auditorium until I went to bed several hours later. The connection between therapist and client often results in a deep, mutual human bond that is akin to a mixture of friendship and love. For me, the greatest challenge of my work was always the struggle for professional objectivity. As hard as I tried to remain detached, I often found myself emotionally affected by my clients and their problems. I would worry about them; sometimes telephone between sessions to check on certain individuals, especially those who were depressed and at-risk for suicide; and often intervene, when appropriate, as their advocate. Routinely, at my clients' request, I would maintain regular phone contact with school personnel on behalf of a troubled adolescent or with a psychiatrist on behalf of a depressed, medicated client. Now I was taking my leave; referring clients to other therapists; paving the way for them; and terminating treatment for those who were ready to discontinue.

Psychotherapy is a profession that specializes in people's pain, in dealing with their feelings of loss, loneliness, anxiety, and despair. Its goals include recovery and healing. When clients get better, they leave. It is the way it must be and should be. Therapy extracts an emotional toll from the therapist, I discovered early on. While packing our possessions into cardboard boxes, I realized that I was indeed ready to move on.

Between client sessions, I sorted clothes, books, papers from personal files, and household items into piles—one for keeping and one for giving to others. Otto and Daniela, as well as a number of our relatives, walked through the house, making claims to various items, including furniture and seventy plants of various sizes and varieties. Even though we gave away half of our furniture and other belongings—transitioning from a thirteen-room house to one of seven rooms—we still had enough to require piles of newspapers and seemingly countless rolls of bubble wrap.

On the longest day of packing, my sister Jo was working at my side. An antiques collector and dealer, Jo is especially adept at the successful and safe preparation of breakables for a move. Outside, it was snowing and blowing; the wind was fierce; and the sky grew dark long before nightfall.

"I'm really proud of you," Jo broke a small patch of silence between us. "I never told you before, but I'm proud of what you did for the Kirchners. I know it was difficult for you and painful, but you hung in there. You've paid a big price," she said, placing a stack of wrapped plates into a large cardboard box.

I found myself unable to respond. Swallowing a few times and looking away, out the window onto the expanse of white yard below, I realized that Jo and I had grown closer because of "Baby Richard." Except for Robert, who has always shared my joys and my sorrows with me, Jo was the only person in my life who regularly asked about the Kirchners, sought to hear details, and both understood and commiserated with their plight. Jo had insisted that Otto and Daniela accept from her the wooden crib and accessories that she had kept from her only son Shane, who was turning ten when Sharon Kirchner was born. Along with the baby furniture and bed linens, she sent them a hand-written note, praising their courage and unwavering love of their son.

"...I feel honored to be able to give you these things from my only son," she wrote. "I can't think of anyone else to whom I would give these cherished possessions, but I want **you** to have them for your new baby." Jo has class.

That day of working alongside my sister became my best day in months.

Otto and Daniela had reconciled in July 1997. In January 1998, they were both looking forward to the birth of their third child, due on Danny's seventh birthday in March. Danny was in first grade, and Sharon, nearly two, was still breast-feeding but in the process of being weaned by her mother. Jessica would be born on March 15th.

His parents worked hard to protect Danny from the devastating image that the media perpetrated about him. "Mentally ill," "scarred for life," "unable to form relationships or to bond with others," "seriously handicapped," and "deprived of the ability to develop as a healthy, normal child" were some of the attributions of mental health "experts" whose prognoses were sought by the media for their fairy-tale stories about "Baby Richard." **None** of the "professionals" knew Danny, but that detail did not prevent them from issuing pronouncements, thereby getting their names and words in newspapers and on the airwaves of radio and television.

Speculating about Danny's social life and issuing other proclamations, including "Danny assuredly is going through his own personal struggle…," Bennett Leventhal predicts:

> "It's not a question of whether he is scarred for life. To me, he is," he [Leventhal] said. "It's a question of how big the scars are, how raw they are." (David Fenner, "Baby Richard 'a model kid,'" *Sunday Southtown*, April 28, 1996)

"The Case for Stability" was published in the *Chicago Tribune* on August 3, 1997, along with the photograph from the previous year of Danny holding his newborn sister. This gratuitous piece, authored by Bennett Leventhal and Lauren Wakschlag, begins by describing "writhing in agony, starting the long, painful healing process all over again," referring to a reopened physical wound with "nerve endings [that] were raw." The authors ask the readers to compare such a terrible wound with the "calamity" and "full-fledged catastrophe" that happened to "Richard."

"…[W]e can only guess how well he might have coped with his torture," the authors continue. With a flare, they conclude:

> It is time to help a child—an innocent child—whose brief history already reminds us, ironically, of a line from Shakespeare's *Richard II*: "Tell thou the lamentable tale of me, and send the hearers weeping to their beds."

My, my. It is difficult for me to respond to this journalistic offering by two professionals who purport to have genuine concern for Danny. Leventhal was fired by Otto Kirchner when he was less available than he had promised and when his behaviors resulted in the loss of Otto and Daniela's trust during the attempted progressive transition of Danny. Leventhal had promised Otto, as a condition of his acceptance onto the three-member team, that he would no longer speak in the media about the case. He was hired to work on behalf of Danny; Otto and Danny became his clients; and he co-authors an article in the most widely circulated newspaper in Chicago about the child! Wakschlag worked behind-the-scenes with the Warburtons... and **perhaps** with "Richard" at some time before his transfer to his natural parents. Otto and Daniela would never be informed about **any** treatment of Danny by Wakschlag, or any other individual for that matter, because their letter of request, addressed to Leventhal and sent by certified mail, was never answered. The letter formally requested "medical records, psychiatric and/or psychological records, to include treatment, evaluation, assessment, or any service(s) rendered [Danny/Baby Richard]." Otto, as the custodial parent of the child, made the written request on October 27, 1995, in an attempt to obtain any relevant and helpful information about his son and his medical history.

As of July 2003, no response has been forthcoming. **Instead**, Leventhal and Wakschlag turned to the newspaper, where they ostensibly lament: "He ["Richard"] has been hurt badly, at a time and in a way that may make it difficult for him ever to trust others easily. He may have trouble ever making solid attachments and feeling secure in them. The last thing he needs is...reopening old but exquisitely sensitive wounds."

The last thing Danny needed was more "professionals" issuing dire published predictions about his future, the state of his mental health, and his emotional wholeness.

It was Leventhal who advised the Warburtons on the day of Danny's brutal transfer. "Inside, the Does began to act out the scene they had rehearsed with the psychiatrist's help, according to Bennett L. Leventhal...," as reported in the *Chicago Tribune's* next-day coverage. "'The boy was brought in and introduced to them [the Kirchners],' said Leventhal, who was on the telephone with the Does throughout the day." (Janan Hanna and Peter Kendall, "Boy begins trip in tears, ends it calmly," May 1, 1995) The psychiatrist—whose involvement with the opposing side lacked the consent of the child's custodial parent—would never inform the Kirchners about his involvement in the transfer event of their son.

How do Leventhal and Wakschlag know about Danny's wounds? you might legitimately ask. Neither one ever spoke to the child or observed him after the incident—his transfer to his father and mother—to which they assign his emotional "scarring." Neither one ever spoke to the child's parents or to me, his therapist, at any time before issuing their public pronouncements about the boy's emotional state.

Otto and Daniela were appalled when they saw this disturbing and distorted article about their son. Otto neither gave his approval nor signed a release for either of these two individuals to go public about his child. He never waived practitioner-client confidentiality. In addition, attorney Mike Foley had earlier written to Leventhal to remind him of his ethical obligations to Otto and Danny:

> ...During the last week, we observed you on a number of television shows publicly commenting on the state of Danny's mental health.... We are sure you are aware that certain ethical and legal requirements of patient confidentiality are implicit in such an engagement [Leventhal's engagement by Otakar Kirchner on behalf of Danny in March 1995]. Mr. Kirchner has advised us that he has not agreed either verbally or in writing to release you from this obligation.... We ask you to explain in writing within ten calendar days how you have been authorized to release confidential medical information about Daniel Kirchner. (January 27, 1997)

Leventhal never responded to this letter, nor did he stop giving opinions about the high-profile child with whom he did not even interact.

Shortly after the publication of the Leventhal-Wakschlag piece, Danny reported to me that several of his classmates said "mean" things to him. Surely Danny deserved better. Surely these two "professionals" should have realized the potential impact of their ominous prognoses upon this real-life child, living nearby in a suburb of Chicago. Regardless of their purpose or motivations, about which we might reasonably speculate, they got themselves into print in a self-promotional manner...at Danny's expense..., all the while, without his parents' approval, presenting themselves as his advocates. They were both involved with the widely publicized "Baby Richard," they emphasize in their article, **before** the child "lost the rounds" that they self-proclaim they fought on his behalf. Their article is more about **them** than it is about this child, whom neither of them ever saw after the 1995 transfer. Lacking both first-hand information and credibility did not deter them from making public their "armchair" diagnosis and prognosis for Danny. They presented their imaginings as real.

Within the context of outrageous media coverage, I find myself reviewing the disappointing outcome of Otto and Danny's joint lawsuit against Bob Greene and the *Chicago Tribune* in 1996. Attorney Mike Foley—on a *pro bono* basis—took up their cause when he realized the ongoing, deleterious effects on Danny and his family from the continuous, vitriolic, and destructive attacks by Greene. Happily married and the father of two young daughters, Mike sympathized with Otto's lamentable predicament and deplored Danny's media image as an object of pity and derision. The Kirchners deserved a cessation of the journalistic bombardment and resultant public hostility. Danny, at the age of five, sorely needed restoration of his dignity and of reality to replace the rampant fantasy speculations about him. Mike sought legal atonement on behalf of Otto for the lies, distortions, and unfounded accusations made by Greene, over and over again, in his widely syndicated columns.

Specifically, in May 1996, attorney Foley filed a lawsuit for defamation and false light invasion of privacy against Defendants Bob Greene, the Chicago Tribune Company, and Chicago Tribune Newspapers:

> ...Defendants claimed that Otakar Kirchner had "broken" his son "like a dog," repeatedly called for the police, courts and child protection agencies to investigate him criminally, accused him of being party to a "crime," an "atrocity", an "unlawful act," and of seeking custody of his son for profit. All are untrue as Defendants now admit. As a result of these culminating acts in Greene's judicially recognized campaign of "journalistic terrorism", Otto Kirchner lost his job, his home, and his previously unsullied reputation....

> ...The Tribune published Otto's telephone records, treated Daniel as an object of public pity and Otto as a subject of public scorn. (Plaintiff's Reply Memorandum

to Defendants' Motion to Dismiss, Circuit Court of Cook County, Illinois)

Because Otto had inadvertently become a "public person" through the highly visible and well-known custody dispute, his grounds for a lawsuit were basically limited to having been wrongly accused of a crime. The power of the press—nearly absolute under the Constitution, Illinois laws, and precedent court rulings—allows journalists and newspapers to mount wide-scale attacks upon individuals, most especially upon "public persons," without the prospect of a successful legal challenge.

Greene and the Tribune responded that they "were merely spouting imaginative and rhetorical opinions." They asserted a "hyperbole" defense.

The lawsuit, on behalf of Danny and his father, clarified that "Bob Greene wrote about **nothing except** the Baby Richard case" for a span of six weeks after the date of the child's transfer to his biological father. "Since there was no news in that time, **Greene created news.** [He] invited Joseph Cardinal Bernardin to mediate between the Does and the Kirchners and treated it as a news item when the Cardinal accepted...." [Emphasis added]

Otto and Danny's petition pointed out that "[i]t was during this period that Greene began labeling the transfer of custody and refusal to provide visitation 'unlawful' and 'a crime' and to call for a criminal investigation [of the Kirchners]." The "baseless accusations of criminal conduct" and of "child abuse" include 33 specific items and 38 of Bob Greene's columns. In several columns, Greene compares the "crime" of Baby Richard to the Oklahoma City bombing and the Smith children drowned by their mother, and in others he compares "Richard" to a hostage, prisoners, and a Holocaust victim.

Although "Greene **admittedly** had no personal knowledge for any of his multiple published statements about what Daniel was feeling, thinking and experiencing [emphasis added]," he wrote as if he knew. Greene made frequent assertions such as "[w]hile it is unconstitutional to inflict cruel and unusual punishment upon even the vilest criminals, it is apparently perfectly acceptable to inflict it upon an innocent child" ("Even Prisoners Can Talk to Loved Ones," *Chicago Tribune*,

June 11, 1995). Calling for state-agency intervention, he wrote:

> What has happened in these 24 days since Richard was taken
> away? There are child-protection agencies in this state that
> are mandated to find out the answers to questions like that.
> ("Is It Really Such A Joke?" *Chicago Tribune*, May 24, 1995)

And, Greene "reported on a proposal [he] had made to Otto's attor-
ney to have Cardinal Bernardin see the boy, to 'assure people he's
OK.'" ("Hope For Richard—If He Is Permitted It," *Chicago
Tribune*, June 7, 1995)

In September 1996, the presiding judge dismissed Otto and
Danny's lawsuit. The ruling was a profound disappointment to
those of us who love Danny. It gave life to the old Gypsy curse:
"May you have a lawsuit in which you know you are in the right."

Of course, Bob Greene kept on writing...and things kept getting progressively worse for the Kirchner family.

Mulling over recent events, I am stunned and dismayed by the incredible contradiction between Greene's fantasy-based journalistic bombardments and my first-hand personal experiences. As an ongoing frequent visitor to the Kirchners' home, I always look forward to my time there. Theirs is a home filled with quiet happiness and the

Danny (six) poses with one of his Christmas gifts at my home in December 1997.

Otto and Danny, sitting across the table from Daniela and Sharon, celebrate with Robert and me our last Christmas dinner as Illinois residents; it is a bitter-sweet occasion.

laughter of children. I wonder why it is not a crime for one columnist, and the newspapers that publish and syndicate his writings, to work toward the destruction of an innocent family, and with no accountability and no repercussions. They sell newspapers and increase their readership by turning a normal little boy into a public curiosity and a pathetic creature and by making serious, hateful, and admittedly false—"hyperbolic"— accusations against his parents, all under the pretense of being the child's advocate!

On February 26, 1997, I received a certified-mail letter from the American Psychological Association, dismissing the October 1995 complaint against me. For sixteen months I wondered and worried about the status of this matter. The complaint, by Dr. Marlin Hoover, stated, "I have no direct knowledge of this case, and rely only on information offered in the newspaper…[,] the accusations raised by the columnist, Bob Greene…." Absent any evidence of an ethical violation of any kind, the A.P.A. decided that no hearing would be held and no further action would be taken.

Daniela (with Sharon on her lap), Danny, and I pose at Daniela's baby shower in January 1998. Jessica arrived on March 15th, one day before Danny's seventh birthday.

It hardly matters any more, as Robert and I are irreversibly involved in our plans to move away from the debris of "Baby Richard." With the relocation, of course, will automatically come the end of my practice of psychology. I remember when Otto Kirchner told me many months ago, "I no longer have the heart to play the violin"—for which skill he had practiced since the age of four, including seven years of music academy training. Now, with genuine empathy, I no longer have the heart to work as a therapist, for which profession I worked my way through college for eleven intense years—five full-time and six part-time.

Disillusioned and angry beyond words, I resolve to move on, to create a new life, and to continue to assist the Kirchner family as much as possible. Although I could not know at the time— as I relocated to Florida—I would never hear from the State of

Illinois Department of Professional Regulation about their findings related to the flood of complaints made against me as the result of Bob Greene's columns attacking me. Of course, no news is always good news in this type of matter. If there had been a shred of evidence of anything inappropriate on my part, the "imminent" hearing about which Investigator Battiste informed me would indeed have been held. Bottom line, I no longer cared.

I remember the plaque, displayed in a colleague's office, that so impressed me:

> **"The Courage of Integrity"**
> **...Choosing right over wrong, ethics over convenience, and truth over popularity...these are the choices that measure your life. Travel the path of integrity without looking back, for there is never a wrong time to do the right thing.**

I continued to support Otto, Daniela, and Danny, as their advocate and friend, after nearly everyone else abandoned them. When attorney Heinemann stepped aside, after having lapsed into a good guy/bad guy mode—with himself as the former and his client Otto as the latter—I stepped forward, at the Kirchners' request, to represent them to the media. I was swept by one columnist into the rubble left by an unprecedented level of continuous media bombardment. I became part of the collateral damage. Refusing to regret my decision, I chose to embrace it fully and loyally.

Feeling as if I have received a huge blank canvas and a new set of paints to create a wholly revised, more colorful scene for my future, I gratefully embraced a Florida life-style as a happily anonymous newcomer. Robert and I adjusted easily to our new environment. We set about the business of making friends and trying out new pursuits in a warm, sunny climate.

One year after our relocation to Florida, columnist John Kass shared his insights and evaluative perceptions about Baby Richard as it contrasted with another Chicago-based child custody dispute. Baby T, an African-American baby who was born with cocaine in his system, had been placed, when only eight days old, in the foster care of white parents, a popular alderman and his wife, an appellate court judge. Later, the child's mother, a "recovering black drug addict," proved that she had overcome her drug addiction, and a judge subsequently awarded her custody of her three-year-old child.

After asserting that "What's missing [in the Baby T case] is...making fun of people because of their looks and their accents," Kass continued:

Don't you remember the Baby Richard story?

...It was a consuming passion of columnists.... talk show hosts and broadcast news directors.... Daniela and Otakar Kirchner[,] were subjected to a media feeding frenzy and they were the entrée.

And their crime? They wanted to raise their own son....

Otakar wasn't an African-American drug addict. Instead, he was a violinist from Eastern Europe—the kind of species left unprotected by journalistic adherence to political correctness.

And his baby was white. White America might pity a black cocaine baby [Baby T], but the white middle class won't identify as strongly....

...Otakar was fitted with a clown suit by the Chicago media and got slapped around like a chump for wanting to raise his boy.... [h]e got slimed....

...[T]he Warburtons turned [the handover] into an ugly public spectacle. They invited the TV cameras to show us the hysterical child, hands outstretched, screaming for his adoptive parents.

...[I]nstead of being criticized for manipulating a child's fear, the Warburtons were the ones who were applauded.... ("In Baby T case, media circus didn't come to town," *Chicago Tribune*, March 10, 1999)

This unusual and belated spurt of journalistic support for Otto and Daniela meant little to them or their daily lives. They had long before chosen to ignore the newspapers in a determined attempt at emotional self-protection.

Meanwhile, I knew, Otto was still widely perceived as a child abuser by many and as a criminal by many others. After all, that's what the public read in the newspaper coverage. Many of my clients and acquaintances called these "realities" when they would talk about "Baby Richard," almost invariably referred to as "that poor child."

"The advertisement is the most truthful part of a newspaper," Thomas Jefferson opined many generations ago. More recently, Norman Mailer observed, "Once a newspaper touches a story, the facts are lost forever, even to the protagonists." It seems to me that, in sync with both of these sentiments, after a newspaper touches a story dozens—or hundreds—of times, as in Baby Richard, the distortions are magnified in a geometric proportion. Certainly the basic facts were lost. And more....

If there were a Ripley's Believe-It-Or-Not category for "Person Most Betrayed by Lies," Otakar Kirchner would be a prime contender. He became the innocent victim of his mother's broken promise to reclaim him, of his aunt's lie to Daniela, of the lies about his infant son's death, of the lie in the would-be adoptive parents' affidavits, and of years of groundless allegations, intended distortions, and outright lies in the media. As columnist John Kass observed, Otto's only crime was simply wanting to raise his own son.

I realized that any of my other clients—especially those involved in litigation related to divorce, child custody, or similar matters—could be victimized in a similar manner. They, too, could be sacrificed on the altar of commercial media interests—for increased sales of newspapers or for capturing a coveted superior market share on television. In fact, just about anyone could fall victim if the circumstances are right.

Danny learned to swim while visiting us in Florida. In August 1998—six months after our move—the Kirchners drove to our condo in Ormond-by-the-Sea to enjoy their two-week vacation on the beach of the Atlantic Ocean, twenty-six miles from our home. Accompanying Otto, Daniela, and the three children were Daniela's parents, recently arrived from Slovakia. We held pool parties at our house and a collective birthday celebration for all of us who had observed the official passage of another year since we had been together. The pink and purple frosting on our shared cake spelled out "HAPPY BIRTHDAY, EVERYONE!" The Kirchners spent part of each day walking the beach and jumping into the giant waves lapping onto the sand. They built sandcastles together and, when the ocean tides got too strong for safety, they swam in the oceanside pool.

Grandma Greta tearfully thanked us for her last opportunity to spend time on the ocean. "I'm sure I won't ever have the chance again before I die," she said in English, with a little help from Daniela. "I love it!" she said, all on her own.

"We can't get Danny out of the water," Otto would say, winking and smiling at his seven-year-old son. "He's going to turn into a fish!" Danny would grin.

The family drove to Disney World; at the Magic Kingdom they took pictures with Mickey Mouse; and they all came away with suntans and souvenirs. Robert and I hosted a farewell barbecue party at our house on the evening before their departure for home.

Otto and Danny (seven) meet at the edge of the pool at our Ormond Beach condo after Danny's first successful unassisted swim across its length.

The Kirchner family, including
Grandma Greta, enjoy the
Atlantic Ocean beach at
Ormond-by-the-Sea, Florida.

On the lanai of our Palm Coast
home, Danny and his dad await
the imminent arrival of our
"Birthday Cake for Everyone."

Missing them more, of course, after they returned to Illinois, I would accelerate my shopping trips to toy stores and to children's clothing aisles in department stores. It helped me feel more connected.

I continued to enjoy bits and pieces from their lives through exchanged photographs and frequent phone conversations.

"I just heard the song 'Butterfly Kisses' on the radio," Otto shared with me one evening. His voice wavered, and I knew that he especially related to the words about the love of a daughter:

> ...I thank God for all of the joy in my life.... Oh, and most of all, butterfly kisses.... With all that I've done wrong, I must have done something right to deserve her love every morning and butterfly kisses at night....

Privately sentimental, Otto is always visibly moved by lyrics and stories about children.

Daniela confides to me her worries about every prospective new event in Danny's life. How will he do? Will people recognize him as "Baby Richard"? Will they relate to him in a menacing manner if they do recognize him? She remembers all too well the reactions of people, ranging from curious to hostile, during his earliest months with her and his father. The unwelcome attention continued, albeit progressively less frequently, across years. Daniela's first impulse is always to shield him, but she also knows that he must learn to make his own way. Fortunately, Danny has always been self-assured and an extravert. He initiates contact and conversation with children of all ages, and he seems consistently drawn more to the older children in his environment.

Robert and I continue to visit the Kirchner family in Chicago three or four times every year. Our arrival is always greeted with spontaneous hugs and kisses, no matter how long between visits. Most of the time, all three children are waiting for us, watching through their front window. They always have plans for our playing with them, board games lined up or bicycles ready for rides up and down the sidewalk. "Try to catch me!" Sharon will yell as she jumps onto her bike and speeds away, glancing over her shoulder to make sure that one of us is chasing her or pretending to run after her. Danny demonstrates for us his most recent accomplishment with his hockey stick or in his skating ability. Jessica follows the lead of her older siblings, shyly peeking to ensure that she is also being watched for her agility or grace.

During one of our visits when Danny was nine, and he sat between Robert and me on his living room sofa, he turned to me with a quizzical expression. "Karen, were you my doctor?" he asked.

"Yes, Danny, I was—when you first came to live with your parents."

"I thought so," he affirmed, nodding with a knowing smile. After a short pause, he continued, "Are you a vet?"

Laughing at the incongruity of his question, I responded, "No, Danny, I'm not a vet—I'm a psychologist. Do you know what that is?"

He answered in the affirmative.

Most of the greeting cards and notes that I send to him and his family are covered with pictures of animals of all kinds. Danny had recently studied occupations in school, I discovered, and he wondered how I fit into the scheme of vocational pursuits. Because of my obvious love of animals, he had assumed that I might be a veterinarian. By this conversation, I was reminded that to Danny I was "always there," like a member of his family, and he did not perceive me as his "doctor." We would talk privately about his feelings, and he became conditioned, from his very first week with his parents, to report to me the events of his day. He would make a point of telling me if he had been "bad," such as the rare occasions when he would become defiant with his grandmother. It was as if he was turning himself in, confessing to a misdeed and seeking absolution. Danny was always remorseful after those infrequent times of misbehavior. Usually he would share with me the good news about his life, his most recent play activity with his cousin, friends, or neighbors, or his latest toy acquisition.

Danny's favorite family album took on fuller meaning for him when he traveled to the Slovak Republic in the summer of 2000. While Otto remained at home to work full-time at his waiter job, Daniela took the three children for a two-month vacation to their native country, where Danny and his siblings interacted extensively with their grandparents, aunt, uncle, and cousins. Danny was delighted to spend time again with Mario, a teenager who enthusiastically welcomed his American cousins.

"I like everyone!" Danny announced to his mother. In fact, he asked if his parents might consider moving to Slovakia on a permanent basis.

"Danny wanted to stay," Daniela told me upon their return to the States, on time for Danny to begin fourth grade in the early fall. "He loved playing hockey with the other kids, going to parks, and having fun. He liked the way kids play there; it's easy, safe, and different for him." She concluded meaningfully, "Danny fit in there." As Daniela shared with me the highlights of their extended stay, I found myself thinking that the warm reception and accepting environment in Slovakia were palpably better for Danny, whose everyday experiences as the "Baby Richard" Kirchner have been colored by strangers' gawking, rudeness, and manifestations of hostility. In the country of his biological roots, he is just an ordinary, nice boy, a blood relative, and a happy guest.

At Robert's birthday party, held at Fox's Restaurant in Orland Park during February 2001, Daniela attended with Danny, Sharon, and Jessica. Because it was Sunday, Otto's most demanding workday, he was unable to attend. Danny, handsome in his navy blue suit and crisp white shirt, sat at the head of a long table. Sharon and Jessica, attired in bright red and burgundy velvet outfits respectively, looked beautiful. Daniela, proud of her well-behaved children, met all of Robert's and my relatives. Danny helped Robert cut the large birthday sheetcake, decorated with extra frosting and candy flowers. A highlight of the event was the surprise bagpiper, who arrived with his blaring pipes playing a cacophonous version of "Happy Birthday." The piper finished with "Danny Boy," an Irish favorite, which he dedicated to Danny, who sat a little taller and grinned his delight.

"I didn't even know there **was** a song called 'Danny Boy'," he told me later. "I really like it."

The next day I sent him a CD of the song, performed by an Irish tenor, so that he could hear and understand all of the words of this poignant ballad of his name.

During the following year, his fifth grade at the local public school, Danny did well both academically and socially. Earning straight A's on two of his four report cards, missing that accomplishment by only one or two B grades at the other two grading periods, Danny was proud and his parents were pleased. However, Daniela expressed to me concerns about the behavior of some of her son's classmates that she had observed and found disturbing. She seeks good role models for Danny among his classmates and the older children.

"Some of the kids use bad language and are very rough and rude," she related when we discussed options for his school of choice. "It's time for Danny to attend the Catholic school. I think the children are better behaved there, and they also learn religion and good values in addition to their academic subjects." Otto and Daniela began to save their money for the parochial-school tuition for the following year.

During July 2002, Daniela and the children came, via their minivan, to spend their two-week vacation in Palm Coast. Otto stayed behind, taking advantage of the opportunity to work during the Fourth of July holiday weekend. Money is an ever present and pressing issue for the Kirchner family, as they are working toward extricating themselves from debts incurred during their custody-battle years and Otto's long bouts of involuntary unemployment.

"The children were so good on the way down," Daniela reported, with a mixture of pride and delight, upon their arrival. "They sang to the radio, slept in the back, and played games. They never complained and were no trouble at all. I'm just glad that I know now that I can do this by myself—that I can drive twenty-plus hours with them." We lapsed into conversation about the happy prospect of an annual vacation for the family in Florida, hopefully with Otto able to join them as well, if they can forgo his earned income for a span of two weeks.

Danny was introduced to the game of golf by Robert, who outfitted him with a small starter-set of clubs and an extra golf bag. Daniela, Sharon, Jessica, and I accompanied Robert and Danny to the closest golf course, where we watched the novice and his new mentor hit balls on the range and then try their hand at putting on the practice green. Danny, a natural athlete, enjoyed himself immediately, took direction with an obvious seriousness of purpose, and noticeably improved across the span of two hours. That night and the next morning in the condo, he practiced, determined to sink his putts with greater frequency in the silver metal cup that Robert gave him. He also read four of Robert's *Golf* magazines from cover to cover. At the age of eleven, Danny demonstrated a level of self-discipline and an ability to focus that are more typical of an older youngster. These personality characteristics contribute to his demonstrated success in establishing and maintaining relationships with older children.

Daniela and the children enjoyed a day of fun at Marineland, observing the park's large variety of sea creatures, including tourist-friendly dolphins. The next day Robert and I toured old St. Augustine with them and stopped for a long, lingering lunch at Sunset Grille, overlooking a pristine stretch of beach on the Atlantic Ocean.

Sitting on our blankets and beach towels on the sand, all six of us—Daniela, Robert, and I, along with the children—watched the Independence Day fireworks burst and sparkle over the ocean. In the dark, the massive surf roared just yards away from our claimed spot, and the moon cast a glowing streak of light across the huge expanse of water. Four couples of middle-aged people, settled onto lawn chairs next to us, were enjoying champagne, sandwiches, and candlelight. Obviously, they were holiday beach pros and we were rookies, but we cooed and marveled with escalating levels of enthusiasm over each new firework erupting into hundreds of red, green, white, or golden yellow points of light overhead. It was my favorite Fourth of July ever.

Watching those three children, giddy with joy and glad to be together, and their mother, more at peace than I have seen her in years, I found myself musing over the turbulent paths that they have traveled. It was that night I decided that someday I must and I would write the story of "Baby Richard"—the inside, untold story of this gentle, real-life child, molding a sand castle with his little sisters at the edge of their shared blanket, under a canopy of stars and clusters of sparkling lights.

One joy dispels a hundred cares.

— Confucius

At Robert's birthday party in Orland Park, Illinois, in February 2001,
Danny listens to a bagpiper play "Danny Boy" as a tribute to the nine-year-old.

During their visit with us in July 2002, Daniela opens a birthday gift as Danny and his sisters, taking a break from swimming, gather to participate in the event.

Left to right: Jessica (four), Danny (eleven), and Sharon (six) enjoy the beach at Marineland, Florida.

CHAPTER SEVENTEEN

Judge James D. Heiple

GREETING me at his front door, Judge James Heiple smiles warmly, invites me inside, and helps me remove my bulky, purple winter coat and matching knit scarf. It is Christmastime 2002, in Peoria, Illinois, and the controversial, now-retired Illinois Supreme Court judge has graciously consented to provide me with an exclusive interview. I have flown to Chicago from my home in Florida and driven three hours in my rental car to meet him for this special privilege. I know that in recent years Judge Heiple has avoided the media. He is a private person with an aversion to publicity, especially now that he no longer sits on the Supreme Court. We share a common element in our respective careers—we were both vilified by columnist Bob Greene for our Baby Richard involvement—the judge for authoring the Court's unpopular ruling in the case and I for being the "Richard" psychologist, on the father's side of the conflict.

Perhaps for the reason of mutual empathy for each other's plight, Judge Heiple responded affirmatively to my recent letter, requesting first-hand information from him about the Baby Richard case.

Most striking to me is that Judge Heiple, 69, looks ten years younger in person than in his official photographs, wearing the black judicial robe. Today he is wearing a yellow-and-brown

> **Living well is the best revenge.**
>
> *— George Herbert*

plaid shirt and tan corduroy jeans. He is tall and slender; has thinning, sandy-colored hair; and wears gold wire-rimmed eye- glasses. His gait is quick and agile, reminding me of an athlete. He shares with me that one of his favorite activities is planting a large variety of trees on his local 360-acre tree farm. The phys- ical demands of this work and the sense of fulfillment in being close to nature are rewarding and exhilarating. He owns anoth- er farm as well, one that grows corn and soybeans. The judge employs a farm manager to oversee both farms on his behalf.

We talk in his living room for an hour and continue our con- versation at a nearby specialty restaurant, over a lunch of health food, after which we return to his home for our final discussion. At the eatery, several of the locals recognize him and approach for handshakes and effusive greetings. One of them, a long-time friend, enthusiastically provides us an update on his Abraham Lincoln collection; the man has recently given some of his most prized possessions to his son. It is apparent that Judge Heiple is a well-known and much-respected citizen in his hometown.

"My law clerk informed me that I have been the topic of **sev- enty** of Bob Greene's columns in the *Tribune* and its syndicated newspapers," the judge tells me. "That explains my image— which continues to this day—that I am both an enemy of chil- dren and anti-adoption. Neither characterization is true. Although I rarely read his columns, my clerk chose to keep track of his writings about me. Greene would call my office; I always declined to speak with him; and he would direct my clerk, 'Tell the judge I am writing another column about him tomorrow.'"

This taunting behavior continued across months and then years. Greene targeted Heiple as responsible for the Illinois Supreme Court decision that returned Baby Richard to his bio- logical father, Otakar Kirchner, because of the deception under- lying the unlawful adoption of the child by the Does/Warburtons. Even though this Court ruling was unani- mous, 7 – 0, Heiple received the brunt of the rancor of both the media and the public. The other six Justices maintained a low profile in the case, allowing Heiple to author their decision and failing to remind the frenzied media that each of the seven had an equal voice and vote in the final outcome.

"The Baby Richard case was one of the easiest, least compli- cated cases in my thirty years as a jurist," the judge relates.

"It was a slam dunk—a direct application of the law; but it was the most monstrous case in terms of the publicity and its disastrous effects on my reputation. The case itself was so consistently misconstrued by the media that it was astonishing."

"What does it all mean today?" I ask him.

Without hesitation, Judge Heiple answers, "It showed how a case can be distorted by the media and result in so much damage.

"The press—and most notably Greene—tried to dictate to the court, at each level, what its ruling should be in this case. Early on, the Warburtons, named the Does in the petitions and pleadings, were supported and championed as victims by Greene. The other journalists and reporters accepted his position and advanced it. No one seemed to read the court decision itself; everyone read Bob Greene for **his** 'truth.' It was incestuous, these relationships among the media," he proclaims, shaking his head in disbelief.

"Greene was engaged in 'journalistic terrorism,' as I wrote in the July 1994 order that denied the Warburtons' request for a rehearing of our unanimous ruling from the previous month. They seemed to do all that they could to delay the inevitable. They should have given up that child to his father when Otakar Kirchner asserted his claim to parent his son before the baby was two months old. I always wondered why they were so persistent...."

Judge Heiple describes to me his forty-one years in Illinois law. After earning his law degree from the University of Louisvillle and later a master's of law degree from the University of Virginia, he spent his first eleven years in private practice as an attorney. He was following in the career footsteps of his father, he explains, "a strong man, a lawyer, a banker, and a businessman."

"I was doing general law, with a variety of different cases, and after a decade I grew tired of its mundane aspects. When provided the opportunity to run for election as a Tazewell County circuit judge, I took it. I was elected and served in that capacity for ten years; then was elected to the appellate court for another ten years; and finally, in 1990, I was elected to the Supreme Court, where I served for another decade." He summarizes, with a smile, "I seem to do everything in ten-year segments."

An idealist from his earliest days, Judge Heiple eventually became disillusioned at every level of his career. "I always expected the best of people and was often disappointed," he says. "The court should be above politics, independent of outside forces, and determined to respect and implement the law. I discovered that some judges were influenced by publicity or other pressures. I pride myself on having been genuinely independent, but I have paid a big price and made enemies.

"Although some judges assign their law clerks to write their opinions," he continues, "I worked with an individual clerk on each opinion. The clerk would assist me with legal research and initial drafts, but the final work product was my own. On the Supreme Court, each justice has four law clerks. We hear about 165 cases each year. With few exceptions, taking a case is discretionary—we choose which ones to review. Yet, we accept only four or five percent of the cases that are appealed."

As I am listening, I marvel that "Baby Richard" was one among so few cases selected by the Illinois Supreme Court for its review.

"Until recently, Illinois Supreme Court Justice James D. Heiple was known mainly in legal circles as a competent, outspoken, sometimes acerbic judge," wrote Janan Hanna. "But his position on the 'Baby Richard' case has thrust the Pekin native into the center of an emotional statewide debate." Presenting Heiple's outspokenness as "unusual for a judge," the article continues:

> He has displayed that kind of candor frequently throughout his judicial career.... For the most part, however, judges and lawyers familiar with Heiple say he is a competent judge with a fine legal mind. ("Heiple has a history of not mincing words," *Chicago Tribune*, July 13, 1994).

Today, the judge's spacious home—half of a red-brick, corner-lot duplex in a quiet, heavily treed subdivision of Peoria—reflects the conservatism and simple good taste of a retired widower. His wife of thirty-six years died in 1995, and he has lived alone since that time. For the past several years, he and Cynthia ("Cisty"), a woman who lives in her own home only five minutes away, "have been a couple," the judge tells me. Cisty stops by the house during my visit in order to snap a few photographs, which I have requested, of the judge and me. She is a lovely woman, thin, with short, dark hair, and a ready smile. She is ten years younger than he.

Pointing out a portrait on his den wall, Cisty exclaims, "He **loves** my dog; in fact, he walks him almost every night." The judge beams an admiring glance at the framed picture of a curled-up sleeping beagle, and he explains that he commissioned it from a local artist. "He is so attached to that dog," Cisty adds, with affection in her voice, as she reaches for her coat to leave for home. She reminds the judge about their concert plans for tonight.

I am delighted to have had the opportunity to meet Cisty during my five-hour interview with Judge Heiple.

His living room contains, instead of the expected couch and coffee table, a cluster of large comfortable chairs, assembled facing each other for good conversation. Some are armchairs, some rocking chairs. The adjacent dining area is devoid of a table for eating, making the entire area appear uncluttered and spacious. It holds a massive, wood storage unit and displays a large, colorful portrait of the judge's grandmother, at the age of four, painted in 1864 by Louis Lussier, an itinerant portrait artist, and counted among his most cherished possessions. The large kitchen contains a table and four chairs; it is both cozy and well lit by a latticed window. Downstairs is an office, filled with shelves of books and other publications as well as a desk, computer, and chair. On one of its walls is a painting of his cabin in Canada, to which the judge escapes for six weeks of R & R during the summer months. Upstairs are his bedroom, with an antique four-poster bed and dresser; and a huge den, housing an overstuffed armchair, television set, and more books lining the walls and sitting on various tables. Judge Heiple spends a great deal of his newfound leisure time in reading for pleasure and in researching by computer out-of-print books by his favorite authors.

"While on the bench, I had to read so much—many hours every week—that I avoided reading for pleasure, but now I can enjoy a range of books by a variety of authors," he says, smiling. "I have also taken several local computer courses. As a jurist, I had assistants and law clerks who did the computer work for me, but in retirement I have discovered the expansiveness of the Internet and the incredibly wide world of the computer. It has been wonderful.

"Although I rarely think about the Baby Richard case today—I have put it behind me—it did have a profound impact upon me and my career," he discloses. "I suffered social ostracism and received a bushel basket full of hate mail and death threats, a steady deluge for months. My cousin who had adopted children wrote me a nasty letter, deploring 'my' Baby Richard decision. She was one among many who chose to vent their anger my way.

"Some people expressed their wish that my own children would die so that I would know what the Warburtons went through."

Walter Jacobson, a long-time newscaster for FOX television, criticized Heiple on his news programs and went so far as to display the judge's home telephone number during one of his telecasts. Jacobson encouraged the viewing public to express their rage over the Baby Richard ruling by telephoning the judge at home.

"Many dozens of calls came at a time when my wife was dying of fibrosis of the lungs and she was on oxygen," he relates, frowning. "Although she was a non-smoker her entire life, she contracted this fatal disease. She suffered with it for five years. I most vividly remember walking into the room during one call that she had picked up. The anonymous caller said, 'Your husband is an evil man,' to which I heard her reply, 'Yes, and I am an evil woman.' She had good humor, spirit, and courage, but it was a difficult and painful time."

"Jacobson made an on-air apology for 'crossing the line' after the legal community became outraged at his unprecedented, unacceptable behavior, did he not?" I ask the judge, testing the accuracy of my recall of those events.

"Yes, but of course the damage was already done," he says. "I changed our telephone number but not before the flood of angry, sometimes threatening, calls poured into our home, at the worst possible time in terms of my wife's declining health."

As I listen to his reliving those sad times, I wonder about his wife's last days. On her deathbed, she also fell victim to the media-generated "Baby Richard" hysteria and hatred. Her devastating illness could only have been exacerbated by round-the-clock telephone incursions into their private life. Surely her husband must have felt undeserved guilt and understandable anger in response.

She did not live to see the most tempestuous episode for her husband. In early 1997, during the same month that he became

Chief Justice, Judge Heiple suffered an onslaught of media-fostered criticism, created over a traffic violation and expanding into a proposed impeachment hearing and the voluntary termination of his Chief Justiceship near the beginning of its three-year term. These startling developments were admittedly more the result of Baby Richard furor than of the alleged events that prompted such intense public scrutiny and overreaction.

By an astounding 113-0 vote, the Illinois House created a bipartisan investigatory panel to determine whether cause existed to impeach Heiple for his alleged behavior during a series of traffic stops across several years and for his role in shaping the judicial panel that reviewed the accusations against him. "On a day when even the most mundane of bills generated half-hour debates, the Heiple vote lasted less than five minutes," according to the front-page *Chicago Sun-Times* article on April 15, 1997 (Dave McKinney, "Move to impeach Heiple"). "A historic step," the coverage continues:

> Monday's vote sets up an almost unprecedented battle between two Illinois branches of governments: the Legislature and the judiciary. The rules of battle are untested, and the definition of an impeachable offense is not spelled out in the state Constitution.

In its editorial entitled "Call off Heiple hunt," the *Sun-Times* summarizes "this unhappy episode":

> Anytime Heiple's name is mentioned, almost in the same breath comes a reference to the Baby Richard case in which Heiple wrote the opinion on the court's unanimous ruling. No impeachment proceeding will be free of suspicion that it is little more than revenge for that unpopular ruling. That means no such proceeding will be free of the taint of political meddling in the judicial system—a much more serious offense than anything Heiple has done. (May 6, 1997)

In late January 1997, the Illinois Judicial Inquiry Board filed a complaint against Judge Heiple, accusing him of misconduct during four traffic stops:

On Nov. 14, 1992, in Mason City, Illinois, Heiple was stopped for speeding; when asked for his driver's license, Heiple initially produced his court ID; he also produced an expired insurance card.

On Nov. 24, 1995, in Creve Coeur, Illinois, Heiple was stopped for speeding. He initially produced his court ID and then his driver's license. No ticket was issued.

On Jan. 8, 1996, a Tazewell County deputy sheriff stopped Heiple for speeding. Heiple produced his court ID. No ticket was issued.

On Jan. 27, 1996, in Pekin, Illinois, after stopped by a police officer, Heiple "drove off without permission" and continued three blocks farther to his home. When police stopped him in his driveway, he failed a "field sobriety test," but a Breathalyzer test at the police station showed no alcohol at all. He was charged with resisting arrest but, in a plea bargain, was convicted of two petty traffic offenses—disobeying police and speeding—and he paid an agreed fine of $200.

Hours before the January 1997 complaint was announced, three of Heiple's fellow judges alleged that an order entered by him regarding an administrative appointment did not include their dissents. Their disagreement with the order was based upon their opinion that the appointment violated the State Constitution and the court's rules. Specifically, the order—supported by a majority, Heiple and three other Justices—appointed Justice William Holdridge of the Illinois Appellate Court in Peoria to take over as director of the Administrative Office of the Illinois Courts. This administrative position had always been full-time, and the three dissenting judges claimed that a sitting judge could not perform two jobs—the Illinois Constitution requires that judges "devote full time to judicial duties."

Earlier that same week, Governor James Edgar chastised the Illinois Supreme Court during his State of the State address for its two-year-old ruling in the Baby Richard case. Heiple, prominently the author of the ruling, was sitting in the front row of Edgar's audience. The Governor continued by asserting that he hoped that, during the coming year, the court would resolve "the Baby Richard tragedy."

Earlier that same month, the news broke—on both a local and a national basis—that Otakar and Daniela Kirchner had separated. The story, typically sensationalized by the angle of

Otto's "having abandoned Baby Richard, for whom he had fought in the courts," created another series of public protests and clamor. The media—again led by Bob Greene—reminded the nation about Judge Heiple's role in the unpopular "Richard" ruling, "even more tragic" for the child than before, within the context of the marital separation of his parents.

"A judge or a court cannot be held responsible for events that occur years after a judicial ruling," Heiple says as we discuss the resurrected Baby Richard controversy in 1997. "We cannot be expected to have crystal balls to predict the future. We simply must make decisions based upon the law and not allow ourselves to be influenced by the press or by public opinion. The court must remain independent," he summarizes.

Within that **one month**, Heiple assumed the position of Chief Justice of the Illinois Supreme Court; the media splashed the Kirchners' separation across airwaves and newsprint; the Illinois Judicial Inquiry Board took up the complaint—based on traffic violations—against Heiple for ethics charges; and Heiple's political and media enemies jumped into the fray. It was no coincidence that these events coincided.

In the fullness of time since those charges, there are those today who might revert to cliches such as "a mountain out of a molehill" or "a tempest in a teapot" to describe Heiple's plight. After he was ticketed by police officers on January 27, 1996, it was a mystery as to how his three previous contacts with traffic police surfaced so publicly and became such a heated issue in January 1997, and across subsequent months. Yet, these traffic situations—coupled with the controversial administrative appointment—led to widespread, statewide cries for Heiple's impeachment from the Supreme Court.

Throughout the entire twentieth century, Heiple's was the first impeachment attempt upon an Illinois Supreme Court judge. And, a traffic violation was the impetus—not treason or a major crime or accepting a bribe—that led to an immediate witch-hunt of other alleged offenses by Judge Heiple.

The judge was accused of attempting to avoid the January 1996 traffic ticket by allegedly asking the police officer, "Do you know who I am?"

Heiple's alleged conduct in the traffic incidents was scrutinized vis-à-vis Supreme Court Rule 61, requiring a judge to "observe high standards of conduct in order to preserve the integrity of the judiciary" and Supreme Court Rule 62, requiring a judge to "respect and comply with the law...."

In "State targets Heiple conduct," the *Chicago Tribune's* Ken Armstrong quotes legal experts regarding the situation:

Northwestern University law professor Steven Lubet [said], "On a scale of impropriety from 1 to 10, it's a 2."

"It's inappropriate, but frankly, it's pretty far down the food chain of ethical impropriety," said Patrick McFadden, a Loyola University Chicago law professor. "It's not like taking a bribe. It's not directly related to the courtroom." (January 24, 1997)

When asked about the motivations of his accusers during those troubled times, Judge Heiple candidly tells me, "Although I do not believe that the traffic stop itself was politically motivated, I believe that the ensuing events were orchestrated by my enemies.

"The police officer, running radar, pulled me over for speeding twelve miles over the limit at about 1:00 a.m. on a bitter cold, blustery night when I was returning from my friend Cisty's house to my own. He was looking for drunken drivers. I had fallen asleep at Cisty's house and had not been drinking at all. She had awakened me and I headed for home. No one was on the streets at that hour. A police car appeared, its lights flashing, and pulled me over. After I gave the officer my papers, he returned them to me and—I thought—he said 'Go on.' I drove away toward home, but—to my surprise—I saw him in my rear view mirror, still following me. In my driveway, he confronted me again. Two other squad cars—with four officers—arrived immediately with their sirens blaring. The first officer asked why I had run from him. I told him that I thought he'd said, 'Go on,' and he exclaimed that he had said, 'Hold on.'

"The officer directed me to walk—heel to toe—the concrete line in my driveway," the judge continues. "He then directed me to close my eyes and touch my finger to the end of my nose. 'You touched the **bridge** of your nose, and you've failed the sobriety test,' he announced."

Judge Heiple then describes for me the ensuing scene. The officer informs him that he will write up citations for the violations. "On that night, I neither said nor did anything to avoid a ticket. Prior to being handcuffed, I told the officer to write up any tickets he wanted while I would wait in the kitchen. It was very cold outside." One of the newly arrived, back-up officers jumps in front of him to prevent him from moving. Before he realizes what is happening, the judge is pushed onto the hood of his car, handcuffed, and then shoved into the police vehicle. Judge Heiple continues, "On the way to the police station, the officer started to explain my legal rights. At that point, I was angry and asked him if he knew who he was talking to. I neither needed nor wanted my legal rights explained."

It didn't take long for the media to jump in.

"During the handcuffing encounter, I feared physical violence," he tells me. Listening to the judge describe his ordeal, I am wondering what I would do in such circumstances, as—with a chill—I realize that the police have both power and prerogative.

"Overreaction" is the best and kindest word for the police officers that comes to my mind as I envision the early-morning scene that culminated in a humiliating, hands-on arrest of a respectable and respected sixty-three-year-old man who has spent his career in the practice of law.

Predictably, Bob Greene launches another series of vehement columns, highly critical of the judge, including one entitled, "Heiple suddenly finds time to think of Joe and Richard." Recycling Baby Richard and Baby Joe—"those poor children," "those voiceless children"—-Greene continues his tirade against the judge who authored the Illinois Supreme Court's decisions in both cases.

"Regarding the allegation that I threw my weight around and said, 'Do you know who I am?' in order to avoid a ticket, that simply isn't so," the judge adds. "The Pekin Police knew who I was without my mentioning it. My entire decades-long legal and judicial career had been in that little town of 30,000 people. I had lived within five blocks of the police station for the previous twenty-five years. They thought they had a trophy drunken driver in their clutches and wanted to make the most of it. Unfortunately for them, I was stone sober. At the initial stop when I handed the officer my driver's license, he would already know my identity by the time we had our conversation through my open car window." Judge Heiple shakes his head as he recalls the painful incident. "It was a misunderstanding that led to a series of events that I could never have anticipated."

In "Heiple a victim of judicial witch-hunt," the *Sun-Times's* political columnist, Steve Neal, reviews the situation:

> Heiple is under attack because he was the author of the unpopular Baby Richard decision..., which angered the baby's adoptive family and public opinion.
>
> Even though legislators have cited other reasons for the impeachment probe, it all comes back to Baby Richard. If Heiple hadn't written the decision, he wouldn't be paying this price.... Heiple wouldn't be under siege....
>
> Heiple shouldn't be punished because you or I don't agree with him. He isn't guilty of high crimes and misdemeanors. This judicial lynching is absurd. (April 16, 1997)

Such attacks on a judge "could weaken an independent judiciary" and threaten "the constitutional structure of this nation, which has well served our citizens for more than 200 years," writes Neal, who quotes a U.S. Court of Appeals decision in another, relevant case. "'When a judge is threatened with a call for resignation or impeachment because of disagreement with a ruling, the entire process of orderly resolution of legal disputes is undermined.'"

Illinois former Governor James Thompson, having returned to practice as a lawyer, assumed legal representation of Heiple. In May 1997, Heiple testified for five hours before a special House investigative committee, empowered to recommend his impeachment or to decide that censure for misconduct and his resignation as Chief Justice would be punishment enough. The Illinois Courts Commission—with the power to reprimand, censure, suspend, or remove a judge who is found guilty of misconduct—had censured Heiple the previous week.

"Although I did not realize it before the fact, Thompson arranged with key legislators my stepping down as **Chief** Justice," explains Heiple. "He encouraged me to accept this alternative, and after considerable thought, I reluctantly agreed. The prospect of impeachment was avoided. I remained on the Supreme Court, and Judge Freeman, next in the rotational sequence for Chief Justice, assumed that position much earlier than expected." Judge Heiple voluntarily vacated the top judicial post in the state.

Thus, Judge Charles Freeman became the first African-American Supreme Court Chief Justice in the history of the State of Illinois.

"I refused to resign from the Supreme Court entirely; I had done nothing impeachable; and I was unwilling to allow my political and media enemies to prevail over my demise," Judge Heiple tells me. "Now in retirement, I live a good, satisfying life and look back with pride on a long and fulfilling career…, in spite of disillusionments along the way."

"The basic purpose of marriage is to have children and raise a family," he shares with me. "I have very traditional values and I support adoptions. I believe strongly in the importance of family. Divorce was never even an **option** for me." Now a widower of nearly eight years, Heiple has one daughter, Rachel, who is a school teacher and librarian in Michigan, and two sons, Jeremy and Jonathan, both of whom are practicing attorneys in Peoria. The judge is the grandfather of Jeremy's five children, four boys and a girl; the oldest boy is an adopted child. "I spend as much time with my family as allowed by all of our busy schedules," he relates.

"I would like to meet Danny and his parents one day," the judge announces. "You know, I've never met any of them. I feel good about having a part in the reuniting of that family."

"I'm sure that can be arranged, your honor. I'll talk to them about it…," I assure him.

With his two large farms, a duplex home, a cabin in Canada, and three vehicles, including a 1976 classic Mercedes, Judge Heiple is always busy. Perhaps his favorite place is the shiny red Pennsylvania Railroad caboose that he had installed on forty feet of rail in the middle of his tree farm, to which he retreats occasionally for an overnight in the woods. Engaged in a wide variety of hobbies to the extent that, "Like many other retirees, I wonder how I had time for a job," he laughs; "I have so much to do."

"Living well is the best revenge, your honor," I offer.

"Exactly!" he replies.

This evening he and Cisty are attending a local Christmas concert. After expressing my gratitude for his time, candor, and graciousness, I leave, feeling an even greater rapport with and respect for the Honorable Judge James Heiple.

Retired Judge James Heiple and the author pause during their interview about "Baby Richard" in his Peoria, Illinois home in December 2002.

> **For what a man sows, that he will also reap.**
>
> — *Galatians 6:8*

The Real Tragedy of Bob Greene

> **A puzzle:**
> **If we read Bob [Greene] here,**
> **what do they read in hell?**
>
> — *Neil Steinberg/Ed Gold*

"HE HAS DISAP-PEARED FROM THE FACE OF THE EARTH," Neil Steinberg exaggerates, grinning mischievously and discussing his role as the nemesis of Bob Greene. Neil and I are sitting in his spacious private office at the *Chicago Sun-Times* building on Friday evening during the Christmas season of 2002. Photographs of his family—a pretty blonde wife, two young sons, and his father—are prominently displayed; memorabilia fill the room; hundreds of books occupy the shelves; and piles of newspapers and magazines cover his desk and nearby table. I have come to hear what he has to say about Greene now that the 24-year veteran columnist has been forced into resignation by Neil's rival newspaper and Greene's employer, the *Chicago Tribune*.

Neil greeted me as I got off the elevator, my "visitor" badge pinned to the lapel of my thick, purple winter coat, which I had retrieved from a storage closet in my Florida home for the frigid Chicago air. He is a stocky man, dressed in casual clothes, with a strong handshake and a friendly smile. He has short brown hair, a bit disheveled; brown eyes; and a round, boyish face.

As he sits behind his state-of-the-art computer and we talk, Neil looks away now and then, avoiding prolonged eye contact, a mannerism that is characteristic of shy individuals. Although he speaks rapidly, he is impressively articulate, employs an esoteric vocabulary, and laces his sentences with references to literature and Greek mythology. He uses words like "avatar" to describe Bob Greene, as in "He was the self-anointed avatar of Midwestern values."

"Bob has been gone now for three months and no one I know has seen him or heard from him," Neil elaborates on his original assertion about Greene's disappearance from public view. "You know, I have a career that's **more** than being the arch-enemy of Bob Greene," he exclaims. "But after Bob was cashiered, a lot of reporters contacted me for information and my reaction. My name, it seems, has gotten irrevocably connected with his, and particularly now during his time of disgrace, people are interested in my historical and current perspectives about him."

"How did you get started as his journalistic rival, his major critic and arch-enemy?" I ask Neil.

"Years ago I would read press releases that came in and crossed my desk. A couple days later I'd read a Bob Greene column in which he would write major portions of that release. I was kind of offended by it. He was just repeating press releases." Neil tilts back in his chair and clasps his hands behind his head. He is reminiscing about the birth of his unique role as the "Bob Watch" reporter.

For two years, using the pseudonym Ed Gold, Neil wrote a monthly column in the Chicago *Reader*, aptly named the "Bob Watch" and fittingly subtitled "We read him so you don't have to." Dripping with sarcasm and parodying Greene's saccharine and maudlin style, Neil's columns are so humorous and sophisticated that they stand on their own merits. He delivers on the subtitle: when you read a "Bob Watch," you can—and probably should—forgo the original Greene offering, which is invariably characterized by "mind-numbing repetition," clichés, pedestrian ruminations, sanctimony, and emotions that vacillate from superficial to histrionic. The "Bob Watch" columns are sidesplitting funny, incorporating hyperbole, metaphor, and allegory to ridicule Greene's writings. To me, they are as intelligent and erudite as Greene's are simplistic and mundane. The Public

Defender in the Baby Sarah custody dispute would explain to me that Greene's parade of columns about that case "revealed the level of insight of a sixth grader."

"It's like he's beating a drum—and doing it badly," Ted F., one of my intellectual male clients once told me when describing Bob Greene's columns. "If he had a sophisticated thought, it would die of loneliness. That guy is obviously as much of a concrete thinker as you can find. Abstractions are lost on him so he reverts to emotional ranting and raving about the most prosaic subjects."

Fashioning himself as "the voice of voiceless children," Greene wrote hundreds of columns for the *Tribune* about cases in which he took the position that the system—typically the courts—had abused a child. His heart would purportedly break and he wanted to help break the hearts of his readers as well. He filled his columns with references to "unjust," "cruel," and "destructive" court rulings to the point that he often seemed to be screaming from the page, "How could they do this to a poor, defenseless child?" This question became the theme of dozens, and then hundreds, of his writings.

Yet he sold newspapers. Greene was syndicated in approximately 200 papers throughout the country during his most feverish coverage of Baby Richard. The *Tribune* received an amazing level of reader response, at its highest during his "Richard" crusade, the vast majority in support of his attitudinal positions. He managed to achieve placement of his Sunday column in a more visible, prominent position in the newspaper, page 2 of the main news section, during the early stage of his long, tiresome, and destructive Richard tirade, which spanned not only months but years.

The actual content of Greene's columns was limited; the majority of his coverage consisted of repetition, reminding, rehashing, reheating, and rebuking. His columns were based on emotion, not intellect; they were intended to evoke feelings in his readers rather than a circumspect and rational thought process.

Sharing opinions with Neil Steinberg, I confess to him that I rarely read Bob Greene before I became involved in the Baby Richard case. "I had read only a dozen to twenty of his columns in all of his years with the *Trib*," I tell Neil, "because I found him boring, focused on the trivial, and so flat-footed in his approach that I never bothered with him." It was only after my first session with Otto and Daniela Kirchner in February 1995 that I read some Greene columns, usually those that were sent to me by family members or friends.

"I was amazed and appalled that he could write so much from his own imaginings and fantasies and present that as real and as factual," I disclose to Neil, who is smiling broadly and nodding in agreement. I decide to explain to him the happy reality of Danny's situation, so starkly different from Greene's fabricated version. "He wrote about Danny and how he was undoubtedly abused and longing for his adoptive family—without ever speaking to the child, his father, his mother, or me, and I was the only professional person who interacted with the boy after his transfer. Before long, four-year-old Danny had only a dim memory of those people and didn't even speak about them after a few weeks with his natural parents. Bob Greene kept writing, though, about fantasized material; and he kept up the journalistic chant that the child needed to be reunited with the other family, with his adoptive brother. He created among the public a widespread sense of urgency for Danny's reunion with the other child. There are so many other issues that he could have championed, to do some real good for unwanted and needy children, but he chose instead to 'beat a dead horse,' as the poet said, about one child who was very much loved."

"It's difficult to write a newspaper column," Neil confides, leaning forward. "I found that out and even felt some short-lived sympathy for Bob. But he did it the easy way. He just kept repeating the same topic, phrases, citations, and whole paragraphs, which saved him from having to do the hard work, creative thinking, and research required of most columnists."

Although the "Bob Watch" continued across two years of Greene's Baby Richard period and then ended, it was later renewed by Steinberg during June, July, and August of 2002. On September 14, 2002, Greene resigned from the *Chicago Tribune* after an internal investigation by the newspaper editors confirmed allegations of his sexual misconduct with a seventeen-year-old high school student whom he met in connection with his job for the paper. Aside from the moral implications, Greene's violations constituted a breach of professional ethics. The decision-makers at the *Tribune* would have been compelled to deal with the incongruity and hypocrisy inherent in his writings about "defenseless" and "abused" children in the wake of public disclosures of his own abuses with a vulnerable teenaged child. Greene's little secret, which turned into a big secret years later, caught up with him. It took significantly more than a decade, however, and he thereby benefited from fourteen years of receiving a top-level salary as a widely syndicated columnist and news commentator before his personal and professional offenses were disclosed.

All of the time that Greene wrote about the Baby Richard case, castigating the biological father with unprecedented venom and volume, he was keeping his own secret. He had already exploited a teenage girl "in the worst possible way," as he himself would probably have described the misconduct if the offender had been someone else. He had already been guilty of sexual misconduct when he ranted about Baby Richard's "abuse" by the Illinois Supreme Court and by his father.

When the news broke on Sunday, September 15th, it ran from coast to coast. The *Chicago Tribune* printed on its front page:

To our readers

Chicago Tribune columnist Bob Greene has resigned and will no longer appear in the pages of the newspaper. The resignation is effective immediately.

Greene's resignation was sought after he acknowledged engaging in inappropriate sexual conduct some years ago with a girl in her late teens whom he met in connection with his newspaper column. The acknowledgment came in response to an anonymous complaint to the Tribune last week. The complaint prompted an inquiry by Tribune editors and officials. Greene was suspended by the newspaper following initial inquiries into the allegation. He resigned Saturday night after the investigation was complete.

Greene's column appeared on page 2 of the Sunday main news section and three times a week in Tempo.

Greene's behavior was a serious violation of Tribune ethics and standards for its journalists. We deeply regret the conduct, its effect on the young woman and the impact this disclosure has on the trust our readers placed in Greene and this newspaper.

Ann Marie Lipinski, Editor (September 15, 2002)

Now, if Bob Greene had a journalistic clone, he could write and write and write in newspaper columns filled with shock and surprise, righteous indignation, and expressions of horror and outrage about the self-inflicted "fall from grace" of the long-standing arbiter and protector of good, solid family values. Like an excerpt from *Dante's Inferno*, it would seem a fitting end, an avenging punctuation mark, for the man who made a fortune as the self-proclaimed crusader for kids.

CNN ran a succinct message about Greene's demise on its scroll on September 15th, along with blurbs about international terrorists and other lead stories. Judge James Heiple had aptly accused Greene of "journalistic terrorism" for his over-the-top and grossly distorted Baby Richard coverage. The irony in CNN's juxtaposition of Greene's termination and terrorist updates was not lost on those of us who were intimately involved in "Richard."

If there is a God who savors any interest in human trivia, S/He would be watching as the news of Greene's ouster reaches Otto and Daniela Kirchner and me. Robert and I are visiting Daniela and the three Kirchner children when Otto telephones from work to tell us about Greene's demise. From the living room, coincidentally, Danny laughs loudly, out of hearing and unaware of the breaking story, while Robert, Daniela, and I shake our heads in sync with each other.

"He did it to himself," Robert declares.

"What a coincidence it is that we are here with you and your children, Daniela, as we learn about the fall of Bob Greene," I whisper to her as we sit around her kitchen table. "This is the first time all year that we have been in your home, and we are able once again to share in the impact of Bob Greene, this time, though, at **his** peril, not **yours**."

Danny bounds into the kitchen, looking for a snack. He grabs a cheese-covered cracker, whirls around, and returns to the other room to resume his play. Danny is grinning broadly today. He loves company, and this evening two visitors from the Slovak Republic—one of his teenage male cousins and his best friend—are staying in the Kirchner home. They have come to the States to work and to see the sights around Chicago for a period of six weeks. Aunt Daniela is housing them and driving them around, as needed.

My only regret today is that Robert and I will miss seeing Otto because he returns home from work late, after a long night shift at the restaurant. We would talk later by telephone about this latest development on the news.

Greene's firing—more accurately, forced resignation—seems to beg the questions that begin with "What if…?" During our car ride back to John and Lynn Moriarty's home, Robert's brother and sister-in-law—our hosts during our one-week visit—we recite for each other a series of rhetorical questions.

What if the editors of the *Tribune* and the public knew about Greene's transgressions a decade or more ago? What if Greene had been fired before he was able to indulge his Baby Richard obsession at the expense of Otto, Daniela, and Danny Kirchner? What would their lives be like now?

More than any other feeling, I am experiencing a profound sense of relief. It is unlikely that Greene will be able to renew his journalistic attacks on this defenseless family. If he finds another forum, such as another newspaper that might hire him, would he attempt a repeat performance about "Baby Richard" and retool his assaults upon the child's biological parents? If he did resume his attacks upon them, would they be credible when the public considers **him** as their source, now appropriately and justly discredited by his own wrongful actions?

"It will be difficult for Greene to try to reestablish himself as a champion of 'abused' children," I say to Robert as we are packing for our return trip to Florida. "He will need to reinvent himself in some other direction."

Across subsequent months, the Bob Greene story is featured in major publications as well as on television and radio programs.

"Bob Greene Gets Spiked" portrays the "strange fall of a veteran columnist whose private life could not live up to his public voice." The author alludes to the "buzz of outrage and glee" that followed Greene's admission to "a sexual liaison over a decade ago with a teenage girl...." It continues:

> The news has rippled out from Chicago across the country to readers of the...papers in which Greene's column ran. To understand the apoplexy it created is to understand what Greene had come to represent. He wrote for people hungry for moral clarity, for nostalgia, for a softer world. And in that respect, he did his job. It's just that he did not personally reside in that world.

> In the spring of 1988 a 17-year-old Catholic high school senior working on a class project visited the Chicago *Tribune* with her parents to interview the much loved columnist. Greene turned the incident into a charming but forgettable column. A while later he asked the girl to dinner and then to a hotel, where they engaged in some kind of sexual activity. (Amanda Ripley, *Time*, September 30, 2002)

Fourteen years later, the young woman, in her early thirties, called Greene several times for "unknown" reasons. In June 2002, Greene contacted the FBI and "said that he felt threatened." The FBI interviewed the woman, who denied making threats. The agency found "insufficient evidence" to pursue the case. "The Tribune received an e-mail describing the affair but not naming Greene," writes Ripley. "Tribune executives tracked the woman down and then brought the allegations to Greene. He confessed and offered his resignation."

Loren Ghiglione, dean of Northwestern University's journalism school, is quoted as saying:

> Here's somebody working for the most powerful news organization in Chicago. What he did was an abuse of personal power and an abuse of the newspaper he worked for.

Describing him as "spokesman for the baby boom generation," Debra Pickett of the *Chicago Sun-Times* presents Greene's reaction to his forced resignation:

In an e-mail to the Associated Press on Sunday, Greene, a longtime crusader against the exploitation and abuse of children, said there had been "indiscretions in my life that I am not proud of." He did not offer specifics and, in a telephone call, declined to discuss the matter further....

"I don't have the words to express the sadness I feel," Greene told the Associated Press. "I am very sorry for anyone I have let down, including the readers who have for so long meant so much to me." (*"Tribune* columnist Bob Greene fired over 'inappropriate sexual conduct'," September 16, 2002)

Greene was married for thirty-one years to Susan Koebel, since 1971; they had two children, a girl and a boy. In 1984, the bestseller *Good Morning, Merry Sunshine*, his account of the joys of fatherhood during his daughter's first year, was released. "Many of his colleagues didn't know he was married or a father," according to the *Sun-Times*.

Susan Koebel Greene, at the age of 55, died in January 2003 from heart failure after having been treated for more than one month for "a respiratory illness." Her death came four months after her husband's publicly disclosed and admitted sexual misconduct with a teenager; the sudden termination of his job; and announcements from a series of women that he had had affairs with them. It is likely, of course, that Susan Greene suffered profound humiliation in addition to her physical ailment.

In 2000, Greene appeared on *The Oprah Winfrey Show*, discussing tortured children, and he returned several times to the show in order to campaign against child abuse. He was carrying his most successful theme, across years of columns, onto one of the country's most popular daytime television programs.

Steve Dahl, co-author of Neil Steinberg's "Bob Greene Watch," the 2002 weekly segment on WCKG-FM, registered his surprise over Greene's termination, according to the *Sun-Times's* Debra Pickett. "'I always thought he'd get fired just for being a bad columnist,' Dahl said."

It would appear that Dahl used the appellation "columnist" in a purposeful manner. Referring to Greene as "a journalist" would be akin to calling the guy who paints your garage "an artist."

Steinberg's Ed Gold reviewed the *Tribune* computer archives—"at the usurious fee of $1.25 per minute"—in order to perform an analysis of eleven years, from 1985 to 1995, of Greene's writings. He discovered that "A solid 35 percent of his entire output"—59 of 167 columns during 1995—were about Baby Richard "with zero practical effect other than making certain people think that by focusing on one white boy who has two sets of parents fighting to love him, they were exercising supreme compassion." Continuing this research, Gold found that although Greene's favorite topics included Elvis, Michael Jordan, and his home state of Ohio, "More than a third—723 [of 1,923 columns across 11 years]—involve children, ...other wee ones Bob has used to cynically fill his columns with pages of court transcripts and letters of reader outrage." Gold offered:

> ...You can view the full scope and horror of Bob Greene's world, the sad spectacle of his near-autistic fixation, suffocating narrowness, and tedious, head-crushing repetition....

> The year 1996 stretches ahead of us, filled with promise and mystery. Only two things are certain: Bob will continue to boldly explore the bedpan ocean of his soul. And the *Tribune* is going to make a fortune on-line. ("Bob Watch," The *Reader*, December 22, 1995)

Years later, the *Tribune's* public editor expounds upon Greene's ouster in "A trust bestowed, a trust betrayed":

> As [my colleague John] Kass summed it up: "Her parents trusted the Tribune enough to bring their daughter here to interview a top columnist. A bit later, the columnist and the girl were in bed together." ...By comparison with some of the ethical problems editors face, Bob Greene's case was clear-cut. Trust bestowed. Trust betrayed. (Don Wycliff, *Chicago Tribune*, September 19, 2002)

Newsweek highlights the story in "A Writer's Fall from Grace":

> ...It was an operatic tale: a man who made his name opining on the lost innocence of high school, the horror of

child abuse and the redeeming love of a good family had destroyed his career because of a tawdry encounter in a downtown hotel with a 17-year-old high-school student.

His behavior shocked the city, and roiled the newsroom....

On Friday, the Chicago Sun-Times ran a piece detailing another woman's supposed affair with Greene.... "It was pretty traditional, normal sex," the woman alleged.... (Seth Mnookin, September 30, 2002)

At the time of his resignation, Greene was the *Tribune's* "most popular and best-read columnist, even if his public bent for nostalgia and small-town Midwestern values were derided as syrupy and sappy by some critics and younger readers." (Jim Kirk & Monica Davey, "Breach of trust ends Greene's career at Tribune," September 16, 2002). Greene's weekly commentary on WGN-TV was also summarily cancelled.

"I have read **all** of the coverage about Bob's demise," Neil tells me as we sit across from each other over his sprawling desk. "Even his detractors are shaking their heads in amazement and feeling, perhaps, a twinge of regret over the loss of Bob's warped world. Who will we make fun of now?"

In "Anatomy of Bob Greene," Steinberg analyzes the "relentless nostalgist" whose writing had "an obvious falseness that he [Greene] seemed to believe was accepted as real." Neil presents his views with his characteristic pungent clarity:

There is no shorthand to explain Bob Greene, no code.... [T]here is no simple way to describe the deeply weird Midwestern world that Bob Greene built through his columns.... That world shattered like a glass Christmas tree ornament hit by a brick last Sunday, after...his forced resignation....

Perhaps the most distinctive Bob characteristic was repetition....

He would latch onto a subject—particularly tales of tortured children he gleaned from trailer park America—

and worry them like a dog with a beefsteak.... [T]he Baby Richard saga[,] prompted more than 100 columns from Bob, each day repeating large blocks of background, lines like "the only family he has ever known" burning into the memory of his readers as certainly as Homer's "wine-dark sea" and "rosy-fingered dawn."

That this world could come crashing down in a sex scandal—with a high school girl, no less—was a shock to his fans and a delightful surprise to his detractors....

Bob is married, with two kids, one of whom he celebrated in the 1984 bestseller *Good Morning, Merry Sunshine*, the book that began the trend of writers commoditizing their children....

Steinberg, an insider within the world of journalists, discloses that "[Greene's] goatish pursuit of young women was an open secret." He explains, "Everyone seemed to know women who had stories of Bob creepily singing his love song at them. I myself knew four...." Radio talk shows received calls from women claiming to have been Greene's fans who wound up as "despoiled groupies."

"So far," writes Steinberg, "the Trib has refused to entertain the issue of whether this was the first complaint or, like the Baby Richard columns, one in a chain of 100." (*Chicago Sun-Times*, September 19, 2002)

Bob Greene was promoting his twenty-first book in Nebraska when he got the phone call from his employer that resulted in his immediate return to Chicago, a brief suspension with pay, and the loss of his job. At the age of fifty-five, Greene's thirty-three-year career came to an abrupt end.

Within five days, an e-mail was sent to the Tribune outlining his sexual misconduct with a teenager in 1988; an internal investigation was held at the newspaper, including a meeting with the young woman and two meetings between Greene and his superiors; and he offered his resignation, which was accepted. "He used his position for personal gain," Ann Marie Lipinski explained; "it's that simple."

In a compelling exposé of the man behind the image, "The Sad Saga of Bob Greene" focuses upon the columnist as calculating, hypocritical, "ethically bankrupt," and a loner—with apparently only one, now-retired friend at the Tribune. Quoting from the *Reader's* Q & A from an interview by Beth Fletcher on the occasion of Greene's thirtieth birthday in 1977, the article relates that he "displays a militantly ignorant approach to literature":

> "I never read anything," he tells Fletcher. "I've never read a word of Hemingway.... I certainly never read any f— —' Shakespeare. All I ever read in my life was newspapers."

The interview continues with Greene complaining about the years of acclaim that he received from a "column about the Israeli athletes, which he calls 'the Jew column'," saying, "'I wish I'd never written it'." To invitations from Jewish organizations, "askin' me to come talk to them about being a Jew, which I won't do," Greene responds:

> I say, "My religion ain't Jewish, my religion is bein' a newspaperman." And when they say, "Oh, that was a beautiful column," I say, "That's right, it was a beautiful column. Period. I wrote it in ten minutes, drunk. And I felt nothing." The only thing I felt was that this had better get good play because it's a hell of a newspaper column."

"...[I]n public comments Greene [also] made it clear that sometimes he did not believe what he wrote. He was just finding an angle...[to] draw attention, promote his career." Greene wrote about himself in *Merry Sunshine*: "I have always been a pathologically ambitious person; it is probably the one quality that defines me most clearly." In 1988, the year that he exploited the teenager who eventually caused his ruin, Greene reportedly earned $750,000. That is before he no doubt started making really big money.

In addition to being "pathologically ambitious," Greene was tacky and arguably slimy. He started the "Ms. Greene's World Pageant" many years ago when he wrote for the *Sun-Times* and he continued it later at the *Tribune*. He invited female readers to send in photos of themselves for the "competition." "[T]he contest was referred to in-house as 'Bob's Dating Service'." (Marcia

Froelke Coburn and Steve Rhodes, "The Sad Saga of Bob Greene," *Chicago* Magazine, March 2003) One might reasonably raise the question, What was the contest prize?

"How far can a man fall?" begins the April 2003 *Esquire* article about Greene. "Imagine very far—and then, in the case of this man, keep going."

The author, Bill Zehme, attempts a redemptive portrayal of the disgraced columnist. Elevating Greene's self-perpetuated demise to the level of "a heartland Greek tragedy, rife with cruel ironies and tortured plot turns from beginning to astonishing end," Zehme virtually glorifies the man. The author discloses that he has been the only person to socialize with Greene outside the confines of his home—or to communicate with him regularly—during the weeks following the termination of his "friend's" career: "...I had become his primary link to the outside world." However, Zehme writes, "I had not laid eyes on him in his new aftermath. I hadn't seen him up close, in fact, for just about **five years**, and that had been mere happenstance, a bumping into at a drinking establishment [emphasis added]." In spite of the obvious tenuousness of his sporadic historical relationship with Greene, Zehme works hard in his article to elicit sympathy and forgiveness for the fallen columnist.

"I didn't admire myself," Greene is quoted as saying to Zehme. The author relates the tale of Greene's heartbreak in revealing to his sixteen-year-old son and twenty-year-old daughter the circumstances of his having lost his job. Greene appears as the victim in this portrayal, while the exploited young woman appears as the guilty aggressor.

"With Greene, clues into his shuttered soul must be sought out, since a pathological oath of privacy has kept him from revealing in print—much less in person—the details of his real life...," Zehme explains. To many, this commitment to privacy is not difficult to understand when considered in light of the numerous skeletons from Greene's closet that appeared after the news broke about his job-ending wrongdoing:

They had come out of the woodwork, the women had, in that third week of September. The ones he had attempted to charm and the ones he had successfully charmed—

they phoned in to Chicago radio shows or wrote in to media Web sites, and they recounted their experiences with him back when they were in their twenties.... ("The Confessions of Bob Greene")

These alleged exploitations of women by Greene in his personal life were paralleled by his exploitations of the weak and defenseless in his professional life, in his columns. "Bob Greene's demographics were exactly the kind we wanted," a former editor is quoted in the *Chicago* article; "they were basically women, 25 to 50, who spent the money and bought the products." So, Greene wrote about children—white children who were victims, in his view, of the courts or of society—the "voiceless" and the "abused." He wrote and wrote and rewrote about them. He pulled heartstrings with his passionate approach, much like a mini soap opera in print.

With sure-fire, low-risk, no-lose, safe and easy topics such as Elvis, Michael Jordan, and nostalgic yearnings for a nicer, gentler, more caring America of yore, he interspersed these favorite subjects with children, the same names and cases, beginning with Baby Sarah in 1990. In the mid-nineties, when his readership reportedly began to decline and the number of newspapers that syndicated his column began to plummet, Greene embarked upon his virulent Baby Richard campaign, and he hit the bonanza. The response from readers was overwhelming, from across the country.

Thus, Greene exploited Baby Richard and the real-life Danny Kirchner, turning him into a pathetic figure, under the implicit guise of loving him more than his biological parents did and of knowing better what was good for him and his emotional well-being. He called upon child protection agencies to look into his circumstances; he urged Cardinal Bernardin to investigate the child's situation in his birth parents' home; and he accused Danny's father of "child abuse." It often took a careful reading of his columns to discern that, bottom line, the "abuse" was attributable to the father's decision to claim and parent his son.

Greene demonized Otakar and Daniela Kirchner, presenting them as totally unworthy and unfit to parent their son. He repeatedly called Daniela the woman who did not want her child, and he lambasted Otto in countless ways and by creating a variety of angles. Greene frequently reminded his readers that the lower court had found the biological father "unfit"—without clarifying that it was a technicality, rather than character defects, upon which that finding was based. As early as 1993, appellate court Judge Tully wrote, in his dissenting opinion, "The charade of terming the [Kirchner] father 'unfit' because he failed to immediately seek legal advice is preposterous and an insidious appendix to the already confused state of the law in such cases."

In his campaign to discredit and malign Otto, Greene even went so far as to publish, four years after-the-fact, the biological father's phone records during the month that his son was born. In that same column, Greene acknowledged, "This doesn't belong in the newspaper, or on the radio or television or in the arena of public opinion...." ("167 phone calls that demand an answer," *Chicago Tribune*, March 5, 1995)

Danny and his family, powerless to stop the accusations and the attacks upon them, paid a big price, while Greene earned a big salary and a greatly expanded reputation. He was sought out by journalists from across the country for his "facts" about Baby Richard and for his opinions, which his professional colleagues typically adopted into their own reporting. They accepted him as the self-fashioned definitive "Richard" expert. They probably did not realize that his "inside" information was from inside his own head. Having **never** interviewed either birth parent or Danny, Greene presumed to write from very little to no first-hand information. When he finally interviewed me one day, after he had already written **dozens** of columns as a "knower" about the state of Danny's mental and emotional health, he ignored the information that he got from me. He just continued his already established themes of the child's deteriorating mental health, deep longings and suffering, and his victimization at the hands of his parents, in a living hell. He whipped the public into a frenzy of sympathetic, indignant, and angry response. In reality, Greene was the victimizer, of course, by creating the hostile, threatening environment within which the real child and his family were compelled to live.

"Everything that deceives may be said to enchant," Plato asserted more than two thousand years ago. Our human nature often impels us toward believing the worst in other people, particularly if it is served up by a supposedly credible source.

Not content with asserting his distortions, misrepresentations, and imaginings as real, Greene actually created news instead of appropriately confining himself to reporting it. He hid in the Warburtons' basement on the day of Baby Richard's transfer, which was captured in multi-national media coverage, so that, as a witness to their tearful final moments, he could grab a graphic exclusive on the child's pain in what should have been the privacy of his home. He later stood on the Warburtons' front lawn, presenting himself as weeping and providing interviews for other reporters. He made himself a part of the vibratingly distressful scene of the four-year-old being wrenched from his adoptive mother's arms in full view of large parts of the world. He initiated, on his own, an arrangement with the beloved Archbishop of Chicago, Cardinal Bernardin, to mediate and oversee a reunion between the child and his adoptive family. Greene wanted to be the creator of another huge Baby Richard media event, this one with his name on it. He turned his alleged readers' responses into "news" and fodder for his columns, most of them bemoaning in the most extravagant terms the "Baby Richard tragedy," "sin," "outrage," and "cruelty."

> Greene, forty-eight, admits he can't shake the heart-wrenching scene he witnessed April 30 when he was invited into the adoptive parents' home....

> "If I go to sleep thinking about him [Richard] and I wake up thinking about him, am I supposed to then come in and pretend that something else interests me more that day? Because it didn't and it hasn't," Greene says. ("Bob Greene's Richard File," *Columbia Journalism Review*, September/October, 1995)

What appears here to be a caring self-disclosure by Greene reminded me of an unwholesome preoccupation with the young and the vulnerable of a middle-aged man, such as I had worked with in psychotherapy. Why is he obsessing about this little boy as his first, last—and probably frequent—thoughts of the day? I wondered. Later, I came to believe that Greene's "obsession" was perhaps more akin to his calculating approach to the piece that he dubbed "the Jew column," about which he admitted he felt nothing and wrote it while drunk. "...[M]any journalists came to think that the [children] pieces had taken on an aura of shtick." ("The Sad Saga of Bob Greene") His Baby Richard body of work, in my opinion, became his "mythical shtick."

In my naïvety, functioning within a life-long idealistic belief in the inherent integrity of professionals, I believed that Greene would stop his rampage once he knew the truth about Danny. Once he becomes aware that the child is indeed thriving and that his memory of his former adoptive family is foggy and diminishing, I thought, he will move along to other topics. Once he knows how destructive his journalistic ravings have become for the child's real life, I hoped and believed, he will stop his tirade, or perhaps even write that his published imaginings—if not admitting them to have been misguided and uninformed—were exaggerated. Instead, to my dismay, he ratcheted up the pathos in his columns another notch or two and continued full steam ahead.

Sadly, Greene influenced important people at all levels of government and from various other walks of life to jump onto his "Richard" bandwagon. He beckoned the governor, the courts, the legislature, and state agencies to intervene in the case on his chosen "side" of the bitter win-lose conflict over the child. He was largely successful in activating people in this easy, low-risk cause. The Illinois Supreme Court, however, maintained its integrity, in spite of "public clamor generated by an irresponsible journalist"—words describing Greene that were incorporated into its 7 – 0 ruling in favor of "Richard's" deceived father.

Imagine, however, how much good could have been done for other children—those of all races, ethnic backgrounds, handicapping conditions, and illnesses; those abused, neglected, unwanted, and homeless—if equivalent efforts had been put forth on their behalf. Baby Richard—although admittedly a precious child— was **one** healthy, white, male child, loved and wanted by two sets of parents who fought tooth-and-nail to be allowed to raise and to cherish him. Think of all of the children who could have benefited from one hundred columns, syndicated in nearly 200 newspapers, with their millions of readers potentially responding in effectively benevolent ways. Think of all of the prominent people—literally hundreds of them—who could have done something constructive and redemptive for those children. As one journalist pointed out in the aftermath of Baby Richard, "It is a disgraceful excuse for political leaders who have the power to improve the lives of the many...instead...to focus on the fate of a few." Long-term Herculean efforts were put forth by a multitude for one little boy who was indisputably loved by parents.

Envision yourself picking up your morning newspaper and reading a column about your own child—or the child of your loved one, friend, or neighbor—asserting that he is sliding into mental illness and living in hell, an abused hostage-like creature. The material is written by an author who has **never** witnessed the child or his family in action, and he has no mental health training or experience. You would likely be appalled, indignant, and perhaps furious. Repetition of these same assertions in tomorrow's newspaper, in the one after that, and then in another series of papers would not make the statements any more valid or true. This scenario, created by Bob Greene, is what happened with Baby Richard and the real Danny Kirchner.

This is the real tragedy of "Baby Richard"...and of Bob Greene, who exploited and victimized the real Danny for his own selfish purposes, beguiling others to join him and diverting attention from meaningful, worthwhile causes that could have benefited so many children in need. The real tragedy is that Greene was not dispatched closer to the time of the sexual misconduct that precipitated his fall, thereby preventing him from doing so much damage to so many guiltless victims of his "pathologically ambitious," ruthless diatribes.

"I was surprised that she got married!" Debbie proclaims during our forty-minute phone conversation on May 9, 2003. She is referring to Sandra McClurg—not her real first or last names, for the sake of her privacy—the woman who revealed the scandal that resulted in Bob Greene's "fall from grace." Now thirty-two, Sandra was involved as a teenager in up-close-and-personal exploitation at the hands of Greene in 1988. She chose to remain silent about her painful experiences with the columnist across the span of fourteen years.

"She threw away your letter," Debbie explains to me after she identifies herself as Sandra's roommate, confidante, and close friend. "I got your phone number from the letter and decided to call you to set the record straight about what happened to Sandra. She is avoiding all interviews with the media," Debbie continues, "and she said she doesn't want to speak with you directly either. The whole situation is **so** difficult for her...."

Although Sandra's name has not been published anywhere because of her age at the time of the incidents with Bob Greene that have been widely termed "sexual misconduct admitted by him," I was able to discover her identity as part of my research for this book. In my letter to her, sent through her attorney, I informed Sandra that, as a woman and as a person who was also a victim of Greene's, albeit in an entirely different way, I sympathized with her plight. The columnist exploited her in a personal, sexual manner during the summer after her graduation from high school, when he was already over forty, married and the father of two young children at home. I became the victim of four of his Baby Richard columns, in which he attacked my integrity, credentials, motives, and competence because I was on the "wrong side" of the conflict.

Debbie explains that she understands, on behalf of her dear friend, the need to clarify and correct some of the ambiguities and inaccuracies in media coverage about the pivotal events that resulted in Greene's forced resignation from his job and his forfeiture of other related professional activities. "You know, Sandra doesn't even really believe in love or marriage since her relationship with Greene. She's been turned off to sex, and she doesn't trust men after Greene. Sandra attributes these feelings to her experience with him. She used to say that she wasn't going to get married at all. That's why I was surprised when she married Charles Smith two months ago. [Not his real name]

"Sandra's attorney sent her to a special psychiatrist for post-traumatic stress disorder," Debbie adds. "The psychiatrist said that Sandra suffers from symptoms of the disorder, like flashbacks, her attitude toward sex, eating problems, and drinking. She **used** to be a big drinker but not any more."

In my pursuit of a personal conversation with Sandra, I spoke on the telephone on three occasions with her father, Judge McClurg [not his real name]. He shared with me the happy news about his only child's wedding on March 5, 2003, in Las Vegas.

Forty people from the Chicago area flew out to attend the celebration, he told me, and Debbie added that the judge and his wife paid the expenses. "It was a nice, short wedding," Debbie tells me; "it was fun." In addition to the core of forty people, others attended, including Sandra's college friends and her classmates from Ireland, where she studied for a master's degree in Irish literature and politics. Sandra and Charles honeymooned in Vegas for one week after the wedding ceremony, according to her father.

"She first told her parents that she and Charles were going to get married in Hawaii, but she changed her mind," Debbie says. "Sandra travels to Vegas frequently, so she decided to have her wedding there. She didn't get married in Chicago because of all of the media looking for a story. They have really been after her since the Bob Greene news broke in September. For a long time, there was someone parked in front of her apartment building, looking for news. For a week, there was an investigative reporter parked outside her parents' house.

"If she could take it back, she would," asserts Debbie, referring to the explosion of media and public interest in the details of the "sexual misconduct" that halted Greene's career when he was ostensibly at the pinnacle of achievement as a writer and public figure. "She feels horrible about what she put her parents through—not about his actual demise," Debbie clarifies, "but the media being after them all of the time. She's mostly concerned about her parents; she's very close to them. Her father has cancer and she worries about him." Judge McClurg also told me that he was upset over members of the media looking for him in his courtroom or chambers for more details to "the story." Sandra has consistently declined interviews, and her father has also been adamant in his desire to avoid more publicity.

"I have known Sandra since we were fourteen and starting high school," Debbie explains. "She is strong-willed, brave, loving, caring, and wonderful," she continues, extolling the virtues of her friend. Sandra is also generous, as Debbie and her three children occupy one apartment of the three-flat owned by Charles; the newlyweds reside in another apartment in the building; and Charles's grandmother and her chihuahua live in the third. "I am separated from my husband, and Sandra is letting us live here rent-free. Sandra is highly intelligent, can speak several languages, and is teaching my daughter German."

According to Debbie, Sandra blossomed into a strong, independent woman during her years after high school: "She turned from an ugly duckling virgin into a 'get out of my way' person.

"She was ugly in high school," Debbie clarifies. "Greene had a picture of Sandra and him framed with the column he wrote about her. She weighed about ninety pounds and had a boy haircut. The picture is still here in her office. Greene sent her a graduation card that said, 'Barbara Walters has nothing on you; Happy Graduation; Love, Bob'."

Debbie continues, "She never kissed a boy in high school; she never drank a beer. Sandra was the high school yearbook editor; she designed its cover. She's like a Renaissance artist; she designs and paints well. After she graduated from high school, Sandra got a job as a secretary at the Daley Center.

"She believed every word that came out of his mouth," Debbie says, alluding to Sandra's gullibility when it came to Bob Greene, twenty-four years older than her inexperienced friend. "We used to call her Pollyanna; she was so naïve. Greene took her to bars; she would get drunk; and then he took her to a hotel room," Debbie relates. "She has the receipts, a pile of evidence. She idolized him and especially admired his book *Be True to Your School*. Greene was teaching her how to become a reporter. He was her mentor. Her parents knew nothing about what was going on. They were busy with their own careers at the time. Greene would take her home in a cab. She says she can't remember a lot because she was drunk; she got drunk her first time with him. Sandra saw him through that summer. And she is **still** screwed up from it all."

Sandra's parents had taken her to meet Bob Greene during her senior year in high school. She was doing a project for her journalism class and wanted to interview him. To their surprise, he granted the interview and then wrote an innocuous column for the *Tribune* about the high school girl who came to visit him. Judge McClurg explained to me that he never knew what was going on between Greene and his young daughter. She had led a sheltered life, attending a Catholic school for girls and not yet involved in dating. The judge found out "shortly before the news became public," he told me, adding that he is "very angry" about Greene's exploitation of his daughter.

After graduating from St. Mary's University in Winona,

Minnesota, with a bachelor's degree in theatre arts, Sandra earned two master's degrees, one in English literature from St. Xavier University in Chicago. "She went to Ireland with just a backpack," Debbie says in admiration of her friend. "She still goes there to participate in summer programs. She's a writer now; she writes fiction. Sandra is trying to get a book published, but she lost a book deal recently. Sandra sent Greene a couple of her books to read. He would send her his new books, signed. In fact, she still has them in her office, even after her mother tried to get rid of them."

Sandra continues her involvement in psychotherapy. "She has severe depression, still sees a psychiatrist, and takes medication," according to her father. Debbie explains that Sandra had trouble with an eating disorder as well as a historical problem with drinking. "She met Charles at AA a couple of years ago," Debbie relates, "but she doesn't go any more; she says it's 'not her.' At her wedding, we teased her when she got tipsy from her first glass of champagne. She doesn't hold liquor well.

"Sandra worked for a while at Cabrini Green, and the irony is that she met Bob Greene's wife, who was also working there. Sandra had so many jobs and moved around so much. She was taking acting and comedy lessons. She did some stand-up comedy. She worked on a couple of movies filmed in Chicago, behind-the-scenes, as an extra and on the props crew. Sandra doesn't seem to like working on a job for more than six months; she gets bored. Because of her parents—her father is politically active—and her own contacts, she's friends with a lot of political people and journalists. About three years ago she moved back home with her parents when she got pancreatitis; she had been living in Marina City. She couldn't drive or work for some time. She started to go to AA and met Charles.

"Her sponsor at AA and her therapist recommended a fresh start for Sandra," explains Debbie. "So she filed for bankruptcy on her own; started driving again, with her doctor's approval; and went to work for Barnes and Noble." Specifically, in January 2002, Sandra filed for bankruptcy; she was living with her parents at the time; and her debt totaled just over $14,000. The court finalized her bankruptcy in May 2002.

"At the book store, Sandra got an advance copy of Greene's new book about North Platte. She called him to say she liked it and to wish him good luck. It had nothing to do with money," Debbie emphasizes. "Sandra wanted to put her past behind her, to move ahead...."

Although they reportedly spoke by telephone "at least once a year," this time Greene was unreceptive to Sandra. Before long, "Sandra got a phone call from the FBI," Debbie describes the critical event that would result in the columnist's ouster. "I was in the room at the time; at first she thought it was a joke.... Greene claimed he felt threatened by Sandra. The FBI determined that she had done nothing wrong related to Greene.

"I don't know who sent the e-mail to the Tribune," Debbie continues. "It may have been the collaboration of three close friends of Sandra's—guys who were like brothers to her. Anyway, Ann Marie Lipinski e-mailed Sandra back, and she agreed to meet with Lipinski and a man at the Tribune. Sandra is very credible and articulate. Just one e-mail and one brief meeting with Lipinski and a guy took Greene down," Debbie summarizes.

Ironically, Greene's last column would appear on September 11th. Executives of the newspaper contacted Sandra on that day.

During the internal investigation conducted by the Tribune executives from September 10 through 14, 2002, the meeting with Sandra was held and Greene was summoned to two meetings. "He offered his resignation and we accepted it," Lipinski announced.

"...Greene virtually vanished from sight, although he sent a statement to the Associated Press saying there were 'indiscretions in my life that I am not proud of. I don't have the words to express the sadness I feel...'." ("The Sad Saga of Bob Greene")

Sandra's attorney, Kathleen Zellner, has discontinued pursuit of legal action on behalf of her client against Greene. "Sandra never wanted money," Debbie asserts. "She has money through her parents and her husband."

Perhaps she wanted justice or emotional restitution of some kind.

Greene's detractors and others who are unconvinced that he has become the victim of a "raw deal" might argue that now, in poetic justice, some prominent journalist should spew out 100 columns about the scandal. "Live by the sword, die by the sword." If the core passages borrow from Greene's style, they might read something like the following:

She was just an innocent. A naïve teenager, an only child, she was sheltered and protected by her loving parents across seventeen years. Unsuspecting and enthusiastic, parents and daughter went to meet the over-forty, married columnist, the girl's hero, to get a simple interview for her high school journalism class project. Her parents couldn't know—and wouldn't know for many years—that pleasant encounter exploded into exploitation, the very worst kind, the sordid kind, the kind that forever touches and scars the soul of a young girl. Trust turned into ugly trysts—sexual misconduct by the columnist, through the summer—that would torment the girl for more than a decade, souring her on men and sex and marriage and sending her into a long depression and psychotherapy.

It was his secret—only it was followed by more and more secrets—that finally erupted into the light of scrutiny, by the columnist's employer and the heretofore trusting public, who had misguidedly looked to him for "the truth." The long cloak of secrecy had sheltered him for fourteen years, while he pretended, day by day, to be in the printed word what he could **not** be in reality—an ethical, congruent man, an ardent protector and defender of children. He raised his phony, hypocritical, and calculating "cause" to the level of a resounding, righteous rant from the pages.

She was just an innocent....
(More tomorrow about the details of the affair.)

Greene, it appears, believed himself to be untouchable, beyond the reach of real harm. "He did it to himself," my husband concisely announced on the Sunday when the startling news broke as we sat in the warmth of the Kirchners' home, surrounded by the chatter and giggles of children. He admitted to doing the deed with Sandra as well as "other indiscretions," and he called the FBI on the young woman, without having informed his employer. His own actions, first in 1988 and then in 2002, triggered the events that led to his departure from the journalistic scene and from his twenty-four year job at the *Trib*. Some might say that it was the combination of his exploitation of a teenager and his arrogance that resulted in his self-destruction.

"Sandra was very upset about the *Esquire* article [about Greene]," Debbie reveals. "She went to the store and got all of the copies of the magazine, and in a fury she bought them and then tore them up." Judge McClurg had told me that Sandra was very upset about the *Chicago* magazine article as well. "Anything written about the incident reopens the wounds for Sandra," he explained.

"I'd like to be there to throw dirt on his grave!" Sandra exclaims during the first minute of her exclusive interview with me. In a startling reversal of her original decision, Sandra telephones me to discuss some aspects of her encounters with Bob Greene. On a warm evening in September 2003—with Greene still unemployed and maintaining a low profile—the young woman who effected his sudden ouster from the *Tribune* is ready to talk, at least to me, about her feelings. Sandra is now responding to the letter that I sent her months ago.

Confirming the media-reported "sexual misconduct" of the columnist, Sandra offers, "I **was** a virgin when I got involved with him. He was my hero when I met him." She is quick to add that she revised her attitude toward Greene during the ensuing months and years as she realized the devastating effects on her emotionally from her intimate relationship, at the age of seventeen, with the "much older, married man with children at home."

"Debbie told you the truth…," Sandra relates. "My phone call to Greene was intended to congratulate him on his new book. He called the FBI on me…. I was just trying to move on with my life; my therapist advised me to call him to be able to do that. I never wanted money from him." Later, after Greene's forced resignation, Sandra connected with attorney Kathleen Zellner. "The only real thing that I would have wanted from him was a joint confidentiality agreement which did not happen," she shares with me. "I really DID do this for myself."

These days Sandra is completing her third book—which she calls "my third baby"—with the hope that it will be published during coming months. It is a work of fiction, unrelated to her sorry episode with the *Tribune* columnist. She also drives her father to his regularly scheduled chemotherapy treatments. Her voice breaking, Sandra explains, "I can't talk about this. My father has been so involved with my recent problems that he hasn't been able to fight his cancer...." She deeply regrets the incursions into his life by the media after the eruption of the news of Greene's sudden demise onto the public scene.

"Good luck with [your] book," Sandra writes in a follow-up e-mail message. "I haven't had the best year, but I have always had my writing...." In addition, of course, Sandra had the courage to speak up for herself when she was confronted by the FBI and *Tribune* executives.

After the Bob Greene scandal broke, a series of women came forward to offer information about their affairs with the fallen columnist. One of them, Susan Taylor from the Milwaukee area, first provided Neil Steinberg and then *Chicago* magazine with an account of her relationship with Greene. In May 2003, I interviewed Susan by telephone, and she was forthcoming and open about her encounters. "In about 1983," when she was twenty-three or twenty-four, she wrote Greene a fan letter about a column on breast implants. She referred to her own; Greene called her; and they met. According to Ms. Taylor, Greene asked to see her breasts; they went to a room at the Marriott together; and she saw him "a few times after that."

Confirming that "it was an affair," Ms. Taylor reveals, "I've been too naïve in my life." She believed what Greene told her, including his confession that he "felt guilty" about his infidelities, "for stepping out on his marriage," as Taylor terms it. "He told me he went into therapy," she says; "he admitted to adultery as a real problem for him."

"It is not always what a person says that counts, but rather what he does that ultimately counts," wrote Rabbi Allan Blaine. Greene's behavior speaks for itself and can be regarded as a measure of the relative value and validity of his writings about "exploited" and "abused" children.

Greene preferred "voiceless" children as his subjects. Sandra McClurg found her voice, albeit years later, to unmask the columnist. Baby Richard—Danny—still a pre-teen, will hopefully have found a voice through the pages of this book, a restoration project for the child's reputation and image.

In the end, it appears that Bob Greene has also been struck down by the "Baby Richard curse," ironically not for his shameful, exploitative "Richard" coverage but—dramatically and justly—for his more private misdeeds and his arrogance.

Today, Greene is working on a comeback to the media world. Addressing Bill Zehme's journalistic attempt to exonerate Greene, fashion him as a victim, and elevate him to a reinstated position, Neil Steinberg writes "Beat a monster when he's down? No problem." Unapologetic for criticizing Greene's "sham persona" and "hyperventilated prose," Steinberg asserts:

> [I'm] proud that... I was drawing attention to the falsity of his world, the insularity.... Proud to contradict a man who... made a habit of lingering over child abuse stories, massaging the details, day after day, in a fashion that some thought was caring, but others, myself included, viewed as practically sick....
>
> He's a horror movie monster. He cannot be killed. Oh, you can try. Like one of those horror movie monsters, he can be shot and stabbed and poisoned and crushed. He looks dead. The movie's almost over, everyone relaxes, and the hero leans down to take a good look at the prone creature, when it suddenly springs up and grabs him.
>
> Don't underestimate Greene. He'll be back. Zehme's act of kindness, picking him out of the gutter and wiping the dust off, is the first step.... Keep the wooden stake and the mallet handy. (*Chicago Sun-Times*, March 7, 2003)

Let's hope Neil is wrong.

The man who reads nothing at all is better educated than the man who reads nothing but newspapers.

— Thomas Jefferson

> Happiness is salutary for the body
> but sorrow develops the powers of the spirit.
>
> — *Marcel Proust*

CHAPTER NINETEEN

The Story of Daniela

We live, as we dream—alone.

— *Joseph Conrad*

WALKING past three small, homemade shelters for the local feral cat population, I approach the front door of Enid Shortell's home in Richton Park, Illinois. Enid and her husband Peder have been friends and supporters of the Kirchners since the first week of their becoming next-door neighbors in late 1995. Enid and I are getting together today for lunch and conversation about her relationship with the family whose private lives burst into the public spotlight on many occasions across a span of years. Enid and her family became nearby, daily witnesses and self-initiated protectors of their beleaguered neighbors from early on.

It is a cold, damp, and windy day in February 2003, during a typical Chicagoland winter. Yesterday Enid was released from the hospital after three days of observation and tests for an abdominal injury that she sustained when she fell on ice on the front deck of her house. She had been stretching to feed three homeless cats for whom she constructed plastic-wrapped, cushioned box-shelters when she slipped and took a hard fall. A thin-faced, black and white cat watches me approach through the picture window from inside the house. He is snugly nestled into the thick back-cushion of the living room couch.

Enid and Peder both greet me at the door and invite me into their home. Enid is a plain woman, wearing no make-up, but her sparkling eyes give her a youthful, vital appearance. The small living room is cheerful and warm, furnished with dark wood tables and animal-friendly, fabric-covered pieces, surrounded by pale orange, sponge-painted walls. Two German shepherds nuzzle each other on the floor, while three cats of varying colors stroll around them, and the couch cat jumps down to inspect me with a perfunctory sniff of my pant leg. Peder explains that these are some of their fluid number of cats that hovers around ten; one recently became ill and had to be euthanized. "The dogs are great, but I prefer a good tom cat any day of the week," Peder offers, as a striped cat brushes against him on her way to the kitchen and her food dish. Enid and Peder have had all of the cats spayed and neutered by their local veterinarian. The Shortells' menagerie is rounded out by a resident bird as well as two horses, stabled nearby.

Enid could qualify as the president of the Daniela Kirchner fan club. "I admire her so much," she tells me, "after everything she has been through. She is strong, loyal to her family, and a fantastic mother to her kids.

"The neighborhood has been divided ever since Otto and Daniela lived here," she continues. "They stayed to themselves and only came to the block party when we specifically invited them. Even though they moved away almost four years ago, some people on our block still do not speak to other people because of the way that loyalties split over the Kirchners." Enid explains that she and her husband were good friends of Loren and Stacy Heinemann until about the time of the dissolution of the friendship between Loren and Otto. Enid and Peder became not only close friends but—as it turned out—allies of Otto and Daniela and they remained loyal to them. Now the Heinemanns and Shortells generally avoid contact with each other.

"Some of the neighbors complained to me that the Kirchner children were naked when they were playing in their child-sized pool in their own backyard," Enid recalls. "I thought this was no big deal, an overreaction—Danny was five or six and Sharon only one or two years old. But I explained to Daniela that this could be a problem in America. She was surprised to hear this, but she always dressed the children in swimsuits after that.

"Danny played with all girls in this neighborhood, my own daughters and some others on the block," Enid explains to me.

"There weren't any boys in the immediate area." As I share her early recollections about Danny, I remember having observed his metamorphosis into a gentler little boy, sometimes preferring a cuddly stuffed animal to a power action figure. Enid continues, "I would call Danny 'Dan Dan the Sunshine Man' because he was **always** smiling, vibrant, and active. It seemed like he never stopped going. All day long he was on the move, playing and having fun. From the first day that they came to live here on Thanksgiving weekend of '95, I got to know him and his parents. In fact, Danny was at our house while his parents were moving in," Enid relates as she and I are sharing reminiscences while sitting in the comfort of the Bakers Square Restaurant one mile from her home.

Enid and Peder's daughters—Shoshannah, now nineteen; Leah, seventeen; and Alisa, fifteen—played with Danny almost every day during his first months in their neighborhood. They played basketball, using the hoop mounted over Danny's garage door, in good weather, or Nintendo games indoors. "Danny had incredible eye-hand coordination, even at the age of four," Enid, a former kindergarten teacher of four years, shares with me. "He was very bright, athletic, and sure of himself."

In the Shortells' backyard is a large playhouse, equipped with kid-sized table, chairs, stove, and other furniture. "Danny loved playing in that house," Enid smiles as she remembers those times. "He was comfortable with my girls, but he would even play in there alone if they were in school or elsewhere. He had so much energy, I asked myself, 'Does he ever slow down?'

"Danny would ring our door bell and ask for Shoshannah most of the time, even though she was seven years older. He seemed to prefer her company even though she was the oldest of my girls. She almost always stopped what she was doing to play with him."

Forthright and outspoken, Enid is a "what you see is what you get" person. She is relaxed, animated, and self-disclosing as we converse over our lunch of salad and cornbread. She and I first met at Danny's sixth birthday party at Chuck E. Cheese's Restaurant, and we had brief conversations from time to time after that. Today we are discussing our common experiences as well as our unique histories within the Baby Richard saga. Enid's countenance grows solemn as she lapses into memories of neighborhood turmoil and ambiguity.

"For weeks at a time after the Kirchners moved next door, we would see a van sitting out by the street curb during the day. Sometimes the driver would flash a photo in front of the house.

"Daniela seemed guarded with me for a long time and, after a while, I found out why," she tells me. "Sometimes I would give her rides to work. One Saturday morning in the car she changed. We started talking like friends for the first time. I came to realize that she had been afraid to trust anyone after all of the media hype about her and the constant scrutiny she had to endure. For months, I even had strangers coming to **my** front door, asking if 'Baby Richard' lived here. One time a woman knocked on my door and said, 'You're the lady who knows that little Richard.' At first I thought she meant the famous singer and then I realized she meant Danny. I would just tell them nothing and send them away. At various times, we also saw cars driving by frequently, going very slow, and sometimes the driver would take pictures of the Kirchners' house. It was scary. We always had to have our guard up."

"Did you ever call the police to report these things?" I ask her.

"No, we didn't," she answers, "but that's because of the response that we got when Stacy Heinemann and I went to the police department to report threats that had been directed at Loren and their family. The police officer seemed disgusted and said that he couldn't do anything for us. I think he was pro-Warburton," Enid explains. As she describes this disconcerting experience, I find myself wondering whether the sense of professional brotherhood between police and firefighters may have contributed to the dismissive attitude of the officer. "After that, I felt 'what's the use' in reporting these strange things?"

Enid describes the investigative reporters as relentless. "Especially after the news of Otto and Daniela's separation broke, the media were here in full force, trying to get a story. They asked questions about Otto, where he was, what he was doing, whose car he was driving. They were also looking for some evidence of child abuse or neglect related to Danny. The question of Daniela's competence as a mother was foremost. I told them that she is a dedicated, wonderful mother and that Danny was just fine. The press quashed these stories, though. They seemed disappointed with what I had to say."

The previous year, Annie Gowan, a free-lance writer working on behalf of *The Washington Post*, interviewed Enid several times during the media's focus on the one-year anniversary of Baby Richard's transfer. Ms. Gowan also contacted me twice for updates on Danny's progress and to obtain a photo of him with his newborn sister, all of which I provided her. However, her story never appeared anywhere. "After all of that time and effort," Enid laments, "they didn't bother to print the truth about how well 'Baby Richard' was doing. They were seeking bad news and didn't find it. No story."

In her follow-up letter to me, Ms. Gowan wrote:

...[A]fter much consultation my editor and I decided to put the story of the Kirchners and their past year on hold....

I continue to believe that Otakar and Daniela's story was never rightly told by the local Chicago media who, in their biased coverage, demonized them simply because they were immigrants.... (June 11, 1996)

Years later, Ms. Gowan would tell me that the controlling reason for the death of her story was the refusal of Kim Warburton, who had originally consented, to give an interview. "Although I believed that she had created the whole situation out of stubbornness, there was no story without her input," Gowan discloses. Once again, the Kirchners' circumstances and Danny's normalcy were not considered sufficient as newsworthy.

Enid describes her own first awareness of the Baby Richard case, long before she met the Kirchners. "I felt **so** sorry for the adoptive mother from the media coverage. Before I met Danny, I expected him to be a timid, frightened child. But he was well adjusted, confident, and happy from the very start. There was no quietness or fear in him. I've never seen him sad about anything. He'd ride his bike up and down the sidewalk. He was always outside playing, summer and winter. And he'd run full steam out of the house to greet his mother when she returned from work, he was so excited to see her.

"And Danny was the light of Daniela's life. You could just see it. Daniela took the children with her to church every Sunday. She protected them from her marital problems with their father.

In fact, she never said anything against their father to the children. She worked hard to keep things as normal for them as possible during their separation. That Christmas Eve, Daniela asked Peder to play Santa Claus, to come to the house and give out the presents. Peder dressed up in the Santa costume that she provided, and he worked hard to fool the kids so that they wouldn't recognize him. They had a nice Christmas," she concludes, smiling her approval. Peder, who has a kind, gentle, round face and a nurturing personality, was undoubtedly the ideal candidate for this Santa impersonation.

It was Enid who paved the way for Danny's admittance to the public school kindergarten program. "I was worried about his safety and concerned about how the teachers and the other children would treat him," Enid explains. "I asked Otto and Daniela for permission to meet with the principal of the school. With their approval, I told her about Danny's situation. I asked her for anonymity for him and protection from harm. That was during the time that lots of strangers were coming to our neighborhood, looking for him. The principal already knew before I arrived that there was a problem. She said, 'I'll have to go to the superintendent with this one.' She was a wonderful woman. She admitted Danny without the required birth certificate. She prepared the teachers to protect Danny from any attempts at intimidation, and she kept his file, sealed in her own office, to ensure his privacy."

Enid occasionally intervened between Danny and his grandmother during daytime hours when Daniela was at work. "Once in a while, Danny would get stubborn and refuse to obey Greta," she relates. "Sometimes he wouldn't fully understand her because of the language difference. I would tell him that Grandma was working hard to take care of him and his baby sister, and he would then relax and go along with her wishes." Greta was invaluable to the young family of her daughter, according to Enid, who admired the older woman's round-the-clock efforts to help out with the two children and the house.

Describing Daniela "like a bear with her cubs, making up for lost time with her son," Enid is similarly protective of her friend and the Kirchner family. "I am glad that Otto is Danny's father. They had their marital problems, but Otto was always a good father to his children." Enid and her husband gave the

Kirchners the used car that Peder's father had given them. "They needed it more than we did. Their car broke down and they had no means of transportation," she recalls; "it was a very difficult time for them."

The Shortells also gifted their next-door neighbors with a clothes dryer. "Daniela would be hanging clothes on the line outside, even in the cold of winter," Enid says, "so we wanted to make her life a little easier. She was always doing things to the house to make it nicer, like putting in a new floor and cabinets in the kitchen."

Enid and Peder continue to play out the return of Santa Claus every year for the Kirchner children. Observing traditions of their native country, Otto and Daniela celebrate on Christmas Eve by furtively putting gifts under their Christmas tree while the children take their baths. When the children return to the living room, they are disappointed to have missed seeing Santa, a feeling that is rapidly overcome and replaced by the excitement of unwrapping presents. The next day, another bag of gifts mysteriously appears at the Kirchners' back door, left by a forgetful Santa Claus who had to double back during the night to deliver them. Enid and Peder seem to enjoy their annual holiday ritual as much as its recipients, Danny, Sharon, and Jessica.

As I drop off Enid in her driveway, under the watchful eye of her couch cat, again peering through the front window, we pledge continued contact with each other. We share a tacit pact of loyalty and commitment to the family who is so publicly misrepresented...and yet so private.

"They took me for a stupid immigrant...and I was," Daniela confesses to me as we revisit her ill-advised and painful excursion into adoption in America, specifically as governed by Illinois law. She is describing her personal encounter with Kimberly and Jay Warburton in the days preceding the birth of her son, Daniel, who would become "Baby Richard" across years of court documents and media accompaniment.

"When I met with them, I went to see if they would be a nice family for my son," Daniela recalls in a low and slow voice. "It's hard for me to talk about this," she murmurs, her eyes moist, although I am already well aware of her acute discomfort and lingering pain. "We met in a restaurant, and I remember feeling disappointed with them. They were not well educated, as I hoped. She was working part-time for a lawyer and he was a fireman. My beauty school teacher's lawyer told Kim about me and the baby. They were interested in adopting him, and so we met to talk about it. I explained that the baby's father and I were drug-free and alcohol-free, and we were both healthy, with no mental problems in our families. I did most of the talking. I told them that the baby's father worked on Lake Shore Drive and that he wanted this child. I also said that I was afraid that he would raise the baby with another woman, who would hate the child. I wanted to prevent that from happening." Daniela stops to clear her throat. She looks both wan and weary as she relates her memories to me while we are sitting at her kitchen table. I am sipping hot tea after sharing a roast chicken dinner with her and the three children, who, after enjoying their dessert of home-made brownies, have gone to Danny's bedroom to play together on his computer.

Although Daniela had shared with me the basics of her background when I was her therapist during the latter stages of the Kirchners' legal battle to regain Danny, she takes this occasion, during my February 2003 visit, to disclose more details related to her personal struggles. Even now, after nearly twelve years of marriage to Otto and eight years of raising her son, her feelings of loss, remorse, and despair from those first four years of Danny's life in another home are close to the surface. She shakes her head solemnly and continues, "I felt so alone and I made a terrible mistake. They took advantage of my condition...."

"I came to this country for freedom," Daniela proclaims with a spurt of enthusiasm as she reaches back in her memories to her teenage years. "I was fed up with not having freedom in my communist country. I like to travel, for example, but travel was limited in Czechoslovakia to only socialist countries. I applied for a visa to the United States and was turned down. They were probably afraid that because I had a good profession—I was already a licensed esthetician in my country after completing four years of training—I would come here and not return. I decided then and there that I would keep trying and if I got a visa, I **would** stay," she says with the determination that I have come to know as one of her most compelling personality traits.

At the age of twenty-one, after her second application for a visa, Daniela Janikova was indeed successful. She packed up her personal possessions to start a new life in the States, leaving behind a loving and supportive family. Her mother and father would miss her, but they also wanted for her the opportunity for a better life with more options than were available to a young woman in their country. As the baby of her family, Daniela had two older siblings, a brother and a sister who were twins, six years older. Her father was a quality controller and her mother worked in a bank, and they enjoyed a middle-class life in a condo. Daniela and her parents envisioned trips between the two continents, from time to time, to visit each other.

Speaking no English but feeling confident in her ability to learn the language, Daniela arrived in the U.S. and moved in with her mother's brother, Uncle Joe, and his wife, who lived in Berwyn, Illinois, a suburb of Chicago. There was a large Czech and Bohemian population in the area, and it seemed to be an ideal place to start her new life.

"It was hard to stay with my uncle and aunt," Daniela recalls, "because they had big problems with each other. It was very tense and I was uncomfortable. I met Otto during my first year here; I was still twenty-one. Otto was my first real boyfriend and the love of my life. He taught me how to be a waitress, and he hired me at the restaurant where he was the manager."

Soon after Daniela began her new job, working with Otto on a nearly daily basis and then dating him for one month, they decided to live together. Otto split up with Maria, his long-time girlfriend, also from their native country, and Daniela moved her sparse belongings from her uncle's home into Otto's apartment on Lake Shore Drive. Within months Daniela became pregnant. She was happy about the news, and Otto was ecstatic.

"Maria was still around," Daniela tells me with anxiety in her voice. "She called me during my first trimester. She said, 'Otto just wants this kid, not you. And **I'm** not taking care of someone else's bastard child.' I remember thinking that the baby would be hated or even harmed in some way if he went with Otto and Maria. She **said** that she wouldn't take care of him."

At Christmas of that year, Daniela discovered that Otto had bought Maria an expensive gift. She found a credit card receipt.

"Once Otto, when angry, told me that he just wanted the child, that I was like a mailbox for the baby, and that I could just give him the child and go back to Czechoslovakia," she says, wincing from the distressful memory. Although she loved him, Daniela felt insecure and unsure about Otto's commitment to her.

During Daniela's third trimester, the pivotal call came from their native country: Otto's grandmother was dying. If he wanted to see her, he must come immediately. Otto and Daniela discussed the situation, and both decided that he should go to be at his grandmother's side during her last days or hours of life. She had raised, nurtured, and loved him when his parents separated and left him behind to embark upon new lives for themselves.

"While he was there, Otto's aunt called me to say that he was honeymooning with Maria. I believed her and I was completely devastated," Daniela discloses as she relives her despair. "I felt so **alone**. I was crying all day long. I kept thinking, 'how could the love of my life do this to me?'"

Daniela, who had left her waitress job to study at a nearby beauty school toward the goal of attaining licensure in Illinois as an esthetician, broke down in tears the next day. One of the teachers, a mature woman with children of her own, asked the overwrought student the cause of her weeping. Daniela explained the situation. Her advanced stage of pregnancy was already apparent, but she revealed the story of the phone call from abroad, her apparent abandonment by the father of the child, and her feelings of confusion and futility. The teacher comforted Daniela by assuring her that she should not be with such a man anyway. The best thing for the baby would be to give him up for adoption to a nice home with people who could offer him a good life. Daniela was learning English and could communicate only on an elementary level; she had no job, no money, and no medical insurance; and her living situation was precarious. The teacher encouraged her by stating that her own adult daughter might be interested in adopting the baby.

On the following day, the teacher initiated another conversation with Daniela about her predicament. "Don't be selfish," she counseled; "think of the future of this baby. Do what is best for him. He should have a home with people who can provide for him."

Feeling torn between her desire to mother her own child and her acute awareness of her inability to support herself and a baby, Daniela seriously considered the teacher's words. "At first I thought, 'no way,' but then I thought more about her advice. I respected her," Daniela relates as she recalls her own vulnerability and intense need for emotional support. The teacher indicated that her daughter was not interested in adoption, but her attorney friend knew a woman, his former part-time secretary, who wanted to adopt Daniela's baby. It would be easy with no agencies involved, no red tape.

Soon Daniela was meeting the Warburtons at a restaurant so that they might get to know each other. During their conversation she gave a weak consent to the proposed private adoption of her baby. No money would exchange hands; the couple would simply come to the hospital to claim the child and take him home with them. They said that they wanted a playmate for their three-year-old son Johnny. Although Daniela would have preferred a couple with more education as the adoptive parents of her child, she comforted herself with the knowledge that they had a home in the suburbs and were already a family of three. She worked to quell her fears about her baby becoming a secondary, lesser child for this couple, professedly a playmate for their biological son. She worked to quiet her inner voices that kept telling her that she should keep the child after his birth.

Not knowing anyone well enough to discuss adoption in Illinois, she wondered about how it worked. In Czechoslovakia, through twenty-one years, she knew only one child who had been adopted—a handicapped gypsy girl from an orphanage, whom a neighborhood couple had met and for whom they felt sorry.

"**Everyone** knew about her because adoption was rare," Daniela explains to me. "It was seldom done through a legal process and it mostly occurred within families, like in Otto's case, where his grandparents just raised him after his parents left and moved away. Otherwise, sometimes people would adopt a child from an orphanage, but I knew of only the one example in my whole life."

After their restaurant meeting, the Warburtons called Daniela to talk more about their proposed adoption of her baby. "They asked if the father would sign adoption papers," she recalls. "I told them, 'No, he won't.'"

They asked about the hospital that had been chosen for the baby's birth. "I told them St. Joseph's," Daniela continues, "and they asked, 'Does he know about the hospital?' I said, 'Yes, of course!' They then suggested that I change the hospital to Alexian Brothers in a suburb close to their home."

Daniela also changed her doctor two weeks before her due date. The Warburtons recommended the new doctor to her. With a switch in her attending physician and in the hospital for the delivery, the father would be unable to find his baby.

"I was still struggling with the decision, confused and lonely, having constant second thoughts about the idea of his adoption, but a situation occurred that settled it for me. My aunt and uncle separated one week before Danny's birth. My aunt ran away to another state; she was afraid of my uncle and made me promise not to tell him her whereabouts. My uncle told me that I could live with him, to clean and cook, but I could not bring a baby into his house. He said, 'No way, I won't hear him crying.' I felt I had no other choice, nowhere else to go. I didn't even have enough money for food," Daniela remembers with sadness in her voice.

Although Otto made many attempts to speak to her, she avoided him, convinced that he wanted only the child and not her. She rehearsed in her imagination Maria's words from months ago—the dire prophecy of Maria's purposeful rejection of the baby whom she acknowledged Otto wanted, although she herself did not and therefore she would refuse to care for him. Daniela convinced herself that the best option for the child was his adoption by this Schaumburg couple; the Warburtons were forceful and determined. The beauty school teacher also guaranteed her that this was the best alternative for the baby's sake. She wanted what was best for him. He deserved her unselfish act on his behalf.

Never having told her mother about her pregnancy, Daniela had no one else with whom she could discuss this important decision. "My mother would never even approve of me living with Otto before marriage," Daniela discloses. "She is very religious and believes strongly about these things. I was ashamed and afraid to tell her that I was pregnant."

During their months of living together, Otto and Daniela had gotten two marriage certificate applications, "but he never asked me to marry him and they expired," she explains. "I never connected with the ethnic community for a number of reasons," she relates, "so I had no interaction or support from that source either."

Because of the escalating conflict between her uncle and aunt, coupled with her desire to avoid Otto, Daniela presented herself at the Greenhouse, a shelter for abused women. She intimated that the father of her baby had abused her so that they would not turn her away. "When they asked if I was physically abused, I said 'No, just verbally.' They let me stay; they knew I couldn't go anywhere else without money."

While at the Greenhouse, she got a phone call from the Warburtons' attorney, saying that the adoption could not go through without the father's consent. "He will never consent," I told him. He said that he would advise his clients not to proceed with the adoption. Later he called back, reporting, "The adoptive parents want to do this even under these circumstances." The Warburtons' attorney discussed with Daniela the possibility of accusing the biological father of being unfit, perhaps an alcoholic or a gambler. If successful, this approach might prevent him from claiming his child. Daniela left the shelter and went directly to the hospital when her baby's birth was imminent.

Daniela had been sick through most of her pregnancy, also experiencing intense mood swings. In contrast, her delivery of the baby was relatively easy. "It was a natural birth on my due date with no complications...at Alexian Brothers Medical Center. In fact, like a lot of mothers, I can't even remember the pain," she declares. After eleven hours of labor, her 7-pound, 12-ounce, brown-haired baby boy was born.

Daniela named him Jesse, upon the recommendation of the Warburtons, who, within days and without her knowledge, would change his name to Daniel. She was not surprised that her baby was a boy. Although she had never sought to know the gender of her baby before his birth, both she and Otto were convinced that their baby would be a boy.

"They showed him to me and put him on my stomach. He was so beautiful. He looked exactly like Otto," recalls Daniela. She held, cuddled, and fed their baby during the following three days. She insisted that the baby remain in her room, never leaving her side.

The next day, when Daniela was checking out of her room, the baby began crying uncontrollably. "It was like he knew what was going on," she says, pausing for a long minute. "I looked at his eyes as I was taking him to the nursery, and he seemed to be saying, 'Why are you doing this?' I was crying, too, and thinking, 'I am doing this for **you**.'"

That was Daniela's last opportunity to see her baby. On the fourth day, the Warburtons came and took him. "I remember feeling so alone and so **empty**," she continues in a soft voice. "They encouraged me to pass the word through the ethnic community that the baby died right after his birth." She would not be speaking with Otto, she reasoned, and this plan sounded feasible within the turmoil of her whirling emotions.

The following day she went to the Cook County Social Service Coordinator's office and signed away her parental rights. "Strangers gave me a paper to fill out," she explains; "there was no counselor, no options, no explanation, no time for me to think." She left blank the space on the form for the father's name.

Compounding her pain and confusion, the beauty school teachers and students had held a baby shower for her shortly before her due date. Daniela was unfamiliar with the concept of baby showers, but she was grateful for the outpouring of happiness and good wishes from the well-intentioned women who knew nothing about the imminent, swift, and privately-arranged adoption of her baby.

"I had received all of these things for my baby and wanted him to have them, so I tried to call the Warburtons on their beeper number. I was going to give them the shower gifts, but they had changed their number and I had no way to reach them. It was then that I realized what I had done."

The sudden awareness of the enormity of her decision was like a flood of grief, regret, and despair for Daniela. She had felt like a cork on a wild sea during the weeks before the birth of her son. Now she felt even worse.

"I had hoped for some kind of continued contact," she reveals. "I knew I could probably never see my baby, but I thought that the Warburtons would tell me from time to time how he was doing. I then went to the hospital to get his birth picture so that I could remember him by it, but they had taken that, too. It hurt my feelings so badly. His picture was gone and I had **nothing**."

During the negotiations stage between the Warburtons' and the Kirchners' representatives in spring 1995, when the court-ordered transfer of Danny was under discussion, Kimberly told Daniela that Danny's birth picture had been destroyed in a flood of their basement. "I felt hurt all over again because of what that picture meant to me, especially after the years I lost with my child."

While Daniela felt alone and emotionally raw after the departure of her baby with his would-be adoptive parents, she would experience another loss soon after this saddest event in her young life. Seven weeks later, "my uncle kicked me out of his house," she tells me as she vividly remembers her fear of the unknown, without money or a place to stay. She was afraid of becoming one of the homeless. "He asked me where my aunt was staying, and I refused to tell him because I gave her my word to keep her secret. I told him that I couldn't break my promises. He insisted that I give him her phone number, but I wouldn't. He got angry and said, 'Then get out right now!'"

Daniela asked her uncle if she could wait until the next day because she had nowhere to go. He refused, adamant that she leave immediately. "I packed up my few possessions and left. I felt that Otto was responsible for my miseries and so I decided to go to his apartment to ask to stay for a while. I had no key, but the security guard recognized me and let me in."

Not having eaten much for a series of days, Daniela describes herself as "skin and bones." She was so tired when she arrived at Otto's apartment that she immediately fell asleep on the bed. When Otto came in, Daniela awoke. "He came to my side and asked, 'Are you hungry?' I said I was, and we left to go to an all-night restaurant to eat. It was nearly midnight."

Ironically, it was also Mother's Day…and the weekend of Daniela's twenty-fourth birthday. "Right away Otto asked me what happened to our baby," she relates. "I told him the truth about our son and I started crying. He said, 'Don't worry—we'll get him back.' I didn't trust him at first, and I was afraid for the baby. Would it be good for him to drag him back from the other house? I suggested that we could have another baby, but Otto said, 'No, we'll get him back.' He was focused on the baby, and then I was, too."

During the weeks that Daniela avoided Otto and refused to speak to him by phone when he called, Maria had insinuated herself into his life again. Although they did not live together, they were spending time with each other. Once Otto knew that his son was alive and well—and living in Schaumburg—he readily chose Daniela, the mother of his child, and once again he broke up with Maria.

Otto and Daniela joined forces to regain their son. Otto contacted a lawyer, Loren Heinemann, immediately after he received a recommendation for the attorney from a customer at his restaurant and within days of his Mother's Day reconciliation with Daniela. Otto became the sole plaintiff in the lawsuit that ensued when the Warburtons not only refused to return his son but also fired their attorney, Tom Panichi, after he recommended that they do so. Under Illinois law, Daniela's legal rights to her child were lost upon the fourth day after his birth, when she signed the consent for his adoption. However, she became the silent partner in the lawsuit, and their mutual pact to regain their son both sealed their relationship and established the primary path of their lives together. Everything for both of them would revolve around their baby.

"It was the beginning of a nightmare when the Warburtons left the hospital with my baby, with Otto's and my baby," Daniela explains. From that day on, her worst real nightmare would be less painful and terrifying than her waking-hours realization that, within the span of a handful of days of torrential emotions, loneliness, and desperation, she had irrevocably lost her child.

Otto and Daniela married in September 1995, four months after their mid-May reunion. Daniela completed her program at the beauty school; easily passed her state examination; and became a licensed esthetician.

Having been a runway model for clothes in her native country, she also decided to enroll in a nearby modeling agency program. After she successfully finished her training, Daniela's portfolio was reviewed by an executive of the modeling agency. "She said my eyes were dead and that I could model only for legs; I had pretty legs," Daniela recounts. "She was right—there was no life to my eyes; they looked empty and showed my inner feelings. That was the end of my modeling career," she says with resolve. Knowing Daniela well, I experience the chilling realization that the modeling agency official—like her predecessor at the beauty school—joined the small but powerful ranks of authority figures in Daniela's life who misguided her into dead ends. I also know that those lifeless eyes reflected her prolonged mourning for her lost baby.

"One of the most miserable days of my life came in 1992 when the judge approved the adoption because he declared Otto unfit for not coming forward in the first thirty days after Danny's birth," she shares with me. "The judge said to me, 'You are young and can have other children.' But I didn't want 'other children'; I wanted **this** child."

Years later Daniela would become an American citizen. "It took a long time, partly because the INS lost my file and I had to start all over again, but at least I could work, with my green card," she explains. With both European and American training and licensure, she readily landed a job in an upscale beauty salon in downtown Chicago.

Daniela would never interact with her uncle or her aunt again. The aunt divorced her husband and, although Daniela has not heard from her aunt since the spring of 1991, she believes that the woman never returned to Illinois. Her uncle remarried and settled with his second wife in a Chicago suburb. Daniela's mother maintains minimal contact with her brother "out of family obligation," according to Daniela, but she herself has not spoken with her uncle since he summarily expelled her from his house and she narrowly avoided becoming homeless. Daniela thus lost the only family members she had in this country.

In some ways, Otto and Daniela were alone...together. But from Mother's Day 1991, neither ever wavered in their determination to reclaim their son; to love, cherish, and parent him; and to make up for lost time.

They had no way of knowing how much lost time it would be....

Dismissed and condemned by the media as "the woman who did not want her child," she has steadfastly avoided either self-promotion or self-defense. Until now Daniela's story has remained untold.

As we might expect
in a business that often
treats children like commodities,
success in the private adoption marketplace
is not always measured
by moral, legal, or ethical standards.

—Jeffery Leving

Lessons Learned– Baby Richard's Impact

There is an
undeniable genetic bond
that exists between children
and their biological parents.
That natural bond...
provides the most
solid foundation
for a child's development.

— *Byron P. White*

A RECIPE FOR PAIN AND CHAOS

Take a couple who has a three-year-old biological son and who has not been seeking to adopt a child. Add a young, naïve, and impoverished immigrant woman, nearly nine months pregnant, who is drowning in despair and confusion. Mix in her healthy, newborn, white male baby—free for the taking. Combine these ingredients with bitter yet digestible lies and cloves of deception. Leave out the boy's father—the victim of betrayal all around since the age of four—who has always wanted his child.

Stir in a horde of attorneys—like many cooks in the kitchen. Blend in, across time, four large court decisions and seven smaller ones. Fold in a ruthless, prominent columnist looking for an easy, low-risk, and heart-tugging story to sensationalize. Salt with a governor whose political need is to appear compassionate and child loving. Pepper with a variety of legislators with their own agendas. Sprinkle in liberally reporters and journalists of all flavors.

You have the makings of "Baby Richard"—with lots of servings. Everyone will take a portion and there will still be lots of leftovers to go around, remarkably for months and even years. When there is nothing else to serve up, it can be reheated—with the addition of only one or two new ingredients—into an entirely palatable offering by journalists and reporters who do not even know how to cook.

"Baby Richard" is a recipe for how **not** to adopt a child. None of the parties to this invalid adoption received the benefits of professional assistance or counseling related to the process of adopting a baby. The biological mother knew nothing about adoption in her new country or in her state of residence. The biological father knew nothing about the proposed, attempted adoption of his only child until after the mother's rights were forfeited under the law and the baby was living with his would-be adoptive parents. Those adoptive parents, in spite of "both a legal and moral duty to surrender Richard to...his father... [when] Richard was then less than three months of age[,] ...selfishly clung to the custody of [the child]" (Illinois Supreme Court finding, rendering the adoption proceedings "wholly defective"). The adoptive parents did not receive pre-adoption counseling or training. They did not inform the child that he was adopted or that he had biological parents who were fighting for him (in the courts) until after his fourth birthday. The child was not even allowed to meet his mother or father until more than three months after the state's highest court ruled that he should be turned over to his father "forthwith" (immediately). He was not allowed to meet his mother or father until they appeared to take him home with them. His departure and his visible suffering were turned into a media spectacle, attended by a mob of unruly and threatening onlookers. It was a fortuitous opportunity for limelight for the adoptive parents, their various attorneys, and media representatives who styled themselves as "Richard advocates."

Lies. Deception. Fraudulent affidavits. Within the quick, independently arranged and executed adoption, only the adoptive parents, their attorney, and the biological mother were involved. The mother, alone and desperate, lacked an attorney, family assistance, money, medical insurance, counsel of any kind, or knowledge about adoption. She was vulnerable, malleable, and confused. In this condition, she gave up her four-day-old child to a couple who would soon enjoy the benefits of almost unlimited resources—both financial and legal—not only to continue their fight to keep him but generally to obscure from the public the realities of their complicity in the ultimately invalidated adoption.

> It would be a grave injustice not only to Otakar Kirchner, **but to all mothers, fathers and children,** to allow deceit, subterfuge and the erroneous rulings of two lower courts, together with the passage of time resulting from the Does' persistent and intransigent efforts to retain custody of Richard, to inure to the Does' benefit at the expense of the right of Otto and Richard to develop and maintain a family relationship.... [Emphasis added] ("Conclusion," Illinois Supreme Court, January 1995)

Honesty is a key issue in the lessons to be learned from Baby Richard. If adoption is done properly—with **full knowledge, consent,** and **integrity** on the part of all of the adults—everyone wins—ultimately and especially the child. Adoption agencies work to ensure these three ingredients for all adoptions that are undertaken under their auspices. With "Richard," at the very least, full knowledge was lacking by the mother; consent was not only lacking but not even sought of the father by the adoptive parents or their legal representative; and the reader is left to assess the level of integrity of the adoptive parents and their attorney.

The dusty cloud of furor and revenge that was kicked up by the losing parties to the lawsuit fogged over the real issues and unnecessarily raised anxiety and fear among aspiring and established adoptive parents, their relatives, and other supporters. Journalists joined in to add their targeted, big kicks to increase the obfuscating cloud as well. Nearly everyone on the public stage jumped into the "misery pool," most of them misapplying and misappropriating the "Richard" outcomes.

FATHERS' RIGHTS

The widely publicized (and widely misinterpreted) Baby Richard case powerfully illustrates the torment and heartache that can result from the possible callous disregard of a father's rights....

...[T]he Illinois Supreme Court demonstrated...to disenfranchised single fathers all over the United States— that the law, although often imperfect, and almost never swift, sometimes fulfills its promise. (Jeffery Leving, *Fathers' Rights*, 1997)

"Baby Richard set fathers' rights on an upward trend," Leving declares during 2003, as he reflects on the case. "Although the media didn't pick up on it at the time, it was the ideal prototype of a loving father's triumph in gaining his son and the ability to parent him.

"Justice shouldn't be a luxury...for fathers...or anyone," asserts Leving with obvious conviction in his voice. The Chicago-based attorney whose specialty is the promotion of more equitable treatment for fathers vis-à-vis their children, Leving represented Juan Miguel Gonzalez in the Elian Gonzalez case in 2000. Six-year-old Elian had been rescued at sea off the shores of Florida, shortly after his refugee mother died amid her courageous attempt to obtain sanctuary in a free country. His Cuban father testified, on behalf of his asserted right to reclaim his son, to the U.S. Senate Judiciary Committee. In spite of forceful protests originating from Miami's Cuban population and then expanding throughout the country, Elian's biological father prevailed and returned to Cuba with his son. Jeffery Leving has also provided significant input into legislation involving fathers' rights, including an Illinois joint custody bill, signed into law in 1986. This law created as a legal standard the presumption that the maximum involvement of **both** parents is in the best interest of their child.

It was attorney Leving who—although not directly involved in the Baby Richard case—first perceived its relevance to the arena of fathers' rights and the example that it provides:

The...case offers fathers valuable (if ominous) insights. While we applaud the courage and wisdom of the judges who finally did the right thing, we realize that few fathers have the resources and resolve Otakar exhibited.... Too often, ...expedience triumphs over justice. We see that the legal and family service professionals who operate within, and preside over, the adoption process often exclude fathers from adoption and child-rearing decisions. Terminating a natural father's parental rights...requires only minimal effort and, even when accomplished illegally, rarely brings disapproval or reprisal.

Citing the "little respect for fathers or fatherhood" among social agencies, "a wide cross section of our judiciaries," and a majority of citizens, Leving points out:

A broader, more distressing perspective emerges when we examine the overwhelmingly negative public reaction spurred by the decision to return Baby Richard to his natural father. Rather than being hailed as a heroic figure for his arduous, determined pursuit of his parental rights, Otakar was cast as some kind of demon, publicly vilified and privately detested. Instead of being commended for bringing an end to what some have called "a state-assisted kidnapping," the justices...were scorned and abused by much of the media and the populace. (*Fathers' Rights*)

Since 1995, however, the fathers' rights movement has gained credibility, momentum, and support across the country. More fathers today are fighting for the opportunity to parent their children in meaningful and lasting ways. Otakar Kirchner became a public figure—unwillingly but necessarily in his circumstances—and became the ideal model of perseverance and commitment, amid great adversity, for other fathers who want to avoid disenfranchisement from their children.

ADOPTION TODAY

In spite of many negative ripple effects of Baby Richard, its legacy includes positive impact. Not only has Illinois, through "Richard"-inspired legislation, instituted a putative fathers' registry for men who want to assert their parental rights to their offspring, sixty percent of the fifty states followed Illinois' lead and now have such registries. The state of Illinois has expedited its adoption process, making such proceedings a priority on the schedules of its courts. The state also requires unwed mothers to disclose the identities of their babies' fathers, if known. In addition, the courts must ensure that genuine efforts are undertaken to locate fathers in order to ascertain whether they will consent to the adoption of their children before they lose their rights to parenthood.

"Until the 'Baby Richard' law, birth mothers had all of the stress of adoption," explains Julie Tye, president of The Cradle. "Now the burden of decision-making is shared by the birth father. He can register within thirty days if he wants to assert his rights to his child rather than allow the baby to be adopted."

Although nationwide public debate and state legislatures focused upon the advisability of a uniform law to govern adoptions, replacing the patchwork assortment of differing statutes among the fifty states, the result has been "increased awareness" rather than the passage of such a law. However, states across the country reassessed—and in many cases revised—their adoption laws in the wake of Baby Richard.

Today, as before, there is no uniformity in adoption requirements between and among the states. As a general premise, however, "when a child is placed for adoption, the consent of the birthfather will always be required when such father has undertaken the normal responsibilities expected of fatherhood...whether the child is born in or out of wedlock." The procedures and time elements for terminating the birthfather's parental rights vary from state to state. Likewise, the requirements on birth mothers vary. As of 1998, "37 states [including Illinois], or more than two-thirds of the country, allow a birthmother to sign a consent within three days or less after birth." (Christine Adamec, "State Adoption Laws," National Council for Adoption *Adoption Factbook III*, 1999)

In 2002, the state of Florida passed a unique and controversial law that requires unwed mothers who cannot locate or identify the biological fathers of their children by a required exhaustive search to disclose by publication the intimate details of their past sexual encounters. The purpose of these disclosures is to provide notice to biological fathers about their children so that they might assert their rights to parenthood and halt adoption proceedings. Proponents of the law have cited the rights of fathers to parent and/or financially to support their children, and they have asserted the likelihood of increased father-paid child support and resultant decreased state aid for dependent children. Opponents have cited the preeminent rights to privacy of women—and of their sexual partners—and have asserted that better ways might be used in order to provide biological fathers with notice about their children. The Baby Richard case was referenced and used as an example by individuals on both sides of the heated debate.

"Unfortunately, the field of adoption is as fragmented today as it was during the Baby Richard case," Julie Tye laments. "If people adopt privately or through an agency, there is a wide difference in expectations for services and for outcomes. Some people undergo years of fertility treatments with disappointing results. They can make poor decisions out of desperation and eagerness for a baby. The adoption system is unregulated in many ways."

Open adoption during recent years is a more frequent option that Tye supports. In an open adoption, there is sharing of information and/or contact between the adoptive and biological parents of the adopted child. "It is more common today and usually more healthy," Tye asserts. "The nature of the relationship between the biological parents and the adoptive parents is established based upon the comfort level of everyone. Usually there is little—or no—direct contact between the biological parents and the child, perhaps until the age of eighteen, but medical and other information is exchanged between the sets of parents. The adoptive parents are typically less worried, and the element of secrecy is removed. Probably the worst thing for a kid is to keep a secret [from him]."

Continuing, Tye explains, "The child needs his or her questions answered." Open adoption allows for that need to be addressed. "**Some** connection to the birth family is maintained, but the nature of the relationship needs to be what works for **all** of the individuals involved. Forcing it to be a certain way is no good," she summarizes.

In my own small family, one of my four maternal cousins is an adoptee; today he is a Catholic priest and the head of his order. My only paternal cousin was informally adopted by our grandparents, who raised him from his infancy. Although his mother continued regular contact with him, our grandparents raised him as their son and made all of the decisions related to his upbringing.

In my husband's large nuclear family, among their twenty-four children, one girl and three boys were legally adopted. As one of eight biological children, Robert grew up in a household of ten children, as two cousins, at young ages, had come to live permanently in his home when their own parents became unable to raise them properly. Although not legally adopted, both the boy and the girl were raised, nurtured, and financially supported by Robert's parents; the girl became a Catholic nun.

My own attitude toward adoption has remained unchanged since the day when, at the age of six, I learned that my only cousin at the time had been adopted by my Aunt Laraine and Uncle Ronald. I was delighted to see their joy in having a baby, and I remember thinking that adoption was a wonderful way of making a family. Today I would urge individuals or couples who desire to parent a child seriously to consider adoption as a viable option. However, I would as ardently encourage them to become involved with a reputable adoption agency or a professional counseling service for both legal and psychological reasons in order to enhance and ensure the success of the adoption process for themselves and their child.

Adoption in America today is characterized by a paradox. Although there are many people seeking babies for adoption, there is a growing number of children who continue to remain immediately available for adoption. The apparent contradiction is attributed to the fact that most people who want to adopt are seeking healthy infants, preferably white babies, while most of the children who are awaiting adoption are older children of color, many with siblings. Some have emotional, physical, or mental disabilities.

"President Bush was dismayed by the surprising statistic that only one percent of out-of-wedlock births are placed for adoption...." (*National Adoption Report*, National Council for Adoption, Summer-Fall 2002) "This unhealthy trend" is partly due to "pregnancy counseling that overlooks adoption or presents it inaccurately," NCFA President Patrick Purtill explained to the President.

According to the National Center for Health Statistics:

> The placement of children for adoption has never been common, but over the past few decades it has grown increasingly rare. Between 1989 and 1995, just under 1 percent of babies born to never-married women were relinquished for adoption.... In the early 1970's, almost 20 percent of babies born to never-married white women were relinquished for adoption, compared with only 1.7 percent of such babies born in the first half of the 1990's. (*Advance Data*, Centers for Disease Control and Prevention, U.S. Dept. of Health and Human Services, May 11, 1999)

"In 1996, domestic adoption of infants comprised only 0.6 percent of 1996 live births, and 1.9 percent of births to unmarried women... [T]hese statistics show that more than 98 percent [of unmarried women] elect to parent the child." (*Adoption Factbook III*) More likely than not, in my opinion, some of the 98 percent of unmarried women make other arrangements for their babies, such as placing them with a grandparent.

"There are 1.5 million adopted children in the United States, over 2% of all U.S. children," according to the Evan B. Donaldson Adoption Institute. "In 1995, about 500,000 women were seeking to adopt a child, and 100,000 had applied with an agency." That same year, "an estimated 1.3% of women adopted one or more children, a decline from 2.1% in 1973."

After Baby Richard and the widespread misconceptions that resulted from it, many people turned to international adoptions, especially for healthy infants. In 1997, *CNN Chicago* reported that "the numbers of international adoptions have risen to their highest level ever...most from mainland China, Russia and Korea." ("Baby Richard," January 21, 1997) The actual statistics for 2002 for the top five countries of origin for international adoptions are China (Mainland), 5,053; Russia, 4,939; Guatemala, 2,219; South Korea, 1,779; and Ukraine, 1,106. From the top twenty source countries combined, 19,139 adoptions were effected. (U.S. Department of State, Office of Visa Processing, September, 2002)

"Intercountry adoptions comprised 17.2 percent of unrelated adoptions in 1996, up from 10.5 percent in 1992.... [I]n 1996, intercountry adoptions comprised over one-fourth of all unrelated adoptions in each of twelve States...." The number of foreign adoptions grew dramatically from 9,384 in 1995 to 11,316 in 1996 and "reached an all time high of 12,596" in 1997. (*Adoption Factbook III*) Although there is no reliable way to measure the impact of the Baby Richard case upon these statistics, many adoption agencies reported experience with prospective adoptive parents who cited the "Richard" case and then turned to foreign countries for babies.

"A growing number of children are now placed through independent adoption—with estimates ranging from one-half...to two-thirds of infant adoptions." Independent adoptions are defined as adoptions "in which birth parents directly place children with adoptive parents, sometimes with the assistance of facilitators, doctors, clergy, or attorneys," as opposed to private adoptions that are arranged through "for-profit or non-profit agencies." ("Private Domestic Adoption Facts," the Evan B. Donaldson Adoption Institute, 2003)

In the Baby Richard travesty—an independent adoption— there was a healthy, white, male infant, an American citizen, born to a young and healthy set of parents...free for the taking...after the passing of a three-day window period, at which time his mother irrevocably forfeited her parental rights. His would-be adoptive parents came upon a fortuitous and rare opportunity. They took him and, at least figuratively, ran; they changed their phone and beeper numbers; and they resolved to fight to keep him. When they left the hospital with four-day-old "Richard," they knew his father wanted him, but they hoped that a lie about the baby's death would prevent the father from claiming his son. When the child was only two months old, his biological father came forward, and his mother, deeply regretting her hasty and uninformed decision, wanted him back.

"They had the truth, their child, and justice on their side," Adrienne Drell would tell me during 2003 when she and I met to review our Baby Richard experiences. As a reporter with a law degree, Adrienne covered court cases for the *Chicago Sun-Times* for thirteen years before she was assigned the "Richard" case. "It was amazing to me that the case took on a life of its own," she tells me. "I thought, 'It's just a single court case,' but the activities outside of court made it so different."

Adrienne attributes Baby Richard's unprecedented rise to prominence to Bob Greene, "who fanned the flames and made it his special project. At first, I thought he must be hard up for material, but then he got both an increased readership and a national reputation from it." It had the ingredients of a "grabber" story—a baby boy; four parents fighting for the child; the role of the state; the rights of children; a bitter conflict among opposing forces at every level; and differing, impassioned court opinions.

Attorney Bruce Boyer was the only **self-initiating** volunteer among a number of individuals, including myself, who donated their services to the Kirchners and their son across their years of struggle. Boyer, after reading the 2-1 appellate court decision in favor of the Does, telephoned Loren Heinemann in order to assert his willingness and desire to work on Otto Kirchner's appeal to the state's Supreme Court.

"It was a dead wrong, arrogant, and dangerous decision," Boyer explains to me, years after his *pro bono* involvement. "I was deeply offended by the ruling and feared the precedent it set for other children."

If the lower and appellate court rulings had been allowed to stand, according to Boyer, they would have paved the way for wealthier couples successfully and easily to claim the children of less advantaged biological parents. Unless and until a poor, or even indigent, parent is found unfit, he or she maintains the right to keep and to raise his/her own child. The Illinois Supreme Court, by reversing the appellate court's "Richard" decision, reaffirmed the right of biological mothers and fathers to parent their own children even if more advantaged individuals would like to claim those children for adoption.

"I got hate mail and harassing calls for my involvement," Boyer shares with me. "I especially remember one person who asked, 'How can you sleep at night after what you did to that child?' For me, **that** was the **point**—I could only sleep at night if I petitioned the Court to do the right thing to protect **all** children from potential removal from their natural parents." Boyer filed an *amicus curiae* brief in support of Otto Kirchner, and Heinemann deferred to his more knowledgeable colleague, allowing Boyer to address the Supreme Court justices during the oral presentations on the case.

MEDIA MAYHEM

"Something evil happened in Chicago, Illinois, on April 30, 1995" begins the article entitled "The Tragic Case of 'Baby Richard'" in the NCFA *Adoption Factbook III*. Authored by Dennis Prager, it decries the Illinois Supreme Court's decision that "devastated" the child. Writes Prager, "...Danny was given to his birth father, whom he had never met, and removed to Iowa."

Danny has never been to Iowa. Prager then states that "fools drew this conclusion after visiting him..." and that it is "literally impossible—that Danny is 'doing fine.'" He further asserts:

> ...The smiling Danny you have seen in those home videos is a child who has no choice but to smile. He knows that he has to "be good." Or else, who knows what will happen to him? He believes that he wasn't good enough for his original family, so he has to be even better for his captors.

In his book, from which this abridged version is printed, Prager continues:

> For as long as human beings care about children, let the names [five Illinois Supreme Court justices] be remembered as the five judges who induced mental illness in a happy and healthy four-year-old boy named Danny....

It is obvious to most of us that the civil rights of Danny...were as violated as were those of black slaves....

...Danny's *life* was permanently ruined. (*Think a Second Time*, 1995)

For such alarmingly inaccurate, hyperbolic, and damaging accusations, Prager—absent first-hand sources of any kind—cites mental health professionals who never met Danny.

It is interesting and illuminating to note that Prager arrogates to himself the role of a knower about Danny Kirchner, although he also never met the child, never spoke to either of the child's biological parents, and never spoke to me—the only mental health professional who interacted with Danny. Yet, he quotes—as his authoritative source—Bob Greene, who shares Prager's history of lacking any first-hand contact with the boy or his family. "'Not to be overly dramatic, but this is how mental illness begins,'" Prager quotes Greene, who attributes this statement about Danny to "one child psychologist," unidentified by name.

That this article is still promulgated in the NCFA *Adoption Factbook III*, with its incorrect facts and outrageous assertions of "reality," absent first-hand sources, is distressing and infuriating. Perhaps the editors of the *Adoption Factbook III* revisions, if any, and of "Factbook IV" will correct this error in judgment. The child to whom the presumptuous, ignorant, and uninformed are attributing mental illness and other permanent defects has been and is living a normal, healthy life—not in Iowa, as erroneously stated, but in Illinois. The major point here is that Danny is entitled to live that normal, healthy life without being compelled to endure the damaging effects of such baseless assertions and allegations, all made by persons who neither met him nor spoke to **anyone** who could properly address these issues.

One of the most lamentable lasting effects of "Baby Richard" is the generally accepted belief that the child is scarred for life, unable to experience a normal, healthy emotional development. This is absolutely not true! Not a single one of the individuals who made such an assertion ever interacted with Danny Kirchner! **Not a single one.** The media created and perpetuated the story line about Baby Richard and found "experts" to advance it.

...Well, news fans, here's one of those dirty little secrets journalists are never supposed to reveal to the regular folks out there in the audience: a reporter can find an expert to say anything the reporter wants—**anything!** Just keep calling until one of the experts says what you need him to say and tell him you'll be right down with your camera crew to interview him.... It's how journalists sneak their own personal views into stories in the guise of objective news reporting....

It happens all the time. (Bernard Goldberg, *Bias*, 2002)

Everyone who interacted with Danny—including a number of reporters and journalists such as Adrienne Drell—has reported that he appears "normal," "happy," and "well-adjusted." Danny's teachers describe him as a bright, self-confident child, who is extraverted and makes friends readily. None of Danny's teachers has reported any problems, either academic or social. As his psychologist and therapist, I have attested to his stable personality, his continuously relaxed, happy disposition, and his ease and success in establishing interpersonal relationships.

In addition to this microcosmic view of the child himself as the innocent victim of dire predictions by those who never met him, most of whom were seeking publicity for themselves, the macrocosmic view is also important to consider. "The real scandal is what happened to Judge Heiple," attorney Mike Foley believes. "It's not too often you see public persons exercise that level of courage," he continues, referring to Heiple's lead role, on behalf of a unanimous Supreme Court, in authoring and explaining the "Richard" decision. As the sacrificial lamb of the Court, Heiple narrowly avoided impeachment hearings by stepping down from his position as Chief Justice. Yet, Heiple—and the Court—stood firm in spite of the barrage of bitter criticism from the media, state legislature, governor, and the public.

"If the independence of the Supreme Court had been successfully compromised, that would have been the worst travesty of justice," according to Foley. "We went through a period in our country where hunting people and destroying them became a spectator sport. Otto Kirchner became a dry run for that. Then there was Heiple on the state level and Bill Clinton on the national level."

Heiple's retrospective viewpoint parallels that of Foley. "Bob Greene took a strong position in his columns as to how the Court should rule, and he wrote outraged, punishing columns when it didn't follow his direction," Heiple relates. "We were doing our jobs. The court must follow the law regardless of its popularity or unpopularity."

Ultimately, the integrity of the Illinois court system and its Supreme Court justices prevailed. Among the other heroes of the "Richard" saga are those attorneys who contributed their time and expertise—absent any financial remuneration—because of their personal beliefs in justice. Bruce Boyer—with the support of Thomas Geraghty, Annette Appell, and Zelda Harris from the Children and Family Justice Center of Northwestern University—prepared and filed the *amicus curiae* brief at the Illinois Supreme Court level, and Boyer wrote the briefs, on behalf of Otto Kirchner, at the U.S. Supreme Court level. Mike Foley represented Otto and Danny Kirchner in their ultimately unsuccessful lawsuit against Bob Greene and the *Chicago Tribune*, which attempted to pave the way for Danny to begin a private life. Susan Haddad and Paul Bargiel represented the Kirchners in their ill-fated attempt to restore Daniela's legal rights to her son. Although Ms. Haddad was unable to obtain Danny's medical records from his former adoptive parents, she eventually got what should have been a routinely issued birth certificate for the child from the governmental office that controls official documents.

There are so many *What ifs?* that must be asked in the aftermath of Baby Richard. What if, rather than being lured into an independent adoption, which she didn't even understand, Daniela had gone to an adoption agency? The agency would have provided her counseling and options, and it would have insisted on the biological father's consent, which would not have been given. What if Daniela had an attorney...or even understood adoption? What if the Warburtons had followed the advice of Tom Panichi, who filed untrue affidavits on their behalf but who advised them to return the baby when his father first came forward? What if Bob Greene had not written 100-plus columns about the case? Or, what if he had taken the opposite position in those many dozens of columns— for example, by continually decrying the "attempted kidnapping" of a child who was wanted by both of his birth parents? What if the *Chicago Tribune* had discovered Greene's sexual misconduct at the time of its occurrence six years before his Baby Richard rampage? If he had **then** been fired, or forced into resignation, as he was in 2002, the "Richard" case would probably have received limited, ordinary, and even-handed coverage by the media.

Baby Richard should have been a private case...between two sets of parents...on behalf of a baby. An appellate court judge wisely initiated the pseudonym "Baby Richard" on the child's behalf. Until that point, he was called "Baby Boy Janikova," his mother's maiden name.

The coverage of Baby Richard lapsed into bad taste and bad judgment early on...and just kept getting worse. It was the incipient stages of an era during which anything could become newsworthy in mainstream newspapers, including subjects and treatments of topics heretofore reserved for the tabloids and other publications specializing in sensationalism.

The power of the media to mislead and to destroy is an important lesson from "Baby Richard." The greatest danger to the real Danny was the Baby Richard hysteria and mythology created by a frenzied media, interested in commercial advantage or a coveted exclusive. In this story that seemingly wouldn't end—the media lowered the bar for standards of journalistic integrity and decorum. Baby Richard "sightings," reported by gawkers in super markets, were elevated to newsworthy. Trespassers, listening at the door of "Richard's" family home, were dignified by anonymity and headline coverage. The privacy of an innocent four-year-old child was violated and invaded on a daily basis, seriously threatening his safety and security and robbing him of a normal life. Allegations regarding his "ruined" mental health and his "flight into mental illness" were reported widely by irresponsible, ethically marginal, armchair "professionals" and media representatives hungry for a dramatic, attention-getting angle. They turned a real child into a curiosity, at the least, and into a genuine victim. He was considered fair game and those of us who cared about him and worked to shelter him were powerless.

In modern-day American society, we espouse and cherish certain values as absolute and inviolate. Our valuing of human life and our responsibility to protect young children, as deserving innocents, are two examples. Daniel Kirchner, as Baby Richard, became the exception. It is perhaps understandable, though not laudable, that the media hounds, responding to the adoptive parents' invitation, came out in full, fierce force to film close-up Danny's pain on the day of his transfer. However, it is inexcusable that a group of journalists continued to invade his privacy on a wholesale basis and painted him as pathetic, irreparably damaged, and doomed, for their public. I know of no other example of this type of media assault upon a little boy or girl. Early on, the coverage of "Richard" disintegrated into such bad taste and irresponsible journalism that almost no one seemed to discern its uniqueness. It was neither politically correct nor morally defensible, but its inappropriateness went unnoticed. In my research, I have found nothing in written form that decried the damning portrayal, by certain members of the media, of the child himself. Shame on the media who were involved in this travesty, victimizing a little boy!

From subtle to overt, the coverage was relentlessly negative toward the Kirchner parents. An underlying theme was the attitude that if Danny was indeed irreparably damaged, this outcome would only serve his father right! When Otto Kirchner was quoted, the sound bites invariably captured some incidental ungrammatical usage of English, a borrowing that didn't translate well from his native language—or from the other three languages in his repertoire. Photographs and news clips typically showed him holding or smoking a cigarette or positioned in a most unflattering way. After all, he was the bad guy, the "evil alien," and he should look like it.

Within the widespread campaign designed to trump the Supreme Court rulings and prevent Otakar Kirchner from claiming his son, Mrs. Brenda Edgar, the governor's wife, wrote a private—and public—letter to Danny's father:

Dear Mr. Kirchner,

As a mother who would do anything for the well-being of my children, I am writing to ask you to be a great hero to your son.

As his father, don't punish him for adult mistakes. Don't wound him or make him cry. Love him so much that as an adult, you endure the pain of the choices made when he was a baby. Spare him any pain.

Please make this sacrifice for your son.

Sincerely,

Brenda Edgar

("Mrs. Edgar's Plea: Don't Take Richard," *Chicago Sun-Times*, January 27, 1995)

Not only was the full content of this letter published on the front page of the newspaper, but a photograph of it was printed. Written on the stationery of the "Executive Mansion, Springfield, Illinois," the letter appeared as an official document...in what should have been a private matter. It was presumptuous, of course, for the governor's wife to insinuate herself into a child custody dispute between two sets of parents. Even many of those who sympathized with her sentiments—patronizing as they were—questioned the appropriateness of her having elevated this written missile to the level of the "Executive Mansion." Of course, her picture also appeared on page one as the companion to her "heartfelt" letter. She was successful in capturing a rare level of attention and media coverage for a governor's spouse.

Five weeks later, Bob Greene, possibly competing for the "bad taste" award, published in his column the telephone records of Otto Kirchner "from his home" for the one-month period before his son's birth. "Only" five calls to Daniela's home were recorded, Greene asserts. He reveals other information—

calls to the former "girlfriend"—that he intends to discredit Otto. In a civil lawsuit, this journalistic invasion of privacy is both unusual and alarming. Greene admits that these records "were subpoenaed but never placed in evidence" during the Baby Richard court proceedings. Yet, Greene takes it upon himself to disclose to the public what he admits to be inappropriate to newspaper material:

> ...This doesn't belong in the newspaper, or on the radio or television or in the arena of public opinion. It belongs in a courtroom—which the prevailing justices will not permit to happen....

> ...This voiceless child will simply be taken away.... ("167 phone calls that demand an answer," *Chicago Tribune*, March 5, 1995)

What ever happened, you might ask, to the droves of powerful and prominent people who got themselves quoted and covered conspicuously in Baby Richard media coverage after the real child went to live with his father and mother? The profound concerns and professed love for the child from the vocal and the visible came to a screeching halt at the Warburtons' street curb, when Danny Kirchner entered the van that carried him home. In spite of dozens of legislators who hastily passed the "Baby Richard Act" and the very public interventions by the governor and many others in government, the media industry, and the entertainment world, none of these individuals contacted Danny's parents to wish them well or to offer encouragement, assistance, or support for them or their young son. Did Baby Richard cease to merit their continuing concern when he changed his residence? If these individuals' professed love and concern were genuine, why did these feelings and their expressed commitment to his best interest not arrive with Danny at his birth parents' home? Many of these individuals opted instead to criticize and to lament—getting more publicity for themselves—rather than becoming constructive and helpful for the real child.

THE POWERFUL BIOLOGICAL BOND

During the earliest stages of formalized interactive media, the *Chicago Sun-Times* conducted a series of "Morningline" phone-in polls related to the "Richard" case. On the day the news broke of Otto Kirchner's victory at the Illinois Supreme Court level, the *Times* initiated a poll of its readers, published within its story "Dad Wins Fight for His Son" (Tom Seibel, June 17, 1994). To the question, "Should the rights of biological parents outweigh those of adoptive parents?" the vast majority of responders, 91.7%, said "No," while only 8.3% said "Yes." Clearly, the public—as determined by this sampling—championed the side of adoption over biology.

An element left out of nearly all of the coverage about Baby Richard is the powerful bond of biology that is felt by many—if not most—adoptees and that should be factored into both the story and the reality of Danny. The child would have undoubtedly wondered about his natural parents as he grew up in his adoptive parents' home if his father had given up on the fight for him. Very likely, Danny would have longed to meet them, to get to know them, and to be able to understand his biological and cultural heritage.

In a unique column about this aspect of "Richard," journalist Eric Zorn changes his formerly adamant position about the child:

> As wrenching as this is for a newspaper columnist to admit, I've come to suspect in the last several days that I may not be supremely qualified to issue ringing pronouncements on the "Baby Richard" case....
>
> ...I had the gut reaction.... Don't traumatize the boy by taking him out of a home where he is now healthy and happy.
>
> I included this viewpoint in my Tuesday column and received objections from a source that surprised me: adults who had been adopted as children....
>
> We are not, they said, taking into account the enduring power and importance of biological ties, ties we [non-adoptees] take for granted.

The columnist continues by quoting from the many phone calls he received:

> "...[W]hen you're adopted, you go through life with a missing piece to your puzzle. At some level, you don't know who you are."

> "I had an idyllic childhood with my adoptive parents, but I always felt there was a hole inside me.... It was low-ebb kind of grief and anger—why didn't my natural mother and father want me?"

Zorn refers to "'the primal wound,' a trendy term that refers to the anguish some say infants inevitably experience when they are separated from their birth mothers and put up for adoption."

Explaining his change of heart, the columnist states, "It is the mysterious but powerful bonds of blood...that makes the Baby Richard case more complicated and more subtle than...it seemed to me when I first applied my experience and prejudices to it." ("'Baby Richard' not open and shut case," *Chicago Tribune*, July 7, 1994)

"Where is she?" asked the three-year-old adopted daughter of Byron P. White, an assistant editor for the *Chicago Tribune*. She was asking about her birth mother.

> The fact is, despite how much we might love our daughter..., it one day will matter to her that she is adopted.

> That is the humbling reality that faces adoptive parents, though some of us try to deny it and make selfish decisions as a result....

> There is an undeniable genetic bond that exists between children and their biological parents....

With the wisdom of a mature adoptive parent—at the time of his published article, involved with his wife in the process of adopting their second child—White evaluates the Baby Richard "ordeal":

...[A]lso apparent through the saga was the Warburtons' intent to deny how important biological parents are in the development of a child....

They might have told Danny that he was adopted, White continues, and might have allowed him to build a relationship with his birth father. "...[A]long with love, a child's discovery of 'who I am' and 'where I fit in' is a critical part of his or her development." He emphasizes a harsh reality:

> For our daughter—and other adoptive children—that discovery includes crossing a hurdle that children who live with their biological parents do not have to [cross]. It is the struggle that has begun to reveal itself in our 3-year-old's simple question: "Where is she?"

The author's unselfish approach to his own child is reflected in his self-disclosures:

> ...[T]he realization that it is critical for our daughter's well-being to consider, at times, the importance of her biological roots above our own needs and emotions has become clearer....

> As we watch our daughter mature, though we are elated she is ours, we increasingly regret that she did not have the option of growing up with her birth parents. It pains us that she will have to contend with the inevitable sense of rejection and abandonment that comes from not having been raised by the people responsible for giving her life.... ("Family matters—Adoptive parents face the inevitable question," *Chicago Tribune*, August 13, 1995)

Danny Kirchner will be spared the problems of wondering, or trying to figure out, why he is growing up with adoptive parents; why his natural parents gave him up to others; and who he is by birth and genes. He started to understand his own unique situation when he was four years old. His adoption was set aside as illegal at the ultimate level of the state's court system. His would-be adoptive parents had "mere possession" of him, to

During our September 2002 visit to the Chicago area,
Robert and I gather together on their sofa with Danny and his sisters.

which they clung beyond reasonableness, and for which they were responsible for the expenditure of huge sums of both private and public moneys.

"We must consider the effect on the child who will one day learn that his biological father was defrauded and prevented of any opportunity to win his custody in a scheme which involved the adopting parents and their attorney...," wrote Justice John Tully in his dissenting opinion at the appellate court level. Fortunately for Danny, he will not have to grapple with this realization or with the bitterness that likely would have accompanied it.

Danny has been granted the right and privilege to grow up with his birth parents and his two younger sisters; to know not only his biological relatives but his ethnic history and roots; and to realize that his parents fought long and hard to reclaim him. He has visited his parents' country of origin, and he has acquired the richness of becoming bi-lingual and bi-cultural, like his mother, father, and sisters. He appreciates his cultural background and he identifies with it. He is part of something bigger than himself. Danny knows, understands, and feels that reality.

He is blessed.

Danny holds his first "real" golf club. He often practices his putting on the living room carpet during the winter months.

On my return visit to Chicago in December 2002,
we celebrate the holiday together in front of the Kirchners' Christmas tree.

"WHAT DO YOU KNOW ABOUT BABY RICHARD?" I ask Danny Kirchner in the privacy of his room during my February 2003 visit. I realize that I have neither mentioned "Baby Richard" to him before nor have I discussed his unique situation as the icon of adoption gone tragically awry. He and I have not talked about his former life with the Warburtons or his transition to his parents' home and care for years. Although his formal therapy with me ended in late 1995, I have seamlessly continued to be a regular part of his life, like an extended family member, on an uninterrupted basis for eight years. Danny never spoke of his former life in my presence after 1996.

"Obviously it's me," Danny responds with a charming, slightly mischievous smile. He is sitting on his swivel chair in front of his desk, which supports his

CHAPTER TWENTY-ONE

Danny

Our need for play
is mysterious,
...akin to our need
for dreaming....
It is how we process
what happens to us,
and how we communicate
what we are processing.
It is how we breathe air
into our emotions
and how we find out
what we are feeling.
As any good
psychotherapist knows,
play and emotional health
are synonymous.
In fact psychotherapy
is a kind of play,
and play a particular kind
of therapy.

— *Mark Epstein, M.D.*

computer and holds an array of books and discs. He is facing me
as I am sitting on his twin-sized platform bed, taking notes as
we begin our conversation about his past, present, and future.

Danny's bedroom is white on white, from the walls to the
laminate furniture. In addition to the bed and desk set, there is
a large shelf unit that houses his games and a few stuffed animals. In one corner of the room, three hockey sticks rest against
the wall. The carpeting is beige and lends a sense of warmth to
the room. His bedding is awash in Pokemon figures against a
white background, and replicas of these figures have been pasted by his mother around the room as a near-ceiling border. The
colorful action characters look as if they are jumping and flying
around the room.

At five-feet-two-inches, Danny is now as tall as I am. Next
month he will turn twelve. He is a handsome, athletic child, with
hair that has turned from bright blonde to honey blonde as he has
matured. It is now styled in a medium-length crew cut, a bit longer
toward his face. Danny, self-possessed and poised, maintains good
eye contact; he smiles readily; and he thinks before he speaks.

Asking him how he feels about my writing a book about him,
I note that he appears both pleased and eager. He replies, "Fine;
my parents told me about it." When I ask him if he is comfortable talking about his past, he says "Yes," and his body language
corresponds. He seems relaxed and anxious to talk about himself. It has been a long time since we spoke privately about serious matters. In recent years, our interactions have revolved
around play, swimming, and beach activities in Florida and
around meals and games of various kinds in Illinois. We have
visited amusement parks together and toured St. Augustine. We
have played board games and Uno, a favorite card game. Often
I have run up and down the sidewalk in front of his home while
Danny and his sisters rode their bikes in a home-made escape
game, accompanied by shouted challenges and squeals.

"Some kids in school saw things on the Internet," he offers.
"They knew I was Baby Richard. Once I saw papers about Bob
Greene; I thought he was the green monster. Who was he any-
way—an attorney?"

"No. He was a writer for the newspaper who mostly wrote for
the other side," I tell him. "Did you ever look for information
about yourself on the Internet?"

"No, I haven't," he responds.

"What else do you know about yourself?"

"I got stolen when I was a baby," he continues. "There was a big argument about who I should stay with and about the truth. The other people—I don't know their names—wanted to keep me."

"They were called the Does in the court papers, Danny," I inform him. "What do you remember about them?"

"Not much about **them**. I remember a closet in the living room with a big crack at the bottom. There were toys in there. I remember creaking and noises from the closet door. And bubble gum and eating doughnuts. I don't like doughnuts any more; I think I must have eaten too many of them there. I don't remember them ever cooking; there was a lot of fast food. They left me alone when they went out. I remember they had a dog," he adds. "And one time I went around the other houses, putting things that I made about Joker from *Batman* in the neighbors' mailboxes.

"I didn't get presents for Christmas," Danny continues, sadness in his voice. "I got up from bed and went to the Christmas tree, but there were no presents for me. They were eating and already unwrapped their presents. So I went to hide in a corner and I cried. I still get nightmares every year at Christmastime now. In my dream I'm looking for presents and there aren't any for me, so I go into the corner and cry. All of a sudden the room gets red all around me. Then I wake up and I'm sweating. I'm scared, but then I know it's a nightmare and I'm okay again."

"Danny, I find it hard to believe that they wouldn't give you presents on Christmas. You know how much I like to give presents, so I think that everyone else does, too. Are you sure this really happened?" I query him.

"Yes, it did," he affirms. "I remember it. I was very sad and disappointed." Danny was not yet four years old during his last Christmas with the Warburtons. Yet this holiday memory is obviously vivid and real for him. It is also significant that his only recurring nightmare involves his life with the adoptive parents.

"Do you remember the day of your transfer to your parents?"

"Yes!" Danny answers. "I was playing gator golf with the other boy. I didn't know who was coming; I asked who they were. They didn't tell me. They told me that the house I was going to would be scary and terrible, and the people would be mean."

"Were you scared?" I ask.

"Yeah! But then I remember they had a stuffed dog in the car," he relates. He is referring to the stuffed animal that Daniela was using as a puppet during the one-hour van ride to his new home in Mokena. She used it to get him to talk to her and to divert his attention from the frightening public transfer that he had undergone moments before.

"What else do you remember about first coming to your parents?"

"My Formula One race car. I remember the house and the glass table, and I remember you," he recalls from his first hours in the Kirchners' home. "Also, later, my bike and coloring on the back porch on a table and chairs out there.

"Some kids stole my Formula One car, though. They took it behind a pine tree and ruined it, with hammers," Danny recalls, shaking his head and frowning. I also remember this event well. One day when I arrived for my usual visit, an agitated Danny greeted me to report how some neighbor boys with mean faces had hammered his child-size car into pieces while they looked at him from a safe distance. He watched, helpless to prevent the older boys from accomplishing their malicious destruction of his favorite toy.

"Why do you think they did that?"

"Probably they were jealous," he speculates, and I accept his answer with a nod, while I remember that this hurtful act appeared at the time to be a type of protest by the children against Baby Richard. Their mutterings, overheard by Danny's father as he approached to intervene, moments too late to salvage the car, revealed the children's true motivation. They were likely acting out the disapproval and anger of their parents during the height of Baby Richard hysteria directed against the Kirchners.

"When you were little, do you remember anyone saying anything nasty or mean directed at you?"

"No," he responds. I feel relieved that he has apparently forgotten the painful incidents during his kindergarten and earliest elementary school years that he had shared with me when they occurred. While in kindergarten, for example, Danny was hurt and angry when one of the boys in his class approached him to say, "Your mother is very stupid." He was also surprised because, as he related, "The boy never even met my mom.

He heard it from his parents." Today he claims no memories of these early upsetting events.

"Do you remember the other boy at your first house?" I am asking him about Johnny, his former adoptive brother.

"Only a little," he says. After a thoughtful pause, he continues, "I remember playing gator golf with him, lazer tag, and video games. Once I fed ducks in a lake with him," he concludes.

"What do you remember about Justin from your old apartment, when you first came to live with your parents?"

"I remember that he had a dart board and I remember a little about his apartment. That's about it," he sums up.

"What about Mario during that first summer?" I ask, eliciting memories of his older cousin, who had come from Slovakia to spend three months with his Aunt Daniela and her new family.

"He had red hair and he was fun. We went fishing together, rode our bikes, and went to a pub one time and ate sandwiches there."

"What do you remember about me?"

"I remember that you would always play with me," he says, smiling.

"Did you know that I was your doctor when you first came to live with your parents? That I was there to help you all become comfortable with each other and to make your settling in as good and as fast as it could be?"

"No, I didn't know that. You were just always there. I never thought about it," he confesses with the candor of an eleven-year-old.

"Do you remember when Cicka was born?" I query, realizing that she was born one month before his fifth birthday.

"No, I just know that I went to the hospital to wait there. Then I went home with Veronica and Lali's family."

"Do you recall saying to me, 'I have my own baby!' when I came to visit your family on the day she came home from the hospital?"

"No, did I say that?" he asks with a giggle, grinning broadly and leaning forward.

"Yes, you did. You were very excited," I explain to him.

"Danny, how do you feel about being Baby Richard?"

"It's **really** strange that something like that would happen to **me**," he summarizes. "But I don't think about it. My parents and I never talk about it."

"What would you want to tell the other people?"

Danny pauses to reflect and then replies, "I'd say it wasn't very nice of them to lie to the public about me. I think they were very mean. I wouldn't want to see them ever again."

We lapse into a question-and-answer format as I probe his feelings and attitudes toward his family and himself....

KM: "What do you like best about your mother?"

D: "She still buys me stuffed animals, and if I want something a lot, she gets me that stuff."

KM: "What do you like best about your father?"

D: "He likes to play sports, especially soccer, and he likes to take me to Odyssey Fun World and to arcade games."

KM: "What do you like best about Cicka?"

D: "She doesn't take anything of mine and she doesn't break any of my things."

KM: "What do you like best about Jessica?"

D: "I don't know; she's so little, I can't say."

KM: "If you had a magic wand, what would you change about your mother?"

D: "She wouldn't be so worried about my grades, testing me all of the time, and going into so much detail."

KM: "With that magic wand, what would you change about your father?"

D: "He wouldn't have to work so much and he could spend more time with me."

KM: "If you had that magic wand, what would you change about your life?"

D: "That's simple for me. I would become a professional soccer player. I would also have a little race track with go carts to drive on."

KM: "If you had one wish that would come true, what would it be?"

D: "I'd ask for **unlimited** wishes," he says, laughing.

KM: "That's very clever. What would be your first wish?"

D: "I'd ask for six million dollars."

KM: "What are your plans for your future?"

D: "To get a good job; retire at thirty-five; and go on lots of trips. Oh, and I'd like to buy a house for my mother."

KM: "Do you consider yourself happy or unhappy?"

D: "Happy, except for waking up so early for school; I'm up at 6:30 in the morning. But I like school. I'm friends with the whole class practically."

KM: "What have been some of your happiest times?"

D: "At Odyssey Fun World, on the slot machine I got three sevens and won 500 tickets. At basketball practice one time I scored every shot I took."

KM: "What have been some of your unhappiest times?"

D: "Leaving my last school after fifth grade to go to my new school for sixth grade, for this year. A lot of my friends were at the old school."

Finishing up our conversation, I take this opportunity to remind Danny that he has continued to be very special to me from that very first week. "I know," he assures me with a maturity level beyond his years. It becomes an unforgettable interaction for me—closure to a long journey of peaks and valleys as well as a first step toward a new future for him and for me.

Although Danny shared with me additional memories regarding his life with the adoptive family, both at the time of my therapeutic interactions with him and during today's conversation, I have purposely omitted them. Absent the ability to confirm them, I have decided that it would do no one good to reveal them in this book. The bottom line is that Danny's memories reflect his former life as less than idyllic. Yet, unsurprisingly, at the age of four his memory started to dim early on, and, like most people, he remembers only snatches and glimpses of events from his first years of life.

A well-rounded seventh grader, Danny today earns mostly A grades, along with a couple of B's. Although his mother wishes for straight A's, which he has achieved on several report cards in recent years, she and his father are pleased not only with his academic progress but also with his level of effort. Danny is conscientious about his studies, but his mother interrogates him daily about his schoolwork and any homework that he has been assigned. He has been promoted to the eighth-grade math class, one year ahead of his age mates, and it is his favorite subject.

"Danny is a very bright boy," Mrs. Gayle Osterberg, one of Danny's teachers, tells me during the spring of 2003. "As their religion teacher, I get to know the kids more than some of the other teachers. We talk about personal things and values in my class. Danny is such an extravert. When he transferred here at the beginning of the school year, he tried very hard to make friends. He experienced some isolation at first, but now he has a lot of friends," she explains.

"He's really a good-hearted kid," she continues. "I've never seen him be mean to anyone."

"What stands out about Danny?" I ask her. "If you had to choose one thing that makes him stand apart from the other kids, what would that be?"

"He's so happy—always smiling or laughing," she responds. "He seems very glad to be here. He's a sweetheart," the teacher concludes.

During our conversation, Mrs. Osterberg is unaware of Danny's personal, early history as the "Baby Richard" of yore. Danny and his parents have striven to keep his courtroom and media-created identity private, disclosed to others on a need-to-know basis only.

"He's a very, very good child," DeAnn Schulte reports to me in another telephone conversation about Danny. Miss Schulte is his social studies and homeroom teacher. "He's independent and competent," she continues, "and he's socializing well with the other kids. Danny takes his academics seriously; he understands the cause and effect of having to work hard to achieve something."

She offers the observation, "He has a very masculine manner about him and that's good. You can see it in his walk; he's a very confident child."

Danny continues to play soccer, which sport he started during fourth grade, and last year he scored goals in nearly every game. He plays basketball for his school team and street hockey with his neighborhood friends. Danny is a serious competitor, who loves to win and works hard to excel. His father regularly expresses pride in his son and demonstrates ongoing support of his athletic efforts.

Danny took flute lessons during the fifth grade. He decided to discontinue last year in favor of his other activities, including his athletics. His current interests include Pokemon games and movies as well as a variety of computer and video games. With his own computer, he spends "too much time," according to his father, in pursuit of personal achievement in these games, always striving to rise to the next skill level. Since he was four, his attention span and powers of concentration have been noteworthy.

Having read all four *Harry Potter* books, Danny has eagerly anticipated the release of the fifth book of the series. "In fact, I have read every one of the books **twice**," he proclaims enthusiastically. "I will probably read the fifth one two times also." His favorite television programs are *SpongeBob SquarePants* and *The Fairly OddParents*, cartoon programs on the Nick at Nite channel.

Danny regularly plays with his little sisters—Sharon, seven, and Jessica, five—demonstrating patience and understanding of his younger siblings. He has always preferred the older children from his neighborhood environments as his favorite playmates. Currently his best friend is fifteen-year-old A.J., who lives two doors away from the Kirchners' southwest suburban townhouse. A.J. and his two brothers—Kippie, thirteen, and Jayme, eight— are home-schooled by their mother.

"Because I know them and they are so well-behaved and so polite, I like Danny having them for friends," Daniela informs me as we discuss her son's social life. She makes a point of getting to know each of his potential playmates before he is allowed to pursue a relationship.

Daniela transferred Danny from the public school, located only two blocks away from their home, to the five-year-old Catholic school, fifteen minutes away by car, beginning with the 2002–03 school year. Although she or Otto must now frequently make the one-half-hour roundtrip drive, they prefer their children in a parochial school. "I think the children are better behaved in the Catholic school," Daniela explains her rationale to me. "They also teach values there in addition to the academic subjects; I want that for my children. It's worth the distance and the driving to give them this kind of education," she summarizes.

Perhaps most noteworthy of Danny's personality characteristics, he is self-confident. When his mother, sisters, and he visited Robert and me last summer for their two-week vacation, we held a series of pool parties in our backyard. At one of these events, Ed and Jean Moriarty—the parents of three adult children and grandparents of eight young children—joined us for dinner and fun. When Danny was introduced to them, he arose from his seat on the couch, walked over to greet them, initiated handshakes, and—with the poise of a typically older boy—said, "It's very nice to meet you." My brother-in-law later remarked that, throughout the day, he was impressed with Danny's good manners and his maturity.

On another day during this vacation, Robert took Danny to the driving and putting ranges at our local golf course to introduce him to the game. Danny was intent on doing well, as he asked questions and worked on his swing and stance with assistance from Robert. Later, he read several *Golf* magazines "from cover to cover," according to his mother, and he practiced his putting for hours. He could explain the construction of a golf ball and tips for good golfers from his reading. Then eleven, Danny was already reading for information and self-improvement.

Like almost all older brothers, he sometimes evidences frustration and exasperation with his little sisters when they become bothersome or stubborn, but he is usually protective of them and sensitive to the differences between them and himself due to their ages and gender. He looks out for them and often interprets little Jessica's needs to others, after explaining on her behalf, "She is shy."

In contrast, Sharon needs no interpretation, as she is exceptionally bright, articulate, assertive, and prone to willfulness. "She will be a handful," Daniela predicts, "because she already knows her own mind and she wants what she wants." Sharon describes her sister with a sigh, "Jessica is a copy cat; she copies everything I do." Sharon is as assertive and verbal as Jessica is quiet and passive. However, both girls learn quickly, and both love books and computer activities. They enjoy coloring and making small creative objects out of everyday household items, such as a duck fashioned from cut-and-paste appendages to a cardboard paper-towel roll. During the past year, their favorite play activities revolve around Barbie dolls and accessories of all types.

Before she began first grade last fall, Sharon taught herself to read both English and Slovak, using workbooks that her mother bought for her and working along with Danny on some of his schoolwork and learning games. She and Danny compete with each other on flash cards and similar educational materials that present questions to elicit correct answers. She strives to be the first to give the right answer and often beats him, to her own delight.

Sharon regularly complains of boredom in school. While she is already reading at an advanced grade level, her classmates are learning three- and four-letter words. She can add most two-digit numbers "in her head," without the use of paper and pencil. She loves learning new things and actively seeks both competition and challenge.

Jessica begins kindergarten in the fall of 2003. Before then, she is home during the day, either with her father or her mother. Although Otto works full-time and Daniela two days per week, they arrange their schedules so that one of them is with the children at all times. They do not utilize babysitters. In a special circumstance, cousin Lali or his wife Alena will watch the Kirchner children for a short time. Otto and Daniela plan their schedules so as to avoid relying upon others for childcare assistance. This shared attitude is born of their European models and reinforced by their unique history of unprecedented intrusions into their private lives and dozens, if not hundreds—no one was counting—of threats from strangers attacking their decision to fight for and parent their son. Their understandable fear of physical violence or kidnapping prompted from them an extraordinary level of surveillance and protectiveness of their children, dating from Danny's first media-saturated day with them in April 1995.

Daniela monitors all of the children's activities and screens television programs for their appropriateness. She prevents them from viewing violent programs and movies. They are not allowed to use certain words, such as vulgarities or the word "stupid." The children are not allowed to drink soda pop of any kind. Historically, they were each allowed one glass of soda when I would visit, as a special treat in deference to my preferences. Currently, their choices are limited to juices, water, milk, or chocolate milk. Daniela prepares and serves nutritious, cooked meals, while Otto is more indulgent of the children's preferences and typically serves foods like fried chicken, french fries, and desserts on "dad's days" while mom is at work.

All three of the children are basically healthy except for the typical colds and flu that seem to spread among youngsters in school. Danny has been plagued by earaches during the past year. Fortunately, he and Sharon need very little time to get caught up on their missed schoolwork when their illnesses necessitate absences from school.

In good weather, Danny, Sharon, and Jessica play in their large fenced backyard, which is filled with children's play things, from a sandbox to a swing set, as well as a child-size plastic pool during summer months. The Kirchners chose this rental house because of its adaptability to their children's needs. A priority of theirs was a safe, secure yard, easily visible from the kitchen window and back door.

Daniela uses creative means, required by her limited budget, to furnish and decorate the house to make it pleasant and homey. Blue is the primary color of the first-floor living room, kitchen, and powder room. She has sponge-painted the walls in shades of pastel blue and white; bought a large medium-blue throw rug for the multi-purpose living room, which serves also as a family room and a playroom; and hung two-tone blue, sheer curtains around the windows. Live plants in various types of containers serve as the primary decorations. The one-car garage has filled up with spillover toys and stuffed animals, stored in boxes, to avoid clutter throughout the compact two-story, three-bedroom townhouse. The girls' shared bedroom and Danny's bedroom contain their respective favorite and more recently-acquired possessions, while their older, ignored items are available, upon request, from the garage. A significant percentage of the Kirchners' income has been invested in fulfilling nearly every request of their three children for the latest toys and kids' crazes, ranging from computer activities to athletic equipment.

"Play is a child's work," according to the famous Swiss developmental psychologist Jean Piaget. It is the activity that is spontaneous and natural for a healthy, intelligent child. Today, for American children it is also often educational as well. Play helps create and reinforce bonding between children and also between children and the adults who engage in play activities with them.

Play became the focus of my interactions with Danny while I was his therapist during his first year with his biological parents. Over crayons or puppets, board games or books, he would freely share his thoughts and feelings with me. He never saw my professional office or crossed its threshold. Working with him in a home environment enhanced our interactions, increased his level of comfort, and ensured his continuous security and safety. Not only was he thereby protected from voracious reporters and cameramen but also from voyeuristic public scrutiny and harassment by strangers. For my therapeutic interactions with Danny, I avoided the more artificial environment of a confining professional office in favor of a real, natural, and flexible home setting.

Danny's remarkably fast and facile adjustment to his birth parents and their home is attributable to a variety of factors and conditions. On a daily basis during his first ten days in his parents' care, I observed his progressive, comfortable integration into a new family unit. My role was to advise and assist; to assess his ongoing progress; and to provide him with the opportunity to express and discuss his feelings. For months I visited three or four times per week, averaging a three-hour period of time with Danny and his parents. Through my intimate involvement in his daily life and activities, Danny experienced many times more hours than he would have in conventional, once or twice weekly, office sessions of fifty minutes. I observed his family interactions in good times and bad times, on good days and bad days, and in their everyday pursuits, ranging from meals to all types of play and recreation.

Why did Danny adjust and settle in so quickly and well? Throughout history there are myriad accounts of young children who suddenly transition from their first parental caretakers to another caregiver. War, famine, political upheaval, death, serious illness, and other less dramatic yet compelling reasons have resulted in children's removal from their first home to another. If the people on the receiving end are responsible, caring, and nurturing individuals, the children have typically not only survived but thrived. Danny, at the age of four, transferred from the only home that he had yet known to his biological parents, who deeply loved and desperately wanted him. He realized from his first day that he was indeed their birth child, and that realization, because he was bright and self-confident, impressed him in profound ways. The impact of the biological bond between parents and child was significant.

Otto and Daniela virtually gushed their delight over every new, small revelation about their son. When he finished eating a meal or demonstrated the ability to work a computer remote control, it did not go unnoticed. They spoke about it in his presence; they praised him; and they were generous with hugs and other affectionate gestures.

One of them—if not both—was with him on a 24/7 basis. He never had a babysitter, and his mother even slept by his side in his bed nightly during his first months in his new home.

Otto and Daniela wanted more than anything else in life for him to be happy and to love them, and to make up for lost time. They behaved in ways that some would label "spoiling him." They tried to provide him with anything and everything that he wanted. His bedroom was filled with toys, games, athletic equipment, and stuffed animals that they had bought across four years of waiting for him, planning for him, and yearning to meet him. They regularly took him to amusement parks, beaches, and arcade games facilities. They steadfastly avoided power struggles and, instead of attempting control or using "discipline," they reasoned with him when he became stubborn or they negotiated a change in behavior. They allowed him to make decisions, to choose from presented alternatives, and to act out his feelings without fear of an angry response.

A good example involved eating patterns. They served him nutritious food, mostly home-cooked meals for lunch and dinner, but he could eat as much or as little as he desired. Fortunately, he was a good eater and learned to like the meals that they presented. However, if he left the table to engage in play, he was allowed to do so, and then return—or not—as he chose. On numerous occasions, I observed Otto taking his son's plate into the living room so that Danny could finish eating while sitting on the floor or the couch. It was a family version of the Burger King motto, "Have it your way." His parents often asked him what he would like for dinner, and if possible, they would cook his preferred foods, even if it meant a special trip for them to the grocery store.

Otto and Daniela allowed Danny to take the lead, to set the course in many ways. He was allowed to play outside for long hours; to invite his friends into his home; and to go often to the neighborhood park or another fun place, limited only by their financial resources. They rarely said "no" to anything. They set limitations on behaviors that might lead to injury, of course, but otherwise there were few rules in his house. At first he would jump up and down on the living room furniture, but they soon explained that he might hurt himself and he should no longer do this. Instead, they promised to take him to Odyssey Fun World, where he could jump in the appropriate places, such as its enclosed room filled with large, colorful rubber balls. Within two days, he was jumping as much as he liked at the indoor amusement park.

Some time during Danny's second week with his birth parents, he fell in love with them. He was calling them "Mom" and "Dad" with ease and naturalness. He was initiating affectionate contact with both of them on a nearly daily basis.

To Danny, his former home had gone bad in some way. For weeks there had been weeping, sadness, and anxiety in the adoptive parents' home. People were coming over to say "goodbye" to him, to express regret and commiserate with the adults, and sometimes to cry. Danny didn't quite understand it, but he was frightened by it.

In my opinion, his adoptive parents were more bonded to the fight for him than to the child himself. This is not to suggest that they lacked parental feelings for him, but they acted out their feelings for themselves more. His transfer to his biological parents could hardly have been more threatening to Danny. It could not have been more public; it was unsafe, undignified, and uncaring; and it was terrifying for a young boy. It was carefully orchestrated by the adoptive parents and their attorneys to be sensational…, at four-year-old Danny's expense.

If we revert to the Biblical wisdom of King Solomon, who demonstrated more their qualifications to be adjudged the child's real parents? If putting his welfare above their own is the standard, the Warburtons fell short by jeopardizing his well-being in such a calculating, public, and garish manner. Sagely, Judge Tully wrote, "The only evidence in the record indicating the 'fitness' of the Does is that they defrauded the court by knowingly acceding to an adoption where they knew the natural father had been deprived of any rights.…" Even at his young age, Danny sensed that his adoptive parents did not do right by him.

Many people have expressed disbelief over reports by Danny's birth parents and by me that he never asked for his adoptive parents. Although he spoke about them from time to time, he never asked for them in my presence or in my therapeutic contacts with him. He probably did not want to disappoint his "new," "real" parents by asking for "Johnny's parents," as he soon came to call them. More significantly, he did not want to return to that house, where there was a "huge" mob of strangers screaming "bad words" like "Monster!" as well as a lot of big, frowning policemen. "Johnny's parents were mad and sad," according to Danny, and he was not anxious to experience more of that atmosphere of pain, grief, loss, confusion, and anger. In his new parents' home, by contrast, he experienced peace, quiet, joy, and celebration, not to mention toys of every variety, shape, and size; new playmates; and indulgence of his every whim. Instead of being a playmate for an older child, he was always center stage, the only child, and the recipient of continuous attention, concern, and solicitousness. He immediately became the epicenter of his parents' universe..., and he realized that.

For me, there are two remaining mysteries related to the issue of the depth and genuineness of Danny's adoptive parents' love for him. First, why have they failed—or refused—to provide the child's medical records—in spite of requests from attorneys and the child's new pediatrician? Second, why have they never telephoned me to ask how he was doing or to request an opportunity to see him? I had given them all of my phone numbers, clarifying that I would be working with Danny, as his therapist, on an ongoing basis; they could call me any time. To this day, across eight years, they have never called me.

Daniela has evolved into a methodical mother, who plans everything for her children. "She reads books and magazines about different trends for children and then she really gets into it," Otto reports with mixed feelings about her zealous pursuit of the "latest" and "best." With a curious blend of frustration and pride, he refers to Daniela as "kids crazy—she will do anything for the kids. It's hard for me to keep up with it all," he confesses. Every month or so, she focuses on a new development or an expert's recommendation, such as the total elimination of sugar from the children's diet or the emphasis upon fresh fruit and vegetables.

For Sharon's seventh birthday, Daniela made an elaborately decorated, blue satin Cinderella gown as one of the child's presents. Because she could not afford to buy the dress that Sharon admired at the local store, Daniela bought the materials, cut the pattern, and sewed the dress secretly through two nights, until nearly dawn, so that her daughter would not be disappointed. After pizza, lemonade, and birthday cake with her siblings and three neighbor children, her father carried the unique gown, covered by a long plastic garment bag, into the party room at Odyssey Fun World—Sharon's site of choice for her celebration—and it became the highlight of her day.

Otto is as indulgent with his children as his wife is structured and organized. He continues to be his "best self" as a father. Daniela acknowledges, "Otto has a hard time expressing his feelings in words. His parents left him when he was little, and his grandparents didn't talk about love or feelings. He can say 'I love you,' but it's hard for him to say it even to me." With his children, however, he is frequently and openly affectionate. They jump onto his lap, reach to be picked up, and stroll by to give and get hugs on a regular basis. He is generous in his praise and in providing them with their preferences. He cooks meals to order on his days at home, complete with desserts of choice. During my most recent visit, he allowed the children to eat strawberry whipped-cream cake, popsicles, and chocolate ice cream bars across a five-hour period. When I asked Danny if he and his sisters would eat like this if his mother were at home, he promptly replied, "No way! But Dad gives us what we want."

One of my most amusing memories of Otto's first weeks as a father involved his giving directions to his home. He used Chuck E. Cheese's Restaurant and Toys Я Us as landmarks to his house, as opposed to the usual corner gas station or street names. If he had $3, he would take Danny to the toy store to select a new addition to his overflowing collection of action figures. Visits to the toy store were as frequent as trips to the grocery store.

While Otto and I sat talking at his kitchen table recently, after the children adjourned to watch television in the living room, Jessica came bouncing to her father's side, silently presenting him with her injured yellow teddy bear and its severed satin bow. Continuing his conversation with me, Otto grabbed the sewing box from the adjacent cabinet, threaded a needle, sewed the bow back onto the bear's neck, and, with a hug, returned it to Jessica. She left the room as quietly as she had appeared, but smiling and cradling her repaired bear in her arms.

Otto is comfortable with being "Mr. Mom," readily engaging in all aspects of child care with his children. While he served them their dinner, he would kneel on one knee next to Sharon and Jessica when they spoke to him so that they would be at eye level. Because of this leveling approach, Jessica spoke more during dinner than at any other time during the day and evening. Otto is especially sensitive to his children's needs and vulnerabilities, and he is neither reluctant nor ashamed to make accommodations in his own behavior to make them more comfortable.

On Mother's Day 2003, Daniela and I spoke by phone during the evening. Sharon made and served her mother breakfast in bed; Otto cooked lunch for the family; and Danny prepared a simple dinner for his mother. A.J. and Danny were playing together in the background, while the girls were watching a videotaped movie. Theirs was a home like a myriad of others but for Daniela it was a crowning day. She has endured, learned, and matured, traveling difficult paths to become a mother. Today was her special day indeed.

Although their styles are different in many ways, Otto and Daniela respect each other's approach to the children. They both try to avoid conflict in their presence. They try to shield all three of them from exposure to potentially disturbing situations, both in everyday life and on movie, television, or computer screens. Their co-parenting is effective, with one parent assuming the lead role at any given time. This approach is not only made possible but created by their rotating schedules with the children. While Otto works, Daniela is in charge at home; while she works, he is in charge.

Although, like all parents, the Kirchners occasionally fall short of their own expectations for themselves, they work hard at being good parents. Amid the challenges of daily life, sometimes their patience runs thin, or personal or marital tensions spill into their parenting, but they have both excelled as parents from the first weeks when they became an instant family of three with a four-year-old son. Danny's development has been steadfastly healthy and normal, as well as nearly problem-free. The Kirchners' greatest challenges have come from external sources, most notably from the media blitz that continued across months and years and that created for them a pervasively hostile environment. They struggled continuously to protect Danny—and then his sisters—from the effects of their unwanted celebrity—and notoriety.

Otto and Daniela's mutual commitment to their children as their continuous first priority has resulted in their creating and maintaining a family of individuals who are loving and loyal to each other. All three children are happy, achieving, and well adjusted. If the Kirchners' approach to their parenting has been so effective and successful, especially when viewed within the context of the truly unique challenges in their lives, their behaviors and priorities as parents are likely to be effective for others as well.

What are these behaviors and priorities?

As a generalization, they decided that Daniela would remain at home with her children five days per week, working only two days at the beauty salon, while Otto would work the conventional five days per week, taking care of his children on the two days that his wife is at her job. One of them is with the children on a full-time, weeklong basis. This schedule limits their social life and leisure time; as a couple, they are willing to accept this trade-off. With interactive time as the underpinning of their parenting, they have purposefully incorporated a series of other priorities as well.

1) **Maintain perspective.** Having struggled—through a painful four-year custody battle and a miscarriage—to have a family, they do not lose sight of the big picture. They never take their children for granted; they perceive them as a gift, as their greatest joy. Their basic attitude is reflected in the wisdom of a former First Lady: If you bungle raising your children, I don't think whatever else you do well matters very much.
— Jacqueline Kennedy Onassis

2) **"Don't sweat the small stuff."** Like the books by Dr. Richard Carlson which promote the attitude of accepting almost everything as "small stuff," Otto and Daniela approach their parenting in a relaxed, accepting manner. They take most things in stride, avoid catastrophizing, and focus on one day at a time. They realize that the little things with their children are usually the most important—and most remembered—things in life.

3) **Spend interactive time with the child(ren).** In addition to being physically present, they play with the children, engage in a variety of activities with them, and converse with them. For example, both Otto and Daniela actively participate in the games at the indoor amusement park with the children. Daniela crawls through the tubes, climbs ladders, and jumps over the obstacles with her daughters in the Exploration Adventure room, while most of the other mothers sit at the sideline and watch. Otto competes with Danny in various games and sports, both at home and at amusement centers.

4) **Ensure time with each child.** They are careful to share themselves with each child, paying attention to each one. Even while Daniela was breast-feeding each of the two girls, she would assure Danny that she would spend time with him as soon as she was finished, and she always fulfilled her promise. He did not compete or act out for attention; he always received his share, at his parents' initiation.

5) **Respect the child(ren) & expect them to respect each other.** Otto and Daniela demonstrate their respect for the children in a variety of ways. They talk to them in a manner that conveys their valuing of each child as an individual with his or her own needs, thoughts, and desires. They both speak softly and rarely raise their voices. They remind the children to behave toward each other with caring and understanding.

6) **Look for the child's unique qualities & nurture them.** From their first week with Danny, Otto and Daniela were vigilant in seeking to determine his unique personality characteristics and abilities. They both pointed these out to him, to each other, and to others in his presence in order to nurture his individuality and self-esteem. They foster the individual talents and personality traits of each child. For example, Sharon, who learns quickly and easily on her own, has been encouraged to master a series of educational, paper-and-pencil and computer workbooks. Each child has his/her own well-defined, special place in the family.

7) **Recognize the differences between children.** As in many families, the three Kirchner children are very different from each other. Otto and Daniela avoid pressuring any of the children to be like another. They express their acceptance of each child's idiosyncrasies and unique personality. As an example, Jessica is quiet and shy, while both Danny and Sharon are assertive, verbal, and initiating. Her parents assure Jessica that she is "okay" just the way that she is; they avoid pushing her to become more outgoing.

8) **Take them seriously.** Both Otto and Daniela accept the children's fears, angers, interests, and desires as legitimate and important. They avoid making light of the things that are meaningful or serious for the children.

9) **Listen.** They listen to what their children have to say. They value the children's opinions and want to hear about their experiences and reactions to everyday events.

10) **Communicate well.** From Danny's first day with them, his parents made special efforts to communicate clearly and on his level of understanding. They explained to him what to expect. If they went out with him, they told him where they were going, why, and when they would return, as well as what he might expect to experience during their outing. Otto would describe the concept of days in Danny's terms, such as, "You will sleep three times and that next day we will go to the park."

11) **Express love often.** The Kirchners make a point of expressing love and affection freely and often. The children learn both to reciprocate and to initiate such expressions with their parents.

12) **Praise often.** Daniela is especially adept at providing frequent and sincere praise. She often and enthusiastically says, "Good job!" whenever one of the children completes a project, or part of one. The results are visibly positive in the children's reactions. Genuine praise reinforces the child's success and contributes to his self-esteem. Frequent praise is much more effective than the most infrequent criticism. It's best to "catch the child doing something right" and then thanking him, or at least acknowledging him, for it.

13) **Celebrate.** Even with limited resources, the Kirchners always celebrate special occasions with the children. They combine American traditions with borrowings from their native country, such as at Christmas, and they observe rituals and have fun together many times throughout the year. Daniela frames photographs of special occasions, and these pictures are displayed throughout the house as reminders of special times.

14) **Encourage.** From supporting Danny in his various athletic activities to encouraging Jessica to try a new food, both Otto and Daniela are cheerleaders for their children to take some risks and to accept challenges. They both try to encourage without being pushy or imposing their wills upon the children. As succinctly expressed by Rudolf Dreikurs, "Children need encouragement like a plant needs water."

15) **Maintain a sense of humor.** Realizing that it is important to smile and to laugh, especially at oneself from time to time, Otto and Daniela express humor in their parenting. Otto especially uses humor if one of the children becomes stubborn or demanding in order to defuse the situation and to lighten the mood. It always seems to work. The children like to laugh and they respond well to humor even when they are intent on getting what they want.

16) **Make requests, not demands.** The Kirchner parents ask their children to do certain things in a way that communicates their wishes without demanding compliance or threatening punishment. They use "please" frequently, which usually gets the desired response and models good manners for the children. A light and polite approach is more effective and pleasant for everyone.

17) **Negotiate choices & consequences.** An effective technique that communicates respect of the child as an individual with his own will, negotiating is a creative means to achieve a win-win result. "If you help me carry in the groceries and put them away, I can play that game with you before dinner" is a legitimate overture to which the child can respond by being helpful to his mother while attaining a desired outcome for himself as well.

18) **Engage in family decision-making.** Especially in recent months, Daniela has frequently engaged the children in collectively deciding important matters, such as how they will spend the day together. Often the children and she will vote if there is a difference in preferences. She structures the choices in such a way that she is comfortable with any of the possibilities that she has presented as options. This type of decision-making is a good learning experience; it is "fair"—an important concept to children; and it builds family cohesion.

19) **Avoid physical punishment & threats.** Neither Otto nor Daniela believes in physical punishment, such as spanking, and they avoid all such contact with the children. Occasionally a "time out" of a specified duration will be imposed but typically only after the child has been given a count of three, or another reasonable amount of time, to comply with the parent's wishes. There should be no surprises with discipline, such as punishment meted out in anger or in exasperation which the child cannot anticipate. He should be told the consequence and given an opportunity to avoid it **before** it is imposed. This way he has actually chosen to accept the punishment if he is disobedient, and the situation turns into a learning experience for the child.

20) **Teach values & manners.** Daniela is especially attentive to the importance of teaching her children certain
values and manners. She takes the children to Sunday
Mass with her every week; Danny and Sharon attend
Catholic school; and the children are given books and
other materials that teach them to value good manners
and family loyalty. She speaks to them about the importance of being polite, and she reinforces their expressions of good manners by verbally acknowledging them.

21) **Seek & give alternatives.** Both of the Kirchner parents routinely present their children with alternatives
related to topics ranging from their vacation destination to the choice of food for dinner. They also present
them with alternatives related to their education and
recreational activities. The children benefit in a variety of ways from this ability to make choices; it is
empowering and builds self-esteem.

22) **Strive for self-discipline.** The best discipline is education, and self-discipline is always better than parent-
imposed discipline. The Kirchners, with their typical
relaxed approach, encourage self-discipline in their children. They communicate that the children are capable of
doing the right things and making the right choices.
Both Danny and Sharon are good about doing their
homework, often offering information about their having
completed their assignments before their mother asks.

23) **Protect the children from conflict & worry.** Both
Otto and Daniela deserve high grades in this area of
parenting. They share the belief that children should be
spared from witnessing conflict or sharing in the worries of their parents. They both work hard to shield the
three children from awareness of adult problems. It is
amazing that Danny was protected to the point of being
nearly oblivious to the continuous fall-out that resulted
from his unique and highly-publicized situation.

24) **Provide rewards.** One of the most visible characteristics of the Kirchners' parenting is the frequent provi-
sion of rewards to all three of their children. They use
every opportunity to give a present or buy a desired
toy. Most of their discretionary income is spent on their
children's personal possessions. They also use special

treats, such as ice cream or the privilege of staying up later than their usual bedtime, in order to reward certain behaviors by the children. Danny and Sharon are allowed to manage their own money, within limits, so that they will learn its value and good decision-making at an early age. They use rewards for good behavior rather than punishments for bad, or undesired, behavior—the "carrot rather than the stick" approach.

25) Know the people in each child's life. This guideline has become an imperative for the Kirchners. They screen every prospective friend of their children and all of the adults with whom they interact. Daniela allows her children to play only with children whose behavior and manners appear appropriate to her.

Again, the Kirchners are not perfect parents—like the rest of humanity—but they have striven to be at their best for their children—always their first priority. Indulgent, nurturing, and protective, they foster a sense of security, and they work hard to keep their children happy, healthy, and comfortable. A good example is found in Daniela's successful commitment to breast-feeding Sharon for two full years, while also working full-time for most of that period. She weaned Sharon shortly before the birth of Jessica, whom she also breast-fed, until the baby weaned herself after one year. Daniela was convinced that, despite its special challenges for her, this choice would prove more healthful for her daughters and contribute to the bond between mother and child.

Perhaps more than any other trait, Otto and Daniela avoid power struggles with their children. Because they are relaxed and flexible, the children tend to respond in kind. "It is a surprising but accurate paradox: control is gained by giving it up," according to Frank Main, Ed.D. The Kirchners' control is not the kind that robs the children of their independence, self-esteem, or decision-making ability, but the type that provides a structure and limits within which the children are allowed to function with autonomy and ease. In the words of psychologist Carl Jung:

Where love rules, there is no will to power; and where power predominates, there love is lacking. The one is the shadow of the other.

Many have said and written that parenting is the most difficult job of all, but it is also the most important. Otto and Daniela Kirchner, who have endured incredible hardships and powerful challenges along their arduous journey into parenthood, have come to know and value this truism as the central focus of their lives.

**Well, all I know
is what I read in the papers.**

— Will Rogers

**You can fool too many of the people
too much of the time.**

— James Thurber

As two people who have been the most often and most viciously pre-judged and criticized parents by the media in my life experience, Otto and Daniela Kirchner are paradoxically counted among the best parents I have ever known. Portrayed as the callous woman who did not want her child, Daniela bears no resemblance in real life to her media-promulgated image. Otto, in his own words "accused of nearly everything except murder," has emerged as a model father, who never wavered in his fierce commitment to claim and parent his son in spite of an epic court battle and an unprecedented level of media and governmental pressures, threats, and impediments.

The media indeed fooled too many of the people, and, in so doing, nearly destroyed the lives of this innocent, harmless, and defenseless family.

> **Map out your future, but do it in pencil.**
>
> — *Jon Bon Jovi*

Conclusion: Today

> **You will find
> as you look back upon your life
> that the moments
> when you have really lived
> are the moments
> when you have done things
> in the spirit of love.**
>
> — *Henry Drummond*

HELPLESS. HOPELESS. The hour that I admitted to myself that I was indeed helpless to do anything significant to effect the Kirchner family's fate or to change the tide of public opinion against them, I was overcome by a sense of hopelessness that I had never known before. In the airport terminal of Atlanta, Georgia, on my way back home from a short vacation with Robert at our condo in Florida, I realized that I was powerless to make a difference. It was that hour when a voice in my head said that Robert and I must move away from the source of what had become for me a pervasively toxic environment in Chicagoland. I also resolved to try to convince the Kirchners to accompany us in changing our geography and our futures together.

"'Baby Richard's' father leaves home"! announced the headline in *USA Today*. The article described Otto and Daniela's marital separation as an abandonment of the child by the father who fought so hard for his son and now "left his son behind." As their recent therapist and current friend—"like family," we described each other—I knew that they had been separated for many weeks. It took the media nearly four months to discover their private situation and, of course, only minutes to make it public—throughout the Midwest and across the country. I also knew that—in the wake of complicated marital problems and a myriad of external pressures from every angle—Daniela had asked Otto to move out of their home, but none of the news stories included that detail. Otto and Daniela needed some time and space apart, I knew, as sometimes occurs within a marriage. Once again, however, Otto was made to look like the bad guy in a big way. The media's disclosure of the Kirchners' marital separation coincided with the investigation of the earlier traffic violation of "Baby Richard Judge" James Heiple, which would generate public furor throughout the state and a movement to impeach the Chief Justice of the Illinois Supreme Court. Heiple's media image was coupled with the Kirchner separation. The judge was again widely blamed and cursed for the return of Baby Richard to his biological parents, this time with the additional allegation of "proof" that it had been "wrong."

It was January 1997, nearly two years after the gut-wrenching transfer of Baby Richard from his adoptive mother's arms to his biological father and mother, amid sobbing spectators, rolling and clicking cameras, and a contingent of uniformed police officers. In all of that time, the story would not go away. Columnist Bob Greene—and others—used, or created, every small opportunity to remind the public about the child, most of the coverage lacking first-hand information and, therefore, any real credibility. It was presented as factual, however, rather than as the imaginings of its authors or the hearsay reports from people who also lacked real information. Sociologists have written about the common phenomenon of rumors, which start and proliferate when people lack knowledge about the facts of an event. Similarly, journalists originated stories about "Baby Richard," asserting his status as living in an abusive, traumatizing condition and as being an emotionally scarred child. Greene—leading this movement—provided regular updates on how many days passed since "Richard" last saw his adoptive parents or brother. He passed this angle along to readers as news...over and over and over again. "Another sundown is on its way, the 25th sundown since he [Baby Richard] was taken...." (May 24, 1995) Amazingly, with seemingly countless other examples along the way, Greene actually wrote, "Since the day

Richard was put into that van...819 days have passed...." (July 27, 1997) **819** days!

This Separation Story, I knew, would also take on bigger-than-life proportions. It would create the opportunity for journalists to use Otakar Kirchner as an example in their broad-brush articles, decrying the state of marriage, loyalty, fatherhood, and justice, and raising questions again about the "best interest" of Danny Kirchner/Baby Richard now that his father had left the family residence. **Any** of my other clients, I mused, could separate—even divorce—without making the front page of the newspaper or CNN headlines, no matter how many children they had fathered or adopted. In fact, during the late nineties, the marital separations of movie stars and other celebrities were typically relegated to miniscule coverage amid the center pages of the paper, no longer considered either shocking news or priority material. Yet again, with the Baby Richard case, in contrast, people's sensitivities were elevated; their thresholds of disdain and disgust were low; and the media converged to discover and to disseminate the dirt. Reporters from all forms of the media swooped into the situation, hoping to find some sordid detail or—better yet—neglect or abuse of the child known far and wide as "Baby Richard." A number of these journalists were themselves the divorced parents of children, but they chose to overlook the hypocrisy inherent in their sensationalizing this story about the Kirchners' separation as especially shocking news.

I became ill—literally. As soon as I returned home to Palos Park, I took to my bed with severe flu symptoms. I telephoned Otto and Daniela, at their respective residences, to offer support. Otto was being followed regularly by media representatives and unidentified strangers in vans, very likely private investigators. Daniela was avoiding everyone outside of the privacy of her home except for her colleagues and customers at the beauty salon and her next-door neighbors, Enid and Peder.

That was the beginning of the end for me. Although the Kirchners would reconcile during the summer of that same year, never again to separate from each other, the media would ignore and avoid a reconciliation story. No one would seem interested in hearing or reading good news about this couple...or about Baby Richard.

Unfortunately, Otto and Daniela would remain steadfast in their disinclination to consider relocating to another state. In countless conversations with Robert and me about a prospective move, they expressed fear that they would be unable to find good jobs in Florida. Both of them were working in acceptable jobs during the latter part of 1997—after Otto landed a job as a waiter that fall— enabling them to provide a decent, comfortable, suburban life for their children. They were both reluctant to risk losing that life, for which they had struggled, sacrificed, and worked so hard.

Robert and I moved in February 1998, one year after the media frenzy over the Kirchners' trial separation. It took twelve months to sell our house in Illinois, find a suitable home in Florida, and make the necessary arrangements for a permanent relocation. I spent months concluding my therapeutic involvements with clients, transferring some to other psychologists and terminating therapy for those who were ready, satisfied with their progress.

Across time, within our sunny, green environment, my memory banks healed over, much like a scab over a wound.

Today, the Kirchner family lives in a far southwest suburb of Chicago. They rent a two-story, three-bedroom, 2-1/2-bathroom townhouse with a big fenced backyard for the three children's safe and private play area. They are surrounded by young families with children, SUVs, and mortgages.

Now in his sixth year with the same employer, Otto continues to work full-time as a waiter in a family-owned Italian restaurant in another suburb. On his days off, he sleeps, cooks, and interacts with his children. For Otto, pleasure has become the absence of pain. But he has attained his heartfelt goal since he was only four years old—a family.

Daniela works two days each week at an upscale suburban salon. She has cultivated a regular, steady clientele for her European-style facial treatments. Daniela has blossomed into a gentle, radiant, and selfless mother, who has earned a second chance with her firstborn child and has joyfully given birth to two exquisitely lovely daughters. She plays with all three children at their own levels, whether that means wearing her pink Power Rangers costume and cavorting around with her caped and masked son or sitting on the floor with her daughters surrounded by Barbies. She never forgets for a minute the importance of healthy, happy children, safe and secure under her own roof.

Otto and Daniela commute a considerable distance but, like hundreds of thousands of others, they are willing to drive many miles to and from their work sites in order to afford better housing than their dollars would provide them in other, closer-to-Chicago suburbs. They continue to arrange their work hours so that one of them—or both—is with the children on a 24/7 basis. Their social life nearly exclusively revolves around their children. They still consider their home a sanctuary and a refuge from the outside world.

Now twelve, Danny is becoming more independent and assertive, as are his other pre-teen friends. Having ended the 2002–03 school year with 5 A's and 2 B's, his articulated goal for this year is to rank academically at the top of his seventh grade class. He plans to play basketball for his school team again, and he is also interested in trying ice hockey as a new athletic challenge and in playing golf next summer. He loves computer and arcade games, cards, and board games of all kinds; and being with his family. Danny also regularly participates in the local library's arts-and-crafts program. Most notably, he is a good boy, soft-spoken, happy, content, polite, confident, and caring. He still prefers and seeks the company of older kids. Fifteen-year-old A.J., his best friend for the past two years, will soon move to Florida with his family, but he and Danny plan to continue their relationship through e-mail and occasional visits with each other, especially during the summer months.

Danny informs me that he considers his "Baby Richard" past "strange." It has remained peripheral to his real, everyday life, as if he had a childhood disease that he knows he suffered but cannot recall except in an amorphous, fleeting manner. He remembers little from his former life as an adopted child and he is disinterested in it. Fortunately, Danny remains impervious to his public status as a celebrity, icon, symbol, tragic figure, and strange combination of a modern-day fairy tale and soap opera character. He feels totally and completely "Daniel Richard

Kirchner," his own person, with the dream of one day becoming a professional athlete.

Sharon, at seven, is a beautiful and charming little girl with waist-length blonde hair, soulful brown eyes, and a smile that reveals the loss of her front teeth. She regularly awaits the Tooth Fairy, her latest lost tooth tucked under her pillow at night. I believe that Sharon is intellectually gifted, although I may be biased in my admiration of her abilities. I have known her since the first day her parents carried her home from the hospital when I arrived to meet and cuddle the new arrival with the eagerness of a grandparent or a loving aunt. Before beginning first grade, Sharon was reading both English and Slovak with ease, and she remembers facts from flash cards and workbooks on a level to rival a third- or fourth-grader. Strong-willed, precocious, and verbal, Sharon is also assertive and enthusiastic. She and Danny continue to compete as peers, especially when they are sharing the use of his computer.

Five-year-old Jessica is an especially attractive child with porcelain skin, big brown eyes, flowing blonde hair, and an impish smile. She intently watches everyone and everything in her environment, speaking quietly and seldom, and she looks out for herself in significant ways. Jessica, without being told, regularly dresses herself in her pajamas in preparation for bedtime, and she will ask for her favorite foods or a special treat in a soft voice, or whisper, but with fervor and determination. She is generally passive, allowing her older brother and sister to take the lead and sometimes to provide interpretation of her needs and preferences to others on her behalf. Jessica copies Sharon's behaviors and models herself after her older sister.

Both girls are devotees of all things Barbie—dolls, furniture, accessories, cell phones, cars, and clothes. Their bedroom looks like a toy store room. Decorated in various shades of pink, it is filled with stuffed animals of every species, color, and size.

During recent weeks Daniela has redecorated Danny's bedroom. She has painted his walls a shade of pale blue and bought him a new bunk bed, the type with a sofa-bed on the bottom and a bed on top. The new furniture can accommodate three or four children comfortably and is intended for sleepovers. Creative and frugal, Daniela pasted cut-out Pokemon figures, Danny's favorite theme, around his room as a ceiling border and as an accompaniment to his Pokemon comforter.

On a weekly basis we talk by phone. Daniela regales me with updates on the children, and I discuss with Danny and Sharon their progress in school and at play. To date, Jessica declines invitations to speak on the phone with everyone; she prefers in-person interactions. Both Sharon and Jessica continue to call their father "Da Da," a term of endearment from their babyhood years.

During the past twelve months, we have seen each other four separate times. In trips to the Chicago area, I have visited them on three occasions during the year, and they visited Robert and me in Florida for their two-week vacation. All in all, we spent twelve days together, having fun and playing in a variety of settings, ranging from arcade games at Odyssey Fun World to sightseeing together in northeastern Florida. Robert and I never tire of conversations with them, into which we always interject comments that extol the virtues of Florida living in the persistent hope that one day they will relocate to our neighborhood. I continue to dream and to scheme toward that goal.

Although my life plan—my script for myself—always featured a life-long working career, through a combination of compelling circumstances and choice, I have embarked upon an early-retirement lifestyle. These days I take courses in mahjongg, computer skills, calligraphy, dancing, floral arranging, and boating. After eighteen months of at-least-weekly golf, I have realized that I am not one iota better at the game than when I first stepped onto the lush-green, three-par course nearby. Today I golf only when I decide to indulge a fleeting masochistic whim. Instead, I have chosen to opt for the gym, where I work out—under the direction of a personal trainer and body builder—three times every week and watch television news from my treadmill. I read books ranging from Stephen Hawking's works on cosmology to biographies and the occasional novel. Robert golfs, fishes, boats, swims, and cooks regularly. We watch movies and travel together, most recently cruising around Cape Horn and visiting Chile and Argentina. We now have time for friends and hobbies.

The square footage of our two-story Palm Coast house equals the square footage of one floor of our previous, Palos Park home.

We have downsized or—as many reorganized companies euphemize—"right-sized." We have acquired the nearly obligatory swimming pool in our backyard, along with a heated spa and screened lanai. Living on a saltwater canal that connects with the Intracoastal Waterway and eventually with the Atlantic Ocean, we watch dolphins swim by and pelicans dive for their lunch. Indoors, we enjoy the daily antics of Tom Riley and Stephanie Ann. Tom is a well-adjusted, friendly orange tabby; Stephanie is a vocal, neurotic but regal tortoise-shell cat.

The fastest growing of 67 counties in Florida—and fifth in the nation—Flagler County is being discovered by people from every state and other countries as a special, sunny, and safe place to live. Palm Coast enjoys water all around—ocean, river, lakes, and canals—and a slower, friendlier pace of life. In our small, old-fashioned movie theater, the owner often does double duty by selling tickets and concessions. He will even carry the rewashable, red plastic glasses of soda and bags of popcorn into the auditorium for customers who need assistance. We are just beginning to see a rush hour "in these parts."

It's a good life…, not the one that I had worked and hoped for but a suitable replacement. "Most people are about as happy as they make up their minds to be," Abraham Lincoln said five generations ago. He was probably right.

Although unplanned and unanticipated, my involvement in "Baby Richard" at first consumed, then diverted, and eventually transformed my life.

"Life is too serious to be taken seriously" was Robert's motto when I met him more than three decades ago. To me, it seems to apply today….

Since the day I met Danny Kirchner, sitting on his king-size bed covered with 101 Dalmatians, my practice of psychology transitioned into home visits and play-based interactions. My career veered, deviated, and swerved onto another path entirely. For the Kirchners, I became therapist, adviser, confidant, spokesperson, ally, friend, advocate, playmate, supporter, and "family." I became a regular "set-another-plate-at-the-table" visitor, not really a guest but "always there," as Danny would remember me years later.

Since the day I met Danny, I have regularly found myself roaming through toy stores more often than clothing boutiques. I cannot recall a time when there has not been a stuffed animal, action figure, toy, or game in my car trunk or closet, destined for Danny on the next special—or everyday—occasion. Turning frequently to the Weather Channel, I wonder whether Danny and his sisters will be playing in their backyard or on the front sidewalk with their friends today.

Since the day I met Danny, the fabric of my life has more color, vibrancy, and texture than any time before.

Since the day I met Danny, nothing has been the same.

Since that day, I have shared with his parents a sense of responsibility for his emotional well-being. I also share their pride in him as the unique, loving and lovable boy that he has become.

Since I met him, there has never been a day that I have not thought about Danny.

I don't think there ever will be.

**A hundred years from now
it will not matter what my bank account was,
the sort of house I lived in,
or the kind of car I drove...
but the world may be different
because I was important
in the life of a child.**

— Anonymous

THE COURT DECISIONS

> [The Baby Richard] tragedy
> is the wrongful breakup of a natural family
> and the keeping of a child by strangers
> without right.

If...the best interests of the child is to be
the determining factor in child custody cases...,
persons seeking babies to adopt
might profitably frequent grocery stores
and snatch babies from carts
when the parent is looking the other way.
Then, if custody proceedings
can be delayed long enough,
they can assert that they have a nicer home,
a superior education, a better job or whatever,
and that the best interests of the child
are with the baby snatchers.
Children of parents living in public housing
or other conditions deemed less than affluent
and children with single parents
might be considered particularly fair game.
The law, thankfully, is otherwise.

— *Justice James Heiple, Illinois Supreme Court*

> **...[T]his adoption [of Baby Richard] was improper, illegal and fraudulent and it should be vacated by this court.**
>
> — *Justice P. J. Tully, Appellate Court*

5-1/2 PERCENT. The odds of the Illinois Supreme Court taking up the appeal of Otakar Kirchner to reclaim his son were about 95 to 5 **against**. They didn't deter Otto, however, who was convinced that the state's highest court would vindicate his unceasing struggle to win his son, for whom he fought through the cumbersome "quagmire of a judicial system," in the words of the Appellate Court. That court referred to the "shamefully" long time that the case took until its own ruling. The child was then nearly two and one-half years old. That court, by a two to one decision, ruled for the adoptive parents.

If the Illinois Supreme Court had not accepted the Baby Richard case, thereby dooming it to be counted among the other 94-95% of its rejected cases, the outcome for Danny would have been very different. The adoptive parents would have been allowed to keep him, even though they were involved in the deception that robbed Danny's biological father of his rights and of the opportunity to parent his son. The child would have grown up as an adopted child, alienated from his loving natural parents through a mixture of deceit, technicality, public opinion, and an erroneous court decision.

The 2 – 1 Appellate Court ruling paved the way for the Supreme Court's discretionary decision to accept Otakar Kirchner's appeal. The Appellate Court basically created new law—the constitutionally exclusive job of the legislature—when it "held that...it would be contrary to best interest of child to disturb judgment of adoption once child had lived with adoptive parents for more than18 months...." The court's attempt to set a new standard, a new time limit upon the inviolability of adoption, triggered the Supreme Court's taking up the case for review.

When Danny was three years and three months old, the Illinois Supreme Court issued its unanimous, 7 – 0 decision, overturning the lower courts:

> As for the adoptive parents, they will have to live with their pain and the knowledge that they wrongfully

deprived a father of his child past the child's third birthday. They and their lawyer brought it on themselves. (June 16, 1994)

Having struggled with my alternatives in writing this book, I have chosen to include most of the written Order of the Illinois Supreme Court that denied the Does' petitions for a rehearing—a reconsideration—of its June 16, 1994 ruling, which found in favor of Otakar Kirchner. His son, Baby Richard, was to be returned to him; the lower courts' rulings for the adoptive parents were reversed. This Order was filed on July 12, 1994.

I have also included a large portion of Justice John Tully's dissenting opinion. Tully was the dissenter in the Appellate Court's 2 – 1 ruling in favor of the adoptive parents. My rationale for its inclusion is that it forms the basis, including the finding of facts, upon which the ultimate Supreme Court ruling was decided.

Although I realize that many people are disinclined to read court opinions—and some are intellectually intimidated by them—I believe that this Supreme Court Order and Justice Tully's previous opinion qualify as exceptions to this generalization. They are readable, written in layman's language, and—more important—they are interesting! Together they illuminate the key issues and controversies surrounding the Baby Richard case. They clarify the relevant facts, as determined by the highest court in the state. They capture many of the human interest aspects of Baby Richard's situation and the pertinent details concerning both his biological parents and his would-be adoptive parents. They also present an understandable overview of the court process that spanned nearly 3-1/2 years. I encourage the reader to continue, with an open mind regarding legal documents, to read and ponder the Illinois Supreme Court's majority decision and rationale.

I have condensed the Supreme Court Order and Justice Tully's opinion, based upon my own evaluation of the most relevant and interesting portions. The reader who is interested in reviewing the documents in their entirety or the lower courts' rulings is encouraged to contact the Clerk of the Illinois Supreme Court in Springfield, Illinois, from whom these documents are available.

(The following is quoted directly from the Illinois Supreme Court's July 12, 1994 Order)

...JUSTICE HEIPLE, writing in support of the denial of rehearing:

On Thursday, June 16, 1994, this court reversed a decision by a divided appellate court.... Our reversal was the result of the failure of the courts below to correctly apply Illinois law in terminating the natural father's parental rights. This cause is now before the court on petitions for rehearing filed by the adoptive parents and the guardian *ad litem* for the child. The following is offered in support of today's order denying rehearing.

I have been a judge for over 23 years. In that time, I have seldom before worked on a case that involved the spread of so much misinformation, nor one which dealt with as straightforward an application of law to fact.

As was made clear in the [June 16th] majority opinion [of the Illinois Supreme Court], a conspiracy was undertaken to deny the natural father any knowledge of his son's existence. It began when the biological mother, 8-1/2 months pregnant, was misinformed that the father, her fiance, had left her for another woman. She left their shared home.... At the behest of the adoptive parents and their attorney, the mother gave birth at a different hospital than she and the father had planned to avoid the father's intervention; the mother surrendered the baby to strangers four days after his birth; and then falsely told the father that the child had died. All of this occurred in the space of less than three weeks.

The father did not believe the mother, and he immediately began an intensive and persistent search and inquiry to learn the truth and locate the child. On the 57th day following the child's birth, the father learned of his son's existence and of the pending adoption.... [H]e hired a lawyer and contested the adoption of his son by strangers. One may reasonably ask, What more could he have done? What more should he have done? The answer is that he did all that he could and should do.

The [June 16th] majority opinion [of this Court] pointed out that the adoptive parents should have relinquished the baby at that time. That is to say, on the 57th day. Instead of that, however, they were able to procure an entirely erroneous ruling from a trial judge that allowed the adoption to go forward. The father's only remedy at that stage was a legal appeal which he took. He is not the cause of the delay in this case. It was the adoptive parents' decision to prolong this litigation.... Now, the view has been expressed that the passage of time warrants their retention of the child; that it would not be fair to the child to return him to his natural parents, now married to each other, after the adoptive parents have delayed justice past the child's third birthday.

For a fuller and more detailed account of the father's efforts and the underlying facts, one may refer to the dissenting opinion authored by Justice Tully in the appellate court decision.... I would further add that Justice Rizzi grossly misstated the law.

If, as stated by Justice Rizzi, the best interests of the child is to be the determining factor in child custody cases..., persons seeking babies to adopt might profitably frequent grocery stores and snatch babies from carts when the parent is looking the other way. Then, if custody proceedings can be delayed long enough, they can assert that they have a nicer home, a superior education, a better job or whatever, and that the best interests of the child are with the baby snatchers. Children of parents living in public housing or other conditions deemed less than affluent and children with single parents might be considered particularly fair game. The law, thankfully, is otherwise.

In 1972, the United States Supreme Court...ruled that unmarried fathers cannot be treated differently than unmarried mothers or married parents when determining their rights to the custody of their children.... The courts of Illinois are bound by that decision.... [I]n 1990, a unanimous Illinois Supreme Court pointed out that when ruling on parental unfitness, a court is not to consider the child's best interests, since the child's welfare is not relevant in judging the fitness of the natural parent; that only after the parent is found by clear and convincing evidence to be unfit does the court proceed to consider the child's best interest and whether that interest would be served if the child were adopted....

Under Illinois law, a parent may be divested of his parental rights either voluntarily (e.g., consenting to an adoption...) or involuntarily (e.g., finding of abuse, abandonment, neglect or lack of sufficient interest...). ...[T]he adoption laws of Illinois are neither complex nor difficult of application. These laws intentionally place the burden of proof on the adoptive parents. In addition, Illinois law requires a good-faith effort to notify the natural father of the adoption proceedings.... We call this due process of law. In the case at hand, both the adoptive parents and their attorney knew that a real father existed whose name was known to the mother but who refused to disclose it. Under these circumstances, the adoptive parents proceeded at their peril.

The best interest of the child standard is not to be denigrated. It is real. However, it is not triggered until it has been validly determined that the child is **available** for adoption. And, a child is not available for adoption until the rights of his natural parents have been properly terminated. Any judge, lawyer, or guardian *ad litem* who has even the most cursory familiarity with adoption laws knows that....

Columnist Bob Greene apparently does not care. Rather[,] columnist Greene has used this unfortunate controversy to stimulate readership and generate a series of syndicated newspaper columns in the Chicago Tribune and other papers that are both false and misleading. In so doing, he has wrongfully cried "fire" in a crowded theatre, and has needlessly alarmed other adoptive parents into ill-founded concerns that their own adoption proceedings may be in jeopardy. In support of his position, Greene has stirred up contempt against the Supreme Court as an institution, concluding one of his columns by referring to all of the Justices with the curse, "Damn them all." *Chicago Tribune*, June 19, 1994, Tempo Section, page 1.

Greene's implicit objective is to secure justice for a child. With that ethical and moral imperative, of course, no one could disagree. Greene, however, elevates himself above the facts, above the law, and above the Supreme Court of Illinois. He arrogates to himself the right to decide the case.

In support of his objective, Greene brings to bear the tools of the demagogue, namely, incomplete information, falsity, half truths, character assassination and spurious argumentation. He has conducted a steady assault on my abilities as a judge, headlining one of his columns "The Sloppiness of Justice Heiple." Another was entitled "Supreme Injustice for a Little Boy." He has shown my picture in his columns with bylines reading, respectively, "Justice Heiple: Ruling takes boy from home," and "James D. Heiple: No justice for a child."...

Make no mistake about it. These are acts of journalistic terrorism. These columns are designed to discredit me as a judge and the Supreme Court as a dispenser of justice by stirring up disrespect and hatred among the general population.

Lest we forget the place from which he comes, let us remind ourselves that Greene is a journalist with a product to sell. He writes columns for a living. His income is dependent on writing and selling his columns to newspapers. He cannot secure either sales or earnings by writing on subjects that lack impact or drama. So, he must seek out subjects that are capable of generating wide public interest. An adoption case involving two sets of parents contesting for the custody of a three-year-old boy is a ready-made subject for this type of journalist. So far, so good.

The trouble with Greene's treatment of the subject, however, is that his columns have been biased, false and misleading. They have also been destructive to the cause of justice both in this case and in the wider perspective. Part of Greene's fury may be attributable to the fact that he staked out his views on this case in a published column that appeared on August 22, 1993.... Subsequently, ...the Supreme Court had the audacity to base its decision on the law rather than on his newspaper column. So much for his self-professed moralizing.

That Greene has succeeded to a limited degree cannot be denied. I have, indeed, received several pieces of hate mail with such epithets as idiot, jerk, etc. The Governor, in a crass political move, announced his attempt to intervene in the case. And the General Assembly, without meaningful debate or consideration, rushed into law a constitutionally infirm statute with the goal of changing the Supreme Court's decision.

Both the Governor and the members of the General Assembly who supported this bill might be well advised to return to the classroom and take up Civics 101. The Governor, for his part, has no understanding of this case and no interest either public or private in its outcome. The legislature is not given the authority to decide private disputes between litigants. Neither does it sit as a super court to review unpopular decisions of the Supreme Court. We have three branches of government in this land. They are designated as the legislative, the executive, and the judicial. Legislative adjudication of private disputes went by the wayside generations ago. Moreover, this case cannot be decided by public clamor generated by an irresponsible journalist. Neither can it be decided by its popularity or lack thereof. This case can only be decided by a court of law. That is a judicial function pure and simple. For the Supreme Court to surrender to this assault would be to surrender its independence, its integrity and its reason for being. In so doing, neither justice to the litigants nor the public interest would be served. Under the circumstances, this case looms even larger than the child or the two sets of contesting parents.

Many law suits are painful matters. This case is no exception. Capital cases, for instance, demand the forfeiture of the life of the defendant. Damage suits take money away from some people and give it to others. No one ever claimed that both sides walk away from a law suit with smiles on their faces. No member of this court ever entertained any thought that the decision it rendered in this case would be easy to accept by the losing litigants. Such an event would be incredible.

As for the child, age three, it is to be expected that there would be an initial shock, even a longing for a time in the absence of the persons whom he had viewed as parents. This trauma will be overcome, however, as it is every day across this land by children who suddenly find their parents separated by divorce or lost to them through death. It will not be an insurmountable trauma for a three-year-old child to be returned, at last, to his natural parents who want to raise him as their own. It will work itself out in the fullness of time. As for the adoptive parents, they will have to live with their pain and the knowledge that they wrongfully deprived a father of his child past the child's third birthday. They and their lawyer brought it on themselves.

This much is clear. Adoptive parents who comply with the law may feel secure in their adoptions. Natural parents may feel secure in their right to raise their own children. If there is a tragedy in this case, as has been suggested, then that tragedy is the wrongful breakup of a natural family and the keeping of a child by strangers without right. We must remember that the purpose of an adoption is to provide a home for a child, not a child for a home.

Although Justices McMorrow and Miller ruled as part of the unanimous Supreme Court decision in favor of Otakar Kirchner, they dissented in this Order, writing, in part, the following:

I vote to allow the petitions for rehearing. I believe that the petitioners [the Does] should be afforded another opportunity to present further argument on the specific legal and factual errors they believe this court has made in its decision....

Justice Freeman [also one of the seven-judge unanimous decision, wrote his own opinion,] specially concurring in the denial of the [Does'] petition for rehearing:

I wholeheartedly concur in the court's decision to deny rehearing in this case.

In the weeks since the publication of this court's opinion in this case, there has been a tremendous public outcry.... We are constrained to interpret and apply the law as it is enacted by our legislature. This remains so, even in the midst of strong public opinion, media attention, and legislative action which comes now, only in the wake of what has been popularly deemed an unpopular decision. Our role is clear, and we possess no authority to deviate from our mandate. To now entreat, and further, require that we either rewrite or apply a law enacted based upon the testing of public opinion, results in an unworkable restructuring of the three branches of government....

In light of our findings, no purpose can be served by allowing rehearing in this case....

Justice Heiple, writing for the Court, and Justice Freeman, adding his own rationale for his part with the 5 − 2 majority, were addressing the state legislature's hasty passage of the "Baby Richard Law," an amendment to the Illinois Adoption Act. The legislature, in an attempt to prevent Otakar Kirchner from claiming his son and thereby circumventing the Supreme Court's authority, passed the new law in order to compel a best interest hearing on behalf of a child whose adoption was successfully contested in the court system. The law was too late to force a different outcome for Daniel Kirchner.

Thirteen months prior to the preceding Supreme Court Order, the Illinois Appellate Court affirmed the lower court's judgment that validated the adoption of Baby Richard by the Does. Justices Rizzi and Cerda concurred; Presiding Justice Tully dissented and wrote his opinion, with which conclusions the Supreme Court later agreed.

(Again, this opinion is condensed here in order to present the most relevant and interesting portions. I have taken the liberty to correct the spelling of the mother of Baby Richard from "Daniella" to "Daniela" throughout my quotations of the original document.)

Presiding Justice Tully, dissenting:

The majority [of this Appellate Court], in its misguided fervor to champion "injustice," has patently distorted and slanted the actual facts of this case on a number of important points.... [T]he following clarifications are necessary to a just analysis of this case....

...[I]n a most egregious departure from all evidence presented in the record, the [Appellate Court] majority [of two justices] declares: "Otakar was content 'to just let his child be born' without any interest, concern or responsibility...[,]" ...and "Otakar was apparently content to go on with his life never truly knowing whether he had a child who was living or had a child who had died."... The following presentation of all the facts will clearly demonstrate that the majority in this case has employed judicial sophistry in creating an untruthful scenario of the "big, bad and unfit" biological father in this case.

I. STATEMENT OF FACTS

The birth mother, Daniela, was single and 24 years old at time of becoming pregnant. She immigrated to the U.S. from Czechoslovakia in August 1988 to live with her uncle. In November 1989, she began living with petitioner, Otakar, at his Lake Shore Drive apartment. She first found out she was pregnant in June 1990. Her due date, March 16, 1991, was also the eventual date of Baby Richard's birth. Otakar was informed of the baby's due date and delivery arrangements were scheduled for St. Joseph's Hospital in Chicago.

Otakar, also an immigrant from Czechoslovakia, returned to his homeland in January 1991 for two weeks in order to visit his ill grandmother. During this time, Daniela received a phone call from Otakar's aunt in Czechoslovakia informing Daniela that Otakar had resumed dating his former girlfriend, that they were still in love and acting as if they had never broken up. She reacted to this phone call by ripping up the marriage certificate...previously obtained by Daniela and Otakar.... Daniela then gathered her belongings and moved from Otakar's apartment to a shelter for women in an apparent state of desperation and confusion.

At the time, she was eight months pregnant and not working. She spoke with...Ms. Scholes, who said she had two options: (1) put the baby up for adoption or (2) wait for the father to return and see what he says.... This triggered the process which culminated in the destruction of the family planned by Daniela and Otakar. (Would not counseling have better helped Daniela to deal with this emotional period, rather than pressure...to consent to adoption?)

Daniela then met with the adoptive parents, the Does, and told them she wanted a two-parent family for her baby.... She was then contacted by the Doe's [sic.] attorney, Tom Panichi. Daniela told him she knew the name of the birth father but refused to give it because she did not want him to have any rights to the baby...[and] that she planned to tell the father that the baby had died at birth. This encounter with Daniela should have been a warning signal to both Panichi and the Does of Daniela's dubious emotional state.

At this time, Daniela knew Otakar was back in the United States because she had called him at work. She called him on Valentine's Day 1991 and said: "I just want to remind you to call somebody who you love." She then hung up the phone without giving Otakar a chance to respond. She told the Does that Otakar had her number at the shelter and that she did not feel safe. This behavior would perhaps be indicative of a scorned, pregnant woman, who began to question her feelings for Otakar.

Thereafter, Daniela moved to her uncle's house in Hillside, Illinois....

After the birth of Baby Richard on March 16, 1991, she avoided Otakar and she refused to accept his phone calls. The baby was delivered at a hospital near the uncle's suburban home instead of St. Joseph's Hospital as planned. Otakar did not know where the baby was delivered and went to St. Joseph's Hospital in search of Daniela and the baby. Daniela told her uncle to tell Otakar that the baby had died and he obliged. She remained living at her uncle's house until May 12, 1991, when she resumed living with Otakar. At this time she confessed all of her prior falsehoods about the death of the baby and how she had consented to the baby's adoption.

On March 19, 1991, three days after Baby Richard's birth, the adopting parents, the Does, filed a petition to adopt Baby Richard, falsely alleging that the father of the baby was "unknown" and that the address of said father was unknown. In their amended petition to adopt, count I alleged that the parental rights of the natural mother...were terminated on March 20...after she voluntarily consented to allow her son...to be adopted. Count I further alleged that the natural father, Otakar Kirchner, was an *"unfit parent"* under...the Adoption Act...in that he: (a) failed to show a reasonable degree of interest in the child within the first 30 days of life; (b) abandoned the child; (c) engaged in open and notorious fornication. The fornication allegation was later dropped from the petition....

Otakar asserted an affirmative defense under the Adoption Act, which provides that impediments beyond a father's control are a defense to his showing a reasonable degree of interest in the child within 30 days after birth. Specifically, Otakar asserted as a defense the deception of the birth mother in representing to Otakar that Baby Richard had died at birth and in hindering all contact with her after the birth.... Upon finding out about the adoption on May 12, 1991, Otakar contacted an attorney and promptly moved on June 6, 1991, filing an appearance challenging the adoption of his infant son by the Does. Thus, Otakar exhibited a "reasonable degree of interest" in his child within 30 days of finding out about the existence of the child as well as his adoption, and after the impediment had been removed.

Otakar testified that during eight months of Daniela's pregnancy, prior to her leaving his apartment, he paid for all household expenses and maternity clothes and other expenses relating to the pregnancy. Moreover, he fully supported Daniela so that she did not have to work during the pregnancy. During his first week in Czechoslovakia, he and Daniela talked to each other every day, then Daniela stopped answering the telephone. During their final overseas phone conversation, Daniela accused Otakar of honeymooning with his ex-girlfriend. When he returned to his apartment in Chicago, the keys and a torn-up marriage license were thrown on a table. She had never told him she was considering adoption. He had recently allowed her to purchase a car on his credit card. They got back together for a day at Otakar's apartment and Daniela "was talking like nothing had happened." Otakar listened to the baby moving inside and they discussed the baby's birth. The next day she called him at work and said she did not know her feelings toward him. Then she said she did not want to see or talk to Otakar anymore. This was sometime around February 28th, just two weeks before Baby Richard's birth.

On the due date, March 16th, Otakar called St. Joseph's Hospital and went there personally looking for Daniela but she was not there. On March 20, four days after the baby's due date, Otakar spoke with the uncle who said the baby had died. He had absolutely no knowledge of the adoption or Daniela's plans to consent to adoption. At the end of March, he left a message on the answering machine at her uncle's house that he did not believe that the baby had died. He then started driving to the uncle's house everyday looking for evidence of a baby. On at least one occasion he was stopped by police and questioned about his loitering around the uncle's house.

A customer from the restaurant, managed by Otakar, contacted Senator Paul Simon's office to find out if a death certificate had been issued on the baby, but the search was only valid for the City of Chicago, not the suburbs, where the baby was delivered. Otakar also testified that other friends confirmed Daniela's story that the baby had died.

Otakar tried calling Daniela four or five times a day but she would not pick up the phone. He also tried sending her $500 in cash through their mutual friend, Selva. He did not speak to her again until after the baby was born[,] around March 25th, when he talked to her briefly in the hospital. (Apparently, Daniela had called him from the hospital, but Otakar did not know which one.)

The attorney who handled the adoption for the Does, Tom Panichi, testified that he knew that Daniela was reluctant to furnish the name of the birth father. He also knew she had continued contacts with the father and that she was planning to tell the birth father that the baby had died.... Daniela later told the Does that she thought a child should be raised by a two-parent family.

It should be noted that under Illinois law, in order to serve notice of an adoption to the father by publication, the attorney must inquire as to the address of the father. Panichi signed a notarized "Affidavit for Service by Publication" wherein he stated under oath that the father "on due inquiry cannot be found so that process cannot be served upon defendant." Panichi later testified that he failed to make any effort to ascertain the address of Otakar, who was then still living in the same apartment on Lake Shore Drive. He never asked Daniela about her address prior to living with her uncle. Daniela also told Panichi that the birth father would never consent to an adoption, whereupon Panichi told her the only other "remedy" would be to find unfitness. Panichi testified: "[Daniela] led us to believe that she was going to be able to control [Otakar] for [sic.] not coming forward by still secreting the birth and the whereabouts [of the baby.]"

When the Does filed their petition for adoption they alleged that "the biological father is unknown " and that "the address of said father is unknown." Subsequently, the Does filed their "Amendment to Supplement Petition for Adoption" wherein they again asserted that the father was unknown and his whereabouts were then unknown. The first petition was personally signed by the Does and the amended petition was signed by the Does' attorney, Panichi, on their behalf. At this time, both the Does and their attorney knew this to be untruthful. They had both been told by Daniela that she knew the name of the father and his whereabouts. Hence, the adoption petition filed was fraudulent and illegal and the subsequent adoption decree entered thereon was void. During the initial adoption hearing, prior to Otakar's involvement in the case, Daniela informed the court that she did not know the identity of Baby Richard's father. This was stated in the presence of the Does and their attorney, all of whom knew this to be false.

Daniela's Uncle Joe testified and corroborated the stories of both Daniela and Otakar. Daniela originally lived with him prior to moving out to live with Otakar. Sometime in February 1991, Daniela returned to live with him, during which time she delivered a baby. He knew that the baby was born alive and had not died.... After the baby was born, at the request of Daniela,

Uncle Joe told Otakar that the baby had died. Otakar left several messages on the answering machine at the uncle's house, but Daniela refused to take Otakar's calls.

The couple's mutual friend, Selva, testified that she worked in the pastry shop at the restaurant complex managed by Otakar and she knew about the baby as well as about the birth arrangements at St. Joseph's Hospital. She did not know that Daniela wanted to put the baby up for adoption. Prior to the birth of the baby, Otakar gave Selva $500 to give to Daniela, but Daniela refused to take it.... On May 12, 1991, Daniela moved back to Otakar's apartment and explained to him what had happened with the baby.

II. FINDINGS OF THE TRIAL COURT

...On May 8, 1992, Otakar's parental rights were terminated [by the trial judge] based upon his unfitness and the adoption decree favoring the Does was entered on May 12, 1992.

The trial judge apparently did not take into consideration the fact that Otakar was hindered from showing an interest in the baby within the first 30 days of birth **as a result of** the scheme propagated by Daniela. Moreover, it should be noted that both the adopting parents, their lawyer and the social worker who arranged this adoption were all aware of Daniela's "plan" to defraud Otakar of his rights to the baby and that she was well aware of his location at all times pending the adoption proceedings. Yet no effort was made by the adopting parents, their attorney or the trial court to locate the biological father in this case. Upon discovering the adoption, Otakar promptly moved within the statutory 30-day period to challenge the adoption and assert his rights as the biological father of the child....

...[I]n the instant case, there was no evidence presented to the trial court on the adoptive parents, in order to provide for a proper "best interests" analysis. The only evidence in the record indicating the "fitness" of the Does is that they defrauded the court by knowingly acceding to an adoption where they knew the natural father had been deprived of any rights.... [A] best interests analysis was never performed by the trial court in this case. Moreover, ...no evidence was presented by counsel for either party regarding the best interests of Baby Richard.

The entire finding of unfitness in this instance rests upon the trial judge's finding that Otakar should have contacted a lawyer within 30 days of the due date instead of trying to make contact with the birth mother and searching through her garbage for evidence that the child was in fact alive.... [T]he entire majority decision [of this Appellate Court] rests upon the fact that the biological parents have had no contact with Baby Richard since his birth.... Nothing in the record reflects the current care and security of Richard, the background of the Does or even the long-term and latent psychological effects on Baby Richard when he realizes the course of events which led to the termination of his natural father's parental rights....

...It must be reiterated that the adopting parents and their attorney knew that the father could be located, but no attempt was made to do so. Moreover, Daniela told their lawyer of her plans to tell Otakar that the baby had died. While we should not totally discount the best interests of the child in this case, we cannot ignore the gross injustice perpetrated upon the biological father in this instance. This is not a case of a disinterested father or a man intending to leave his girlfriend "in the lurch." He lived with and cared for Daniela throughout her pregnancy, paying for all rent, food and medical necessities. He also made delivery arrangements for Baby Richard. It was only as a result of the meddling of Otakar's relatives that the relationship between the biological parents became severed. Daniela decisively and improvidently reacted to the hearsay information that Otakar was seeking his former girlfriend. It has been medically proven that women often react in an unusually emotional and volatile manner even to ordinary everyday occurrences during pre-natal and post-natal care, much less such a severe blow dealt to her in her eighth month of pregnancy. There is no evidence in the record that the information given to Daniela was even remotely true and it seems extremely doubtful given their subsequent reconciliation.

The interests of the child are but one factor to be considered in a case of such a delicate nature. We must consider the effect on the child who will one day learn that his biological father was defrauded and prevented of any opportunity to win his custody in a scheme which involved the adopting parents and their attorney, not just the biological mother. Moreover, during the initial adoption hearing, the trial court did not require any proof of the biological father or his whereabouts.... The potential damage of allowing the birth mother to solely control the termination of parental rights is immeasurable and the social costs too great. Even the biological mother herself is a sorry victim in this case. Her actions were entirely instigated by the interference of Otakar's relatives and a vicious unproven rumor which called into question her future relationship with Otakar and her prospective ability to care for the baby as a single mother and as a new immigrant in a foreign culture....

...Severe sanctions should be imposed upon parties and their counsel for concealing information regarding the whereabouts of the natural father.... The entire process should take no more than six months, unlike the instant case, where the process took two and one-half years....

The natural father in this case did what a reasonable man could be expected to do within the first 30 days of Baby Richard's life. Through the entire pre- and post-natal period, he held himself out as the father of Baby Richard, he never abandoned the baby and he even begged Daniela's uncle for information about the baby, culminating in his desperate search through garbage cans for discarded diapers or formula. One can visualize the pain and anguish this father was experiencing. One would not expect him to immediately run to an attorney at this point, when he had still hoped for an amicable reunion with Daniela. We have here two young people from a foreign country thrust into a situation where they were in love, but due to the interference of family and "well-meaning" social agencies, they end up losing legal right to their child. This case is not so different from the concepts promulgated by the Third Reich when it ruthlessly selected children at random and informed parents: "This child may live, but this other child must be forever removed because of religion or ethnic origin."

...This child should be reunited with his biological parents....

Unlike the Baby Jessica case, this case involves two loving biological parents who remained together except for the brief period of time when Daniela became confused about her relationship. It was during this period that she signed her baby away. Otakar's rights were never protected. He never left her. He provided for her support throughout the pregnancy and even tried to send her money through an intermediary. He pled with her uncle to speak with Daniela and even searched through garbage cans for evidence of the child. He did everything a reasonable person could have done except obtain the services of an attorney. However, within the first 30 days of Baby Richard's life, Otakar did not know the adoption process had commenced. The attorney for the Does could have easily ascertained the whereabouts of Otakar and yet he filed an adoption petition alleging that the biological father was "unknown." In so doing, the Does and their attorney filed a patently false document. A judgment for adoption cannot be entered on the basis of a false or fraudulent petition. Hence, this case warrants an outright reversal of the trial court's ruling....

There is no doubt that the rights of the biological parents were improperly obliterated by the lower court. The charade of terming the father "unfit" because he failed to immediately seek legal advice is preposterous and an insidious appendix to the already confused state of the law in such cases. If the biological father did not know when or where the child was born, when did the 30-day period for measuring fitness begin to run? If Otakar was informed the child had died, then the 30-day period could not have begun until May 12, almost two months after the baby's birth, when Daniela informed Otakar of the adoption. Until this point, there existed an impediment to Otakar exhibiting a reasonable degree of interest in Baby Richard.... Based upon all of the foregoing, this adoption was improper, illegal and fraudulent and it should be vacated by this court....

It is interesting that the [Appellate Court] majority, without blinking, has deemed itself all-knowing in this instance and has assumed a sacrosanct role formerly reserved for Divine Providence. The tradition of adoption in our society was created in order to provide a place of love and care for abandoned, unwanted and orphaned children. Baby Richard was never abandoned or unwanted. American society should not be so devoid of humanity, fairness and just plain good common sense.

For all of the aforementioned reasons, I respectfully dissent from the majority view.

The Illinois Supreme Court's rejection of the Does' petition for a rehearing of its June 1994 decision in favor of Otakar Kirchner was not surprising, from a pragmatic standpoint. "The state's highest court typically accepts at most 2% of petitions for rehearing," according to Wayne Russell. As the Chief Deputy Clerk of the Supreme Court for the past twenty years, Russell maintains the records and statistics of the court. In 2002, one such rehearing was granted from 52 petitions. In 1994—the year of the Baby Richard petitions—one rehearing was granted from 55 petitions.

"It is **very unusual** for a case to make its way to the Illinois Supreme Court five times," Mr. Russell assures me as we discuss the uniqueness of Baby Richard. Between 1994 and 1997, the highest state court ruled on aspects of the case five times: the adoption/custody dispute; petition for rehearing; subsequent petition for rehearing based upon the new, hastily-enacted amendment to the Adoption Act; request for mental health expert(s) to be required to oversee Richard's transfer to his biological parents; and petition to stay a lower court's ruling that threatened to reopen the custody dispute when Daniela sought to restore her parental rights.

"I remember the case well," Russell summarizes for me; "it was extraordinary."

The Baby Richard decision was appealed to the United States Supreme Court **twice** by the adoptive parents. Specifically, the Illinois Supreme Court's ruling that overturned the adoption and awarded the child's custody to his biological father was appealed in August 1994, and again in spring 1995— after the state Court's third ruling in favor of Otakar Kirchner. (In addition, the adoptive parents twice petitioned judges of the U.S. Supreme Court to stay the Illinois Supreme Court's order that directed them immediately to turn over Baby Richard to his biological father. Thus, they made **four** unsuccessful trips to the nation's highest court.)

Predictably, the U.S. Supreme Court did not take up the adoptive parents' appeals. The highest court of the land accepts an even lower percentage of cases than does the Illinois Supreme Court. From approximately 7,000 petitions annually, the United States Supreme Court accepts eighty to ninety cases, less than two percent.

Losing the ultimate fights for "Richard" in the state's and nation's highest courts, the Warburtons (a.k.a. Does) would turn to a new battlefield. Buttressed and protected by their battery of twenty-plus attorneys, they would take their case to the media, where they would fare considerably better than in the legal system. The Warburtons would be championed by powerful celebrities, vocal politicians, prominent journalists, and clamoring citizens from coast to coast.

Although the forceful and widespread public campaign would still prove insufficient to change the final outcome for Daniel Kirchner, joyfully and permanently reunited with his birth parents, it would wreak devastation upon his new family for years to come....

All media work us over completely.
They are so pervasive in their
personal, political, economic,
aesthetic, psychological, moral, ethical,
and social consequences
that they leave no part of us
untouched, unaffected, unaltered.

— *Marshall McLuhan*

BEFORE WE MET — MEDIA TRUMP CARD: 1994 – 95

IT took **ten** anguished months for Otto and Daniela to meet their firstborn child Danny after the Illinois Supreme Court's first ruling that granted Otakar custody of "Baby Richard." Using the effective buffers of a willing media, sympathetic legislators, government officials, and a cadre of manipulating attorneys, the Warburtons distanced themselves and Danny from his birth parents and placed seemingly limitless impediments in the way of a first introduction between child and parents.

> All successful newspapers are ceaselessly querulous and bellicose. They never defend any one or anything if they can help it; if the job is forced upon them, they tackle it by denouncing some one or something else.
>
> — *H. L. Mencken*

The public furor generated over the Supreme Court decisions and the mountain of misinformation and misinterpretation can hardly be exaggerated. Dozens of journalists from every medium cover the case, while talk shows and call-in programs feature the story. Bob Greene pounds out column after column of whiny, condemnatory, and regurgitative accusations against the Court and the biological parents. Greene's coverage was described as "both false and misleading" by Judge Heiple in the Court's "Richard" decision of July 1994: "Greene brings to bear the tools of the demagogue, namely, incomplete information, falsity, half truths, character assassination and spurious argumentation."

Remaining anonymous by using the pseudonyms John and Jane Doe—consistently employed throughout the Baby Richard court documents—Jay and Kimberly Warburton go public, in person, starting at the top of the media food chain, with an exclusive appearance on Barbara Walters' nationally televised *20/20* program on August 19, 1994. Promoted by ABC as the first public appearance of Mr. and Mrs. Doe, the show is billed as "an effort to save their son" from Otakar Kirchner, the boy's biological father. Maintaining their assumed names, which adds to the melodrama and uniqueness of this highly-publicized debut of the Chicago-suburb couple, Jay and Kim Warburton take their case to the American public, now that they have lost their legal battle in the Illinois Supreme Court the previous month. An ABC press release explains that the Does "feel they must now tell their side of the story in order to bring wider attention to the case." The Kirchners are not invited to the program.

"My heart just absolutely bleeds for the [adoptive] parents. I've got a headache, I'm so angry," asserts a female caller's voice before the Does' interview begins on *20/20*. "Outrage, frustration – radio talk show callers inflamed over an Illinois Supreme Court decision that to many seemed heartless and threatened to destroy a child's happiness...," Barbara Walters begins.

"With this decision, if it's allowed to stand, basically adoption's on its ear, not only in Illinois but across the nation," Mr. Doe proclaims to Barbara Walters, who is the adoptive mother of a daughter. "...The child could be five years old, ten years old, possibly all the way up until eighteen..., and a biological mother or father could come back and say, 'I didn't know.'" The adoptive father, concealing the critical fact that this court-reversed adoption was based upon deceit and the Does' untruthful affidavits, hyperbolically and erroneously interprets the Court's ruling to the viewers in a manner to alarm and to arouse sympathy.

Mrs. Doe vows to "exhaust every legal remedy that there is" to keep the child. "...We were simply asked to love a child that no one else wanted...," Mrs. Doe tearfully appeals to Walters and the viewing public. Predictably, the would-be adoptive mother chooses to ignore and deny the biological father's continuous love and "wanting" his child across the three-plus years during which he vigorously challenged their adoption of his son. Of course, they also omit acknowledgement that they were involved in the initial deceptions upon which the child's adoption took place. Walters avoids such references as well.

Meanwhile, hostilities—destined to span more than three years—have broken out among the three branches of Illinois government over the Baby Richard dispute.

In early July 1994, the Illinois legislature passes amendments to the state's Adoption Act—less than three weeks after the Supreme Court's "Richard" ruling. Passed by a bi-partisan vote in both the House and the Senate, the bill goes on to receive an equally rapid and dramatic signature by Governor Edgar, on a Sunday. He points out that he has vocally and visibly supported the new legislation. The Illinois House voted 77 – 21 in favor, swiftly advancing the measure to the Senate, which passed it by a 42 – 4 vote after Edgar called a special, emergency session on it.

Referred to as the "Baby Richard" bill, it is "aimed at keeping a 3-year-old boy with the parents who adopted him at birth," reports the *Chicago Sun-Times*, whose coverage continues:

> "To take a child away from the parents that child knows, that to me would be an extremely traumatic experience for the child and could have devastating impact for years to come," said Edgar, whose staff plans to ask the Illinois Supreme Court to review its decision to turn the boy known as Baby Richard over to his biological father....
>
> The [emergency] session on Baby Richard legislation was needed because senators had passed an adjournment resolution that prevented them from voting on other matters until later this month....
>
> The governor believes the timing is critical because he wants the Baby Richard measure...to become law quickly. (Ray Long, "Senate Passes 'Richard' Bill," July 2, 1994)

The new law calls for a "best interest" hearing to determine the temporary or permanent custody of a child after an adoption petition is denied or an adoption is revoked. It establishes a registry for unwed biological fathers who want to assert a claim of paternity; they must register within thirty days of their child's birth or forfeit their claim unless they can prove they were unable to do so through no fault of their own. The birth mother is also required to sign an affidavit to identify the birth father.

The affidavit includes penalties for lying or providing intentional misinformation. The measure sets a one-year limit for biological parents to challenge court rulings that allow a baby to be adopted. It also requires an expedited process in the courts so that cases do not drag out because of the judicial system. The law applies to all "pending" and future cases in an overt attempt to influence and in fact to overturn the Supreme Court's "Richard" ruling.

Legal experts are divided on the potential impact of the new law on the Baby Richard case. Some opine that it will be determined to apply because the adoptive parents have requested a rehearing of its decision by the Supreme Court. The Does will assert that the "Richard" case is therefore still "pending" and the law therefore applies; if successful, they will obtain a "best interest" hearing for the child to determine the custody issue. Other experts believe that, because the highest state court has ruled on the case, it is no longer pending and a "best interest" hearing would therefore be unavailable. The case would be closed, except for a potential U.S. Supreme Court reversal, an unlikely event for a domestic dispute.

Many legal experts and columnists address the pivotal issue—the violation of the constitutionally guaranteed division of powers among the branches of government. If the executive branch—the governor—and the legislature can reverse a judicial ruling retrospectively, this would pose a serious threat to constitutional protections and requirements. Some observers criticize the "rapid-fire response" by the governor and the General Assembly to the controversial and unpopular "Richard" ruling. It reminds me of the humorous—yet applicable—aphorism:

> People who love sausage and respect the law
> should never watch either one being made.

> — Lowell D. Streiker

In an unprecedented act, Governor Edgar, through his attorneys, petitions the Illinois Supreme Court to rehear its Baby Richard decision. The governor is officially entering into a domestic conflict between two sets of parents, turning the dispute into an issue between the executive and the judicial branches of state government. He joins the adoptive parents; Patrick Murphy, the Cook County Public Guardian; and Edward J. O'Connell, the child's guardian *ad litem*. Edgar is quoted as saying:

> I think we all think the Supreme Court decision was wrong.... But this legislation now...allow[s] this [custody] hearing to be held, which we think would give the adoptive parents the opportunity to show that they should retain custody [of Richard]....

> If we had not tried to do something to save this child from what I think could be a tragedy the child maybe could never overcome, I think we would have been held derelict in our duty.... (Mark Caro, "Bill signed on child's best interest in custody talks," *Chicago Tribune*, July 4, 1994)

In the article, Edgar "denied that election-year politics may have played a role," and "he attributed the legislature's speediness to a widespread sense of urgency."

The *Chicago Sun-Times* covers the story on page one:

> Edgar flew to Chicago to sign the bill, ensuring maximum publicity....

> ...Using that standard [the child's best interests], the child [Richard] should remain with his adoptive parents, he said.

> Jeffery Leving, a fathers' rights attorney, said determining the best interests of a child is a subjective judgment. In custody hearings, the side with the most money to litigate often wins, he said. "An unwed father with limited resources is at a disadvantage."

> ...Edgar signed the bill in front of cheering adoptive parents and restless toddlers at the Parent and Infant Development Center.... (Jim Ritter, "'Baby Richard' Measure Signed," July 4, 1994)

Within days of Edgar's signing the "Baby Richard" measure into law, Judge Heiple, in a one-paragraph order, denies the governor's historic request to get involved in the legal case, now before the Court for a requested rehearing.

> The order and the swiftness with which it came caught the attorneys...by surprise....
>
> ...[Edgar] vowed to try to change the decision [of the Court].... Edgar has called the court's decision "terrible," "wrong" and "a tragedy."...
>
> "This result [the Richard ruling] casts a frightening chill over Illinois' entire adoption process...," Edgar stated....
>
> But it was to no avail. It took Heiple less than four hours to slam the door on the governor....
>
> Edgar had attached a 17-page brief to his request [for the Court to rehear its decision]....
>
> Public opinion seems overwhelmingly in favor of the adoptive parents. In the last weeks, the Supreme Court clerk's office has received more than 100 calls a day. Fewer than 10 have supported the decision. (Jan Crawford Greenburg, "Court gives Edgar fast 'no' on 'Richard' plea," *Chicago Tribune*, July 8, 1994)

Edward O'Connell makes a formal proposal on behalf of Baby Richard to both sets of parents. It includes allowing the child to remain living with the adoptive parents; granting the biological father visitation rights with the child; requiring Otakar Kirchner to pay child support to the adoptive parents; and relinquishing all further legal battles by both sides to the dispute.

Meanwhile, the adoptive parents continue to refuse numerous requests to provide photographs of the boy to his biological father. Otto and Daniela have never seen their son, either in person or in photos. They long to see what he looks like; they want to know something about him. O'Connell admits that his proposal "would probably end up leaving nobody totally happy." Otto responds that he has already won in Court. Why would he voluntarily relinquish custody of his only child after having won such a lengthy court battle to obtain the right to raise him?

The startling coalition between the governor and the legislature in publicly and vehemently opposing the state Supreme Court gives rise to an especially virulent strain of media maliciousness directed against Otakar and Daniela Kirchner. Many journalists jump onto the bandwagon of public opinion by championing the adoptive parents and fashioning them as modern-day martyr figures and tragic victims.

Columnist Eric Zorn clamors:

>...The best strategy for Baby Richard's adoptive parents to pursue now is to invite a media circus—a full-blown, front-lawn festival of mini-cams..., of interviews and intrusions, of stakeouts and stand-ups....

>...[Y]es, Governor Finger-in-the-wind [Edgar] has made a belated and politically opportunistic entry in the case....

>Now that the adoptive parents have lost in the Illinois Supreme Court and are facing long odds, they owe it to the boy to change tactics....

>And, it's a long shot, but maybe the judges will feel it too. ("Media glare could help Baby Richard," *Chicago Tribune*, July 5, 1994)

During the same week that the "Baby Richard" law becomes effective, a Chicago rally is staged to support the adoptive parents in their continuing fight. Using a "Hear our voice" battlecry, the more than 200 demonstrators carry picket signs outside the State of Illinois Building. The group consists of legislators, members of several state delegations of the national DeBoer Committee for Children's Rights, and dozens of adoptive parents. Since August 2, 1993, the day on which "Baby Jessica" DeBoer left her adoptive parents to live with her biological parents after a long court battle, the DeBoer Committee has provided powerful and well-organized support for adoptive parents across the country. Early on, the Committee has embraced the cause of the "Richard" adoptive parents. Organizers of the rally present the first "Hear My Voice" award to Elizabeth Edgar, accepting it on behalf of her father, the governor, who is recovering from emergency heart bypass surgery. Elizabeth Edgar asks supporters of the adoptive parents to persevere and "not get discouraged."

The DeBoer Committee throws its strong support behind this fund-raising campaign, begun by a life-long friend of the Does/Warburtons. Contributions are solicited from across the country "to help pay for legal bills." Additional fund-raising activities include a car wash, golf outing, and walkathon. In the adoptive parents' neighborhood and adjacent areas, citizens sympathetic to them festoon their front-yard trees with blue ribbons-and-bows as symbols of their protest against Richard's biological father.

Jenner and Block, the mammoth Chicago-based law firm, announces in November that—on a *pro bono* basis—a horde of its attorneys will jump in to assist Richard Lifshitz and his partners in new and continuing attempts to pursue legal remedies on behalf of the Does/Warburtons.

In spite of widespread and broad-based political and media efforts, as well as a vociferous public outcry, the Illinois Supreme Court denies a rehearing of their Baby Richard decision on July 12, 1994.

Edgar issues a public statement:

> This is a dark day for justice and human decency in Illinois. The highest court in this state has committed a travesty.... [T]he court has decreed [Richard] should be brutally, tragically torn away from the only parents he has ever known.... Frankly, I cannot imagine how the justices who prevailed in this case will be able to sleep at night. (Jan Crawford Greenburg, "No words barred as Edgar and Heiple trade jabs on 'Richard'," *Chicago Tribune*, July 13, 1994)

The Court temporarily postpones enforcement of its decision, however, until the adoptive parents have exhausted their rights to an appeal to the United States Supreme Court. The child may remain with them until that time.

Otto and Daniela, avoiding public contact as much as possible, work to keep up their spirits. They have won their son, but they are still unable to meet him, to see a picture of him, or to discover anything about him. They wonder about his real name and about his favorite toys, foods, and routines. They continue to speculate about his physical appearance. Is he blonde, like his mother and like his father when he was Danny's age? Is he tall or short or average in height? Is he healthy? Is the care provided him by the adoptive parents truly loving and healthful? Is he treated as if he is important or is he a second-class citizen in his family, relegated to the position of a playmate for the adoptive parents' biological son? Is he the object of the frustrations, disappointments, and anger of the adoptive parents? After all, Otto and Daniela reason, the Warburtons knew that they might lose him from his first week in their home. Would they have steeled themselves to this possibility? How would it have played out in their daily interactions with him, in their decisions on his behalf?

How soon, or late, will it be before they are allowed to meet him? Daily Otto and Daniela talk about every aspect of having a son who will **someday** be with them. They buy toys of all sizes and shapes and a menagerie of stuffed animals, and they place each new item with loving anticipation in a visible place, as a purposeful, constant reminder that Danny will experience the happiness of playing with it...someday. Daniela's favorite is a two-foot-tall, shaggy white dog with wide eyes and a big black nose. She often sleeps with it to convince herself that her son will soon enjoy that opportunity, at her side.

Spurred by the Baby Richard case, a national commission debates a proposal that would unify the patchwork of varying state adoption laws. The National Conference of Commissioners on Uniform State Laws urges legislators from all fifty states to enact specific reforms related to adoption.

> Under the proposed Uniform Adoption Act, birth mothers would have eight days to change their minds after putting a baby up for adoption.

> ...[T]he model law would give biological fathers 30 days to claim their parental rights after adoption proceedings begin. Courts would have to try to give fathers notice

that an adoption was about to take place....

Adoption records would be sealed, but registries could be established by states to facilitate efforts by willing children and their natural parents.

Supporters of the reforms include groups with an interest in stable adoptions that are not open to legal attack after a child has lived with adoptive parents for years.... (Michael Briggs, "Baby Richard Ruling Slated," *Chicago Sun-Times*, November 7, 1994)

Although the proposed Act is debated across the nation, it fails ever to receive the support necessary to prevail as a consistent, nationwide set of standards for adoption.

Adrienne Drell attempts to interject reason and balance into the raging public debate over Baby Richard and to suggest the lessons from it:

Despite the public clamor, Kirchner has supporters. They include legal experts, the president of the state's largest bar organization and family law specialists who are troubled that Richard's adoption proceeded without his father's knowledge....

Jane Rutherford, a professor at DePaul University College of Law and past president of the Association of American Law Schools Family Law Section, compared the adoption to "kidnapping, because you knowingly are taking someone's child without their permission.

"I hold the adoptive parents culpable because they may have been taking advantage of a woman who wanted to keep her child but was not given any options...."

The Cradle is the largest private adoption agency in the Chicago area and has placed 13,000 children in its 71-year history. In each case, the mother has been required to disclose the name of the father. ("Legal Experts Back Ruling on 'Baby Richard'," *Chicago Sun-Times*, July 10, 1994)

"People really misunderstand what the Baby Richard case was about," Julie Tye, long-time president of The Cradle, would tell me in an interview in 2003. "Just last week one of my board members brought it up, in sympathy with the adoptive parents. At this agency, we would never have allowed that adoption, based upon the initial facts," Ms. Tye declares. "Adoption is treated as a legal transaction; it's not—it's much more than that. And sadly, a white baby—especially a boy—is perceived as a commodity. The Baby Richard case completely missed the human needs of all of the parties involved.

"We saw lots of angst from adoptive parents here because of 'Richard.' And we had to do a lot of education with adoptive parents," she continues. "Adoption agencies were not surprised at the Supreme Court decision, but most of the public didn't want to be confused with the facts. A lot of people turned to international adoptions out of fear after Baby Richard. If they use a good agency, though, there is never disruption or successful contest of an adoption."

Tye believes, from her many years of experience, that people in crisis lack the ability to make informed decisions. "That's what happened to Daniela," she states. "Social work professionals should always be involved in helping a birth mother reach her decision regarding adoption of her child. Daniela lacked counseling, support, and even knowledge about adoption. The system failed these people," she summarizes.

The Warburtons, seemingly undaunted by their loss in the state court system, decide to take their case to the U.S. Supreme Court. In August 1994, they file a petition asking the nation's highest court to decide whether Baby Richard has a constitutional right to maintain a family relationship with his adoptive parents and sibling. Patrick Murphy also files an appeal to the highest court, asserting a protectable liberty interest in the child's maintaining his established familial relationships and asking whether his unmarried father had the right to veto his adoption. Murphy argues that the boy is entitled, under the due process clause of the Fourteenth Amendment, to a hearing to determine his best interests before he is removed from the only family he has known. The petition is filed on the last day allowed by the Illinois Supreme Court before time runs out on the Warburtons' keeping the child from his father. In another highly visible demonstration of his support of "Richard's" adoptive parents, Governor Edgar joins the other petitioners in seeking the U.S. Supreme Court's reversal of the Illinois Court's ruling for Otakar Kirchner.

On November 7, 1994, the U.S. Supreme Court announces that it will not get involved in the case.

Loren Heinemann, on behalf of his client, files a petition on the same day with the Illinois Supreme Court. The petition asks the Court to declare unconstitutional the new "Baby Richard" law, which may still require a state lower court to conduct a custody hearing in order to determine the child's best interests vis-à-vis with whom he should live. Within hours, Patrick Murphy asks for the custody hearing "under the new law or previous laws." Murphy also files an emergency request for the Does to be given temporary custody of the child, saying he "will suffer irreparable harm" if he is removed from their home. If granted, this petition will successfully keep "Richard" with the adoptive parents until further court decisions to the contrary.

"Like it or not, as of today, they're going to be dealing with Otto forever," Heinemann announces, referring to the legal reality of the Does' defeat at the U.S. Supreme Court level.

"Although I missed out on his infancy," Otto declares, "I am happy that I will now be able to share my son's childhood."

Kirchner's petition argues that the new "'law is unconstitutional because it changes the rules in the middle of the game,'" Heinemann clarifies, and "'it goes against the traditional separation of powers doctrine in the U.S. Constitution that prohibits the legislature from changing a final judicial decision.'" (Jan Crawford Greenburg, "U.S. justices leave 'Baby Richard' to state court," *Chicago Tribune*, November 8, 1994)

The Does' most recent petition seeks to convince the Illinois Supreme Court that the case was not final when the "Baby Richard" law went into effect. They argue that their appeals, subsequent to the Court's ruling, kept the case alive and still "pending."

Richard Roeper, taking an anomalous position among his journalism colleagues, displays the courage to state categorically, "Baby Richard...belongs with his biological parents." He concludes his well-reasoned opinion:

Despite any other allegations that have been forwarded in the press, the stated reason that a Cook County judge found Kirchner unfit was that he had failed to demonstrate a reasonable degree of interest during the 30 days after the child's birth. The evidence suggested otherwise— but it took two years for the case to reach the Illinois Supreme Court, which reached the correct legal decision that Otto's rights had been improperly terminated.

And now the U.S. Supreme Court has let that ruling stand.

The biological father of this child never did anything wrong, never did anything to warrant what he has gone through for more than three years. [The child] belongs with his biological parents. ("Baby Richard Facts, Law Back Biological Parents," *Chicago Sun-Times*, November 15, 1994)

Large, prominent ads appear in the *Tribune*, exhorting the public to assist the anonymous adoptive parents with their legal fees:

Please help "Baby Richard" remain with the only family he has ever known!

...Last week, the U.S. Supreme Court refused to hear the case....

...To help this family with their overwhelming legal bills, please send contributions to: **The Baby Richard Legal Defense Fund...[address].** (November 20, 1994, et al.)

In my neighborhood, Robert and I encounter individuals who are thrusting around blue plastic pails to collect contributions for the Does. They stand on street corners and in shopping malls. They entreat passersby to donate whatever they can.

Before Christmas, Otto and Daniela—through Heinemann— request the adoptive parents to allow the child to receive gifts from them. They also ask, once again, to see photos or videotapes of him. He will be four years old in three months, and they have yet to see what he looks like or to be apprised about his personality, his health, or his emotional state. Their feelings are bubbling from recent events; they weep, sometimes alone and sometimes together; and they laugh with joy over the prospect of getting closer to some resolution of their prolonged agony. The holiday season is important, especially this year, the fourth of his life and of their fight to have him with them.

"No!" comes the answer to both requests—no gifts, no pictures. Because he has not been informed that he is an adopted child, he should not receive presents from his natural parents, the Does' responding attorney asserts. He ignores the Kirchners' proposal that Danny be given their presents "from Santa." They cannot see or have pictures of him, without a court order, "because that would compromise his privacy."

During Christmas week 1994, Judge Stephen Yates rules that John and Jane Doe have the legal right to seek permanent custody of "Richard," opening the door to a lower court hearing on the issue of his best interest: Who is better fit to raise him—the adoptive parents, the only parents he has known, or his biological father? Yates denies Otakar Kirchner's challenge, which asserts that the Does have no legal standing because of the Illinois Supreme Court's having invalidated the adoption in June. The Does claim that they have legal standing because "Richard" was in their physical custody when the adoption occurred.

The Illinois Supreme Court decides to take up the case once again; it will decide both sides' issues. Heinemann has requested the Court to invalidate the applicability of the new "Baby Richard" law, thereby precluding another round of lower court involvement, and to grant a writ of habeas corpus. The writ would require the Does to turn the child over to his biological father, in accordance with the Court's June and July rulings months ago.

During these months, Bob Greene publishes a series of columns in support of "Richard's" remaining with his adoptive parents. As an example, he poses the question of the child's lamentable fate "if the [Does'] lawyers fail":

> What will happen to him if he is handed over to the man he has never seen, and to the woman who cared so much about him that she blithely said that he was dead after she placed him for adoption?

He'll probably live. He'll probably survive. As we noted in a recent column, a child can be broken like a dog. A child, regardless of what he or she feels or wants or begs for, can be broken and made to adapt. ("Richard is left to cope on his own," *Chicago Tribune*, November 9, 1994)

After the holidays, I am preparing to leave the school district for which I have worked on a full-time basis for fifteen years. I have never met the Kirchners; I know well what Otto Kirchner looks like, as I have seen him on TV news programs and in numerous photographs in various publications; but I have never seen a picture of Daniela in any medium. The story plays prominently across Christmas and into the New Year 1995.

In school lunchrooms and offices, which I frequent during the course of my job responsibilities, teachers and support staff buzz about "Baby Richard." "What will become of that poor child?" "How could the Court give a kid to an unfit father?" "Can **anything** prevent Richard from having to go to those awful people?" "Will **one** of the courts yet spare him?"

Generally avoiding discussion with others about "Richard," I secretly wonder if there is more of a story than is being disclosed. What is going on with both sets of parents behind the scenes? What is **really** going on with the child?

More than anything else, I wonder why one child has been receiving so much non-stop attention and publicity. Privately, I am tired of hearing about the story. Little did I know that all that has transpired in the Baby Richard case would turn out to represent round one in a long series of rounds yet to come...for the child, for his parents, and for me.

On January 25, 1995, after my farewell party, I leave my school district office forever, carrying my last box of personal possessions and three live plants to my car. Buoyant but nostalgic, I drive home to a quiet, at-home dinner with Robert, over which we excitedly discuss the prospect of our new life with more time for each other and less stress in our everyday lives. During the day, the Illinois Supreme Court rules, using twenty-eight words addressed to the Does/Warburtons:

You are hereby ordered and directed to surrender forthwith custody of the child known as Baby Boy Richard,

also known as Baby Boy Janikova, to petitioner Otakar
Kirchner.

Evening news programs on television highlight the announcement with animated, excited coverage. After having listened to
the lawyers present their respective arguments to the Court, the
adoptive parents were driving back from Springfield when they
heard an account on their car radio. Otto and Daniela Kirchner
are overcome by joy...and relief.

In a ruling described as "stunningly swift," the Court
announced its order within hours of the concluding statements by
attorneys in the case. Governor Edgar calls the ruling "Shocking.
Outrageous. Heartless. Incredibly inhumane...." Edgar further
announces, "I know I am joined by millions of my fellow citizens
in being disgusted and pained by this heartbreaking decision."
(Adrienne Drell, "Court's Decision Brings Vindication and
Outrage," *Chicago Sun-Times*, January 26, 1995)

On the day after this Supreme Court's third ruling on behalf
of Otakar Kirchner, the news breaks that Daniela Kirchner is
expecting the couple's second child.

> "I am so overjoyed and I can't even jump," said Daniela
> Kirchner, who is expecting the new arrival in August.
> "This is really, really great. I am so happy our first baby
> will live with us and our new little boy or girl. We will
> make room for them both."

> "At long last we can be a family," her husband said.
> (Adrienne Drell, "Court Backs Birth Father," *Chicago
> Sun–Times*, January 26, 1995)

Drell's front-page article quotes Otakar's reaction to the
Court's decision: "The miracle finally happened.... I feel like
[the] most happiest father right now. I feel like my child was
born just now."

Meanwhile, the Does consider fleeing the state with
"Richard," according to their lead attorneys, who "talked [them]
out of doing so." Attorney Jerold Solovy exclaims, "Never in my
40 years of practice have I seen the court issue an order in the
same day as arguments without an opinion."

Patrick Murphy says, "This is the most dispassionate, cold-hearted decision I have seen from a court in 31 years." Murphy had argued to the Supreme Court that it was the Does who took Richard "to see Santa Claus and who stayed up all night with him when he had colic." Chief Justice Michael Bilandic interrupted him, "Whose fault is that?" Some of the justices expressed concern that their earlier rulings were being disregarded.

The Does' attorneys and Murphy immediately announce their plans to request a rehearing of the Illinois Supreme Court on this ruling and to petition the U.S. Supreme Court for a stay of the order. They will need to wait until the written opinion of the Court is issued before they request another rehearing.

Behind the scenes, private investigators are attempting to gather discrediting information about Otakar Kirchner for use in a "best interest" hearing if the Does ultimately prevail in yet obtaining a favorable ruling by the U.S. Supreme Court. That Court, however, turned them down once before and less than three months ago. If they do succeed—a long shot by anyone's estimation—the lower court in Illinois will conduct a hearing to determine the child's custody...all over again.

It's not over.

For me, it was just beginning. On Sunday, January 29th, four days after the Illinois Supreme Court issued the writ of habeas corpus, Loren Heinemann called me at home. It had been only four days since I left the security of my school district job in favor of my private practice.

"Will you consider becoming the mental health professional to work with my clients and their child as he transitions to their home and care?" he asked. "Think it over." Heinemann clarified that the process would no doubt be long and difficult. There was no money at all for fees—I would need to donate my time and services. He added, "And, you will be on the **wrong side** in terms of public opinion."

How could I resist?

Comedy is tragedy plus time.

— Carol Burnett

Otto and Danny enjoy a laugh and a hug
in February 2003, during my late winter
visit to their home.

> It is the end that crowns us, not the fight.
>
> — *Robert Herrick*

EPILOGUE

When **Auggeretto Battiste**, investigator for the Illinois Department of Professional Regulation, was interviewed in 2003, he informed me that my case had been closed years ago. "You only wanted what was best for that child [Baby Richard]," he told me, "and you were largely responsible for his doing so well. I recommended no further action in the Department's investigation.... You **should** be writing a book!"

Bruce Boyer is the Director and Clinical Professor of the Child Law Clinic at the Loyola University Chicago School of Law.

Adrienne Drell is doing research and writing, under a two-year grant, for the Children and Family Justice Center at Northwestern University's Law School. She will soon begin teaching at the Medill School of Journalism for Northwestern.

Reportedly, **Bob Greene** is trying to make a comeback to rejoin the ranks of working journalists. He will need to reinvent himself after his nationally publicized and admitted sexual misconduct with a teenager, which pre-dated his self-promoted image as the guardian of Midwestern values and the "voice of voiceless children." The teenager remained voiceless for fourteen years before she came forward in 2002 to expose Greene to his employer and his public.

Mike Foley and his wife Donna practice law in their own firm, Foley & Foley. Mike represents public and private schools as well as civil rights cases. Donna is a criminal defense attorney in federal court. They live in Chicago with their daughters Katharine (Katie) (16) and Rebecca (13).

Susan Haddad, a sole practitioner in the city of Chicago, specializes in family law cases.

William J. Harte, a veteran attorney with nearly five decades of successful experience, continues to practice law and oversee his own firm in Chicago.

As of February 2003, **Loren Heinemann** was working as a plant manager of a manufacturing company. His wife Stacy works as a secretary at a dentist's office on a part-time basis. They reside with their children—Lexi (9), Barron (5), and Cameron (4)—in Richton Park, Illinois.

Demonstrating that "Living well is the best revenge," **Judge James D. Heiple** has settled in Peoria, Illinois, after his retirement in December 2000 from the Illinois Supreme Court and from thirty years as a judge.

Judge Gay-Lloyd Lott, a jurist since 1995, was transferred to the Law Division of the Cook County Circuit Court during the spring of 2003.

Thomas Panichi has been a Cook County Circuit Court judge since November 1994; he is assigned to the Sixth District in Markham, Illinois.

Enid and Peder Shortell live in Richton Park, Illinois, with their daughters, Shoshannah (19), Leah (17), and Alisa (15); they are greatly—and happily—outnumbered by their resident animals.

Neil Steinberg, the unabashed nemesis of Bob Greene, is a columnist and member of the editorial board at the *Chicago Sun-Times*. He is working on his fifth book. Neil and his wife Edie have two sons, Ross (7) and Kent (5).

In June 2003, **Justice John Tully** remembers his critically important dissenting opinion in the Baby Richard case: "I could tell from the record that the lower court made the wrong decision regarding that father and his child. I had to spell that out." Tully has served on the Illinois appellate court for thirteen years.

Robert (Jay) and Kimberly Warburton (f.k.a. John and Jane Doe) live with their sixteen-year-old son John in Schaumburg, Illinois.

There must be conclusions.

— William Shakespeare

ABOUT THE AUTHOR

DR. KAREN MORIARTY has worked as a teacher, counselor, administrator, and consultant in Illinois public schools and as a licensed clinical psychologist in private practice. She earned advanced degrees, including her doctorate, from Northern Illinois University. She has contributed a variety of articles about human resources to professional publications and a chapter about negotiations for a textbook. *Baby Richard — A Four-Year-Old Comes Home* is her first book, written "because it's a story that had to be told."

Karen is married to Dr. Robert V. Moriarty, also a licensed clinical psychologist and former college president. They reside with their feline companions, Stephanie Ann and Tom Riley, in northeastern Florida.

QUICK ORDER FORM

Fax orders: 217-258-3407. Fax this form.

Telephone orders: Call 866-MARCH 16 (866-627-2416) toll free. Have your credit card ready, please.

e-mail orders: babyrichard.com *or* babyrichard.net

Postal orders: Open Door Publishing Inc.
P.O. Box 664 · Mattoon, IL 61938 USA

Baby Richard — A Four-Year-Old Comes Home · 557 pages / 20 photos

Number of books ordered _____ @ $21.95 per book (US)
$31.95 per book (CAN)   *(total)* $_____

Shipping & handling @ $5.95 per book (US)
$10.00 per book (International)   *(total S & H)* $_____

Sales tax: Please add 6.25% ($1.37 per book)
for books shipped to **IL** residents   *(total tax, Illinois only)* $_____

Prices subject to change without notice.   **TOTAL $_____**

Shipping: If you prefer **priority mail** (US residents only), please add $2.50 per book. If you order **10 or more** books, please telephone 866-627-2416 to request current information on a reduced rate for shipping & handling.

Name _____

Address _____

City _____ State _____ Zip _____

Tel _____ e-mail _____

Payment: ☐ **Check** ← *(US Funds Only)* → ☐ **Money Order**

☐ **Credit Card** *(please check one below)*

☐ Visa   ☐ MasterCard   ☐ American Express   ☐ Discover

Card number_____ Expires _____ /_____

Name on card _____

Please make out check or money order payable to OPEN DOOR PUBLISHING INC.
A photocopy of this form may be used for ordering